Photoshop® 7: The Complete Reference

Photoshop® 7: The Complete Reference

Laurie Ann Ulrich

McGraw-Hill/Osborne
New York   Chicago   San Francisco   Lisbon
London   Madrid   Mexico City   Milan   New Delhi
San Juan   Seoul   Singapore   Sydney   Toronto

McGraw-Hill/Osborne
2600 Tenth Street
Berkeley, California 94710
U.S.A.

To arrange bulk purchase discounts for sales promotions, premiums, or fund-raisers, please contact **McGraw-Hill**/Osborne at the above address. For information on translations or book distributors outside the U.S.A., please see the International Contact Information page immediately following the index of this book.

Photoshop 7: The Complete Reference

1234567890 DOC DOC 0198765432

Book p/n 0-07-222312-X and CD p/n 0-07-222313-8
parts of

ISBN 0-07-222311-1

Publisher	**Technical Editor**	**Computer Designers**
Brandon A. Nordin	Don Day	Maureen Forys, Jeffrey Wilson, Happenstance Type-O-Rama
Vice President & Associate Publisher	**Freelance Project Manager**	
Scott Rogers	Laurie Stewart	
Acquisitions Editor	**Copy Editor**	**Series Design**
Megg Morin	edilogica	Peter F. Hancik
Senior Project Manager	**Proofreaders**	**Compositor**
Betsy Manini	Sachi Guzman	Happenstance Type-O-Rama
	K.J. Malkovich	
Acquisitions Coordinator	**Indexer**	
Tana Allen	Jack Lewis	

This book was composed with QuarkXPress™ 4.11.

I dedicate this book to my family and friends. I don't know where I'd be without their understanding, support, and humor, and I hope I never ever have to find out.

Contents at a Glance

Contents

Part III

Building Original Artwork

Part IV

Photoshop on the Web

About the Author

Laurie Ulrich—an artist through heredity and education, a teacher by nature, and a writer since she was old enough to pick up a crayon—is a web designer, graphic artist, and computer trainer. She is the author and co-author of more than 20 books on computer software, including the recently published titles *The Web Design Virtual Classroom* (McGraw-Hill/Osborne, 2001), *How to Do Everything with Office XP* (McGraw-Hill/Osborne, 2001), *Photoshop Web Graphics fx & Design,* (The Coriolis Group, 2001), and *Troubleshooting Excel 2002* (Microsoft Press, 2002). Laurie has written hundreds of computer training manuals for universities and corporate training centers, and in the last decade, she has trained more than 10,000 people to make more creative and effective use of their computers. In the early 1990s, after spending way too many years working for other people (including jobs managing computer training centers and running computer systems), Laurie started her own firm, Limehat & Company, Inc., putting her experience, ideas, and contacts to good use. Her firm provides consulting, training, web design, and web hosting, focusing on the special needs of growing companies and non-profit organizations.

When not writing about or teaching people to use computers, Laurie can be found supporting a variety of animal rights organizations—through protests, writing educational articles, and contributing to various Internet sources for animal rights information. She also enjoys her family, gardening, antiques, old houses, and adding to her collection of books. You can find out more about Laurie and her interests, skills, and experience at www.planetlaurie.com, and she welcomes your e-mail at laurie@planetlaurie.com.

About the Contributors

Robert Fuller is a web developer, author, and educator. He is currently "Web Guru" at Philadelphia's Limehat & Company, Inc. (which means he drinks a lot of coffee and pushes his responsibilities off on interns). A veteran of New York's Silicon Alley, it's been his great pleasure to take that experience into the classroom. He's trained thousands of students from such schools as Pratt Institute in his native Brooklyn to Temple University in his adopted Philadelphia.

Robert has developed online courses in web design, and has been published on other related topics that include programming and graphic design for the Web. He is the author of both the Dreamweaver® 4 and HTML Virtual Classroom books for McGraw-Hill/Osborne.

Dorothy Burke has been an independent computer consultant and trainer since 1988, following careers in sales, customer service, and writing. Although she now concentrates on teaching Lotus Notes and Lotus QuickPlace (she's a certified Lotus Notes instructor), she has taught courses in Microsoft, Quark,

Corel, and Adobe software products, as well. In addition, Dorothy develops applications in Lotus Notes and for the Web. Dorothy has co-authored 16 books on Microsoft Windows, Word, Excel, PowerPoint, and Lotus Notes. She is currently involved in delivering online training.

Bob Hires is the owner of HiRES Graphics, a graphic design firm that has been operating in the Philadelphia/Southern New Jersey area for more than 12 years. A graduate of the Pennsylvania Academy of the Fine Arts, Bob became involved in computer graphics in the Early 1980s. Since then he's been involved in a wide range of projects, from computer game design to print graphics to web site design. His past work includes projects for many financial companies. His recent projects have focused on ePhilanthropy including a web site design for the National Philanthropic Trust and GivingCapital Inc. Bob has taught Photoshop and other computer graphics programs at Moore College of Art and Design in Philadelphia since the early 1990s. Additionally he has served as President of the Macintosh Business Users Society for a 5-year period. Feel free to visit Bob's web site at www.hiresgraphics.com, or contact him by e-mail at bob@hiresgraphics.com.

About the Technical Editor

Don Day extended his love for traditional photography into the digital realm with the introduction of Photoshop 1.0 in 1989, and he remains passionate about Photoshop 7.0 in 2002. He has worked at Adobe since 1993, first providing Technical Support for Photoshop, and currently working in Photoshop Quality Engineering. He has taught classes in Photoshop and Computer Graphic Design and has provided technical reviews of other books on Photoshop. An Adobe Certified Expert in Photoshop since version 4.0, he also helps develop the Photoshop ACE exams.

Acknowledgments

I'd like to thank Megg Morin for giving me the opportunity to write this book, and for her unflagging support and encouragement throughout the process. I must also thank Tana Allen for her organization, attention to detail, and positive attitude. Working with these women has been a great experience. My technical editor, Don Day, was also an invaluable resource to me, and I thank him from the bottom of my heart for his insightful, thorough, and technically impeccable contributions to this book.

Special thanks go to Scott Wellwood and Gwyn Weisberg at Adobe for their help. Scott filled in many pieces that were crucial, and the CD included with this book would never have come together without Gwyn's help along the way!

Thanks must also go to Laurie Stewart and Kari Brooks, who are responsible for the final editing, and to Maureen Forys and Jeffrey Wilson, who laid out the book. Many long nights (and weekends that should have been vacations) were spent producing this book, and I thank them for their hard work and dedication.

Finally, I want to acknowledge my contributors—Robert Fuller, Dorothy Burke, and Bob Hires. I've had the pleasure of working with Dorothy and Bob for the better part of a decade, and I'm honored to have their experience and expertise in my book. As for Robert, I have to thank him not only for his expertise and the three excellent chapters he contributed to this book, but for putting up with my stress-induced whining and being tired and crabby. Even if he never does the dishes, he's a wonderful partner in both life and work (which are NOT the same thing, no matter what people tell you), and I don't know what I did to deserve his love and support. It must have been good, whatever it was!

Introduction

*P*hotoshop 7: The Complete Reference is written for Photoshop users of all levels, and it was my goal as the author to provide coverage that's both comprehensive and accessible. There's no sense providing reams of information if it's not accompanied by relevant examples, clear and concise explanations, and practical advice. In writing for such a diverse audience, I tried not to talk down to the veterans, while not speaking over the heads of the neophytes. I have covered all of Photoshop's major uses, from photo retouching to creating original artwork, and from designs intended for print media to graphics bound for the Web. Hopefully, there's something for everyone here.

If you've never seen Photoshop before, you'll find thorough coverage of all of Photoshop's tools and features, providing the strong foundation you'll need to master the application. If you've used Photoshop before and have taught yourself everything you know, you'll find useful insights into the inner workings and intentions of Photoshop's many features, and will undoubtedly find ways to do things faster, more easily, and with better results. If you're a Photoshop veteran with years of experience and training in Photoshop, you'll find coverage of what's new in Photoshop 7 and will no doubt pick up some useful tips and suggestions along the way. If nothing else, the book provides a logically indexed and easily accessible resource for any technical question you might have, and you'll find the information both accurate and easy to digest.

To provide a logical flow and structure, the book is divided into four parts, each containing a series of chapters with a consistent theme or related topic. The parts are

- Part I: Getting to Know Photoshop
- Part II: Editing and Retouching Images
- Part III: Building Original Artwork
- Part IV: Photoshop on the Web

Throughout these parts, there are a total of 20 chapters, plus an appendix that explains what can be found on the CD that accompanies this book. Each chapter begins with a short descriptive paragraph on the chapter's title page, helping you to find the chapters that interest you. Each chapter also ends with a summary, so you get a sense of what you should have learned. The order of the chapters is intended to build—in terms of complexity and in terms of the way a typical Photoshop image is developed. The book starts with an introduction to the interface and the application tools, so that you know what's available to you and how to use the software. In the subsequent chapters, the key features and procedures involved in creating, editing, formatting, and applying special effects to images are covered, in what I hope is a logical and practical sequence.

As you read *Photoshop 7: The Complete Reference*, you'll spot some consistent elements. First, there are Notes and Tips throughout the book, providing a quick dose of information in the form of suggestions and warnings. You'll also notice the abundance of images—figures referenced in the text that demonstrate a feature in use, a dialog box or palette, or a photo or drawing that's being created, edited, or to which a special effect is being applied. The examples are diverse, but are primarily photographs—some professionally taken, others shot by amateurs. There are color photos, black and white images, and vintage sepia-tone pictures, as well. They provide a strong cross-section of the types of images you, the reader, will encounter as you use Photoshop for both personal and professional projects.

I hope you enjoy this book and that it helps you in your use of Photoshop. I enjoyed writing it, and as someone who uses Photoshop every day, I enjoyed honing my own skills as I developed examples for the book and investigated new and improved features. Please let me know if you have suggestions for future editions; if you have any questions about Photoshop, you can contact me via e-mail at laurie@planetlaurie.com. I thank you for buying this book, and I look forward to hearing from you!

The Complete Reference

Part I

Getting to Know Photoshop

The
Complete
Reference

Chapter 1

Getting to Know Photoshop: What It Does Best and What's New in Photoshop 7

One of the most common remarks one will hear about any application as powerful and rich as Photoshop is, "I didn't know you could do *that*!" Therefore, before embarking on a complete tour of the Photoshop 7 interface and delving into its enhanced and new features and tools, it's a good idea to take a step back. In this chapter, we'll look at what exactly Photoshop does, to which specific tasks it's well-suited, and how it's changed in recent versions to meet the changing demands of the increasingly diverse group of graphic designers and artists in the world. For those of you who are familiar with previous versions, this chapter also provides an opportunity to find out what's new and exciting in this latest release of Photoshop—if you're new to Photoshop, *everything* will be new and exciting!

What Is Photoshop?

Photoshop is an image editor. It can also be an image *creator* (but even after you create the image, the vast amount of your time will be spent editing it). The real reason Photoshop is considered an image editor, though, comes from the fact that the software's original and sole purpose was to edit and retouch photographs. The photos would have been created with a camera and then brought into Photoshop for reworking, as shown in Figure 1-1.

Figure 1-1. At one time, cropping and retouching would have been the only reason to use Photoshop.

Over the years, however, Photoshop's purpose as an application has changed and expanded to reflect and meet the needs of its audience. The tools that were designed to retouch, redesign, and apply special effects to photographs can now be used to create and edit a wide variety of other images, and the needs of those image types are now fully supported. Of course, the images you're still most likely to edit in Photoshop are photographs—big surprise—but it truly doesn't end there.

You can edit any type of image in Photoshop, including clip art, line art, drawings, or paintings. They can be images created in Photoshop or in an illustration and graphics application such as Adobe Illustrator or CorelDRAW. The file format of the images you can edit is virtually unlimited, as well. You can edit bitmap images (PSD, BMP, JPG, or GIF, just to name a few), and you can also edit vector-based files such as those created in Illustrator or CorelDRAW. Of course, the destination of the images after you edit them can affect the choices you make when you save your files, but there again, you have a very wide range of formats to choose from.

You can also scan original items, such as drawings and paintings that were done by hand, and tinker with them using Photoshop's own drawing and painting tools, as well as its special-effects filters. There is literally no end to what you can do with Photoshop and where the images you create and edit with Photoshop can end up—in any number of printed locations, viewed electronically, or functioning as graphic content and links on a web page, as shown in Figure 1-2.

Figure 1-2. *Photoshop: It's not just for photographs anymore!*

What Photoshop Does Best

Of course, like any diverse and powerful tool, Photoshop does some things better than others. Photo editing is its mainstay and major strength. You can clean up an old or damaged photo by removing scratches, scuffs, stains, and creases—version 7 even contains a new tool, the Healing Brush, just for this purpose (see the "Major Changes" section later in this chapter). Photoshop also provides tools that allow you to remove content, replace content, and add new things that weren't in the original image at all. As shown in Figure 1-3, you can cover unwanted portions of a photo with more appealing stuff.

You can also apply artistic and special-effects filters to photos, which turns a photograph into what looks like a watercolor painting, or you can blur unimportant background content in favor of more important items in the foreground (see Figure 1-4). Photoshop offers an extensive and easily customized group of tools for changing the appearance of an image or any portion thereof.

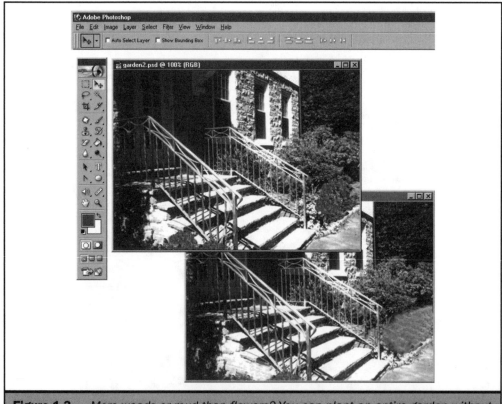

Figure 1-3. *More weeds or mud than flowers? You can plant an entire garden without leaving your desk.*

GETTING TO KNOW
PHOTOSHOP

Figure 1-4. *Background becomes just that—a diffused foundation for what you really want people to notice.*

Photoshop is also great for creating original artwork that requires fine detail and subtle effects—shading, shadows, a three-dimensional look, the appearance of a light source on a glossy surface, or any realistic effect that you can't easily create with drawing applications such as Illustrator or CorelDRAW. While initially intended for use on photos, Photoshop's tools help you even if your image contains no photographic content at all. Some other things that Photoshop does well follow:

- Creating images for the Web and optimizing the quality and online loading time
- Creating print-ready color separations for books and magazines
- Scanning original artwork
- Creating original artwork that looks drawn or painted by hand
- Editing images captured with a digital camera
- Editing digital video, frame by frame
- Adding text to photographs and original artwork
- Creating animations and rollovers (interactive images) for web pages

You can take images from a variety of sources and bring them together in Photoshop, applying special effects and editing their content as needed. The use of Photoshop's extensive set of tools also makes it possible to combine drawn, scanned, or digitally captured content with original artwork and text. Figure 1-5 shows an image consisting of original artwork and text.

What Photoshop Doesn't Do Best

By now, it may be sounding like if you have Photoshop, the only other application you might need is a word processor! But there are some things that Photoshop doesn't do well, despite its extensive tools and features. To create the following media, you'd be better off using an application like CorelDRAW or Adobe Illustrator, as these applications were designed for specific kinds of artwork:

- Line art such as logos consisting solely of solid color, simple shapes, and crisp, straight lines that will need to be resized for different advertising purposes (see Figure 1-6)

- Schematics and other line drawings that require absolutely straight lines and clean edges

- Books, brochures, flyers, pamphlets, and similar text-heavy documents (although, you can dress them up with graphics created in Photoshop)

- Charts, graphs, tables, or overhead slides

- Digital video or animations such as cartoons or movies

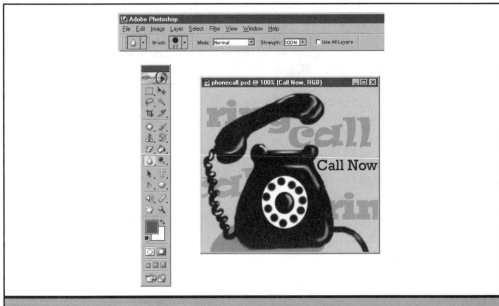

Figure 1-5. *Create an image and add your own original brush strokes and text.*

Figure 1-6.   *A logo made up of solid shapes and straight lines doesn't require Photoshop's power.*

Other Adobe Products to Consider

Adobe Illustrator is a good choice for the things that Photoshop doesn't do well—you'll find a great deal of compatibility between the two applications, including a common look and feel (see Figure 1-7). The consistency can shorten your learning curve if you take up Illustrator after having mastered Photoshop (or vice versa).

If you work with video, you'll find Adobe Premiere a useful editing tool, enabling you to apply special effects, add music, and combine still images with video footage.

For creating page layouts—for magazines, newsletters, white papers, and other text-heavy documents that also include images—you may want to try Adobe PageMaker or Adobe InDesign. With these applications, you can bring together text and images that require precise placement.

And finally, when it comes to pages bound for the Web, you'll want to check out Adobe GoLive, a powerful WYSIWYG (what-you-see-is-what-you-get) tool for designing web sites and pages. With a user-friendly interface that allows you to design your pages graphically, as well as effective tools for writing and editing HTML code, even a novice web designer can produce impressive web pages in very short order.

So with Illustrator, Premiere, GoLive, PageMaker, InDesign, and Photoshop, there isn't any sort of print or electronic visual content you can't create or edit. You can find out much more about these products at Adobe's home on the Web, **www.adobe.com**.

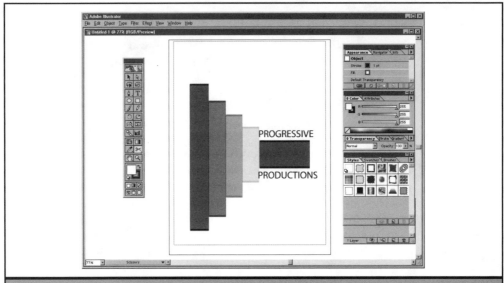

Figure 1-7.   *The Illustrator interface will remind you of Photoshop, and you can use what you know about one application as you master the other.*

What's New in Photoshop 7?

Now we know what Photoshop is best suited for. So what does Photoshop 7 have that version 6 didn't? The changes and additions in version 7 can be found throughout the application, in every thing from the look, feel, and content of the application interface to support for Mac OS X and Windows XP (the latest versions of Mac and Microsoft Windows operating systems, respectively). Some of the changes are major; some are simply cosmetic. You can install version 7 alongside version 6 (or 5/5.5, if you never upgraded to 6), so you can still work in the version that's comfortable for you while you dabble with 7 for a while. Once you're familiar with 7, though, it's a good idea to save your drive space and uninstall your previous versions.

Note   *You will be able to edit your images in both new and old versions, and you should be able to work back and forth between versions with no problem (unless you include elements created by new features that are not supported in previous versions). I tested this with images saved in the native Photoshop (PSD) format, as well as images in JPG and GIF format, saved for the Web.*

What You'll Notice First

When you fire up Photoshop 7 for the first time, the first thing you'll notice if you're familiar with Photoshop are the changes to the toolbox. On Mac OS X, you'll notice the new consistent Aqua user interface; on Windows XP, you'll notice the new look there, too. The buttons now have a 3-D look, as shown in Figure 1-8. There are a few new tools, as well, which we'll go over in Chapter 2. For now, it's the change in the appearance of the toolbox that's most striking.

The 3-D look is continued on the tool option bars—the buttons and options/check boxes that appear there for the selected tool also have an embossed look. In addition, you'll notice a pair of tabs at the far-right end of the options bar, as shown in Figure 1-9. These tabs offer brush presets (see the Brushes tab) and quick access to your files (File Browser). Through the File Browser tab, you can view the contents of your local drive and see thumbnails of your graphic images. From the view of your files, you can open images for editing, rename files, or place files in a new folder.

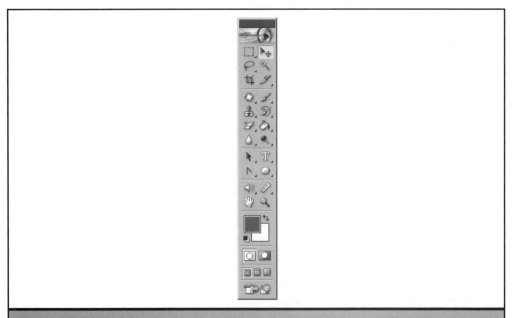

Figure 1-8. *The 3-D look of the toolbox will catch your eye immediately.*

Docking well with Brushes and File Browser tabs

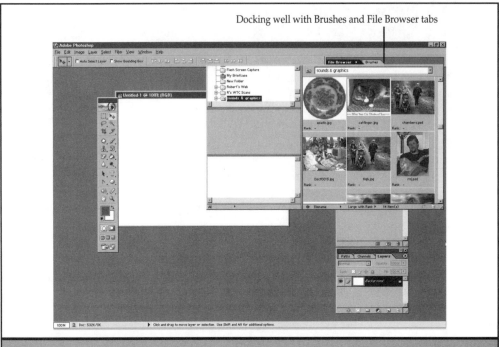

Figure 1-9. *New tabs give quick access to brush options and file management.*

Note *You can leave the Brushes and File Browser tabs docked where they are by default, or you can drag them out onto the workspace to float like your other palettes. If you turn them into independent palettes, you can drag them anywhere on the workspace, minimize them as needed to save space in the application window, and close them, which returns them to the docking well.*

Major Changes

Beyond the immediately noticeable changes to the appearance of the toolbox, the most significant changes involve two areas of the application—new user presets, and new and improved tools and features. In terms of changing the way you work, the ability to create and save presets is extremely important. *Presets* are settings that are applied to tools and workplace environments, allowing you to establish a series of settings and put them into effect at any time.

In version 7, you can create workspace presets and save the arrangement of your palettes, windows, and other onscreen tools for different types of work. For example, you might have a different set of palettes onscreen when you're creating buttons for a web page than you'd have when you're retouching photographs for a brochure. The ability to save workspace presets means you can save the workspace configuration you like best for creating web graphics and apply it whenever you're designing art for the Web. When you're cleaning up a photo, you can switch to that workspace preset, and you've automatically got the tools and palettes you need, in one fell swoop. No more need to go through the palettes and open the ones you need and close the ones you don't. Workspace presets also include the size of palettes, so if you typically expand the size of the Layers or History palette while working on a particular type of image, even that level of customization will be retained if you save the workspace in its most effective state for your working style. You can create and save as many presets as you need (Figure 1-10 shows a small selection in the Window | Workspace submenu), giving each one a relevant name to make it easier to apply it when you need it.

Figure 1-10.   *Save your workspace settings for future use.*

Also new to version 7 is the ability to create tool presets, establishing settings for individual tools so you don't need to keep adjusting options each time you return to a tool. The Tool Presets palette makes it easy to name, save, and apply presets for any tool in the toolbox (see Figure 1-11). For example, you can choose default fonts, point sizes, and text colors for the Text tool, choose specific brush settings for the Eraser, and set up the way the Gradient tool will work automatically. Any tool in the toolbox can be customized and the custom settings saved. You can create multiple settings for individual tools (and for each version of each tool), again making it possible to customize your environment so it's quick and easy to set up for specific projects or projects of a particular type.

The tool and feature-related additions and changes in version 7 expand on Photoshop's already considerable arsenal of intuitive and powerful devices:

Custom Brushes You can create and save your own brushes, customizing everything from the size of the brush to the texture it paints. Using the Brush Presets palette and menu, you can tweak anything and everything about a brush stroke, and then save the settings for future use (see Figure 1-12). There are 11 different brush types, and for each one, a multitude of variations. A slider allows you to set the brush diameter, making it quite simple to maintain a consistent stroke at different widths throughout the editing process for a single project. The ability to save your settings makes it possible to achieve consistency throughout related projects, as well.

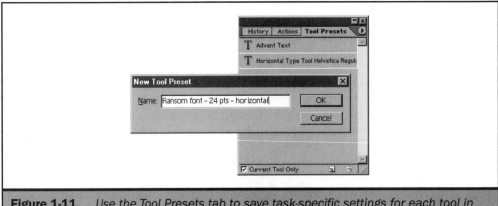

Figure 1-11. Use the Tool Presets tab to save task-specific settings for each tool in the toolbox.

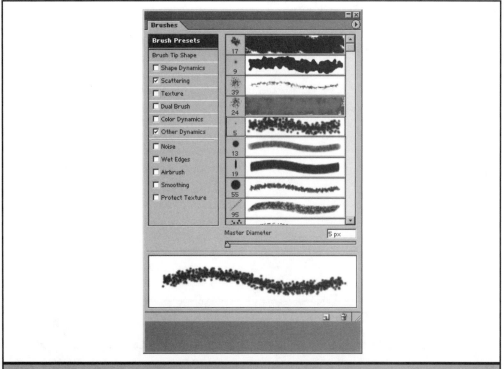

Figure 1-12.   *Set your brush options, and then save your settings.*

Healing Brush   This tool is a big help when retouching photographs. The Healing Brush tool (see it selected in Figure 1-13) allows you to clean up scratches, wrinkles, creases, and other artifacts on a photograph while preserving the texture and any desired noise (spots, dust, scratches) on the original image. You can imagine the benefits of restoring vintage photographs in a way that allows you to keep the textured matting around a picture and the image's overall aged appearance as part of its charm. Previously, if you cleaned up an image with a definite texture of its own, you often lost that texture on the places where you had to paint over a scratch or spot.

Liquify   This feature has been enhanced and now includes the ability to save and load a customized mesh, and use a turbulence brush. You can also see individual layers or look at a flattened image and refer to it while editing your image layer with the Liquify tool. You'll find this new feature in the Filter menu.

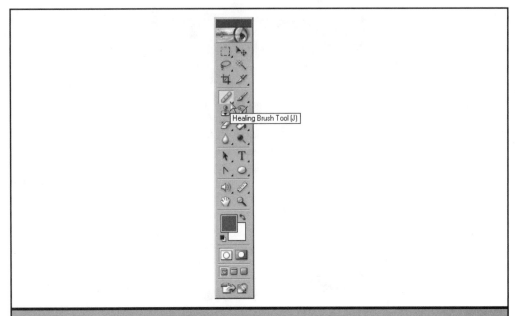

Healing Brush Tool (J)

Figure 1-13.   Use the Healing Brush tool to remove blemishes while preserving the texture beneath and around them.

Picture Package   Photoshop now supports multiple page sizes, and you can print more than one image per sheet of paper, labeling the sheet of images for reference on the printout. You'll find this in the File menu, in the Automate submenu; there, a dialog box helps you choose the image(s) to print (the active image or images in a particular folder), specify the page size, and apply a label (see Figure 1-14).

Web Photo Gallery   Providing both convenience and added security, this feature is found in the File menu, in the Automate submenu. With Web Photo Gallery, you can use new templates for creating web content and apply copyright information to your images. Figure 1-15 shows the Web Photo Gallery dialog box.

Pattern Maker   This is a new plug-in that allows you to create new patterns based on a selected sample. The feature is found in the Filter menu.

Spell Checking   Finally! Photoshop can now spell check your text (see Figure 1-16), and provides the added ability to find and replace text content (see Figure 1-17). This will be a significant benefit to users working with both print and web-bound images, helping to eliminate typos in what you hoped would be your final version of an image. You can access the Check Spelling and Find and Replace Text commands in the Edit menu, or via the Text tool's context menu.

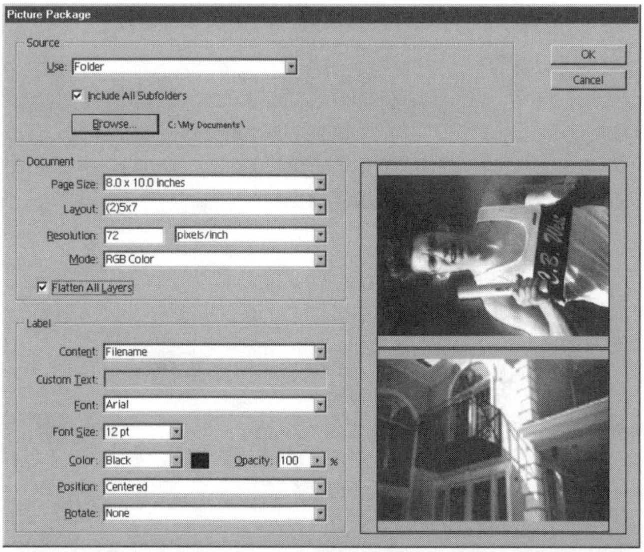

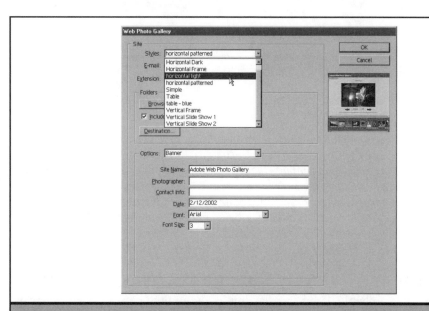

Figure 1-14.   *Picture Package allows printing to a variety of page sizes.*

Figure 1-15.   *Choose from a variety of display styles for your series of images.*

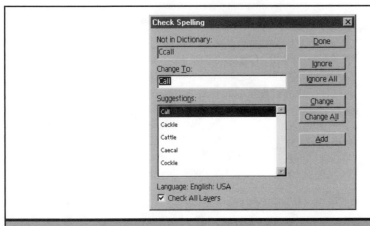

Figure 1-16. *A major convenience and quality-assurance feature: the spell checker.*

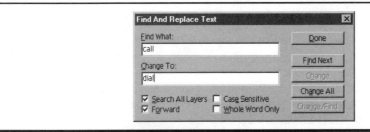

Figure 1-17. *Find and Replace makes it easy to be out with the old, in with the new.*

Note *Errors in printed documents often have a smaller audience than mistakes made in web content, but it's easier to correct a web page—simply edit the image and upload it to the page, replacing the image that contains the error. When it comes to print, however, even if the distribution was smaller, it's harder to retrieve the documents you've mailed or handed out and replace them with corrected materials. With Photoshop 7's spell checker, your margin for error is greatly decreased, although it's still advisable that you manually proof your work in addition to running the spell check.*

Subtle Differences That May Change the Way You Work

The way you work is probably based on a few things—your own personal style, the way you think, your work environment, and the software you use. In the case of the software, this is truly an example of the tail wagging the dog: If the software does something a particular way, even if you would prefer to do it another way, you'll eventually learn to do it the way the software does it, even if that way isn't the most efficient. When software is revised, therefore, the enhancements that give you more flexibility and more stability are the ones that will really change and improve the way you work.

When it comes to Photoshop 7, the following new and enhanced features will probably affect your daily use of the software:

PDF Security   Accessed through the Save dialog box and the PDF save options, you can now assign passwords to PDF files in Photoshop (see Figure 1-18). You can open the secured PDFs in either Photoshop or Adobe Acrobat. This makes it possible to share documents with people, yet you can use passwords to control who has access to those documents. A design prototype (or a document enhanced by Photoshop content) is an excellent example of the sort of Photoshop creation you might want to share in PDF form but to which you'd want to limit access.

Auto Color Correction   More reliable than the previous versions' Auto Levels and Auto Contrast commands, this feature removes color casts, assuring you of consistent and accurate colors in your Photoshop created and/or edited images. You'll find the Auto Color command in the Image menu, in the Adjustments submenu.

Save for Web   This feature, found in the File menu, isn't new to Photoshop 7, but the ability to include ImageReady optimization settings is. You can now include dithered transparency and remap transparency in your options when saving an image for the Web. The dialog box has a slightly different look, and as with all parts of the interface, there's a 3-D look in version 7 (see Figure 1-19).

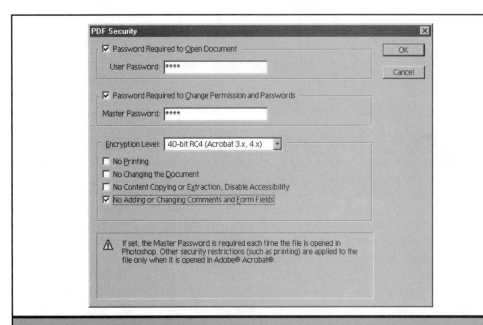

Figure 1-18.   *Thin the crowd that can open your PDFs by applying passwords when you save the files.*

Figure 1-19.   *Your Save for Web options are increased in version 7.*

   *The ability to create and apply presets to tools and the workspace will also significantly influence the way you work. The ability to customize your environment and tools to specific jobs and types of images will save you a great deal of time and aggravation. It may be my favorite new feature in Photoshop 7!*

Summary

This chapter focused on Photoshop's strengths and gave you some insights into the few image creation and editing tasks that might be better served by another application. You also got a sneak peek at the enhancements, new features, and the 3-D interface of Photoshop 7. This should help you choose when and where to use Photoshop for your print and web-bound images, as well as give you a head start in using the new version—whether you're new to version 7 or to Photoshop in general. In the next chapter, you'll take an in-depth tour of the Photoshop interface.

The
Complete
Reference

Photoshop 7

Chapter 2

Understanding the
Photoshop Interface

Imagine moving to a new town or starting work in a new office and not knowing where anything is or how things work. You'd spend a lot of time poking around, trying to figure things out on your own, and while that process might net you some insights, it will waste a good deal of your time and potentially leave you with some significant misconceptions. You might even end up taking the long route to frequently visited places simply because nobody showed you a more efficient path. The goal of this chapter is to make sure you don't waste any time figuring things out on your own. You want to get up and running efficiently and effectively in Photoshop 7, and this chapter will introduce you to the Photoshop interface—the tools, options, menus, palettes, and dialog boxes that you need to find, customize, and utilize in order to master Photoshop. If you're new to Photoshop, this will be a time-saving introduction to a new working environment; if you've used previous versions of Photoshop, you'll quickly be able to see what's new and different in version 7 and get going that much faster. The tour starts here!

The Photoshop Desktop

The first thing you see when Photoshop opens is the Photoshop desktop. The desktop contains a title bar, menu bar, Options toolbar, toolbox, and four palettes. Unless you opened Photoshop by opening an image file, there won't be an image window within the Photoshop desktop until you choose to open a file or start a new one. Figures 2-1, 2-2, and 2-3 show the default Photoshop desktop as it should appear the first time you open Photoshop 7 in Windows, Mac OS 9, and Mac OS X, respectively.

The Photoshop desktop's detail will change as you begin to work. For example, if you click a tool in the toolbox, the Options toolbar changes to offer options for working with that particular tool. When a file is open, the palettes will display specifics about that image and any portion of it that's been selected or clicked. As you can see in Figure 2-4, using the Eyedropper tool (by clicking a pixel in the image to "sip up" the color there) changes the Color palette to show the color sipped up by the eyedropper, and the toolbar shows options for the eyedropper. In this figure, the Navigator palette shows that we've zoomed in on the image to be better able to select an individual pixel within the image. This wasn't done with the eyedropper, but with the Zoom tool (it could also be done with the Navigator palette's slider), which facilitates using the eyedropper.

The Photoshop desktop can be resized and moved; you can also choose from three viewing modes, each one potentially advantageous to a particular task. To resize the Photoshop application window (if you're using Windows), point to border of the window and look for the mouse pointer to turn to a double arrow (see Figure 2-5). Click and drag outward to increase window size, inward to shrink it. Drag a corner to resize both horizontally and vertically at the same time. To move a window, point to its title bar, then click and drag it to a new position. You can drag it aside to reveal a window (from another application) that's behind it, or to expose program shortcuts on your Mac or Windows desktop so you can double-click them to start a new application.

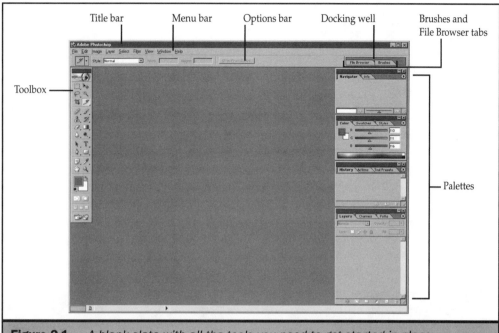

Figure 2-1.   *A blank slate with all the tools you need to get started in place*

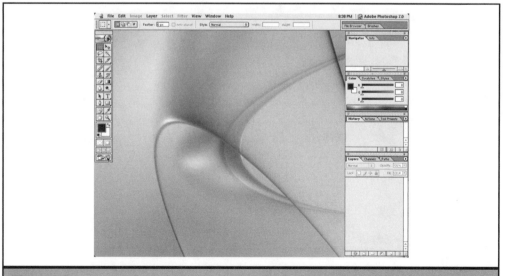

Figure 2-2.   *The Photoshop desktop on a Macintosh (here under OS 9) offers the same tools and features in many of the same places.*

Figure 2-3. *The default Photoshop 7 desktop on Mac OS X*

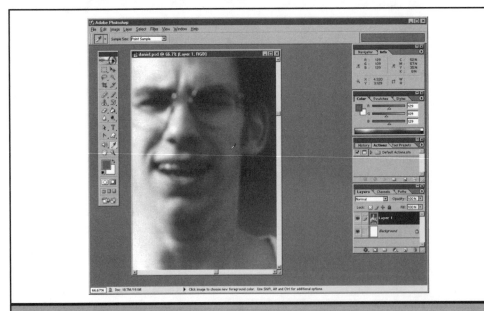

Figure 2-4. *Use the toolbox tools and watch the environment respond.*

If a window is maximized (snapped to the full size of your screen), you can't resize it in this way.

Figure 2-6 shows the Photoshop desktop in transit.

Figure 2-5.   *The double arrow resizes a window—just click and drag to increase or decrease window size.*

Figure 2-6.   *Pick it up and move it—the Photoshop desktop can be dragged anywhere on your screen.*

If you use Photoshop to edit images that will be used in other applications, you might find it helpful to keep the Photoshop desktop small enough to see other applications' windows behind it. If you're editing an image bound for the Web, you may have Adobe GoLive or Macromedia Dreamweaver open at the same time and want to quickly switch back to that application after saving your image in a web-safe format. Clicking an exposed portion of an application's window is a fast and easy way to hop between open applications.

The Photoshop Image Window

Now that we've seen the Photoshop desktop's features change when an image is opened and edited, it's high time we talk about the window that contains that image. The *image window* is a container. You can resize the window by clicking and dragging the window's lower-right corner; you can alter the view of your image by zooming in and out on it and using the Hand tool to move the image around within the window so you can focus on a particular area. Figure 2-7 shows the Hand tool in use and an image viewed at 300 percent magnification.

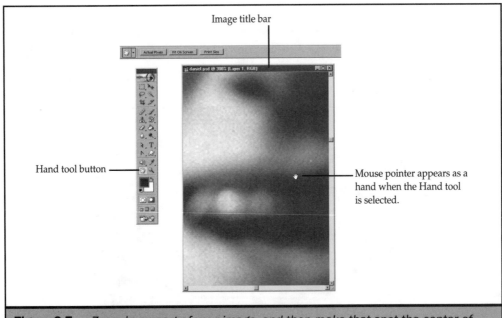

Figure 2-7. *Zoom in on part of your image, and then make that spot the center of your attention.*

Changing Your View of the Image

Two things control the way your image is viewed in the image window: the percentage of magnification you've applied, and the Screen Mode you've chosen. Zooming obviously allows you to get closer to or farther away from an image. The Screen Mode you choose will dictate the onscreen tools that are available and how much of the Photoshop desktop is taken up by the image window. Of course, each image you're working on and each task within the process of creating and/or editing an image will call for different zoom settings and different Screen Modes—the trick is to find the one that gives you the greatest advantage, putting the tools you need within easy reach and the image at a distance from you that suits the tools you're using and how you intend to apply them.

Zooming In and Out on an Image

"Zoom" is a term taken from photography—the camera can zoom in on or out from a subject, bringing the photographer closer to or farther away from the image in the viewfinder. In Photoshop, the Zoom tool works the same way. You can zoom in on or out from an image, making it easy to select and work on small areas or to see more or all of an image. You can zoom in any of three ways:

The Zoom tool (z)   This tool is found in the toolbox. It changes your mouse pointer to a magnifying glass, whereupon you can click any portion of the image and zoom in on that spot, getting closer with each click of your mouse in hundred-percent increments. If you right-click (Windows) or CONTROL-click (Mac) the image while the Zoom tool is active, you can choose Zoom Out, which zooms you out 100 percent. To continue zooming out, you need to keep reopening the context menu and choosing Zoom Out. In lieu of that, you can use the options bar for the Zoom tool (it appears as soon as the Zoom tool is activated) and click the magnifying glass that contains a minus sign (–), turning the Zoom tool from Zoom In to Zoom Out Mode. Figure 2-8 shows the tool in Zoom Out Mode.

The Navigator palette   This palette offers four tools for zooming in or out on an image. It also provides a tool for navigating the image (thus the palette's name). Drag the red rectangle around on the image thumbnail to refocus the portion of the image displayed in the image window. To zoom with the palette, use the tools shown in Figure 2-9.

The View menu   There are five zoom options offered in this menu—Zoom In, Zoom Out, Fit on Screen, Actual Pixels, and Print Size. The names of the commands are pretty self-explanatory, but it's important to note that the Zoom commands simply activate the tool and move your magnification up or down 100 percent.

- The Fit on Screen command makes the image display in its entirety within the image window. It expands the image window to fit within the application window, bounded by the toolbox on the left and the palettes on the right.

- Actual Pixels displays the image at a pixel depth to match your monitor's display resolution. The pixel depth (also referred to as color depth) also affects the view you get when this command is issued—higher resolution results in a larger image (and view); lower resolution results in a smaller image/view.

- Print Size is the size at which the image will print. Choose Image | Image Size to view the document size for your particular image (see Figure 2-10).

Note

The buttons on the Zoom tool options bar (Actual Pixels, Fit on Screen, Print Size) are the same as the View menu's commands with the same names. Like all tool options, these buttons only appear on the options bar when the Zoom tool is active. You'll find out more about all the tools' options as you read through this chapter.

Figure 2-8. *Look at your mouse pointer to see if you're in Zoom In (+) or Zoom Out (–) Mode.*

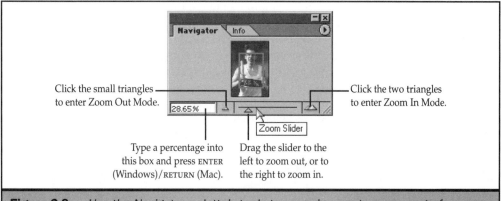

Click the small triangles
to enter Zoom Out Mode.

Click the two triangles
to enter Zoom In Mode.

Zoom Slider

Type a percentage into
this box and press ENTER
(Windows)/RETURN (Mac).

Drag the slider to the
left to zoom out, or to
the right to zoom in.

Figure 2-9.   *Use the Navigator palette's tools to zoom in or out on any part of your
image.*

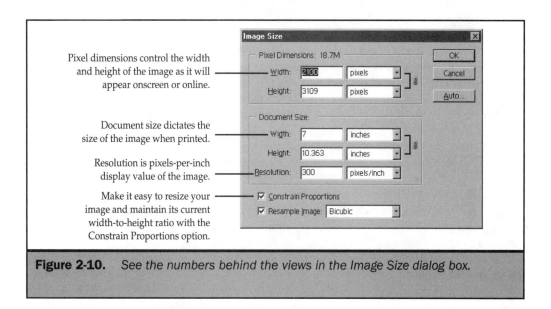

Pixel dimensions control the width
and height of the image as it will
appear onscreen or online.

Document size dictates the
size of the image when printed.

Resolution is pixels-per-inch
display value of the image.

Make it easy to resize your
image and maintain its current
width-to-height ratio with the
Constrain Proportions option.

Figure 2-10.   *See the numbers behind the views in the Image Size dialog box.*

Choosing a Screen Mode

The Screen Modes affect both the image window and the Photoshop desktop, and are
accessed through the toolbox. Figure 2-11 shows the mode buttons (the shortcut key
for all three buttons is F) and Figures 2-12, 2-13, and 2-14 show the three Screen Modes for
viewing your images and Photoshop desktop. The mode you choose depends on what

you're doing—if you need to zoom in very close to the image and want to see a lot of the image, as well, either of the Full Screen Modes will work nicely. Choosing not to include the menu bar is simply a matter of whether or not you anticipate needing to use the menus. Standard Mode gives you more onscreen support—the palettes and toolbar—but these things take up real estate you may want to make better use of by seeing more of your image.

| Note | *In all three modes, the toolbox remains onscreen. This means you can switch between modes as you work. If you happen to turn off the toolbox (Window | Tools), turn it back on to facilitate switching between modes, and of course, to give you access to Photoshop's drawing, painting, and editing tools.* |

Navigating an Image

Moving around an image is done in one of two ways: with your mouse, using the scrollbars to see currently hidden portions of the image from a horizontal and/or vertical perspective; or with the Hand tool. Of course, you won't need either technique if your image is the same size as the current size of the image window. If this is the case, no scrollbars will appear, and the Hand tool, while available, won't do anything.

Assuming either you've zoomed in on your image or the image at its actual size is larger than the image window, you will need to move around in order to view or edit the portions of the image that are currently hidden. Using the scrollbars is easy enough, and you're probably accustomed to them from your use of any other Windows or Macintosh application.

The Hand tool works by allowing you to drag the image around within the image window, as though you were moving a page around on a tabletop. As you move the image within the window, you can zoom in on specific areas if you need to work closely with a particular set of pixels or if you just need to look closely at all parts of an image. If, for example, you're cleaning up a photograph (removing scratches and stains), you can use the Hand tool to visually check all areas of the image after you've zoomed in close enough to spot blemishes (see Figure 2-15). Once you've found a blemish, of course, you can zoom in closer and activate the requisite tool for retouching the photo.

| Note | *The Navigator palette is also useful for navigating an image. If you've zoomed in on an image and want to instead focus on another area—currently showing or hidden—click the image thumbnail that appears in the Navigator palette. You can drag the red rectangle anywhere on the image, and the image in the image window will move in tandem, displaying the portion of the image within the palette's rectangle.* |

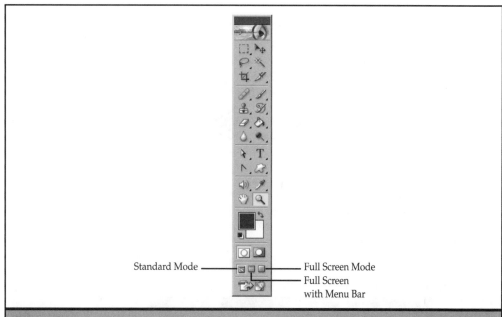

Standard Mode ———   ——— Full Screen Mode
                                     ——— Full Screen
                                         with Menu Bar

Figure 2-11.   *Choose from Standard Mode, Full Screen with Menu Bar, or Full Screen Mode.*

Figure 2-12.   *Standard Mode gives you all your onscreen tools—palettes and toolbars—and allows you to expand the image window to the full size of the Photoshop desktop below the options bar.*

Figure 2-13. *Pick Full Screen with Menu Bar if you'll be needing to get at the menu commands.*

Figure 2-14. *Do you have all the keyboard shortcuts memorized? If you don't need the menu bar, then Full Screen Mode (F) is for you.*

Figure 2-15. *Set your zoom and then use the Hand tool to help you inspect every
pixel of the image.*

Using Photoshop's Menus

Not much mystery here! The menus work by your clicking the menu name and then
making a selection from the list of commands. Some of the commands spawn
submenus, some open dialog boxes, and others go right to work to perform a task.
Some visual clues you should be aware of follow:

- If a menu command is followed by a right-pointing triangle, this means a
  submenu will open when you click or point to the command.

- If an ellipsis (…) follows a command, you know that a dialog box will open as
  soon as you choose the command.

- Check marks indicate that something is turned on or in force. For example, the
  Tools command in the Window menu is checked if your toolbox is displayed.

Keyboard shortcuts—the keyboard equivalent of a command—appear to the right of
the command, as shown in Figure 2-16. If you're a fan of keyboard shortcuts, you can

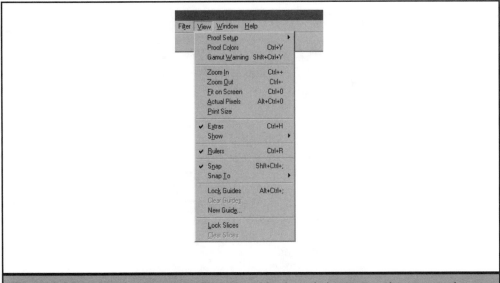

Figure 2-16. *Checks, triangles, ellipses, and keyboard shortcuts—the menus give you quick access to just about anything Photoshop can do.*

skip using the menu next time you need to execute a particular command—just press the combination of keys and the command will execute.

To use a keyboard shortcut, press the first key in the combination, and with that key held down, tap the second key in the combination. If the shortcut you want to use has three keys in it, hold the first, add and hold the second, and then tap the third.

Working with the Toolbox

The toolbox is an essential element of the Photoshop desktop—without it, you can't make selections, paint, draw, retouch, fill, or type on your image. You can turn it off if it's in the way (the Window | Tools command will toggle it off if it's on), and you can move it around by dragging its title bar. By default, it sits along the left side of the Photoshop desktop, and unless you have your image displayed full screen, you can easily keep it alongside your image window so it's not covering anything up. If the toolbar is in the way (and there's nowhere to drag it so it won't be) but you don't want to turn it off, double-click its title bar. This will reduce the toolbox to just the title bar and the Adobe Online button (the picture at the top of the toolbox). To redisplay the full toolbox, double-click the title bar again.

Assuming the toolbox is fully displayed, activate a tool on the toolbar by clicking it with your mouse. In version 7, where everything has a very 3-D look, you'll see the button appear to indent. Figure 2-17 shows the Rectangular Marquee tool selected. Not obvious in the black-and-white figure, the toolbox buttons also display in color when you point to them with your mouse. Figure 2-18 shows the Photoshop 7 toolbox as it appears under Mac's OS X.

You'll notice that some of the tool buttons have tiny triangles in the lower-right corner. This indicates alternative tools that can be activated with that button, as shown in Figure 2-19. If you click the triangle or hold your mouse button down while hovering over a button that has a triangle, a palette of alternative buttons appears, and you can choose one from that palette. Once chosen, that button becomes the default button, at least for the current session.

Tip   *If you want a particular tool to remain displayed beyond the current work session, you need to reset your General Preferences, which are covered in Chapter 3. To edit them, choose Edit | Preferences (Windows or Mac OS 9.x) or Photoshop | Preferences (Mac OS X), and in the General Preferences dialog box make sure that Save Palette Locations is selected.*

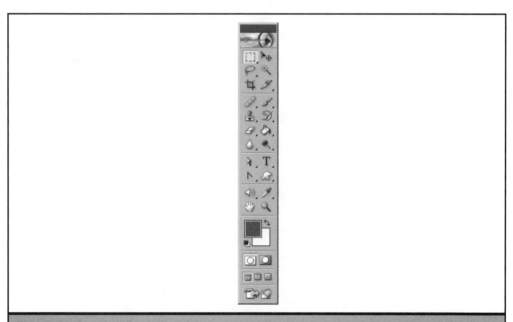

Figure 2-17.   *Click a button to turn on a tool.*

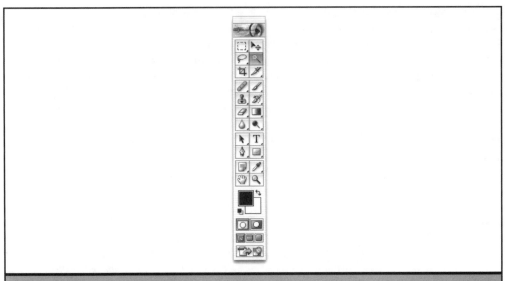

Figure 2-18. *Photoshop's toolbox sports a new look in Mac OS X.*

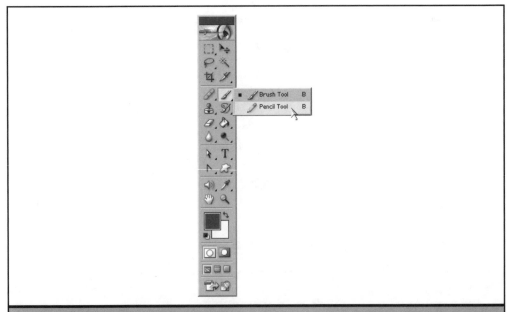

Figure 2-19. *Click the button's triangle to display related alternate buttons.*

Note *Want to know a tool's "official" name? Hover over the button with your mouse pointer (don't click). A tool tip will appear, displaying the name of the button as well as a very useful item—a single letter of the alphabet. The letter you see in the tool tip is the keyboard shortcut for activating that tool. For example, press B to activate the Brush tool or L to activate the Lasso tool. Most of the letters have some mnemonic association to the tool they activate (Move is V, not M [Marquee], but the V makes sense, as the "v" sound in the Word "move" is obvious to the ear), so you shouldn't have too much trouble remembering them!*

Using the Options Bars

As soon as you click any tool in the toolbox (or activate it with its single-letter keyboard shortcut), you'll notice the options bar displays a series of buttons and drop-down lists. These items are the options for the selected tool (see the Eraser tools in Figure 2-20). Of course, the settings that appear the first time you use the tool are the defaults; once you make changes, whatever you've set will remain in force during your current work session (and in the future, if your General Preferences are set to Save Palette Locations), unless and until you change the settings for a particular tool.

Figure 2-20. *Use the options bar to customize the way the selected tool will work.*

It's important to note that the changes you make to many of the tools' options will remain in place even after you close Photoshop, appearing on the options bar when you reopen the application and activate a tool you've used before. For this reason, it's a good idea to look at the options bar before you begin using a tool—you could find that the setting you used last isn't appropriate for the image you're working on now.

At the far end of the options bar is the docking well. It's a space where you can dock palettes (in addition to the two tabs, Brushes and File Browser, which appear in the well by default) to keep them available without taking up space within the Photoshop desktop. Figure 2-21 shows the Color palette being dragged to the docking well—just drag it by the tab and release the mouse button when the palette is over the well.

Note   *If you don't want to devote any Photoshop desktop real estate to the options bar, close it by choosing Window | Options. This will toggle the bar off if it's currently displayed, and bring it back if you've turned it off.*

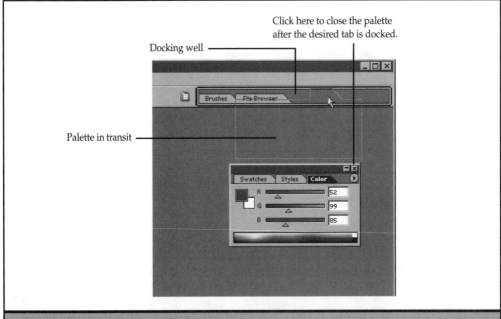

Figure 2-21.   *Drag to the docking well any palette you want to keep close by. Then, if you don't need the rest of the tabs in that palette's group, close the group.*

Selecting the Right Tool for the Job

So with all the options for customizing tools available—making it possible for you to make a tool do just about anything you want, any way you want to—how do you know which tool you need to use in the first place? Well, becoming familiar with the tools and what they do is a great first step to knowing that answer when you're faced with a task or problem. One important thing to remember: There are many ways to do the same things, so while someone might tell you how to do something, it's a good idea to explore alternatives. Some basic things can only be done one way, but when it comes to creating original artwork or retouching photos and other images, you'll find that you can blaze your own trail and come up with some really interesting, effective results.

With that said, let's look at the toolbox and its tools, breaking them down into the following five groups: Selection tools, Painting and Drawing tools, Retouching tools, Type tools, and Color tools. There are other tools in the box, but we'll talk about color later, and we've already looked at the Screen Mode tools.

A tool's alternates can be selected on the options bar for that tool—click the drop arrow next to the button on the far-left end of the bar, and then choose the alternate tool you want to customize and use.

Understanding the Selection Tools

The tools that allow you to select portions of an image (or portions of a layer within an image) are found at the top of the toolbox. From selecting rectangular and elliptical shapes to selecting by color, these tools make it possible to select a single pixel or an entire freeform shaped section of your image. With some practice, you can master all of them, making the rest of the tools that much more powerful. When you can control which part of your image is selected, you can control where the Paintbrush tool paints, where the Fill tool fills, and where the Retouching tools have their effect.

Starting with the top-left tool and working down, the four Selection tools (and their alternatives) are as follows:

Rectangular Marquee (M)   Drag to select a rectangular section of the image. Once selected, a dashed border will border the area. You can use the SHIFT key as you drag to make the rectangle a perfect square; once you've created the selection, drag with the SHIFT key again to add a section to the selection—it can be a contiguous section, or a rectangular/square region anywhere else on the image. To remove a portion of the selected area from the selection, use the ALT (Windows) or OPTION (Mac) key and drag to select the portion to be removed. Figure 2-22 shows a rectangular selection with a subtracted selection in the center, creating a hole in the selection.

Elliptical Marquee (M)   Working just like the Rectangular Marquee tool, this tool selects round sections of an image. You can use the SHIFT key just as you would with the Rectangular Marquee tool—instead of a perfect square, however, the SHIFT key (used while you're dragging a new selection) allows you to select a perfect circle.

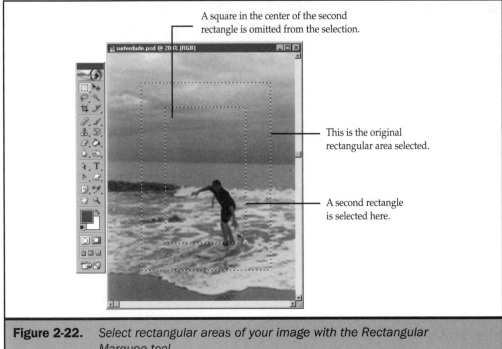

A square in the center of the second rectangle is omitted from the selection.

This is the original rectangular area selected.

A second rectangle is selected here.

Figure 2-22. *Select rectangular areas of your image with the Rectangular Marquee tool.*

Single Row Marquee (M)   Selects a single horizontal row of pixels in your image. As shown in Figure 2-23, a single dashed border appears where you click, spanning the entire width of the image. If you hold the SHIFT key and continue to click other spots on the image, you can select multiple rows, potentially creating a striped effect when you apply another tool (such as the Eraser or Paintbrush) to the selected pixel rows. Displaying the ruler (View | Rulers) will allow you to create the rows (or columns, if using the Single Column Marquee) at regular intervals.

Single Column Marquee (M)   This tool works just like the Single Row Marquee, but selects a vertical column of pixels instead.

Move (V)   This tool does just what the name implies—moves selected content (or the contents of an active layer) when you drag with your mouse. The most common use for the tool is to adjust the position of items within the image—text or a shape or line that's not where you want it. If the Move tool is activated, you can also use the arrow keys to nudge selections or layer content up, down, left, or right. A less common but very powerful use for the Move tool is creating clones. Press the ALT or OPTION key as you drag, and you'll create a clone (duplicate) of the item you're moving, be it an entire layer or a selection within the image or layer. Figure 2-24 shows a series of stacked clones that were created with the Move tool.

Figure 2-23.   *Select horizontal rows in your image in preparation for applying color or effects to the single-pixel strips.*

Figure 2-24.   *Drag with the ALT or OPTION key and create duplicates of your selection or layer.*

Lasso (L)   This tool allows you to create freeform selections, as shown in Figure 2-25. If you hold the ALT or OPTION key and then click and move (as opposed to dragging) the mouse, you can create a selection with straight sides.

Polygonal Lasso (L)   This variation on the Lasso tool creates selections with straight sides, but it doesn't require you to hold the ALT or OPTION key to do it. To select any polygonal shape, just click and move, clicking at each corner in the shape, and coming back to your starting point to close the selection, as shown in Figure 2-26. As with the regular Lasso tool, if you don't come back to the starting point and click, Photoshop will close the shape for you, often with undesirable results.

Magnetic Lasso (L)   The third and final variation on the Lasso tool can be either very handy or very annoying. When you drag to create a selection with this tool, the selection outline hugs the edge of the foreground image, as shown in Figure 2-27. It may hug it accurately, following the edge very neatly, or it may leap inside and outside the edge you wanted it to draw. At each point in the path, a node is created. If a node appears where you don't want it to, press the DELETE key to get rid of it. This only works while you're creating the selection and while the unwanted node is dark.

Figure 2-25.   *Selecting freeform shapes with the Lasso tool allows you to create an entirely new shape to be painted, cloned, or otherwise edited.*

Starting point

Figure 2-26. *Drag to create a freeform selection with straight sides.*

Figure 2-27. *Draw a selection that sticks to the edges of a shape in your image foreground.*

Unlike the Lasso and Polygonal Lasso tools, which both require you to keep dragging from the starting point and back again, the Magnetic Lasso tool works best if you release the mouse when changing direction, clicking and dragging again to continue the selection. You can stop and start as many times as you want until the desired selection is made. Once you return to the starting point or double-click to have Photoshop close the selection for you, the lines connected by points changes to a dashed line and the points disappear.

Magic Wand (W)   To select content of a similar color, use this tool. When you click a spot on an image (or an intentionally chosen pixel, which you'll have to Zoom in to see), the wand goes to work, selecting contiguous pixels that are close to the color of the pixel you clicked on. The options bar allows you to set a Tolerance for the color selection—numbers greater than 32 mean that colors farther from the originally selected pixel will be included in the selection; lower numbers mean the selection will be more restricted, including only pixels very close to the color of the original one. By default, the Contiguous option is on, which means that only contiguous pixels that meet the Tolerance setting will be selected. If you want to include noncontiguous pixels in your selection, turn off the Contiguous option, or hold down the SHIFT key and click elsewhere on the image to tell the wand to select any pixels in that area that are within the tolerance range of the original pixel. Figure 2-28 shows a contiguous range of pixels selected with the default Tolerance setting of 32.

You'll notice on the options bar for all of the selection tools there are four buttons at the beginning of the bar: New Selection, Add to Selection, Subtract from Selection, and Intersect with Selection. These are the button equivalents of some of the results you can achieve with SHIFT-ALT (Windows) or SHIFT-OPTION (Mac) as described earlier as each of the tools was introduced. So, for example, if you want to select a figure-eight shape, use the Elliptical Marquee tool and select a circle or oval. Then click the Add to Selection button on the options bar and select a circle that touches the first one, as shown in Figure 2-29. Voilà! A figure-eight selection is created. You can do the same thing—creating new shapes of all types—with the Rectangular Marquee and Lasso tools.

To turn off any selections you've made, press CTRL-D (Windows) or COMMAND-D (Mac).

Path Selection (A)   Any shape you draw with the Pen tool (covered in the "Working with Painting and Drawing Tools" section, which follows this one) or the various shape tools (with the Paths option set) is a path, and this tool allows you to select it.

Direct Selection (A)   Once a path is selected, this tool allows you to select or edit a segment of the path. As shown in Figure 2-30, a freeform shape drawn with the Pen tool can be edited by selecting the path and dragging the points along the path to change the shape itself.

Figure 2-28.   *Use the Magic Wand tool to select only some of the image, based on color.*

Figure 2-29.   *Use the options bar to create a unique selection; add to, subtract from, and intersect selected areas on your image or layer.*

Figure 2-30.   *Draw a shape with the Pen tool, and then select and edit its path with the Path and Direct Selection tools.*

Measuring with the Rulers

The horizontal and vertical rulers, displayed by choosing View | Rulers, enable you to measure your selections and placements while using the Selection and Move tools. You can also use rulers to help you draw shapes or lines that need to be a specific length or width, and to help you crop your image with either the Crop or Marquee tools. Note that if you crop with the Marquee tool, you need to follow up making the selection with execution of the Image | Crop command. Figure 2-31 shows the two rulers in place and their zero point set to the edge of a rectangular selection (see the guidelines). To set the zero point, click at the intersection of the rulers and drag toward the center of the image until the indicators (one on each ruler) are at the desired spots on both rulers.

If you want to reset the rulers and return the zero points to their default location in the upper-left corner of the image, double-click the box in the upper-left corner where the horizontal and vertical rulers intersect.

Drag out from here to set zero points.

Zero points on both rulers

Figure 2-31.   *Use the rulers to measure your image, selection, or something you're about to draw.*

Working with Painting and Drawing Tools

Tools that allow you to paint and draw allow you to create original artwork and add original content to scanned images and imported graphics created in other applications. Like the editing and retouching tools we will discuss later, the painting and drawing tools can also be used to clean up images, painting out a splotch or re-creating content lost to damage or error. The uses for the painting and drawing tools are limited only by your imagination:

Brush (B)   Called the Paintbrush in Photoshop 6 and earlier versions, the Brush tool is used for painting. You can paint to draw a line, a freeform shape, or to fill in a shape or selected area in your image, as shown in Figure 2-32. As soon as the tool is activated, the options bar offers settings for the size and shape of the brush itself: Mode controls the effect of the brush, Opacity (the amount of paint coverage applied by the brush) is set to 100 percent by default, and Flow controls how quickly paint is dispensed by the brush. Also on the Options bar is an Airbrush tool, which allows you to use the brush with airbrush effects, creating a soft, diffused stroke.

Pencil (B)   Not much mystery here. You can draw thin or thick lines with the Pencil tool, creating straight lines if you hold the SHIFT key as you draw; or you can freeform lines if you want to scribble or create flowing lines as you would with a "real pencil." Many people use the Pencil tool only to target individual pixels when cleaning up choppy edges along a shape's edge. Whatever your purpose in using the Pencil tool, the options bar presents tools for selecting the thickness of the pencil point, and Mode and Opacity settings just like those offered for the Brush tool.

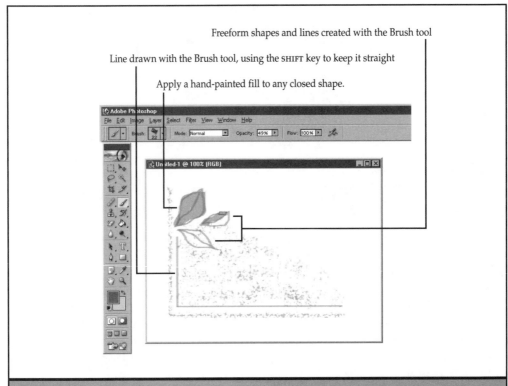

Figure 2-32.   *Use Photoshop's Brush tool to apply paint to your image in a variety of ways.*

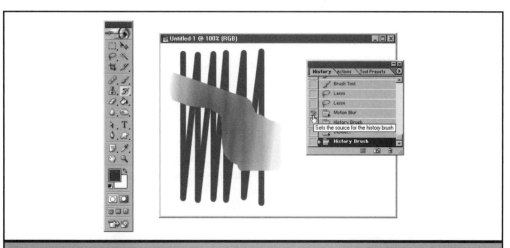

Figure 2-33.   *Turn back the clock and paint in a style or with an effect you applied earlier in your image-editing process.*

History Brush (Y)   Used in conjunction with the History Palette, this tool allows you to go back in time to a brush or effect (such as blur or another filter) you used earlier in your work on the current image and apply that brush style or effect in brush strokes. Of course, you can only go back to a state represented in the History palette. By clicking in the box to the left of the state (a point in time in the History palette), you activate that brush style or effect (see Figure 2-33). Then you go out onto the image and paint, and the style or effect is applied as you paint.

Art History Brush (Y)   As the name implies, this tool is an artistic variation on the History Brush tool. When you choose a point in the image History and use this brush to apply the style or effect applied then, you can also establish settings for different artistic effects, using the Style, Area, and Tolerance tools on the options bar (see Figure 2-34).

The tools in the list that follows create shapes. Before Photoshop version 6, you had to use the Marquee tool to draw rectangles, squares, ovals, and circles, using the Fill tool to create a filled shape. Now there are six variations of Shape tool, each capable of drawing a shape on the active layer, creating a shape layer (created as soon as the shape is drawn, and consisting solely of that shape), or creating a path. When using any of the tools, you can make a shape that's equal in width and height by pressing the SHIFT key while drawing. The six shape tools and their shortcut keys follow:

■ Rectangle (U)

■ Rounded Rectangle (U)

- Ellipse (U)
- Polygon (U)
- Line (U)
- Custom Shape (U)

The Custom Shape tool is one that provides some real artistic freedom for creating original artwork in Photoshop. As soon as the Custom Shape tool is activated, the options bar offers a series of settings, including a Shape palette, as shown in Figure 2-35.

When you go to draw your shape, you have to choose the role that the shape will play in your image. You have three choices: make it a Shape Layer (a shape on its own layer), a Path, or a shape on an existing layer (the Fill Pixels option). The buttons that allow you to make this choice are at the far-left end of the options bar, as shown in Figure 2-36.

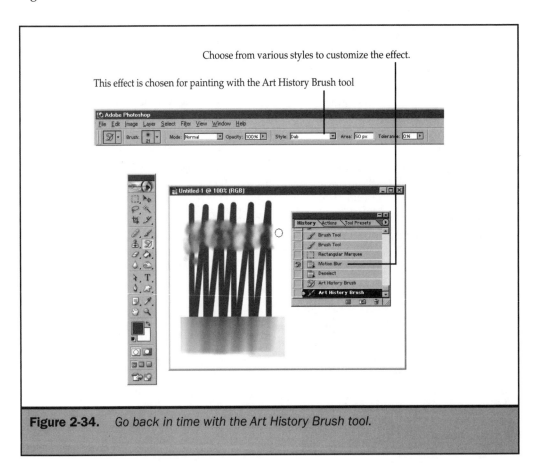

Figure 2-34.   *Go back in time with the Art History Brush tool.*

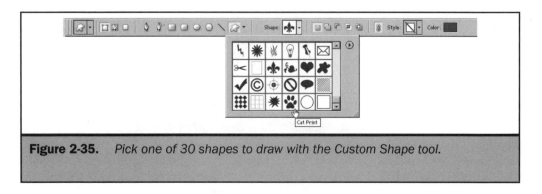

Figure 2-35.   *Pick one of 30 shapes to draw with the Custom Shape tool.*

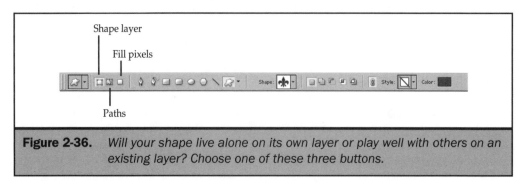

Figure 2-36.   *Will your shape live alone on its own layer or play well with others on an existing layer? Choose one of these three buttons.*

Note

If you opt to draw a shape on its own layer (a Shape Layer), that layer cannot contain anything other than the shape. If you want to add a shape to an existing layer or create a new layer for the shape but retain the ability to add other items to that layer, use the Fill Pixels option on the options bar for any of the shape tools.

We've mentioned paths before, and here are the tools that create and edit them. It would seem that the Pen tool would simply be a variation of the Brush and Pencil tools, but its role is a little more extensive than that. Unlike lines and shapes drawn with the Brush and Pencil tools, the lines and shapes you draw with the Pen tools (Pen and Freeform Pen) create editable paths. You can change the length, angle, and curve of the lines and shapes after you've drawn them, turning, for example, an amoeba into a face. Figure 2-37 shows two shapes, as originally drawn with the pen and then after the path is edited.

Pen (P)   To use the Pen tool, select it, and then click and drag on the image. Click again, and drag in a different direction. You'll see points and anchor points appear as you click and drag, and these are the elements of the path—you can move and delete them later, and add new ones. Figure 2-38 shows a path in progress with the Pen tool.

Freeform Pen (P) Unlike the Pen tool, the Freeform Pen doesn't require clicking and dragging—you simply drag to draw freehand, as you would with the Brush or Pencil tools. As shown in Figure 2-39, once the freeform shape is drawn, its points can be displayed and edited by clicking the shape with the Path Selection tool.

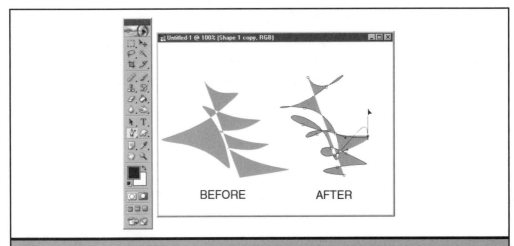

Figure 2-37.   *Drag the points and their controls to change the path anywhere along its length.*

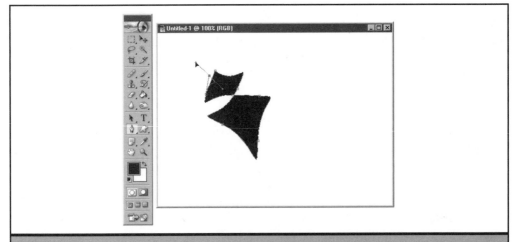

Figure 2-38.   *Draw a closed shape by clicking and dragging to develop a path.*

Figure 2-39.   *Easily drawing shapes of any description, the Freeform Pen's paths can be edited to change the shape you've drawn.*

Add Anchor Point (no shortcut)   Use this tool to add a point to the path. Points may need to be added if you have a long stretch of the path and you need to bend it in the middle.

Delete Anchor Point (no shortcut)   If your hand shook a bit as you used the Freeform or regular Pen tools, you can end up with several points along what should be a long, fluid line with no breaks. Use this tool to remove the unwanted points, or to simply change the shape of any path. By removing points along a curve or on a corner, the shape automatically changes—subtly or dramatically, depending on where the point was and the nature of the shape itself.

Convert Point (no shortcut)   Points either create curves or straight lines. If a point is currently used to create a curve along the path, this tool will change it to a point that creates a straight line, and vice versa. Figure 2-40 shows a Freeform Pen–created shape that's been vastly improved by converting some of its points. To use the Convert Point tool, just select the tool and then click the point you want to convert. When converting a corner or straight-line point to a curve or smooth point, click it and then drag its anchor points to adjust the shape and direction of the line.

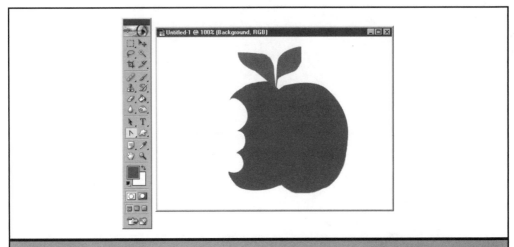

Figure 2-40.   *Smooth jagged edges and add corners where you need them.*

Using the Editing and Retouching Tools

Photoshop's editing and retouching tools enable you to edit scanned images for content and quality, doing everything from removing unwanted periphery to covering unwanted content with something more desirable, from improving an existing image by applying interesting effects and fills to hiding scratches, stains, and mistakes. You can reduce the contrast of an over-exposed photo or make an under-exposed or faded photo brighter. You can take a scanned image that came out too red or too yellow and pump up green or blue to make the image look more realistic. Between the tools set to their defaults and the vast array of controls on the options bar, you can salvage a disastrous image in less time and with less effort than you imagine.

Crop (c)   This tool works very similarly to the Rectangular Marquee tool in that you click and drag to select a rectangular area within the image. The similarity ends there, however; after the selection is made, it can be used to crop the image to include only the content within the selected rectangular area. As shown in Figure 2-41, when the Crop tool is used to select an area, the portions of the image outside the selection are darkened, helping you to imagine how the image will look without that portion. If you like what you see, press ENTER (Windows) or RETURN (Mac) to execute the crop.

You can also crop an image by using the Marquee tool, and then use the Image | Crop command to cut away everything outside the selection.

Figure 2-41.   *Get rid of any unwanted edges with the Crop tool.*

Slice (K)   This tool is used when you're creating graphics for the Web. By slicing a large image (large in terms of physical dimensions, as well as file size), you break it into small sections, which become small files, which will download faster for web site visitors. Figure 2-42 shows an image that will become a large portion of a web page. The image has been sliced into blocks, and the images created from each sliced block (when the file is saved) can be placed in a table on a web page. Using the slices when designing a page is a lot like assembling a puzzle; however, to the site visitor, the image will look like one big picture.

Slice Select (K)   This tool makes it easy to select small slices that can be hard to grab by their borders with your mouse. With Slice Select activated, you can click anywhere inside a slice to select it, and then either drag the slice to move it or click and drag any one of its handles to resize it.

Healing Brush (J)   New to Photoshop 7, the Healing Brush tool lives up to its name. Similar to the Clone Stamp tool, the Healing Brush tool takes a sample from somewhere on the image (you need to ALT/OPTION-click to establish the sample location and choose a Brush size to determine the size of the sample), and then you can paint that sample onto another area. Where the Healing Brush tool differs from and exceeds the restorative capabilities of the Clone Stamp tool is in what is preserved when the Healing Brush tool is used—it removes scratches, dust, creases, and other blemishes, but leaves the texture, lighting, and shading that was originally in place (see Figure 2-43).

Patch (J)   Like patching torn or worn fabric using material from an unseen or unworn portion of the same fabric, the Patch tool lets you take content from one place on the image and patch another spot. Figure 2-44 shows a selected region that needs to be patched—by dragging the selection onto another portion of the image, you tell Photoshop what to use in making the patch.

Note   *When you go to select the spot to be patched, don't be surprised—your mouse pointer will change and look just like the lasso—you use it the same way to select a freeform area.*

Clone Stamp (s)   Copy one portion of your image to another with this tool, after using the ALT or OPTION key to designate which portion to copy. When you ALT/OPTION-click on a place on the image (the size of which is determined by the Brush size you choose), you "sample" the image. Then click where you want to place that sample, and you can cover a scratch, smear, crease, or other eyesore. You can also drag with the Clone Stamp tool, leaving a trail of the sampled section of the image in your wake.

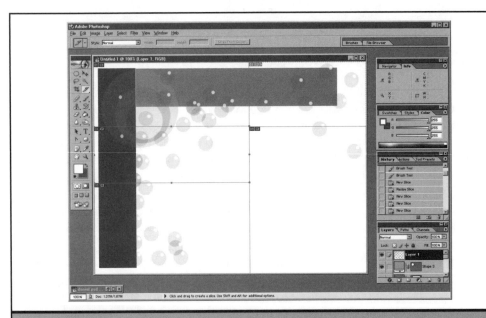

Figure 2-42.   *Slice and dice a large image into manageable blocks for use on the Web.*

The texture, lighting, and shading here (selected by ALT/OPTION-click) will be applied to heal the scratch.

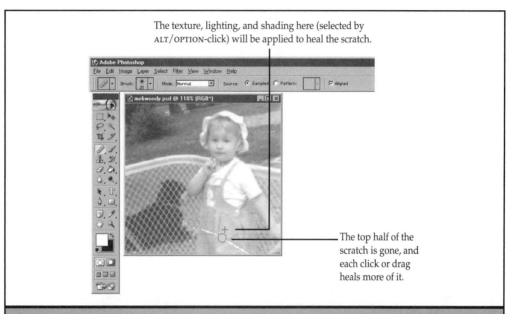

The top half of the scratch is gone, and each click or drag heals more of it.

Figure 2-43. *Maintain the look and feel of an image while healing its wounds.*

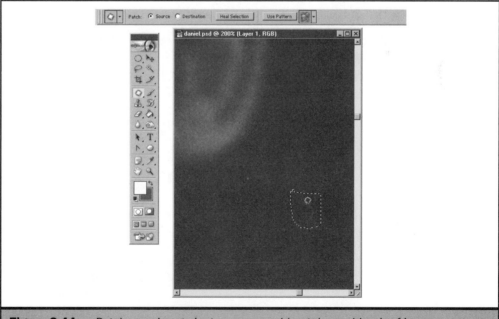

Figure 2-44. *Patch your image just as you would patch an old pair of jeans.*

Pattern Stamp (s) The relationship between this tool and the Clone Stamp is very much like the relationship between the History Brush and the Art History Brush. The Clone Stamp allows you to copy a section of the image to another location in the same image; the Pattern Stamp goes it one better, allowing more creativity. When you choose the Pattern Stamp tool, the options bar acquires an additional option—a Pattern drop-down list, which offers a selection of colored patterns. Choose one, and then click your image with the Pattern Stamp tool—you'll be stamping the pattern onto your image, as shown in Figure 2-45.

Note *Both the Clone Stamp and the Pattern Stamp have an Aligned option (see the options bar while either tool is selected), which makes sure that the same offset is applied to each stamp/stroke made with the tool and allows you to release the mouse after each application of the stamp (whether clicking or painting) without losing reference to the current sampled area. If you turn off the Aligned option, each click or drag of the Stamp tool will reflect the content of the original sampling point.*

Figure 2-45. *Stamp one of the installed or a user-created pattern onto your image, covering blemishes or simply dressing things up.*

Eraser (E)   The most straightforward of the editing tools, the Eraser tool does just what its name implies—it erases. You can choose the size of the eraser by choosing a Brush size on the options bar, choose the shape with the Mode option (Brush, Pencil, or Block), and set the Opacity. You can also use the Erase to History option to restrict your erasure to portions of your image created before a certain point as designated on the History palette. When you erase, it's also important to note that you're only erasing the active layer—if you want to erase everything down to and including the background, merge your layers and then erase the single layer that action creates.

Background Eraser (E)   Another aptly named tool, the Background Eraser tool lets you erase continuously sampled pixels on a layer, leaving transparency in their wake. This enables you to erase the background while leaving items in the foreground untouched. Figure 2-46 shows the Background Eraser tool at work. The grid appears where the sky has been removed from behind the trees that live on the same layer. Note that while using the tool, you need to keep an eye on the crosshair in the middle of the cursor—this is known as the *hotspot*, and it shows you exactly which color is being sampled, which controls which pixels are erased from within the confines of the entire pointer.

Figure 2-46.   *Erase the background on a particular layer without disturbing the content in the foreground.*

Magic Eraser (E)   The Magic Eraser tool works very much like the Magic Wand, but instead of selecting pixels, it erases them. To use the tool, select it, and then click on a pixel in the image—preferably a pixel that's the color you want to erase from the image. After establishing the color, you can drag the eraser across your image to erase only pixels that are the same color as the first pixel you clicked. You can set the Tolerance just like you do for the Magic Wand, and that sets the threshold for the color erasure; higher tolerances will allow the erasure of pixels that are farther from an exact color match, and lower tolerances will restrict the erasure to pixels that are exactly the same as or very similar to the first pixel you clicked with the tool. Figure 2-47 shows only white content being erased.

Note   *The Contiguous option (see the options bar for both the Magic and Background Eraser) is on by default. It confines the erasure to pixels that are touching. If you turn this option off, you can erase pixels all over the image, whether the erased areas are touching or not. The Tolerance setting still ultimately controls which pixels are erased, however.*

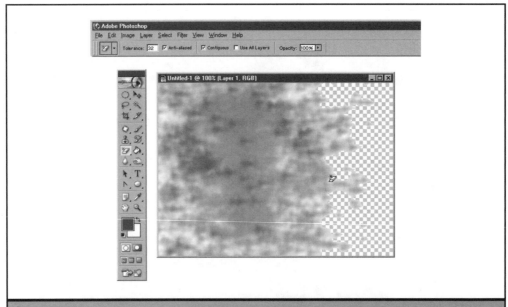

Figure 2-47.   *Choose which color pixels you want to erase with the Magic Eraser.*

The starting color as you drag from left to right

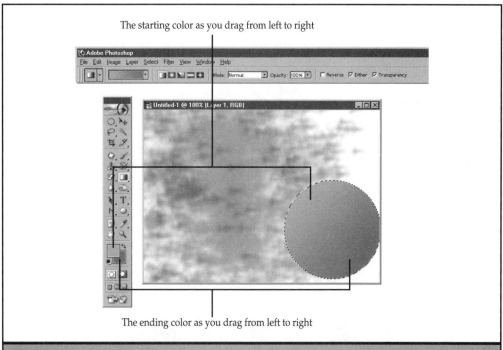

The ending color as you drag from left to right

Figure 2-48.   *Use the options bar to choose the type of gradient (Linear, Radial, Angle, Reflected, or Diamond), and then drag to fill a layer or selection.*

Gradient (G)   This fill tool enables you create a shaded fill, going from one color (the Foreground color in your Color Picker) to another (the Background color in your Color Picker) with a simple drag of your mouse. You can apply the gradient to the entire width and height of the image, filling a layer, for example, or you can select an area and apply the gradient to that region only. Figure 2-48 shows a Marquee-created selection with a gradient fill applied to it.

Paint Bucket (G)   Very simply, this tool fills layers, selected areas, and areas of similarly colored pixels with a solid color. The threshold for "similarly colored" is controlled by the Tolerance setting, and the color it applies is based on the selected Foreground color in your Color Picker.

Blur (R)   Use this tool to reduce the contrast between contiguous pixels in your image, creating a blurred effect. If you hold the ALT or OPTION key as you drag, you can sharpen the image, increasing the interpixel contrast. Figure 2-49 shows the Blur tool being used to make items in the background less sharp, thus allowing a central object to stand out by comparison. You can use the option bar's Strength setting to control the degree of blur you apply as you drag—a low percentage will have a subtle effect, and a high percentage will have a much more dramatic effect.

Sharpen (R)   The opposite of the Blur tool, the Sharpen tool increases the contrast between contiguous pixels. If you hold down the ALT or OPTION key as you drag with this tool, you'll create a Blur effect.

Why make it possible to blur with the Sharpen tool and sharpen with the Blur tool? To save you a trip to the toolbox as you apply effects that are often used in the same image.

Smudge (R)   Like blending chalk or pastel crayon strokes with your finger, the Smudge tool smears pixels in your image as you drag your mouse. The mouse pointer, as shown in Figure 2-50, even looks like a fingertip. You can also set the Strength of the tool, controlling the intensity of the smudged effect, and you can smudge through all layers or just the active one. The Finger Painting option on the options bar allows you to begin each smudge stroke with a dab of the Foreground color set through the Color Picker. If the Finger Painting option is off, each drag with the mouse smudges with only the colors at your starting point.

Figure 2-49.   *Control viewer focus with the Blur tool.*

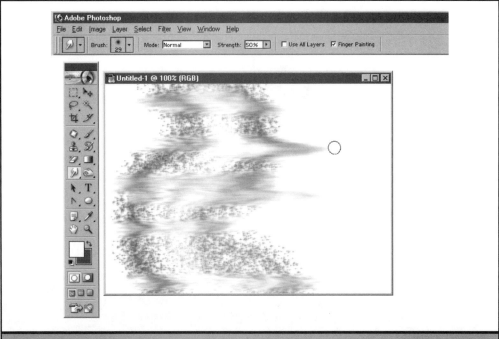

Figure 2-50.   *Diffuse a sharp edge or really smear the colors in your image with the Smudge tool.*

Dodge (o)   The Dodge tool lightens the pixels through which you drag it, and allows you to control which portions of the image are lightened—the Shadows, Midtones, or Highlights. These Range options are found on the options bar, where you'll also find an Exposure option to control the degree of lightening applied, as shown in Figure 2-51. Don't forget to adjust the Brush size to control the number of pixels you lighten in a single drag of the mouse.

Burn (o)   The opposite of the Dodge tool, the Burn tool darkens pixels. Use the options bar to choose a Brush size, choose which Range of colors to darken, and set the Exposure. The Burn tool is great for over-exposed images, revealing detail lost to a bright flashbulb or improper lighting in general.

Note   *You can reverse the Dodge and Burn tools with the ALT or OPTION key. This can save you the time and trouble of switching tools when you have an image with areas that are too dark and others that are too light.*

Figure 2-51. *Details lost forever to a shot that's just too dark? Not with the Dodge tool to lighten them.*

Sponge (O)   Like washing out a watercolor painting by swabbing at it with a sponge, the Sponge tool reduces the color saturation in your image. You can also use it to increase saturation, by changing the Mode (see the options bar) to Saturate. The Flow option controls the intensity of the saturation or desaturation, and the Brush size controls how much of the image you affect with a single drag of your mouse.

Working with Type and Annotation Tools

The Type tools allow you to bring text to your images (as shown in Figure 2-52), adding names, labels, instructions, or creating patterns through the artistic use of repeated or overlapping text. You can type horizontally or vertically, and in both Type and Type Mask Modes, adding legible text to your image on its own layer or removing content in the shape of text. You can type short bursts of text—a single word, a short phrase, or entire paragraphs. You can add text to your Photoshop 7 images with greater confidence, thanks to the inclusion of a spell checker with this latest version. The tools for inserting type are as follows:

- ■ Horizontal Type (T)
- ■ Vertical Type (T)
- ■ Horizontal Type Mask (T)
- ■ Vertical Type Mask (T)

Figure 2-52.   *Type your text and then format it, or apply the options first and then type the text.*

To use the Horizontal and Vertical Type tools, click the image where you want the text to start, and then simply type your text. You can use the ENTER (Windows) or RETURN (Mac) key to create a line break, or keep typing in an uninterrupted string. As soon as you activate the Type tool in any of its variations, the options bar offers settings for choosing the font, style (bold, italic, regular), size (in points), anti-aliasing method (to prevent jagged edges), and color of your text. You can also set the alignment (left, center, or right), handy for text that will run to more than one line.

The Horizontal and Vertical Type Mask tools work similarly, except the text is not placed on its own layer—it becomes a mask on the active layer. You can press DELETE to remove the content within the masked area (exposing the background or layers underneath the active layer), drag the masked area to move the content (leaving a cut-out behind and the text in place wherever you place it), or use one of the painting or drawing tools to change the appearance of the content within the masked area. Figure 2-53 shows an image with portions of it deleted by a type mask, revealing the pattern-filled background behind the image.

The text was cut away, exposing the background pattern.

Painting across the selection only applies paint within the letters.

Figure 2-53. *Use text like a cookie cutter, removing portions of your image. It can also be used to create a mask, or selection, to control the use of other tools.*

The remaining text-related tools allow you to place comments, suggestions, or instructions on an image for others to refer to or as reminders for yourself.

> **Tip**
>
> *Both the Type and Type Mask tools (in all their variations) can be used to type paragraph text to a confined area. Instead of clicking to mark where the text will begin, click and drag a rectangle to designate the area in which text will be typed. When you type the text, it will wrap to fit within the rectangle you drew.*

Notes (N)   Use this tool to place comments or instructions on the image. As shown in Figure 2-54, you can type in a small text window, and then after closing the text window, an icon remains on the image to indicate the presence of a note. To read a note, double-click the icon.

Audio Annotation (N)   If your computer has sound capability and you're interested in leaving audio notes for yourself or others, click this tool and then click the image—preferably on the spot to which your annotation pertains, or in an out-of-the way spot (like a corner) if the annotation applies to the image as a whole. Once you click the image, a dialog box appears, indicating that you should click Start to begin recording (see Figure 2-55). Say whatever you want to say, and then click Stop. As soon as you click Stop, a small speaker icon appears that will play your audio annotation when clicked.

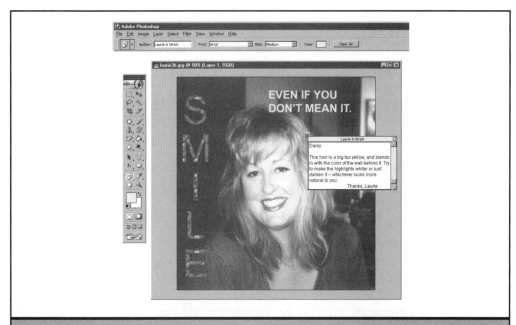

Figure 2-54. *Leave instructions for the next person who'll be working on the image.*

Figure 2-55. *Record comments for yourself or others to listen to as they view and work on an image.*

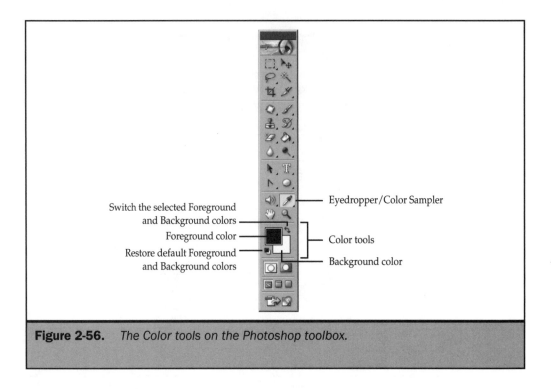

Switch the selected Foreground and Background colors

Foreground color

Restore default Foreground and Background colors

Eyedropper/Color Sampler

Color tools

Background color

Figure 2-56.   *The Color tools on the Photoshop toolbox.*

Note   *When clicking an annotation to play it, be sure you're not using the Audio Annotation tool—use any other tool instead. If you activate the Audio Annotation tool and then click the image (intending to click one of the annotation icons), you may inadvertently miss the icon and open the recording dialog box to create another annotation rather than playing an existing one.*

Using the Color Tools

Photoshop's color tools are very sophisticated, but they're friendly at the same time, making it easy to select colors for any aspect of your image, used in conjunction with virtually any tool. See Figure 2-56 to help you identify Photoshop's color-application tools (the Color Picker, Eyedropper, and Color Sampler) and read on to find out how they work.

Eyedropper (I)   If you already see the color you want to use for your Foreground color on a new selection, shape, or layer in your image, use the Eyedropper tool to sample the color and make it the official Foreground color. As soon as you click the tool and then click the pixel containing the color you want to use, the Info palette displays the RGB (Red, Green, and Blue) levels for the color, and the Color palette displays the same levels along with colored sliders visually showing the three color components (see Figure 2-57). If you want to use the Eyedropper tool to set your Background color, press and hold the ALT or OPTION key when you click to select a pixel—you aren't restricted to pixels in your active image, either. Click any other open image, or on any element within the image window, or even within the Photoshop desktop.

Color Sampler (I)   This tool works like the Eyedropper tool in terms of how it samples a pixel within your image and displays the color's statistics on the Info palette. But instead of the Foreground color changing to the color of the sampled pixel, the Info palette displays an expanded set of statistics (see Figure 2-58), including CMYK (Cyan, Magenta, Yellow, and Black) levels. The Color palette is unaffected by your use of the Color Sampler, as is the Color Picker. What you will see in addition to the Info palette's data are small sample symbols on the surface of your image—one at each position you clicked to sample a color. You can choose to sample a single pixel, or a 3 by 3 or 5 by 5 Average, both of which will use the pixels surrounding the one you click to gather the statistics displayed in the Info palette. You can drag the symbols around to sample a new area, and you can right-click (Windows) or CONTROL-click (Mac) a symbol and choose from a context menu of color choices—Actual color, Proof color, Grayscale, RGB color, Web color, HSB color (Hue, Saturation, and Brightness), CMYK color, and Lab color. You can also Delete the symbol, deleting with it the statistics for that pixel or cluster of pixels, depending on your sampling options.

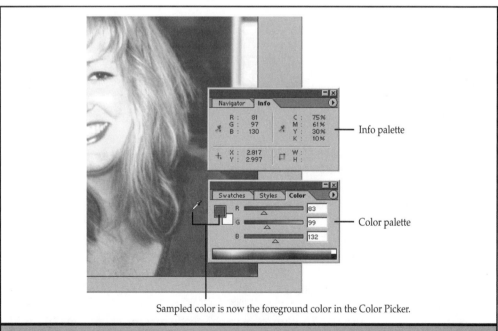

Sampled color is now the foreground color in the Color Picker.

Figure 2-57.   *Pick a color you've already used and apply it to something else in the same image.*

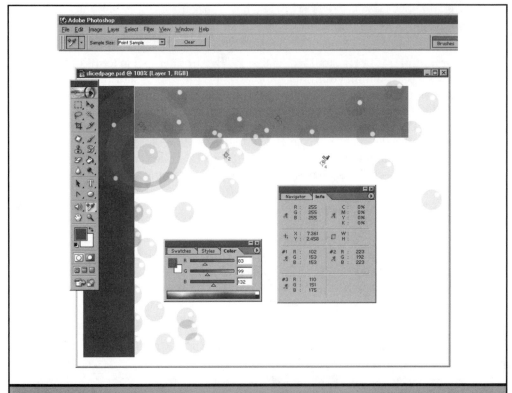

Figure 2-58. *If you want to see all the statistical color data on a particular pixel, click it with the Color Sampler and watch the Info palette.*

Note *Your sampled pixels remain sampled, and the symbols remain on the image (though hidden) even if you click and use another tool and continue to edit the image. As soon as you click the Color Sampler again, you'll see them reappear. If you want to get rid of them, point to one of the samples (your mouse pointer will turn to a small, black arrowhead when you're close enough to the sample), and right-click (Windows) or CONTROL-click (Mac) each one. When the context menu appears, choose Delete. If you prefer an even shorter shortcut, you can also ALT-click or OPTION-click on the symbols to delete them directly.*

Measure (I) Not really a color tool, per se, this tool appears here because it shares a button space in the toolbox with the Eyedropper tool and the Color Sampler. You can use the Measure tool to check the distance between objects in your image, the length or width of items in the image or between items and the edge of the image. As you click (to establish a starting point) and drag, the measurement appears in the Info palette, as shown in Figure 2-59. If you hold down the ALT or OPTION key as you drag, you can click and drag a second line from the first line's end point, creating an onscreen protractor for measuring angles. Of course, as soon as you click and drag from a new starting point (with or without the ALT/OPTION variable) or switch to another tool, the measurement is gone from both the image surface and the Info palette. If you don't need to measure again and want to get rid of a measurement you've already created, drag it out of the image window.

Color Picker (no shortcut)   This is the heart of Photoshop's color tools, at least as far as the toolbox is concerned. There are a lot of color features—preferences, presets, and customization tools—that you'll find out about later in the book. But for choosing a color and applying it to your image, the Color Picker is *it*.

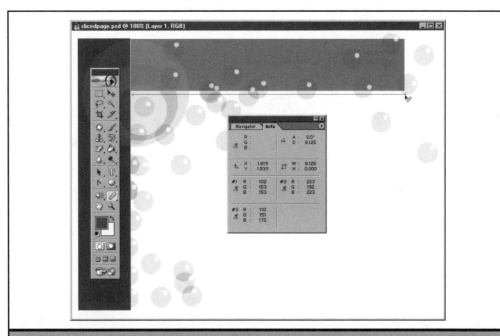

Figure 2-59.   *Use the Measure tool to check space, distances, lengths, and widths within your image.*

The Color Picker consists of four tools:

Foreground Color (no shortcut)   This is the color that will be applied by the Brush, Pencil, Airbrush, Gradient, Shape, and Paint Bucket tools. When you click the Foreground color button, the Color Picker dialog box opens, as shown in Figure 2-60. From this dialog box, you can click the color you want, or you can select a range of colors using the vertical spectrum slider, or you can enter the color levels (using HSB, Lab, RGB, or CMYK models). If you click the Only Web Colors option at the bottom of the dialog box, you will see only the web-safe palette. Click the Custom button if you want to choose from Pantone, Focoltone, and Trumatch colors, among other popular palettes.

Background Color (no shortcut)   The Background color is used by the Eraser tool, the Gradient tool, and the Canvas Size command. Click it to open the same Color Picker dialog box you see if you click the Foreground Color button.

Default Colors (D)   Click this button to return the Foreground and Background colors to Black and White, respectively.

Switch Colors (x)   If you want the current Foreground color to be the Background color (or vice versa), click this button.

Working in Editing and Mask Modes

Photoshop gives you two ways to work: Standard Mode, in which you're editing by adding and deleting image content and changing the appearance of elements within your image; and Quick Mask Mode, in which you're preparing to perform certain editing tasks that require masking off, or protecting, sections of your image. To switch between these modes, click the Edit in Standard Mode or Edit in Quick Mask Mode buttons on the toolbox (see Figure 2-61), or press the Q key, which is the shortcut that allows you to toggle between these two modes.

While you're in Standard Mode, all of the tools and palettes function as I've described them thus far—paint brushes apply paint in the color designated in the Foreground Color box, the Type tool adds text to your image, the retouching tools clean up the image, applying content to obscure problems. When you switch to Quick Mask Mode, however, things change. If you use the Brush tool in this mode, instead of painting in a color, you apply what looks like a red wash to your image. That red wash is a mask; it indicates which parts of your image will not be selected, and therefore protected, from editing once you return to Standard Mode.

Figure 2-62 shows the Brush tool being used to paint a mask over portions of an image, and Figure 2-63 shows the resulting selection that appears when the image returns to Standard Mode. Only the area within the flashing dashed border can be edited in Standard Mode—that is, until you press CTRL-D (Windows) or COMMAND-D (Mac) to remove any selections.

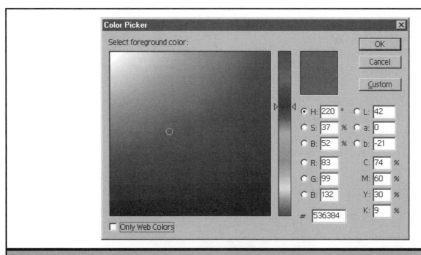

Figure 2-60.   *Choose the color with which you want to paint, draw, or fill your image.*

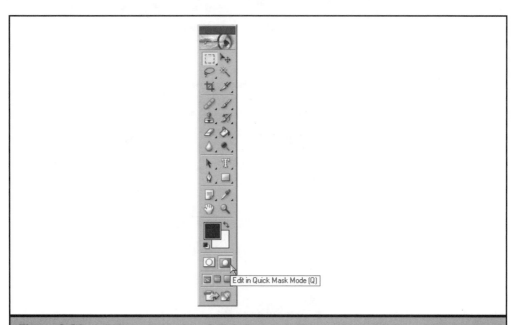

Figure 2-61.   *Editing or masking? Pick the mode that suits your task.*

Figure 2-62. *Paint a mask on with the Brush tool, draw a mask with the Pencil tool, or draw shapes (with the Paths setting in force) to mask areas of the image, allowing all other areas to be edited.*

Figure 2-63. *Back in Standard Mode, what was not masked is now selected, prepared for any editing you want to do.*

| Note | *If you were thinking that color had no role while you're working in Quick Mask Mode, think again! If you want to unmask a masked area in Quick Mask Mode, paint with White. To apply a mask, paint with Black. If your Foreground and Background colors are currently set to Black and White (respectively), click the Switch Foreground and Background Colors button to make White the color you'll paint with, removing masks where you've already applied them. Switch back to Black in the foreground to keep masking new areas.* |

Saving and Applying Tool Presets

New to Photoshop 7 is the ability to save tool *presets*, or sets of preferred options. With presets, you can customize a tool to work the way you want it to work and not have to reset the options each time you use the tool. In addition, you can create multiple presets for an individual tool; for example, save a set of options for when you're working on a particular image, and save another set of options for when you're creating images for the Web rather than print. You can set presets for any tool and save them with names of your choosing. Don't forget to make the names specific, so you can tell your presets apart!

To create a tool preset, click a tool, and then use the options bar to customize its functioning. If it's a tool that uses a brush setting, choose a brush size and style, set an opacity, flow, pressure, tolerance, whatever options are available, and adjust them as needed. When the tool's options are just where you want them, click the Tool Presets palette tab, and then click the Create New Tool Preset button at the bottom of the palette (see Figure 2-64). A dialog box appears, into which you can type a name for your preset. Photoshop will suggest a name based on the settings you chose, but you can edit it as needed to help you identify the preset (and tell it from any others for the same tool) in the future. Click OK to save the name, and you'll see the new preset appear in the Tool Presets palette.

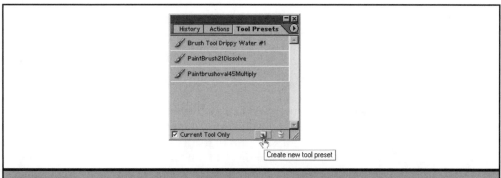

Figure 2-64. *Do you have a special brush you like to use for certain images? Save the brush and options bar settings so you can quickly go back to those settings when you need them.*

To apply a preset, click the tool and observe the Tool Presets palette—the ones that "came with" Photoshop are there, along with any you created. Just click the one you want to use and note the changes in the options bar settings; the preset settings are now in effect, and the tool is ready for your use.

You can always edit a preset by applying it and then deleting the preset (drag it to the trash can in the Tool Presets palette). Adjust the options bar settings and repeat the tool preset creation process—you can apply the same name again because you deleted the incorrect version.

If you click the Tool drop-down list on the options bar (after clicking any tool in the toolbox), you'll notice a Current Tool Only check box. The check box also appears at the bottom of the Tool Presets palette. This box is checked by default. If yours is not checked, you'll see all the tools listed in the Tool Presets palette, no matter which tool is selected on the toolbox at the time.

Viewing and Working with Palettes

Speaking of palettes—and we have looked at quite a few so far in this chapter—you can display any of Photoshop's 16 different palettes (see Figures 2-65 and 2-66, which show the Windows and Mac palettes, respectively)—including the Brushes palette, brought down from the Docking Well—in any combination, in any configuration onscreen, at any time. They can be minimized so that you only see their title bars, resized, stacked on top of each other, and docked in the Docking Well to get them out of the way. Palettes are very important to your successful use of Photoshop—they provide information, options, and controls for the tools and the images you create and edit with them.

Displaying, Arranging, and Docking Palettes

To display a palette, choose it by name from the Window menu. If the palette is already onscreen (but another palette from its group is already on top of it), the one you chose from the Window menu will become the selected palette in that group. If you want to turn a palette off entirely, click the close button in the upper-right corner (for Windows users) or the upper-left corner (for Mac users). You can also click it again in the Window menu to toggle it off.

As far as the palette groupings are concerned—History, Actions, and Tool Presets are grouped, as are Styles, Swatches, and Color, for example—you aren't stuck with these collections. You can move palettes around to form new groups. To move a palette from its current group to another, click and drag it by its tab, releasing it atop the target group (see Figure 2-67). Similarly, you can create a single-tab palette (leaving a palette all by itself) by dragging a palette tab out onto the workspace and releasing it there.

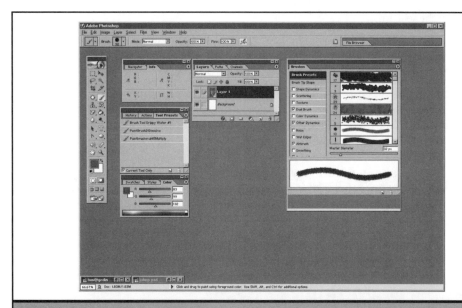

Figure 2-65.   *Probably too many to display all at once, Photoshop's palettes control and display information about every aspect of your image.*

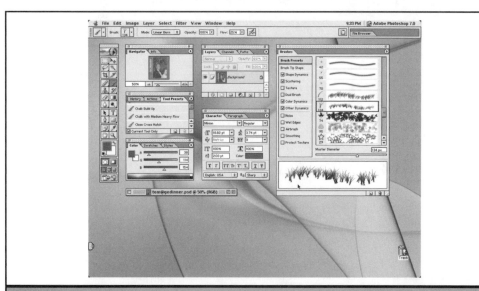

Figure 2-66.   *The complete set of palettes as seen in Photoshop running in a Macintosh environment.*

Consider these additional palette options:

- Moving palettes is easy—just click and drag the palette's title bar (the colored bar above the tabs) and release the palette where it will be available but not overlapping anything else you might need to access.

- Docking palettes (putting them in the docking well) requires use of the Palette menu, accessed by clicking the triangle button on the right side of the palette (see Figure 2-68). The first command is always Dock to Palette Well, and if chosen, the active palette will move to the well, where its tab will appear. To access a palette that's docked, click its tab—the palette displays full size, just below the docking well. To undock, drag the tab back to the desired palette group (or out onto the workspace if you want it to be in a window by itself).

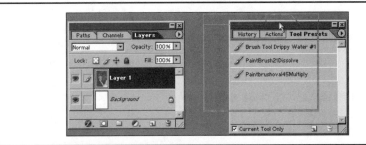

Figure 2-67. *If you want to regroup your palettes, drag them one at a time to their new homes.*

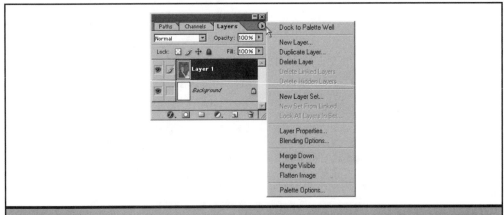

Figure 2-68. *Options for the display, function, and content of a palette are available through this menu.*

- Resize a palette by pointing to any edge or to the lower-right corner of the palette. When your mouse pointer turns to a double arrow, drag your mouse outward to make the palette bigger, inward to make it smaller. Obviously, if you're dragging from a left or right side, you're going to make the palette wider or narrower, and if you're dragging from the top or bottom, you'll make it taller or shorter. For Windows users, dragging from the lower-left corner allows you to adjust the height and the width at the same time by dragging diagonally. Figure 2-69 shows a palette being resized on the Mac, with OS X running.

Note   *You can resize only those palettes that vary in size depending on the information they're displaying—the History and Layers palettes, for example. The Info, Color, Character, and Paragraph palettes cannot be resized.*

- Minimize the palettes by double-clicking the bar across the top of the palette group's box. If the palette is at its full size, double-clicking will reduce it to a title bar and the tab strip. Double-click again, and the palette is back to full size.

Conceivably, you can create a single palette group of all 16 palettes, making it possible to have all of them onscreen at one time, in a very wide window. To activate an individual palette in that window, simply click its tab or choose it by name from the Window menu. When you add the palettes to a palette window, at first they'll be very tightly grouped, and some of them may be illegible because of tab overlap. Simply point to the side of the palette and, when your mouse pointer turns to a double arrow, drag outward to increase the width of the palette and make room for all the tabs to be read.

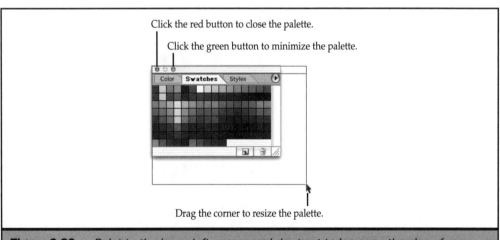

Click the red button to close the palette.

Click the green button to minimize the palette.

Drag the corner to resize the palette.

Figure 2-69.   *Point to the lower-left corner and drag out to increase the size of your palette. Here the Swatches palette is resized in a Mac OS X environment.*

To access options for the palette, click the right-pointing triangle on the right side of the palette. A menu of commands related to tools controlled by or displayed within the palette appears, from which you can make selections.

Saving and Applying Workspace Presets

The way your palettes and toolbox are displayed and arranged can be key to your efficient and effective work in Photoshop. Some people like to have many palettes open at once, and some people like to have just one or two open at a time so as not to clutter their workspace. Further, the arrangement that works for one image or task may not work for another image or task, simply because different jobs often require different tools.

To facilitate this phenomenon, Photoshop now offers you the ability to save workspace presets. Like a tool preset, a workspace preset is a group of settings that can be applied quickly whenever you need them, but instead of applying to the way a tool works, workspace presets apply to the way your workspace is arranged. Say, for example, you like to see only the Layers, History, and Color palettes when you're creating web graphics, and you like to have the palettes, image window, and toolbox close to the center of the workspace so all your tools are close together. In Photoshop 7, you can save that arrangement and give it a name Then by selecting the preset by that name, you can automatically arrange your workspace the next time you're about to work on a graphic bound for the Web. You can also save a workspace preset for working on specific images, specific types of editing, or specific tools—any task or image that you work on repeatedly can have its own workspace preset.

Saving a workspace preset is easy. Just arrange the workspace as you like it, including the position, size, and grouping of your palettes, and then choose Window | Workspace | Save Workspace. In the resulting dialog box (see Figure 2-70), type a name for the workspace. You'll want to choose a name that describes the workspace in some way—the job it's best suited to or the type of images for which you intend to use it—and then click Save.

Once you've created a workspace preset, you can apply it by choosing it by name from the Window | Workspace submenu. Figure 2-71 shows a series of workspace presets in the menu.

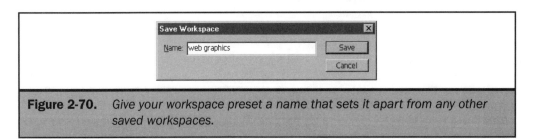

Figure 2-70.   *Give your workspace preset a name that sets it apart from any other saved workspaces.*

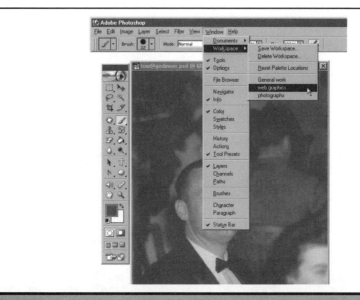

Figure 2-71.   *You can save as many workspace presets as you have different images, tasks, and ways of working.*

Working with Multiple Images

When you have more than one image open at a time, your workspace can get a bit busy and you can get confused. Any number of mishaps can occur if you have too much going on in the Photoshop desktop—accidentally clicking the wrong image window, closing one image when you meant to close the other, pasting content from one image into another when you meant to paste within the same image. Some tips for managing multiple image windows follow:

■ Minimize the image you're not working on. If you're using Photoshop in a Windows environment, click the Minimize button in the upper-right corner of the window, or click the Photoshop icon in the upper-left and choose Minimize from the resulting menu. If you're on a Macintosh running OS 9.*x*, click the window-shade button in the upper-right corner to collapse the window in place. In Mac OS X, you can click the yellow minimize button in the top left of the window and watch the window shrink to the dock. In any case, the image window will be reduced to a title bar; in the case of Windows, the minimized title bar will move to the lower-left corner of the Photoshop desktop (see Figure 2-72). To restore it to its previous size (the last size in which you were working on it), double-click the title bar. Figures 2-73 and 2-74 show the Mac OS 9.*x* and OS X windows as they minimize.

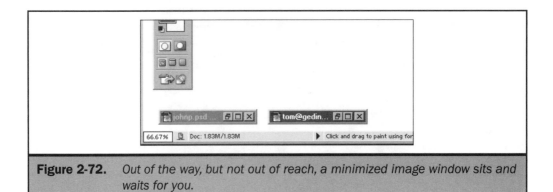

Figure 2-72. *Out of the way, but not out of reach, a minimized image window sits and waits for you.*

Figure 2-73. *A minimized window in Mac OS 9 stays in its place.*

Figure 2-74. *Watch as the window shrinks into the dock in Mac OS X.*

- Make sure your inactive title bar and active title bar colors are very different. If you're a Windows user, this is done through the Display Properties dialog box (right-click or CONTROL-click your Desktop and choose Properties, and then use the Appearance tab to adjust the settings). By default, the active title bar is dark blue, and the inactive title bar is gray. This may not be dynamic enough for you to notice which image window is the active one (should two or more be open), so you might consider a brighter color for the active title bar.

- If you're copying and pasting between two image windows, keep the windows side by side, rather than overlapping. This prevents your accidentally activating (clicking in) the wrong window, which is easy to do if they're stacked and you can't see all of both windows. If you think there isn't room to keep them both open side by side, remember that you can zoom in on the area to be edited in both windows, and then resize (shrink) the image windows so only that area is visible. You can use the Hand tool to move the image around in the small window should you need to edit multiple areas of an image.

Saving Photoshop Files

By default, when you save an image that you created entirely in Photoshop (as opposed to saving a file of another graphic format that was created in another program), the image is saved in PSD format. PSD is Photoshop's default format, and it allows you to keep your layers, paths, channels, and all the Photoshop-specific information with the file. You can save your Photoshop creations in virtually any other graphic file format: JPG, GIF, BMP, PCX, TIF, EPS, TGA. You can also go through a Save for Web procedure that prepares images for use on the Web, saving them in web-safe formats (GIF, JPG, PNG) and allowing you to control their quality and file size for optimal web use.

As soon as you start working on a new image, you should save the file. Choose File | Save, or press CTRL-S (Windows) or COMMAND-S (Mac) to open the Save As dialog box (see Figure 2-75). Give the file a name and choose a place to save it. If you're not going to save it in PSD format, click the Format drop-down list, choose the format in which the file should be saved, and then click the Save button to save the file. If you chose a format other than PSD, you may be presented with an Options dialog box, through which you can customize the way the file is saved in that format. Figure 2-76 shows the Mac OS X Save As dialog box, with its navigation tools displayed.

Beyond establishing a name, location, and format for your saved file, saving early in the creation and/or editing process has another important benefit—it makes it easier and faster to save as you continue to work. Don't forget the Save command's keyboard shortcut CTRL/COMMAND-S. Every time you make a change, add a layer, edit something, delete something—do anything you'd hate to have to do again—save the file by pressing CTRL/COMMAND-S. Even if you're not a fan of keyboard shortcuts (some people find them hard to remember), commit this one to memory so you can quickly and easily save your files at frequent intervals.

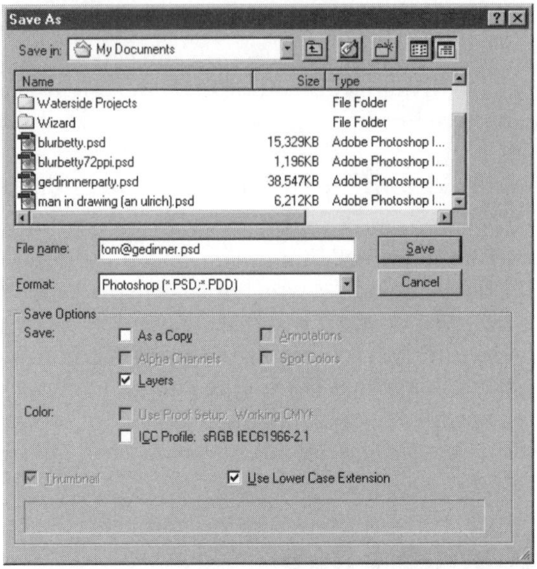

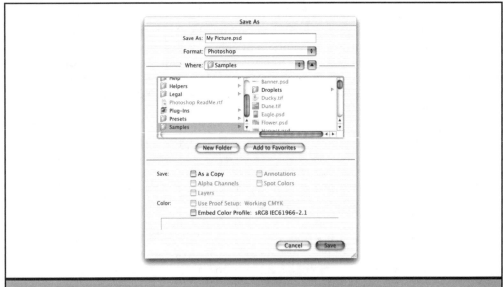

Figure 2-75. *Save early and often to protect your work.*

Figure 2-76. *The new look of the Save As dialog box in Mac OS X*

Using the Save As Command

Once you've saved a file, if you want to change its name, format, or location, you'll have to use the File | Save As command to get the Save As dialog box open again. Once open, you can change the file name, choose another folder or drive to save it to, and even select a different format for the file. As soon as you click Save this time, however, the version of the file you had open is closed, and the new version is left open onscreen. This is done to protect the previous version of the file, based on the assumption that you changed the file's name, location, or format so you'd have two versions of the file and you now want to work on the new one. You can reopen the previous version (File | Open Recent) if you want to work on both versions at the same time.

Note   *While you can choose web-safe formats from the Format drop-down list in the Save and Save As dialog boxes, this is not the same as choosing File | Save for Web. If your image will be used on a web page, don't skip this step. You can read all about creating and saving images for the Web in Chapters 17, 18, and 19.*

Accessing Adobe Online

To visit Adobe's web site and its pages devoted to Photoshop, click the Go to Adobe Online link at the top of the toolbox. Note that your mouse pointer turns to a pointing hand, indicating that this is a hyperlink, and not one of the regular toolbox tools. Of course, you'll need to be connected to the Internet in order to visit the site; but even if you aren't, a dialog box will appear to offer you the chance to access Updates (product updates, additions, and new content) and Preferences (so you can customize the way Adobe Online looks and works for you). See Figure 2-77. If you're not online, click the Go Online button. If you're already connected to the Internet, click the Updates or Preferences button to go to the Adobe site and begin exploring the Photoshop offerings available there.

Activating ImageReady

The toolbox also contains a button you can click to Jump to ImageReady. The shortcut is CTRL-SHIFT-M (Windows) or COMMAND-SHIFT-M (Mac). Click the button (see Figure 2-78) to start the ImageReady application in a new Photoshop desktop. There is no need to exit Photoshop—in fact, you'll find that unless your computer is short on system resources, you can easily keep both applications open and work between the applications, copying content from images in one to images in the other, taking advantage of what each application does best as you edit an image bound for the Web. You'll find out more about ImageReady in Chapters 18 and 19.

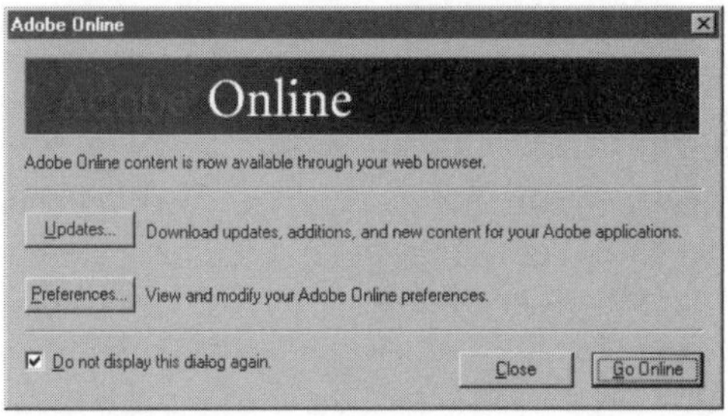

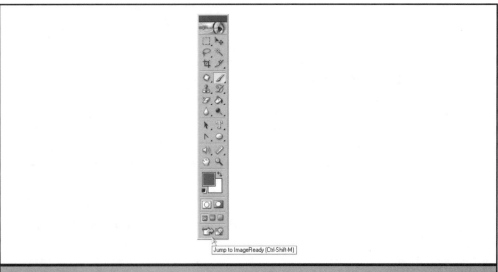

Figure 2-77. Adobe's web site is accessible through the toolbox in version 7.

Figure 2-78. Click here to jump to ImageReady.

Summary

The goal of this chapter was to give you a good foundation for navigating and using the Photoshop interface menus, tools, and palettes, as well as some of the dialog boxes that appear when you use these features. You can refer to the descriptions of individual interface elements as you move through the book and begin to use aspects of Photoshop that are new to you. Of course, all the features discussed in this chapter are also covered in detail in subsequent chapters in this book, where you'll see them used in conjunction with specific images and tasks. Think of this chapter as a road map—use it to start exploring now!

The
Complete
Reference

Chapter 3

Customizing Photoshop's Preferences

Photoshop's default settings for its tools and windows are designed to suit most users and most jobs. While this is great most of the time, you will probably want to adjust the way Photoshop works, at least in one respect or another, at some point. Photoshop's Preferences dialog box provides one-stop shopping for all the changes you need to make; through the Color Settings dialog box, you can customize how colors appear and are applied to just about any kind of image, be it bound for printing or viewing online.

Understanding Photoshop's Default Settings

Photoshop's defaults are based on the needs of the average user who will be producing images for print. The shortcuts, cursors, units of measure, and display settings are designed to provide a working environment that you can use simply. You'll find these settings in the Preferences dialog box, which appears when you choose Edit | Preferences if you're a Windows user, or Photoshop | Preferences if you're on a Mac. In either case, once the Preferences dialog box is open, select General from the submenu.

As you can see in Figure 3-1, the Preferences dialog box offers a list of preference categories that you can change. As you select each one, the dialog box changes to show you the settings for that category. Figure 3-2 shows the Preferences dialog box as it appears for Mac users running OS X.

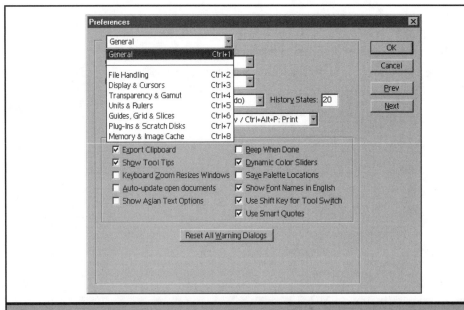

Figure 3-1.   *There are eight different sets of Preferences you can tweak to make Photoshop work your way.*

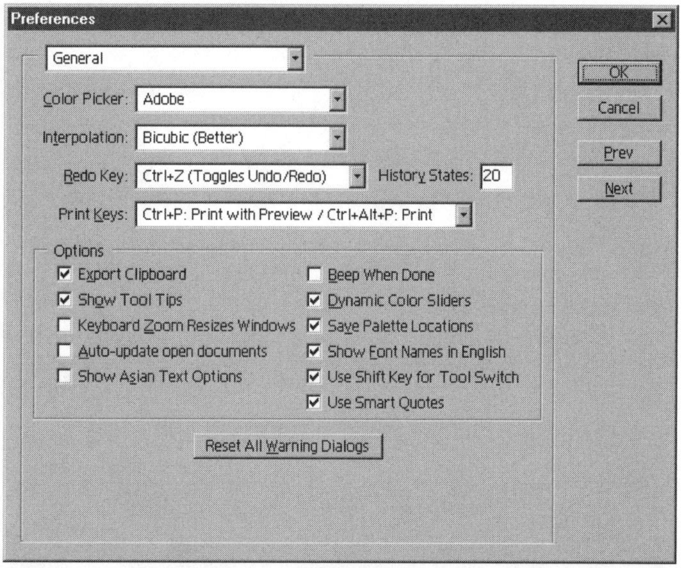

Figure 3-2.   *Look under the Photoshop menu for the Preferences in Mac OS X.*

Note   *The keyboard shortcuts (CTRL/COMMAND and a number) that you see listed next to each of the Preference categories only work while the Preferences dialog box is open, saving you the process of clicking the drop-down menu and selecting a category. Another way to move through the categories is to click the Prev and Next buttons, which can cycle you from General to Memory & Image Cache and back again.*

Changing General Preferences

The General Preferences dialog box, shown in Figure 3-3, offers options for some very important Photoshop features and functionality.

Color Picker   The choice you make here—Adobe or Windows/Macintosh—will determine what you see the next time you click the Foreground or Background Color tools in the toolbox. The default is Adobe, and this choice results in the very useful and informative Color Picker shown in Figure 3-4.

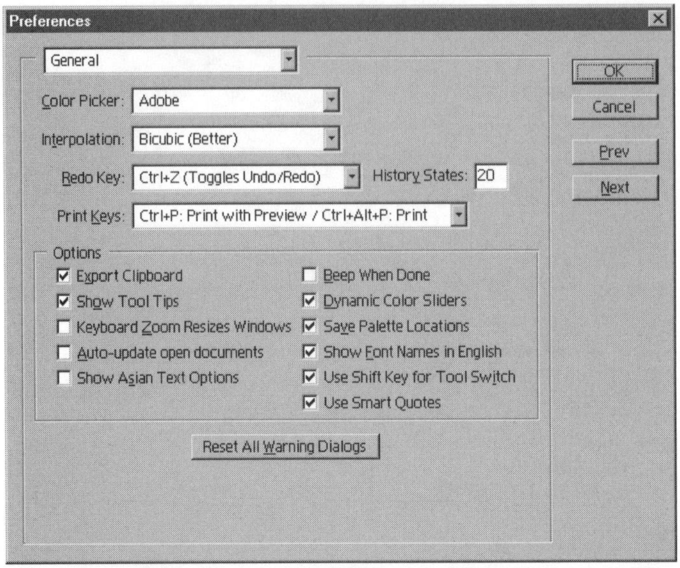

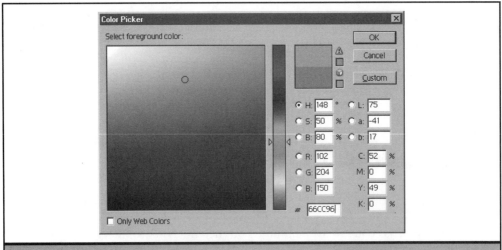

Figure 3-3. Core defaults can be changed through the Preferences dialog box's General category.

Figure 3-4. Adobe's Color Picker offers all the tools you need to select colors for both print and web work.

If you choose Windows, you'll see the same Color dialog box with the basic Windows palette and tools for creating Custom colors. As you can see in Figure 3-5, this is a much more limited tool than the Adobe Color Picker, and I'd advise you to stick with the Adobe option here.

Figure 3-6 shows the Macintosh Color Picker, which is quite useful, but still not a good choice for Photoshop users, especially if you're working with photographs.

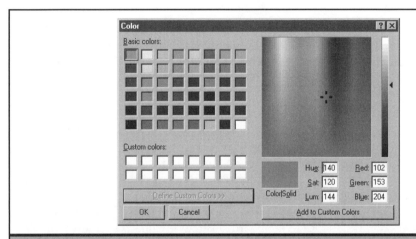

Figure 3-5.   *Windows users will find this Color dialog box rather familiar. Click the Define Custom Colors button to expand the box as it's seen here.*

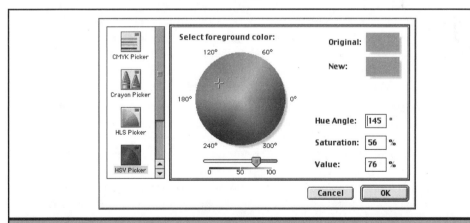

Figure 3-6.   *If you're a Mac user, you've seen this Color Picker before.*

Interpolation   This option determines the way Photoshop will fill in new pixels when you resize or transform an image or portion thereof. Your interpolation options are Bicubic (the default), Nearest Neighbor, or Bilinear.

- The Bicubic option is the default because it creates the smoothest edges by averaging the colors of the eight nearest pixels. This is the most time-consuming of the three interpolation methods, as so much is going on—not only are the colors of the adjacent pixels being averaged, but the contrast level between pixels is being raised to mitigate the blurry look that interpolation can cause.

- The Nearest Neighbor option would seem to do the same thing as the Bicubic option, but instead of averaging the nearest eight pixels, it simply applies the color of the nearest pixel to the new one. For this reason, it's the fastest of the three options, but it also provides the least attractive results—jagged, choppy edges.

- Bilinear interpolation creates intermediate shades of the existing and new pixels, averaging the color of each new pixel with its four nearest neighbors: the pixels above, below, and to the left and right. Bilinear interpolation takes longer than Nearest Neighbor and less time than Bicubic. If you don't have time to wait for Bicubic's superior results, Bilinear produces better results than the quick-and-dirty Nearest Neighbor.

Redo Key   By default, the Redo keyboard shortcut is CTRL-Z (Windows) or COMMAND-Z (Mac). You're probably familiar with this shortcut from your other applications, as it's the Undo/Redo shortcut in virtually all software for Windows or the Mac. As Photoshop only supports a single Undo (you can only reverse the last action you took), there isn't much to be gained by changing the shortcut to either of the offered alternatives (CTRL/COMMAND-SHIFT-Z or CTRL/COMMAND-Y) because you're probably already familiar with CTRL/COMMAND-Z and won't have any trouble remembering it. The shortcut, whether you leave it at the default or choose an alternate, toggles between Undo and Redo—if you've just done something, you can Undo it. If you've just undone something, you can Redo it. Of course, to go back further in time, you'll want to use the History palette.

History States   This setting, which is 20 by default, determined how many steps you can store in the History palette. You might think that raising this number—to 100 steps or some huge number like that—would be the best thing to do. If your computer has a lot of memory (256MB or more), you may want to raise the number. If your computer has very little memory or if you're typically running several programs at the same time you're using Photoshop, you may want to leave it at 20 or even lower it so as to tie up less of your system's resources. If memory is not a problem, it's a good idea to let experience determine the best setting for you—if you find that you're often wishing you could go further back in time than the History palette is allowing you, it may be time to raise the History States level. If you rarely go back more than a handful of steps, then 20 is probably just fine.

Print Keys   This option is set to CTRL/COMMAND-P for Print with Preview and CTRL-ALT-P (Windows) or COMMAND-OPTION-P (Mac) for Print by default. It establishes the keyboard shortcuts for printing and whether or not you see a preview of the image before you print it. If you don't want a preview before you print, change to CTRL/COMMAND-P for a simple Print and use CTRL/COMMAND-ALT/OPTION-P for Print with Preview. This alternative turns the quick, two-key shortcut into a direct path to the Print dialog box so you don't have to view a preview before printing the image. The thinking behind these alternatives is that the longer shortcut (the one that involves the ALT/OPTION key as well as CTRL/COMMAND and the P) is the least-used shortcut, so it should be assigned to the print method you like least.

| Tip |

The print keys as described above represent a change for Mac users. Before Mac OS X, users accessed these application-specific controls within the Print dialog (COMMAND-P). COMMAND-P now brings up Print with Preview dialog box (this was the Print Options dialog box in Photoshop 6), so you still have access to these commands.

Options   An assortment of 11 settings, this group of check boxes controls everything from the way selections that you've cut or copied are handled when you exit Photoshop to whether or not your quotation marks curve toward the text around which they're placed.

By default, the following options are on in Photoshop 7:

Export Clipboard   If you want your cut or copied selections to be available outside of Photoshop (transferred to the operating system's Clipboard when you exit Photoshop), leave this option on. Turning this option off can shorten the lag time when you're switching between applications, but this lag is usually negligible, anyway. Whether on or off, items you've cut or copied in other applications can be pasted into Photoshop and remain available for pasting even if you close Photoshop entirely—this option only controls selections cut or copied in Photoshop.

Show Tool Tips   Leave this option on if you want to see the name and keyboard shortcut (if any) for a tool when you hover over it with your mouse pointer. There is no drag on your system resources if you leave this on, and the tips can be very helpful to new or sporadic users.

Dynamic Color Sliders   This option allows the preview color to change in response to your dragging the color slider in the Color Picker dialog box and in the Color palette. There's no reason not to leave this option on other than if you have a very slow computer (due to lack of memory or an older processor).

Save Palette Locations   While this option is on, Photoshop will remember how your palettes were arranged—which ones were open, where and what size they were—when you last exited the application. When you open the application again, the palettes will be in the same configuration. If you turn this option off,

Photoshop will display the palettes in the default configuration (see Figure 3-7) every time you open Photoshop. Some users like to turn this option off so that when they reopen Photoshop, all the main palettes are open and set up along the left side of the application window. You may want to turn this option off so that your default arrangement is not determined by your last work session.

Show Font Names in English   If English is your preferred language, you'll want to leave this option on so that foreign fonts appear in names you can easily read.

Use Shift Key for Tool Switch   This option is on because it makes using keyboard shortcuts much more convenient. If more than one tool can be displayed in a single spot in the toolbox, this option allows you to press the SHIFT key to switch between them. Because the tools that share a slot have the same single-character shortcut, once you use the shortcut to select the tool, there's no way to switch to the alternate tools in that group without the SHIFT key.

Use Smart Quotes   If you type a lot of inch and foot measurements, you may want to turn this option off so that you can type straight (non-curving) quotation marks after numbers that indicate measurements in feet and inches. If the text you type in Photoshop rarely requires straight quotes, you should leave this option on so that your quotation marks will curve appropriately around the characters they embrace.

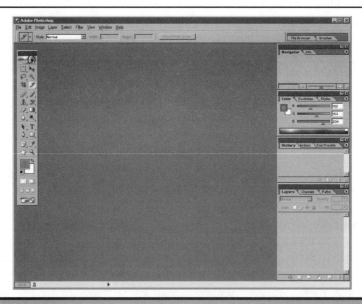

Figure 3-7.   *The four palette groups are automatically displayed when you open Photoshop if you turn the Save Palette Locations option off.*

The following options are off by default, and you may want to leave them that way:

Keyboard Zoom Resizes Windows   If this option is turned on (which it is by default for Mac users), every time you zoom in or out on an image, the image window will resize to match the change in magnification. This can be annoying if you have more than one image open, as zooming in will cause the active window to become quite large, potentially obscuring the other open image windows. Unless the Ignore Palettes option is checked in the Zoom tool's options bar, the expansion will stop when the image window encounters a palette. If you opt to leave the Keyboard Zoom Resizes Windows option on, but while working on a particular image you want the option off, simply press the ALT/OPTION key as you zoom in or out, and you'll toggle this setting off temporarily. Similarly, if the option is off, you can toggle it on with the ALT/OPTION key.

Auto-update Open Documents   This option enables you to work with someone else on the same image file and have their changes, which will update the image file, be reflected in your copy of the file while it's open in Photoshop. This option, which is only useful if you're on a network, is off by default, but if you know someone else may be working on the same image that you are, you may want to turn it on so you are kept apprised of changes that person is making. When a change to the file is made and saved, a prompt appears that you can respond to. There you can choose whether or not to update your working copy to match the file stored on the network.

Show Asian Text Options   If you will be typing in Japanese, Chinese, or Korean, you want to turn this option on so character and paragraph formatting options (through the Character and Paragraph palettes) reflect the needs of these languages.

Use System Shortcut Keys (Mac Only)   Photoshop uses a lot of shortcut keys to speed up operations. If you are using some of them for other system-related duties, turn this option on so Photoshop won't override them.

Beep When Done   For those users who like a prompt of some kind when things happen on their computer, this option (when turned on) can be quite convenient. Beep When Done causes Photoshop to play a beep sound when any task that is represented by a progress bar is completed. If, for example, you work with a lot of huge files (multiple megabytes in size) and find yourself waiting for a filter or other effect to apply, you can go off and do something else in another application and, when Photoshop beeps, you know you can come back and pick up working on your image.

Note   *You know those warning prompts that tell you there's some unpleasant consequence to something you just did? Most of them have a check box ("Don't show this warning again") that you can select to prevent the warning from being displayed in the future. The Reset All Warning Dialogs button will clear any check marks you may have placed in these check boxes, causing the warnings to again display whenever you do something that Photoshop wants to warn you about. This can be a good thing if you were a little too cavalier in choosing not to be warned in the past—most warnings are for our own good, and it only takes a second to read them.*

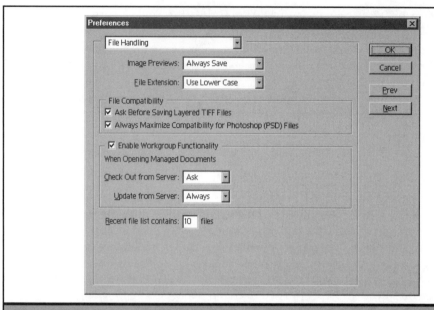

Figure 3-8.   *Press CTRL/COMMAND-2 to open the File Handling Preferences dialog box.*

Understanding Your File Handling Options

The File Handling version of the Preferences dialog box (see Figure 3-8) replaces the Saving Files dialog box found in earlier versions of Photoshop. File Handling refers to the way files are saved, how they're accessed on a network, and the number of recently used files that will appear in the Open Recent submenu displayed by choosing File | Open Recent.

When working with the File Handling dialog box, you'll find the following options—each is listed with its default state in parentheses:

Image Previews (Always Save)   This option, set to Always Save, provides a thumbnail preview of your saved files to help you when opening a file through the Open dialog box (or if you're on a Mac, from the Finder desktop). Saving the preview takes up a kilobyte or two, and you may not like giving up that much disk space (multiply that by the number of files you have saved). You can choose to Never Save, or Ask When Saving, which would give you the best of both worlds for specific images.

File Extension (Use Lowercase)   This option refers to the file's three-character extension (.psd, .tif, etc.), and how they're saved as part of the filename. In its default state, this option would apply the lowercase letters ".psd" to a Photoshop file, rather than ".PSD." The alternative (Use Uppercase) can be a risky choice due to possible compatibility issues: If you upload a file to a Unix-based web server, it won't like uppercase characters, because Unix is case-sensitive.

Mac users will encounter an additional set of four check boxes in the File Handling dialog box; the Mac version of this dialog box appears in Figure 3-9. The options pertain to how files are previewed on the desktop, the Open dialog box, in other applications, and for files created on a Mac and opened later in a Windows environment. The options and their default states, shown in parentheses, are as follows:

Icon (On)   This option indicates that the file will appear as an icon on the desktop, and that the icon will be a preview of the file (rather than a generic application icon).

Macintosh Thumbnail (On)   The image preview will display in the Open dialog box, in thumbnail size.

Windows Thumbnail (On)   If the file is created or last saved on a Mac, this option enables the Windows version of Photoshop to display a thumbnail in its Open dialog box—something that happens automatically for files created and opened in the Windows version of Photoshop.

Full Size (Off)   If you turn this option on, it causes a 72-ppi version of the file to be saved for use in applications that can only open low-resolution Photoshop images.

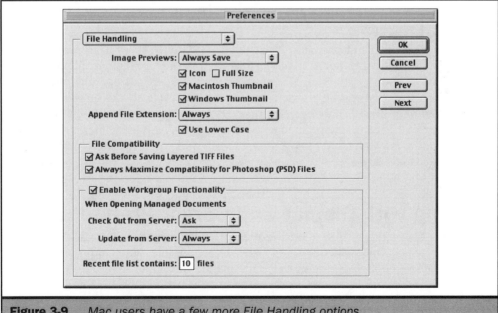

Figure 3-9.   *Mac users have a few more File Handling options.*

In the File Compatibility section of the dialog box, you'll find these options:

Ask Before Saving Layered TIFF Files (On)   If you want to see the TIFF Options dialog box when saving a file that's gone from flat to layered, leave this option on.

Always Maximize Compatibility for Photoshop (PSD) Files (On)   To save a flattened composite with your PSD files, leave this option on. If you opt to turn this off, you may have trouble using your files with future versions of Photoshop, and you may be unable to open PSD files in other applications—even those with the filters in place to do so.

The Enable Workgroup Functionality section (which is activated by default) offers the following options for When Opening Management Documents:

Check Out from Server (Ask)   The Ask option gives you more of a situational approach than the extremes of the alternatives, Never and Always, which refer to whether or not to check out a managed file when it's opened. The process of checking out a file prevents other users from making changes to the file on the WebDAV (Web Distributed Authoring and Versioning) server. You check the file back in when you're finished editing and don't mind others making their mark on the image again.

Update from Server (Always)   If you open a server-managed file, do you want it to be updated to match the version on the server? If so, leave this option set as it is by default—Always. Your alternatives are Never and Ask.

And last, the setting for controlling how many recently used files will appear in the File | Open Recent submenu:

Recent File List Contains (10)   You can increase this to 30, or decrease it to 0. If you share your computer with others and want to prevent them from seeing which files you've had open, or keep them from accidentally opening one of the files you were just editing, you can set it to 0 so the list is always empty. Increasing the default of 10 will enable you to choose from a longer list of files that you've worked with, potentially going back further in time. Increasing the number is also a good idea if you tend to open and work with more than 10 different files in an average single day.

Working with Display and Cursor Preferences

The Display & Cursors version of the Preferences dialog box (see Figure 3-10) offers options for the way colors are displayed after fills are applied, when painting is performed, and when selection pointers, such as the eyedropper, are put to work.

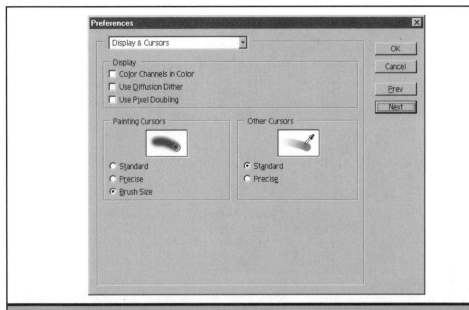

Figure 3-10.   *CTRL/COMMAND-3 will open the Display and Cursor Preferences dialog box.*

The options and their defaults are as follows, beginning with the Display section:

Color Channels in Color (Off)   This option pertains to the display of colors in the Channels palette and how the channels you have set to be visible are displayed in your image. If you turn this option on, the red, green, and blue channels will be displayed in color (the RGB remains gray in the palette). In addition (and more importantly), if you turn this option on, a translucent color wash will appear over your image when you set the visibility of one or more of your channels to off. This makes it difficult to view your image, and it certainly hides the true effect of turning off a color channel. Figure 3-11 shows the red wash over an image where only the Red channel is displayed.

Use Diffusion Dither (Off)   If you're viewing colors on an older or limited monitor and can see only 16 or 256 colors, you might want to turn this option on. When this option is on, Photoshop creates the illusion of 16 million visible colors, and creates a natural-looking diffusion of pixels (called *dithering*). The downside of this option's use is that sometimes the dithering creates harsh edges within your image. The downside of leaving it off is that images can look very ugly if you're viewing them on an 8-bit screen.

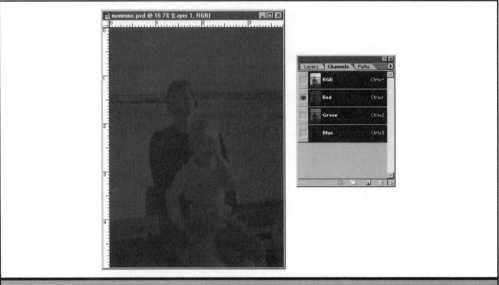

Figure 3-11. *Do you need this much of a reminder that you're viewing the red channel? Probably not.*

Use Pixel Doubling (Off)   When on, this option displays at a lower resolution while moving an image (or portion thereof) to save system resources. If you leave it off, you might notice that a computer with low system resources works slowly while you're dragging a layer or selection because the computer is trying to display the image at full resolution while it's in transit.

The Painting Cursor options are as follows:

Standard (Off)   This option makes the cursor appear as a small icon (a paintbrush, pencil, or an eraser, depending on which tool you're painting with, as shown in Figure 3-12), rather than a simple circle the size of the selected brush or a crosshair. The least useful of the Painting Cursor options, it makes it hard to paint precisely, and doesn't provide any indication of the amount of paint you're about to apply.

Precise (Off)   Choose this to make your painting cursor appear as a crosshair, as shown in Figure 3-13.

Brush Size (On)   The default makes a lot of sense: The cursor appears as a circle sized to reflect the brush size you've selected with the Paintbrush options bar or the Brushes palette. Figure 3-14 shows an 83-pixel brush cursor at work.

GETTING TO KNOW
PHOTOSHOP

Figure 3-12.   *The Standard painting cursor looks like the tool you're using to paint—
here it looks like a paintbrush.*

Figure 3-13.   *The crosshair cursor can be useful for very precise painting.*

Figure 3-14.   *The Brush Size painting cursor allows you to see the diameter of your paintbrush, the thickness of your pencil point, or the size of your eraser.*

The Other Cursors options are:

Standard (On)   This setting displays an icon cursor for all other tools—like the Eyedropper, Marquee, Lasso, Magic Wand, and Crop tools.

Precise (Off)   Like the Precise painting cursor, the Precise setting for all other tools turns the mouse pointer to a crosshair while the tools in question are in use.

Tip

If you're a fan of keyboard shortcuts, you'll be happy to know that you can toggle between Standard and Precise cursors by pressing the CAPS LOCK key. If you're also working in a word processor or other program in which you'll be typing text, beware of this shortcut— if CAPS LOCK is on (due to your toggling between cursor settings), you'll end up typing in all caps when you return to your word processor.

Establishing Transparency and Gamut Settings

The two areas controlled by this version of the Preferences dialog box relate to perception—in the case of *Transparency*, you can choose how a transparent background is displayed, helping the designer (and eventually the viewer, depending on the way the file is saved and then used in print or online) to perceive the background and its role in the appearance of the image. In the case of *Gamut*, this is the term that represents the range of colors that can be viewed and printed accurately, which affects the perception of color. If a color can be viewed accurately but won't print that way, it is considered "out of gamut," or beyond the gamut range.

The Transparency & Gamut dialog box, shown in Figure 3-15, is divided into two sections, and offers a total of five options.

The Transparency Settings options and their default settings (in parentheses) follow:

> **Grid Size (Medium)**   Your alternatives are None, Small, and Large. None can cause confusion, as the background will appear to be solid white and you might forget that it's a transparent layer or a colored fill. Your choice of Small or Large is simply a matter of visual preference.

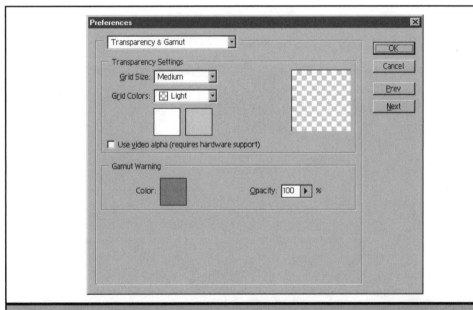

Figure 3-15.   *Press* CTRL/COMMAND*-4 to set your Transparency & Gamut preferences.*

Grid Colors (Light) This option has several alternatives—Light, Dark, Red, Orange, Green, Blue, or Purple—for the color of the grid that represents your transparent background (see Figure 3-16). You can also choose a custom grid by clicking the colored blocks below the option; each one, when clicked, will open the Color Picker, and you can choose the colors for your checkerboard grid.

Use Video Alpha (Requires Hardware Support) (Off) This option is utilized by people who work with video. When on, it displays transparency through your video-viewing device.

In the Gamut Warning section, the options are as follows:

Color (Dark Gray) When Photoshop can't display a color accurately, it is said that the color is "out of gamut." This color setting is your choice for how Photoshop will display the colors that fall out of the gamut range. The default is gray, which may or may not stand out in a given image. Turn on the gamut feature by selecting View | Gamut Warning, and the color you choose by clicking the Color swatch (which opens the Color Picker) will display for your out-of-gamut colors.

Opacity (100%) By setting this to a lower opacity, you can make sure your out-of-gamut display stands out. The color you choose will be applied as a translucent layer on top of the color that Photoshop is unable to display accurately. At 100 percent, the gamut warning color you chose will obscure the color in question.

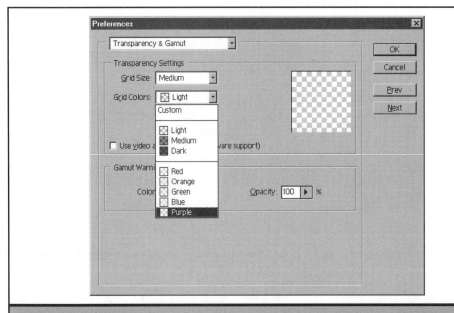

Figure 3-16. *Medium gray too boring for you? Apply a dark, light, or colored grid instead.*

Understanding Your Measurement Options

When you work with the Units & Rulers version of the Preferences dialog box, you're choosing how Photoshop will measure your images and type, and what presets for image print and screen resolutions will be. The defaults are intended to support the average user who's using Photoshop for a variety of tasks—designing graphics or retouching photos—but you may find that the defaults don't work for you, especially if you find yourself resetting them for individual images most of the time. Choose View | Rulers or press CTRL/COMMAND-R to display the rulers. The dialog box is divided into four sections, as shown in Figure 3-17.

In the Units section of the dialog box, you choose how your rulers will measure the image, and how type will be measured. Your options appear below, with their default settings in parentheses:

Rulers (Inches)   Your alternatives are Pixels, cm (Centimeters), mm (Millimeters), Points, Picas, or Percent. Choose the one you feel most comfortable with, or the one that lends itself best to a particular image.

Note   *You can change your measurement method for a specific image or for just a short period of editing time by right-clicking (Windows) or CONTROL-clicking (Mac) the ruler. In either case, a context menu appears, from which you can choose an alternate measurement method.*

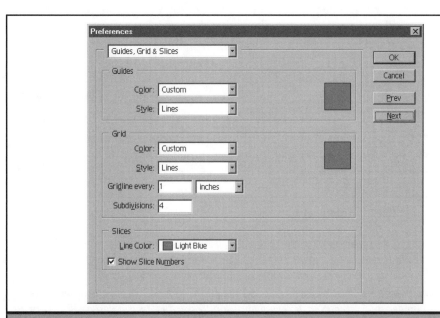

Figure 3-17.   *Use CTRL/COMMAND-5 to open this version of the Preferences dialog box.*

Type (Points) Points is the default because it's the standard type-measurement method in word processors. You can measure type in Pixels or mm (Millimeters) instead of points. You may want to switch to Pixels if you're thinking of the text in terms of designing for the Web.

The Column Size section of the dialog box contains two options and gives you the ability to measure images for use in newspapers or magazines, where they'll have to fit inside or between printed margins. You can set these measurements and also choose *how* they'll be measured by choosing between a variety of measurement methods:

Width (180, Points) The default of 180 points is considered standard for newspaper and magazine columns, but you can change it to meet the needs of your specific text and image. When you finish entering the width, you can choose an alternate measurement method—your alternatives are Inches, cm, mm, Points, or Picas.

Gutter (12, Points) The gutter is the space around the column, and the default of 12 can be increased or decreased as your specific projects require it. You can also change the measurement method to Inches, cm, mm, Points, or Picas.

In the New Document Preset Resolutions section, you can set the defaults for Print and Screen Resolution. The options in this section are broken into two values: the amount and the measurement method used.

Print Resolution (300, Pixels/Inch) You can increase or decrease the resolution within the bounds of your printer's capability, or the capabilities of the printer on which a third party will be printing your image. If you prefer, you can measure the resolution in Pixels/cm. Of course, the higher the resolution, the more detailed the printout will be, and the longer it will take to print.

Screen Resolution (72, Pixels/Inch) If your image is bound for the Web, leave this set at 72, which is the standard for online images. You'll also want to stick with Pixels/Inch for the measurement method, as pixels are the standard unit of measure for web pages and their content.

The Point/Pica Size section allows you to choose how points and picas will be measured if you're working with PostScript or Traditional printing. There are two choices for the size of points and picas:

PostScript (72 Points/Inch)

Traditional (72.27 Points/Inch)

Note *Did you know that there are 72 points in an inch (so a single character that's formatted to 72 points will be 1 inch square, or take up an inch footprint within a word), 12 points in a pica, and 6.06 picas in an inch? Further, because picas are not evenly divisible, it was decided to simply say that a pica as one-sixth of an inch, and a point as one-twelfth of an inch. If you design for the Web, you probably don't care, and even if you design for print, this may fall under the category of Extremely Trivial. If you need to scrupulously measure your type and the space around it, however, these might be vital statistics.*

Customizing the Guides, Grid, and Slices

Photoshop provides guides to help you align content vertically and horizontally within your image, and a grid to help you position things by eye as you drag them with your mouse. Through this version of the Preferences dialog box (see Figure 3-18), you can customize the guides; choose their color and style; and establish the color, style, and position of the grid. The Guides, Grid & Slices dialog box also allows you to choose the color of slices, and to choose whether or not each slice's number appears with it on the image.

Bear in mind that none of these items—the grid, the guides, or the slice lines—become part of the image unto themselves. They appear on top of your image, but do not become part of it. Figure 3-19 shows an image with two guidelines set, and a grid displayed. The guidelines have been used to position a photo within the image, and the grid has helped to draw a rectangle.

Slices are used to break an image into blocks for fast loading on the Web, but the slice lines themselves do not become part of the image as a whole or once it's broken into several smaller images. You want to pick colors, styles, and positions that will make the guides, grid, and slices visible on the surface of your images (you don't want gray lines if you're working primarily with faded black and white photos, for example). When it comes to the grid, you want to set it up so that the grid's coordinates are far enough apart to give you freedom in positioning content, but close enough together to give you tight control, too. Your options for customizing the Guides, Grid & Slices follow.

Note   *To use the grid, first display it by choosing View | Show | Grid. Then choose View | Snap To | Grid. Whatever you've set up for the color and frequency of your grid's coordinates will appear on top of your image.*

To set up the way your Guides look, use these two options:

Color (Light Blue)   Click the drop-down list and choose a color, or click the color swatch to open the Color Picker and make your selection there.

Style (Lines)   You can also choose Dashed Lines, which can be useful if your image has a lot of solid horizontal and vertical lines in it—using dashed lines instead of solid ones can make the Guides stand out.

To control the appearance and frequency of your grid's coordinates, use these four options:

Color (Custom)   Just like Guides colors, you can choose a color from the drop-down list or click the swatch to open the Color Picker.

Style (Lines)   Here, your alternatives are Dashed Lines or Dots. Dots are the least obtrusive on the image, but can be harder to see if your image is very colorful or if you've also selected a subtle color for the grid.

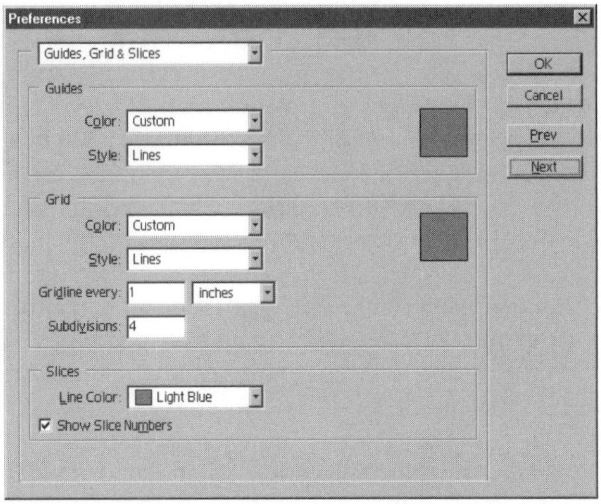

Figure 3-18. CTRL/COMMAND-6 will open a dialog box offering options for your Guides, Grid & Slices.

Figure 3-19. Guides and grids provide a network of vertical and horizontal lines to assist you in creating and editing an image to meet specific positioning and size requirements.

Gridline Every (1/inches) Like all the other measurement-related options (in the Units & Rulers dialog box), your choices for the frequency of the grid (how often vertical and horizontal gridlines appear) are Pixels, Inches, cm, mm, Points, Picas, or Percent. The default, one gridline every inch, allows for quarter-inch subdivisions between gridlines, creating a grid that's not too tight and not too loose. Of course, if you're measuring everything else in pixels or picas (or some other units), then you might want to make the gridline setting follow suit.

Subdividions (4) More subdivisions make for a tighter grid; fewer subdivisions make for a looser, more open grid. How tightly you want to arrange items will dictate this setting.

Your Slice options include:

Line Color (Light Blue) Click the drop-down list to choose a color. There is no swatch for this option.

Show Slice Numbers (On) It's nice to see the slice numbers, if only because if you wanted to divide an image into four slices, when you see that you have five or six slices, you know you've drawn your slices improperly. When drawing slices, if you allow even a pixel-wide gap alongside an existing slice line as you draw the line for the next slice, a tiny slice will be created to fill that gap between the slices you wanted. Figure 3-20 shows a sliced image with more slices than the designer wanted—but thanks to the numbers, it's easy to see which slices can be removed to create the simple two-slices-across–by-two-slices-down arrangement originally desired.

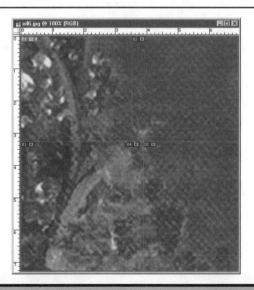

Figure 3-20. *Leave your slice numbers on so you can spot unwanted, extra slices.*

Setting Up Plug-Ins and Scratch Disks

The Plug-Ins & Scratch Disks version of the Preferences dialog box (see Figure 3-21) gives you the opportunity to direct Photoshop to an extra location for plug-in and scratch files. *Plug-ins* are programs that allow other programs to run in conjunction with Photoshop, or that enhance the functioning of the application. *Scratch files* are temporary virtual memory documents that make use of your hard-drive space while Photoshop is running and an image is open. The *Scratch Disk* is the partition or hard drive on which the Scratch Files are stored.

The dialog box offers the following options, each listed below with the default setting in parentheses:

Additional Plug-Ins Directory (Off) While you can see the current location for plug-ins, that path and the Choose button are dimmed in the display. If you turn this feature on, the Choose button becomes available; when you click it, you can use the resulting Browse for Folder dialog box (see Figure 3-22) to pick a secondary location for Photoshop to look for plug-ins.

Legacy Photoshop Serial Number (Blank) Type your Photoshop serial number here for use by any plug-in that requires it.

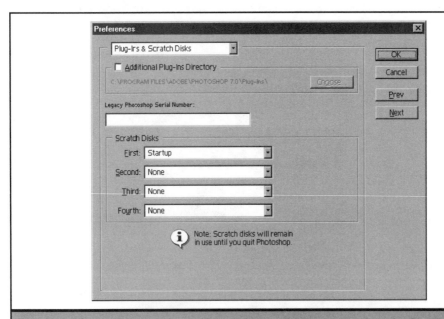

Figure 3-21. Use CTRL/COMMAND-7 to view your Preference options for Plug-Ins & Scratch Disks.

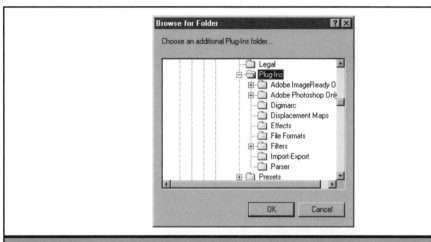

Figure 3-22.   *Pick another plug-ins folder for Photoshop to check when a plug-in is required.*

Scratch Disks   This section of the dialog box allows you to set up four different scratch disks—the first one is set to Startup, and your alternative is the C: drive (Windows) or hard drive (Mac). If you have more than one hard drive on your computer, you can specify the second, third, and fourth drives as your alternate scratch disks by making selections from this option drop-down list:

First (Startup)   Startup refers to the drive that contains the active system folder. For systems with one hard drive, this will amount to the same thing. For systems with multiple drives, you can choose the drive with the most free space as the primary (First) Scratch Disk, the next-largest amount of space as the Secondary, and so on.

Second (None)

Third (None)

Fourth (None)

As it states in the dialog box itself, the areas you designate for scratch disks are only in use while Photoshop is running. As soon as you exit the program, the space on your designated drives is again free for use by other applications.

For best Photoshop performance, set your Scratch Disk(s) to the fastest drive(s) with the most free space. If you're a Windows user running Windows 2000 or XP, the first time you launch Photoshop, you'll be prompted to set your scratch disk to a drive other than your C: drive for best performance (see Figure 3-23).

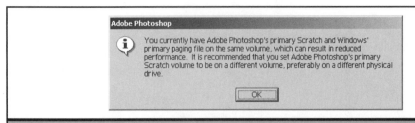

Figure 3-23.   *When you first launch Photoshop on Windows 2000 or Windows XP, you are prompted to set your primary Scratch volume.*

Working with Memory and Image Cache Settings

Having an effective amount of system resources available to you while you're working with Photoshop is essential to your success as a user. Photoshop does a good bit of the work involved in making sure there are enough resources available, and the options found in the Memory & Image Cache version of the Preferences dialog box (see Figure 3-24) are a big part of that. Your options include the ability to establish how much cache is set aside for handling things like all the views of an open image, and a setting for allocating memory for Photoshop's exclusive use. The dialog box is divided into two sections: Cache Settings and Memory Usage.

Cache Settings options and their default settings follow:

Cache Levels (4)   You can increase this setting to 8 and speed up redraws as you change views and move images and their components around in the Image window and within the workspace. The default of 4 is adequate for most users; it means Photoshop can cache (store) up to four *downsamplings*, or views of the image at zoom levels (66.7%, 50%, 33.3%, and 25%). If your computer has a lot of memory (128MB or more) you might want to bump this setting up to 7 or 8, because you have memory to spare and won't see a reduction in performance by allocating that many levels of cache memory to these views. If your computer has very little memory (32MB or less), you might want to reduce the number of levels to 1 or 2.

If you normally work with large, high-resolution images, your cache level should be set to a higher number. If you work with low-resolution Web graphics or other images that will be viewed solely onscreen, a lower cache level may be more appropriate.

Use Cache for Histograms (Off)   If you want Photoshop to use your cache levels to generate the histograms you'll find in the Levels and Threshold dialog boxes, turn this option On. This won't provide the most accurate histograms, but they'll be calculated and displayed much faster.

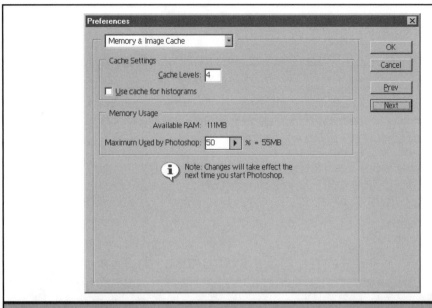

Figure 3-24.   *Press CTRL/COMMAND-8 to open the Memory & Image Cache Preferences dialog box. If you're using Mac with OS 9.x, the dialog box will be the Image Cache dialog box.*

Memory Usage options and their default settings follow:

Available RAM (*nnn* MB)   This number (the *n*s represent your system's available RAM) is based on the total amount of RAM memory you have on your computer, representing approximately 90 percent of your computer's total resources.

Maximum Used by Photoshop (50% = 55MB)   By default, Photoshop will gobble up only 50 percent of this available memory, but you can increase or decrease this percentage as you see fit. If you tend to run other applications at the same time you're using Photoshop, it's not a good idea to designate much more than 50 percent for Photoshop exclusively, as you might see reduced performance (or even crashes) in the other applications. If you're running Photoshop in a Mac OS 9.*x* environment, you can set this option (see Figure 3-25) by selecting the Photoshop icon and choosing File | Get Info | Memory while Photoshop is running.

Note   *When changes are made to the Scratch Disk, Cache, and Memory Usage settings, they won't take effect until the next time you open Photoshop. Obviously, if you need the change to take effect right away, exit Photoshop and reopen the application so you can begin to work with the new settings in place.*

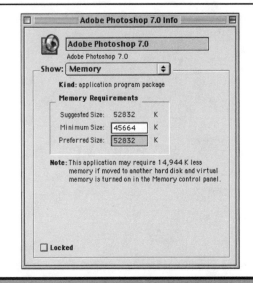

Figure 3-25.   *In Mac OS 9, you use the Memory option of Get Info to allocate memory to Photoshop.*

Customizing Your Color Settings

Different images require different color settings and color management tools. For example, the color settings you would use for a print job would be very different from the settings you'd want in place for an image that's going to end up on the Web. The Color Settings dialog box) gives you the ability to choose your settings and then as needed, customize them for a specific image. If you're using Windows or Mac OS 9.*x*, the Color Settings dialog box is opened by choosing Edit | Color Settings. If you're using Mac OS X, the Photoshop | Color Settings command (see Figure 3-26) opens the dialog box. In any platform, you can press SHIFT-CTRL/COMMAND-K to open the dialog box.

Figure 3-27 shows the Color Settings dialog box with Web Graphics Defaults selected, in Advanced Mode. The option defaults in the Working Spaces and Color Management Policies sections will vary by the setting you choose.

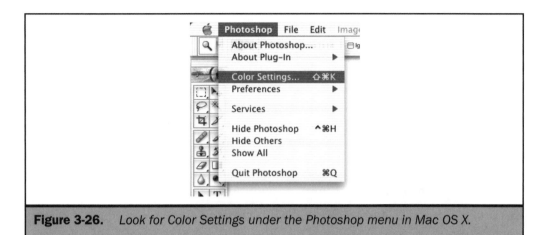

Figure 3-26.   *Look for Color Settings under the Photoshop menu in Mac OS X.*

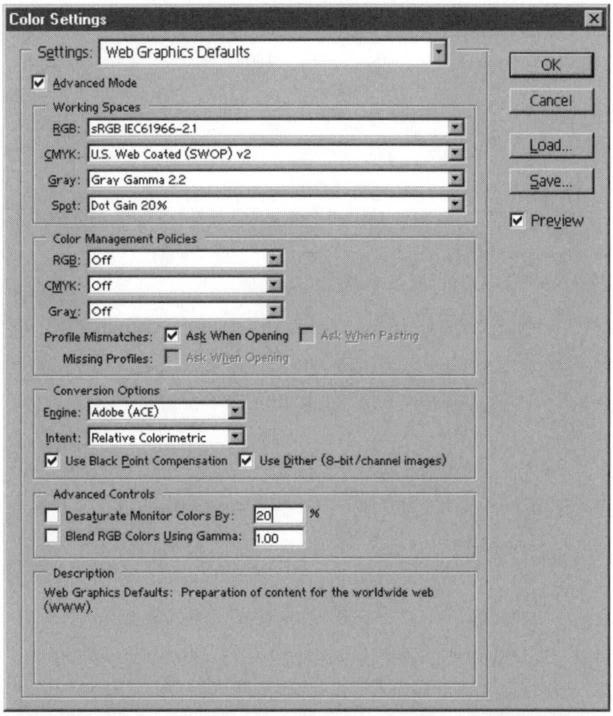

Figure 3-27.   *Color settings for each kind of image or job you have are simple to choose and customize.*

To choose a different setting (and therefore change the option defaults), click the Settings drop-down menu and choose from the following:

Custom Choose this one if none of the other job or environment-specific Settings options meets your needs. Typically, you'll choose the one with defaults closest to your settings goals and then tweak individual options as needed. If none of the settings are even close, just choose Custom and build your settings option by option.

Color Management Off Considered a *passive* color management setting, this option is best for images that will be used in video or onscreen in some other way (other than on the Web). It's also handy if you'll be working with applications that don't support color management—it won't tag documents with profiles. The defaults for this setting are shown in Figure 3-28.

ColorSync Workflow (for Mac OS users only) This option, shown in Figure 3-29, uses the ColorSync CMS with profiles chosen in the ColorSync control panel. If your image will be used in or edited with both Adobe applications and non-Adobe applications on your Mac, this may be the setting for you. Windows or ColorSync versions prior to version 3 do not recognize this setting.

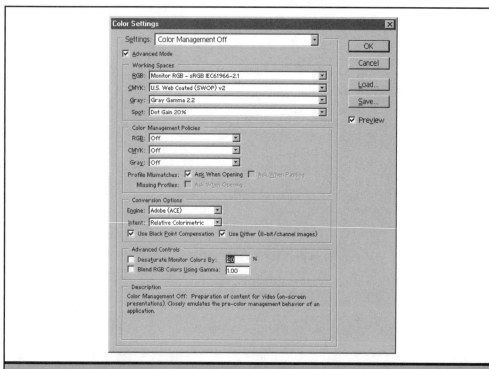

Figure 3-28. *Color Management Off's color settings*

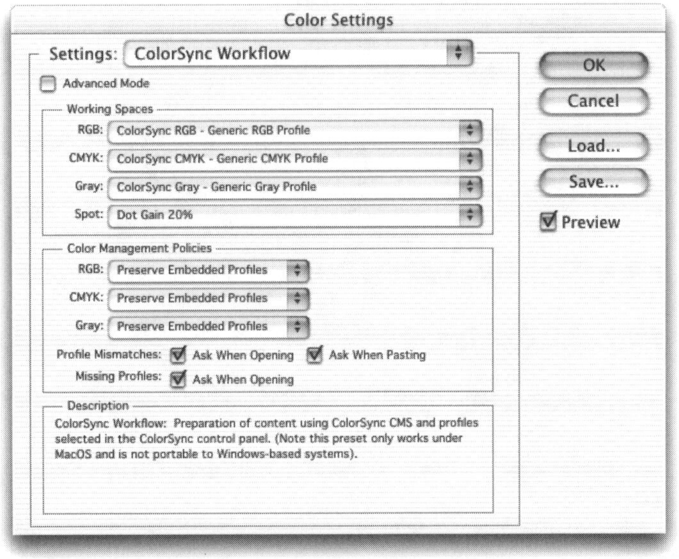

Figure 3-29.   *ColorSync Workflow is an option that only Mac users can select.*

Emulate Photoshop 4   This option emulates (mimics) the color workflow that was used in the Mac OS version of Adobe Photoshop 4. Note that, as shown in Figure 3-30, the RGB setting is Apple RGB, and the CMYK setting is Photoshop 4 Default CMYK.

Europe Prepress Defaults   Prepress conditions in Europe are often different than those that you'd find in the United States. For an image you know is bound for European prepress, make this your choice—its settings appear in Figure 3-31.

Japan Prepress Defaults   Like European prepress, Japan's prepress needs are unique. This option's settings, as shown in Figure 3-32, include Japan's inks for Standard v.2 for CMYK.

Photoshop 5 Default Spaces   This option's settings, shown in Figure 3-33, include Photoshop 5's defaults for CMYK and RGB settings for an average PC monitor. It's not a good choice for prepress work, because the color gamut is quite limited.

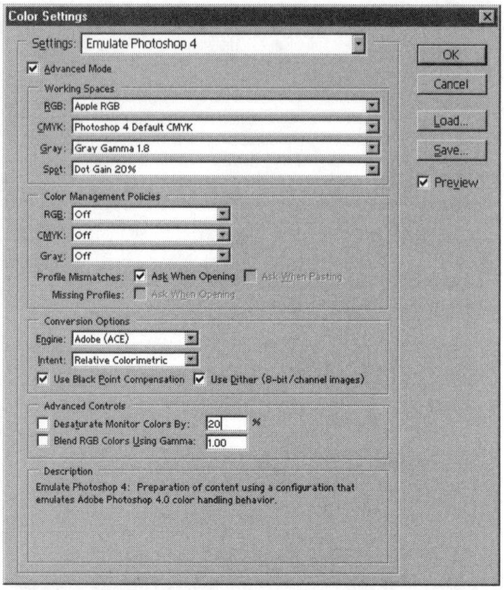

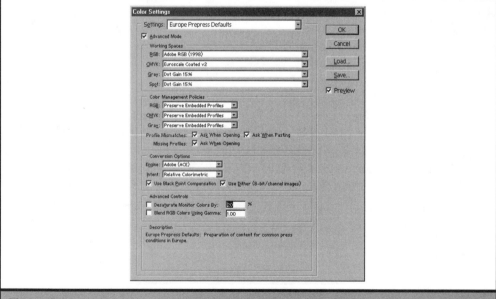

Figure 3-30. *Choose Emulate Photoshop 4 to achieve compatibility with Photoshop 4.*

Figure 3-31. *Meet the needs of European prepress with Europe Prepress Defaults.*

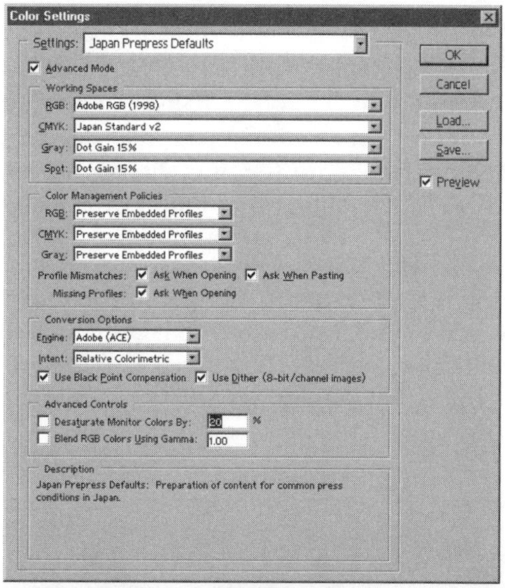

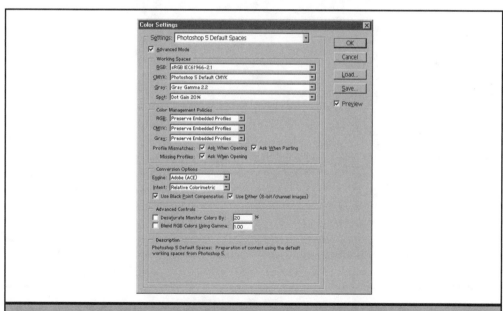

Figure 3-32.   *Prepare your image color settings for Japan's prepress requirements.*

Figure 3-33.   *Photoshop 5 Default Spaces is okay for the Web.*

U.S. Prepress Defaults   If your image will be produced according to U.S. standards for prepress, this is the option for you. As shown in Figure 3-34, it uses U.S. Web Coated CMYK inks, perfect for quality separations in typical prepress conditions.

Web Graphics Defaults   Use U.S. Web Coated CMYK inks, and the RGB settings of an average PC monitor, which enable you to design for an average web site visitor. This option, shown in Figure 3-35, is obviously the best choice for web-bound graphics—note that the Color Management Policies are all set to off by default in this setting.

After you choose a Settings option and customize it, you may want to save the settings for future use on other similar projects or images. To save your settings, click the Save button and give the new settings file a name. You'll see that you're automatically saving to a Settings folder, and that the settings (.csf) files for the existing settings are already there, as shown in Figure 3-36.

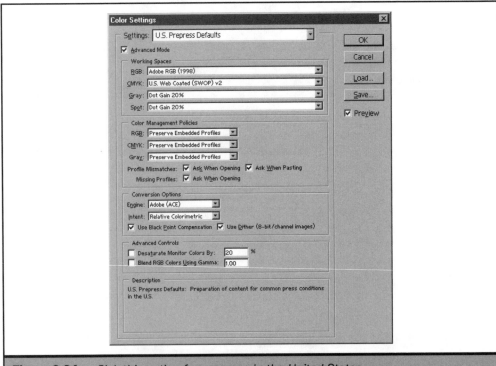

Figure 3-34.   *Pick this option for prepress in the United States.*

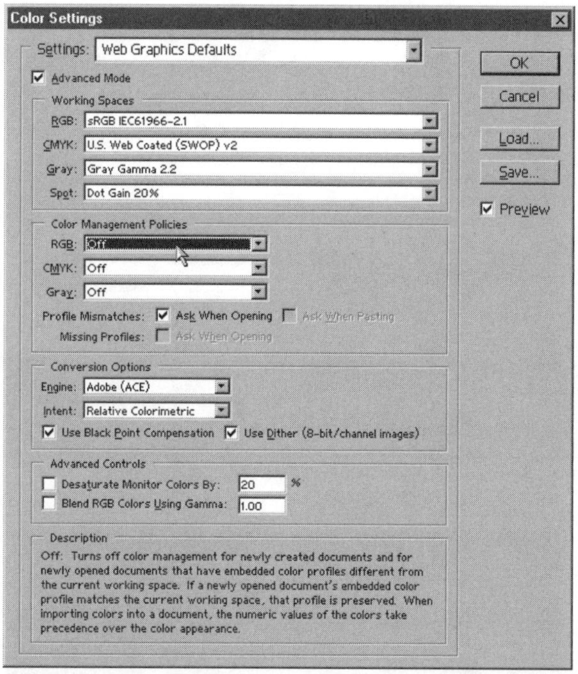

Figure 3-35.   *Doing web work? Web Graphics Defaults offers settings tailor-made for your image.*

Other   This option represents color settings not saved in the Settings folder.

After you save the file, you're asked to provide a description for the new setting. Whatever you type in the dialog box shown in Figure 3-37 will appear in the Description section of the Color Settings dialog box. If you create a new custom color setting, it appears in the Settings menu, as shown in Figure 3-38.

Note   *Want to get rid of a setting you've created in Windows? Click the Save button to open the Save dialog box, and right-click the settings file you want to remove. Choose Delete from the context menu, confirm your intention to delete, and then close the dialog box without saving anything. You may have to restart Photoshop to keep it from trying to apply the deleted settings file to your open image—if in fact it was the color setting you'd applied to the active image or any of the open images. Once you restart Photoshop, the deleted color setting file will no longer appear in the Settings drop-down list.*

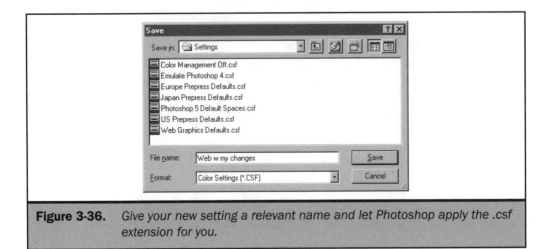

Figure 3-36. *Give your new setting a relevant name and let Photoshop apply the .csf extension for you.*

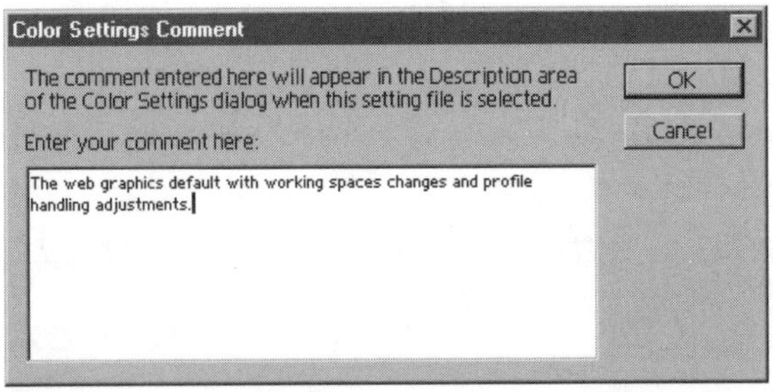

Figure 3-37. *For your future reference, and to help others who may be using your computer to work with Photoshop, provide a description of your new setting.*

Setting RGB, CMYK, Grayscale, and Spot Color Preferences

If you pick a color setting and don't like the Working Spaces settings, you can easily change them by clicking the following drop-down menus:

RGB   Choose a color profile for the red, green, and blue color model. In addition to the default RGB spaces, your options include a wide variety of monitor types, for manufacturers from Epson to NEC, and then some. These options are only available when the Advanced option is selected in the dialog box.

CMYK   Select a cyan, magenta, yellow, and black color profile here. Your options are extensive and include a custom CMYK, which you can create by adjusting options in the dialog box shown in Figure 3-39.

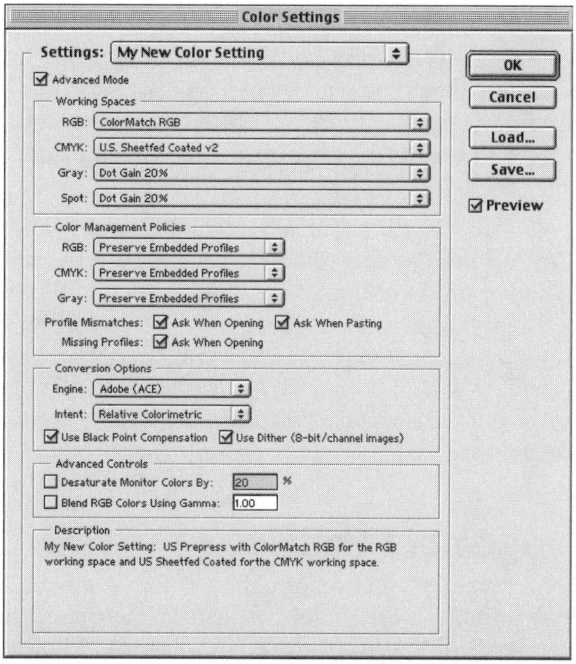

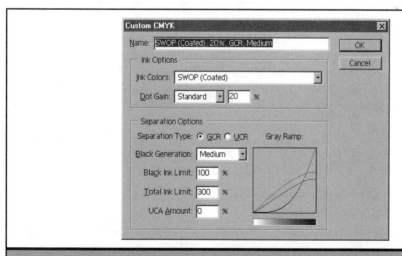

Figure 3-38.   *Your new custom color setting takes its place in the Settings menu.*

Figure 3-39.   *In Custom CMYK, set your own Ink and Separation options.*

Gray   You can pick from several different Dot Gain settings, plus a Custom Dot Gain and a Custom Gamma. It's a good idea to have your printer tested before adjusting this setting, as you won't know beforehand how your dots will be absorbed by certain papers or spread by certain inks in certain printers. You should also be prepared to test a series of different papers until you find the one that gives you the best results on your printer, with that printer set to its most effective setting.

Spot   Set your Dot Gain settings for spot color, preferably after printing and seeing how much the ink has spread and been absorbed by the paper. The dot gain can be set higher or lower than the default (which will be determined by the Settings choice), depending on the printed results. You can set it as low as 10% or as high as 30%, or set a a Custom Dot Gain as high as 90%.

 As soon as you change even one of the Working Spaces, Color Management Policies, or Conversion Options settings, the selected color setting changes to Custom.

Using Color Management Policies

Color management policies allow you to control how colors in a particular color model are managed—you can control how the color profiles are interpreted, how non-matching embedded profiles and working space settings are resolved, and how colors are translated between images. Your Color Management Policies settings are:

RGB   Your options for this setting are Off, Preserve Embedded Profiles, and Convert to Working RGB. If you choose off, color management is turned off for new images and for existing images that don't have embedded color profiles. If an embedded profile is present, the profile is preserved. The other two options indicate your preference for how embedded profiles are handled on existing images—they're either Preserved or converted to the current Working Spaces settings.

CMYK   The three options here are Off, Preserve Embedded Profiles, and Convert to Working CMYK. They work exactly like the RGB options—Off lets the existing situation prevail (and applies no profiles to new images) and the alternatives allow you to choose how profiles and Working Spaces settings are utilized.

Gray   Choose from Off, Preserve Embedded Profiles, or Convert to Working Gray. Like RGB and CMYK, the grayscale settings offer you the ability to work with existing profiles (while not imparting any new ones to new images), to maintain the current embedded profiles, or to follow the options set in the Working Spaces options for Gray.

Profile Mismatches   Some of these options may be dimmed, based on your Color Management Policies selections.

Ask When Opening   If the embedded profile for an image you've just opened does not match the Working Spaces settings, you'll be notified if this option is turned on.

Ask When Pasting   If a profile vs. Working Spaces settings mismatch occurs when colors are imported into your image through an Edit | Paste command or by drag-and-drop, you'll be asked if you want to override the mismatch. Of course, this only happens if this option is on.

Missing Profiles   If your open image has no embedded profiles, you can choose to be prompted (turn on Ask When Opening) and apply a profile then.

Ask When Opening   If this option is on, you'll not only be notified about your image not having embedded profiles, but given the chance to assign a color profile, as shown in Figure 3-40.

Working with Conversion Options

Converting colors between color spaces is done through a Color Management System (CMS) or Color Matching Method. Your options in this section pertain to the Engine that will handle the conversion, and the Intent, which is the method by which colors are converted between color spaces. Your options and their variables are as follows:

Engine   Choose from Adobe (ACE) or Microsoft ICM if you're running Photoshop in a Windows environment. If you're on a Mac, you can choose between Apple ColorSync and Apple CMM (see Figure 3-41). If you have any third-party CMMs installed, they'll also be available here. The Adobe engine is recommended for the majority of users.

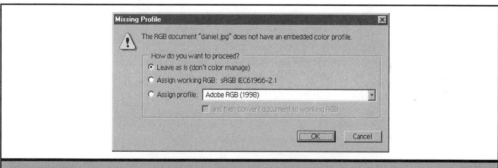

Figure 3-40.   *No profile? Choose what to do when this prompt appears.*

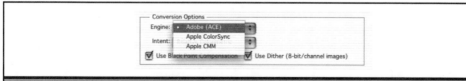

Figure 3-41.   *Your Mac OS X choices for color engine.*

Intent Choose from Perceptual, Saturation, Relative Colormetric, and Absolute Colormetric. Relative Colormetric is the recommended Intent for most users.

Adjusting Advanced Controls

If you need to control how colors are blended and compressed, these settings will give you the power you need to get the results you want. These are your two options:

Desaturate Monitor Colors By (a percentage) When this option is turned on, you can enter a percentage of desaturation to apply to colors when displaying them on a monitor. This can be handy if the range of color spaces requires a gamut larger than the monitor can support. By adjusting the percentage, you can make sure the monitor's limitations are supported by the desaturation level.

Blend RGB Colors Using Gamma The default, or most generally effective setting for this option, is a gamma of 1.00. This setting gives you cleaner edges with few artifacts. When this option is off (regardless of the gamma value set), RGB colors are blended in the image color space, which works well with most other image-editing applications.

Summary

In this chapter, you learned how to view and set preferences for the way Photoshop works and relates to you. You may never have the need to change any or many of the settings in the various versions of the Preferences dialog box, but if you do, this chapter should help you navigate and understand the options available to you. In addition, you learned how to set up the way Photoshop displays and applies color, and we looked at the options available for many different types of output.

The Complete Reference

Chapter 4

Importing Existing Images

P hotoshop's extensive set of image-editing tools is only slightly more extensive than the list of image types that Photoshop can open and edit. From vector-based images created in Adobe Illustrator or CorelDRAW to clip-art images of unknown origin, from scanned drawings and photos to digitally captured photographs and video, you can import virtually any kind of image and put Photoshop's creative arsenal to work, improving the image and saving it in a variety of formats for any number of uses.

Opening an Existing Bitmap or Vector-Based Image

Before you can begin editing an image, you have to open it. If you have the image on your hard drive or on disk and it's in a format that Photoshop can open, you're set—all you have to do is choose File | Open; navigate to the drive, disk, or folder in which the file is stored; and then select and open it. The Open dialog box, shown in Figure 4-1, allows you to look at a list of the file types that Photoshop can open. If you see the format of the file you intend to open in that list, click once on the file you want to open, and then click the Open button. You can also double-click the desired file to open it.

Note
Vector images store the information about the image as a series of mathematical statements that define the width, height, angles, curves, and other attributes of the objects within the image. Bitmap images store the image as a group of pixels, each with its own color depth. Photoshop creates bitmap images, and when vector-based images are opened and saved as Photoshop files, they are rasterized, or converted from being a collection of objects to being a cohesive bitmap image, and become bitmap images.

In a typical Photoshop installation, there are more than 20 different graphic file types that Photoshop can open. These include graphic formats used primarily for the Web (.jpg, .gif, .png) and a variety of formats for print media (.tif, .eps, .bmp, and so on). Figure 4-2 shows the Files of Type drop-down list (the Format drop-down list on the Mac) and a portion of the list of file types Photoshop supports. Table 4-1 provides the complete list.

If you don't see your file's format in this list or on the Files of Type/Format drop-down list, consider reopening the file in the application used to create it and save as one of the supported formats. You can also install a plug-in for the format you want your installation of Photoshop to support. The plug-in manufacturer should provide you with instructions for setting up the plug-in; as soon as the installation is complete, you can restart Photoshop and see the format in the Files of Type/Format drop-down list. Then you can open the file and edit it.

Of course Photoshop opens (and saves) files in its native PSD format faster than it does any other type of file, and the PSD format saves all of the Photoshop attributes—layers, channels, file information, and any document-specific preferences. Not all images you need to open are going to have come from Photoshop, however; it's not a format you'll have saved your image in if you were working in another application to start with.

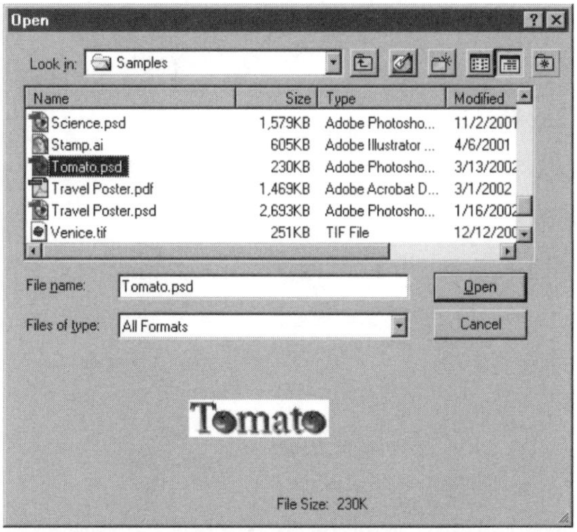

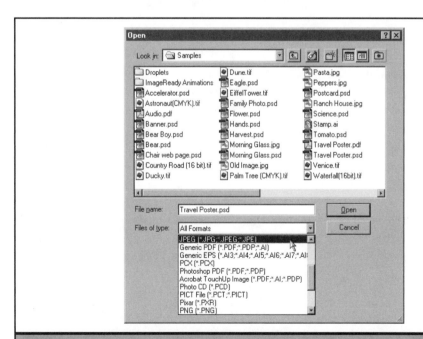

Figure 4-1.   *Use the Open dialog box to select and open the file you want to edit.*

Figure 4-2.   *Click the Files of Type drop-down list to view the formats Photoshop can open.*

Format Name	Common File Extensions (Windows and Mac)
Acrobat Touchup Image	PDF or PDP
Bitmap	BMP
Compuserve Graphics Interchange File	GIF
Encapsulated Postscript	EPS
Filmstrip	FLM
Generic EPS	AI3, AI8, PS
Joint Photographic Experts Group	JPG/JPEG
Paintbrush	PCX
Photo CD	PCD
Photoshop Source Document	PSD
PICT (Picture) File	PCT
PICT (Picture) Resource	RSR
Pixar	PXR
Portable Document Format	PDF
Portable Network Graphics	PNG
Raw	RAW
Scitex	SCT
Tagged Image File	TIF/TIFF
Targa	TGA
Wireless Bitmap	WBMP/WBM

Table 4-1. *Photoshop-Supported File Formats*

Note *Images created and saved in Adobe Illustrator (versions through 9), Freehand, CorelDRAW, and other similar packages create EPS (encapsulated postscript) files. When you open these files in Photoshop, the images are rasterized. The Rasterize Generic EPS Format dialog box, which pops up when you choose to open an EPS file, allows you to control the resolution and size of the image once it's converted to a bitmap file.*

Once the image is open, it has a single layer; all of the image content appears on top of a transparent background. Your editing process may include filling that visible background with a solid color (white to mimic how the image looked while it was in Illustrator, for example), and any number of changes you can apply using Photoshop's tools. You can use the Marquee, Lasso, and Magic Wand tools to select image content, and then cut that content to new layers, or leave everything on a single layer. If you do break things up into separate layers, you may want to flatten the image (Layer | Flatten Image) and get rid of the transparent background if you intend to save the file in a format other than PSD, TIFF, or PDF (all of which support the use of layers).

Note *Windows users can set things up so that any number of graphic file types are associated with and automatically opened in Photoshop. When you double-click a graphic file within the Windows Explorer or My Computer windows, Photoshop will automatically open and the graphic file you selected will open in the image window. To designate Photoshop as the application of choice for a given format, choose Tools | Folder Options from within the Windows Explorer window; use the File Types tab in the resulting dialog box to select the file format and change the format's details. Onscreen instructions will guide you through the process.*

If you haven't installed Photoshop yet, you can also choose file types to associate with Photoshop during the installation process.

Browsing for Files

When you select a file from within the Open dialog box, you see a thumbnail image of the file at the bottom of the dialog box. This helps you select a file without having to open it to see if it's the one you wanted (Figure 4-3 shows a thumbnail displayed for a selected JPG file). Using the Open dialog box to find a file visually can be very time-consuming, however; because only one thumbnail is visible at a time, you would have to click many individual files, viewing their thumbnails one at a time, until you found the file you needed.

In lieu of the one-click-for-one-image approach, it would be nice to be able to see thumbnails of all the images on a particular disk or in a particular folder, wouldn't it? Well, you can view a group of thumbnails, speeding the file selection process considerably. The visual listing is available two ways:

- Choose File | Browse.
- Click the File Browser tab in the docking well.

Once the browser is open (see Figure 4-4), you can navigate a series of folders in the upper left pane, and when you want to see the images in a particular folder, simply click that folder. The image thumbnails appear in the large block on the right, and individual file statistics (for any file you click on from the group of thumbnails) are displayed, including file name, the date created, format, dimensions, and size. Once you've found the file you want to open, double-click its thumbnail image and the file opens in its own image window.

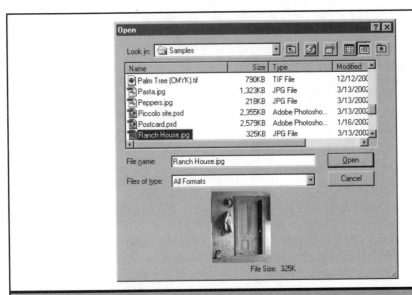

Figure 4-3. *Click a graphic file once to preview a thumbnail of it in the Open dialog box.*

> **Tip** *While Windows provides plus and minus signs to assist you in expanding and collapsing your view of folders and files, the Mac OS provides "twisties"—arrows that twist down to expand your view or twist back to pointing to the right to collapse your view.*

Across the bottom of the browser palette, you can click a series of option buttons that change the way the thumbnails are displayed, and whether or not you see the file navigation tools and statistics or just an array of thumbnails. Figure 4-5 shows the expanded view of the File Browser, and the option buttons are identified.

> **Note** *You can hover your mouse pointer over any of the tools to get a full description of how they work, and you can also hover over the individual thumbnails to see their statistics. This can be handy if you're in expanded view and can't see the statistics in the lower-left block. If your ToolTips don't show when you mouse over the tools (they should, by default), check your General Preferences and be sure the Show ToolTips option is selected. As discussed in Chapter 3, the Preferences command is located in the Edit menu if you're a Windows user, or in the Photoshop menu if you're using a Mac.*

> **Tip** *Right-click (Windows) or CONTROL-click (Mac) any image thumbnail and choose from a series of commands in a context menu. You can open it, delete it, change its rank in the display, rotate it, or display its folder location.*

This folder list includes tools for expanding and collapsing folders and subfolders (click the plus and minus signs to expand or collapse).

The selected image preview appears here.

Click this button to go up one folder level.

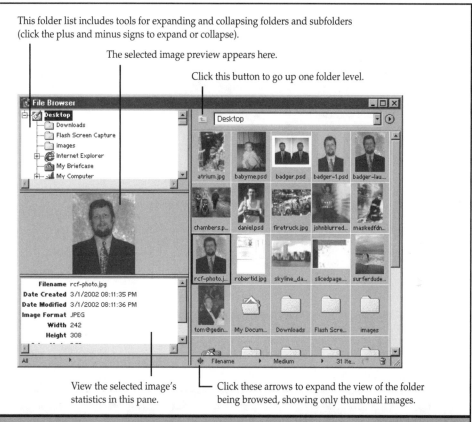

View the selected image's statistics in this pane.

Click these arrows to expand the view of the folder being browsed, showing only thumbnail images.

Figure 4-4.   *The File Browser provides file thumbnails, file statistics, and tools for finding and viewing groups of images in specific folders and drives.*

Using the Open As Command

The Open As command is a Windows version–only feature; it is located in the File menu. The command allows you to take a file with no discernable format (or the wrong extension applied) and open it in the appropriate format. Once the file is open, you can edit it and either save it in the new format or save it as a Photoshop file. As shown in Figure 4-6, there is no Files of Type drop-down list and no All Files option in the Open As drop-down list—you see all graphic files in whichever folder is chosen in the Look In box. Figures 4-7 and 4-8 show the Mac Open dialog box, with both All Documents and All Readable Documents displayed, respectively. Note that the File | Open command serves the same purpose on the Mac as Open As does in a Windows environment.

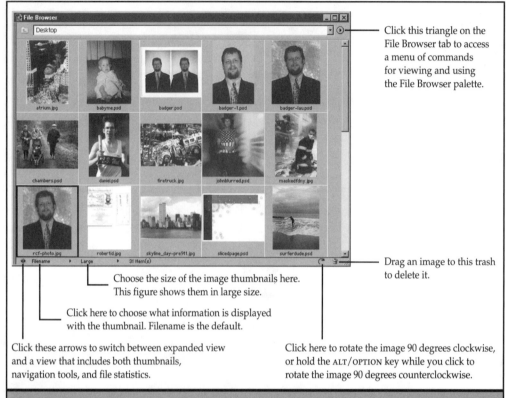

Click this triangle on the
File Browser tab to access
a menu of commands
for viewing and using
the File Browser palette.

Drag an image to this trash
to delete it.

Choose the size of the image thumbnails here.
This figure shows them in large size.

Click here to choose what information is displayed
with the thumbnail. Filename is the default.

Click these arrows to switch between expanded view
and a view that includes both thumbnails,
navigation tools, and file statistics.

Click here to rotate the image 90 degrees clockwise,
or hold the ALT/OPTION key while you click to
rotate the image 90 degrees counterclockwise.

Figure 4-5.   *Expand the File Browser view so you can see more thumbnails at once.*

Note   *The Mac version of Photoshop doesn't offer an Open As command because you can save a file with no extension on the Mac, but not in Windows. Because Windows requires an extension, files will always have an extension, but it may be the wrong one. If a file's extension isn't appropriate for the file in question, Windows won't be able to open it from the Windows Explorer or My Computer windows, and Photoshop may reject it as well (if you use the File | Open command). By using the Open As command, you can open the file in the appropriate format, the one that should be reflected by the file's extension.*

If you're a Windows user, choose the format for the file you're going to open by clicking the Open As drop-down list and picking a format. Then double-click the file you want to open (or click the file once, and then click the Open button), and it appears in an image window. You'll notice that the file's name appears as expected on the image window's title bar, but the file's extension has change to reflect the format you chose from the Open As drop-down list. If you're using a Mac, choose File | Open, navigate to the folder in which your file resides, and double-click the file once you see it displayed in the list.

GETTING TO KNOW
PHOTOSHOP

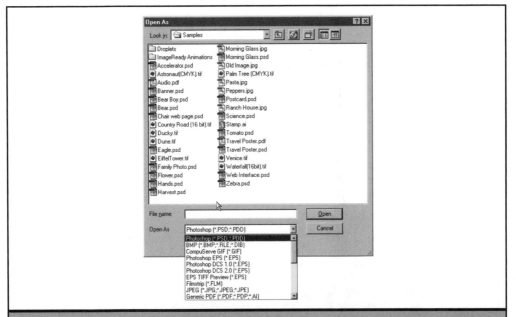

Figure 4-6.   *All files, with any graphic file format, are visible in the Open As dialog box.*

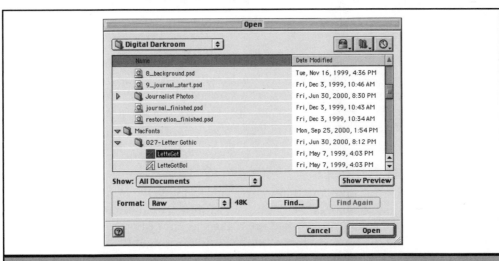

Figure 4-7.   *With All Documents selected in the Mac's Show menu, even fonts will show up in the Formats menu.*

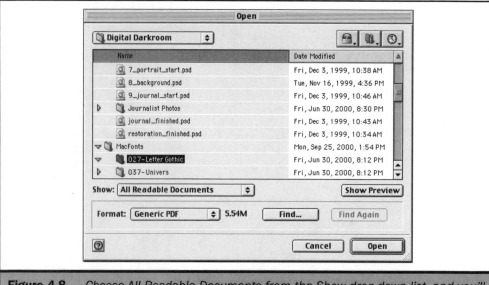

Figure 4-8. *Choose All Readable Documents from the Show drop-down list, and you'll see only files with valid file formats.*

If the file won't open, it may be damaged, or its original format and the one you've chosen are incompatible.

If you're a Windows user and you don't see your file's extension on the title bar, you need to change your file options through the Windows Explorer. Use the Tools menu, and choose Folder Options. Click the View tab and remove the check mark from the Hide File Extensions for Known File Types option. Click OK. When you return to Photoshop, the open file's extension should appear on the title bar.

Opening Recent Images

The File | Open Recent command tucks into a submenu the list of recently used files that used to appear at the foot of the File menu, as shown in Figure 4-9. This feature allows you to re-open a file you worked on in a recent Photoshop session quickly and easily, avoiding the process of searching for and opening it through the Open dialog box.

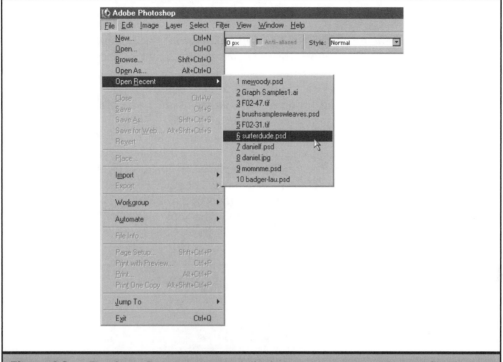

Figure 4-9.   *The Open Recent command displays your most recently used files in a tidy submenu, saving space on the File menu itself.*

If you've moved a file since you last worked on it in Photoshop, however, selecting it from the submenu may result in an error prompt, indicating that the file cannot be found. While the path to the file is not displayed in the Open Recent submenu, it is assumed that the file is where it was when you last worked on it. If the error prompt shown in Figure 4-10 appears, click OK to close it, and use the File | Open command to find and open the file. Note that Mac users will have more luck with this feature than Windows users will. On a Mac, unless the file's been moved to a different drive, selecting a file from the Open Recent submenu will open the file from its new location.

To increase or decrease the number of files displayed in the Open Recent submenu, choose Edit | Preferences | File Handling. In the File Handling version of the Preferences dialog box, change the Recent File List Contains setting, entering any number from 0 to 30.

Placing Images

The File | Place command allows you to insert an image into an existing image or into a blank image window in Photoshop. The formats supported by the Place command are limited to AI, EPS, PDF, and PDP formats, as shown in the Place dialog box in Figure 4-11. Placing an EPS file can be a way to add the EPS content without having to deal with the rasterizing dialog box discussed earlier in this chapter, because as a placed file, it simply becomes a layer in an existing image—the Rasterize Generic EPS dialog box won't appear, although the content will be rasterized as it is placed in the file on its own layer.

Once the file is selected and placed, a large box (called a *bounding box*) appears on your image, as shown in Figure 4-12. The new image is placed on a new layer, and the layer's name is the same as the file name of the placed image. The placed image can be resized by using the handles that appear on the sides and corners of the bounding box. The image can also be skewed or rotated with your mouse pointer—move the axis point in the center of the image to change the axis of rotation. You can also use the options bar to make these changes.

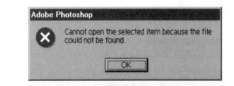

Figure 4-10.   *Files that have been moved since you had them open may not be able to be opened from the Open Recent submenu, even if the file is still listed there.*

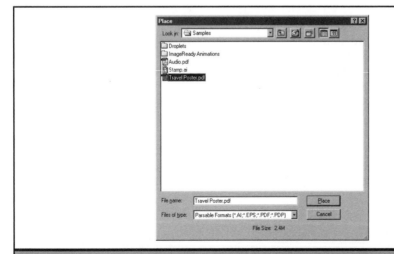

Figure 4-11.   *Find and select the file you want to place in your open image.*

Use these tools to adjust the position, size, rotation, and anti-aliasing for the placed image.

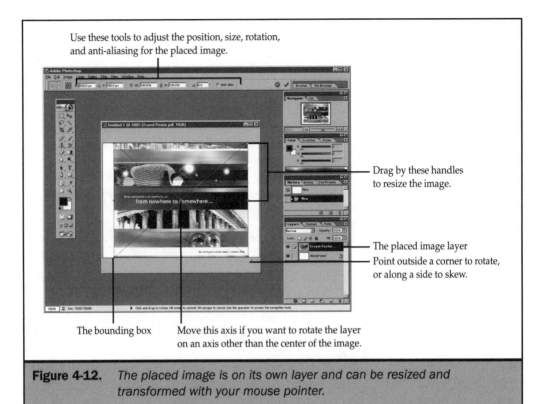

Drag by these handles to resize the image.

The placed image layer
Point outside a corner to rotate, or along a side to skew.

The bounding box   Move this axis if you want to rotate the layer on an axis other than the center of the image.

Figure 4-12.   *The placed image is on its own layer and can be resized and transformed with your mouse pointer.*

Tip   *In addition to moving your mouse pointer on or near handles to display your transformation pointers, you can also right-click/CONTROL-click on any handle to display a list of transformations that can be applied. If you want to skew your content and you're not seeing the skew pointer, CTRL/COMMAND-click on a handle to display the skew pointer; then drag to skew your image.*

If you're placing a PDF file with multiple pages, you'll have to choose which page through the PDF Page Selector dialog box shown in Figure 4-13. You can click the Go To Page button to look at different pages before you choose one. Once you've found the page you want (and you see it in the PDF Page Selector dialog box), click OK. You will see the page appear on its own layer in your image. Like any other type of image, your placed PDF can be moved, resized, rotated, or skewed.

Tip   *If a font in a PDF file cannot be found on your computer, a Missing Fonts dialog box will open. Click Continue to place the PDF page and have Photoshop make font substitutions for the missing font.*

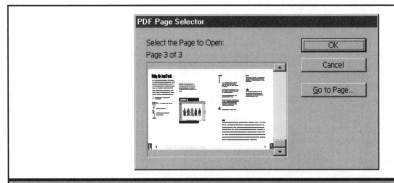

Figure 4-13. *Use the PDF Page Selector to pick which page you want to place.*

After transforming the placed file as needed, you need to confirm your intention to place it. There are a few ways to do this:

■ Click the Commit Place button on the options bar.

■ Press ENTER/RETURN.

■ Double-click the bounding box.

If you forget to confirm in one of these ways, Photoshop won't let you get too far without making a decision about your transformations. As soon as you attempt to click a tool in the toolbox or save the file, you'll be prompted to formally place the file. As shown in Figure 4-14, your options are to Place the file; Cancel, which leaves the placed image in its box, awaiting further transformation or deletion; or Don't Place, which removes the file from your image. Once "officially" placed, the image is a bona fide layer, no longer containing handles or lines across it, and it can be treated like any other layer—you can apply blending options (drop shadows, embossing, etc.), and you can hide or display it as needed.

If you didn't transform the image before confirming its placement, you can use the Edit | Transform or Edit | Free Transform commands to make any changes to the layer's size or rotation. If you choose Edit | Free Transform, you'll see a bounding box appear around the image, and you can use your mouse to make your transformations—scaling, rotating, skewing, and so forth. Note that the Edit | Transform command will open a submenu from which you can choose what you want to do to the image, but again, a bounding box and handles will appear, enabling you to make the change you select from the submenu.

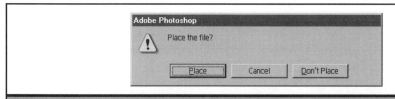

Figure 4-14. *Confirm your intention to place the file by clicking Place in response to this prompt.*

 Before you formally place the image, you can simply press DELETE *or* ESC *at any time to get rid of it. Once you've clicked Place in the confirming prompt, you can throw out the layer containing the placed file by dragging it to the Layers palette's trash can. You can also use Edit | Undo, or go back in time through the History palette, to remove the placed file layer from the image.*

Working with the Import Command

The File | Import command opens a submenu that lists all the devices, such as scanners and digital cameras, connected to your computer that can be used to capture images. If the devices are Photoshop compatible, their installation (or Photoshop's installation, if the devices were already in place when Photoshop was purchased) will add them to this menu and make a connection to the device's proprietary software so that when you choose the device from the menu, that software opens in a new window.

In addition to any Photoshop-compatible devices, the Import submenu may also offer the following commands:

PDF Image This command opens the Select PDF for Image Import dialog box (seen in Figure 4-15) and allows you to extract the images from a PDF file and open them in their own image window within Photoshop. If you choose a PDF file with multiple images, you can choose which image to import, or you can choose to Import All (see the PDF Image Import dialog box in Figure 4-16), which will open a new image window for each image of the PDF file.

Annotations Another Import command that opens PDF files, the Annotations command loads a PDF (via the Load dialog box, shown in Figure 4-17) and looks for any annotations in that PDF. If the PDF has annotations, they will appear in the active image in the spots where they were saved in the PDF from which they were loaded. If there are no annotations in the PDF, a prompt will inform you.

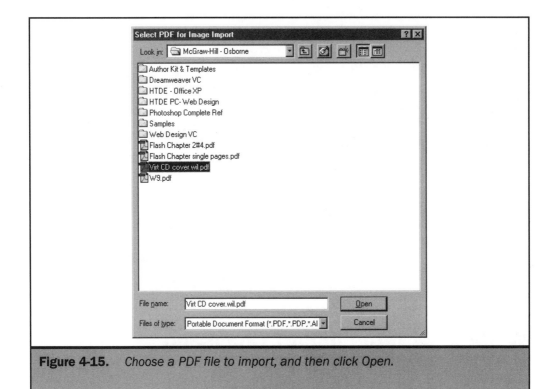

Figure 4-15. Choose a PDF file to import, and then click Open.

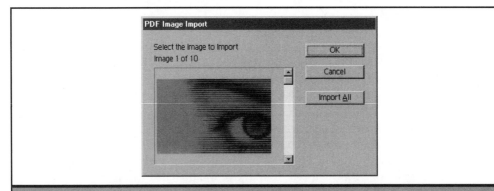

Figure 4-16. Select a single image from the PDF to import, or import all the images as individual image files.

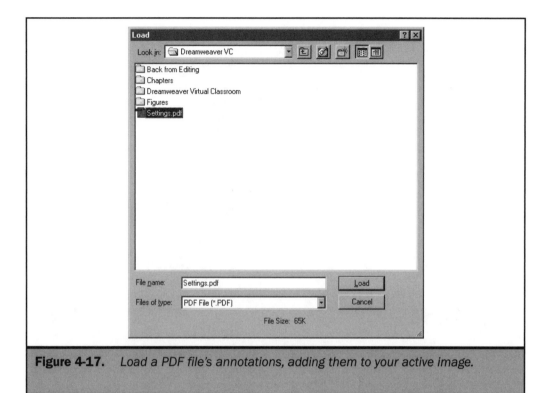

Figure 4-17. *Load a PDF file's annotations, adding them to your active image.*

WIA Support   This command accesses any scanners or digital cameras that use WIA (Windows Image Acquisition) Support; it is available only if you use Windows Me or XP. Macintosh users will not have this command, nor will Windows 98 or 2000 users. If the latter users can see the command, it won't work and will display an error prompt if you select it.

TWAIN/TWAIN Select   TWAIN is an interface that allows you to capture images with a scanner, digital camera, or a frame-grabber for capturing individual frames from video footage. When the TWAIN-compatible device is installed (or if Photoshop is installed after the device is set up on your computer), Photoshop adds this command to the Import menu and provides a connection to the TWAIN device software so you can capture the image or frame. You can start with the TWAIN select command if you have more than one TWAIN device to choose from, or go right to the TWAIN command if you have only one device or have already chosen one. The TWAIN command will open the device software in a new application window.

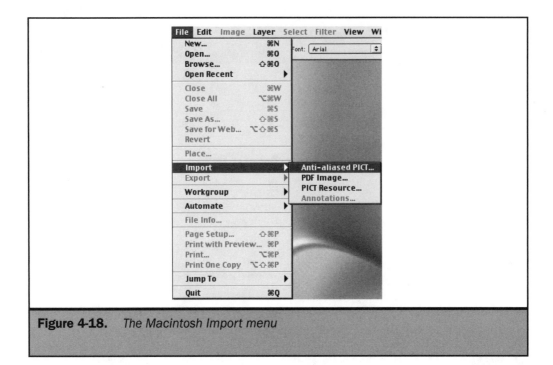

Figure 4-18. *The Macintosh Import menu*

If you're using Photoshop on a Mac, you'll notice that your Import menu has two additional commands, as shown in Figure 4-18. The additional commands are as follows:

Anti-Aliased PICT If you have PICT files you created in MacDraw, Canvas, or any other similar package, you will want to import them with this command from the Import submenu. In the resulting dialog box (see Figure 4-19), you can enter new dimensions for the imported file, being careful to select Constrain Proportions if you need to maintain the file's current width-height ratio. You can also choose between RGB and Grayscale for the file's color mode.

PICT Resource This import module allows you to read PICT resources from files created in another application. In the dialog box that appears when you make this choice from the Import submenu (see Figure 4-20), you can click the Preview button and then scroll backward and forward through the resources. The resource number at the top of the dialog box indicates the position of the resource in ascending order in the resource fork, a Mac OS convention for organizing file information.

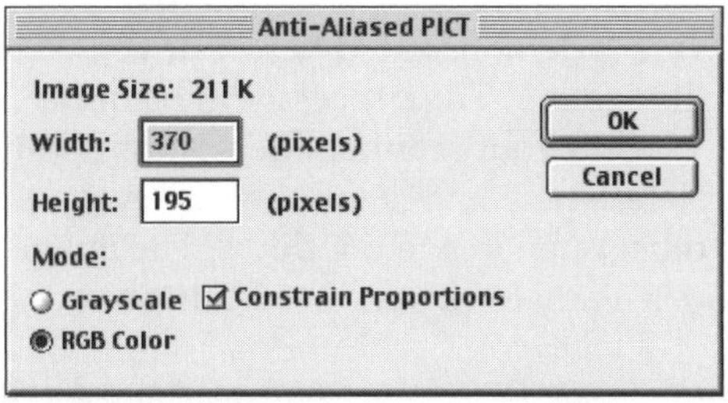

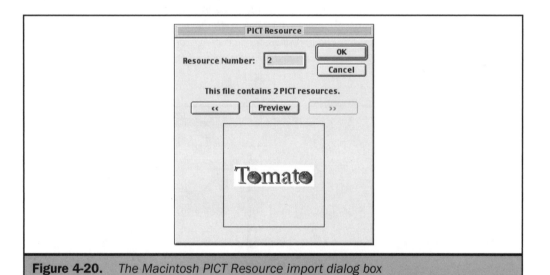

Figure 4-19. *The Macintosh Anti-Aliased PICT import dialog box*

Figure 4-20. *The Macintosh PICT Resource import dialog box*

Scanning Images Directly with Photoshop

If your scanner has a Photoshop-compatible plug-in module, you'll find the scanner's software listed directly in the Import submenu. As you can see in Figure 4-21, the scanner's software opens as soon as you choose it from the Import submenu, and you can then set the scan session's settings for the type of image, resolution, and size. You can preview the image to make sure it appears correctly and that the software is looking at the right region of the scanner's plate, and then do the actual scan. Visioneer PaperPort scanning software is demonstrated here, but your scanner may have come with different software all together. The process will be quite similar, however. For anything that's not clear, consult your scanner and scanning software user guide.

Once the scan is complete, a new image window opens on the Photoshop desktop, appearing on top of any other open image windows. The image has a single layer, as shown in Figure 4-22, and is ready to be saved and edited.

Tip *If you have several small images—say, four or five standard 4 × 6 or smaller photos to scan—scan them all at once. Assuming they're all color images intended for the same use, you can use a single scan setting for the mosaic of images on the scanner's plate, and then you can use the Marquee tool to copy each individual picture and paste it into a new Photoshop image window. Once you copy a selected region (the size of one of the pictures), the size, resolution, and color mode of that selection are automatically used to dictate the size, resolution, and color mode of the new image. Choose Edit | Paste with the new, blank image window active. The copied portion of the scan will appear inside that image window. You can rotate the canvas as needed (Image | Rotate Canvas) if the image isn't facing the right way.*

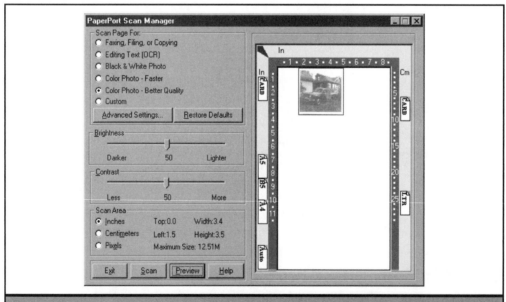

Figure 4-21.   Use your scanner's software to set up the scan, and then scan your image.

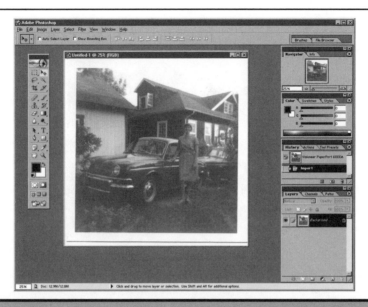

Figure 4-22.   *The scanned image appears in its own new image window.*

Summary

In this chapter, you learned about the wide variety of file formats that Photoshop supports and will open, and how to open them using the Open, Open As, Open Recent, Place, and Browse commands, all found in the File menu. You also learned how to create new Photoshop images by scanning or capturing digital images via the Import command, as well as how to add PDF documents and their annotations to your existing Photoshop images. With these skills, you're able to obtain graphic content from an extensive list of places, and you can begin editing your image.

The Complete Reference

Part II

Editing and Retouching Images

The
Complete
Reference

Chapter 5

Working with Selections, Paths, and Masks

apping out the area of an image that you want to work with or protect from changes is probably the most common task you'll perform while using Photoshop. It's often the first step in the process of any sort of editing you might do; in many cases, selecting an area of your image helps prepare the "canvas" for original drawing or painting, as well. You can select geometric shaped areas, draw freeform selections, or use drawing tools to isolate a section of your image for editing. You can also use related commands to augment, reduce, combine, or invert your selection as needed.

Understanding Selections, Masks, and Paths

Photoshop wouldn't be Photoshop without the ability to create selections, masks, and paths. Editing tools, painting tools, fill and stroke tools—all would be useless or severely limited if you couldn't isolate part of your image and treat that area differently. You couldn't retouch a photograph, selecting the model's eyes and softening the lines around them. You couldn't draw a shape and delete it or fill it with a color or pattern, and you couldn't confine your erasures to a specific area of an image. All you'd really be able to do is draw and paint, drag your mouse to draw shapes, and type artistic text. You'd be hard-pressed to tell Photoshop from Illustrator if you didn't have selections, masks, and paths.

Selecting a portion of your image, be it on a single layer or across multiple layers, isolates that portion and tells Photoshop that the area within the selection (see the dashed border around the selected region in Figure 5-1) is the only area that should be affected by your next action. You can then paint, draw, fill, stamp, or apply a filter or other effect to that area, or delete the area's content altogether. Because a selection was in force, you know that no other part of the image will be affected. This control makes it possible to confine your edits and special effects to very small or specific areas, entire layers, small portions of layers, or only certain pixels within an image. The control is further enhanced by the number of ways that selections can be made—by drawing geometric shapes with the Marquee tools, by drawing freeform shapes with the Lasso, or by selecting pixels with the Magic Wand.

Tip   *Do you find the dashed border of your selection to be distracting? Sometimes when a selection is very small or follows a very complex route around a jagged edge, the dashed lines can make it difficult to see exactly what's selected. To maintain the selection without seeing the dashed lines, press CTRL-H (Windows) or COMMAND-H (Mac) while the selection is in place. The dashed line disappears, but your selection remains in place. You can toggle the display so the lines reappear by pressing CTRL/COMMAND-H again.*

Masks are similar to selections in that they protect part of the image from the use of brushes, erasers, filters, and other special effects. Where masks and selections part company is in how they're created. Selections are created using tools that exist solely for creating selections—the Marquee, Lasso, and Magic Wand tools. Paths can be created with the Brush and Pencil tools, the Shape tools, and the Paint Bucket tool. Selections and masks also differ in terms of what's protected and what's not. When you make a

Figure 5-1.   *Use any of Photoshop's selection tools to designate a portion of the image for editing.*

selection with the Marquee, Lasso, or Magic Wand tools, the portion of the image that's encompassed by the dashed border is the only part of the image you can edit while the selection is in force. When you create a mask, the portion that's literally masked is the part of the image that won't be editable, and this creates some confusion.

To prevent confusion, it's important to note which tools are used for making selections and which tools are used to create masks (in addition to their other roles in the image-creation and editing process). Figure 5-2 shows the toolbox with the selection and masking tools identified.

Many Photoshop users never use masking tools, finding them to be more trouble than they're worth; other users swear by them and wouldn't consider working without them. Most users fall into a middle ground, however, using masks when the ability to select by painting or drawing rather than using the typical selection and path tools is the only way to protect a particular area of an image. Photoshop makes masking your image relatively simple by offering Quick Mask Mode, through which you can use tools like the Paintbrush and Pencil to isolate areas of the image and mask them off in preparation for editing the image. Figure 5-3 shows an image in Quick Mask Mode. The Brush was used to create a mask, and the Eraser can be used to clean up an edge where an unwanted portion of the image was included in the mask.

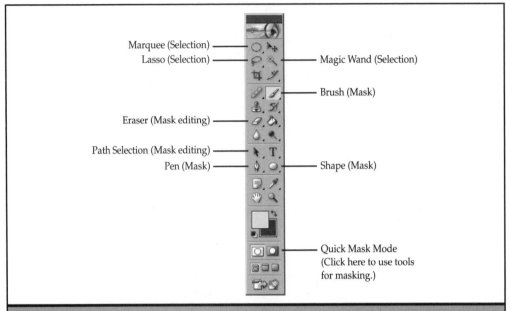

Marquee (Selection)

Lasso (Selection)

Magic Wand (Selection)

Brush (Mask)

Eraser (Mask editing)

Path Selection (Mask editing)

Pen (Mask)

Shape (Mask)

Quick Mask Mode
(Click here to use tools
for masking.)

Figure 5-2. *When it comes to masks and selections, the tools make the difference.*

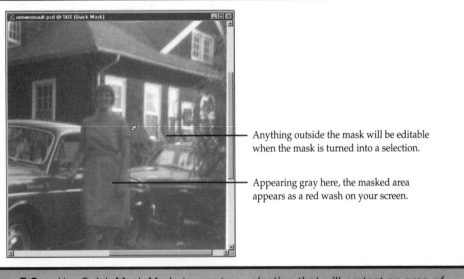

Anything outside the mask will be editable
when the mask is turned into a selection.

Appearing gray here, the masked area
appears as a red wash on your screen.

Figure 5-3. *Use Quick Mask Mode to create a selection that will protect an area of your image.*

This area is protected. ⎤   ⎡ You can draw, paint, and apply
                                  effects and filters to this area.

Figure 5-4.   *As soon as you leave Quick Mask Mode, your selection becomes visible.*

Paths are objects that you draw with the Pen tool or using the Shape tool set to Paths Mode. They live as an object atop an image and can be filled with solid color, a gradient, or a pattern. You can save a path to use over and over again in the same image, or you can create a temporary path to do something quickly and do it only once. Paths can also be converted to selections, enabling you to use the very flexible Pen tool to create a path and then convert it to a uniquely shaped selection. Paths that remain paths (and that aren't converted to selections) come in two basic flavors:

Work Paths   A Work path is a temporary path that, once drawn, appears in the Paths palette as a shape. Work paths can be used as *vector masks*, serving to hide areas within a layer, or you can simply fill the path with color or a pattern. You can paint inside the path or use the Fill or Gradient tool to apply a fill to the entire space within the path's walls.

Clipping Paths   A Clipping path enables you to make parts of an image transparent so they don't show when the image prints, or so the hidden content is invisible when the image is opened in another application such as Illustrator. To create a Clipping path, draw the path, and then save it through the Paths palette menu, as shown in Figure 5-5. Once saved, you can select Clipping Path from that same menu and give the Clipping path a name. Once the file is saved and exported to a program like Illustrator, the content within the Clipping path's confines will be omitted from any printouts of the image. Figure 5-6 shows the portions of an image that will be hidden by virtue of the Clipping path that's in place.

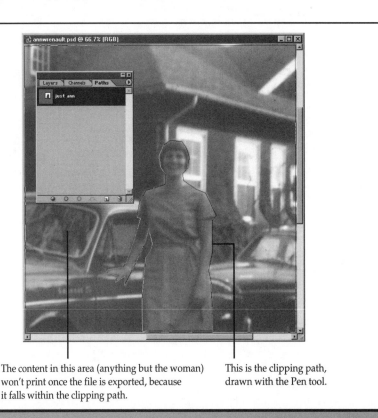

The content in this area (anything but the woman) won't print once the file is exported, because it falls within the clipping path.

This is the clipping path, drawn with the Pen tool.

Figure 5-5.   *Turn your path into a Clipping path to gets rid of unwanted content.*

Figure 5-6. *The content outside the Clipping path is gone now that the image saved as a PSD, PDF, or EPS file is open in Illustrator.*

Selecting with the Marquee Tools

You had a basic introduction to the Marquee tools (as well as the other selection, mask, and path tools) in Chapter 2, but here you'll learn more about them and see examples of the tools in use. As shown in Figure 5-7, the Marquee tool offers these four options:

- ▮ Rectangular Marquee (keyboard shortcut: M)
- ▮ Elliptical Marquee (keyboard shortcut: M)
- ▮ Single Row Marquee
- ▮ Single Column Marquee

You can deselect any selection, be it created with the Marquee, Lasso, or Magic Wand tools, by pressing CTRL/COMMAND-D.

You can draw rectangular, elliptical, or 1-pixel-wide row or column selections with these tools, marking an area for editing within your image. After making a selection using these tools, the next thing you do—painting, drawing, using the solid color or gradient fills, applying a filter, using any special effects or invoking an action—will be applied only to the portion of the image within the selection, and will only apply to the selected area on the active layer. Figure 5-8 shows an elliptical selection within a photograph, the area was selected in preparation for cutting and pasting to a new layer. Now this portion of the image can be moved and edited independently and perhaps added to another image later.

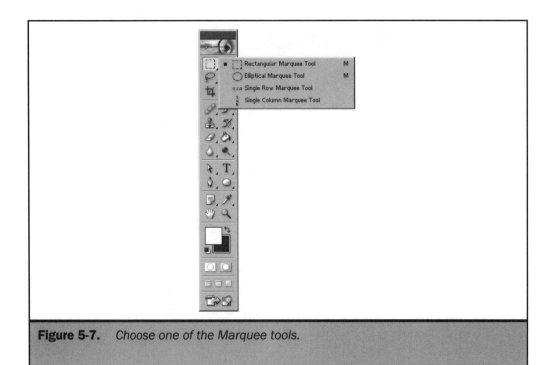

Figure 5-7. *Choose one of the Marquee tools.*

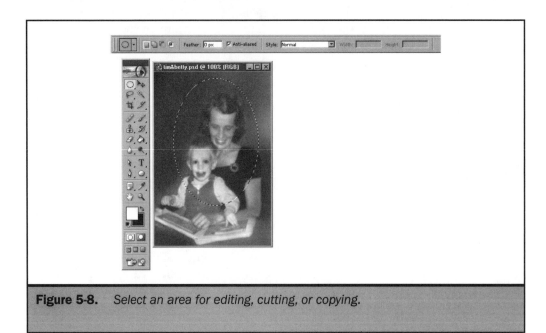

Figure 5-8. *Select an area for editing, cutting, or copying.*

> **Note**   *When you're using the Rectangular and Elliptical Marquee tools, you can use the* SHIFT *key to select a square or circular selection, respectively. When using the* SHIFT *key, be sure to release the mouse before you release the key, or your selection will change to the rectangle or ellipse you'd have drawn if the key had never been pressed at all. By keeping the key down until you release the mouse button, you maintain the equal height and width of the selection, regardless of the direction and distance you dragged your mouse during the selection process.*

> **Tip**   *It's easy to confuse the* CTRL/COMMAND *and* SHIFT *keys and their jobs. In some applications, the* CTRL/COMMAND *key is the one you press to control the shape of your selections or drawings, so you might forget which keys to use while you're working in Photoshop. Note that in Photoshop, if you press and hold the* CTRL/COMMAND *key while the Rectangular or Elliptical Marquee tools are in use, you'll move the active layer instead of drawing a selection on it.*

Selecting a Rectangular Area

To select a rectangular area in your image, click the Rectangular Marquee tool once or press its keyboard shortcut, the letter M key. Take your cursor, which appears as a small crosshair, and click and drag to create a rectangular, dashed box atop a portion of your image, on the layer that you want to edit. You can switch layers after you've drawn the rectangular selection, or you can click the appropriate layer (using the Layers palette) before drawing the selection. Figure 5-9 shows a rectangular selection on Layer 1.

Figure 5-9.   *Draw a rectangular selection on the desired layer.*

If you drew your Marquee (regardless of the shape) in the wrong place, point anywhere inside the selection. When you see a small box accompanying the mouse pointer arrow, you can drag to move the selection.

Once the rectangular selection is drawn, you can click the tool you want to use to edit the selected portion, or you can use the desired menu command to employ a filter, adjust image quality or levels (such as contrast or brightness), or use the Actions palette to apply an action to the selected area. Figure 5-10 shows the same rectangular selection as seen in the previous figure, but now a filter has been applied, changing the appearance of the image within the selected area.

Using the Elliptical Marquee

The Elliptical Marquee works just like the Rectangular Marquee, with one limitation—you can't use it to crop an image. Other than that, however, selecting an elliptical area of your image is the same as selecting a rectangular area.

When you want to select an oval or round area (use the SHIFT key as you drag to make your selection a perfect circle), simply turn on the Elliptical Marquee tool and drag to draw the selection. Once the selection is made, you can apply filters, special effects, or fills to the selection, or use any of the other Photoshop tools to change the appearance of the selected area. As shown in Figure 5-11, you can select a portion of a larger image for use in a new, smaller image that focuses on a portion of the larger one.

Figure 5-10. *Apply a filter while a selection is in place, and the filter affects only the content within the selection.*

Figure 5-11. *Direct Photoshop's attention to an elliptical area within your image.*

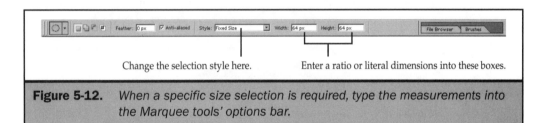

Change the selection style here.   Enter a ratio or literal dimensions into these boxes.

Figure 5-12. *When a specific size selection is required, type the measurements into the Marquee tools' options bar.*

Another feature that works with both the Rectangular and Elliptical Marquee tools is the option bar. There you can enter specific width and height measurements for the selection. If you change the Style setting from Normal to Fixed Aspect Ratio or Fixed Size, Width and Height boxes become available in which you can enter numbers to define the size of the rectangle or ellipse (see Figure 5-12). Note that when you choose Fixed Aspect Ratio, you aren't going to enter dimensions for the selection—rather, you'll enter the ratio, such as 1 and 1 (for a 1-to-1 ratio) or 2 and 1 for a selection that's twice as wide as it is tall.

Selecting Single Rows and Columns

If you need to select a single row or column of pixels in your image, the Single Row and Single Column Marquee tools are your best bet. You can use them to create a simple line on the image. By increasing the Feather settings you can create a wider, diffused effect if you paint or fill the selected row or column. Figure 5-13 shows a bright line "drawn" on the image by selecting a column of pixels, filling the selection with white with a Feather of 3 pixels applied to the selection.

Figure 5-13. *The column of selected pixels becomes a line on the image.*

Figure 5-14. *Multiple row and column selections can be used to create interesting effects.*

Other reasons to use these tools include deleting a row or column of pixels to let the background or another layer beneath the active layer show through. Figure 5-14 shows the results of selecting two rows and then two columns, creating a box. By deleting the pixels in these selected areas, the white background shows through and creates the appearance of a grid or frame (as the surfer is centered within the four intersecting lines).

Modifying a Selection

While your selection is in place, you can choose Select | Modify and choose from four submenu options, which allow you to control the selection, changing, adding to, or subtracting from the selection you created:

Border   This modification adds a buffer zone of selected pixels (the number of pixels is set in the Border Selection dialog box, shown in Figure 5-15) around the perimeter of the existing selection. As shown in Figure 5-16, if you start with a simple selection and use the Border command, the original selection serves as the basis for a new selection, which will act as a border.

Smooth   If you've used the Rectangular Marquee tool, or created an angular selection with the Polygonal Lasso tool, you can round off the corners with this command. Choose Select | Modify | Smooth and use the Smooth Selection dialog box to control the radius of the new smoothed corners. Figure 5-17 shows the dialog box and a polygonal selection that's already been rounded by 50 pixels. You can repeatedly smooth your selection until the desired effect is achieved.

Figure 5-15.   *Enter a number from 1 to 200 to indicate the thickness of the border.*

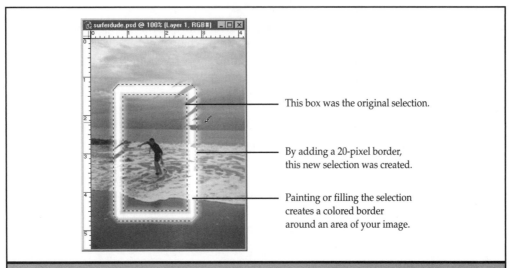

This box was the original selection.

By adding a 20-pixel border, this new selection was created.

Painting or filling the selection creates a colored border around an area of your image.

Figure 5-16. *Turn your selected shape into a soft-edged, rounded border selection.*

Figure 5-17. *Round out the corners of a selection with the Smooth command.*

Figure 5-18.   *Need your selection to be exactly 20 pixels wider and taller? Use the Expand command to create an all-over increase in the size of your selection.*

Expand   You can increase the size of your selection by a specific number of pixels—anything from 1 pixel to 100 pixels, in all directions—by choosing Select | Modify | Expand. In the resulting Expand Selection dialog box (shown in Figure 5-18), you can enter the number of pixels by which the current selection should be expanded.

Tip   *Unlike the Border command, which rounds the corners of any rectangular selection, Expand and Contract do not change the shape of the selection—merely its size.*

Contract   This command does the exact opposite of the Expand command. If you need your selection to be smaller and need that reduction to be by a specific number of pixels, use this command (Select | Modify | Contract) to shrink the selection. The Contract Selection dialog box works just like the Expand Selection dialog box, allowing you to enter any number of pixels (from 1 to 100) indicating the amount of contraction you're looking for.

The Feather command, also found in the Select menu, allows you to soften the edges of a selection. As shown in Figure 5-19, you can enter a number into the Feather Selection dialog box, or you can use the options bar when any of the Marquee or

Lasso tools are active to enter a number of pixels by which to feather the selection. The Select | Feather command can only be applied after a selection has been made—if you use the Feather setting on the options bar (displayed while the Marquee tools are active), you can set the amount of feather before making your selection.

Once the selection is feathered, any fill applied to the selection will stray beyond the edge of the selection, extending that fill by as many pixels as were entered into the Feather Selection dialog box or the Feather setting on the options bar. Figure 5-20 shows a selection that was painted with a semi-opaque solid color—a 10-pixel feather was applied to the selection, creating a soft, sort of fuzzy edge to the colored fill.

Feathering a selection achieves the same result as blurring a mask. The selection boundary (the dashed border) lies at the point where the mask is 50 percent opaque or the image is 50 percent selected. To see a feathered selection more accurately, switch to Quick Mask Mode.

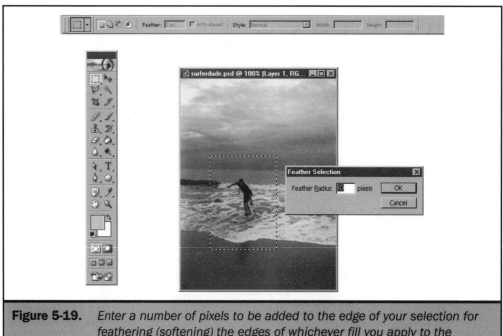

Figure 5-19. *Enter a number of pixels to be added to the edge of your selection for feathering (softening) the edges of whichever fill you apply to the selected area.*

The painting just outside the selection is the result of the Feather setting.

Figure 5-20.   *Soft, muted edges can be achieved by feathering a selection prior to applying a solid, pattern, or painted fill.*

The Transform Selection command works much like the Free Transform command in the Edit menu, except that it applies to a selection, not to content on a layer within the image. When you choose Select | Transform Selection, a box appears around the current selection, and handles on the sides and corners of that box allow you to resize and rotate the selection. As shown in Figure 5-21, the appearance of your mouse pointer as you move around the perimeter of the box indicates what control you can have over the selection. Vertical or horizontal double arrows indicate that you're in resize mode, and a curved arrow, typically displayed when you're on or near a corner handle, allows you to rotate the selection. If you want to rotate the selection on a different axis, drag the axis anchor to any other location on the image—you needn't keep it inside the Transform box.

Note that while the Transform box is displayed, the options bar (shown in Figure 5-22) displays settings for the position of the selection (X and Y for the coordinates), the width (W), height (H), angle of rotation, and horizontal (H) and vertical (V) skew. If you need to make precise changes to your selection, you might prefer to use these settings rather than your mouse.

Figure 5-21. *Transform your selection by dragging outward on side or corner handles to make it bigger. Drag inward to make it smaller, or drag in a circular motion to rotate the selection.*

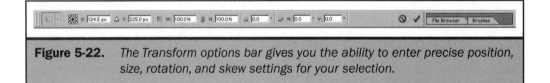

Figure 5-22. *The Transform options bar gives you the ability to enter precise position, size, rotation, and skew settings for your selection.*

To get rid of the Transform box and start over, or if you simply don't want to transform your selection after all, press the ESC key. The box disappears, and any changes to size, position, and rotation that you applied using the box will not take effect.

Cropping with the Marquee Tool

The Rectangular Marquee tool can be used to crop your image. Sometimes it's easier to use this tool for cropping than to use the actual Crop tool. Simply select a rectangular area (or a square, using the SHIFT key) that does not include the unwanted edges of your image. Figure 5-23 shows a scanned photo that was scanned to include the white border around the picture. The border is yellowed, torn, and doesn't contribute to the image, so it should be removed. By selecting the image within that border and then using the Crop tool, the unwanted edge is removed, as shown in the "after" version of this image (Figure 5-24).

Figure 5-23.   *Select the portion of the image that you want to keep after the Crop command is issued.*

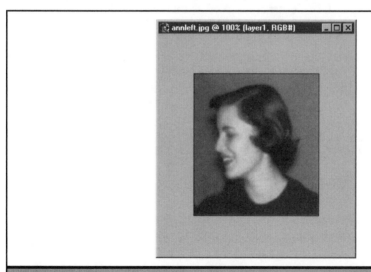

Figure 5-24.   *An undesirable border is removed by cropping it away with the Rectangular Marquee and the Image | Crop command.*

Note

So how does the Crop tool differ from the Marquee tool? If you use the Crop tool to select the portion of your image you intend to keep, you can simply press ENTER (Windows) or RETURN (Mac) to crop away the portion of the image outside the selection. If you regret the move, you can undo it, or use the History palette to go back to the state prior to the crop. If you use the Marquee tool, you have to take the extra step of choosing Image | Crop to crop away whatever's outside the selected area. This can be a good thing, because you're less likely to accidentally choose a menu command than you are to press a key. While an unwanted crop can be undone (as can an unwanted Crop command), you give yourself that wider margin for considering what to crop before cropping it if you use the Marquee tool.

Tip

You can apply the Image | Crop command to freeform and feathered selections, too— you're not restricted to rectangular marquees. The cropping effect, however, will not follow the shape of the freeform or otherwise non-squared selection. Instead, it will crop the image to meet the widest and tallest points of the selected area.

Selecting with the Lasso Tools

The Lasso tools—Lasso, Polygonal Lasso, and Magnetic Lasso—all give you the ability to create freeform selections based on a shape or area you visualize or by following the edges of actual content in the image. Like the Marquee selection tools, the selection is in effect on the active layer only, and you can apply any of Select menu's Modify submenu items (Border, Smooth, Expand, or Contract), as well as the Feather command and the Transform Selection command, also found in the Select menu. Figure 5-25 shows a set of non-contiguous selections, each made with a different Lasso tool.

Another thing the Lasso tools have in common with the Marquee tools is the presence of the New Selection, Add to Selection, Subtract from Selection, and Intersect with Selection tools. You can select areas with all three different Lasso tools (or select with the Marquee tools, and then switch to the Lasso tools as needed) by simply making sure the Add to Selection button is selected before you switch selection tools. If your selections are contiguous, a new shape will be created by the additions of new areas. Figure 5-26 shows the options bar and your options for adjusting the size and shape of your selection.

Drawing Freeform Lasso Selections

When using the standard Lasso tool (keyboard shortcut: L), you simply draw with the mouse pointer in the Lasso shape, creating a closed shape of any size or configuration. You can follow the shape of something in the image, as shown in Figure 5-27, to allow for blurring or sharpening your image, or you can select an area that will stand on its own once you apply a fill or filter to it. Figure 5-28 shows a freeform region to which a filter has been applied.

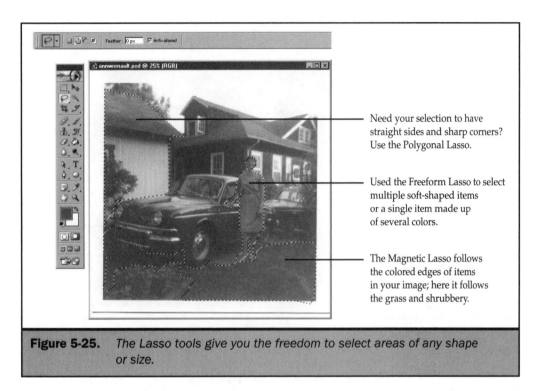

Need your selection to have straight sides and sharp corners? Use the Polygonal Lasso.

Used the Freeform Lasso to select multiple soft-shaped items or a single item made up of several colors.

The Magnetic Lasso follows the colored edges of items in your image; here it follows the grass and shrubbery.

Figure 5-25.   *The Lasso tools give you the freedom to select areas of any shape or size.*

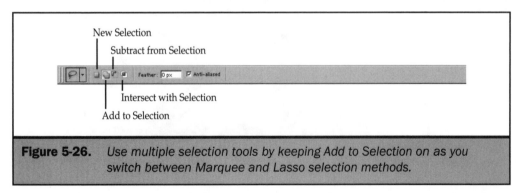

New Selection

Subtract from Selection

Intersect with Selection

Add to Selection

Figure 5-26.   *Use multiple selection tools by keeping Add to Selection on as you switch between Marquee and Lasso selection methods.*

Figure 5-27.   If an area is large enough or has few intricate turns, you can select it with the Freeform Lasso tool. Here, the shadows around her hair would make the color-controlled Magnetic Lasso difficult to use.

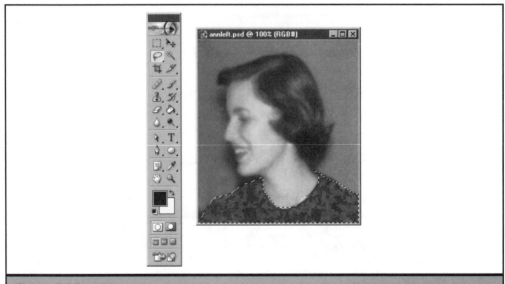

Figure 5-28.   Select an area within your image and apply a filter to it. Here, we've created the illusion of a patterned or textured sweater.

> **Tip** *When creating a selection with the Lasso, be sure you close the shape by coming back to the starting point. If you don't, Photoshop will close the selection for you, creating a straight line back to the starting point—rarely is this the selection shape you were hoping for. Coming back to the starting point needn't be a precise action; just coming close to the point should suffice. If you do require a great deal of precision and want the starting and closing points of the selection to be on or near the same pixel, use any of the Zoom tools to get close enough to see the pixel on which you started your selection and drag back to it to close.*

Working with the Polygonal Lasso

Unlike the standard Lasso tool, which requires that you drag the mouse to draw a selection, the Polygonal Lasso tool works by your clicking the mouse to designate corners and then moving (not dragging) the mouse to create the sides that connect them. Figure 5-29 shows a polygonal selection in progress. To close the shape, you must come back to the starting point and click, or get close to the starting point and double-click to force the closure by adding a short line between your end point and the starting point.

To assist you in closing your polygonal selection, watch the mouse pointer as you come close to the starting point. As shown in Figure 5-30, a small circle appears next to the pointer when you're close enough to the starting point to click and close the shape.

Figure 5-29.   *Angular content within your image calls for the Polygonal Lasso tool.*

Figure 5-30.   *Look for the small circle to appear with your mouse pointer when the starting point is nearby.*

You can ignore the circle and move away so you can keep clicking and moving if you're not ready to close the selection yet. When you are ready to close the shape, you'll find this feature quite helpful.

> **Tip**   *If you end up stuck in Polygonal Lasso Mode and it seems like the lasso is following you—sort of like having adhesive tape stuck to your fingers—you're probably in Add to Selection Mode and didn't realize it. You also probably double-clicked when you only needed to single-click to close your selection, or you triple-clicked instead of double-clicking. If you click too many times as you close a selection, Photoshop assumes you want to continue building the selection with a contiguous polygonal selection, and it doesn't "let go" until you double-click again or come back to your original starting point and click (watch for the little circle next to the mouse pointer). You can also press the ESC key to end the added selection, leaving only the original closed selection.*

Using the Magnetic Lasso

The Magnetic Lasso tool works by following your mouse as you drag, all the while following the edges of content within the image on the active layer. It manages to do this seemingly magical thing by looking for contrasting pixels—where it finds the greatest amount of contrast, it adheres to the pixels, and the selection is created (see Figure 5-31). As you drag, you can click to change direction and have the Magnetic

Lasso follow you as you continue to drag the mouse. As you drag, it continues to look for contrasting adjacent pixels and lays down a lasso line as it finds them.

You can control the standards by which the Magnetic Lasso tool seeks and finds contrasting pixels, raising and lowering the bar for what's considered enough contrast to warrant selection. The controls for this tool are, of course, found on the options bar when the tool is active (see Figure 5-32).

To control the way the Magnetic Lasso works, you can make adjustments to the following settings:

Width   Set to 10 pixels by default, the Width setting dictates the area in which the Magnetic Lasso looks for contrasting pixels as you drag your mouse. If you decrease

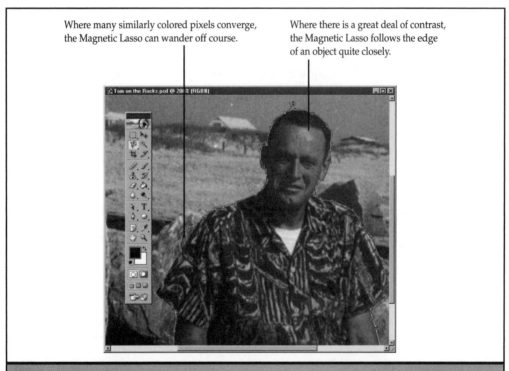

Where many similarly colored pixels converge, the Magnetic Lasso can wander off course.

Where there is a great deal of contrast, the Magnetic Lasso follows the edge of an object quite closely.

Figure 5-31.   *Use the Magnetic Lasso tool to trace the edges of items within your image.*

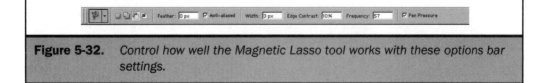

Figure 5-32.   *Control how well the Magnetic Lasso tool works with these options bar settings.*

the number here, you're limiting the range that will be searched; potentially, you'll have greater control and fewer "leaps" away from the actual edge of items as you make your selection. Increasing the number in this setting allows for a search of a wider area around the path your mouse takes and gives you less control over the selection, especially in an image that has a lot of detail and color variations throughout it.

> **Tip**   *If you want to be able to see the pixel Width you've set on the options bar as you drag and use the Magnetic Lasso, press the CAPS LOCK key before starting the selection. Your cursor will change to display a circle, the radius of which will be the number of pixels you entered into the Width setting. You can use the [and] keys to increase and decrease (respectively) the width as you make the selection.*

Edge Contrast   Another setting that allows you to refine and control your selection, Edge Contrast is set to 10 percent by default, but it can be increased (to as high as 100 percent) or decreased (to as low as 1 percent) depending on how much contrast you want the Magnetic Lasso to look for before it makes its selection. A low percentage will make it easier to find an adequate amount of contrast, and your selection can therefore follow edges where there isn't a great deal of difference between pixels. If the items in your image are very similar in color, it's important to reduce the Edge Contrast so the Magnetic Lasso can stick to the outlines you want to follow and not waver when it comes to pixels that are very close in color.

Frequency   This number, set to 57 by default, controls how many fastening points are placed along the selection line created by the Magnetic Lasso. You can reduce it to 0 or raise it to 100. As you can see in Figure 5-33, the fastening points appear each time you click and change direction, and as the Magnetic Lasso tightens to adhere to the edge of an object. The more fastening points you have, the more control you have over the direction your Magnetic Lasso selection line takes. As you drag, if you see that the lasso is heading in the wrong direction or has adhered to the wrong part of the image, before you click again to redirect, move it and the line will hinge on the last fastening point, allowing you to redirect the line. Obviously then, the more fastening points you have, the more control you can potentially have over the Magnetic Lasso selection. You'll find, however, that the default setting is usually fine, as you'll probably apply more anchor points manually than the setting would have applied on its own.

Pen Pressure   If you have a pressure-sensitive stylus attached to your computer and use the Pen Pressure check box (click to place a check mark in the box, turning the feature on), you can control your Magnetic Lasso selection by varying your pressure as you move the pen. If you don't have a stylus, this option will be dimmed on the options bar.

Figure 5-33. *Adjust the frequency to give yourself more fastening points that will stick to your selection as you drag.*

EDITING AND RETOUCHING IMAGES

Tip   *If you're using the Magnetic Lasso tool but need the functionality of the regular Lasso tool for a brief period during the selection process, you can switch to the regular Lasso tool—just press and hold the ALT (Windows) or OPTION (Mac) key while you drag. If you want to turn the Magnetic Lasso into the Polygonal Lasso, press ALT/OPTION and hold it as you click and move your mouse. As soon as you release the ALT/OPTION key, the tool returns to Magnetic Lasso function.*

Working Wonders with the Magic Wand

As opposed to selection tools that require you to draw a shape with your mouse, the Magic Wand makes selections for you, based on a single click on a single pixel. When you click that single pixel, all the pixels that are touching that pixel (or touching a pixel that's touching that pixel) are selected, assuming the color of those pixels falls within a Tolerance threshold setting. Figure 5-34 shows a selection based on the single pixel.

Figure 5-34.   *Click a pixel to sample a specific color.*

By default, the Contiguous option on the Magic Wand's options bar is on. This means that only pixels that are touching the original sampled pixel will be checked to see if they fall within the Tolerance range, and if they do, they'll be selected. If you turn off the Contiguous option, sampling a single pixel will select pixels that fall within the Tolerance range from anywhere in the image. Figure 5-35 shows the same sampled pixel that was clicked in Figure 5-34, but now with Contiguous turned off. The resulting selection is larger and includes clusters of pixels with no physical connection to the originally sampled pixel.

Controlling the Magic Wand's Selections

The aforementioned Tolerance setting determines the standard by which contiguous (or non-contiguous) pixels are judged. The default Tolerance is 32, and this is a good average setting for most selections. If you find that the resulting selection is too large, including pixels you don't think are close enough matches to the sampled pixel, reduce the Tolerance setting. If you feel that you're not getting enough of the pixels in your image, increase the Tolerance setting; more pixels will pass muster and be included in your selection. Figure 5-36 shows the same pixel sampled again, now with the Tolerance setting set to 50 and many more pixels included in the selection.

Figure 5-35. *Turn the Contiguous option off to expand the Wand's magic touch to the entire image.*

Figure 5-36. *Widen your net by raising the Magic Wand's Tolerance setting.*

The Magic Wand's options bar also offers you the ability to select pixels on all of the image layers—just place a check mark in the Use All Layers check box. If you leave this option off (the default setting), only the active layer's pixels will be considered for selection. You can also leave the Anti-aliased setting in its default state (on) to make sure that the edges of your selection remain smooth. You can make use of the Select menu's Feather and Modify submenu commands to control and refine your selection even further, and you'll find that these commands work just as they do for the Marquee and Lasso tools.

Modifying a Magic Wand Selection

Commands that are particularly helpful to the Magic Wand are also found in the Select menu, and you can use all of them before making your selection or after the selection's been made. In the case of one of the commands, you might want to use it in place of the Magic Wand:

Color Range This is the one that might make you forget all about the Magic Wand tool. The Color Range command, found in the Select menu, opens a dialog box through which you can select pixels within your image by clicking on the image with an eyedropper pointer, and by setting a Fuzziness threshold to increase or decrease the number of pixels that meet your criteria for selection by color range. You can select Sampled Colors, or select pixels that are considered red, yellow, blue, cyan, green, and magenta. You can also pick just highlights, midtones, or shadows, or choose to select only the colors that are out of gamut. Once the selection preview (shown in a black box in the center of the dialog box, as shown in Figure 5-37) shows the selection you're looking for, click OK to see the selection applied to your image.

> **Tip** *You can use the Add to Sample and Subtract from Sample buttons in the Color Range dialog box to augment or reduce the number of pixels selected.*

Grow The Grow command expands the selection by expanding the Tolerance value (though the setting won't change on the options bar) so that more pixels fall within the color threshold. Whatever your Tolerance option is set to, that number will be used to control the amount of growth applied by the Grow command.

Similar This command seems like it does the same thing that Grow does, but it adds only pixels that match those that are already selected. If you had the Contiguous option off while you were using the Magic Wand, the Similar command will have the same effect as if you'd made your Magic Wand selection with the Contiguous option on.

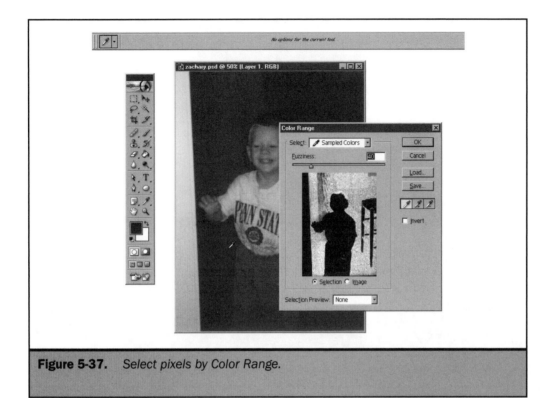

Figure 5-37.   *Select pixels by Color Range.*

Inverting Your Selections

Any selection you make, be it by Marquee, Lasso, or Magic Wand, can be inverted so everything but the original selection is selected. The Select | Inverse command works quickly and simply, making it easier to select an area of the image that's too intricate to be selectable with the Magic Wand, Lasso, or Marquee tools. Just select the portion of the image that you *can* select with any of those tools, and then invert the selection— voilà! The portion you had no way to select all at once is selected. Figures 5-38 and 5-39 show selection before and after inversion. To select the background behind the cat, the Magnetic Lasso was used, and then the Select Inverse command selected everything but the cat.

Figure 5-38. *Use the selection tool that's appropriate for selecting the portion of your image you want to eventually exclude.*

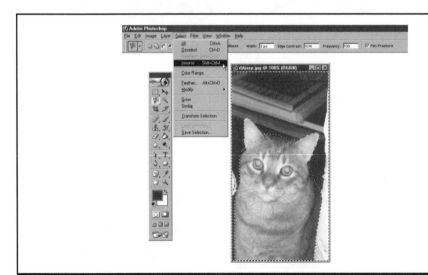

Figure 5-39. *Inverting your selection makes it easier to select a varied or intricate area of the image that defies selection with the Marquee, Lasso, or Magic Wand tools.*

At first glance, you may not think that the selection has changed when you use the Inverse command—chances are, the border around the originally selected area will remain in place, as now this is the border where the selection ends. As shown in Figure 5-39, a border appears around the entire perimeter of the image, showing that the selection now encompasses everything from the edges inward, to the outside edges of the cat.

 If you deselect your selection (CTRL/COMMAND-D or Select | Deselect), you can reselect it with the Select | Reselect command. The shortcut for Reselect is SHIFT-CTRL/COMMAND-D.

Cutting, Copying, and Pasting Selections

Photoshop users select portions of the image for two reasons: to edit the selection, or to cut or copy it to the clipboard for pasting in the same image or in another existing or new image. The selection technique has no bearing on the selection's potential use as pasted content. You can cut or copy and then paste selections created with the Marquee, Lasso, or Magic Wand tools. You can also cut or copy selections created in Quick Mask Mode, which we will discuss later in this chapter, in the section titled "Using Quick Mask Mode."

When you select a portion of your image, you can place that selection on the clipboard with the following keyboard shortcuts:

- CTRL/COMMAND-C copies the selection.
- CTRL/COMMAND-X cuts the selection.

 You can also use the Edit menu's Copy and Cut commands to do the same things.

Using Cut or Copied Content

Once selected and cut or copied, the content on the clipboard can be pasted into the same image, or into another exiting image, or into a new image. You can paste content by choosing Edit | Paste or by pressing CTRL/COMMAND-V. The connection between clipboard content that originated in Photoshop and your next new image file is strong; in fact, when you copy something to the clipboard, its overall dimensions become the default size of the next new image you create. Figure 5-40 shows a selection within an open image. The selection has been copied to the clipboard and, according to the New dialog box, the dimensions of the new image will be the same as the selected region: 559 pixels wide by 630 pixels tall.

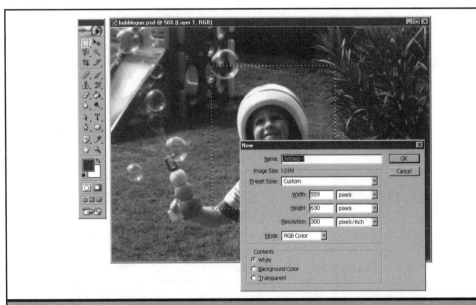

Figure 5-40.   *Your cut or copied selections create custom dimensions for the next new image you create with the File | New command.*

Tip   *A quick sequence of keyboard shortcuts will cut or copy your content and position them in a new image. Select the content to be cut or copied, press CTRL/COMMAND-X (cut) or CTRL/ COMMAND-C (copy), and then press CTRL/COMMAND-N to create a new image. Press ENTER to confirm the dimensions of the new image, and then in the new, blank image window, press CTRL/COMMAND-V (Paste) to paste the cut or copied content onto the new image.*

When you paste content into an existing image, be it the same image from which the selection was cut or copied or an entirely different image, the pasted content is automatically placed on a new numbered layer. If, for example, you're pasting a selection three times, as soon as you paste the selection the first time, Layer 1 will appear (assuming the image didn't already have a layer called Layer 1). The second time you paste the content, Layer 2 is created, and then Layer 3 when the third paste occurs. Figure 5-41 shows three pasted layers, each containing the same selection (a bubble) from within the image.

These separate layers are a good thing. As you'll discover in Chapter 10, it's best to place as many of your visual components on individual layers as possible. This gives you the most control over the placement and appearance of your content, and this control obviously benefits you when you're pasting content into an image. If all the pasted content ended up on an existing layer, or all the pasted content ended up on a single layer, you couldn't move the pasted items around or use the Image | Transform tools to resize, rotate, or skew them. With each pasted item on its own layer, you can move the pasted content into position, resize it if you need to, and apply layer-specific effects (like drop shadows) to the individual layers.

Three of these bubbles are pasted copies of this bubble.

Figure 5-41.   *Each time you paste something into your Photoshop image, a new layer is created.*

Merging Pasted Layers

Once you've positioned and transformed your individual pasted layers as desired, you may want to merge those layers with each other (making one layer out of all the pasted items) or merge them with another layer. You'll find out all about layers and the process of merging them in Chapter 10. In the meantime, you can use the Layers menu, selecting Merge Visible, to make a single layer out of all your pasted content, no matter where you've moved them within the image.

When merging your pasted layers, be sure to make only the pasted layers visible, using the Layers palette's visibility tools to hide the layers that you don't want to merge with, such as the background. Do this before issuing the Layers | Merge Visible command. Figure 5-42 shows the Layers palette and only the pasted layers visible, awaiting the Merge Visible process, which will combine them into a single layer.

Once your pasted layers are merged, you cannot move individual items within the new merged layer. You'll only be able to move the layer as a whole. If, after merging your layers, you find that an individual element within that layer needs to be moved or otherwise transformed, you can cut that one item and paste it, which will create a new layer. Once on its own layer again, the content can be moved, resized, or rotated as desired. If you simply regret merging any of your pasted layers, you can use the Undo command to reverse that step, or use the History palette to go back to the point in time prior to your issuing the Merge Visible command.

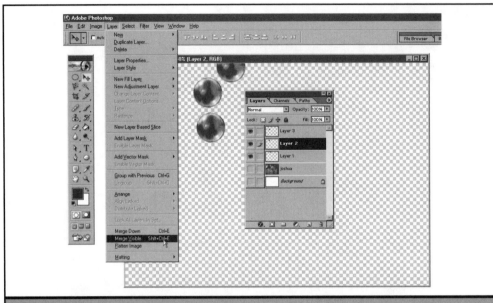

Figure 5-42. *Merge your pasted layers into one layer after you've moved and transformed them as needed.*

Tip

You can use the clipboard to add content from other graphics and illustration applications. Within the other application, select the content you want to add to a Photoshop image, and use the Edit | Copy command or press CTRL/COMMAND-C. Switch to or open Photoshop, open the image that will receive the copied content, and use the Edit | Paste command or press CTRL/COMMAND-V to paste the content. Again, a new layer will be created to house the pasted content (unless you're pasting from another application such as Illustrator, which will give you the choice of pasting as pixels or paths, the latter not creating a new layer). If you want to create a new image based on the content copied from another application, issue the File | New command (CTRL/COMMAND-N) before pasting, and then paste the content into the new file.

Using Quick Mask Mode

Quick Mask Mode makes it possible to paint and draw your selections in the form of a mask, or semi-transparent wash, over the surface of your image. You work in Quick Mask Mode to create the mask (or to edit an existing mask), and then you switch back to Standard Editing Mode where your painted area is converted to a selection in which the portions you'd painted are protected from editing. Everything else in the image is actually selected, ready for editing or special effects. Figures 5-43 and 5-44 show a Quick Mask being created and the resulting selection as it appears in Standard Editing Mode.

Figure 5-43.   *Paint your mask by using brushes, Shape tools, or the Eraser.*

Figure 5-44.   *Back in Standard Editing Mode, the mask becomes the one part of the image that can't be edited.*

Switching to and Working in Quick Mask Mode

To work in Quick Mask Mode, you have to *be* in Quick Mask Mode. It's easy to get there—just click the Quick Mask Mode button on the toolbox. At first, you won't be able to tell that you've changed your working mode, but as soon as you begin using any painting or drawing tools, you'll see what's different. Instead of applying a solid color/pattern or drawing a shape on your image, you're applying a light red wash. Figure 5-45 shows a mask being applied with a small paintbrush, allowing for a very detailed area to be masked—in this case, the iris in a cat's eye.

While you can select a tiny area with the Lasso tool, it's not quite as responsive as the Brush and Pencil tools can be, especially if you're well versed in using those tools for painting and drawing. When it comes to using the Shape tools (the Rectangle, Rounded Rectangle, Ellipse, Polygon, and Custom Shape tools, set to Fill Pixels Mode), yes, you could have used the Marquee tools, but there you'd be more limited in terms of the shapes you could create. Figure 5-46 shows a Custom Shape that's been applied as a mask. Note that on the options bar for the Shape tool, the Fill Pixels button is selected—this creates a mask rather than a new shape layer or path.

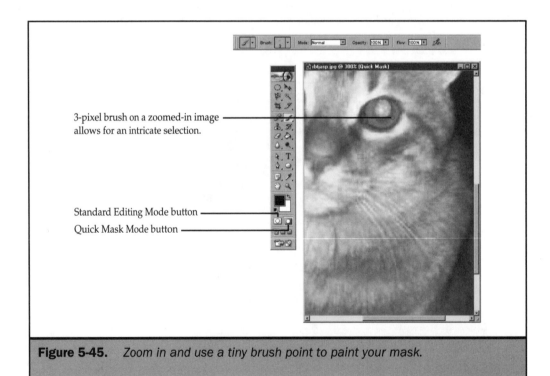

3-pixel brush on a zoomed-in image allows for an intricate selection.

Standard Editing Mode button

Quick Mask Mode button

Figure 5-45.   *Zoom in and use a tiny brush point to paint your mask.*

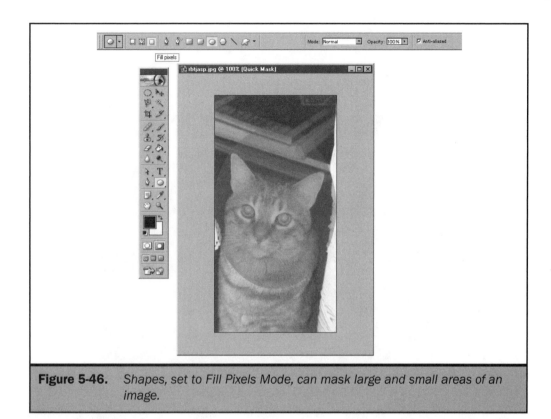

Figure 5-46.   *Shapes, set to Fill Pixels Mode, can mask large and small areas of an image.*

As you draw your mask, using the Brush, Pencil, and Shape tools, you can also apply the Eraser tool, removing areas of the mask. You can also use the Horizontal Type Mask and the Vertical Type Mask tools to make a mask from text. As shown in Figure 5-47, when you type using these tools, the text becomes the only non-masked area on the image.

You can type as much text as you want, creating a legible string of characters, or use many text layers to create a text pattern on top of the image. Either type of mask will turn into an interesting selection, and then an interesting fill or effect when you use the selection to control where new colors, patterns, and effects are applied.

Returning to Standard Editing Mode

After creating your selection, return to Standard Editing Mode by clicking the Standard Editing Mode button, as shown in Figure 5-48. Your mask, which looked like a semi-transparent red wash, now appears as a selection. The portion of the image over which you applied the mask will now be protected, and everything else in the image will be selected and ready for editing.

As soon as you click either Type Mask tool, the entire image is washed in red.

Typing removes the mask.

Figure 5-47. *Create a text mask that runs horizontally or vertically.*

Figure 5-48. *The Standard Editing button takes you out of Quick Mask Mode and displays a selection on your image.*

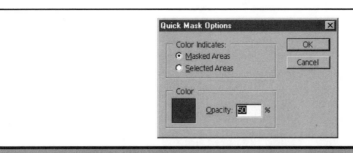

Figure 5-49.   *Customize the way Quick Mask Mode works.*

What if you used the mask to create a selection from the masked area, and not the rest of the image? It's a common mistake to think that what you're painting or drawing on in Quick Mask Mode will be the selected area once you return to Standard Editing Mode. It's also common to use the masking tools to create a mask, intending to turn the masked area into the selection, rather than allowing it to be the protected region of the image. To change the masked area from being protected to being the focus of the selection, use the Select | Inverse command to select the masked area only.

If you want to control how Quick Mask Mode works, you can double-click the Quick Mask Mode button to display the Quick Mask Options dialog box shown in Figure 5-49. You can choose what the colored wash represents—the masked area or the selected area—and also choose the color wash that is applied when you paint or otherwise apply the mask.

If you want to make sure that whatever you mask becomes the selection (rather than the masked area), choose Selected Areas from the Color Indicates section of the dialog box. This will achieve the same end if you use the Quick Mask in its default mode, and then invert the selection afterward.

Understanding and Using Paths

Paths can serve several purposes within your image. They can be visual elements of your image, such as freeform shapes you draw with the Pen tool or shapes you create with the Shape tools. When you add a path to your image for the purpose of adding content, you can use the Paths palette buttons to fill the path with a solid color (see Figure 5-50).

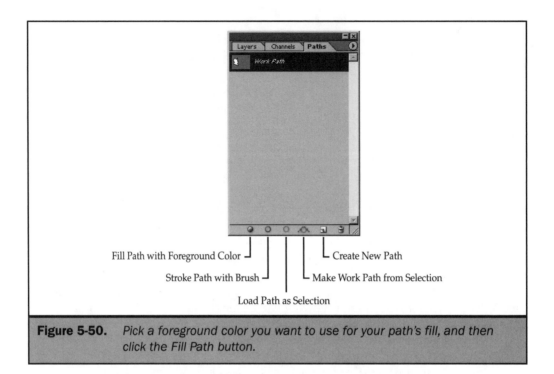

Fill Path with Foreground Color ─┘

Stroke Path with Brush ─┘

Load Path as Selection

└─ Create New Path

└─ Make Work Path from Selection

Figure 5-50. *Pick a foreground color you want to use for your path's fill, and then click the Fill Path button.*

If you want to outline, or *stroke*, the path, click the Stroke Path with Brush button, right next to the Fill Path button. You can also fill a path with a pattern, a fill selected from the History palette, or the colors black, gray, or white. To access these fill options for a path, right-click (or CONTROL-click) the path in the Paths palette, and then choose Fill Path (the Fill Path dialog box appears in Figure 5-51).

If you want your path to appear as an outline (or have your filled path also have an outline), you can choose how the outline will look by choosing Stroke Subpath from the palette menu, or from the context menu that appears when you right-click/CONTROL-click the path in the Paths palette. In the Stroke Path dialog box (see Figure 5-52), you can choose which tool to use in creating the outline. You don't have to draw with the tool—the path's outline will be created in the style of the selected tool.

If your path consists of two or more shapes and only one of them is selected, the Stroke Path command will appear as Stroke Subpath. This simply means that the stroke you set up and apply will affect only the selected shape, not all shapes in the active path.

You can use the Make Selection command to convert paths to selections, as shown in Figure 5-53. From within the resulting Make Selection dialog box (see Figure 5-54), you can choose to Feather the selection (creating a soft edge should the selection be filled with color or a pattern), turn on the Anti-aliased option (to get rid of choppy edges on curves), and choose how the selection will operate in relation to any existing selections. If you already have something selected on the image, you can add to, subtract from, or create an intersection from the selection and path-turned-selection. Whether or not there is already something selected, you can choose to create a new selection, wherein the path will become an independent selection, replacing anything that's already selected at the time.

You can also use the Load Path As Selection button at the bottom of the Paths palette to convert your path to a selection.

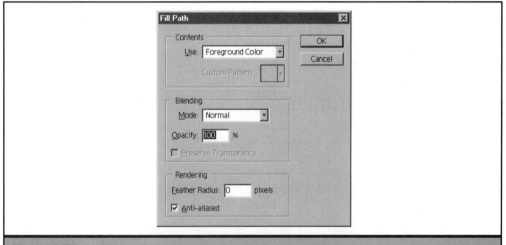

Figure 5-51.   *Choose how your selected path will be filled.*

Figure 5-52.   *Turn your path into an outline, simulating the use (and stylus pressure) of any of 15 drawing and retouching tools.*

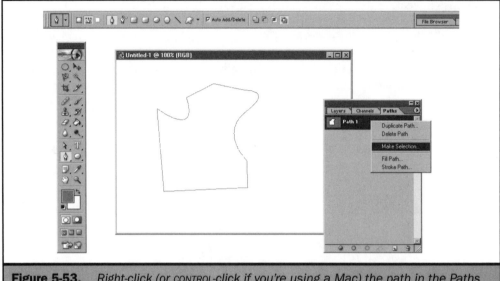

Figure 5-53. *Right-click (or CONTROL-click if you're using a Mac) the path in the Paths palette and choose Make Selection to convert the path to a selection.*

Figure 5-54. *Feather the selection, and then prevent choppy edges with the Anti-aliased option. You can also make your path into a New Selection, or choose how to use it with any existing selections.*

You can reverse the path-to-selection process (or convert a selection that was never a path in the first place) by clicking the Make Work Path From Selection button (fourth from the left along the bottom of the Paths palette). With a selection displayed, display the Paths palette, and click the Make Work Path From Selection button. The selection is converted to a Work path, which can then be saved, converted to a Clipping path, stroked, or filled with color or a pattern. You can also click the Palette menu, and choose Make Work Path. This opens the Make Work Path dialog box, which consists solely of a Tolerance setting (set to 2.0 pixels by default), which allows you to control the sensitivity of the Make Work Path command. You can enter any number between .5 and 10 pixels, the smaller entries resulting in more anchor points along the path.

Paths can also hide portions of your image by converting a path to a Clipping path, a process discussed earlier in this chapter. Clipping paths are created like any other path—with the Pen or Shape tools—but require saving and conversion to a Clipping path. Saving a path and converting it to a Clipping path is done through the Paths palette, shown in Figure 5-55.

Paths are known as Work paths until and unless you save them. If you want any path to appear larger in the Paths palette, choose Palette Options from the palette menu and choose the size you want your path thumbnails to appear—small, medium, large, or None, which means the shape of the path won't appear in the palette at all.

Earlier in the chapter you learned that paths live as an object on top of the image, on the active layer or on a new layer you create expressly for the path. Paths can be manipulated through editing their anchor points or by applying fills and strokes using the Paths palette. You can create and use the two path types—Work paths and Clipping paths—with the Pen or Shape tools. In the latter case, you need to use the Paths button on the options bar in order to make the shape an editable path.

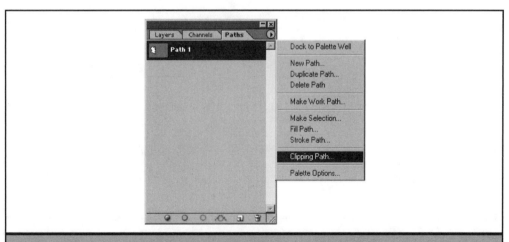

Figure 5-55.   *One-stop shopping for all your paths-related needs.*

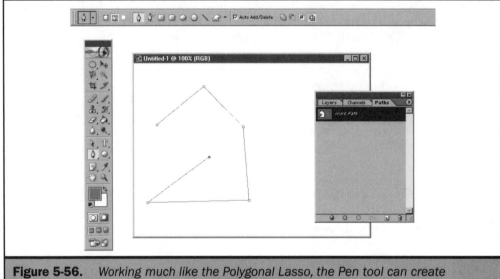

Figure 5-56. *Working much like the Polygonal Lasso, the Pen tool can create polygons of any shape or size.*

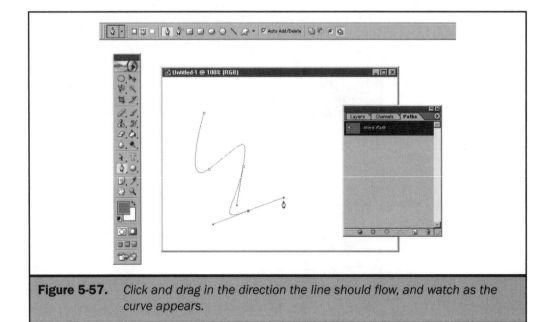

Figure 5-57. *Click and drag in the direction the line should flow, and watch as the curve appears.*

Drawing Paths

So you need a path—to add content to your image, to hide a portion of an image that will be opened in a vector-based graphics package like Illustrator, or to create a selection. The process of creating the path is the same no matter what purpose the path will eventually serve—simply choose your path creation tool and start drawing. Your path creation tools are as follows:

Pen   The Pen tool works in one of two ways—by clicking and moving to create a polygonal shape with anchor points at each place you clicked and changed direction, or by clicking and dragging to create *Bézier curves*—lines that flow from one anchor point to another, the depth and nature of the curve dictated by the direction points associated with each anchor point. Figure 5-56 shows a polygonal path in progress, and Figure 5-57 shows a curved path with anchor and directional points in use.

Freeform Pen   This tool allows you to draw freeform shapes without having to click and move or click and drag repeatedly. Just click and drag once. The path is created as you move your mouse, and it closes as you return to your starting point. Figure 5-58 shows a Freeform Pen path in progress. Note that the mouse pointer is sporting a small circle—this indicates you're close enough to the starting point to close the shape by clicking again. If you want to use the Freeform Pen to trace around content within your image, you can turn on the Magnetic option on the Freeform Pen options bar. Once this option is on, the Freeform Pen works much like the Magnetic Lasso—it adheres to pixels of a certain color or color range, allowing you to create a path that follows the edges of image content. If you click the inverted arrow next to the shape buttons on the options bar (to the left of the Magnetic option check box), you can choose how the Freeform Pen will work in Magnetic Mode. Figure 5-59 shows you your options, which include Width, Contrast, and Frequency options just like those that control the functioning of the Magnetic Lasso.

Shape   There are several Shape tools—the Rectangle, Rounded Rectangle, Ellipse, Polygon, and Custom Shape. Each one can create a path (rather than a shape layer or a filled shape on the active layer) if you click the Paths button before drawing the shape. Your mouse pointer will change slightly from the typical Shapes tool crosshair, and it will acquire a small circle with an X below and to the right of the crosshair. Figure 5-60 shows a new path that was created by drawing several shapes, including a Custom Shape. Observe the Paths palette and see that the places where the ellipses overlap the leaf are not part of the path.

If you drew a path or dragged another image's path onto your image and you're ready for a new path, click the Create New Path button at the bottom of the Paths palette (see Figure 5-61). A new blank path thumbnail appears in the Paths palette, awaiting the shape of the path as you create it with the Pen or Shape tools.

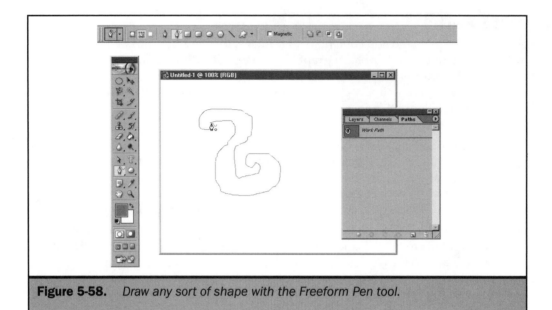

Figure 5-58. Draw any sort of shape with the Freeform Pen tool.

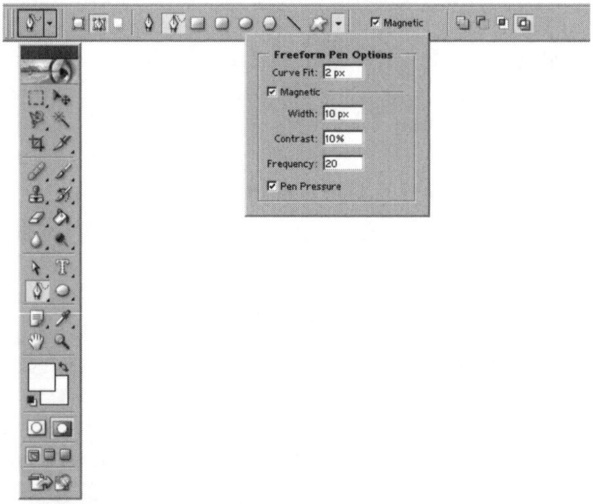

Figure 5-59. Customize the magnetic functioning of the Freeform Pen tool.

EDITING AND
RETOUCHING IMAGES

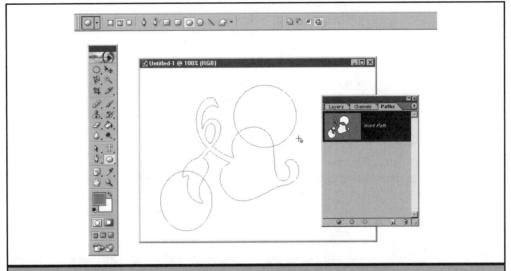

Figure 5-60. *Click the Paths button on the options bar for the Shape tool, and draw a path from a single or multiple shapes.*

Figure 5-61. *The Create New Path tool allows you to start a brand new path, unrelated to any existing paths.*

If you don't create a new path, any path you draw will become part of the active path.

Editing Paths

Any path—be it drawn with the Pen, Freeform Pen, or Shape tools—can be edited to change its shape. You can do this by moving, adding, deleting, or converting the anchor points that define the path's shape. Figure 5-62 shows a path that was made from a variety of tools—the Ellipse tool, the Pen tool (used to create Bézier curves), and the Custom Shapes tool.

The first step in editing a path is to select it. You can click the path by name in the Paths palette and then click the path itself to display its anchor points. If the path is already showing but you can't see its anchor points, click the Path Selection tool once and then click the path—its anchor points immediately appear, and you can begin editing them.

Another way to select a path is to use the Path Selection tool, or the Direct Selection tool, both of which are shown in Figure 5-63. The Path Selection tool allows you to click on a path and display not only the path's anchor points, but a bounding box that can be used to change the path's size and proportions. The Direct Selection tool allows you to select individual anchor points and their direction handles, which makes it possible to change the shape of a selected path.

If you use the Direct Selection tool, the path and its anchor points are selected, and you can begin editing the path by dragging the anchor points and any directional points to change the shape and curve of the path.

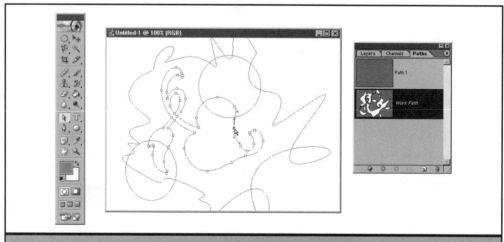

Figure 5-62. *Each part of the path (parts distinguished by the tool used to create them) can be edited individually.*

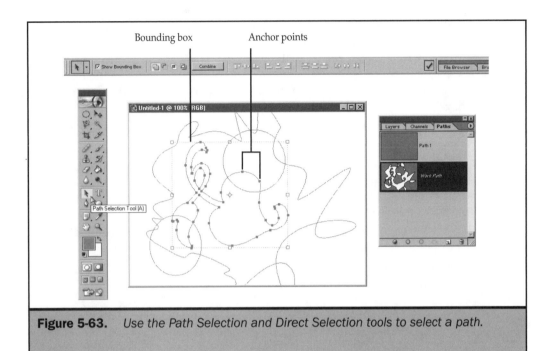

Figure 5-63.   *Use the Path Selection and Direct Selection tools to select a path.*

Once you can see a path's anchor points, there's nothing you can't do to change the path's shape or size. You can add and delete anchor points, changing the shape and direction of the path. You can move anchor points, and you can change the curves that flow between anchor points by dragging directional points. If your path has directional points, you can also edit the path by converting the anchor points from curves to straight lines, or vice versa.

Note *The same tools you use to transform a layer or content within a layer can also transform a path. When a path is selected (and its anchor points displayed), you can scale, rotate, skew, distort, or flip it, using the Edit | Transform Path submenu commands. These are the same submenu commands you'll see when you choose Edit | Transform—the menu command simply changes to Transform Path because a path is selected. You can also use the Free Transform Path command (also renamed within the Edit menu because a path is selected) to make any number of transformations using your mouse pointer in conjunction with the path's bounding box and its handles.*

Adding and Deleting Anchor Points

As you're creating a path, regardless of the technique, you'll find that the path can have as few as two or more than a thousand anchor points—it all depends on the complexity of the path's shape. To edit a path, you have to display the anchor points and begin dealing with those that affect the portion you want to change.

Adding and deleting anchor points will change the path's shape by providing more anchors by which to grab and stretch the shape, or fewer anchors, thus reducing the number of sides and curves that make up the shape. There are two ways to easily add anchor points:

- Click the Add Anchor Point tool on the toolbox, and then click the path at the spot where the new anchor point should go.
- Right-click/CONTROL-click a spot along the path and choose Add Anchor Point from the context menu.

Deleting anchor points is also simple:

- Click the Delete Anchor Point tool on the toolbox; then, on the path, click the anchor point you want to get rid of.
- Right-click/CONTROL-click an anchor point on the path and choose Delete Anchor Point from the context menu.

If you leave the Auto Add/Delete option on (located on the options bar while the Pen tool is active), you can click on a path at any spot and add a point, or if you click an existing point, the point will be deleted.

Moving Anchor Points

You can't move an anchor point from one place to another along the path, but you can drag it and pull the path's shape along with you, changing the shape of the path. As shown in Figure 5-64, even a simple elliptical path can be made more interesting by dragging one or more of the four anchor points that reside along the path. Of course, adding points gives you more options for reshaping the path, as each one can be pulled in any direction.

Redirecting and Reshaping Curves

The directional handles that are attached to anchor points drawn with the Pen tool can be dragged to change the direction and depth of the curves that flow between anchor points, as shown in Figure 5-65. By dragging one or both of the directional anchors, the curved path is changed considerably.

If you want to change the location of a point—not drag it in or out or up or down—delete it and then add a new point where you want an anchor point to be.

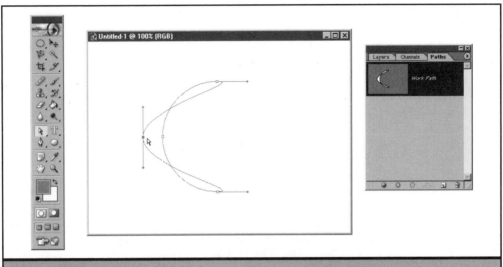

Figure 5-64.   *Click and drag an anchor point to reshape a path.*

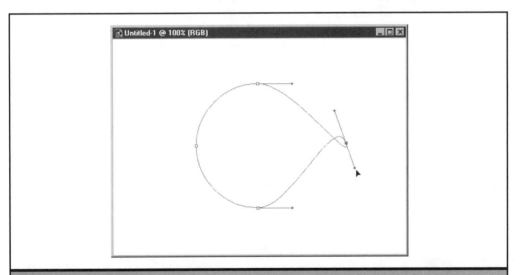

Figure 5-65.   *Change the pitch and direction of the path by dragging directional handles that accompany your path's anchor points.*

Converting Points

You get a rounded path when you draw a series of Bézier curves, each beginning and ending with an anchor and directional points, using the Pen tool. If you need a more angular path, you can delete the rounded path and redraw it with the click-and-move technique, creating straight sides between each anchor point. You can also change some of the curve anchors so the lines flowing from them are straight, or change the straight-line anchors so the lines flowing from them are curved. You can make these changes with the Convert Point tool, shown in Figure 5-66.

To use the Convert Point tool, you can click the anchor point to go from a curve anchor to corner/straight anchor, or you can click and drag a corner/straight point that you want to convert to a curve. The dragging motion of the latter process displays the converted point's directional handles. You can drag the point and/or its handles to change the corner or straight edge to a rounded corner or curved line.

When you use the Convert Point tool, watch for your mouse pointer to turn from an arrow to an inverted V as soon as you're atop an anchor point. When the mouse pointer changes, you can click (or click and drag) to perform the conversion.

Of course, you can convert points back to whatever they were to begin with by converting them again or by adding a point and converting that. Many times, the best way to edit a shape is to add points and convert them to the type of points you need along the flow of the path. Many paths are both angular and curved, and a variety of point types may be required to get the correctly shaped path.

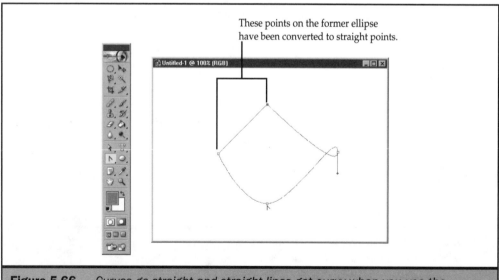

These points on the former ellipse have been converted to straight points.

Figure 5-66.   *Curves go straight and straight lines get curvy when you use the Convert Point tool.*

Chapter 12 contains a complete discussion of applying color and pattern fills to shapes, including paths. If you've created a path and want to fill it with a solid color, you can click the Fill Path with Foreground Color button, found at the bottom of the Paths palette. You can also apply an outline or stroke to a path, by clicking the Stroke Path with Brush button, also on the bottom of the Paths palette.

Combining and Aligning Paths

If you have multiple shapes within a single path (whether they touch, overlap, or share no common points), you can use the options bar that appears in conjunction with the Path Selection tool to change their position and relationship. As shown in Figure 5-67, you can click the Combine button to combine two or more selected paths (selected with

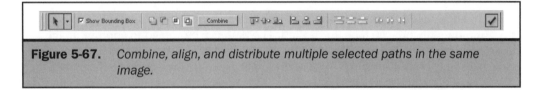

Figure 5-67.   *Combine, align, and distribute multiple selected paths in the same image.*

Figure 5-68.   *Drag the Path Selection tool to draw a box around the paths you want to select.*

the Path Selection tool), or you can use the alignment and distribution buttons to control the placement of the selected paths in relation to each other.

Selecting two or more of your shapes in a single path is simple. Select the path that contains the shapes you want to work with (click the path in the Paths palette). Then click the Path Selection tool and drag it around the portions of the path you want to select. Figure 5-68 shows two shapes in a single path selected, both within the same bounding box, with all their anchor points displayed.

The Dismiss Target Path button (the check mark on the far-right end of the Path Selection options bar) deselects the path on the Paths palette, as well as any selected portions of the path within the image.

Saving Paths

An unsaved path is a Work path, and it has no name. A Work path cannot be converted to a Clipping path, nor can it be duplicated. The path can be copied to another image by dragging it from the Paths palette onto the second image, however. If you need to save your path, simply click the palette menu button on the right side of the Paths palette and choose Save Path. In the resulting Save Path dialog box, type a name for the path and click OK (see Figure 5-69). The name appears on the path in the Paths palette, and you can now access the Clipping Path command, also found in the Options menu.

You can also open the Save Path dialog box by double-clicking the path in the Paths palette, or quickly name the path "Path 1" (or "Path 2" if you already have a Path 1) by dragging the path to the Create New Paths button at the bottom of the Paths palette.

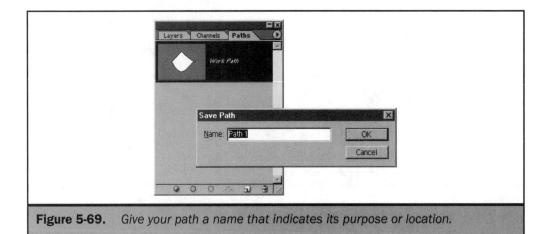

Figure 5-69. *Give your path a name that indicates its purpose or location.*

Figure 5-70.   *Choose which path will become the Clipping path.*

The Clipping Path command, available once your path has been saved, gives you the ability to use a path for obscuring part of an image that's bound for use in a vector-based graphics application such as Adobe Illustrator or CorelDRAW, or in page layout applications such as PageMaker and QuarkXpress. The Clipping Path dialog box, shown in Figure 5-70, gives you the ability to choose the path that will serve as a Clipping path, and to set a Flatness level (to improve the way the image prints). Leaving the setting blank allows the image to be printed using the printer's defaults.

Tip   *If you have a selection in your image and want to turn it into a path, go to the Paths palette and click the Make Work Path from Selection button (the fourth button from the left along the bottom of the palette). The selection immediately becomes a path, converted at the current Tolerance setting. The path can then be edited, saved, or converted to a Clipping path.*

Applying Paths Between Images

Once you've created a path in one image, you can use it in any other image by simply dragging it out of the Paths palette in the active image, and dropping it onto another image. Once the path appears in the second image, you'll see it listed in the Paths palette for that image. Then you can fill it, outline (stroke) it, or convert it to a selection or Clipping path. Figure 5-71 shows a path in transit, being copied from one image to another.

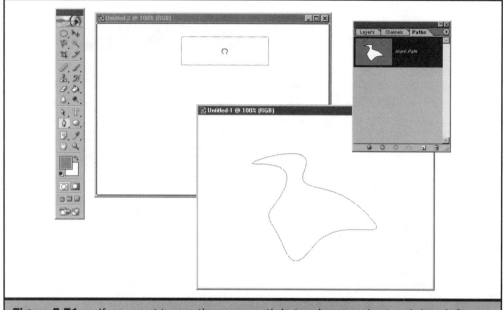

Figure 5-71. *If you want to use the same path in two images, drag and drop it from the Paths palette, depositing it on the image where it's needed.*

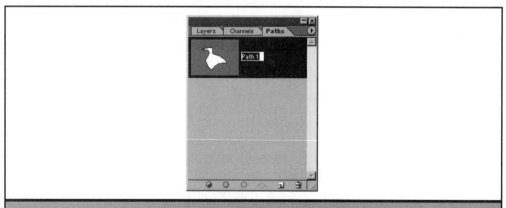

Figure 5-72. *Rename your path by double-clicking its current name.*

You can also drag the path itself—from right out of the image—if you use the Path Selection tool to select and drag the path out of one image window and into another.

If you've saved the path in the original image, the name comes with it when you drag and drop the path into another image. You can rename the path by double-clicking the path name in the Paths palette (see Figure 5-72). When the current name becomes highlighted in a box, type the new name and press ENTER/RETURN.

You can also make copies of paths with Duplicate Path command, displayed by right-clicking/CONTROL-clicking the path in the Paths palette. You can also choose Duplicate Path from the palette menu. Either way, in the resulting dialog box, just type a new name and click OK (see Figure 5-73). This action will result in two paths: the original and the duplicate. If you need only one of these paths, just right-click the one you don't want and choose Delete Path from the context menu, as shown in Figure 5-74.

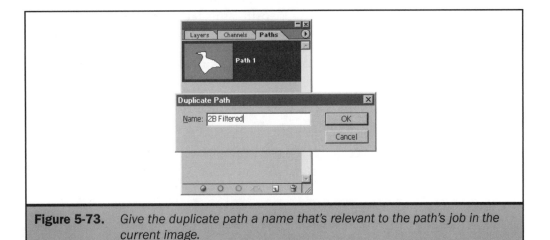

Figure 5-73. *Give the duplicate path a name that's relevant to the path's job in the current image.*

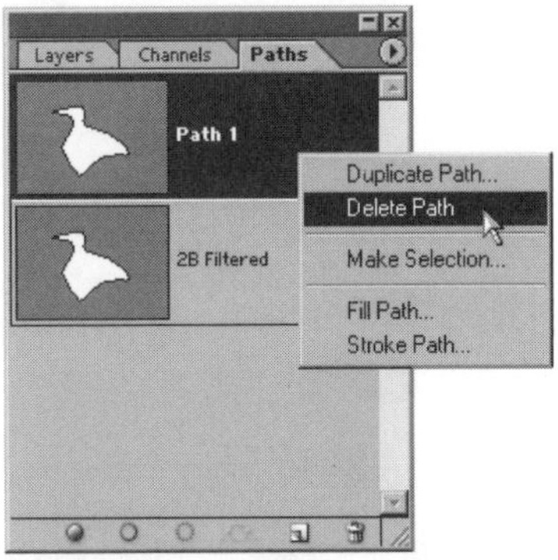

Figure 5-74. *With the redundant path selected, right-click/CONTROL-click and choose Delete Path.*

Summary

In this chapter, you learned to use Photoshop's extensive selection, masking, and path-creation tools, including the Marquee, Lasso, Wand, and Pen tools. You discovered how to protect areas of your image from editing, and how to focus editing and special effects tools on very specific regions within your image. You learned how to select image content for use within the same image or another image, utilizing the clipboard through Cut and Copy commands. You also learned how to base a new image on cut or copied image content, creating a new image that's sized to match the cut or copied content. For more power over your image and the editing process, you also learned to create and edit paths, as well as to use those paths as image content or as another way to select a portion of the image.

In the next chapter, you'll learn about color—how to select and work with color modes, how to apply colors, and how to control the colors used in your images.

The
Complete
Reference

Photoshop 7

Chapter 6

Understanding, Applying, and Adjusting Colors

211

When it comes to Photoshop, color is a complex topic. There are aesthetic issues such as choosing the right color for a piece of original artwork, adjusting the colors in a photo to make sure the items in the picture are the color they should be, and making creative use of color by applying nontraditional colors to familiar objects. Beyond aesthetics, there's the science of color—choosing color modes and models, viewing color channels, and configuring colors for particular tasks and for your monitor. With all that in mind, this chapter's goal is to show you how to apply colors, how to choose color modes, how to adjust colors, and how to make sure you're using the right colors for individual projects.

Applying Colors to Your Image

When you open Photoshop for the first time, the Color Picker on the toolbox displays two colors—a Foreground color (black) and a Background color (white), as shown in Figure 6-1. The Foreground color is applied when you use the Brush, Pencil, or Shape tools, and is applied by the Paint Bucket tool if you click on a selection or anywhere on the active layer. The Background color is revealed when you use the Eraser tool or select an area on the Background layer and press the DELETE key. If you select an area and press DELETE, the color of the Background layer will show through—if it has a color applied. Otherwise, transparency will show through the deleted area.

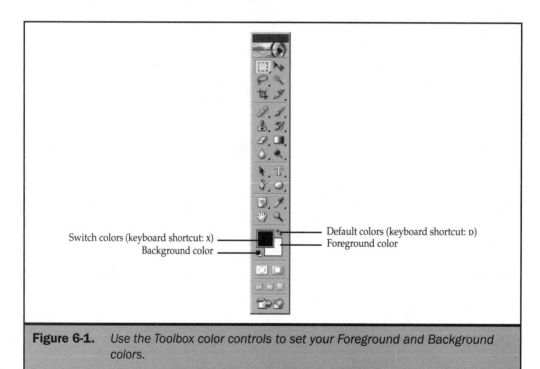

Switch colors (keyboard shortcut: x)
Background color
Default colors (keyboard shortcut: D)
Foreground color

Figure 6-1. *Use the Toolbox color controls to set your Foreground and Background colors.*

The color of your new image background is determined at the time you start the new file—you can choose a White background (the default), a Transparent one, or apply the color that's currently set for the Background color by referring to the toolbox color controls.

If you use the Gradient tool to fill a selection or layer, the gradient will be applied in the direction you drag through it with the tool. Going from left to right, the gradient will start with your Foreground color, and end with the Background color.

Using the Color Picker

To choose new Foreground and Background colors, click the Foreground or Background color boxes in the toolbox color controls. Whichever box you click, that's the color you're resetting. When you click either box, the Color Picker opens, as shown in Figure 6-2 (the Mac version appears in Figure 6-3). You can select any color with your mouse, dragging up and down on the slider (the vertical color spectrum) to find the color "family" you want to choose from, or you can enter specific numbers into the RGB, HSB, Lab, and CMYK color model boxes.

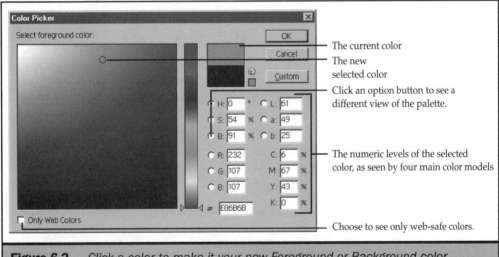

Figure 6-2.   *Click a color to make it your new Foreground or Background color.*

Color models are systems used for analyzing and adjusting colors. Read more about them in the section titled "Understanding Color Models," found later in this chapter.

EDITING AND
RETOUCHING IMAGES

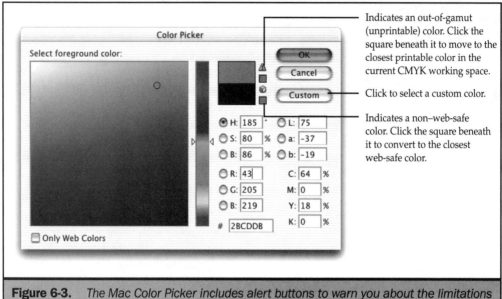

Figure 6-3. *The Mac Color Picker includes alert buttons to warn you about the limitations of certain colors and/or Photoshop's ability to print or display them.*

Tip *If you're selecting a color to use in a graphic that's bound for the Web, be sure to click the Only Web Colors option in the lower-left corner of the Color Picker. The colors you can choose when Only Web Colors is on are considered "web-safe," which means you know that any browser software will support their display. If you know the hexadecimal number of the color you need to use, you can enter it into the # text box within the Color Picker— that color will be automatically displayed and selected.*

Each of the color models—HSB, RGB, Lab, and CMYK—are systems by which colors are expressed numerically. Each system defines colors according to different qualities: levels of specific colors, such as Red, Green, or Blue (RGB); Cyan, Magenta, Yellow, and Black (CMYK); or levels of color saturation and brightness (HSB and Lab). You can view the Color Picker's colors "through the eyes" of these models and their individual levels by clicking the radio button next to any one of the level letters. Figure 6-4 shows the L (Luminosity) view of the Color Picker, with Only Web Colors turned on. The Hue (H) view is the default view, but you may prefer another view if it more closely matches the way you think about colors.

As soon as you click OK to close the Color Picker, you'll see the color you chose displayed in the toolbox color controls. You can use the Switch button to reverse the colors, swapping the Foreground and Background colors, or you can go back to the black and white defaults by clicking the Defaults button.

If you need to select a Custom Color, such as a Pantone, Focoltone, or Trumatch color, click the Custom button on the right side of the Color Picker. The Custom Colors dialog box (Figure 6-5) offers a Book list of custom color manufacturers. When you pick one, the entire spectrum of colors they offer is displayed. You can scroll through the color options by using the vertical slider or by scrolling through the named and/or numbered colors with your arrow keys. You can also type the color number (if you know it), and the color will become selected.

EDITING AND
RETOUCHING IMAGES

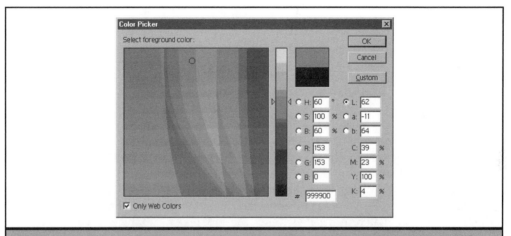

Figure 6-4. *View the Color Picker's palette through a variety of color model perspectives.*

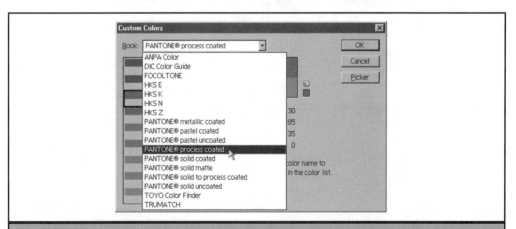

Figure 6-5. *Pick a Custom Color set from the Book list.*

Depending on the book you choose, additional information is also displayed along the right side of the slider:

Lab (*L* stands for luminosity; *a* and *b* represent two color axes) levels are displayed with the following books:

- ANPA Color
- DIC Color Guide
- HKS
- Pantone

CMYK (*c*yan, *m*agenta, *y*ellow, blac*k*) levels are displayed with these books:

- Focoltone
- Toyo
- Trumatch

It's important to note that none of these Custom Color groups are web-safe. You'll see warning of this next to the selected color sample in the Custom Colors dialog box (see Figure 6-6). If you want to find the web-safe equivalent for one of the Custom Colors, simply note the CMYK or Lab levels and enter them into the Color Picker, with the Only Web Colors option on. As soon as you enter the levels, the picker will select and display the closest web-safe match. You can also click the square beneath the web-cube icon to find the closest web-safe match, as shown in Figure 6-7.

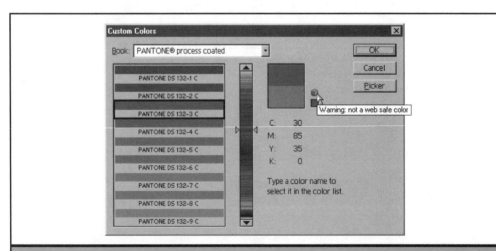

Figure 6-6. *The little gray cube indicates that this custom color is not web-safe. Hover your mouse pointer over the symbol (which changes to a colored cube) to see a warning.*

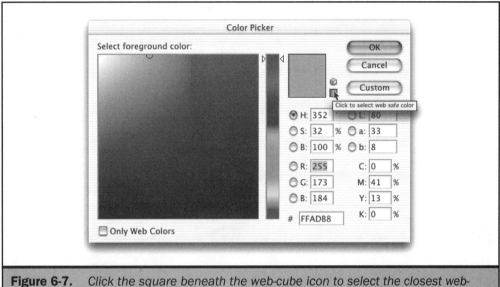

Figure 6-7.   *Click the square beneath the web-cube icon to select the closest web-safe color.*

Note   *If the words "closest web-safe match" give you pause, realize that if you're trying to match print colors when designing web graphics, the person viewing the web site is not likely to be holding a brochure or sheet of letterhead up to the screen, making sure the colors in the logo are an exact match. In addition, all monitors display colors differently—what might look like blue on one monitor might look purple on another. When colors are viewed onscreen, there are very few absolutes in terms of how they'll be seen on different computers, through different web browsers, and to different people. The precision and consistency you may be accustomed to when it comes to printed graphics is simply not possible when graphics are viewed electronically.*

Using the Color Palette to Set Foreground and Background Colors

If you don't need or want to use the Color Picker, you can set the Foreground and Background colors with the Color palette. Of course, this tool requires that you pick the color "by eye," or with a single color model's settings. By default, RGB levels are displayed in the sliders, but if you click the palette menu button, you'll see, as shown in Figure 6-8, that you can change the sliders to display CMYK, HSB, Lab, Web, or Grayscale. You can also change the ramp, which is the horizontal spectrum of colors along the bottom of the palette.

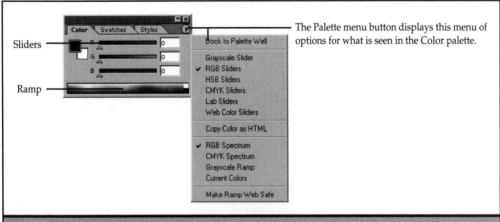

Figure 6-8. *Pick a color model to display, and then drag the sliders to choose a Foreground or Background color. You can also drag the cursor through the spectrum to set new Foreground and Background colors.*

 You can right-click (or CONTROL-click if you're using a Mac) on the ramp to change the spectrum. A context menu appears, from which you can select the spectrum you want to use.

Selecting Colors with the Eyedropper

If the color you want to use for your foreground or Background color is already somewhere in an open image or even somewhere within the Photoshop desktop itself—on a button, palette, or the desktop background—you can select the color quickly and easily with the Eyedropper tool. Figure 6-9 shows the Eyedropper tool at work, and the sampled color (where you see the eyedropper pointing on the image) is also the selected Foreground color.

 By default, the Eyedropper tool sets the Foreground color. To set the Background color, you can ALT/OPTION-click on a color with the eyedropper, or use the tool without pressing ALT/OPTION, thus setting the Foreground color as usual. To make the new Foreground color your new Background color, use the Switch button to swap the Foreground and Background colors.

It's important to note that you may be surprised at the color that appears in the Foreground Color box when you click on a portion of your image with the eyedropper. For example, Figure 6-10 shows a woman standing next to a red car (it appears gray in the figure, but trust me that it's a red car). You'd expect that if you clicked on the car, you'd get the same shade of red in the Foreground Color box. Chances are, however, that you'd get a dark red, brown, or light gray Foreground color. Why? Because of the red we see when we view the image at a low-level zoom (such as Fit on Screen or Print Size), we see a red car. But the car color is made up of many, many pixels, and each one is potentially a different color. The colors that make the red car range from the dark, nearly black pixels where the car is in shadow, to the bright, nearly white pixels where the sun is reflected on the shiny paint. Throughout the portions that are neither in complete shadow nor in bright light, there are many shades of red and brown that go into the "red car" we see.

Figure 6-9. *Sample a color from an image or within the Photoshop desktop, making it the Foreground color.*

Figure 6-10. *Even if something looks like it's all one color, each of the pixels that make up that element of your image may be a different color.*

The net of all this is that you have to be careful where you click when you're using the Eyedropper tool to select a new Foreground color. If you're selecting a color to use in retouching a photo, click on a pixel that's as physically close to the spot you're going to paint over as possible. Figure 6-11 shows the eyedropper selecting a color in order to paint over tiny spots on a piece of clothing. By clicking on pixels right next to the spots, the painted shade, when applied to the pixels that make up the unwanted spots, will blend in with the rest of the fabric, and the repair will be invisible.

To quickly switch to the Eyedropper tool while any painting tool is active, press the ALT/OPTION key. The tool temporarily is suspended in favor of the Eyedropper tool, which you can use to sample and select a color. Release the ALT/OPTION key, and you're back to the tool you were using before you switched.

When you activate the Eyedropper tool, you'll notice that the options bar displays a single option, Sample Size, as shown in Figure 6-12. This option allows you to expand the Eyedropper's sampling area to a 3-pixel × 3-pixel area or a 5-pixel × 5-pixel area and average the pixels in those ranges. The default setting is Point Sample, which means a single pixel will be sampled at the point where you click your mouse while the Eyedropper is active. The 3 by 3 and 5 by 5 options will average the pixels in either a 3-pixel or 5-pixel square area around the spot where you click and display that color in the Foreground Color box.

What would you gain by using either of these alternatives? If you're setting the Foreground color before using the brush to paint over unwanted content in an image, you can avoid your painted stroke showing if you use a color that won't be much darker or lighter than the pixels surrounding the content you're painting over. For example, if you want to get rid of a blemish on a face in a portrait, using the 3 by 3 Average option will enable you to select a skin tone that will blend in nicely when you paint over the blemish. Of course, if the blemish is small you can use the Point Sample option and simply paint only the exact pixels that need to be recolored. If the blemish is larger, using a single nearby pixel to set the Foreground color risks the painted portion standing out against surrounding pixels. Using an average will allow you to paint with a color that covers the blemish and fades out into the surrounding pixels.

Sampling Colors

The Color Sampler tool allows you to view the statistics of specific pixels in an image (up to four sampled pixels per image) or, like the Eyedropper tool, click on pixels to see the information for an average of the surrounding three or five pixels. You can use this tool to see how changes you've made to the overall color of your image are affecting specific areas, or to simply gather information about areas of the image you're about to edit or use elsewhere. The Color Sampler's sample data appears in the Info palette, as shown in Figure 6-13.

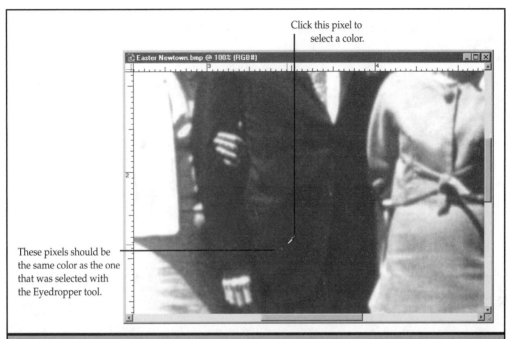

Click this pixel to
select a color.

These pixels should be
the same color as the one
that was selected with
the Eyedropper tool.

Figure 6-11. *When selecting a pixel with the eyedropper, stay in the neighborhood of the pixels that you'll be recoloring—you'll get a closer match that way, and your painted repairs won't stand out.*

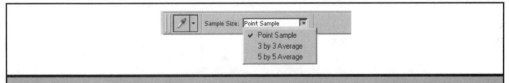

Figure 6-12. *Expand the range of the eyedropper to include an average of the surrounding three or five pixels.*

You can use the sampled-color information you gather to choose colors for your image, and you can also change the data that's displayed by right-clicking the sampled pixels. When you hover over a sampled pixel (while the Color Sampler tool is in use), your mouse turns from an eyedropper to an arrow. When this happens, right-click the sampled spot and choose Actual Color | Proof Color, or choose one of the color models that appears in the context menu (Figure 6-14). The effects of your choice will be reflected in the Info palette for the sample you right-clicked/CONTROL-clicked.

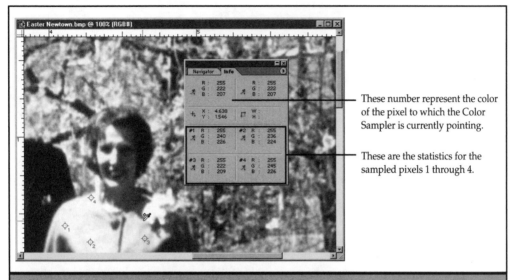

These number represent the color of the pixel to which the Color Sampler is currently pointing.

These are the statistics for the sampled pixels 1 through 4.

Figure 6-13. Click on the image and view the RGB and CMYK levels for a specific pixel or small group thereof. Your sampled color statistics appear in the Info palette.

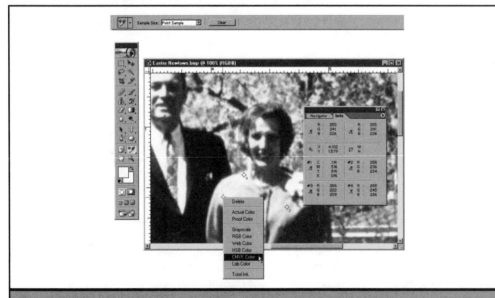

Figure 6-14. Right-click/CONTROL-click a sample and change the type of information you see in the Info palette.

Working with the Swatches Palette

Like having your own display of paint chips or fabric samples for future home decorating use, the Swatches palette allows you to view and store color samples for future use in creating and editing images. You can use the default set of colors, or switch to any of 25 sets of alternative swatches, as shown in Figure 6-15. You can append one group of swatches to another, and add and delete individual colors from any group of swatches.

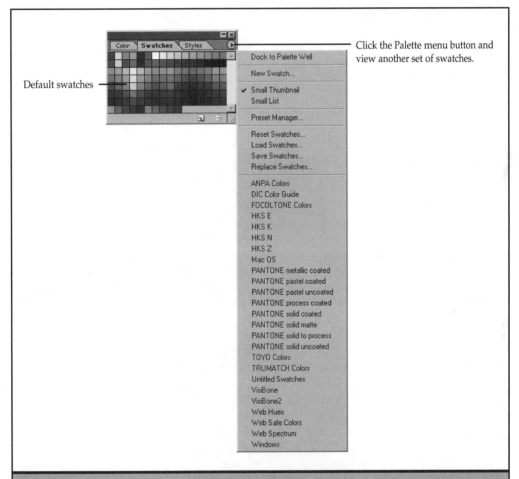

Figure 6-15. *The default swatches and your options for other swatches you can display and use*

To use the Swatches palette, you can click any color with your mouse pointer (the pointer will change to an eyedropper as soon as you hover over the palette), and that color will become the Foreground color, as shown in the toolbox's color controls. If you want to set a Background color using the Swatches palette, ALT/OPTION-click one of the swatches.

As you hover over the swatches, if you pause for a moment without clicking a color, a tool tip appears showing you the name of the color. If you've switched to one of the Custom Color groups, such as Pantone Metallic Coated, you'll see color numbers instead of names. Figures 6-16 and 6-17 show two of the possible tips you'll see displayed over a swatch. In Figure 6-17, the Swatches palette has been resized to show more swatches at once.

To see the color statistics for any swatch, click the swatch and go to the Info palette—the CMYK and RGB levels are displayed, or you can click the Palette menu button and then use the Palette Options command to display settings for changing what information is displayed in the Info palette.

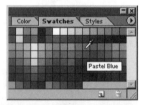

Figure 6-16.   *The default Swatches set has colors like Light Pea Green and Pastel Blue.*

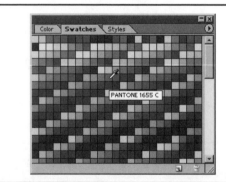

Figure 6-17.   *If you work with Custom Color Swatches, you'll see the color's number as you point to a swatch.*

Adding and Deleting Swatches

Because you can use the Eyedropper tool to select a new Foreground or Background color from within any open image or from anywhere on the Photoshop desktop, you may want to add such a color to the Swatches palette for future use. To add a swatch to the Swatches palette, make sure the color is currently displayed in the Foreground Color box in the toolbox. Then go to a blank spot in the gray area after the last swatch (see Figure 6-18), and when you see your cursor change to a paint bucket, click to "spill" the current Foreground color into that swatch. Immediately the Color Swatch Name dialog box appears, enabling you to name the swatch you've just added. Type a name, and then click OK.

To get rid of a swatch you've added (or an unwanted swatch from the default or any other swatch groups), right-click/CONTROL-click it and choose Delete Swatch from the context menu (see Figure 6-19). You can also ALT/COMMAND-click a swatch and, when your mouse pointer turns to a pair of scissors, click the swatch you want to delete. A third technique is quite simple—just drag the unwanted swatch to the garbage pail icon at the foot of the Color palette.

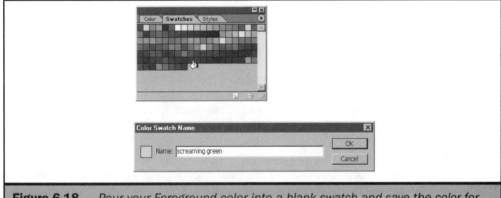

Figure 6-18.   *Pour your Foreground color into a blank swatch and save the color for future use.*

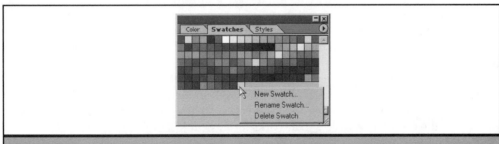

Figure 6-19.   *Choose Delete Swatch to delete the selected swatch.*

Regret that deletion? Click the Palette Options menu button and choose Reset Swatches. In the resulting prompt, click OK to confirm that you want to replace the current swatches with the default colors. If you were deleting swatches from a customized group, you would have to have saved that group as it was before your deletion in order to reload it with the deleted swatch back in the fold.

You can also use the context menu to rename a swatch or to create a new swatch. If you choose New Swatch, the current Foreground color is added to the Swatches palette after you name the color (using the Color Swatch Name dialog box that appears when you choose New Swatch).

You can also click the Create New Swatch button at the bottom of the Swatches palette to add the current Foreground color as a new swatch.

Resetting, Loading, and Saving Swatches

When you're working with swatches, your additions, deletions, and rearrangements result in truly customized groups of swatches. You can save these groups for future use, and to protect yourself in the event that you make deletions or other changes that you later regret—if you've saved a group of swatches and then make a regrettable change, you can reload the saved version.

To save swatches, make sure the displayed group of swatches includes all the colors you want to save, and that any colors you want to get rid of have been weeded out. Then click the Palette Options menu button and select Save Swatches from the menu. The Save dialog box opens, and you can name the swatches (see Figure 6-20). The default file extension for swatches is .aco. The swatch files are saved to the Color Swatches folder, a subfolder of the Presets folder, which is typically located in the folder that contains the rest of the Adobe Photoshop 7 application. It's not a good idea to choose a new folder for your saved swatches—let the software pick the destination for you so the swatches can be found with all the others when you go to load or reset your swatch group later.

Once a group of swatches has been saved, you can switch to it by clicking the Palette menu button and choosing Load Swatches. In the resulting dialog box, you can choose a group of swatches by name; by clicking the Load button, you can display the selected swatches in the palette. Of course, if the swatch group you want is on the menu, you don't need the dialog box to load it—just choose it from the menu and click OK (in response to the prompt shown in Figure 6-21) to replace the current swatches with the one you've selected.

To go back to the default swatches, simply choose Reset Swatches from the Palette menu (see Figure 6-22), and respond by clicking OK in the prompt asking you to confirm the desire to return to the defaults. You can keep switching swatch groups indefinitely, displaying the group of swatches that works for any project or phase thereof.

Figure 6-20. Give your Swatches file a relevant name and save it to the Color Swatches folder.

Figure 6-21. The swatches you choose will replace the ones you're currently displaying in the Swatches palette. Click OK to make the switch.

Figure 6-22. Go back to the default swatches by choosing Reset Swatches from the Palette menu and clicking OK in this prompt.

Tip *You can choose to add a group of swatches to the currently displayed group by clicking the Append button when prompted to OK the switch to a new or back to the default set of swatches. Instead of clicking OK and replacing the swatches, click Append and both sets will appear in the palette.*

Working with the Preset Manager

Another command in the Swatches palette menu is Preset Manager. This command opens the Preset Manager dialog box, as shown in Figure 6-23. Through this dialog box, you can change from seeing color swatches to seeing Brushes, Gradients, Styles, Patterns, Contours, Custom Shapes, or Tools. Whichever you choose from the Preset Type list appears in the Presets Manager dialog box, as shown in Figure 6-24. You can click the Load button once it's displayed in the dialog box to select a group of presets, or you can save a set by clicking the Save Set button. The Save Set button becomes available as soon as you do anything to change a displayed group of presets—rearranging, renaming, or deleting the items in the displayed set.

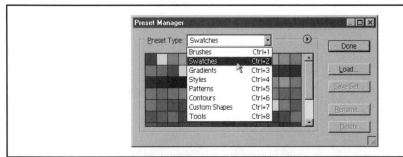

Figure 6-23. Manage your presets, and view all of your options for colors, styles, patterns, shapes, and tools.

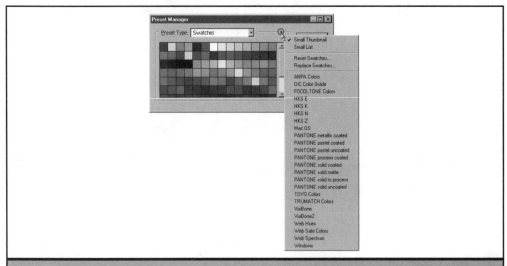

Figure 6-24. Spawned from within the Swatches palette, you can choose to look at much more than solid colors.

You can also open the Preset Manager dialog box by choosing Edit | Preset Manager. When the dialog box opens via this approach, the Brushes presets are displayed, and you can switch to the Swatches presets by clicking the Preset Type drop-down list and choosing Swatches.

Selecting a Color Mode for Your Image

We generally think of images as being either in color or in black and white. It's not that simple, though. First of all, a black and white image is still in color; it's just that it's only comprised of two colors. And don't forget *grayscale*, the term for images that are comprised of various shades of gray. We call non-color photos "black and white," but they're really grayscale.

When you say that an image is a color image, you're opening the door for several questions, one of which pertains to the color mode of the image. A *color mode* is the system by which colors are applied and represented. Another way of putting it: Color modes determine which color *model* is used to display and print images.

You can view and change the selected mode for your open image by choosing Image | Mode. The submenu lists all the available modes and color models you can apply to your image, and there's a checkmark next to the one that's currently assigned.

Understanding Color Models

A color model determines which base colors are mixed to create the colors used in your image. Your color model choices in Photoshop are

RGB   These letters stand for red, green, blue—the three colors used to make all colors for images in this mode. The levels of red, green, and blue in any color are measured in levels of intensity, also known as *brightness levels*, ranging from 0 to 255. The higher the numbers, the lighter or brighter the color, so a dark color, like a navy blue, would have no red or green, and blue level of only 102. A bright sky blue, on the other hand, would have a red level of 153, green of 204, and a blue level that's as high as it can go—255. RGB is supported by all computer monitors (they, too, show colors based on this model).

CMYK   These four letters stand for cyan, magenta, yellow, and black. If your image is in CMYK Mode, all of the colors in the image will be a percentage of one or more of these four colors. For example, a bright yellow might be almost all yellow, with just a touch of cyan. A bright blue might be 87 percent cyan, 69 percent magenta, and 0 percent yellow and black.

HSB   These letters stand for hue, saturation, and brightness. Yet another way to measure a color numerically, these levels indicate the color, amount of color, and amount of light (white) in the color. Black's HSB levels are all 0. White has a hue of 0, saturation of 0, and brightness of 100, the highest level possible for this model. Obviously, lighter and brighter shades of any color will have high S and B levels.

Grayscale   Believe it or not, there are 256 shades of gray. In a grayscale image, each pixel can have a brightness value as low as 0 (black) or as high as 255 (white). The values in between these extremes are the shades of gray (such as 128, which is a "middle" gray) that make up the grayscale.

Indexed Color   Based on a color lookup table (aka CLUT), Indexed Color Mode uses up to 256 colors. If you switch to this mode and a color in the image is not found among the 256 color contenders, the closest match will be substituted. Using indexed color can reduce file sizes, because less color information is saved with the file. You won't see a reduction in quality, however, but you may encounter limitations in terms of your ability to edit images in Indexed Color Mode. If you need to edit an image and find indexed color too limited, switch to RGB for the editing phase, and then go back to Indexed Color Mode before saving the file.

Lab Color   Lab Color Mode is based on the colors' lightness (L), which can be as low as 0 or as high as 100. The *a* and *b* in "Lab" represent the color axes on which the color mode is based. The *a* axis is red-green, and the *b* axis is blue-yellow. Both axes can range from –128 to +128, crossing at the zero point. Lab Color Mode is great for working with photo CD images and for printing to PostScript Level 2 and 3 printers.

Bitmap   When you convert to Bitmap Mode (after preparing to do so by switching to Grayscale Mode first), your image is reduced to two colors, black and white. This reduces file size, as there is much less color information saved with the image. Why convert to grayscale first? You need to remove the hue and saturation information from the pixels and retain the brightness values. As many of the editing tools will be disabled if your image is in Bitmap Mode, you want to edit the image in grayscale and then make the conversion to bitmap.

Duotone   As the name implies, this mode reduces your grayscale image to duotone (two colors), tritone (three colors), and quadtone (four colors) using two to four custom inks.

Multichannel   This mode works with 256 levels of gray in each channel. When you switch to this mode, channels become spot color channels, and the grayscale information is based on the color values of the pixels in each channel. If you convert a CMYK image to Multichannel Mode, you'll end up with cyan, magenta, yellow, and black spot channels. Switching to RGB leaves you with cyan, magenta, and yellow spot channels. Converting an RGB image to multichannel also creates cyan, magenta, and yellow spot channels.

| Tip | *If you delete a channel from an RGB, CMYK, or Lab image, the image is automatically converted to Multichannel Mode.* |

Switching Modes

To change color modes for your image, simply choose Image | Mode and select a mode from the submenu shown in Figure 6-25. Some of the options in the submenu may be dimmed, based on the settings in place for the open image—namely, the mode that's currently applied.

Through the Mode submenu, you can also change the bits per channel setting (choosing 8 or 16, the latter resulting in a much larger file size due to more color information being saved with the file), assign a color profile to the image, or convert from one profile to another. Note that the Color Table command will only be available if the image is currently in Indexed Color Mode.

If you change from 8 bits per channel to 16, a limited set of tools will be available. If you want the full set of tools, settings, and commands to be available, stick to 8 bits per channel.

More image data, in the form of increased bit depth, is achieved when you scan and edit images in 16-bit mode. With more bit depth, you give Photoshop more to work with, resulting in richer and finer effects from image adjustments, editing, and the use of filters.

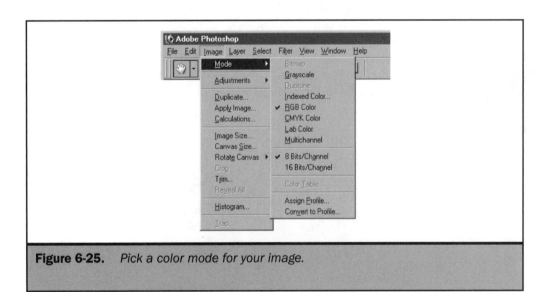

Figure 6-25.   *Pick a color mode for your image.*

Understanding and Working with Color Channels

The Channels palette displays a channel for each of the colors in the mode selected for your image. For example, if your image is in RGB Mode, you'll have four channels: RGB (the composite channel), red, green, and blue. If your image is in CMYK Mode, you'll have five channels: CMYK (the composite channel), cyan, magenta, yellow, and black. Figure 6-26 shows the CMYK channels for an open image. The Lab Mode also displays a composite channel (Lab), plus lightness, a, and b. When you switch to any mode through the Image | Mode submenu, the channels palette will change (usually after a prompt asking you to confirm your intentions to change the mode, and perhaps to flatten the image to facilitate the change) to display a channel for each component of the mode you've selected, plus, for RGB, CMYK, and Lab color, a composite channel that represents all the channels together.

You can use keyboard shortcuts to display and hide channels. CTRL/COMMAND-~ (tilde) displays all channels, CTRL/COMMAND-1 displays the red or cyan channel, CTRL/COMMAND-2 displays the green or magenta channel, CTRL/COMMAND-3 displays the blue or yellow channel, and CTRL/COMMAND-4 displays the black channel. When a single channel is left visible, the image appears in grayscale, regardless of which color channel is selected.

The channel that includes all the colors (the RGB or CMYK channel) is automatically displayed when all the individual channels are displayed. It turns off (the eye icon disappears from that channel in the palette) if any one of the channels is hidden.

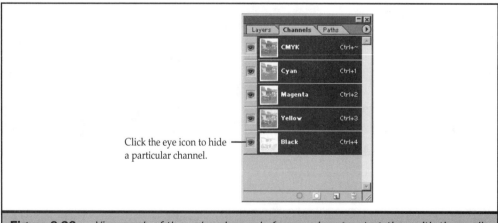

Click the eye icon to hide a particular channel.

Figure 6-26.   *View each of the color channels for your image—together with them all displayed, or one at a time, with all but one hidden.*

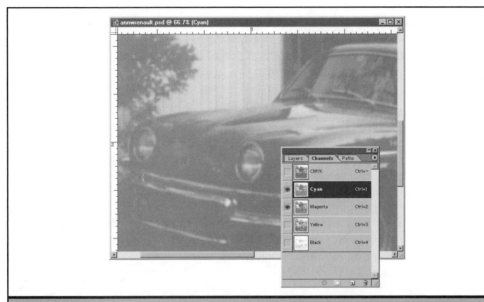

Figure 6-27.   *With some channels hidden, only the displayed channels' colors are visible in the image.*

You can do a lot more with the Channels palette than displaying and hiding channels. You can edit your image, working with only one channel at a time, or with some or all of them. When you hide one or more channels, any editing you then do on the image will apply only to the channel/s that are visible (as shown in Figure 6-27). To edit a channel, use the Brush, Pencil, or other painting/editing tools or filters, applying the following colors:

■   White applies the selected channel's color at 100-percent intensity.

■   Black completely removes the channel's color wherever you paint or otherwise apply it.

■   Use a shade of gray to apply the channel's color at a reduced intensity—the brighter the gray (the more white in it), the more intense the channel color applied.

Displaying and Hiding Channels

To display a channel, make sure the eye icon appears next to the channel in the Channels palette. If you want to hide a channel, click the eye icon to the left of the channel. By toggling the eye off, you can hide the channel as well. Note that the composite channel cannot be turned off directly—it responds to the appearance of the other channels, and is only visible if all the other channels are visible, too (see Figure 6-28). As soon as you hide a single channel, the composite's eye disappears. If you have hidden one or more channels and want them all back, click the visibility box for the composite channel. As soon as the eye icon appears next to that channel, all the other channels will be redisplayed, too.

 You can select channels that aren't visible, and make visible those that aren't selected.

Mixing Color Channels

You can use the Channel Mixer to change a color channel, applying a combination of color channels displayed in the Channels palette. This can help you increase the quality and clarity of grayscale images, and to apply tints to images. To use the Channel Mixer, select the composite channel, and then choose Image | Adjustments | Channel Mixer. In the Channel Mixer dialog box (shown in Figure 6-29), you can adjust the channels for the mode you're using, increasing and decreasing their intensity by dragging the sliders to the right or left, respectively. The Constant slider applies a black or white fill, at an opacity you set by dragging the slider. Negative Constant settings add a black fill, and positive Constant settings add a white fill.

 Use the Monochrome setting to apply the same levels to all of the channels, resulting in an image that consists of only shades of gray. You can then adjust the sliders until you get the color balance you're looking for. It's helpful to keep the Channels palette onscreen during this process, and to increase the size of the thumbnails to Large (choose Palette Options from the Palette menu).

If you want to save a mixture of channel data, click the Save button in the Color Mixer dialog box. You'll see a Save dialog box appear, through which you can name and save a .cha Channel Mixer file, which should be saved to the Photoshop 7.0 folder (the default location). You can also load existing channel mixer files by clicking the Load button and then selecting a file from the Load dialog box.

Figure 6-28. *Hide any channel and you hide the composite channel as well.*

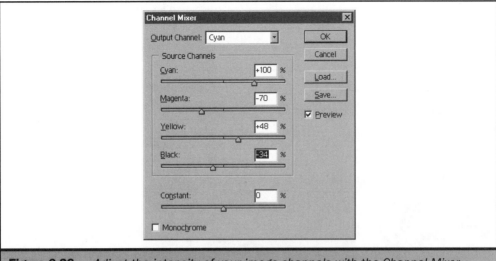

Figure 6-29. *Adjust the intensity of your image channels with the Channel Mixer.*

> **Tip** *Keep the Preview option on so that your changes are reflected in the image—really the best way to make sure you're making the right adjustments for your particular goals. Of course, you want the image window to be positioned so that you can see most, if not all, of the image while the Color Mixer dialog box is open. The changes won't actually be applied to the image file until and unless you click the OK button. If you don't want any change to take place, click Cancel.*

Adding Alpha Channels

Alpha channels are selections you store in order to edit or protect parts of you image. To create an alpha channel, simply select a portion of your image, using the Marquee, Lasso, or Magic Wand. Alternately, you can use the Select | Color Range command and dialog box. Once the selection (however you created it) is in place, click the Save Selection As Channel button at the bottom of the Channels palette (see Figure 6-30). An alpha channel (called Alpha 1, if it's your first) appears in the palette, with the shape of your selection displayed in the thumbnail.

Once the alpha channel is selected, you can edit it using any painting, drawing, or editing tools. You can also apply filters to the alpha channel. It's important to note that all channels, including alpha channels, are 8-bit grayscale images; all 256 shades of gray can be displayed within them. You can rename an alpha channel by double-clicking the Alpha 1 text (or some other, subsequent number). A box forms around the name, and you can retype it at that time. If you double-click the alpha channel (not the name, but the highlighted channel or thumbnail in the palette), a Channel Options dialog box appears (see Figure 6-31), through which you can again change the channel name, choose what the mask Color Indicates (Masked Areas is the default, but you can change to Selected Areas or Spot Color), and choose the color wash that will appear in the mask.

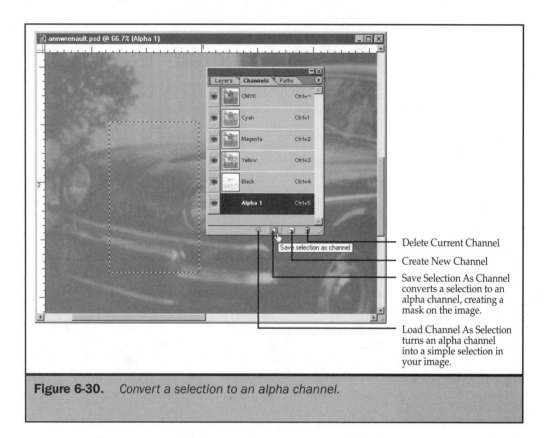

Delete Current Channel

Create New Channel

Save Selection As Channel converts a selection to an alpha channel, creating a mask on the image.

Load Channel As Selection turns an alpha channel into a simple selection in your image.

Figure 6-30. *Convert a selection to an alpha channel.*

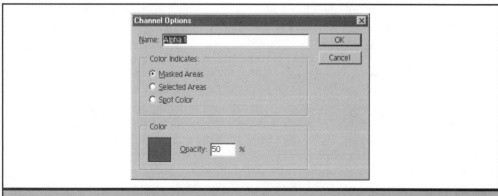

Figure 6-31. *Customize the mask that your alpha channel creates.*

Figure 6-32.   *The New Spot Channel dialog box allows you to choose the Color and Solidity applied to the selection.*

Working with Spot Channels

Spot channels are typically used to apply custom colors to an RGB, grayscale, or CMYK image—they are not part of the core color channels for an image. To create a spot channel, select an area within your image (using any of the selection tools or commands), and then choose New Spot Channel from the Channel palette's menu. The New Spot Channel dialog box appears (see Figure 6-32), through which you can name the new channel, and choose the color that will be applied to it. To change from the default red, click the color box, and make a new selection from the Color Picker. You can enter a new Solidity setting (50% is the default), which adjusts the opacity of the spot channel.

You can split the channels of a flattened image into multiple images. When you choose Split Channels from the Channel palette menu, your main image will close, replaced onscreen by individual grayscale images for each of the channels in the original image. Each image will have the same name as the original file, plus the channel abbreviation (if you're using Windows), or the full channel name if you're on a Mac. Why would you split channels? You may need to keep channel information available for an image that will lose that information when it's saved in a format that doesn't support channels.

Tip   *If you don't have enough space for a composite image on the removable disk or CD to which you're saving, you can save individual channels to different disks/CDs and then reopen all of the files and merge the channels back into a single image.*

Working with the Color Table

When you're working with an image in Indexed Color Mode, you can use the Color Table (Image | Mode | Color Table) to view a table of all the colors currently used in your image, and to edit those colors—for special effects or to assign transparency to one or more colors in the table.

To edit a single color in the table, click the color once. The Color Picker opens, and you can pick a different color there. Once you click OK, the selected color replaces the color you clicked originally in the color table.

If you want to change multiple colors, you can make the changes individually if the color boxes in the table aren't contiguous. If they are contiguous, they're considered a range of colors, and you can have Photoshop build a gradient in the color table starting with the first color in the range, and ending with the last color in the range. The designation of "first" and "last" is based entirely on the direction you drag your mouse. As soon as you release the mouse after selecting the range of color blocks, the Color Picker opens, and you can select the starting color of the gradient-to-be. Click OK, and the Color Picker reopens immediately, at which time you can select the ending color for the gradient. As soon as you click OK to close the second appearance of the Color Picker, the selected range of color blocks in the table is changed.

If you want to designate a color as transparent in the image, click the eyedropper button (see Figure 6-33), and then click on the color that should be made transparent. The image window will reflect the adjustment, and you can decide if you've achieved the desired result before clicking OK to commit to the changes. If you don't like the effect, use the eyedropper to make a different color transparent, or click the Cancel button to leave the Color Table without making any changes.

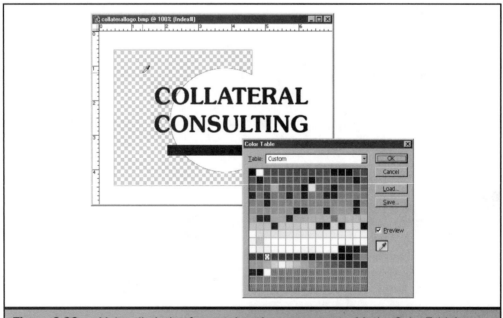

Figure 6-33.   *Make all pixels of a certain color transparent with the Color Table's Eyedropper tool.*

> **Tip**   *If you know which pixels you'd like to make transparent but can't find the right block in the Color Table to make it happen, use the Color Table's Eyedropper tool to select a pixel in your image directly. You can click on a spot in the image while the Color Table dialog box is open, and the corresponding color block will become transparent in the table.*

A Color Table is also visible in the Save For Web dialog box, which appears when you choose File | Save for Web. If your image will be saved in GIF or PNG-8 format, a Color Table appears on the right side of the Save For Web dialog box, as shown in Figure 6-34. The buttons along the bottom of the table give you control over the table and the colors in it.

If any of the colors in the Save For Web Color Table have a tiny white circle on them, that tells you they're web-safe colors. When you hover your mouse pointer over these blocks in the table, a hexadecimal number (such as #FFFFFF) will appear in a tool tip. The non–web-safe colors will display their RGB levels when you hover over them. As soon as you save the image, the colors will be changed to the closest web-safe match.

The number of colors you see in the Color Table is dictated by the choice you make from the Settings drop-down list, seen in its entirety in Figure 6-35. For example, if you choose GIF 128 Dithered, the resulting Color Table will have 128 colors in it, and the colors will appear more blended than the No Dither version of GIF 128. Similarly, the GIF 32 and GIF 64 will offer a 32-color and a 64-color Color Table, respectively. PNG-8 128 Dithered will give you a 128-color Color Table, with colors blended nicely.

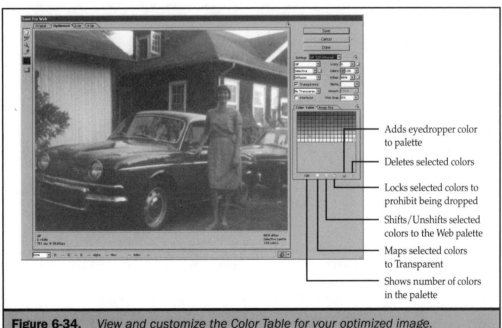

Adds eyedropper color to palette

Deletes selected colors

Locks selected colors to prohibit being dropped

Shifts/Unshifts selected colors to the Web palette

Maps selected colors to Transparent

Shows number of colors in the palette

Figure 6-34.   *View and customize the Color Table for your optimized image.*

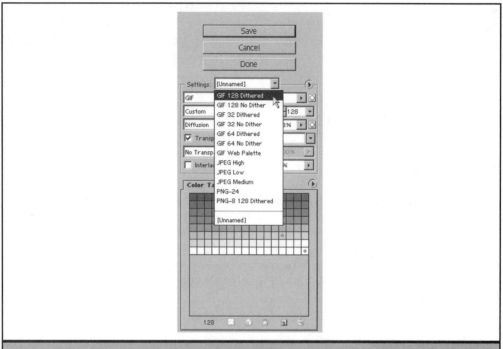

Figure 6-35. *Select a set of saved optimization settings from this drop-down list.*

Note

If the word "Dither" is new to you, don't worry. You'll find out all about it in Chapter 17, which pertains to optimizing graphics bound for the Web. In short, dithering reduces the blocky, choppy appearance along edges in your images. When an image is dithered, the choppy edges on the perimeter of the image and/or where different colors meet within the image are filled in by pixels colored to match or blend in with adjoining pixels. Sounds great, eh? There's one caveat. Dithering increases file size, which can be a problem when you're saving images for the Web—larger files take longer to load, and that's a web no-no in most cases.

In order to use the color table, you can click on colors in the table, and then use the buttons along the bottom of the table. For example, if you want certain colors to be transparent, click the color block for those colors (one at a time) and click the Maps Selected Colors to Transparent button. As shown in Figure 6-36, when a particular shade is mapped to transparent, the pixels colored that shade seem to have been deleted. If you make a color transparent in error, click it again (at the end of the table, as shown), and reclick the Maps Selected Colors to Transparent button—this will toggle the transparency off for that color, and the color block will return to its original location in the table.

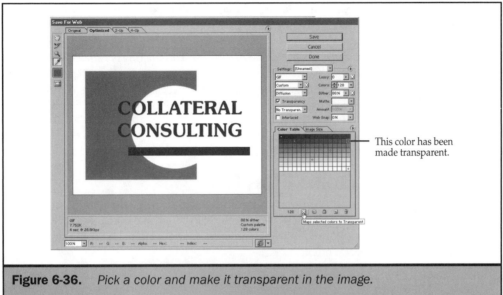

This color has been made transparent.

Figure 6-36. *Pick a color and make it transparent in the image.*

Figure 6-37. *An extra step makes it harder to accidentally delete a color you wanted to keep.*

As you hover over the color blocks in the table, the RGB levels are displayed as a tool tip. Use this to make sure you're selecting the right color for transparency, web-shifting, deletion, and locking.

To delete a color, simply select it by clicking it, and then click the trash can button at the bottom of the Color Table. A prompt will ask you if you want to delete the color(s)? and your response will either be Yes or No, as shown in Figure 6-37. To lock a color so it cannot be deleted or made transparent, click the color block and then click the Lock Selected Colors button, also at the bottom of the Color Table.

Full coverage of the options found on the right side of the Save For Web dialog box are covered in Chapter 17. Your selections in the Colors option (with increment and decrement arrows) will allow you to raise or lower the number of colors shown in the Color Table for the file format settings you've put in place.

While ImageReady is covered in Chapters 18 and 19, it's worth noting here that if you're using ImageReady and working with Color Tables, it's possible to confuse the Color Table palette with the Color palette. Remember that the Color Table optimizes colors for use on the Web; the Color palette displays color options and applies colors to an image through the use of fill, painting, and drawing tools.

Using Special Color Effects

There are a series of Photoshop commands you can use to change the colors and brightness levels in your images. These tools are not so much meant for retouching or correcting colors, but to apply interesting visual effects with color. The commands you can use to create these special effects are:

- Invert
- Equalize
- Threshold
- Posterize
- Gradient Map
- Desaturate

You'll find the commands in the Image | Adjustments submenu. Their availability in the menu will depend on what's going on in your image—if you don't have a gradient map adjustment layer created and selected, for example, the Gradient Map command won't be available in the Image | Adjustments submenu. You'll also find the command unavailable if you're working with an image in 16-bit, Multichannel, or Indexed Color Mode.

Adjustment layers are discussed in Chapter 10. A gradient map adjustment layer is a layer that is added to facilitate the application of a gradient to a shape or selection within an image.

Inverting Colors

The Invert command works quite simply—it takes each color in the image and swaps it with its opposite, based on the brightness level for each pixel within the 256-color scale. For example, if a pixel currently has a value of 250, it is changed to a 5. In less mathematical terms, imagine a color wheel. Picture each color and the color opposite it on the wheel—black becomes white, dark blue becomes yellow, red becomes cyan, and so on. Figure 6-38 shows two states of an image—before the inversion process, there is a navy blue squiggle drawn on a white background. After inversion, the blue squiggle is light yellow, and the white background is black.

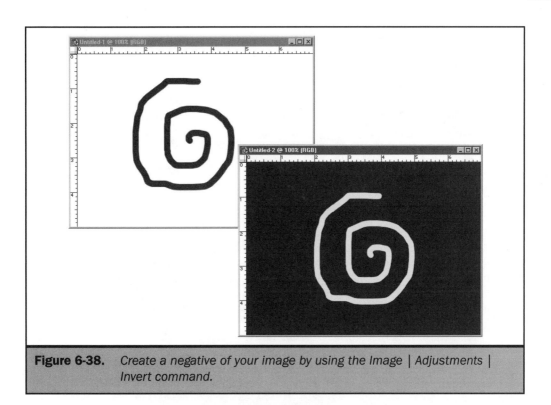

Figure 6-38. *Create a negative of your image by using the Image | Adjustments | Invert command.*

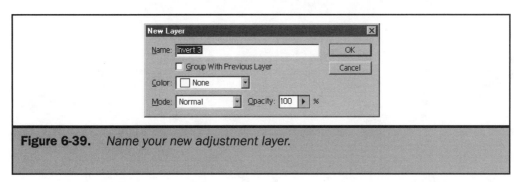

Figure 6-39. *Name your new adjustment layer.*

To access the command, you can also choose Layer | New Adjustment Layer | Invert. This command will create a new layer that serves to perform the color inversion. If you take this approach, a dialog box opens through which you can name and customize your new layer (see Figure 6-39) and as a result, you'll maintain two layers—one before the inversion, and an invert layer that shows the image colors inverted (see Figure 6-40). You can use the visibility options (click the eye icon) next to either of the two layers to determine whether or not you see the original colors or the inverted ones.

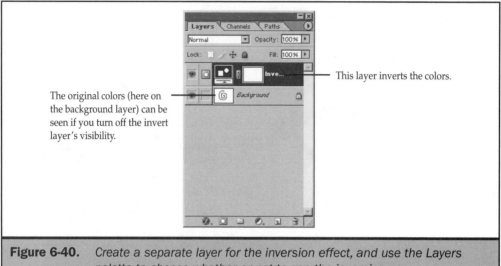

The original colors (here on the background layer) can be seen if you turn off the invert layer's visibility.

This layer inverts the colors.

Figure 6-40.   *Create a separate layer for the inversion effect, and use the Layers palette to choose whether or not to see the inversion.*

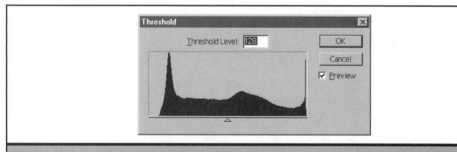

Figure 6-41.   *Choose the standard by which all colors in the image are measured—those that are brighter than the threshold will be turned white, and all those darker than the threshold will be turned black.*

Tip   *Choose the color that will appear on the adjustment layer's thumbnail by clicking the Color drop-down list.*

Working with Color Thresholds

The Image | Adjustments | Threshold command converts images to black and white, but doesn't change the image's color mode. When you apply this command to an image, a dialog box appears (see Figure 6-41) through which you can set the threshold that will dictate which colors are converted to black and which ones are converted to white.

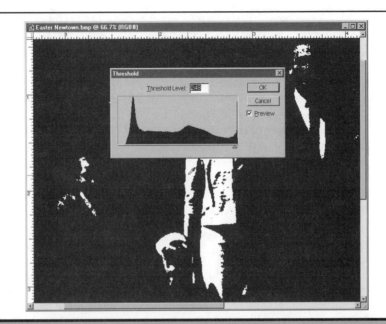

Figure 6-42.   *Need to find your image highlights? Drag the threshold to the far right, and then back it up slowly until white appears.*

As you drag the threshold slider, you're adjusting a histogram of luminosity levels for the pixels in the image. If the Preview option is on, you'll see your results applied to the image itself. When you see the effect you wanted to achieve, click the OK button, and the threshold level is applied to the image directly.

You can also use the Threshold command to locate highlights and shadows by setting the threshold to one of two extremes (all the way to the left to find shadows, and all the way to the right to find highlights) and then slowly dragging it back toward the middle until the highlight or shadow you seek is revealed. Once this happens, you can use your mouse pointer to sample the color (by clicking with the eyedropper directly on the revealed highlight or shadow pixels), thus making that color the new Foreground color. Figure 6-42 shows highlights being revealed, and a color sampling in process. You can also SHIFT-click the pixels in your image, and then through the Info palette, view the color levels before and after the Threshold command was applied.

Equalizing Colors

Finally, a command with a name that clearly reflects what it does. The Equalize command, found in the Image | Adjustments submenu, makes the brightness values of pixels in your image more evenly distributed over the range of brightness levels from 0 to 255. When the command is issued, the brightest and darkest pixels are found in the composite image, and the colors are remapped, making white the brightest value and black the darkest. The pixels that fall between these two extremes are then equalized—the range of brightness established by the lightest and darkest pixels distributed over the rest of the image.

When you choose Image | Adjustments | Equalize, the equalization will take place without any further intervention from you—unless you have a selection made in the image at the time that the command is issued. If you do, then a dialog box appears, asking if you want to equalize the selected area or the entire image based on the selected area (such as a face, as shown in Figure 6-43).

If you choose to apply it to only the selected area, the dynamic effects of this command are immediately evident, especially if you're working with a very faded photo like the one shown in Figure 6-44. In this image, the car and the woman are clear and more brightly colored, and the rest of the image (the parts that were not equalized) remain dull and faded. By spreading brightness levels evenly over the entire image, the photograph's original brightness is restored.

Of course, the effects of the Equalize command will vary with each photograph, depending, of course, on the colors, brightness, and darkness found in the image. If your image is already very vivid or already has a lot of bright and dark, the results of equalizing the image might be unpleasant, or if the image has a lot of noise in it—spots and textures from aging or damage—you may find that those blemishes are accented

Figure 6-43.   *Equalize just a selection or equalize the entire image based on the bright and dark extremes found in the selection.*

by the equalizing process. Figure 6-45 shows a black and white photo that now, because of the Equalize command, has a very bright face and a noisy background—all due to the exaggeration of the signs of age and a less than ideal exposure in the original photo.

Figure 6-44.   *Dull and faded become bright and vivid again.*

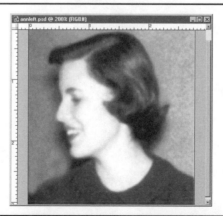

Figure 6-45.   *Equalizing an image can also have negative effects on the quality of your image.*

Once you've applied the Equalize command, you'll find a new command in the Edit menu: Fade Equalize. When you choose this command, a dialog box appears (see Figure 6-46) through which you can control the opacity achieved by fading the results of the initial Equalize command.

Posterizing Images

The Posterize command, located in the Image | Adjustment submenu, allows you to apply multiple brightness values for each channel in an image. When you set the number of tonal levels and click OK (in the Posterize dialog box, shown in Figure 6-47), the pixels in each of your image's channels will be mapped to the nearest matching level. If, for example, your image is in CMYK Mode (and therefore has four color channels), the default number of four tonal levels will result in four colors for each of the four channels.

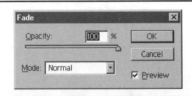

Figure 6-46. *Fade the effects of the Equalize command by choosing Edit | Fade Equalize.*

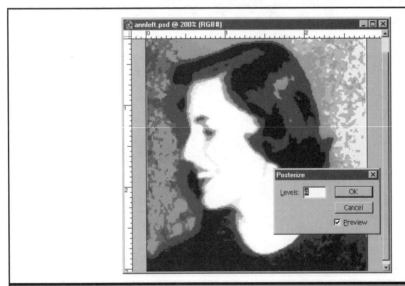

Figure 6-47. *Set the number of tonal levels for your Posterize adjustment.*

My students have called Posterize the "psychedelic effect," and I agree that it's a good descriptor for the effects it often has. Figure 6-48 shows the same image with a portion thereof that has been Posterized with 15 tonal levels. Of course, the more levels you set, the less bizarre the color effects will be, because more colors will be applied. You can set from 0 to 255 levels, and tinker with different levels (making sure Preview is selected in the Posterize dialog box) to find the perfect level for your image goals.

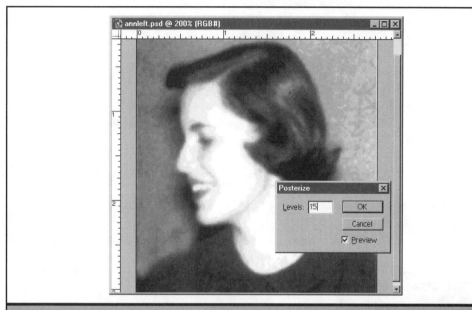

Figure 6-48. *The selected area has been Posterized with 15 tonal levels, resulting in a much more subtle effect.*

Creating a Gradient Map

The Gradient Map command maps the grayscale tones of an image to the colors of a specified gradient fill. For example, if you specify a two-color gradient, shadows will map to one of the endpoint colors of the gradient fill, highlights will map to the other endpoint color, and midtones will map to the shades between the two endpoints. Figure 6-49 shows the gradient map applied to a portion of an RGB image.

Your gradient options include:

Dither   Use this to add noise to a smooth gradient fill, reducing the banding effect that non-dithered images can exhibit.

Reverse   This changes the direction of the gradient fill, which reverses the gradient map as well.

Figure 6-49. *Dramatic color effects are applied through the use of a gradient map, affecting an entire image or just a selected portion thereof.*

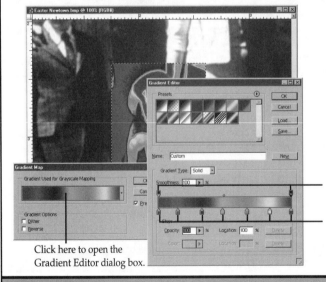

Click here to open the Gradient Editor dialog box.

Drag these boxes to control where the opacity changes along the span of the gradient as it's applied to the selection.

Drag these boxes along the sample gradient to control how the gradient flows from starting to ending color.

Figure 6-50. *Pick a gradient fill to apply, and choose where the swap from starting to ending color will begin.*

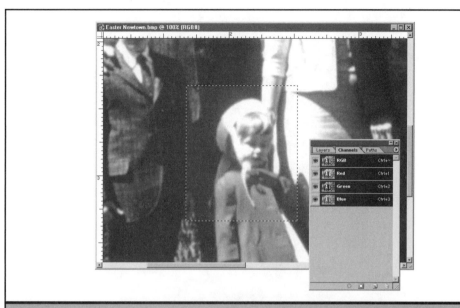

Figure 6-51.   *The Desaturate command lets you take away the color in your image, but not the color information associated with the image color mode.*

You can choose from an array of gradient fills if you click the triangle on the right side of the displayed gradient fill shown in in the Gradient Map dialog box, or click the gradient itself and select a fill and customize its application through the Gradient Editor dialog box (see Figure 6-50).

Desaturating Colors

Just as the Sponge tool can essentially wash the color out of an image, the Desaturate command is used to convert a color image to grayscale, keeping the same color mode. An RGB image will maintain three color channels (red, green, and blue), but equal values of each color will be applied to each pixel, making it look like a grayscale image.

You use the Desaturate command to achieve grayscale effects without losing the color channels and the ability to manipulate the image through them. Figure 6-51 shows a selection of an image to which the Desaturate command has been applied. Note that the Channels palette still shows the complete set of RGB channels for this image.

You can also use the Hue/Saturation command (also found in the Image | Adjustments submenu) to desaturate an image. Simply drag the Saturation slider down to –100, as shown in Figure 6-52. Of course, this dialog box can also be used for increasing the hue, saturation, and lightness (brightness) as well. If you leave the Preview option on, you can see how the changes you make to the settings will affect your image before you approve the changes by clicking OK.

Use the Colorize option to set the hue of the image to the current Foreground color (assuming it's not black or white).

Figure 6-52. *Saturation can be reduced to create a grayscale look while maintaining the color info the image originally had.*

Figure 6-53. *Get rid of ruddy skin tones, blue grass on a lawn, or the faded yellow of an improperly stored color photo by adjusting the color balance.*

Adjusting Color Balance and Tone

Use the Color Balance command (Image | Adjustments | Color Balance) to adjust the levels of cyan, magenta, and yellow. You can enter color levels and drag the sliders to adjust individual levels (see Figure 6-53). In the Tone Balance section of the dialog box, you can choose to make your adjustments affect only the Shadows, Midtones, or Highlights. The Preserve Luminosity option is on by default, which maintains the brightness of the pixels in the image.

Another way to adjust the tones in your image is to work with the Curves dialog box (Image | Adjustments | Curves). You can use this box, shown in Figure 6-54, to adjust the entire range of tones in your image, manipulating any point in the range from 0 to 255, or 0 percent to 100 percent, depending on how the gradient is set, maintaining as many as 15 other constant values. To adjust the tonal range and color balance, point to the curved line on the grid and drag it—up, down, left, or right—and watch the Preview effect on your image. You can also click along the line to add anchors, making it possible to adjust smaller portions of the curve as a whole.

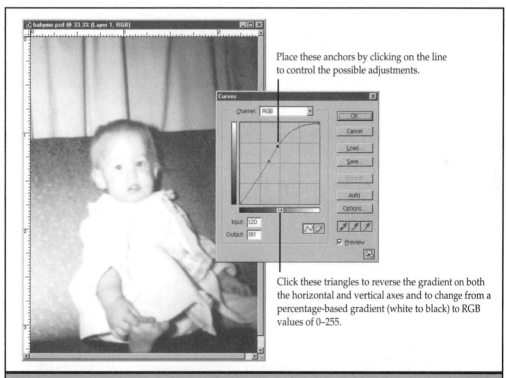

Place these anchors by clicking on the line to control the possible adjustments.

Click these triangles to reverse the gradient on both the horizontal and vertical axes and to change from a percentage-based gradient (white to black) to RGB values of 0–255.

Figure 6-54.   *Drag the curve to adjust the tones in your image.*

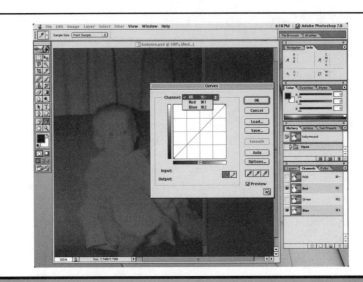

Figure 6-55. *By SHIFT-selecting the channels ahead of time, you can apply levels or curves adjustments to two channels at once.*

The graph on which this line is plotted is like any other type of graph, at least in terms of the parts of the graph and how they work. The horizontal axis works like a value axis in a graph that plots numeric values; in this case, the original intensity values of the pixels are plotted along this axis. The vertical axis represents the new color values. If you want to change only certain color levels in the image, choose which channel you want to adjust (SHIFT-click the channel) on the Channels palette (see Figure 6-55).

Make the grid more detailed by holding down the ALT/OPTION key as you click the grid. ALT/OPTION-click again to toggle back to larger squares in the grid. Larger squares represent fourths, as in quarter-tones, midtones, and three-quarter tones. Smaller squares represent tenths.

You can achieve further mouse control as you click along the curve line to lock spots along the curve, preventing changes to the pixels they represent.

Adjusting Color Levels

The Levels command (Image, Adjustments, Levels) allows you to set the highlights and shadows in an image by dragging three Input Levels sliders to adjust the Levels histogram. You can use the Channel drop-down list to choose which channel you want to adjust (or SHIFT-click the channels you want to adjust in the Channels palette before issuing the Levels command). The sliders, as shown in Figure 6-56, represent shadows, midtones, and highlights.

Figure 6-56.   *Use the Levels histogram and sliders to adjust the levels of highlights, shadows, and midtones in your image.*

As you drag the Input Levels sliders (note that only the midtones slider can be moved independently), you'll see the levels of light and dark change in the active image. You fine-tune the process by mapping pixels (black, gray, and white) using the Set Black Point, Set Gray Point, and Set White Point eyedroppers. After clicking the eyedropper buttons (one at a time), you can click on pixels in your image; again, you'll see your image change to match the new tonal range you've set.

The Output Levels slider controls shadow and highlight values. Dragging the shadow slider to the left (it's all the way to the right by default) reduces the shadows in your image, and dragging the highlight slider to the left (it's all the way to the right by default), reduces the highlights in your image.

You can save levels (creating .alv files) and load saved levels, using the Save and Load buttons, respectively. You can also click the Auto button to automatically adjust the image levels based on the settings in the Auto Color Correction dialog box. To access the Auto Color Corrections dialog box, click the Options button to view and change the settings that dictate how the levels and other adjustment commands work. Through this dialog box (shown in Figure 6-57), you can change the algorithm that will be used to make overall tonal changes in your image. The Algorithm options follow:

Enhance Monochromatic Contrast   Use this to make sure all channels are clipped the same way. This algorithm will maintain the overall color and brightness ratios throughout your image. The Auto Contrast command utilizes this algorithm, making use of its uniformity.

Enhance Per Channel Contrast   Used by the Auto Levels command, this algorithm creates more dramatic effects by maximizing the color range for each channel, adjusting each channel individually. Color casts may appear or disappear based on the use of this algorithm.

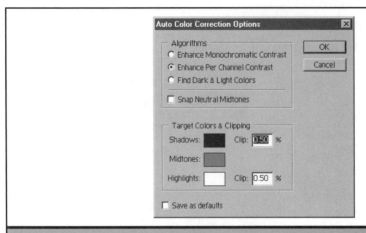

Figure 6-57. Change the way levels and the Adjustments submenu's automatic commands are applied through the Auto Color Correction Options dialog box.

Find Dark & Light Colors The Auto Color command uses this algorithm, relying on its ability to locate the average darkest and lightest pixels in an image and bases changes to color and contrast on them. Clipping is minimized with this algorithm.

The Snap Neutral Midtones option asks Photoshop to find an average neutral color and adjust gamma values to make the color literally neutral.

Also located in the Auto Color Corrections dialog box are Shadows, Midtones, and Highlights color boxes. When clicked, these open the Color Picker so you can choose new colors for these three levels. You can click within the image as well as inside the Color Picker when choosing a Shadow, Midtone, or Highlight color. As you make your selections and OK them in the Color Picker, you'll see the results in your image.

Using Auto Levels

The Auto Levels command, also located in the Image | Adjustments submenu, does just what its name implies—it automatically adjusts the highlight, shadow, and midtones levels in your image. When you issue the Auto Levels command, the sliders you see in the Levels dialog box are moved automatically to set highlights and shadows, defining the lightest (highlight) and darkest (shadow) pixels in each color channel as white and black, respectively. Then the automation continues as the middle pixel levels are proportionately distributed between the new levels of light and dark.

Because Auto Levels adjusts all of your color channels, you may notice a change in overall color cast in your image. If the change is undesirable, you can use other color correction tools, such as the Color Balance command, to make any necessary adjustments.

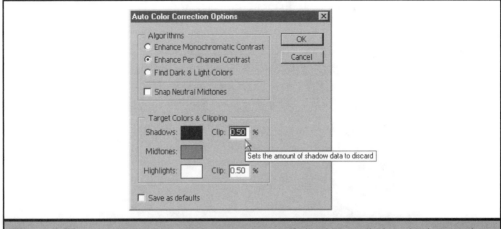

Figure 6-58. *Increase or decrease the amount of clipping applied to shadows and highlights, thus controlling the effects of the Auto Contrast command.*

Using Auto Contrast

More automation can be found through the Auto Contrast command. Located in the Image | Adjustments submenu, this command automatically adjusts the contrast in your image. The command works by mapping the darkest and lightest pixels in the image to black and white (respectively), resulting in lighter highlights and darker shadows.

Because there is no dialog box associated with this command, it's important to understand the defaults by which it operates. The command clips the white and black pixels by .5 percent, ignoring the first .5 percent of both extremes. This makes the results of the Auto Contrast command less stark than they might be. If you need to control the clipping of black and white values, you can open the Auto Color Correction Options dialog box, accessed by clicking the Options button in the Levels dialog box (choose Image | Adjustments | Levels). In that dialog box, shown in Figure 6-58, edit the Clip levels for Shadows and Highlights, and then click OK.

Whether you tinker with the clip settings or not, you'll find the Auto Contrast command a good first step in correcting photos and other continuous tone images. The command is so effective you may not need to do anything else at all to adjust the contrast in your image.

Using Auto Color

New to Photoshop 7, the Auto Color command automatically adjusts the colors and contrast of any RGB image based on the existing content. This is a departure from the Auto Contrast and Auto Levels commands, which rely on the channels and their histograms for highlights, shadows, and midtones. The Auto Color command does operate based on the settings in the Auto Color Correction Options dialog box, though, so you can make adjustments to the settings there to control how the Auto Color command affects your image. Figures 6-59 and 6-60 show an image before and after the use of the Auto Color command. Even in the black and white view of these images, you can see how the image is improved.

Figure 6-59.   *Before Auto Color, the image is dull, with very little contrast and no bright colors.*

Figure 6-60.   *After Auto Color, the image has improved contrast, and the colors are much more vivid.*

Controlling Brightness and Contrast

If you want to control the brightness and contrast of your image directly, not relying on any automatic commands and their dependence on the Auto Color Corrections Options dialog box, you can use the Brightness and Contrast command found in the Image | Adjustments submenu. The command opens a dialog box, as shown in Figure 6-61, that offers two sliders: One adjusts brightness, the other adjusts contrast.

You can make a selection before issuing the command, in which case only a portion of the image will be adjusted, as shown in Figure 6-62. When you drag the sliders, dragging to the left reduces the levels; dragging to the right increases them. You have the ability to adjust the values from –100 to +100.

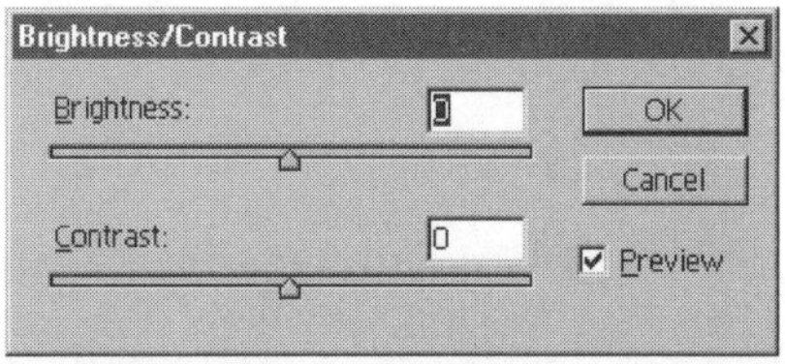

Figure 6-61. *Simple sliders adjust the brightness and contrast of your image.*

Figure 6-62. *Does only part of your image seem to fade away? Select that region and adjust the contrast and brightness accordingly.*

One caveat to using the Brightness and Contrast command to adjust your image quality—you may lose some image quality in the process of adjusting these levels (in either direction), which can have a negative impact on printed output that requires great depth and detail.

Replacing Colors

This command allows you to create a temporary mask for certain colors, after which you can replace the masked colors. Through the Replace Color dialog box, you can use the Transform sliders (see Figure 6-63) to adjust Hue, Saturation, and Lightness. You can use the Fuzziness slider (or type a value into the Fuzziness box) to control the tolerance of the mask. The fuzzier the setting, the more the mask will allow related colors to be included in the color replacement. A low fuzziness setting will be more restrictive.

Click the Image option to see the image in the Preview window. This is helpful if your image is obscured by the dialog box.

To select the color that will be replaced, you can click in the Preview window, or you can click in the image itself. If you want to include multiple areas in the mask, you can SHIFT-click with your mouse, clicking on additional spots in the image—this can help you expand the colors that are changed when you click OK to apply your Replace Color settings. If you want to reduce the masked area, thus reducing the scope of the color

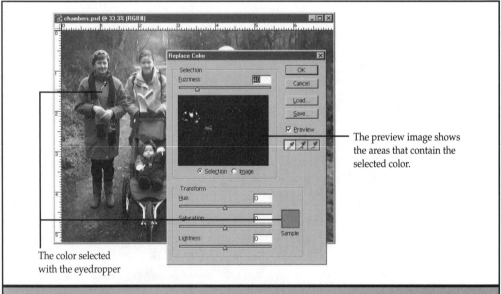

The preview image shows the areas that contain the selected color.

The color selected with the eyedropper

Figure 6-63. *Use the Replace Color feature to select and mask colors in your image and change them to a new color.*

replacement, ALT/OPTION-click the unwanted but currently selected spots to remove them from the mask.

Adjusting Selective Colors

To use this command, you must first select the composite channel in the Channels palette. If you don't have the channel displayed, the command won't be available in the Image | Adjustments submenu. Once the channel is selected, open the Selective Color dialog box and choose the color you want to adjust. Click the Colors drop-down list and make your selection (see Figure 6-64).

Next, choose a Method—Absolute or Relative—from the two options at the bottom of the dialog box. If you choose Absolute, you'll be using absolute values to adjust the colors in the image. Imagine a pixel that's currently 10 percent cyan. It will become 25 percent cyan if you drag the Cyan slider to +15 percent. The color percentages for each pixel will be used to determine the new colors, based on how much you add or take away using the dialog box sliders for Cyan, Magenta, Yellow, or Black.

If you choose the Relative method, that same 10-percent-cyan pixel will become 16.5 percent cyan if you drag the Cyan slider to +15 percent. Increasing the cyan level by 15 percent will add just 1.5 percent cyan to the pixel, because 1.5 is 15 percent of 10 percent. Note that the Relative method cannot be used to adjust white, because it contains no percent of any color.

It's important to note that Selective Color corrections utilize a color table that contains the level of each process ink needed to build a primary color. As you decrease or increase the level of a specific ink, you can selectively (thus the command's name) adjust a specific color. For example, if you only want to increase the amount of cyan in the blue components of an image but leave the cyan in the green components alone, you can use Selective Color. Select Blue from the Color list and then drag the Cyan slider accordingly.

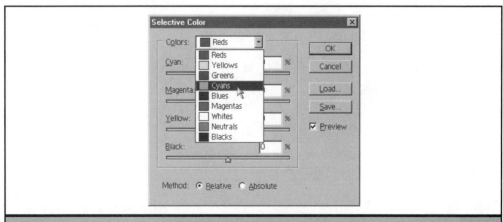

Figure 6-64. *Choose the Selective Color you want to adjust.*

Although the Selective Color command offers CMYK sliders to adjust your color, you can also use the command to edit RGB images.

Working with Variations

This is a very handy feature also located in the Image | Adjustments submenu. (If you don't see it there, you may need to install the plug-in.) The Variations command allows you to view a series of thumbnails, each showing a different color or contrast effect. As shown in Figure 6-65, you can click the Lighter thumbnail to see how adding more white to the image will affect it. If you want to see what will happen when you bump up the Blue component, you can click the More Blue thumbnail. At any time, you can click the Original thumbnail to bring all the thumbnails back to their default state. You can view the effects of compound changes—lightening, adding more yellow, adding more red, or whatever combination you'd like to preview. The Current Pick thumbnail (located next to the Original thumbnail, and also in the two other sections of the dialog box) shows the effects of the thumbnail you just clicked. The Current Pick thumbnail is repeated in all three sections of the dialog box so you can see the results of your selections right alongside the other options.

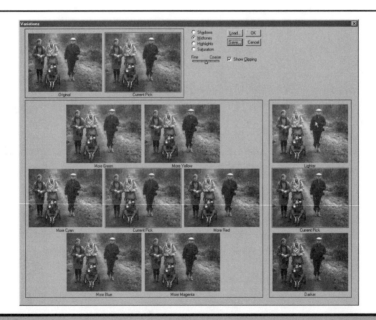

Figure 6-65. *Preview the effects of lightening or darkening your image, or adding more green, yellow, cyan, red, blue, or magenta.*

At the top of the dialog box you can choose what aspect of your image will be changed by the addition of a color or the change to lighter or darker. Click the Shadows, Midtones, Highlights, or Saturation option, and then drag the Fine/Course slider to choose between a subtle or garish result. The slider default is right in the middle. After choosing how your adjustments will affect the image, you can set about previewing the Variations thumbnails as you make your selections to add more color (red, blue, green, cyan, yellow, or magenta), more white (lighter), or more black (darker). Once you like the way the Current Pick thumbnail looks, you can click OK to apply the changes to your image, or click Cancel to end the preview and close the Variations dialog box.

Note *You can save your Variations settings by clicking the Save button. This will create an .ava file that you can name appropriately and save to whichever folder you desire. If you want to open a previously saved set of variations, click the Load button.*

Summary

In this chapter, you learned to apply color. You looked at how different color modes interpret and store information about colors. You learned to adjust colors, contrast, brightness, and to use automatic tools to adjust the levels of those elements in your images. You also learned how to reduce file sizes by changing color modes, and how to view only certain colors within your image as an integral part of the editing and retouching process.

Chapter 7

Making Artistic Use of Photoshop's Painting and Drawing Tools

Y ou can use Photoshop's painting and drawing tools to both add original content to your images and retouch existing content. Through a vast array of customization tools, you can make the brushes, pens, pencils, and erasers do your bidding with ease. In this chapter, you'll learn to operate the tools, take advantage of their options, and through a varied set of sample images, discover new ways to paint, draw, and enhance your images with Photoshop.

Using the Brush and Pencil Tools

The Brush and Pencil tools are simple to operate, requiring only a steady hand with whatever pointing device you're using and a working knowledge of the seemingly endless selection of brush and pencil options, found on the tools' options bar and on the Brushes palette. Through these options and settings, you can easily customize the way the brush and pencil apply color and texture to your images.

The basics of using the Brush and Pencil tools were covered in Chapter 2— just click the tool (or press the B key) and then drag your mouse across the image, making certain the appropriate layer is active (see your Layers palette) before you start. Figure 7-1 shows a variety of brush and pencil strokes on a white background.

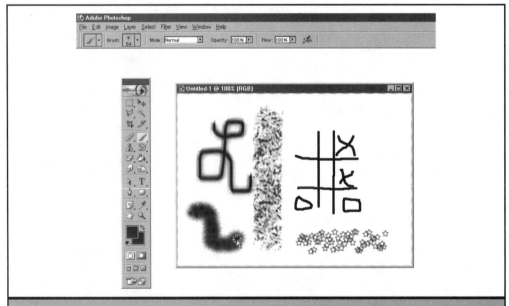

Figure 7-1.   *From simple lines to exotic effects, you can apply color and texture with the Brush and Pencil tools.*

It's important to note that the only difference between the Brush and the Pencil is that the Brush is intended for painting soft lines, and the Pencil is assumed to be a tool for creating hard, crisp lines, even when a textured or thick point is used. This is the same as the way you'd use real, physical brushes and pencils—you wouldn't apply color to a wall or a piece of furniture with a pencil (unless you're a kid, and then you're likely to get in trouble). Rather, you'd use a paintbrush to get a soft, thick coverage of color. You'd use a pencil to draw a picture, or to create crisp, straight lines for a schematic or a border. Photoshop assumes you'll apply the same logic when choosing a tool for use on your images, and the brush defaults for the Pencil tool reflect a pencil's natural characteristics, despite the word "brush" appearing on the options bar and Brushes tab/palette.

One other minor difference: When the Pencil is active, the Airbrush option disappears from the options bar, replaced by the Auto Erase option (see Figure 7-2). Auto Erase allows you to paint the current Background color over parts of your image currently filled or painted with the Foreground color. In general, this is the only pencil-specific feature you'll encounter as you work with the options bar and Brushes palette. When it comes to using the Pencil tool, the word "Pencil" will appear only on the tool itself (in the toolbox); don't be confused by the references to brushes when you're setting up the way the Pencil will work.

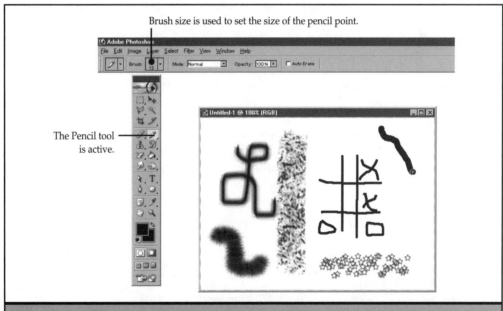

Figure 7-2.   *The Pencil may seem to get little attention, given all the reference to brushes, even when the Pencil tool is active.*

> **Note** When using the Pencil with the Auto Erase feature on, remember that the color you're drawing over determines the effects of the tool. For example, if you draw on an area that's currently colored with the Foreground color, the Auto Erase feature kicks in (assuming you turned it on)—the pencil strokes will erase the Foreground color, revealing the Background color. If, on the other hand, you draw on an area that doesn't contain the Foreground color, the area will be painted with the Foreground color, as though the Auto Erase feature is not in use.

Choosing a Brush Size

The first thing you'll probably want to do when preparing to use the Brush or Pencil tool is choose the size brush/pencil to paint with. The paint job you intend to do will dictate the size that works best. A small (as small as 1 pixel) brush works well for intricate brushwork, and large brushes (as big as 2500 pixels) work well if you have a lot of area to cover quickly. There are textured brushes, brushes with diffused edges, and brushes that apply recognizable shapes such as leaves or flowers. Figure 7-3 shows the list of brushes, and just a few of the brush styles available.

The list of brush styles below the Master Diameter slider starts with a simple 1-pixel-wide line, culminating in a variety of textures and effects, each with a name you can view if you pause your mouse pointer over the sample stroke in the list. With names like Oil, Heavy Flow, Dry Edges, and Charcoal Large Smear, you can get a good sense of the effect even before you use the brush. A sample of a quick stroke appears on the left side of the list. Its resulting brush effect on the image is shown in Figure 7-4. Note that the selected style is only 39 pixels, but the stroke seen on the image is much larger—this comes from dragging the Master Diameter slider to increase the brush size after choosing the brush style.

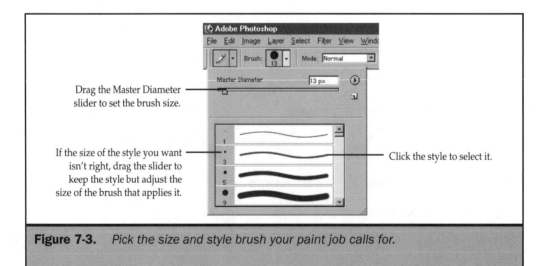

Figure 7-3. Pick the size and style brush your paint job calls for.

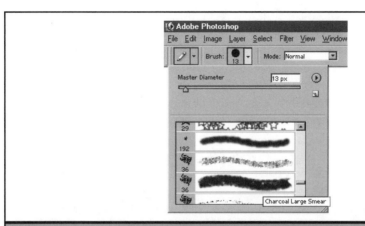

Figure 7-4.   *Choose a brush style by sight or by name.*

Tip   *You can choose how your brushes will appear in the Brush menu by clicking the menu button. When the menu displays, choose from Small Thumbnail, Large Thumbnail, Small List, or Large List, as well as Stroke Thumbnail, which is the default. Text Only is another choice, and shows the brush names only—there's no sample of the effect any of the brushes achieve. If you choose to stay in a graphic mode, you can still see the names of the brushes by hovering over them with your mouse pointer and displaying the ToolTips.*

Picking a Painting or Drawing Mode

Once you've chosen a brush/pencil size and style, you may want to make further adjustments, controlling how the color is applied and how the painted area looks. Your choices, located on the Brush options bar (shown in Figure 7-5), are easily set by making selections from drop-down lists. The default settings work for most situations, but you can achieve interesting effects by making adjustments.

The first setting on the options bar is Mode, which determines how the paint will be applied and the effect it will have on the image. This setting is also known as the *blending mode*, as it refers to how the paint will blend in with the existing color and content on the active layer. The default mode is Normal. Whichever mode you choose (even keeping Normal as the setting), consider the following formula:

base color + blend color = result color

To understand the parts of this equation, remember that the *base color* is the color of the active layer—the color over which the paint will be applied. The *blend color* is the color you're applying with the brush. The *result color* is what you get when you apply the blend color to the base color. Obviously, the blending mode with which you apply the new color will affect how the blend color looks, affecting the result color dramatically. Of course, the settings you employ elsewhere on the options bar (Opacity and Airbrush, particularly) also affect the way the paint looks, but the blending mode has significant impact. Your blending mode choices are:

Normal   This mode paints each painted pixel to make it the result color (the color you chose for the Foreground color on the Color Picker).

Dissolve   This works the same as Normal Mode, except that the paint is applied as though the color were dissolving on the edge of soft brush strokes (see Figure 7-6), which shows the same color and opacity applied in Normal Mode (on the top) and Dissolve Mode (on the bottom).

Behind   This mode paints the transparent areas of a layer only, and is obviously applicable only on layers with Lock Transparency turned off. As shown in Figure 7-7, this mode gives you the look of paint applied to the back of a clear surface like glass or a sheet of plastic.

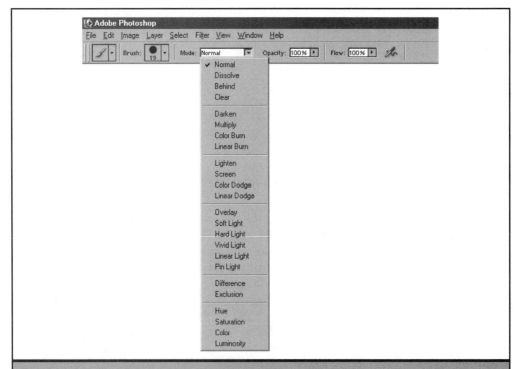

Figure 7-5.   *The Brush options bar offers tools for changing the way the paint is applied, such as whether or not you can see through it, and how quickly the paint flows from the tool.*

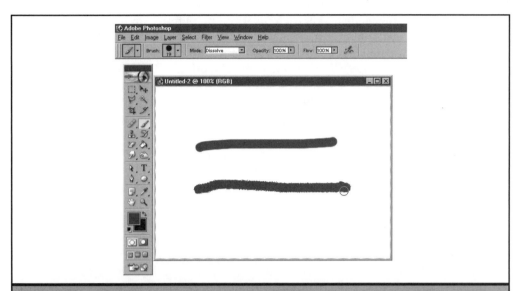

Figure 7-6.   *Dissolve Mode uses a random method of applying paint to pixels, using both the base and blend colors.*

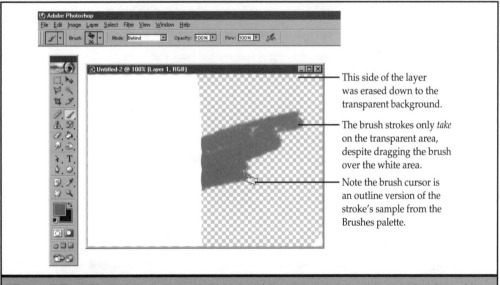

This side of the layer was erased down to the transparent background.

The brush strokes only *take* on the transparent area, despite dragging the brush over the white area.

Note the brush cursor is an outline version of the stroke's sample from the Brushes palette.

Figure 7-7.   *The brush stroke only shows on the transparent areas, making it useful to apply the Eraser (erasing to a transparent background) first.*

Clear The Clear Mode makes each pixel you paint transparent, or clear, thus earning its name. You can use Clear Mode on tools other than the Brush, such as the Paint Bucket tool, the Pencil, the Fill command, and the Stroke command. As with Behind Mode, Lock Transparency must be off in order to use this mode. Figure 7-8 shows the effects of the Clear Mode—paint has been applied across existing painted strokes of a different color, on a transparent field.

Darken This mode refers to the color information in each channel and selects the darker color when comparing the base and blending colors. Pixels that are lighter than the blend color are replaced, and the pixels that are darker than the blend color are left as is. Use Darken if you want to apply a light color and darken a base color that's already darker than the color you're painting with, as shown in Figure 7-9.

Multiply Use this mode to create a darker color by multiplying the base color by the blend color, based on the color information in each channel. When you use Multiply Mode and paint with colors other than white, you create increasingly darker colors as you paint over and over in the same spots (see Figure 7-10), much like applying layers of translucent color and overlapping the same or different colors: The more you paint or draw in the same spot, the darker your colors become.

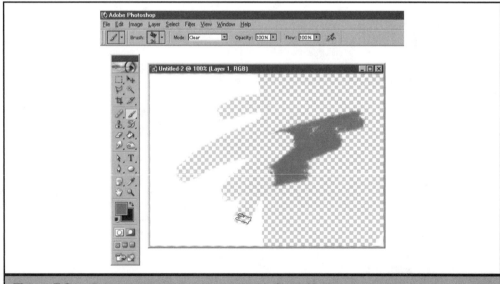

Figure 7-8. *Paint to create transparency with Clear Mode.*

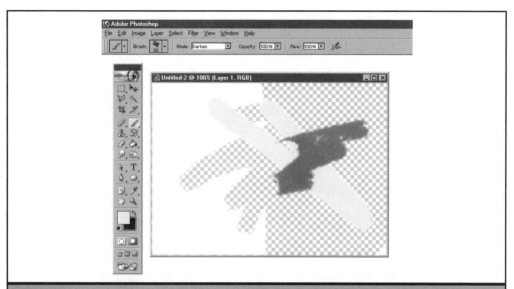

Figure 7-9.   *Apply a light yellow over a blue (all appearing in shades of gray here), and where the yellow crosses the blue, the blue is darkened.*

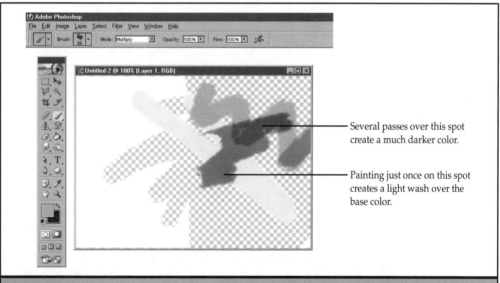

Several passes over this spot create a much darker color.

Painting just once on this spot creates a light wash over the base color.

Figure 7-10.   *Paint over an existing color and multiply the base and blending colors.*

Color Burn   This mode darkens the active layer (wherever you paint on it) by increasing the contrast between base and blend colors. You can use this blending mode to get a more stark, high-contrast effect, as shown in Figure 7-11.

Linear Burn   This mode works much like Color Burn, but it uses the color information in each channel to reduce the brightness levels of the base color.

Lighten   If your base color is lighter than your blend color, the base color is chosen as the result color, and vice versa. If the blend color is lighter, that becomes the result. If there are pixels in the painted area that are darker than the blend color, they're changed to the result color, and pixels that are lighter than the blend color don't change at all. You can use this mode to achieve an eraser-like effect—wiping out darker colors in favor of a lighter one. If you paint with a color that's already in the image, that color is unaffected by the new paint, but whatever's darker is replaced with white, and transparent areas are filled with the painting color.

Screen   Unlike Multiply, which creates darker colors where paint overlaps, the effect of Screen Mode is a lighter color. Screening with black doesn't change the color, and screening with white gives you white. For a good visual analogy, imagine aiming dueling overhead projectors (with color slides on them) at the same spot on the wall. Unlike overlapping slides on the same projector, which would produce darker colors where they overlap, the two projected images would appear lighter at their common target.

Color Dodge   For an extreme brightening effect, use Color Dodge Mode. This mode takes the color information in each channel and then brightens the base color (and thus, brightens the result color) by decreasing the contrast. If you paint with white or very light colors, you increase the effect.

Linear Dodge   The results of this mode are very similar to Color Dodge, but instead of reducing contrast to achieve added brightness, the brightness level is directly increased.

Overlay   This mode works like Multiply or Screen in that overlapping colors maintain highlights and shadows. The base color mixes with the blend color to give you a result color that has the same light or dark quality of the base color.

Soft Light   Imagine shining a soft, white light on something—the shadows and highlights are increased by the light source, but the effects are subtle (see Figure 7-12). Changes to color in this mode are based on the blend color, and the lightness or darkness of that color determines the lightening effect. If the blend color is lighter than 50 percent gray, this mode produces an effect similar to the Dodge tool. If the blend color is darker than 50 percent gray, the Burn tool's effect is mimicked.

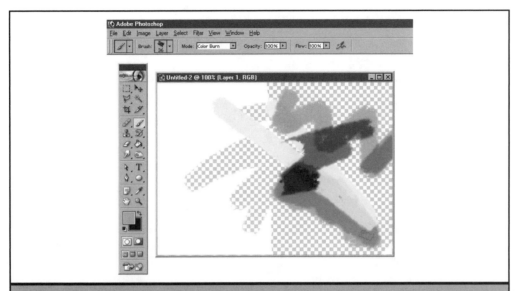

Figure 7-11.   *Darken your colors by increasing the contrast between base and blend colors.*

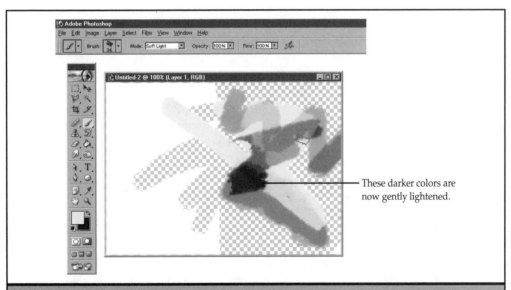

These darker colors are
now gently lightened.

Figure 7-12.   *A gentle, diffused lightness can be achieved with Soft Light Mode.*

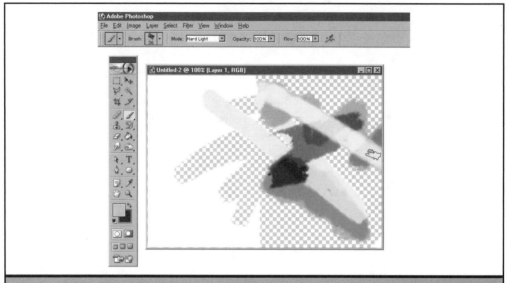

Figure 7-13. *Hard Light Mode is very aptly named—no softness or diffusion here.*

Hard Light Having the opposite effect of Soft Light Mode, Hard Light creates a harsh, bare-bulb lighting effect on your image. The blend color is used as in the case of Soft Light, but the effects are much harder and not subtle in the least, as shown in Figure 7-13.

Vivid Light This mode will lighten (dodge) or darken (burn) as you paint by adjusting the contrast in relation to the blend color. When the blend color is lighter than 50 percent gray, Vivid Light Mode will lighten the image by reducing contrast. Conversely, if the blend color is darker than 50 percent gray, a darkening effect occurs from the increase in contrast.

Linear Light The same way Vivid Light bases contrast adjustments on the blend color, Linear Light Mode adjusts brightness based on the blend color. A blend color that's lighter than 50 percent gray will result in a lighter effect, achieved by increasing the brightness level. If the blend color is darker than 50 percent gray, brightness will be decreased, resulting in a darker effect.

Pin Light In Pin Light Mode, if your blend color is lighter than 50 percent gray, any pixels darker than your blend color are replaced with the result color. If there are pixels lighter than the blend color in the path of your paintbrush, they are not changed. On the other hand, if your blend color is darker than 50 percent gray, any pixels lighter than your blend color are replaced. If there are pixels darker than the blend color in the path of your paintbrush, those don't change, either.

Difference   Use this blending mode to invert lower layers based on the levels of brightness in the layer on which you're painting. This mode takes the color information in each channel and takes the blend color from the base color or the base color from the blend color—it all depends whether or not the base is brighter than the blending color, or vice versa. The results can be quite dramatic, in a sort of color-negative effect, as shown in Figure 7-14.

Exclusion   This mode has virtually the same effect as Difference Mode, with lower contrast levels.

Hue   Working with the HSL (hue, saturation, and luminosity) color model, this blending mode gives you a result color that has the luminosity and saturation of the base color and the hue of the blend color.

Saturation   Again using the HSL model, Saturation mode gives you a result color with the luminosity and hue of the base color and the saturation of the blend color.

Color   Yet another combination of the HSL color model's components, this blending mode gives you a result color with the luminance of the base color and the hue and saturation of the blend color. You'll find this mode works well when you're changing the tint of a color image or when you're adding color to a monochrome image.

Luminosity   This mode gives you a result color with the hue and saturation of the base color and the luminosity of the blend color.

Figure 7-14.   *Light becomes dark, dark becomes light, and colors appear as their opposite with the Difference blending mode.*

EDITING AND
RETOUCHING IMAGES

Setting Opacity and Flow

As you move from left to right across the options bar, the next Brush setting you see is Opacity. The Opacity setting controls whether or not you can see through the paint you apply. It is set by typing a percentage or dragging the slider that appears if you click the drop-down list triangle to the right of the text box (see Figure 7-15).

An opacity of 100 percent is completely dense, and nothing can be seen through it. An opacity of 50 percent allows some of the underlying content to be seen, but dimly. An opacity of 1 percent (the lowest you can go) applies virtually no paint, and the underlying content is barely obscured. Figure 7-16 shows three brush strokes of the same size and style—from left to right, the opacity is set to 100 percent, 50 percent, and 10 percent. As you can see, the lower the percentage, the more transparent the paint is, and the more subtle the effect of the painting.

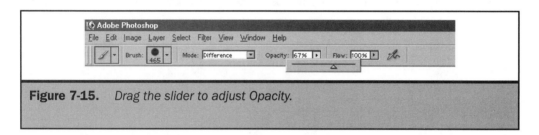

Figure 7-15.   *Drag the slider to adjust Opacity.*

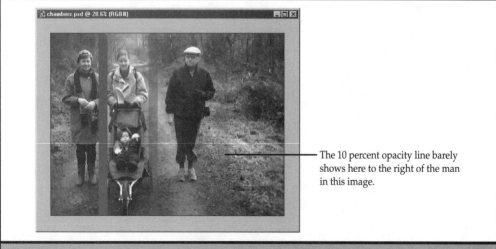

The 10 percent opacity line barely shows here to the right of the man in this image.

Figure 7-16.   *Let your image show through by reducing brush Opacity.*

As you continue to move across the Brush options bar, the next setting is Flow. Flow controls the speed at which the paint is applied by the Brush tool. The default is 100 percent, and you can again type a percentage or use the slider to increase or decrease the setting. If you leave the Flow set to 100 percent, you'll see 100 percent of the paint on the image (dependent on your other settings, of course). For example, if your Opacity is set to 50 percent, you won't see thick, dense coverage. If, however, you reduce Flow, and Opacity is set to 100 percent, you'll see less paint applied to the image, as though the brush were running out of paint as you drag it across the surface of your image. Figure 7-17 shows three brush strokes from top to bottom: one at 100 percent, one at 50 percent, and one at 10 percent. Note that the stroke at 10 percent looks like the opacity is set low, but as you can see on the options bar, it's not.

You'll find that setting either or both the Opacity and Flow settings at a low percentage results in a softer, more transparent effect. You can use this technique to apply a typically dynamic blending mode in a way that's not as stark or harsh as it might be if your Opacity and/or Flow were set to 100 percent. Conversely, if you're using a subtle blending mode (such as Soft Light), you may want to keep your Opacity and Flow settings higher so the effects of the mode aren't so subtle they're missed.

Figure 7-17.   *Control the flow of paint from your brush with the aptly named Flow setting.*

Using Airbrush Mode

The last setting on the Brush options bar is the Airbrush. It's not so much a setting, however, as it is an optional tool. Instead of painting with a regular brush, you're using an airbrush, a device that sprays paint onto a surface. The Airbrush option turns your brush into such a device, giving you a softer brush stroke with translucent edges, and often a thicker finish to the stroke, as shown in Figure 7-18. In this figure, a line on the left (painted with the Airbrush turned off) is a uniform thickness and opacity, and has solid edges. The line on the right, which was painted with the Airbrush turned on, has soft, diffused edges, and the paint thickens toward the end of the stroke as though extra paint sprayed out of the airbrush at the very end.

You can achieve an exaggeration of this effect by clicking your mouse to apply a dot of paint and then holding the mouse button down. With the Airbrush option on, the dot gets larger and larger (still with a diffused edge) as though you were holding a felt-tip marker on very porous paper—the paper would absorb the ink and make a fat spot rather than a sharp dot. Figure 7-19 shows the dot that will result with the Airbrush option off, and below it, the larger, softer spot that is created by dispensing ink in one place with the Airbrush on.

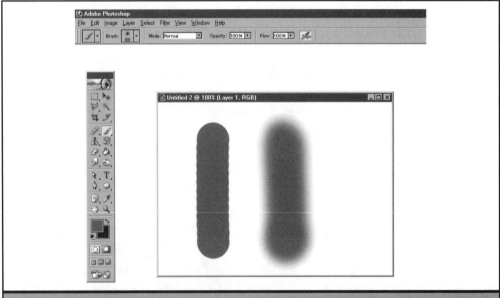

Figure 7-18.   *The airbrushed line resembles the line you'd get if you used a spray can to apply a streak of paint.*

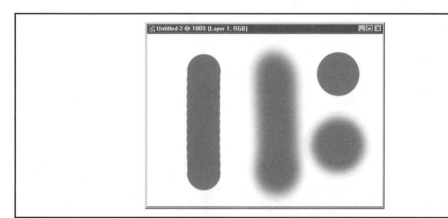

Figure 7-19.   *Even a single dot of color becomes a large, soft spot with the Airbrush.*

Note   *Even if you don't use the Airbrush option, you can achieve a soft line with the Soft brush styles. For example, if you paint a line with the Hard Round 5 pixels brush style, you get a solid line with clean, solid edges and no extra paint flow after you stop moving your mouse. If you use the Soft Round 5 pixels brush style, the same thickness of line now has soft edges and a diffused look. If you don't turn the Airbrush option on, however, that's the end of the airbrushed effect—your painted strokes won't have the spray-can look at the end of the stroke or when you press the mouse and apply paint continuously on a single spot.*

Tip   *If you choose a brush style that starts with the word Airbrush, the Airbrush option is automatically turned on as soon as you click that style in the Brush drop-down list or on the Brushes palette. If, on the other hand, you turn the Airbrush option on and then choose a Hard style for your brush, the Airbrush option remains selected, but the airbrush effects are barely noticeable, diminished by the hard traits of the brush style.*

Working with Brush Sets

The Brush tool's style list (displayed by clicking the Brush drop-down list on the options bar), displays a basic set of styles by default. The default bristles are varied enough for most jobs, but some of the more interesting styles aren't part of the set. The default set contains more than 60 brush styles, from a thin, hard, 1-pixel line to styles that include scattered star shapes, the look of fur or grass, and scratchy-looking styles that mimic drawing or painting on rough paper. Figure 7-20 shows a series of brush strokes painted with the more interesting styles in the default set.

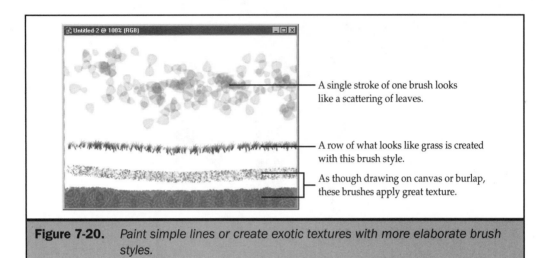

A single stroke of one brush looks like a scattering of leaves.

A row of what looks like grass is created with this brush style.

As though drawing on canvas or burlap, these brushes apply great texture.

Figure 7-20. *Paint simple lines or create exotic textures with more elaborate brush styles.*

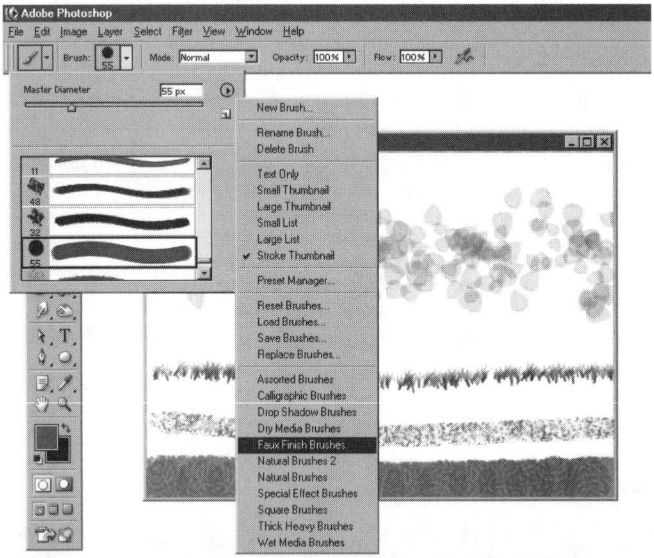

Figure 7-21. *Choose from the list of alternate brush sets on the Brush menu.*

Figure 7-22. *Replace or Append to the current set of brushes.*

Loading Brush Sets

If you want to add more brush styles to the Brush drop-down list, click the Brush button on the options bar. When the list of default bristles (along with the Master Diameter slider) displays, click the menu button on the right. This displays the options menu shown in Figure 7-21. From the menu, choose one of the specialty sets, such as Faux Finish Brushes or Special Effect Brushes, from the bottom section.

Once you've made your selection, a prompt appears (see Figure 7-22) asking if you want to replace the default bristles set with the new set, or if you want to add the new set to the existing set so you'll have all of them to choose from. I prefer to use the Append command to add the new set, but if you don't like scrolling through a long list of brush styles or know that there are a very small group of styles all in one set that you'll be using , then click OK to replace the current set.

Working with the Brushes Palette

Located in the docking well by default, the Brushes tab can be clicked to display a series of Brush tool options (see Figure 7-23), or brought down onto the screen to become a full-fledged palette (see Figure 7-24), displaying those same tools. There's a lot of redundancy between the Brushes tab/palette and the Brush tool and options bar, but there are some features that are unique to the tab/palette (which I'll refer to as the Brushes palette from now on).

First, the Brushes palette offers two modes: Brush Presets and Brush Tip Shape. Depending on which one you choose, you'll have a completely different view of your available brush styles. The Brush Presets view looks very much like the Brush tool drop-down list on the options bar in terms of the display of brush styles—you see pixel sizes and samples of the brush strokes in a scrollable list. The Master Diameter slider is below the list instead of above it, and as a bonus, you can see a sample of the style you've selected at different pixel sizes in a large preview area at the bottom of the palette.

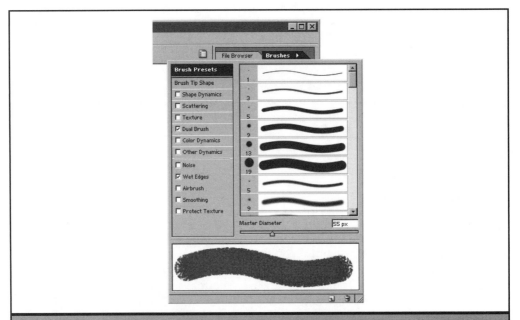

Figure 7-23. When clicked, the Brushes tab displays a variety of brush and pencil customization tools.

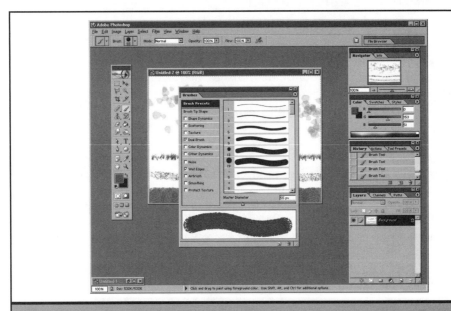

Figure 7-24. Drag the Brushes tab down onto the desktop to use as a Brushes palette offering the same tools.

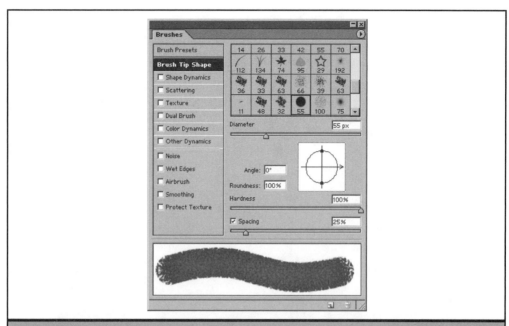

Figure 7-25.   *The Brush Tip Shape view allows you to adjust the size, shape, and angle of the tip of the brush or point of the pencil.*

If you click the Brush Tip Shape button at the top of the palette, the graphical list of styles is replaced by a set of brush tips, representing all the same styles shown in the Presets view, of course, but this time displayed as single dots rather than strokes (see Figure 7-25). The Diameter slider allows you to change the pixel size of any selected tip shape.

You can also adjust the Angle of the brush tip, the Roundness percentage (adjustable via the text box or by dragging on the black dot anchors in the schematic box), and the Hardness and Spacing (both of which are adjusted with a slider or by typing a percentage into their respective text boxes).

Note that the Spacing option can be turned on or off; if it's off, the Spacing slider is dimmed and cannot be adjusted. The Spacing option controls the distance between dots in a single stroke of the brush or pencil—if you increase the spacing, it's as though the brush or pencil is skipping or moving in a halting fashion across the page, as shown in Figure 7-26. Decreasing the Spacing percentage creates a smoother line, because the dots are closer together along the line you paint with the brush or draw with the pencil.

If you've dragged the Brushes tab down from the docking well and turned it into a palette, and now you want it back in the well, click the Palette menu button and select Dock to Palette Well. The palette returns to its original tab orientation.

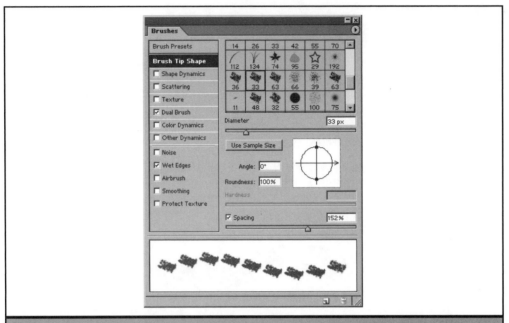

Figure 7-26. *Create a more textured line that skips along its length by increasing the Spacing for your brush tip.*

Working with Brush Options and Dynamics

The left side of the Brushes palette—whether you're in Brush Presets or in Brush Tip Shape mode—offers a series of options, each preceded by a check box. Each option comes with a series of settings in the form of sliders, more check boxes, and text boxes, which you can display by clicking on the option name (placing a check in the box doesn't display the options).

Each of these options' settings alters the appearance and/or function of a particular brush or tip:

Shape Dynamics This option offers six sliders, some of which may be dimmed depending on which brush style you've selected and the settings you've put in place for the other sliders within the Shape Dynamics display. Figure 7-27 shows the available options, including Size Jitter, Minimum Diameter, Tilt Scale, Angle Jitter, Roundness Jitter, and Minimum Roundness. As their names indicate, these options allow you to make your brush or pencil create a variety of effects, as shown in Figure 7-28. With no Shape Dynamics set (the top line), the line you paint or draw will be quite straight and plain. With jitter, tilt, spacing, and angle settings adjusted (see the bottom line), the line becomes more textured, as there is more variety in the strokes that make up a single line.

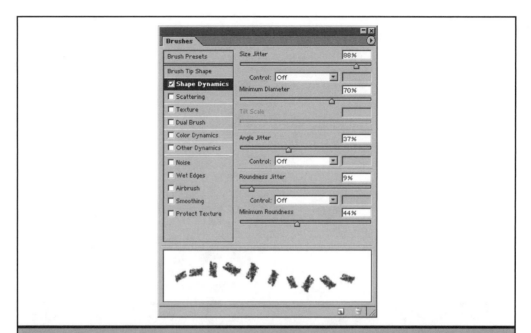

Figure 7-27.   *Drag the sliders to increase or decrease the degree of jitter, size, scale, and angle of your brush shape.*

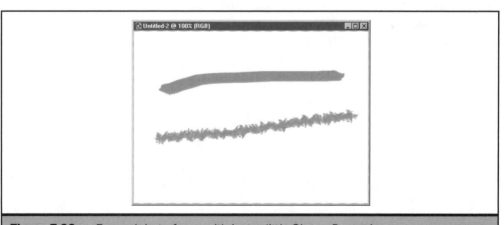

Figure 7-28.   *From plain to fancy with just a little Shape Dynamics.*

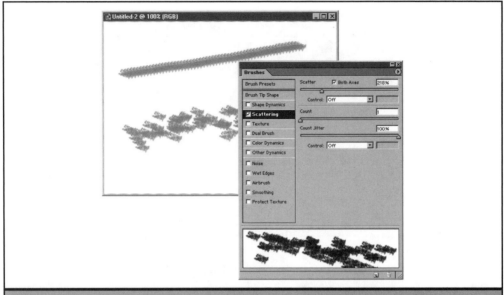

Figure 7-29. *Control the distribution of marks within your brush stroke through Scattering.*

Scattering   Here you have three sliders and two drop-down lists, accompanied by text boxes into which settings can be typed. The Scattering options allow you to control how brush marks are spread out throughout your stroke, how many brush marks will occur within a length of brush stroke, how the marks will vary, and how much jitter will be applied to the stroke. Figure 7-29 shows a line without any Scattering set, and one with Scattering turned on, plus the Scattering settings you can use to achieve the bottom line.

> *The Control settings (for the Scatter options and in the rest of the options you'll see for the Brushes palette) allow you to choose between Off, Fade, Pen Pressure, Pen Tilt, and Stylus Wheel, and are useful only if you're using a pressure-sensitive tablet. The choice you make will dictate the appearance of the brush marks—Fade will make the number of brush marks fade from whatever you've set for the count down to 1 in a series of steps. The remaining options will give you the ability to control your strokes based on the features of the pen that comes with your tablet.*

Texture   Through this option, you can apply a pattern to the brush—click the arrow next to the pattern thumbnail to see a palette of patterns. You can also control the Scale of the pattern, the blending Mode (just like the blending Modes available on the options bar, but a somewhat shorter list), the Depth, Minimum Depth, and Depth Jitter of the stroke. The settings appear in Figure 7-30. There's also a Texture Each Tip option, which is off by default. If you turn it on, the entire set of options becomes available; while it's off, the Minimum Depth and Depth Jitter options are unavailable.

Tip   *Use the Invert option to allow the tones in your selected pattern to determine the low and high points in the texture that your brush applies. By inverting the process, the dark areas of the pattern are the high points, and the light areas are the low points—the opposite of what happens when Invert is not on.*

Dual Brush   With this option, you can create brush marks with two different brush tips—a primary tip and a secondary tip, each with its own settings. The primary tip is selected through the Brush Tip Shape version of the Brushes palette, and whichever tip shape you choose (and whatever size you set with the diameter slider) will dictate the basis of the dual brush effect. The secondary tip is controlled by the settings you see when you click the Dual Brush option, as shown in Figure 7-31. The controls for the secondary tip include Diameter (the size of the stroke), Spacing (distance between marks in the stroke), Scatter (distribution or spread of the marks in a stroke), and Count (the intervals at which the marks are spread). All four of the secondary tip settings in the Dual Brush display are adjusted with sliders, or you can type numbers into the text boxes.

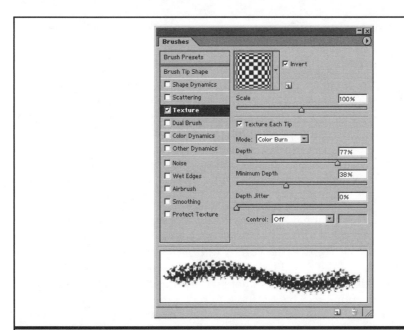

Figure 7-30.   *Create a textured stroke by applying a pattern and controlling the scale and depth of the pattern's detail.*

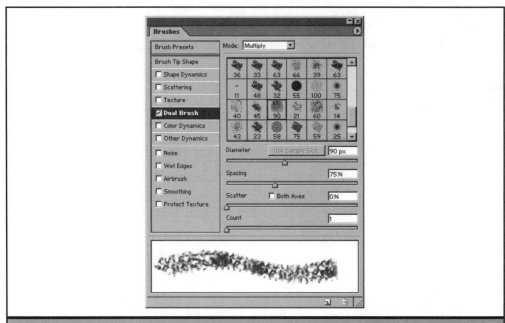

Figure 7-31.   *Paint with two brushes at once and control the appearance of the secondary tip with the Dual Brush option.*

Color Dynamics   This option controls how color is distributed over the distance of a single painted stroke. If Color Dynamics is on, you can control how the currently selected Foreground and Background colors are included in the stroke, and you can adjust the HSB (Hue, Saturation, and Brightness) levels of the jitter brush mark variance applied to the stroke. The Purity option controls saturation of color throughout the stroke, not just with respect to the jitter, which is controlled by the Saturation Jitter setting. Figure 7-32 shows the Color Dynamics options and, within the image window, a colored stroke that reflects the current settings.

Other Dynamics   This option (see Figure 7-33) allows you to control the Opacity Jitter (the variety of Opacity settings throughout the marks in a single brush stroke) and the Flow Jitter (the variety of flow settings throughout a single stroke). Note that only if the Brush tool is active on the toolbox will the Flow Jitter options (including Control) be available. If the Pencil is active, Flow is a moot point, and the option will be dimmed. In both jitter settings, you can use the slider or type a percentage, and if you're using a pressure-sensitive tablet, use the Control settings to adjust how the pen pressure, tilt, or stylus wheel affect the appearance of the stroke.

Note the variations in color (here they appear as several shades of gray).

The more jitter you apply, the more extreme the color variations will be.

Set the colors that will be used in the stroke by changing the Foreground and Background colors as desired.

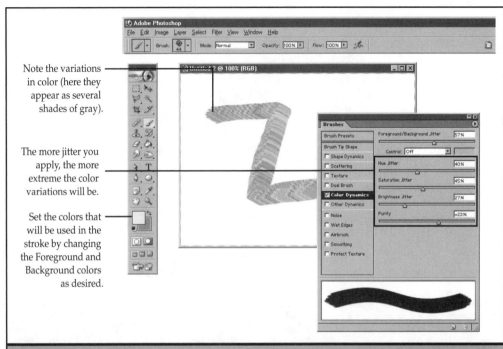

Figure 7-32. Use both the Foreground and Background colors in a single brush stroke.

Figure 7-33. Apply varied opacity and flow throughout the length of your brush strokes with Other Dynamics.

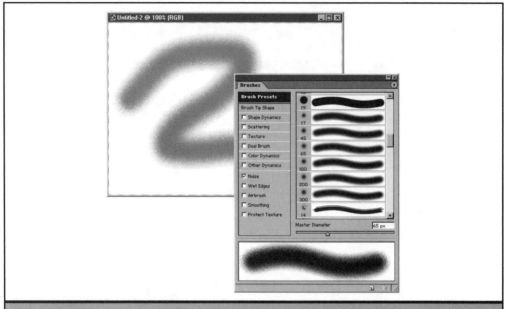

Figure 7-34.   *Add some Noise to soft or airbrushed strokes.*

Noise   Turn this option on to add the appearance of spray-can spatter to the edges of any of the Soft or Airbrush brush styles. Figure 7-34 shows the Noise option on for the Airbrush Soft Round 65 style. Where you'd have a soft, diffused edge to the stroke, now there's a speckled, spattered look working away from the center. Note that if you add Noise to a Hard style, there will be little or no effect.

Wet Edges   Like watercolor paint applied with a great deal of water, this option makes paint collect around the edges of the brush stroke, as shown in Figure 7-35.

Airbrush   Just like the Airbrush option on the Brush options bar, the Airbrush option in the Brushes palette allows you to create the effect of an actual airbrush as you paint. Your strokes will have a diffused edge. If you hold the brush still and hold the mouse button down, you can allow the paint to pool and look as though it's bleeding into the paper.

Smoothing   Most useful if you're working with a stylus or pen and tablet, Smoothing softens the curves on a hand-painted line. If your eye-hand control isn't great and your attempts to draw curves end up looking jagged or more angular than you want, turn this option on to smooth out the kinks. If you're painting with a regular mouse or trackball, you may experience a short delay between when you release the mouse button after dragging to paint a stroke and when the stroke appears on the image.

Protect Texture   You'll want to turn this option on if you're going to work with a variety of brush tips but want the same texture settings to apply to all of them. It allows you to create a level of consistency throughout all your strokes, no matter which brush tip you use to create them.

Once you've customized your brush strokes and tips with the Brushes palette settings, you're ready to paint. You can also use the Palette menu to change the view of strokes and tips shown in the palette—choose Text Only, Small Thumbnail, Large Thumbnail, Small List, Large List, or Stroke Thumbnail (the default).

Tip   *If you want to go back to square one, before you tinker with any of the options in the Brushes palette, choose Clear Brush Controls from the Palette menu. Conversely, if you love your settings and want to apply them to other tools (like the Pencil, Eraser, or Clone Stamp tools), you can choose Copy Texture to Other Tools, also found in the Brushes palette menu.*

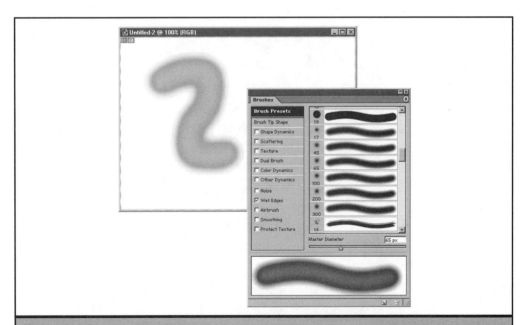

Figure 7-35.   *Use Wet Edges to add the appearance of very watery paint.*

Creating a New Preset Brush

Once you've used the Brushes palette and/or Brush options bar to customize a brush, you can add that particular brush with its particular features (size, texture, noise, scatter, and jitter settings—anything you can apply via the palette or bar) to the list of Brush Presets. This means that you can use a very specific brush again in the future simply by selecting it from the Brush Presets or Tip Shape lists, and know that all of your settings will be in place once again. You'll be able to adjust the size of the brush to meet specific needs, but all that will require is an adjustment on the slider.

To save a brush as a new preset brush, make all your changes and settings adjustments, using as many of the options bar and Brushes palette options that you need. Then, use one of the following methods to add it as a new preset:

- Click the Create New Brush button at the bottom of the Brushes palette or the top of the Brush tool drop-down list (see Figure 7-36).

- Display the Brushes palette menu and choose New Brush.

- Right-click/CONTROL-click the current preset and choose New Brush from the resulting context menu.

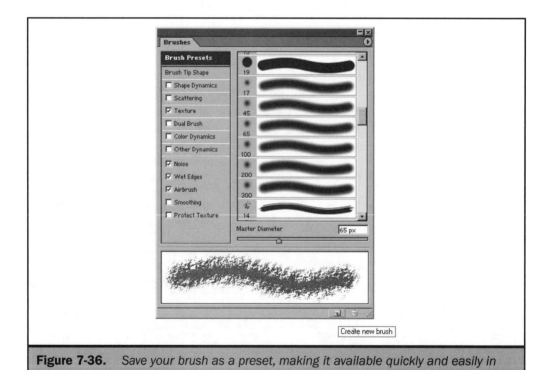

Figure 7-36.   *Save your brush as a preset, making it available quickly and easily in the future.*

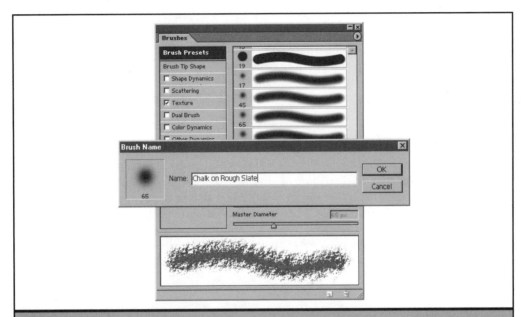

Figure 7-37. *Give your new brush preset a name that describes its appearance and/or purpose.*

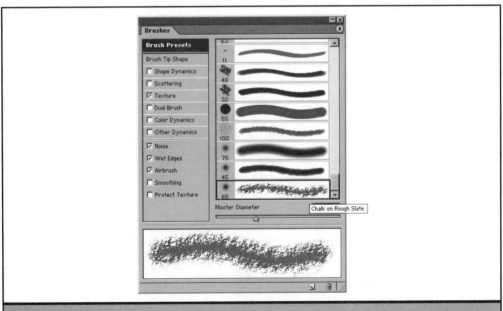

Figure 7-38. *Voilà! Your preset is now listed and easily accessible to use again and again.*

As a result, a dialog box opens (see Figure 7-37) through which you can give the new brush a name. Don't be alarmed if the thumbnail of the brush that appears in the dialog box doesn't match your customized brush—what appears in the dialog box is the existing preset on which your custom brush was based. As soon as you click OK, you'll see your new brush in the list of presets, and it will appear as it did in the Brushes palette preview. Figure 7-38 shows a new brush (with a very descriptive name) in the Brush Presets list.

Renaming Brush Presets

After you've added a brush to the presets list, you may need to rename it. To do so, just right-click/CONTROL-click the brush preset in the Brush Presets list, and choose Rename Brush from the context menu (see Figure 7-39). The existing name appears in a dialog box, and you can edit it or replace it outright. Click OK to save your changes.

You can also double-click your preset brush in the list to open the Brush Name dialog box, or choose Rename Brush from the Brushes palette menu.

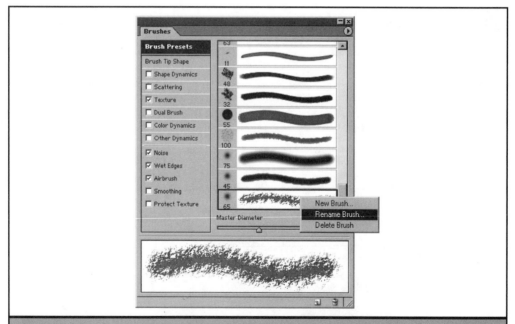

Figure 7-39.   *Choose to rename a brush preset if you don't like the name or spelled it incorrectly.*

Deleting Brush Presets

As easily as a brush can be created (after its settings are established), you can make it go away. You can delete a brush preset with any of the following methods:

- Right-click/CONTROL-click the preset in the list and choose Delete Brush from the context menu. A prompt will ask you to confirm your intentions.

- Select the preset by clicking it once with your mouse, and choose Delete Brush from the Brushes palette menu (again, a prompt will ask you to confirm).

Once you've deleted a brush, you can get it back only if the brush's settings (and its preview) are still visible in the Brushes palette. If you see the brush preset you just deleted still displayed in the palette, you can recreate it (assuming you have "deleter's remorse" and want it back) by clicking the New Brush command in the Brushes palette menu or clicking the Create New Brush button at the bottom of the Brushes palette.

Creating Your Own Custom Brush Sets

If you've added some of your own brush presets, deleted others, renamed presets, etc., and you want to make the current group of presets something you can use in the future, you can save the brush set, making it loadable at any time you need it. Simply display the Brushes palette options menu and choose Save Brushes. A Save dialog box, as shown in Figure 7-40, appears. Through the dialog box, you can name and save a new .abr file for your own custom set of brushes.

Figure 7-40. *Give your presets a name that describes what's unique about your custom presets, or that describes when or how you'd use these particular brushes.*

Once you've saved the set, you can load it by choosing Load Brushes from the Palette options menu (see Figure 7-41). This opens a Load dialog box that lists all the .abr files in the Brushes folder. The Brushes folder is typically a subfolder of the Presets folder, which is found in the Photoshop 7.0 folder. As soon as you choose a set of presets to load, click the Load button, and they're displayed in your Brushes palette, ready for selection and use.

Working with the Preset Manager

You can use the Preset Manager dialog box (opened by choosing Preset Manager from the Brushes palette menu or from the Edit menu) to perform several of the tasks you can also access individually from the Brushes palette options menu. You can Load saved presets, Save presets (with the Save Set command), Rename a brush preset, or Delete a preset you no longer want. When you've finished working with the dialog box (shown in Figure 7-42), click the Done button to close the box and maintain any changes you've made to the displayed presets.

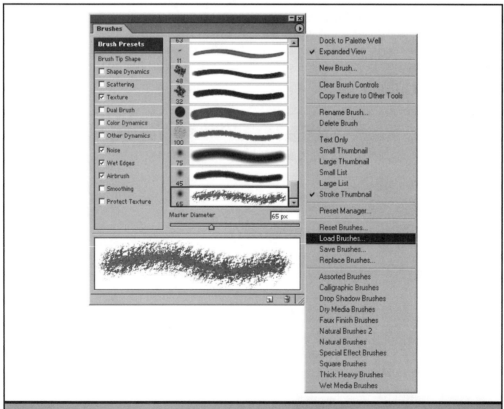

Figure 7-41.   *The Brushes palette menu offers tools for both saving and loading saved brushes.*

If you click the Preset Manager options menu (see Figure 7-43), you can also change how the brush presets (or any other group of presets, which you can select from the Preset Type drop-down list) are displayed. Choose from various Thumbnail and List sizes, or stick with the Small Thumbnail default view.

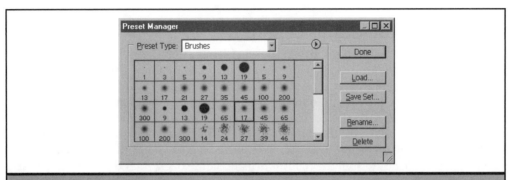

Figure 7-42.   *One-stop shopping is available through the Preset Manager dialog box.*

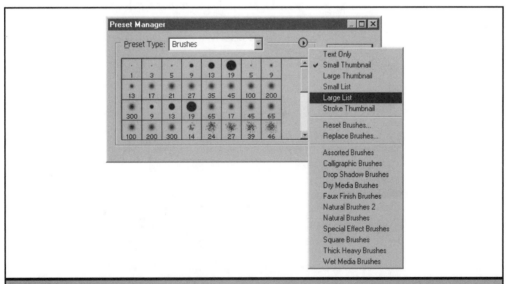

Figure 7-43.   *Customize the view of your current batch of presets.*

You can also right-click/CONTROL-click any brush preset in the dialog box and choose to Rename or Delete it, and if you don't like the order in which the presets appear, just point to and then drag the individual preset boxes around in the box—release the mouse when the I-beam cursor is where you want the box you're dragging to be positioned.

Resetting and Replacing Brushes

After you've displayed multiple brush presets (using the Append button to add selected presets to those already displayed) or switched to a new preset entirely, you can go back to the default set by using the Reset Brushes command. This command, found in the Brushes palette options menu, results in a prompt that asks you to confirm your intention to replace the current presets with the default brushes (see Figure 7-44). If you click OK, the default set comes back and any presets you were viewing disappear (they can always be redisplayed later by loading them again). If you click the Append button, the default brushes come back, added to the custom sets you are currently viewing. Of course, Cancel closes the prompt and makes no change to the displayed set of brush presets.

Why would you want to view only the default presets? Perhaps you've opened all the presets and now your list of available brushes is so long you have to scroll forever to find the one you want. Perhaps you deleted a brush that's only in the default set and you want to see and use it again. In either case, it's easy to display only the brushes you need or all the brushes available simply by using the Preset Manager dialog box or the Palette options menu.

Figure 7-44. Do you want to add the default set or view the default presets instead of the presets you're displaying now? Use this prompt to make your choice.

Working with the History and Art History Brush Tools

Both of these brushes, which you can adjust as you would the Brush tool in terms of their style and tip shape (as well as selecting a blending mode from the options bar), rely on information from the History palette (see Figure 7-45) to determine what effect the brushes have on your image. You can go back to a previous state in your image development history with the History Brush, using it to control which parts of the image are reverted to the previous state, or you can apply an effect from a previous state with the Art History Brush.

Tip   *The History Brush is quite simple to use, and in theory, so is the Art History Brush. You may find, however, that mastering or finding a really good use for the Art History Brush is a little more difficult—in most cases, instead of applying a previously used effect via the brush, it's much easier to simply select an area and apply the same effect/filter you used before.*

The History and Art History Brush tools

If you want to apply this filter with a brush, select the column to the left of the state and then use the Art History Brush.

Figure 7-45.   *Paint back to one of these states with the History Brush, or pick a state where you applied a special effect or filter and paint that with the Art History Brush.*

Going Back in Time with the History Brush

Have you ever wished you could turn back the clock on your image editing but only in a particular area of the image? If you rely solely on the History palette for your time travel, your entire image will be taken back in time to whichever state you click on in the palette—before you applied a filter or applied a blending option, or before you smudged, dodged, or burned your image or a portion thereof. But what if you only want to unsmudge, undodge, unburn, or unfilter *part* of the image, reverting just one area to the way it was before?

That's where the History Brush comes in handy—it uses the History palette, yes, but you can paint the areas you want to take back in time, and only those spots are reverted to a History state you specify. To use the History Brush, just click the tool to activate it and click the column to the left of the state in the History palette *prior to* the state where the unwanted effect was applied. Then paint over the portion of the image you want to take back in time. Figure 7-46 shows an image where a portion of it was turned into a painting via the Watercolor filter. As indicated in the figure, the area selected for the filter's effects included part of the image that should have been left alone. In Figure 7-47, an "after" version, the History Brush has been used to go back in time to a point before the Watercolor filter was applied, but only the parts that were painted with the History Brush have been "unfiltered."

Note you can resize the brush or reshape its tip using the options bar and/or Brushes palette before or during the process, or use different sized or shaped brushes throughout the time that the History Brush is active. You can continue to use the History Brush on as many places as you want to revert.

Figure 7-46.   *The Watercolor filter has been applied to the image within this rectangular marquee.*

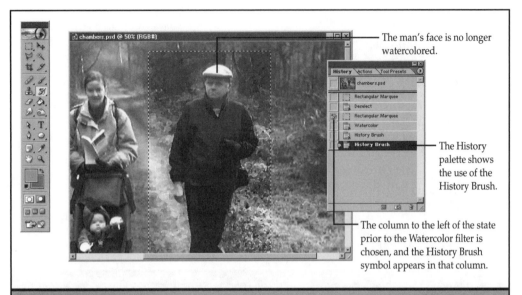

The man's face is no longer watercolored.

The History palette shows the use of the History Brush.

The column to the left of the state prior to the Watercolor filter is chosen, and the History Brush symbol appears in that column.

Figure 7-47. *By using the History Brush, the man's face is back to a pre-filtered state, as though the filter was never applied, yet the filter is still in effect where it should be.*

Tip *You can find out all about applying and customizing filters in Chapter 13.*

Using the Art History Brush

This tool, the companion to the History Brush on the toolbox, is difficult to master. What you might want to do with it is often easier to do with other tools. First, consider what the tool does: It paints an effect—a filter, a blending option, a retouching tool's results—on part of your image via a brush. So if, for example, you apply the Watercolor filter used in the History Brush example, you could conceivably paint that filter onto another part of the image, right? Well, yes, sort of. Figure 7-48 shows what happens when you use the Art History Brush to select a state in history and paint the effect applied during that state with the brush.

While the Art History Brush is active, the options bar offers tools for controlling the effects of the tool. As shown in Figure 7-49, you can set a Style (defining the nature of the brush strokes), an Area (to determine how many pixels are affected by the stroke), and a Tolerance setting, which controls where the strokes can be applied. A low tolerance (0 percent is the default), allows you to paint anywhere, and a high tolerance restricts you to areas that are drastically different from the area where the selected state's effect was originally applied.

Here's where the Watercolor filter was applied using a selection tool to confine the effect, and the Filter | Artistic | Watercolor command.

The History palette shows which state was selected for Art History brushing.

Painting the filtered effect gives a quite different result from simply applying the filter directly.

Figure 7-48. *Brushing on an effect is often quite different from applying the effect to a selected area of the image.*

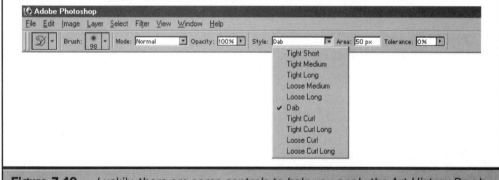

Figure 7-49. *Luckily, there are some controls to help you apply the Art History Brush to achieve the effect you're looking for.*

The Art History Brush can be good for creating special effects, and it can also be useful if you master the right brush sizes and tip shapes for certain effects. Figure 7-50 shows the use of the Glass filter, painted with the Art History Brush. By using the brush to apply the filter, rather than using the filter itself again, the rippled-glass effect can be customized quickly and easily by changing the brush settings throughout the painting process. A similar effect can be achieved with some of the Blur filters.

The Art History Brush was used to apply the glass effect here.

The Glass filter was applied directly here.

Figure 7-50.   *Painting a filter's effect with the Art History Brush can give you more freedom to apply the filter with different brush styles and shapes, achieving results the filter couldn't give you on its own.*

In many cases, however, it's just easier to select a new area (maybe even using the Brush tool to create a mask, and then converting that mask to a selection) and apply the filter or effect again. Only trial and error will serve to determine which situations call for which techniques, and sometimes your "errors" will end up being the most educational and artistically profitable moments you spend using Photoshop.

Making Creative Use of the Eraser Tools

Many people may think of the Eraser as a tool to be used simply for getting rid of mistakes—rubbing out an unwanted shape or line, removing colors, or reducing the size of an area that was drawn or transformed improperly. It is a tool for erasing things, mistakes being one of the things it can get rid of. However, it can also be used to erase *creatively*, meaning you can use it to remove content as a sort of reverse drawing tool. Instead of applying color in a certain shape or design, you can remove color in a deliberate, artistic way, exposing either an underlying color or a transparent background layer. Figure 7-51 shows the results of using the Eraser tool to remove part of a shape, revealing a photograph on another layer beneath it.

Tip   *Read all about layers in Chapter 10.*

EDITING AND
RETOUCHING IMAGES

Drawing with the Eraser

You use the same technique for drawing with the Eraser that you use when you're erasing to remove a mistake or unwanted content. Cick the tool to activate it, and then make sure the right layer is selected—the one with the content you want to erase—bearing in mind that you cannot erase content on a text layer (a layer created with the Type tool) or on a Shape layer (a layer created by using the Shape tools). With the correct and erasable layer selected, drag your mouse on the image, removing the content as you go. You can hold down the SHIFT key as you drag to erase lines at a 45- or 90-degree angle, or you can just drag freehand, creating whatever shapes or lines you like. Figure 7-52 shows several different eraser effects.

When you prepare to erase, remember that you can use the Brush drop-down list to choose a brush style, or you can use the Brushes palette to choose a brush preset or adjust your brush tip shape. Erasures can be textured if you use some of the more exotic brushes— they needn't be solid strokes.

When the Eraser tool is active, you have Mode, Opacity, and Flow options on the Eraser options bar—just like the options you have when the Brush tool is active. Of course, the Mode options are not the same. You can choose from three: Brush, Pencil, or Block (see Figure 7-53). Brush Mode allows you to use any of the brush presets and tip shapes, Pencil Mode will erase crisp hard lines (of any width you want, by using the Diameter slider to adjust the size of the pencil's point), and Block gives you a square tip you can use to erase single squares (by clicking without dragging) or to erase along a choppy edge if you're zoomed in tightly on a shape that's not aliased.

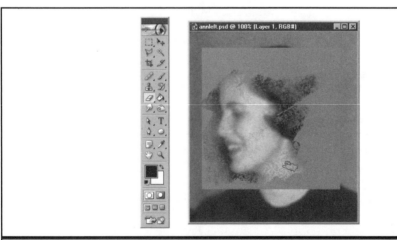

Figure 7-51. *Use the Eraser tool as though it is a drawing tool, not just a tool for rubbing out mistakes.*

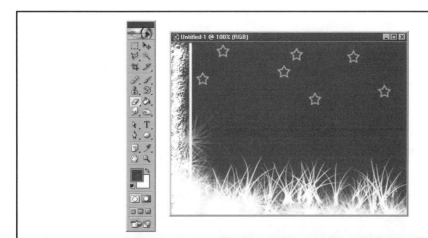

Figure 7-52.   *Use the same interesting brush presets you used with the Brush and Pencil tools to erase content in exciting patterns and textures. Here, a white background is revealed by the Eraser tool using six different brush presets.*

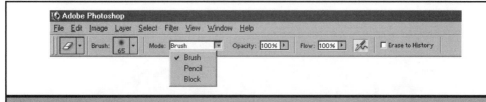

Figure 7-53.   *Use the familiar options bar settings to control the effects of the Eraser tool.*

Note   *If you switch to Block Mode, the Opacity, Flow, and Airbrush options are dimmed on the options bar. If you switch to Pencil Mode, Flow and Airbrush are not available. Only Brush Mode makes all three options available.*

One option that's not on the Brush option bar but that the Eraser tool does offer is Erase to History. This option makes the Eraser work very much like the History Brush in that you can click on a state in the History palette (clicking to place the History Brush symbol in the box on the left side of the palette) to establish how far back in history you'll be erasing. Then, after adjusting the brush size/shape, drag with the Eraser tool and watch as the effects of any steps taken after the selected History state are erased. Figure 7-54 shows the stroke of the eraser wiping out the results of a filter that was applied earlier in the editing process.

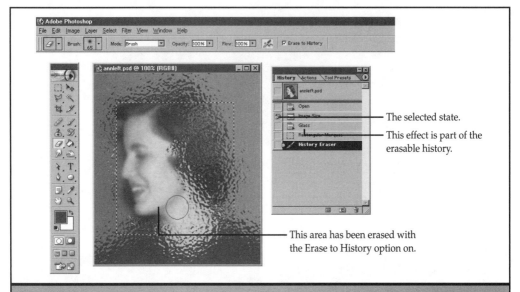

Figure 7-54.   *The Erase to History option lets you pick a point in the image history and erase everything back to that point.*

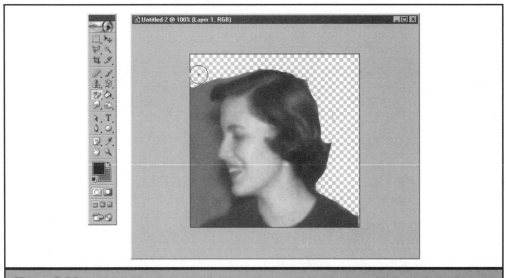

Figure 7-55.   *If your Background is transparent, you'll see the grid show through when you use the Background Eraser tool.*

Erasing Image Background Color

The Background Eraser tool enables you to erase pixels on a selected layer, leaving transparency in your wake (see Figure 7-55). If your Background has a color, that's what will show through when you use this tool.

When you activate the Background Eraser tool, the options bar offers five options, enabling you to control the effects of this specialized eraser:

Brush   Rather than the list of brush styles you're accustomed to finding when you click the Brush drop-down list, you'll find a series of controls (see Figure 7-56) that allow you to adjust the Diameter, Hardness, Spacing, Angle, and Roundness. You can use the Size and Tolerance settings at the bottom of the dialog box to adjust how your pressure-sensitive tablet and pen work.

Limits   This mode setting offers three alternatives: Contiguous, Discontiguous, and Find Edges.

- Contiguous restricts the erasure to pixels that are touching the first pixel you clicked on when you started erasing—the first pixel becomes the *sampled pixel*, and it dictates which pixels are considered erasable and which ones are not (the Tolerance setting on the options bar also controls this).

- Discontiguous erases the color you first click on as you begin erasing (also referred to as the *sampled color*) no matter where the pixels that fall within the Tolerance range are located.

- Find Edges helps you maintain the clean edges of shapes as you erase around them.

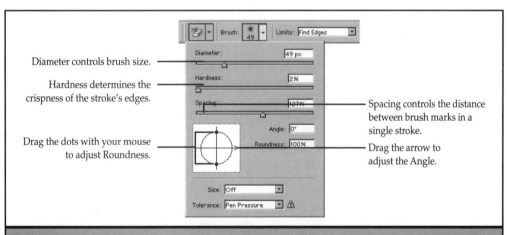

Diameter controls brush size.

Hardness determines the crispness of the stroke's edges.

Drag the dots with your mouse to adjust Roundness.

Spacing controls the distance between brush marks in a single stroke.

Drag the arrow to adjust the Angle.

Figure 7-56.   *Customize your Erase to Background tool using these tools—they're quite similar to the Brushes palette tools.*

Tolerance Use this option to set the threshold for erasing pixels that are a close match for the sampled pixel. The setting is adjusted via a slider. The higher the Tolerance (drag to the right), the wider the range of pixels that will be deemed to be a match.

Protect Foreground Color If you want to protect all pixels that are the same color as the current Foreground color (the one showing in the toolbox), turn on this option. You can also turn this option on and then reset the Foreground color by clicking that box on the toolbox and making a new selection from the Color Picker.

Sampling This option offers three alternatives for how colors are sampled (selected for erasure) as you use the Background Eraser tool:

- Continuous keeps resampling pixels as you drag. It is a good choice if you're working with a photograph. This is the default.

- Once erases only those pixels that match the first pixel you clicked on when you began erasing. This option is best for erasing areas filled with a solid color.

- Background Swatch limits the erasure to pixels that match the currently selected Background color.

Note *The Background Eraser's pointer looks different from the regular Eraser. Instead of a plain circle (sized to match the Diameter setting you established), the pointer also has a crosshair in its center, helping you spot the pixel that's serving as the sampled pixel for further erasure.*

Using the Magic Eraser Tool

This alternative form of the Eraser tool erases all the pixels that match the first pixel you click on with the tool. If the Background is selected at the time, the Background is converted to a new layer and all the matching pixels on that layer are made transparent. If you're working on a layer with locked transparency, all the matching pixels on that layer are changed to the background color. If you're on any layer other than the Background and the layer you're on is not set to locked transparency, the pixels that match the first one are erased to transparency. Figure 7-57 shows the results of the Magic Eraser tool, which quickly removed all the like-colored content with a single click of the mouse.

When the Magic Eraser tool is active, the options bar (see Figure 7-58) offers the following five options you can use to control how magically the eraser works:

- Set the Tolerance, which establishes the threshold for matching pixels to the sampled one.

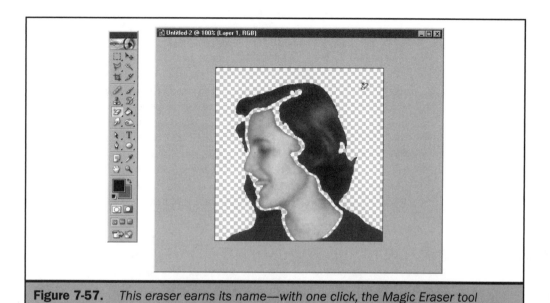

Figure 7-57.   *This eraser earns its name—with one click, the Magic Eraser tool
erases all the pixels that match the sampled pixel.*

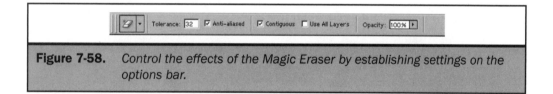

Figure 7-58.   *Control the effects of the Magic Eraser by establishing settings on the
options bar.*

- Turn on Anti-aliased to keep your curves and edges smooth.
- Use the Contiguous option to erase pixels that are touching the one you sampled.
- Turn the Use All Layers option on to make the tool work on all layers simultaneously.
- Set an Opacity so you can leave some of the color behind (lower opacity) or erase the pixels entirely (100-percent opacity).

Working with the Pen Tools

While the Pen tool has and will be discussed in this book as a tool for creating work and clipping paths and creating closed shapes, it can also be used to draw lines and curves that can end up looking as though you created them with the Brush or Pencil tools. Because the Pen affords you more control over the direction and path of the lines (and because you can edit the line after drawing it and don't have to draw freehand, as you must with the Brush or Pencil), the Pen tool may become your tool of choice for drawing on your Photoshop images. Figure 7-59 shows a set of lines that were drawn with the Pen tool. One of them has a brush stroke applied to it, showing you that you can use the Pen to create the line, and then additional tools can be applied to give the line the look of having been drawn with the Brush tool.

 Read more about the uses for the Pen tool in Chapters 5 and 11.

Drawing with the Pen Tools

The Pen tool is quite simple to use, and there are several ways to use it. You can draw curves as well as straight lines with the Pen tool, as shown in Figure 7-60, or you can draw freehand lines with the Freeform Pen tool, as shown in Figure 7-61.

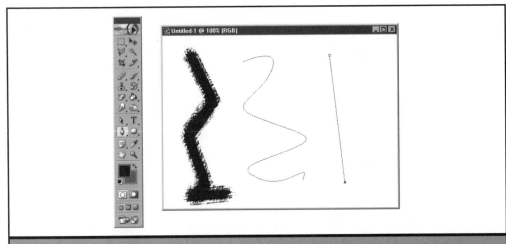

Figure 7-59.   *The Pen tool creates thin lines that can be stroked with any brush preset you select.*

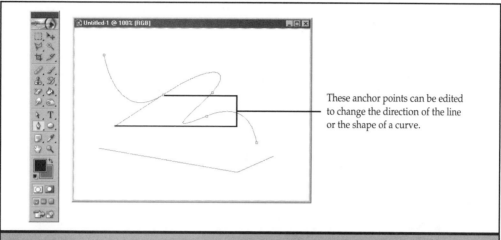

These anchor points can be edited
to change the direction of the line
or the shape of a curve.

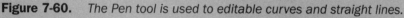

Figure 7-60.   *The Pen tool is used to editable curves and straight lines.*

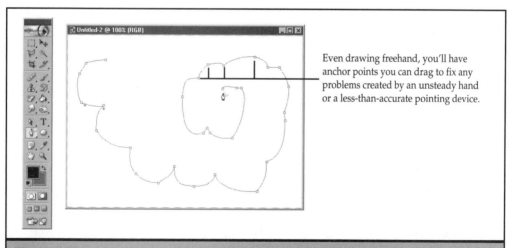

Even drawing freehand, you'll have
anchor points you can drag to fix any
problems created by an unsteady hand
or a less-than-accurate pointing device.

Figure 7-61.   *The Freeform Pen enables you to write and draw freehand with your
mouse or other pointing device.*

Drawing Curves

To draw curves with the Pen tool, first click the tool to activate it, and then click on the
image to start the curve. Immediately after clicking (which creates your first anchor point),
drag to see the direction points appear, as shown in Figure 7-62. The farther you drag from

the starting anchor point, the longer the direction points will be, and the deeper the curve you'll end up with. To draw a simple arc, move (don't drag) your mouse to the spot where the arc should end, and click again—the line will connect the starting anchor point to the ending anchor point, and each of the anchor points will have its own set of direction points that you can drag to change the direction and depth of the arc. Figure 7-63 shows a completed arc, with directional points at each of the line's anchor points.

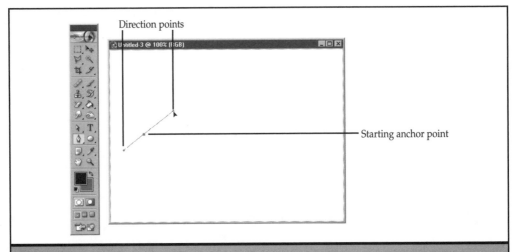

Figure 7-62. *Click to start the curve, and drag to set the depth of the curve by establishing the length of the curve's direction points.*

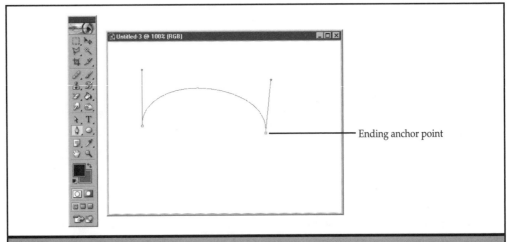

Figure 7-63. *Click again to end the curve, and drag the ending anchor point's direction points to make final adjustments to the curve.*

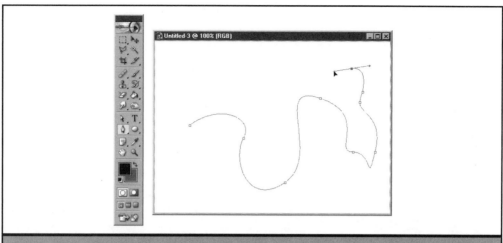

Figure 7-64.   *Each click creates an anchor point, and as you drag, you take your
curve in a new direction.*

If you want to draw a curve that has multiple "bumps" such as an S-curve, a figure-8,
or something more abstract, continue to click to create the anchor points between each
bump, and drag the direction points that appear at each anchor point. You can drag and
then click again in any direction you want, and the connecting lines will respond to the
clicks and movement of your mouse or other pointing device. Figure 7-64 shows an
elaborate curve in progress.

*Don't get frustrated if you feel like you're completely uncoordinated with this tool.
Drawing this kind of curve, known as a Bézier curve, is difficult to master. Take the time
to experiment, first just letting things happen without planning the appearance of the
resulting curves, and then with specific goals in mind, seeing if you can make them
happen. The more you practice, the quicker you'll master the Pen tool.*

Drawing Straight Lines

A straight line is easy enough to create with the Brush or Pencil tools—just press the SHIFT
key as you drag the mouse, and the line is automatically set to a 45- or 90-degree angle,
and it's perfectly straight. So why would you use the Pen tool to create straight lines?
Because you can create them more easily, and edit their direction and length afterward,
and you can draw multiple-segmented lines that look like Zs or Ws. Figure 7-65 shows a
complex segmented line created with the Pen tool.

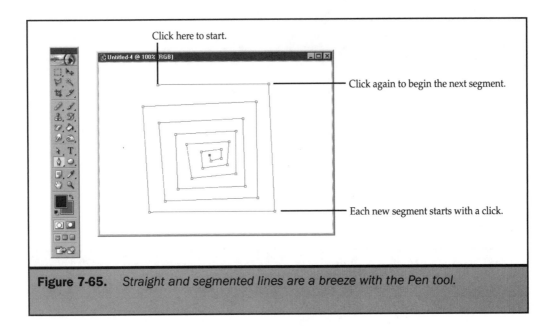

Figure 7-65. *Straight and segmented lines are a breeze with the Pen tool.*

To draw a straight line with the Pen, click the tool to activate it, and then click on the image where you want the line to start. An anchor point (with no direction handles) appears where you click, and as long as you don't drag (as you would if you were drawing a curve), the line that connects your starting anchor point to the end or next section of the line will be straight. You can continue to click and move and click again until the line you want appears onscreen.

To constrain your straight line to a 45- or 90-degree angle, press and hold the SHIFT key as you click and move the mouse to create your line segments.

Drawing Freeform Lines

Freeform lines require the Freeform Pen tool, which you can activate by clicking the triangle in the lower-right corner of the Pen tool, or by holding the mouse button down on the Pen tool for a few seconds to display the optional tools. You can also click the Freeform Pen tool on the options bar that is displayed when the Pen tool is selected.

After selecting the Freeform Pen tool and activating it, it's easy to create your freeform line—just click on your image to start the line, and drag as though you were writing with a pen. Remember that like drawing curves, it takes practice to develop the hand-eye coordination required to end up onscreen with what you see in your mind. Don't be discouraged if your first freeform lines just look like messy squiggles. Unless, of course, that's what you were looking for in the first place!

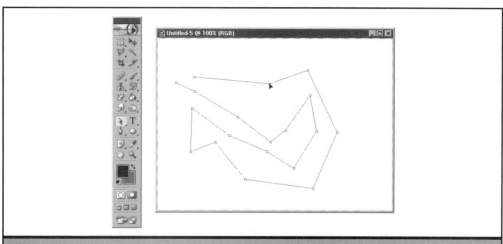

Figure 7-66.   *Drag an anchor point up, down, left, or right, and the line or segments attached to it move in response.*

Editing Your Pen and Freeform Pen Lines

The beauty of using the Pen and Freeform Pen tools to draw lines (rather than the Brush or Pencil tools) is that you can edit the lines after you've drawn them. If you use the Brush or Pencil tool to draw a line, and you don't like the curve, direction, or length of the line, you have to delete or erase it and start over. Not so with lines you draw with the Pen tools. Those anchor and direction points that appear with each of your respective clicks and drags show their real purpose, enabling you to change just about any aspect of the line. Figure 7-66 shows a selected line and one of the anchor points being moved to change the angle of the line.

To make the anchor and direction points available for editing, click the Direct Selection tool, which is the alternative to the Path Selection tool. You can also use the Path Selection tool to select the line and its anchor and direction points, but you'd have to switch to the Direct Selection tool in order to move any of the individual points.

After activating the Direct Selection tool, use it to move any anchor or direction point—just click and drag on an anchor point to move it, or on any direction point to change the curve of the associated curve or segment thereof. Figure 7-67 shows a selected curve and its anchor points being adjusted.

Adding and Deleting Anchor Points

If you need to adjust your curve or add segments to a straight line, you can add points along the lines, giving you more places from which to adjust the appearance of your lines. To add an anchor point, switch to the Add Anchor Point tool, shown activated and in use in Figure 7-68—just click where you want to add the point.

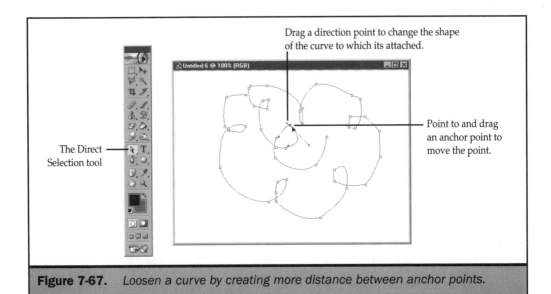

Figure 7-67. Loosen a curve by creating more distance between anchor points.

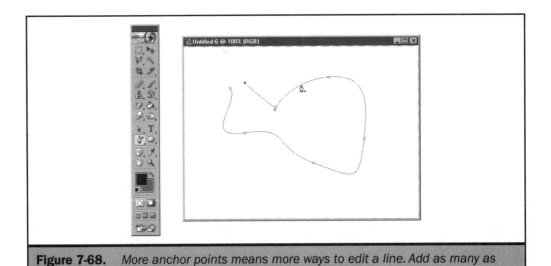

Figure 7-68. More anchor points means more ways to edit a line. Add as many as you want with the Add Anchor Point tool.

If the new anchor point should function as a curve anchor, click anywhere along the line, and an anchor point with direction handles will appear. To control the length and effect of the direction handles, drag after clicking to create the anchor point, and the direction points will lengthen, enabling you to create a deeper curve. If you want a shallow curve, don't drag too far from the anchor point you add.

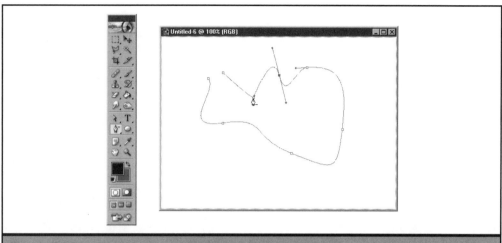

Figure 7-69.   *The tiny minus sign that accompanies the arrow-head cursor reminds you that you're about to delete an anchor point.*

After adding points, you may want to get rid of one or more of them. You may also want to get rid of anchor points that were part of the line's original configuration—perhaps a segmented straight line has more segments than you wanted, or maybe your curve has too many bumps. Whether the anchor point was created during the line's original drawing or afterward with the Add Anchor Point tool, it can be easily removed with the Delete Anchor Point tool. Just click the existing anchor point you want to get rid of, and it's gone. Figure 7-69 shows the tool in use, and an anchor point about to be deleted.

 If you've left the Auto Add/Delete option turned on in the Pen tool's options bar, simply clicking an existing anchor point will delete it; clicking along any length of pen-drawn line will insert an anchor point.

Converting Anchor Points

To change original or added anchor points from curves to straight points (or vice versa), use the Convert Point tool shown in Figure 7-70. Activate the tool, and then click an anchor point. If the point was a curve anchor, it becomes a straight anchor, and if the point was a straight anchor, it becomes a curve anchor when you click and then drag the anchor—it's the dragging in this latter case that makes the formerly straight anchor into a curved one.

 Learn about additional uses for the Pen tool, and find out more about editing lines drawn with the Pen tools in Chapter 5. The use of the Add, Delete, and Convert Point tools is discussed in detail.

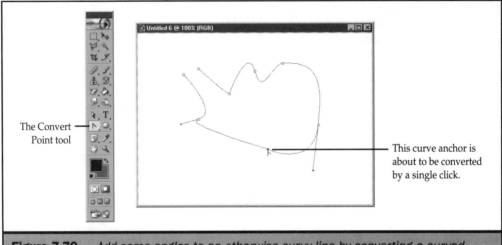

Figure 7-70. *Add some angles to an otherwise curvy line by converting a curved anchor to a straight one.*

Applying a Stroke to Your Lines

Photoshop considers the lines you draw with the Pen tool to be *paths*—lines that can be used to select or confine effects you apply to portions of your image. Until you apply a stroke (in this case, a Brush stroke) to the path, the line you've drawn with the Pen or Freeform Pen won't show in your image—you won't see it when you print, and it won't show if the image is saved in another format (such as .jpg or .gif for the Web) and viewed onscreen.

Applying a stroke is simple, but it requires a few extra steps. This may make you want to use the Brush and Pencil tools exclusively for drawing lines, even considering the editability of lines drawn with the Pen tools. The extra steps require you to display the Paths palette, make a menu selection, and establish a brush preset ahead of time. If that doesn't sound like too much trouble, read on.

Choosing a Brush Preset

Before applying a stroke to your path, you want to choose which stroke will be applied. You'll do this with the Brushes palette, or by activating the Brush tool and using the Brush styles drop-down list. In either case (the former offering more tools for customizing the stroke), choose a brush preset, set the diameter of the stroke, and apply any special effects—Noise, Wet Edges, a change in Opacity, or changes to Spacing and Jitter. You'll also want to use the Color Picker to change the Foreground color, if the color currently displayed on the toolbox isn't the one you want used for your line. Figure 7-71 shows a brush preset selected, ready to be used on a line drawn with the Pen tool.

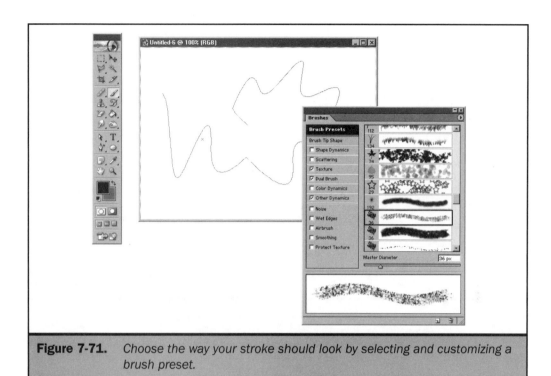

Figure 7-71.   *Choose the way your stroke should look by selecting and customizing a brush preset.*

Note   *The Brushes palette's tools will be dimmed as long as any of your Pen tools are active. To make the Brushes palette and its controls accessible again, switch to the Brush tool. After you've selected a preset and applied any special effects to the stroke, you can go back to the Paths palette and proceed to apply the stroke to your line.*

Using the Paths Palette

With the stroke you want to apply selected, go to the Paths palette and click the options menu button. From the menu, choose Stroke Path (see Figure 7-72). If your image has several individual lines on it, all drawn with the Pen tools, the command will appear as Stroke Subpath, because each individual line is considered part of a single overall path.

After issuing the Stroke Path command, a dialog box appears, as shown in Figure 7-73. Through this dialog box you can choose the tool you want to use to stroke the path (the default is Brush). Assuming you want to apply the brush preset you've selected previously, click OK to accept this default. Of course, you can also choose from the entire list of drawing and editing tools, but if you choose any of the others, the stroke you get will be based on the current settings for those tools—based on their last use or based on their defaults, depending on your setting in the General Preferences dialog box. If you have Save Palette Locations selected, your tools go back to their default settings each time you exit Photoshop. If you have this option off, your last settings are saved each time you exit.

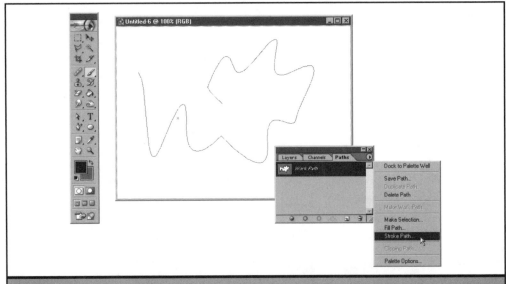

Figure 7-72. Choose Stroke Path (or Stroke Subpath) from the Paths palette options menu.

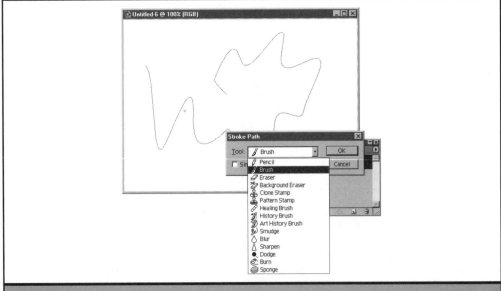

Figure 7-73. The Stroke Path dialog box allows you to choose which drawing or editing tool you want to use to apply the stroke.

Note   *The Simulate Pressure option in the Stroke Path dialog box pertains to pressure-sensitive tablets and the pens that are used with them. If the option is on, the pressure that is exerted on the pen when drawing the path is reflected in the thickness of the stroke applied to the line.*

Tip   *If you have your tool preferences set to save the last settings (with Save Palette Locations on in the General Preferences dialog box), the last settings you used for the tool you choose in the Stroke Path dialog box will be applied. To check your settings, choose Edit | Preferences | General. Note that if you're using Mac OS X, the Preferences command will be located in the Photoshop menu.*

Once you've applied a stroke to the line, you can no longer edit it. You can display the anchor points, but you can't change the stroked portion of the line, so there's no point in dragging them anywhere. Further, Photoshop still retains a work path (you can see it in the Paths palette shown in Figure 7-74) based on the line(s) you've drawn. Unless you have a use for the path, such as converting it to a selection or saving it and changing it to a clipping path to remove unwanted content from an image that will be saved as a .tif file, there's no reason to keep the path. To get rid of the work path (but retain the lines you've drawn and stroked), drag the Work Path to the trashcan icon at the bottom of the Paths palette.

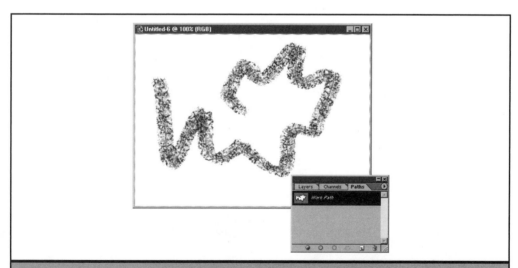

Figure 7-74.   *Use the Paths palette to get rid of the Work Path that remains even after you've stroked the path and turned it into the equivalent of a line drawn with the Brush or Pencil tool.*

Summary

In this chapter, you learned to use the Brush, Pencil, History Brush, Art History Brush, Eraser, and Pen tools. You are now able to create original artwork, apply color to photos and drawings, and add exciting color, pattern, and texture effects to your images. This chapter introduced the Brushes palette, and showed you how to customize brushes and pencils, adjusting their size, style, and shape to control the effects of the tools. You also learned how to customize the tools, creating your own brushes and saving them for future use.

The Complete Reference

Chapter 8

Cleaning and Editing Photographs

By its very name, Photoshop tells you that its primary function is to deal with photographs—applying special effects to them, correcting or changing their colors, and repairing and restoring them. Whether you're scanning prints or working with a photo captured with a digital camera, Photoshop provides the tools you need to remedy just about any problem, from scratches to missing content. In this chapter, you'll learn to use the tools specifically designed for repairing photos, and you will discover ways to use Photoshop's drawing and painting tools to add and restore content as well.

Mastering Image Cleanup

Virtually any photograph you've scanned or captured with a digital camera can be improved. You learned about adjusting color in Chapter 6. You can apply what you've learned to improve an image from a color standpoint, and then use what you learn here in this chapter to repair actual damage—the sort of stains, scratches, tears, and effects of aging and improper storage that are seen in the photo in Figure 8-1.

The principal Photoshop tools you'll use to repair an image are located in the toolbox; they include the Healing Brush, Patch tool, and Clone Stamp tool (see Figure 8-2). You can also use the regular Brush and Pencil tools, as well as the Eraser tool, to add and remove content.

Figure 8-1.   *A damaged photograph may seem beyond help, but Photoshop gives you the tools to restore it to its original condition.*

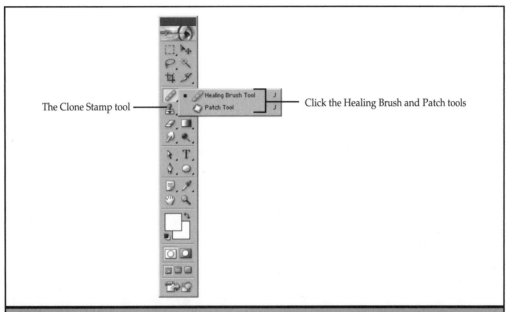

The Clone Stamp tool   Click the Healing Brush and Patch tools

Figure 8-2. *Your primary repair tools enable you to paste clean portions of the image over the damaged areas.*

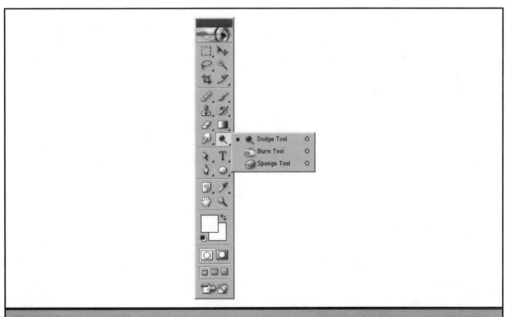

Figure 8-3. *Brighten, darken, or change the amount of color in your photograph with the Dodge, Burn, and Sponge tools.*

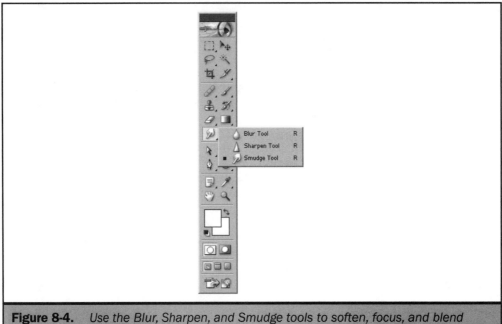

Figure 8-4.   *Use the Blur, Sharpen, and Smudge tools to soften, focus, and blend portions of your image.*

To adjust the quality of the image—brightening a photo where the camera's flash wasn't sufficient or the lighting was wrong, darkening a photo that's overexposed, sharpening areas that need more focus, blurring areas that need to fade out—you can use the Dodge, Burn, Sponge, Sharpen, and Blur tools, respectively (they're shown in Figures 8-3 and 8-4). You can also use the Smudge tool to gently blend adjoining portions of the image—smudging away a blemish, for example.

The tools you'll use can all be customized with their respective options bars, enabling you to achieve subtle effects or very dynamic ones. While each of the tools in the toolbox was generally described (and many were demonstrated) in Chapter 2, the tools you'll use to improve the appearance of your photographs will be covered in much more detail in this chapter.

Adjusting Image Quality

Printed pictures that you scan into Photoshop can have a lot of problems—some problems that were part of the image to begin with, and others that the scanning process creates. If your printed photos are old or have been stored improperly (allowed to dry out, exposed to too much moisture and covered with mold, stored loose in a drawer and exposed to dust and abrasion), you have one set of problems to deal with: scratches, spots, stains, cracks in the emulsion coating on the image, even rips and tears. If your scanner doesn't do a great job, or you scanned the image at too low a resolution and didn't acquire enough visual information with the image, then you can compound the problems or create new ones: choppy edges, clumsy blends between colors, or general noise in the form of dots and unclear content. Also, by scanning at too low a resolution (lower than 300 pixels per inch), you may not have enough detail to work with in cleaning up the image. If your image is bound for the Web, don't skimp on the scan—you can always reduce the resolution later (using the Image Size command in the Image menu) before optimizing the image for the Web.

If you capture your photos with a digital camera, you can run into problems there, too. Even though you're eliminating the "copy-of-a-copy" effect, the digital capturing process can add noise and distortion to the image, and many digital cameras don't create the sharpest, cleanest image possible. Digital video cameras can take still images, but rarely with the kind of quality you'd get from a reasonably good 35-mm camera or a good digital camera.

Once an image is sitting in front of you in the Photoshop image window, however, it's not really that important how the problems occurred. The key is to solve them by choosing the right tool or tools to improve the quality of the image. In the following sections, you'll learn to use the tools that can fix photographer errors, repair the damage caused by inappropriate storage, and smooth out the bumps that a low-end camera or scanner can add to the mix.

Shedding Light with the Dodge Tool

The Dodge tool is known as one of Photoshop's "toning tools" (the Burn tool is the other one). *Dodging* lightens an image or portion thereof, adding light to an image that's too dark, or bringing hidden content out of the shadows. Figure 8-5 shows an image that's in dire need of the Dodge tool, and Figure 8-6 shows the results after the image has been dodged.

The Dodge tool's options bar (shown in Figure 8-7) offers four choices for customizing how the tool is used and its effects applied to your image. You can choose any brush for the tool, applying the lightening effect with a simple solid brush tip or with one of the textured or specialized brushes if you want to both lighten and add visual interest. You can also choose which parts of the image will be lightened; choose Shadows, Midtones, or Highlights from the Range drop-down list. The Exposure option uses a slider to adjust a percentage. The higher the percentage, the more drastic the Dodge tool's effects. You can also click the Airbrush button to apply the Dodge tool with soft-edged, diffused brush strokes. This can be useful if your image has a soft, out-of-focus look already, or if it's your intention to attain that look through tools you'll use after you've dodged the image.

Figure 8-5. *Faces from the past needn't be so dark—this image needs dodging to bring out these people's features.*

Figure 8-6. *Now we can see what these people look like, as their features are no longer hidden in the shadows.*

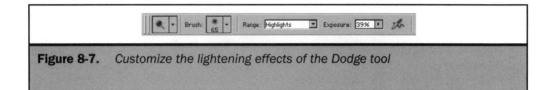

Figure 8-7. *Customize the lightening effects of the Dodge tool*

Figure 8-8. *Brighten a single spot quickly and uniformly by clicking once on the spot you want to lighten.*

EDITING AND
RETOUCHING IMAGES

To use the Dodge tool, just click the tool (or select it from the group that includes the Burn and Sponge tools), and then paint your image with the tool. You can lighten large areas with a very large brush (use the Brush setting to increase the size of the brush tip), or lighten small, very specific areas. If you use any of the selection tools to confine the Dodge tool to a certain area, you can either leave part of your image dark or make sure you're lightening only the areas that need it. Figure 8-8 shows a face being lightened by using a brush tip that's the same diameter as the face itself—this prevents lightening the surrounding content. By not using a smaller brush in an area selected with the Lasso tool, you don't have any overlapping strokes that can result in too much lightening.

Tip *If you're not sure which size Brush to use, make sure to set the proper Brush size (Edit | Preferences in Windows or Photoshop | Preferences if you're on Macintosh OS X) and then adjust the Brush size using the Master Diameter slider on the Dodge tool options bar. You can also use the square bracket keys ([and]) to increase and decrease size. Then hover over the area you want to lighten. If the brush is close to the size of the area, you're ready to start lightening. If it's too small or too large, go back to the Brush slider, and make the appropriate adjustments.*

Figure 8-9.   *Too much Dodge tool can hide the very details you sought to reveal.*

You can paint with the Dodge tool, creating overlapping brush strokes to lighten some areas more than others—it's not required that you try to lighten an area with a single stroke with a very large brush or a single click with a brush sized to match the area to be lightened. Be prepared, however, to use the History palette to undo some of your dodging if you go over an area too many times and create the look of an overexposed photo. Figure 8-9 shows what can happen if you're too aggressive with the Dodge tool, through painting over a spot too many times, or by setting too high an Exposure setting on the options bar.

Removing Glare and Overexposure with the Burn Tool

The Burn tool—the opposite of the Dodge tool—darkens areas of the photo that are too bright or where there's too much light. Figure 8-10 shows an image of a baby who was too close to the flash. By using the Burn tool (its results are shown in Figure 8-11), the glowing skin is darkened slightly, and the glare is diminished. You can use the Burn tool for photos that were literally overexposed, where the subject was too close to the flash, or where lighting was too bright—people facing into the sun or light bouncing off of shiny surfaces.

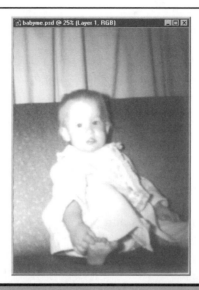

Figure 8-10.   *You may want to tone down any area that's too bright or where there's an unpleasant glare.*

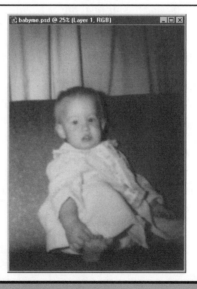

Figure 8-11.   *The Burn tool takes the glare down a few notches, creating more even lighting throughout the image.*

You don't want to use the Burn tool to reverse the effects of too much dodging—if you dodge an image and regret it, use the History palette to go back in time before the dodging was applied. If you can't do that, you can try using the Burn tool; however, chances are you won't end up with the same color or tone you had before you dodged the image. Once the color information has changed in the pixels, it's not easy to recover that information.

Using the Burn tool is easy. Select the tool, set the brush size and other options bar settings (they're the same as the options you have for the Dodge tool), and begin painting. You can set your Brush size to the same diameter as the area you want to darken (like the size of a face or some other area within your image), or you can use any of the selection tools to confine your burning to a specific region. Like the Dodge tool, there's the risk of darkening an area too much by painting over it too many times or using too high an Exposure setting.

Apply the Burn tool in small strokes, and be prepared to wait a few seconds to see the result if you're using a very large brush—sometimes the computer takes a while to display the results if the system resources are low. Always wait, though, before continuing to paint with the Burn tool (the same rule applies to the Dodge tool)—if you keep painting and your first strokes haven't shown up yet, you'll end up darkening the image more than you wanted to.

The more separate strokes you apply, the more History states you'll accumulate, making it easier to go back to very specific stages in the burning (or dodging) process. Don't hold the mouse button down and do all your dodging or burning in a single, long stroke—if you do and then realize you've gone over an area too much, using of the Undo command or going back a single state in the History palette will remove all of your tone adjustments, not just the last, unwanted stroke.

Saturating and Desaturating with the Sponge Tool

The Sponge tool enables you to increase or decrease the color saturation in your image. You can apply the tool to both grayscale and color images. When the tool is active, the options bar (shown in Figure 8-12) allows you to choose a Brush size and shape and to select one of two Modes—Saturate or Desaturate. You can also set the Flow for the tool, controlling how fast the Sponge tool applies its effect and how much color is added or taken away. The Airbrush button also appears on this options bar; with it, you can make sure your Sponge strokes have soft, diffused edges.

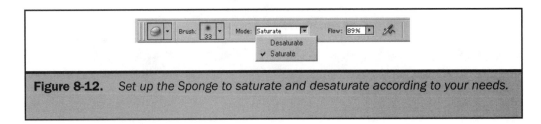

Figure 8-12. *Set up the Sponge to saturate and desaturate according to your needs.*

Figure 8-13. *Intensify the colors in your image with the Sponge tool.*

To use the Sponge tool, simply activate the tool and then paint on your image—stroke over the areas that need more or less color saturation. Your options bar settings will dictate how subtle or dynamic the effects are. A lower Flow setting will create very gentle saturation or desaturation, and a high Flow setting will make a more dramatic impact on the image, and could result in an almost psychedelic look, so be careful. Figure 8-13 shows an image with the Sponge tool used to saturate a portion of the image. The colors are brightened, appearing in the figure (which is in black andwhite) as an area that looks brighter than the rest of the image.

Tip *You can intensify colors in other ways, using features found in the Image | Adjustments submenu. Many of these features were discussed in Chapter 6. However, rather than dealing with selected areas of an image or specific color levels or channels, the Sponge tool allows you to add or take away color by painting with your pointer, easily and quickly adjusting all the colors in the path of the brush.*

Adding Focus with the Sharpen Tool

Even a photo that was sharp and crisp when it was first printed can lose some of its detail over time. Both new and old images can lose some clarity in the scanning process, and digital cameras can fail to capture adequate sharpness from the beginning. No matter what caused the problem, however, you can take a fuzzy image and add some focus with the Sharpen tool. The Sharpen tool allows you to paint the desired focusing effect onto the portions of your image that need it. Figure 8-14 shows a photo that needs some sharpening; a portion of it has been sharpened, where indicated.

The Sharpen tool's options bar (shown in Figure 8-15) contains settings for choosing a Brush size and shape, a Blending Mode, the strength of the sharpening effect, and an option to include all layers of the image when the tool is applied.

You'll notice that the Mode list is much shorter than it is when you're using the Brush tool—you have just six options, plus Normal, which is the default. The pixels you sharpen are intensified—they're made brighter, darker, lighter, or changed according to their hue, saturation, color, or luminosity, depending on the Mode you choose. If you aren't sure which Mode will give you the effect you're looking for, experiment—you can always undo it if you don't like the results.

Note   *The set you can apply to the Sharpen tool is discussed in detail in Chapter 6.*

Sharpening was applied to this area with the Sharpen tool.

Figure 8-14. *Sharpening an image can be like putting on a better pair of glasses to look at it—detail is restored, definitions emphasized.*

Figure 8-15. *Control the Sharpen tool's effectiveness with the options bar settings.*

The Strength setting allows you to turn the intensity of the tool's effect up or down. A low percentage will sharpen subtly, and a high percentage will sharpen more dramatically. The default setting is 50 percent, and even that can be a bit much in some cases—if you paint over a spot more than once, you may notice stray, odd-colored pixels appear, as the sharpening effect reduces image quality rather than improves it. Figure 8-16 shows the undesirable effects of oversharpening an image. The same result can appear with the use of the Sharpen filter, which is covered in Chapter 13.

If your image is a composite of several photographs and each of them is on a different layer, try the Use All Layers option. It's off by default, but if you turn it on, it saves you having to turn on individual layers and sharpen them one at a time, or having to merge your layers before you sharpen the image overall.

Softening the Image with the Blur Tool

More often than not, the Blur tool is used to soften parts of an image so that other parts of the image stand out as they are. Figure 8-17 is a perfect example of this. The Blur tool has been used to diffuse the content surrounding the man in the center of the image. With the surrounding content blurred, the man is the first and perhaps only thing you notice in the image. You can still see that he's surrounded by people sitting at or standing by dining tables, but these peripheral items are reduced to a very limited supporting role in the image.

These bright pixels resulted from passing over the same spot too many times with the Sharpen tool.

Figure 8-16.   *Sharpen with care: You can create visual noise on the image by sharpening the same spot more than once or with too great a Strength setting in use.*

Figure 8-17. *Make something stand out by blurring everything else.*

You can also use the Blur tool to soften sharp edges, achieving the opposite effect of the Sharpen tool. Instead of intensifying the color or shade of pixels you paint with the tool, you're bringing the pixels to closer levels of brightness and depth. Figure 8-18 shows the Blur tool used to soften a sharp edge where a solid-colored shape meets a white background. By blurring the edge, any aliasing (choppy edges) that existed along curves are smoothed out; the stage is set for much softer blending options, such as drop shadows, embossing, or glows, which might be applied later.

Using the Blur tool is no different from using the Sharpen, Dodge, or Burn tools—just click the tool to activate it. After setting the Brush size, Mode, Strength, and deciding whether or not to blur all the layers, you can simply paint the blurred effect over portions of your image. You can confine the blur to a specific area by making a selection first (use the Marquee, Lasso, or Wand tools) and then painting within the selection.

Tip *If you want to blur a very small or intricate area, zoom in on the image using the Zoom tool or the Navigator palette. Then, using a Brush size that gives you the degree of control and the amount of blurring you desire, paint the area to be blurred. To see your results as you work, choose Window | Documents | New Window, and keep that window's view of the document zoomed out. Or you can simply zoom out on the single image window when you're finished to check your results as they'll appear when the image is viewed on paper or onscreen.*

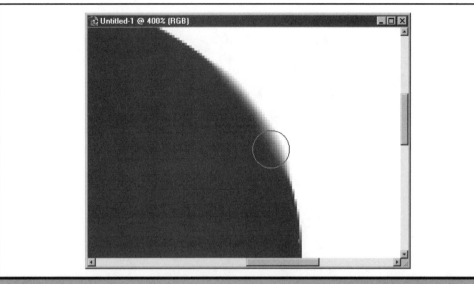

Figure 8-18.   *Soften edges to eliminate choppy curves and to create a gentler transition between contiguous colored areas in your photo.*

Repairing Spots, Stains, Scratches, and Tears

Disaster strikes. You open your photo album and find that the one remaining picture of your great-grandmother as a young girl has been damaged, seemingly beyond repair. If it's your photo or you're the artist being asked whether the picture can be saved, take heart—even images with missing content due to tears, rips, stains, and other forms of damage—can be restored to their original glory.

Photoshop's Cloning, Pattern Stamp, Healing Brush, Patch, and Smudge tools can work wonders to recreate missing content, cover up spots, stains, scratches, and cracks, and to generally clean up an image that looks as though it's been to hell and back. Figure 8-19 shows just such an image—this photo has a multitude of problems. And as you can see in Figure 8-20, they're all fixable.

Cloning Sections of Your Image

The Clone Stamp tool is a great choice if you want to cover up a damaged portion of your image. The tool's name gives you a clue to its benefit in these situations: You clone one area of your image and place that clone somewhere else. For example, if you have a portrait that's been damaged, you can clone part of the person's skin and stamp that cloned sample onto the portion of the face that's damaged. As long as you clone an area that's the same color and texture, the repair should be invisible. Figures 8-21 and 8-22 show a figure before and after cloning to get rid of a scratch on the portrait face. The cloned area is indicated in the first figure, and you can see how it covered the scratch in the second figure.

Figure 8-19.   *Stored in a drawer and scuffed by other objects stored in that same drawer, this photo sports several problems.*

Figure 8-20.   *The image has been miraculously restored.*

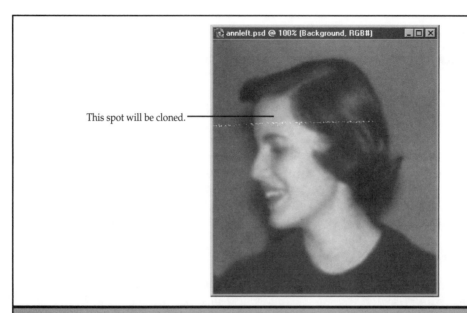

This spot will be cloned. ——————

Figure 8-21.   *Clone a clean spot near the blemish you want to get rid of so you know that the content you're cloning is a close match for the target area.*

Figure 8-22.   *The Clone Stamp removed the portion of the scratch that spanned the woman's forehead and hair.*

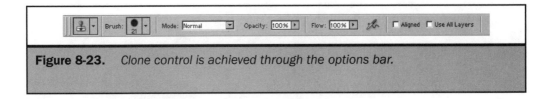

Figure 8-23.   *Clone control is achieved through the options bar.*

To use the Clone Stamp, activate the tool and then use the options bar (shown in Figure 8-23) to choose the Brush size, Mode (the same Blending Modes discussed in Chapter 6—and this time they're the full set, not the six that you can use with the Blur and Sharpen tools), Opacity, and Flow. You can leave the Aligned option on (it's on by default), which will cause each successive click of the Clone Stamp to resample a portion of the image that's the same distance from the sampled spot and the place where you're clicking. If you turn Aligned off, the content you're stamping will come from the original cloned location.

If you want to use the Clone Stamp to clean up an image with multiple layers, you may want to turn Use All Layers on. This option will allow you to clone any visible content without regard for which layer it's on.

Note that the Opacity and Flow settings work the same for this tool as they do for any tool that applies content with a brush. The Opacity can be set to 100 percent, which will apply the cloned content at its full depth—none of the underlying content will be visible through what you stamp onto the image. Reducing the opacity when using the Clone Stamp is normally done to create special effects rather than for repair or restorative purposes, because if the stamped content isn't fully opaque, it won't completely cover the area onto which it's stamped. The Flow is also set to 100 percent by default, and this allows the brush to apply the cloned content fully and quickly with each click and stroke of your mouse.

Once the tool is active, you need to sample an area of the image, selecting the content that you want to stamp onto another area of the image. To do this, press and hold the ALT (Windows) or OPTION (Mac) key and click once on the content you want to clone. Release the key, and then begin clicking to place the cloned content on the portions of your image that have spots, stains, or other content you want to cover up. Note that when you click with the ALT/OPTION key down, your brush has a crosshair in the middle of it—the crosshair indicates that you're sampling a precise area of the image, showing you from which area of the image you're sampling.

You can also use the Clone Stamp tool to remove unwanted content from your image—not stains and spots, but people, trees, garbage cans, cars, puddles, mud, or anything you wish hadn't been in the picture when it was taken. You can also remove content that while it's not unwanted or undesirable, is distracting from the intended subject of the picture. With Photoshop, instead of cutting parts of the picture off entirely, you can simply stamp the unwanted content out of the picture—replacing it with background, other people, or a nice potted plant. When it comes to using the Clone Stamp to get rid of content on a large scale, you have to clone and then stamp content that exists elsewhere in the image (or in any other image that's open at the time), such as shown in Figures 8-24 and 8-25, another set of before and after images. Shrubbery and grass—content that is already part of the image—replace the boy in the foreground of the first image. It's as though he was never there.

Figure 8-24. *Content needn't be undesirable for you to want to remove it—it might simply be distracting from the intended subject of the photo.*

Figure 8-25. *The boy in the foreground is replaced by shrubbery and grass.*

Tip *To avoid the creation of a patterned effect, make sure the Aligned option is on—this will prevent your stamping the same exact sampled content onto a large area you want to edit. You'll have to resample more frequently to make sure you're getting the content you want to use with the Clone Stamp tool, but the results will be more realistic if the Aligned option is in use.*

Using the Pattern Stamp Tool

While the Clone Stamp tool applies content from somewhere else in the image, the Pattern Stamp tool applies preset patterns, creating a brand new fill for portions of your image that need an interesting background, or to cover up something you don't want. If your image doesn't have any content you can clone, using a pattern might be just the ticket—it can cover unwanted content, and it adds visual interest, as you can see in Figure 8-26.

When you activate the Pattern Stamp, the options bar displays the same options you saw when you used the Clone Stamp tool—with some important additions. The most important option on the Pattern Stamp options bar is, of course, the Pattern drop-down list. From the list, shown in Figure 8-27, you can choose which pattern you're going to stamp onto an area of your image.

Once your pattern is selected and your other options (Mode, Opacity, Flow) are set, you can begin stamping the pattern—you can also paint the pattern on with long strokes. If you want to make sure that the pattern is applied uniformly, no matter how often you release the mouse as you drag (or literally stamp, by repeatedly single-clicking your mouse), make sure the Aligned option is on.

Figure 8-26. *Use the Pattern Stamp to apply a preset pattern to areas of your image.*

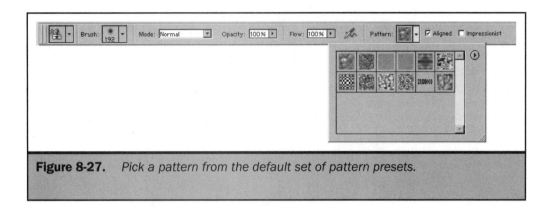

Figure 8-27.   *Pick a pattern from the default set of pattern presets.*

The Impressionist option applies the selected pattern in a splotchy, "impressionistic" way.

Displaying and Using Added Pattern Presets

The default list of patterns that appears in the Pattern drop-down list is rather short, and the patterns aren't that great, frankly. You'll probably want to append the list with other presets, or create your own patterns, which is discussed in the next section. To display additional pattern presets, click the Pattern option menu (on the right side of the Pattern drop-down list) and choose from one of the sets of pattern presets at the bottom of the menu (see Figure 8-28). As soon as you make a selection, a prompt appears asking if you want to replace the current patterns with the preset group you just selected (click OK to do this) or to Append the new group to the existing set. I usually choose Append, so I can easily compare the patterns in the default set to the patterns in any sets I choose to display in addition to them.

If you don't think you can really see the individual patterns well enough in the Pattern drop-down list, click the Pattern options menu button and choose Large Thumbnail from the list of options.

Restoring and Saving Pattern Sets

To restore the patterns displayed in the Pattern drop-down list to the default set, choose Reset Patterns from the Pattern option menu. A prompt will appear asking if you want to replace the current patterns with the default patterns; clicking OK will do just that. If you choose to Append the default patterns, they'll be added to whatever set of pattern presets was currently displayed. This can be a good choice if earlier you opted to display a new set of presets instead of (not in addition to) the default set.

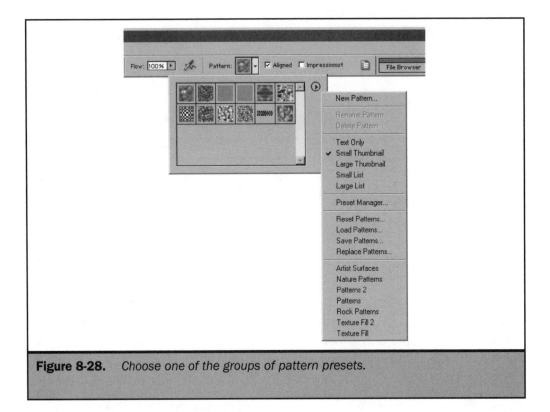

Figure 8-28. *Choose one of the groups of pattern presets.*

If you add and delete patterns (those you create or unwanted patterns from a set you chose to display) and want to save the custom set of patterns you've created for use in the future, choose Save Patterns from the Pattern option menu. In the resulting Save dialog box, you can name the set (creating a .pat file); from then on, that set will appear in the list of presets in the Pattern options menu. Note that the pattern set you save should be saved to the Patterns folder, which is typically found in the Presets folder, a subfolder of the Photoshop 7.0 folder.

Creating New Patterns

What if none of the preset patterns are appealing to you? You can create your own patters quite easily by selecting a rectangular section of your image, and using the Edit | Define Pattern command. When you use the command, a dialog box opens, through which you can name your new pattern (see Figure 8-29). After you name the new pattern, it will appear in the Pattern drop-down list when you use the Pattern Stamp tool.

To use your new pattern, simply click the Pattern drop-down list (when using the Pattern Stamp tool), and click once on the pattern. You can then apply the pattern in spots by clicking your mouse, or apply it in strokes by dragging your mouse. The size of the spots will be the size of the brush in use at that time. The patterns you create can be used to cover content in other images, such as grass patterns used to cover muddy spots on a lawn, or a pattern created from pavement used to "pave" another image.

If you decide later that you don't like a pattern you've created (or any of the patterns that are part of Photoshop's installed preset groups), you can right-click/CONTROL-click the pattern in the Pattern drop-down list and choose Delete Pattern from the context menu. Be careful in doing so, however, as there is no confirming prompt that appears to give you a chance to cancel the deletion. You'd have to redisplay the preset group that contained the deleted pattern in order to get it back; or, if it was a pattern you created from a Marquee-selected sample, you'd have to recreate it.

> **Tip**
>
> *Although the New Pattern command appears in the context menu displayed when you right-click/CONTROL-click the patterns in the Pattern drop-down list, choosing New Pattern will result in an error prompt. The prompt informs you that the pattern already exists, which is helpful, but doesn't explain why the command is in the menu in the first place—it doesn't work even if you have a Marquee selection in the image at the time.*

EDITING AND
RETOUCHING IMAGES

Figure 8-29.   *Use the Rectangular Marquee tool to select the area that should become your new pattern, and then give the pattern a relevant name.*

Working with the Healing Brush

The Healing Brush is new to Photoshop 7, and it's a great addition. It enables you to repair scratches, spots, and other blemishes on an image, and to have the repair disappear seamlessly into the surrounding pixels. The Healing Brush is very much like the Clone Stamp tool, except the Healing Brush does something extra: When you paint the sampled content onto the blemish, the texture, shading, and lighting of the target area is preserved. This makes it much easier to repair a photo using its own content as the source material for the repair—especially if the lighting and texture in the damaged area is not the same as any other area of the image. Figures 8-30 and 8-31 show before and after versions of the same photograph. In the first image, there are stains across the top third of the photo, caused by water damage; in the second image, the stains have been "healed" using nearby content. If the Clone Stamp had been used, there wouldn't have been such an effective cover-up because there is so much detail and variety in the tones and textures throughout the image.

It's a good idea to zoom in on the image when healing an intricate image. By zooming in, you can take the damaged area and deal with sections of it individually, rather than trying to fix it all in one piece.

Figure 8-30. *Removing these stains will require applying content from somewhere else in the image—but where?*

Figure 8-31. *The Healing Brush to the rescue—the differences in shading are adjusted, making for a seamless correction.*

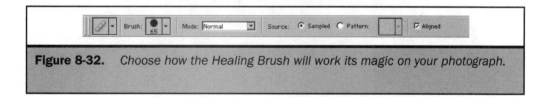

Figure 8-32. *Choose how the Healing Brush will work its magic on your photograph.*

To use the Healing Brush, first activate the tool, and then check the options bar (shown in Figure 8-32) for any settings you wish to adjust. As found within virtually all of Photoshop's repair tools, there's a Brush setting you can use to choose the size and shape of the brush with which you'll paint the healing effects onto the image, and a Mode drop-down list. The different Blending Modes have been covered elsewhere in the book (namely in Chapter 6), but you will probably find that the default, Normal, works best. Its results are quite predictable. Given the automatic texture and lighting match that the Healing Brush applies to the target area's pixels, you shouldn't have to tinker with this too much.

In addition to Brush and Mode settings, you can choose whether or not the Healing Brush will apply Sampled content or a Pattern. If you choose Sampled, the tool will work by sampling a portion of the image and painting that content on another area of the image. If you choose Pattern, the drop-down list next to that option becomes available, and you can choose from the default set of patterns and paint those onto any portion of your image. Because you're painting the pattern on with the Healing Brush, however, the pattern's texture and lighting effects are changed to mimic the surrounding pixels. Figure 8-33 shows the Bubbles pattern, which was painted on the boy's helmet with the Healing Brush. The bubbles are the same color as the helmet (yellow, with some green brought in from the grass behind the boy's head), rather than their default blue-gray.

After making any adjustments to how the Healing Brush will work, you can sample an area of your photo by pressing the ALT (Windows) or OPTION (Mac) key and holding it as you click on the image. Your brush will display a crosshair in the middle, indicating that you're sampling content rather than applying it.

Once you've sampled part of the photo for use by the Healing Brush, paint or dab (with quick mouse clicks) over the blemished area, and you'll see the sampled content applied. A second later, the painted area changes, and you'll see the lighting, shading, and texture change to match the pixels surrounding the original damage.

The selected pattern is grayish-blue bubbles.

When painted across the helmet, the pattern take on the colors and shading of whatever's in its path.

Figure 8-33. *Paint a pattern onto your photo with the Healing Brush, and watch the pattern's texture, shading, and lighting effects change to match the surrounding pixels.*

*Use the Aligned option to make sure that as you paint one or more strokes with the
Healing Brush, the content you're applying is resampled as you drag. This makes it
possible to paint, stop, and then paint some more (with as many stops and starts as you
need), without the Healing Brush going back to the originally sampled pixels as the source.*

Patching Images

The Patch tool is also new to Photoshop 7, and it makes it extremely easy to cover up
problems such as unwanted content or the signs of age and damage. Like its companion,
the Healing Brush, the Patch tool matches the patch content to the pixels in the damaged
or unwanted area, enabling you to create seamless corrections for virtually any problem,
anywhere on the image.

To use the tool, you can take one of two patch approaches—working from the
Source (where the problem is) or the Destination (the content you'll use as the patch).
I prefer to work from the Destination, as this is conceptually similar to the Clone
Stamp and Healing Brush tools, as well as in the way they repair images and cover
up content.

On the other hand, the nature of the problem itself might dictate that you
take the Source approach. If the damaged area is an odd shape, you may prefer
to select the damaged area (the Source) with the Patch tool, and then drag the
selection to the area that should be used as the patch (the Destination). The choice
is up to you, and you can experiment with the Patch tool on your own to see which
approach you prefer.

To patch using the Destination approach, click the Patch tool to activate it, and then
click the Destination radio button on the options bar (shown in Figure 8-34). This tells
Photoshop that you're going to select content (or use content that's already selected)
and place it on top of the damaged or unwanted portion of the photo.

Next, select an area to serve as the patch by dragging the Patch Tool to draw a
selection. If you used another selection tool to select the patch prior to activating the
Patch tool, that selection can also be used. Figure 8-35 shows a damaged photo and a
selected area ready to be used as the patch.

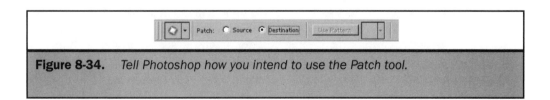

Figure 8-34.   *Tell Photoshop how you intend to use the Patch tool.*

Figure 8-35. *Draw a patch that's roughly the same shape as the area you want to cover up. It's a good idea to make the patch slightly larger than the damaged or unwanted area.*

Tip   *You can use the Feather option to make sure there are no hard edges to your patch—the diffused edge caused by feathering will help the patch blend in.*

Your next step is to point to the selected area and drag it onto the damaged area. Magically, the content blends into its new location, taking on the texture, lighting, and shade of the surrounding pixels. A seamless cover-up is achieved, as shown in Figure 8-36.

The Patch tool also offers you the ability to patch with patterns—applying patterned areas to your image, covering up anything you don't want to see anymore, or simply adding a patterned area to the image. To patch your image with a pattern, select the Patch tool and use it to select the area that will be patched. Next, click the Pattern drop-down list on the options bar, and click once on the pattern you want to use. To finally apply the pattern, click the Use Pattern button. As shown in Figure 8-37, the pattern is applied, taking on the color, texture, and lighting of the patched area.

Figure 8-36. *The selected area was dragged onto the scratch, and the scratch disappeared.*

Figure 8-37. *The edges of the pattern "shirt." Under his arms it's darker, matching the shading on the original shirt.*

As you're selecting your Source or your Destination area, you can use different keyboard shortcuts to add to or subtract from your selection:

- SHIFT-drag on the image to add to the selection. This needn't be an area contiguous to the existing selection.

- ALT-drag (Windows) or OPTION-drag (Mac) to subtract from the selection. This requires that you draw the shape to be subtracted somewhere within the existing selection.

It's best to use the Patch tool to fix problems that involve a very small portion of your photo. If you want to use it on larger areas, make several small patches rather than trying to patch a huge area all at once—you'll find that your results are more seamless and effective.

Blending with the Smudge Tool

Using the Smudge tool is a lot like finger painting; in fact, there's a Finger Painting option for the tool, which makes the effect even more like the results you get when you drag your fingers through wet paint. As shown in Figure 8-38, the Smudge tool drags color from the point where you start dragging and pulls that color along, eventually smudging the colors through as you drag with the mouse. You can use this tool to blend areas of your image, making small strokes that run perpendicular to the two areas' common edge, or by stroking along the edge where two colors meet. You can also use the Smudge tool to literally wipe away small blemishes by dragging properly colored pixels' colors onto the pixels you want to affect.

To use the tool, simply activate it. Choose a Brush size and adjust the Strength. The higher the Strength percentage, the more dramatic the smudge effect—keep it near or below 50 percent for the most subtle effects. And, as needed, change to a different Blending Mode if you want your smudge to adjust darkness, lightness, hue, saturation, color, or luminosity. The default Normal Mode is usually fine for most smudging jobs.

The two remaining settings, Use All Layers (which you've seen before on other retouching tools) and Finger Painting, control which portions of your image are smudged and the nature of the smudge effect, respectively. The Finger Painting option starts the smudge with the currently selected Foreground color, and then it smudges the pixels you drag through as you continue the stroke. Figure 8-39 shows the Smudge tool's effect with the Finger Painting option on.

Photos can be vastly improved by adjustments to their color, brightness, and contrast. Chapter 6 provides detailed coverage of the Image | Adjustments submenu, which contains a variety of commands you can use for this purpose.

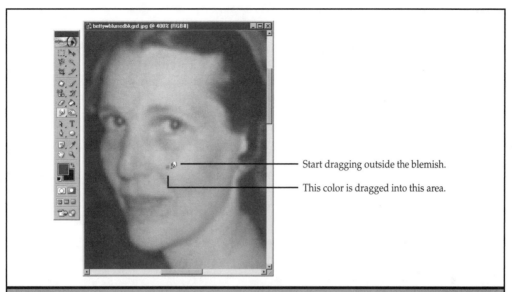

Start dragging outside the blemish.

This color is dragged into this area.

Figure 8-38.   *Smudge away a blemish as though applying touch-up paint with your fingertip.*

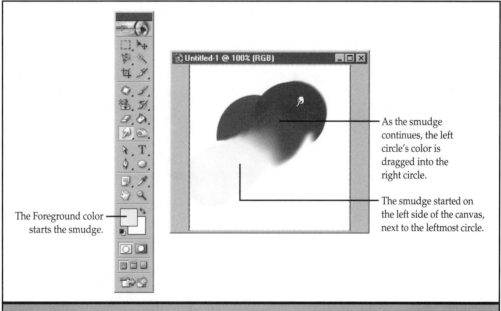

The Foreground color starts the smudge.

As the smudge continues, the left circle's color is dragged into the right circle.

The smudge started on the left side of the canvas, next to the leftmost circle.

Figure 8-39.   *Drag the Foreground color through your image with the Finger Painting option.*

Summary

In this chapter, you learned how to use Photoshop's retouching tools to modify the spots, scratches, stains, tears, and missing content that you may have thought rendered a photo unusable. You also learned to adjust overall image quality and, in specific areas, improve and change the appearance of an image.

The
Complete
Reference

Chapter 9

Resizing and Cropping Images

W hether an image was scanned, photographed digitally, or painted digitally, it does not necessarily come in the size and shape you want for your project. Its dimensions might be too large in height or width to fit your needs, or the file size could be too large in bytes. The image could be oriented incorrectly, such as being in a portrait (vertical) orientation instead of being in landscape (horizontal) orientation. The background could be so busy it takes away from the subject of the image. All of these problems, and maybe more, are likely to be true if the image was not one you took yourself, because you had no control over what was captured. Fortunately, these problems can be fixed, and with Adobe Photoshop you have the tools to do it.

Changing the Print Size of Your Image

Images—or more properly called *bitmap* or *raster* images—may be photographs or digital paintings. Like mosaic paintings, images are made up of bits of color called *pixels*. If you think of each image being broken down into a grid, the pixels are the rectangular "dots" formed at the intersections of the rows and columns, as on your computer monitor. Each pixel has a color value assigned to it, which allows for subtle degrees of shading and coloring in the image.

A bitmap image contains a fixed number of pixels. Unlike graphics that use mathematical objects called *vectors* to build the lines and curves needed to create pictures, a bitmap image loses detail and appears jagged when you scale it onscreen to a larger size. You must therefore handle it differently from vector graphics when you want to change the dimensions of your image.

Changing Pixel Dimensions

Pixel dimensions are the number of pixels along the width and height of the bitmap image. How an image displays onscreen depends on the pixel dimensions and on the size and settings of the computer monitor used to view the image. You must therefore consider the monitor when preparing images for viewing onscreen, such as on the Web.

For example, computer monitors typically display a screen area of 640 × 480, 800 × 600, or 1024 × 768 pixels, depending on the video card installed on the system and the amount of RAM on the card. In the case of 800 × 600, it means the screen displays 800 pixels horizontally and 600 pixels vertically. With this screen area setting on the monitor, an image that is 800 pixels wide × 600 pixels high would cover the entire screen. These dimensions are typical of a 15-inch monitor, so on a larger monitor screen each pixel will appear larger. However, for larger screens that are set for a screen area of 1024 × 768 pixels or even 1280 × 1024 pixels (such as a 21-inch monitor), the image would appear smaller and wouldn't take up the full screen area.

Keeping all this in mind, you might want to change the pixel dimensions of your image to fit the size of monitor and screen area you think most users would have. If you set the pixel dimensions to 1024 × 768, the whole image won't be seen on a monitor that is typically 800 × 600. Making the image 800 × 600 will allow it to be seen on both 15-inch and larger monitors.

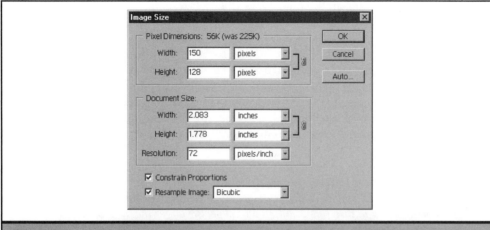

Figure 9-1.   *Once you change the dimensions, the new file size appears at the top
with the old file size in parentheses.*

To change the pixel dimensions of your image, choose Image from the menu and
then select Image Size to open the Image Size dialog box (see Figure 9-1).

If you select Constrain Proportions at the bottom of the dialog box, Photoshop
preserves the current ratio of pixel width to pixel height. Then, whenever you change
either the height or the width, the other dimension automatically updates to maintain
the proportions. Therefore increasing the width of a 20 × 10 image to 40 pixels causes
an automatic change in the height to 20 pixels.

You should select Resample Image and specify the interpolation method you want
to use (if you don't want to use the default method already shown). *Resampling* occurs
any time that you change the pixel dimensions. Decreasing the number of pixels, or
downsampling, deletes information from the image. Resampling up, or increasing the
number of pixels, adds new pixels. For image quality, it is generally better to start with
too much data and downsample your image than to not have enough pixels and
resample up to achieve the image you want.

The interpolation method assigns color values to any new pixels created when
the image is resampled, based on the color values of existing pixels in the image. The
default interpolation method is set in the General Preferences dialog box, which you
open by choosing Preferences from the Edit menu and then selecting General (in Mac
OS X, choose Photoshop, then Preferences, and then General). The available types of
interpolation include the following:

■ Nearest Neighbor is a fast but less precise method recommended for preserving
hard edges and producing smaller files, but it can result in jagged effects if you
distort or scale an image.

■ Bilinear is a medium-quality method.

■ Bicubic is a slower but more precise method that produces the smoothest tonal
gradations of the three methods.

Under Pixel Dimensions in the Image Size dialog box, enter the Width and Height in pixels (to use a percentage of the current size, change the measure to Percent instead) and then click OK.

Because you may get a poorer image quality from resampling—loss of detail or sharpness—you could apply the Unsharp Mask filter to the resampled image. Avoiding resampling is better. The best way is to make sure you start by scanning or creating the image at a high enough resolution. If you do need to resample an existing image by changing the dimensions or resolution and are unsure of the results, try using a copy so you preview the effects your changes make onscreen or in printed output without affecting the original.

Do you notice your file sizes becoming too big? The size of your image file, measured in kilobytes (KB) or megabytes (MB), is proportional to the pixel dimensions of your image. The more pixels, and therefore detail, in an image, the larger the file size will be and the more disk storage it will consume. You may find, too, that larger image files take longer to print and edit. Onscreen, larger files take longer to load and refresh. Consider changing the resolution or reducing the pixel dimensions to reduce your file size.

Adjusting Resolution

You measure image resolution in pixels per inch (ppi), based on the number of pixels displayed per unit of printed length in an image. A high-resolution printed image generally gives you more detail and subtler color transitions in your final output than a lower-resolution image. It contains more pixels than a low-resolution image, and the pixels are smaller. However, increasing the resolution of an image originally captured at a low resolution probably won't increase the image quality; it's better to scan the image again at a higher resolution. Using too low a resolution for a printed image causes *pixelation* (the output has large, coarse-looking pixels).

While pixel dimensions control the amount of detail in an image, image resolution controls how much space the pixels are printed over. The two are dependent on each other. If you change the image resolution but keep the same number of pixels in the image, the printed size will be changed. If you want to keep the height and width dimensions of your printed output, any change to the image resolution means changing the total number of pixels in the image.

To set the resolution of your image, open the Image Size dialog box (see Figure 9-2) by choosing Image Size from the Image menu. Enter a value in Resolution, which is measured in either pixels/inch or pixels/cm. Then click OK to close the dialog box and apply your changes. If you increased your resolution, the image will probably look larger on your screen.

What resolution do you choose? Your best bet is to stick with the resolution of the output device. Monitor resolution is measured as the number of pixels, or dots, per unit of length on the monitor, which is dots per inch (dpi). If you are producing an image for onscreen use, most monitors have a resolution of 72 dpi or 96 dpi. (Setting the resolution higher doesn't improve the image, although you may use a lower setting for quick loading if you don't need quality.)

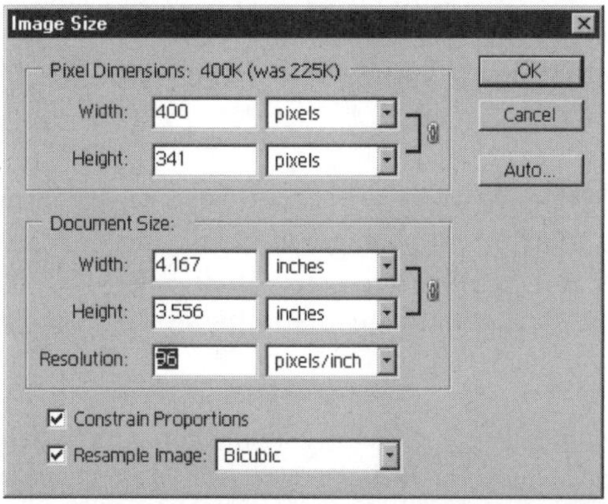

Image Size   [X]

Pixel Dimensions: 400K (was 225K)

Width: [400]   pixels ▾

Height: [341]   pixels ▾

Document Size:

Width: [4.167]   inches ▾

Height: [3.556]   inches ▾

Resolution: [96]   pixels/inch ▾

☑ Constrain Proportions
☑ Resample Image: [Bicubic ▾]

[OK]
[Cancel]
[Auto...]

Figure 9-2.   *Increasing the resolution also increases the size of the file.*

In setting the resolution of an image that you will be printing, you need information about your printing device and its output. Laser printers, ink jet printers, and imagesetters measure resolution as the number of ink dots per inch (dpi). Resolutions for these printing devices vary based on the quality of the device, with typical resolutions of 600 dpi or 720 dpi for laser printers, 300 dpi to 720 dpi for ink jet printers, and 1200 dpi or higher for imagesetters (check your printer documentation to be sure).

That doesn't mean that you set the resolution to 600 ppi (pixels per inch) if you have a 600 dpi laser printer. In a printed image, you also have to consider screen frequency. Because printing devices cannot print continuous tones, they break down images into a series of dots that give the illusion of continuous tones. By varying the size of the dots, the printer creates the appearance of gray tone or color variations. This is called *halftoning*. In order to print a continuous tone image, a halftone screen is applied to the image. The screen organizes the dots into lines. The number of lines per inch (lpi) on the screen, which is the *screen frequency*, helps set the quality of the image. You should check your printer documentation to find the screen frequency for your device before you set the resolution for your images. With your printer information in hand, let Photoshop help you determine the correct resolution for your images. When you have the Image Size dialog box open, click on the Auto button. Enter the screen frequency for your device and then select the Quality you want: Draft sets the resolution equal to the screen frequency, Good sets the resolution at 1.5 times the screen frequency, and Best sets the resolution at twice the screen frequency. When you click OK, the new resolution is set for you in the Image Size dialog box.

Using Auto in the Image Size dialog box only helps you set the resolution. It doesn't set the halftone screen for printing. You do that in the Halftone Screens dialog box that is available from Print with Preview.

Although most printers use halftone screens to print images, there are other screening techniques available. Consult your printer documentation or service provider for recommendations in setting the image resolution if you are using one of these devices.

Changing Document Size

When your intention is to print your image, you will probably find it easier to specify the image size in terms of its final printed size, such as $4\frac{1}{2} \times 5$ inches. This makes it easier for you when you place the image in another application, such as a desktop publishing program.

Tip   *How should I size my images for working within a desktop publishing program? To avoid having to resize the image in your desktop publishing program, set the document size as close as possible to the dimensions the image will have on the published page. Not only will this save you time in working with your layout, it will decrease the file size of your publishing file if the original image was larger than its final printed form. Also, you may want to have a higher resolution version of the image for printing and a lower resolution version for working onscreen.*

The printed width and height dimensions, combined with the resolution, make up the document size. These factors determine the total number of pixels in the image. If you increase the document size by increasing the width, the pixel dimensions automatically increase. The same thing occurs when you change the resolution. This automatic adjustment occurs as long as you have resampling enabled.

When you turn resampling off, any modifications you make to the print dimensions or the resolution won't change the total pixel count. Instead, Photoshop updates the other value(s). For example, with resampling on, decreasing the width of an image from 4 inches to 3 inches might change the pixel dimension from 288 to 216 pixels wide, a loss of 72 pixels. With resampling off, the same change wouldn't affect the pixel dimensions, but it might instead increase the resolution to 96.

To change the document size, open the Image Size dialog box (see Figure 9-3) by choosing Image Size from the Image menu. Deselect Resample Image if you want the pixel count to stay the same, and then enter the Width and Height values under Document Size. You can use inches, centimeters (cm), millimeters (mm), points, picas, columns (as specified in the Rulers & Units preferences), or percent as the units of measurement. Click OK to apply your changes and close the dialog box.

Tip   *If you want to return to the original values in the Image Size dialog box, hold down ALT/OPTION and click the Reset button.*

You can view the print size onscreen by choosing Print Size from the View menu or by clicking Print Size in the options bar when you are using the Hand tool or the Zoom tool. Of course, this is only an approximate print size, matching the dimensions in the Document Size section of the Image Size dialog box. The resolution and size of your monitor will have an affect on how it appears onscreen.

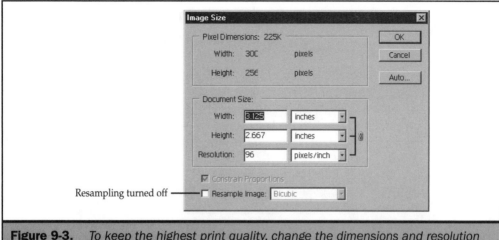

EDITING AND
RETOUCHING IMAGES

Figure 9-3.   *To keep the highest print quality, change the dimensions and resolution with resampling turned off, turning resampling on only when needed.*

Increasing Canvas Size

The workspace on which you create your artwork is called the *canvas*. When you work with images, you don't always see the canvas because the image covers all of it. But if you need to add text above an image, where are you going to put it? Photoshop allows you to increase or decrease the size of the canvas. If the image is on the background layer, the color of the canvas you add will be the same as the background color in the toolbox. However, if the image is on another layer, the added canvas is the color of the background layer. Just remember that if you reduce the size of your canvas, you'll be cutting off part of your image at the same time.

Setting New Width and Height

With a new Photoshop file, you set the size of the canvas at the same time you name the file. To adjust the canvas size for an existing file, you need to open the Canvas Size dialog box (see Figure 9-4) by choosing Canvas Size from the Image menu.

You may set the size of your canvas in percent, pixels, inches, centimeters (cm), millimeters (mm), points, picas, or columns. Select the unit of measurement you want to use and enter the Width and Height values. If you check Relative, you can use plus (+) and minus (–) with numbers to indicate how much to modify the current canvas dimensions. For instance, entering –2.5 in the Width will reduce the width of the canvas by 2.5 inches. Click OK to apply your modifications to the canvas size and close the dialog box.

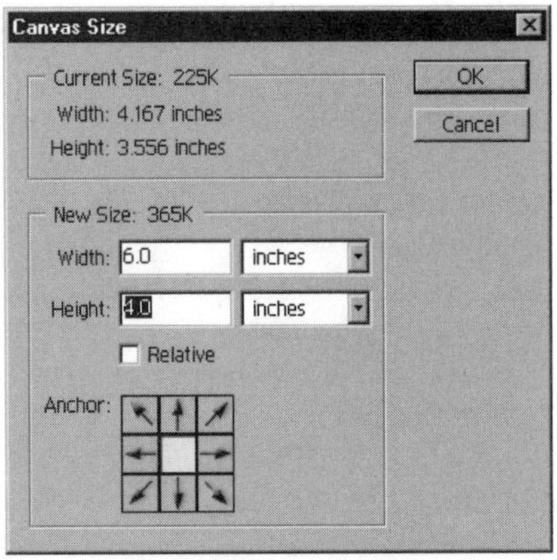

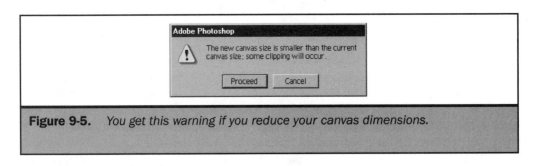

Figure 9-4. *The current dimensions of the canvas and file size display at the top of the dialog box, so you know the starting point for your modifications.*

Figure 9-5. *You get this warning if you reduce your canvas dimensions.*

Because reducing the size of the canvas may cause part of your image to be cut off (called *clipping*), Photoshop warns you of the potential problem and gives you the option to proceed or cancel your changes (see Figure 9-5). You might want to consider using a duplicate of your image to test how the clipping will affect it before you apply the new dimensions to your image, but you can always use the History palette to return to a previous state.

Using Anchors to Control Canvas Effects

When you increase or decrease the dimensions of the canvas for an existing image, Photoshop automatically adds or subtracts equal amounts from the width or height. For example, if you add 2 inches to the width, Photoshop adds 1 inch to the canvas on each side of the image. However, if you subtract 2 inches from the width, Photoshop will cut off 1 inch on either side of the image.

Where Photoshop adds to or subtracts from the canvas depends on the anchor. The default anchor is the white box in the middle (see Figure 9-6), as you can see in the Canvas Size dialog box. To change the anchor position to add more canvas on top of the image, for instance, click one of the arrow boxes in the anchor box to show where you want the image in relation to the canvas you are adding. To add to or subtract from the canvas on the right of the picture, you would click on an arrow box on the left side so it is replaced by the white anchor box. Watch the arrows; they show to which sides your changes will apply.

Once you have entered your dimensions and selected your anchor, click OK to apply your modifications and close the Canvas Size dialog box. In Figure 9-7, you see a baby picture that is the beginning of an adoption announcement. Adding canvas at the top (see Figure 9-8) gives you room to place text without covering the baby's picture.

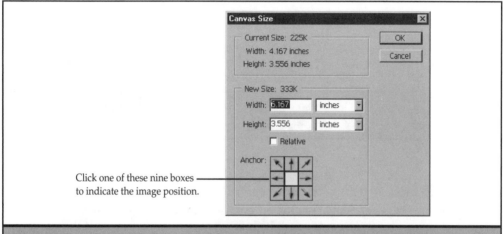

Click one of these nine boxes to indicate the image position.

Figure 9-6.   *With the default anchor, new dimensions are added or subtracted equally from all sides of the image.*

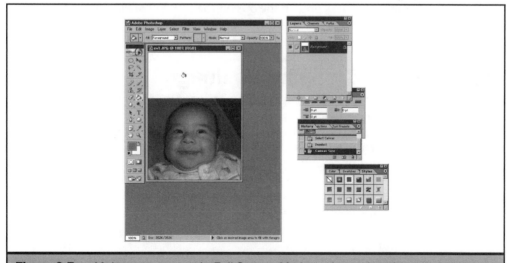

Figure 9-7.   *Make sure you are in Full Screen Mode and can view the menus when you fill the canvas area.*

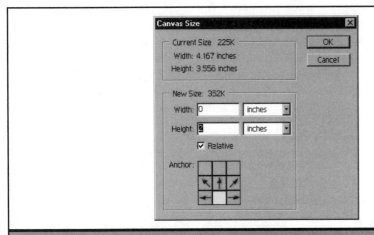

Figure 9-8. *Clicking the middle anchor box on the bottom row indicated that the extra canvas was to be added to the top of the image, as shown in Figure 9-7.*

Back-Filling the New Canvas Area

The canvas you add to an image retains the color attributes or transparency of the original canvas, or background layer, if the image was on another layer. If the image was on the background layer, the new canvas is the same color as the Background color on the toolbox.

Did you forget to set the Background color before adding the new canvas? To fill the canvas with a different color, you start by choosing the Foreground color you want to use. Select the Paint Bucket tool, and on the options bar, set Fill to Foreground (see Figure 9-7). Then click in the canvas area.

Trimming and Cropping an Image

Some images may have too much background or an inappropriate background. You may need to focus on one individual or group or a particular object while eliminating the extraneous stuff around it. One way to do this is to crop the image, which removes the unwanted background and centers the person or object in the middle of the image. It's almost like taking scissors and cutting off the unwanted portions of a picture.

Trimming, on the other hand, trims pixels that are either transparent or match the color of a particular pixel. It therefore removes any unwanted background and places the person or object in the middle of the image.

Using the Crop Tool

The Crop tool gives you the flexibility to select the area you want to include in the final image and also to adjust the size, shape, and position of the cropped area.

Before you begin cropping, you need to think about resampling. When resampling occurs during cropping, it is as if you combined the Image Size command with the Crop tool. Remember, resampling either adds or subtracts pixels when you change the dimensions, and then the interpolation method assigns color values to any new pixels created when the image was resampled.

To keep resampling from occurring while you are cropping the image, you need to make sure all text boxes in the options bar are empty, as in Figure 9-9. Click the Clear button to clear all the text boxes. On the other hand, if you want resampling to occur while you are cropping, enter values for the Height, Width, or Resolution in the options bar (the cropping marquee that you draw with the Crop tool is then restricted to this size).

With the image active, select the Crop tool and drag it over the image to form a rectangular cropping marquee (see Figure 9-10). Did you want to make the cropping marquee bigger or smaller, or adjust the shape? You fix it by dragging any one of the handles on the marquee to scale it to the size you want. Hold down the SHIFT key as you drag a corner handle to constrain the proportions.

Would you like to move the marquee over a little? Position the pointer inside the bounding box and drag the marquee to a new location. The size of the marquee will not change.

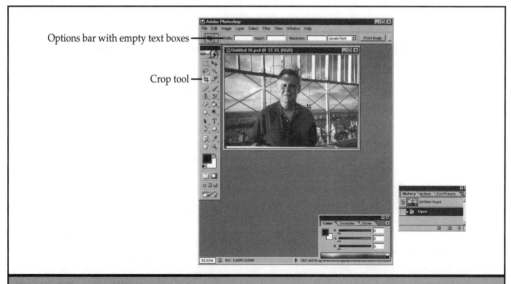

Figure 9-9.   *To avoid resampling, leave these boxes empty. To crop the image to a specific size, enter the dimensions in the options bar.*

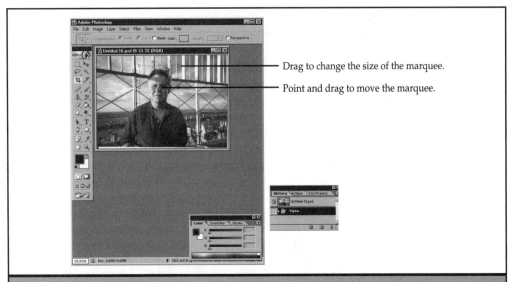

Drag to change the size of the marquee.

Point and drag to move the marquee.

Figure 9-10. *The marquee marks the area you want to save; everything else gets discarded from the image.*

The cropping marquee rotates, too. Place the pointer outside the bounding box until it changes to a curved arrow, and then drag. The marquee rotates around the center point, which acts as the pivot point. By moving the center point (drag the circle at the center of the bounding box), you change the rotation to make it off-center, as in Figure 9-11.

After the cropping marquee is correctly sized and positioned, do one of the following to complete cropping the image:

- Press ENTER/RETURN.
- Click the Commit button on the options bar.
- Double-click inside the cropping marquee.

Press ESC or click the Cancel button on the options bar to cancel the cropping.

To get the same dimensions and resolution in your image as another image, open the image that has those attributes, select the Crop tool, and click Front Image on the options bar. Make your image active to apply these attributes.

Normally, you delete the area outside the cropping marquee, but it is possible when using the Crop tool to hide a cropped area. By selecting Hide in the options bar you preserve the cropped area in the file (note that Hide isn't available for images that contain only a background layer). The hidden area becomes visible again when you move the image with the Move tool. The Shield option on the options bar is normally selected (it's the default), so when you're cropping an image, the shield shades the area of the image to be deleted or hidden (see Figure 9-12). You can even specify a color and opacity for the shield. The area outside the cropping marquee displays in the same color and opacity as the cropping area when the shield is deselected.

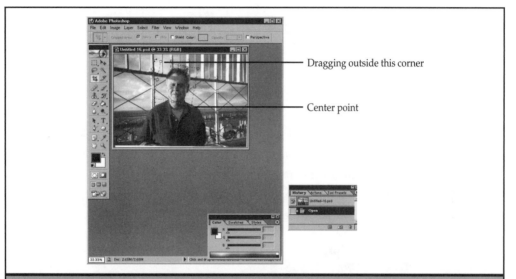

Dragging outside this corner

Center point

Figure 9-11. *By moving the center point to one corner, the marquee rotates around that corner.*

Figure 9-12. *The cropping shield accentuates the area you are keeping.*

Working with the Image Menu's Crop and Trim Commands

In order to crop an image using the Crop command, you need to first select the area of the image you are keeping. You do this using any of the Marquee tools except non-rectangular shapes such as the ellipse, which only crop to the rectangle that contains the shape (if you apply a Feather to the selection, the image is cropped to the outermost pixel of the feather). Then choose Crop from the Image menu.

Need to crop several images to the same size? With the Crop command, you can set a fixed size with the Marquee tool, then click once and drag the marquee until it's positioned where you want it. Now use the same dimensions for all the images.

Choose Trim from the Image menu to trim pixels from the image. When the Trim dialog box opens (see Figure 9-13), you need to choose one of these options:

Transparent Pixels   Trims transparency at the edges of the image, which results in the smallest image that doesn't contain transparent pixels.

Top Left Pixel Color   Removes an area that matches the color of the upper left pixel in the image.

Bottom Right Pixel Color   Removes an area that matches the color of the lower right pixel in the image.

After you select which portion of the image to trim—Top, Bottom, Left, Right—click OK to apply the trim and close the dialog box.

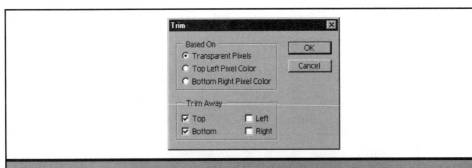

Figure 9-13.   *These settings remove the transparent pixels from the top and bottom edges of the image.*

Rotating the Canvas

Images don't always arrive in the layout that you want to use. For example, the picture you just received might have been scanned in a portrait (vertical) orientation because it fits best on the scanner in that position, even though it's a horizontal image and should have been in landscape orientation. If you want to rotate an image's orientation, you *could* select the entire image and rotate it. But unless the canvas and the image are square, you may end up with part of the image outside the canvas. That's when you need to rotate the canvas instead.

Choose Rotate Canvas from the Image menu and then select one of the following options from the submenu:

180°   Rotates the canvas half a turn.

90° CW   Rotates the image a quarter turn in a clockwise direction.

90° CCW   Rotates the image a quarter turn in a counterclockwise direction.

Arbitrary   Rotates the image by the angle you enter (from –359.99 degrees to +359.99 degrees) in the angle text box in the direction you choose (CW or CCW), as shown in Figure 9-14.

Flip Canvas Horizontal   Flips the canvas horizontally, along its vertical axis.

Flip Canvas Vertical   Flips the canvas vertically, along its horizontal axis.

> **Tip**
>
> *Need to straighten out a crooked scan? Using the Measure tool, drag along the edge that should be vertical or horizontal. Then choose Rotate Canvas from the Image Menu and select Arbitrary from the submenu. The correct angle will already be entered for you. Just click OK.*

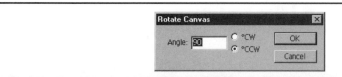

Figure 9-14.   *Enter the exact degree of rotation you want, as well as the direction.*

Summary

In this chapter, you learned how to change the size of your image, as opposed to scaling an image. Changing the size involves either setting new pixel dimensions to control the number of pixels in the image or adjusting the print dimensions to set the width and height of the printed image. You also learned how resolution plays a part in changing the dimensions of the image. To eliminate unnecessary or unwelcome portions of the image, you learned to crop or trim the image. The canvas size is another aspect that you learned to control by setting the size, adding to or subtracting from it, or rotating it.

The Complete Reference

Photoshop 7

Part III

Building Original Artwork

The Complete Reference

Chapter 10

Creating and Working with Layers

When the very first versions of Photoshop shipped, the product didn't include the ability to create and work with layers. Combining images was a frustrating procedure where you had no ability to change your mind about anything. You either got it right the first time or started over—there was little room for mistakes. This was not a working method that promoted creativity and spontaneity.

The introduction of layers freed users to create images the likes of which had never been seen before. Having images on separate layers that could be overlapped without destroying information on either layer is one of the keys that helped make Photoshop the world standard that it is today.

Understanding the Layers Palette, Layers, and the Layer Menu

Layers and the processes of creating, using, and maintaining them are controlled using three sections of the Photoshop interface: the Layers palette, layers themselves, and the Layer menu.

By understanding how each works and how they interact with each other, you'll soon be creating complex images in new, exciting ways. Each of these three key points in understanding how to work with layers is discussed in detail next.

Understanding the Layers Palette

The first step to being able to work with layers and create composite images like a professional is to open and understand the Layers palette. It's activated by choosing the Show Layers command from the Window menu. If Layers is already checked, then the palette is already active.

You can position the Layers palette anywhere on the screen that feels comfortable. Photoshop will remember, from session to session, where you placed it and will bring it up in the same location each time, even with a dual-monitor configuration. Since most likely you will be using it often, it's best to find a place that you can put it and leave it open and active. Alternatively, you can choose the command Dock to Palette Well from the Layers palette menu to attach it to the far-right side of the options bar. From there you can click its tab to activate it when needed. This is a useful option when screen space is limited.

Additionally, you may find that you need to resize it during the course of a project. The Layers palette can be stretched to enlarge or contract its physical size by clicking and dragging the box in the palette's bottom-right corner.

As shown in Figure 10-1, the Layers palette gives you access to six areas of control: Blending Modes, the Layers palette menu, Opacity/Fill controls, locks, layers, and shortcut icons.

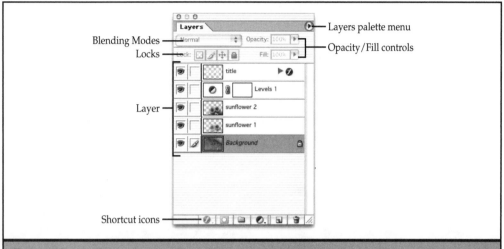

Blending Modes
Locks
Layer
Shortcut icons

Layers palette menu
Opacity/Fill controls

Figure 10-1.   *From the Layers palette you have access to most of the commands you'll need to effectively create and use layers.*

BUILDING ORIGINAL
ARTWORK

Blending Modes

Blending Modes affect how a layer displays in relation to the layers beneath it in the stacking order. Only one mode can be applied to a layer at a time. These 22 modes can create a wide range of visual effects.

Blending Modes are covered in detail in Chapter 7. As shown in Figure 10-2, the Blending Modes are:

Normal   The standard mode used to display layers.

Dissolve   In this mode, lowering the layers will dissolve the layer into non–anti-aliased noise.

Darken   Compares the pixels in the selected layer to the underlying layer's pixels and displays only the darkest pixels.

Multiply   Multiplies the color information from the selected layer with the color information from the underlying layers. The result is always a darker color.

Color Burn   Darkens pixels in underlying layers based on the color of the pixels in the selected layer using a change in contrast.

Linear Burn   Darkens pixels in underlying layers based on the color of the pixels in the selected layer by reducing brightness.

Lighten   Compares the pixels in the selected layer to the underlying layer's pixels and displays only the lightest pixels.

Screen   Compares the selected Layer's colors to the underlying layer's colors and multiplies the inverse to create a new lighter color.

Color Dodge   Lightens pixels in underlying layers based on the color of the pixels in the selected layer by decreasing contrast.

Linear Dodge   Lightens pixels in underlying layers based on the color of the pixels in the selected layer by increasing brightness.

Overlay   Multiplies or screens the pixels in the underlying layer based on the color of pixels in the selected layer.

Soft Light   Lightens and darkens the pixels in the underlying layer based on the color of pixels in the active layer.

Hard Light   Multiplies and screens the pixels in the underlying layer based on the color of pixels in the active layer.

Vivid Light   Burns and dodges the pixels in the underlying layer based on the color of pixels in the active layer.

Linear Light   Burns and dodges the pixels in the underlying layer by increasing or decreasing their brightness values based on the values of pixels in the active layer.

Pin Light   Replaces pixels in the underlying layers with pixels from the active layer based on brightness values.

Difference   Compares the color in the layer to the color in underlying layers and displays a new color which is the mathematical difference between the two.

Exclusion   An effect similar to Difference, but created with much less contrast.

Hue   Displays only the hue or color information of the layer.

Saturation   Displays only the layers saturation, or color intensity, information.

Color   Displays both the layer's hue and saturation information.

Luminosity   Displays only the layer's luminosity, or light and dark, information.

Understanding the Layers Palette Menu

Clicking the arrow button in the upper-right corner of the Layers palette accesses this menu. As shown in Figure 10-3, the Layers palette menu enables you to perform almost all of the major tasks involved with the creation, maintenance, and management of layers.

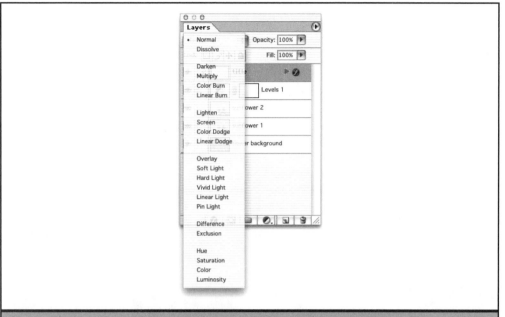

Figure 10-2.   *The Layers palette contains a drop-down list of Blending Modes that affect how a layer displays.*

Figure 10-3.   *The Layers palette menu includes controls for creating and managing layers.*

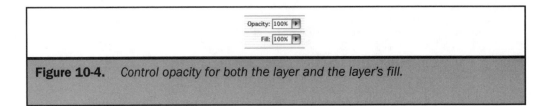

Figure 10-4. *Control opacity for both the layer and the layer's fill.*

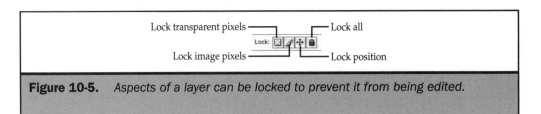

Figure 10-5. *Aspects of a layer can be locked to prevent it from being edited.*

Adjusting Opacity and Fill Controls

Layer Opacity and Layer Fill Opacity are both controlled from the Layers palette (see Figure 10-4). You can either type in new numbers or use the pop-up opacity sliders to alter a layer's opacity.

Understanding Locks

The Layers palette provides the ability to lock any combination of three different aspects of a layer so they cannot be edited. As shown in Figure 10-5, the locks are:

> **Lock transparent pixels** Any transparent areas of the layer are locked and can't be edited.

> **Lock image pixels** Any non-transparent pixels are locked and can't be edited.

> **Lock position** If selected, the layer cannot be repositioned.

> **Lock all** Locks all three aspects of the layer.

Understanding Layers

The actual layers in the Layers palette are displayed as a list. The order of the layers in this list determines how the image displays. Layers at the top of the list are closest to the view. This list is sometimes referred to as the *layer structure* or the *stacking order*. Moving layers to new positions on the list is called *stacking*. Each layer, as you can see in Figure 10-6, has a unique name, an attached thumbnail image, and icons related to its type and visibility.

You can change the size or remove entirely the layer thumbnail by selecting Palette Options from the Layers palette menu and choosing a radio button to make your selection in the resulting dialog box.

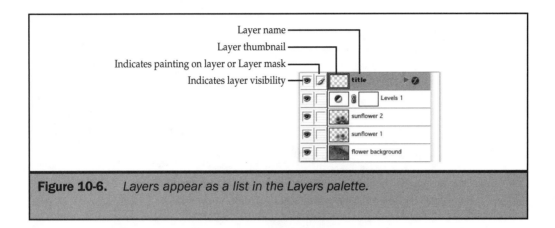

Figure 10-6.   *Layers appear as a list in the Layers palette.*

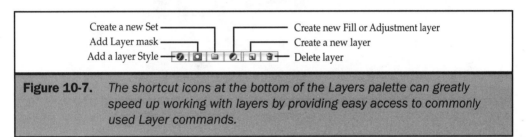

Figure 10-7.   *The shortcut icons at the bottom of the Layers palette can greatly speed up working with layers by providing easy access to commonly used Layer commands.*

Understanding the Shortcut Icons

The shortcut icons and their drop-down lists are located at the bottom of the Layers palette. They provide you with quick access to many commonly used commands that are otherwise available from menus and dialog boxes. Using them can speed up your Photoshop work.

As shown in Figure 10-7, the six shortcut icons are:

Add a layer style (italic letter "f" within circle)   Attaches any of ten Layer styles to the selected layer and provides access to advanced blending options.

Add layer mask (circle within rectangle)   Attaches a Layer mask to the selected layer. This can be used to make a variety of transparency effects.

Create a new set (folder icon)   Layer sets aid with the organization and management of large numbers of layers.

Create new fill or adjustment layer (black/white circle)   Create any one of eleven Adjustment layers or three Fill layers.

Create a new layer (page icon)   Creates a new blank layer.

Delete layer (trashcan icon)   Deletes the selected layer.

Figure 10-8. *The checkerboard pattern of the transparency grid.*

Understanding Layers and the Layer Menu

Perhaps the best analogy for layers is that they're like working on overlapping sheets of transparent plastic. Imagery can exist on different layers. Even though layers can affect each other and how they display, most layer changes can easily be undone. The secret is that even though images overlap, they are on different layers that don't affect each other in any permanent manner.

Layers display their transparency through a gray checkerboard pattern called the *transparency grid*. You can see the transparency grid in Figure 10-8. This is a sort of visual metaphor used to display which areas of the layer are transparent.

The final major piece of the layers puzzle is the Layer menu. Almost all of the commands used to create, control, and manage layers are included or repeated in this menu. As shown in Figure 10-9, the fifth menu in the menu bar is the Layer menu.

Understanding Layer Types

As Photoshop has evolved from its earlier versions, the need has grown for the product to support more than one type of layer. Currently there are seven different layer types that you'll need to understand to get the most out of layers.

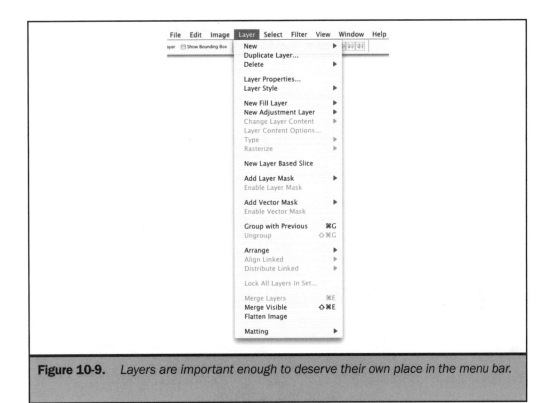

Figure 10-9.   *Layers are important enough to deserve their own place in the menu bar.*

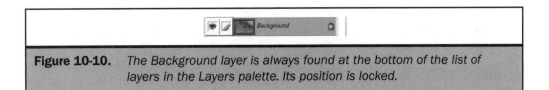

Figure 10-10.   *The Background layer is always found at the bottom of the list of layers in the Layers palette. Its position is locked.*

Understanding the Background Layer

Almost all images, whether they are scans, digital photos, or stock photography, start with the Background layer (see Figure 10-10). On Background layers you can paint, clone, adjust colors, and perform almost all Photoshop functions; however, there are some things that cannot be done on a Background layer. These are related to the Background layer's two limitations—it is opaque and cannot be repositioned. This being true, no Photoshop function involving transparency or translucency will work. Nor will you be able to use the Move tool to change the Background layer's position.

You can create a document without an official Background layer by choosing Transparent as the Content type when creating a new layer. Instead of a Background layer, the new document will contain Layer 0 instead.

Using Image Layers

Image layers are the most common layer type and are the default type created when a new layer is generated. Image layers are where you will paint, draw, and manipulate photographic and other image information—they are the original default layer type. As shown in Figure 10-11, the paintbrush icon to the left of a layer's thumbnail in the palette indicates that you are editing the layer.

Understanding Type Layers

Type layers are created when you use the Type tools from the toolbox. Type layers contain text information that Photoshop understands as being vector-based. This means that these layers can be scaled, warped, and transformed with little or no loss of image quality. As you can see in Figure 10-12, a Type layer is identified by the capital "T" that appears in the layer's thumbnail icon in the Layers palette.

When using the Type tools to work on type layers, the options bar changes to provide access to text controls and commands such as font, font size, paragraph alignment, anti-aliasing, and more. The Text tool and Text layer options (see Figure 10-13) are discussed in detail in Chapter 14.

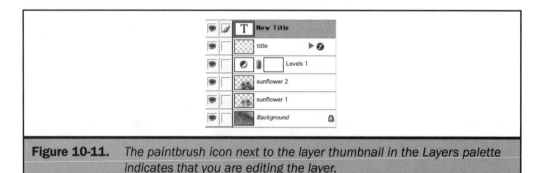

Figure 10-11.   *The paintbrush icon next to the layer thumbnail in the Layers palette indicates that you are editing the layer.*

Figure 10-12.   *A capital "T" in a layer's thumbnail indicates that the layer is a Type layer.*

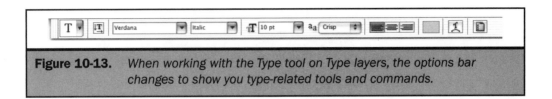

Figure 10-13.   *When working with the Type tool on Type layers, the options bar changes to show you type-related tools and commands.*

Working with Shape Layers

Creating Shape layers is one of the newer functions of Photoshop. Shape layers are vector masks that display some information from a solid color or other type of Fill layer—that is, the shapes that are generated as Shape layers are understood by Photoshop as a series of mathematically described points and straight and curved lines that connect them. They are Bézier paths, like the graphics created by Adobe Illustrator, that clip the information on the layer (in Photoshop 6 they were called *layer clipping paths*). This being the case, Shape layers can be transformed in any number of ways with no loss of image quality. This powerful ability makes Shape layers very versatile.

The six tools that automate the Shape layer creation process are:

Rectangle   Creates any size rectangle or square.

Rounded Rectangle   Creates any size rectangle or square whose corners are rounded off. You can set the amount of rounding.

Ellipse   Creates any size circle or ellipse.

Polygon   Creates shapes with any number of straight sides of equal sizes. The fewest number of sides is three, a triangle; the highest number is 100.

Line   Creates straight lines. You can chose the line width and include arrowheads at either end of the line.

Custom Shape   You can create you own shapes and save them to this library of saved custom shapes.

You can see the six tools in Figure 10-14.

Shape layers are a clever use of vector masks masking a Fill layer. The thumbnail icons, as shown in Figure 10-15, provide insight into how this masking works.

The icon on the left is the Fill layer; double click this thumbnail to call up the Color Picker. You can use the Color Picker to assign any color you desire. The right-hand thumbnail icon is the Vector mask that defines what area of the Fill layer is visible and what is masked out.

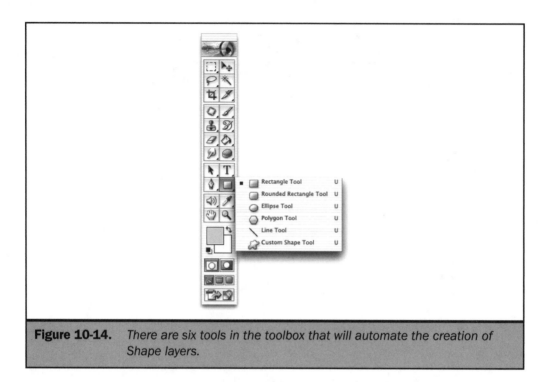

Figure 10-14. *There are six tools in the toolbox that will automate the creation of Shape layers.*

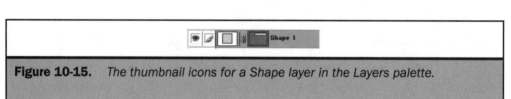

Figure 10-15. *The thumbnail icons for a Shape layer in the Layers palette.*

Using Adjustment Layers

If you understand the analogy that layers are like sheets of transparent plastic that can be stacked atop each other, then imagine Adjustment layers as colored sheets that can be put between layers. They change the color of layers that are beneath them in the stacking order.

What's brilliant about Adjustment layers compared to just adjusting image color normally is that Adjustment layers are not cumulative—you can readjust the settings after applying them. You cannot do this with normal image adjustments. Just double-clicking the thumbnail for the layer in the Layers palette will bring up the adjustment's dialog box. You can use the dialog box to adjust the Adjustment layer's settings. Normal image adjustments do not provide this sort of versatility.

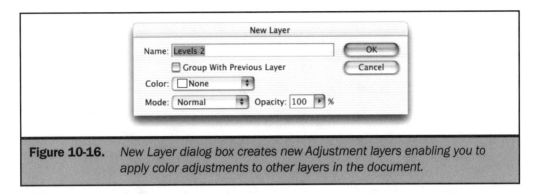

Figure 10-16. *New Layer dialog box creates new Adjustment layers enabling you to apply color adjustments to other layers in the document.*

Photoshop often has more than one way to accomplish a desired result. When given more than one way to do something, always choose the method that can be undone. Always give yourself the opportunity to change your mind at a later date.

If you create an Adjustment layer while an area of the image is selected, a mask will be generated automatically. The adjustment will then only affect that selected area.

The options for creating an Adjustment layer are like those for creating any other layer, as you can see in Figure 10-16. However, the choice Group with Previous Layer is key to getting control of Adjustment layers. If this option is not chosen, then an Adjustment layer will affect every layer beneath it in the stacking order. If Group with Previous Layer is chosen, then the Adjustment layer will affect only the layer that is directly underneath it in the stacking order. This is incredibly useful in helping adjust the color in your images because each layer can be individually controlled. Your Adjustment layer options are as follows:

Name Use this to assign a unique name to the Adjustment layer.

Group with Previous Layer This command groups the new Adjustment layer so the adjustment only affects the layer direct beneath it in the stacking order.

Color Use this command to assign a color to the layers to help visually organize the Layers palette.

Mode There are up to 22 Blending Modes for new Adjustment layers, but the number of Blending Modes may vary depending on the image's color mode—for example, CMYK images will have fewer Blending Modes available than would be available for an RGB image.

Opacity This option controls the opacity of the new Adjustment layer.

Color adjustments are covered in detail in Chapter 6. Not all color adjustments are available as Adjustment layers. As you can see in Figure 10-17, there are 11 types of adjustments that can become Adjustment layers. Briefly, they are:

Levels Adjusts an image's values using triangular arrows representing the black, neutral gray, and white points on a linear graph (called a *histogram*). The

BUILDING ORIGINAL ARTWORK

position of the arrows enables you to set the images black, neutral gray, and white points.

Curves   Enables the adjustment of a range of colors using a gamma ramp. A *gamma ramp* is a graph that uses a curved line to compare and adjust input to output—that is, what the tonal values were compared to what you are changing them to. Curves can control a more specific range of tonal values compared to levels.

Color Balance   Shifts colors in an image toward one of six colors. These colors can be adjusted separately for the image's three tonal ranges: shadows, midtones, and highlights. Choosing to protect the image's Luminosity can prevent the image from becoming lighter or darker as the color is adjusted.

Brightness/Contrast   Controls brightness values in an image; lightens, darkens, or alters the contrast.

Hue/Saturation   Enables colors to be altered using the Hue, Saturation, and Brightness (HSB) color model. Very versatile.

Selective Color   This adjustment uses the process color palette of cyan, magenta, yellow, and black (CMYK) to affect images.

Channel Mixer   Enables the transfer of information between channels.

Gradient Map   Maps a color gradient onto an images luminosity values.

Invert   Reverses the color values of the colors.

Threshold   Separates the image into pure black and pure white using an adjustable break point. This gives you much more control of the conversion than switching the color mode to Bitmap.

Posterize   Limits the number of levels used in the image.

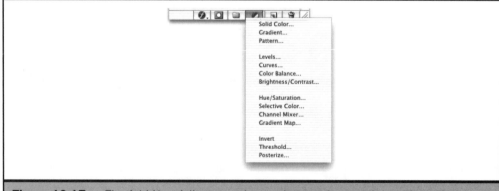

Figure 10-17.   *The Add New Adjustment Layer shortcut icon and drop-down list*

Understanding Fill Layers

Related to Adjustment layers are Fill layers. Using Fill layers with other layers, grouping them, and changing their opacity settings can make Fill layers versatile tools for creating many different special effects. As you can see from Figure 10-17, they are located in the same shortcut icon drop-down list as the Adjustment layers. There are three types of Fill layers:

Solid   Creates a new layer filled with any color.

Gradient   Creates a new layer filled with any gradient from the currently available list of gradients.

Pattern   Creates a new layer filled with any pattern from the currently available list of patterns.

You can create a new custom pattern by selecting an area of an image with the rectangular marquee tool set for 0 pixels of feathering then choosing Define Pattern from the Edit menu. You'll be prompted to name the new pattern, and the pattern will then be included in the list of patterns.

Fill layers can be changed from one type to another after their creation by using the Layer menu command Change Layer Content. For example, you can change a Pattern Fill Layer to a Gradient Fill Layer. This same command can be used to change an Adjustment layer from one type to another.

Accessing Style Layers

Style layers don't stand alone; they are always attached to another layer. As you can see in Figure 10-18, they can be attached to Image, Text, or Shape layers and automate the inclusion of special effects such as drop shadows and glows. They are all effects that are generated using layers. Any Image, Text, or Shape layer can have one or multiple style layers attached. More complex effects can be achieved by using multiple style layers and you can automate their application by saving the settings to the Style palette.

Figure 10-18.   *Styles can be attached to any Image, Text, or Shape layers.*

Working with Layers

To get the most out of all the different layer types, you'll need to be able to work with them effectively. You'll find as you get started that most likely the things you can do with layers are the things that interested you in learning Photoshop in the first place. Layers are the key to creating composite photographs combining two or more photos to make a new image. They make adjusting colors easier, are absolutely necessary for dealing with text, and are how some of Photoshop's more spectacular special effects are made. Once you understand layers, a new world of image processing will open up to you. In this section, you learn how to create, alter, use, organize, and manage layers.

Creating New Layers

You've seen how important layers are to working with Photoshop. So it should be no surprise that there are several ways to create new layers. Both the Layer command from the Layer | New menu and the New Layer command from the Layers palette menu will bring up the New Layer dialog box (see Figure 10-19). From the dialog box, you can preset many of the new layer's properties including the name, color, Blending Mode, and opacity—very similar to the options available for Adjustment layers. Alternatively, you can hold down the ALT (Windows) or OPTION (Mac) key and click the fifth shortcut icon (page icon).

Giving layers unique names that describe their contents can help you organize a complex layer structure, as well as make it easier for yourself and others to edit the document.

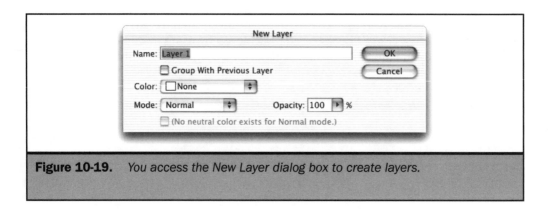

Figure 10-19.   You access the New Layer dialog box to create layers.

Of course there are other ways that a new layer can be created:

New Layer shortcut icon   Clicking the fifth shortcut icon, the page icon, creates a new layer without accessing the New Layer dialog box.

New via Copy   With an area of a layer selected, you can choose Layer | New | New via Copy to duplicate the information in the selected area to a new layer.

New via Cut   With an area of a layer selected you can choose the Layer | New | New via Cut to move the information in the selected area to a new layer.

New Layer from Background   Converts the Background layer into a normal layer.

Paste   Unless there is an active selection, cutting and pasting will almost always create a new layer. This is often how images are moved from one document to another.

Drag and drop   Use the Move tool to drag a layer from one document to another.

Place   From the File menu, use the Place command to enable the creation of a new layer from an Illustrator (.ai) or Acrobat (.pdf) file. Since both of these file formats are based upon PostScript, a vector-based programming language, the Place command will enable you to scale and position the image before the new layer is created. After scaling and positioning, pressing the ENTER (Windows) or RETURN (Mac) key will complete the process.

There are also alternative layer types, each of which is created in a different manner:

Text layers   Text layers are created using one of the Text tools.

Shape layers   Shape Layers are created by either using one of the six Shape tools or by using the Pen tools.

Adjustment layers   Adjustment layers can be created using commands in the Layer menu, or by using the fourth shortcut icon's drop-down list.

Fill layers   Like Adjustment layers, Fill layers can be created using commands in the Layer menu, or by using the fourth shortcut icon's drop-down list.

Activating a Layer

Only one layer can be selected at a time. When you are first getting started, using layers can cause some confusion. If you perform a process and nothing appears to have happened, one of the first things to check is whether or not you have the correct layer selected. You can tell which layer in the Layers palette is currently active because the layer's name is highlighted in a bold font, the paintbrush icon is shown to the right, and the highlight color fills the layer's name field. See Figure 10-20.

Keep the Layers palette visible and check it often. This can prevent a lot of confusion and save time. Since you can view one layer while editing another, keeping track of which layer is currently active is key to creating what you want. ALT-click/OPTION-click the eyeball icon to make only that layer visible.

BUILDING ORIGINAL ARTWORK

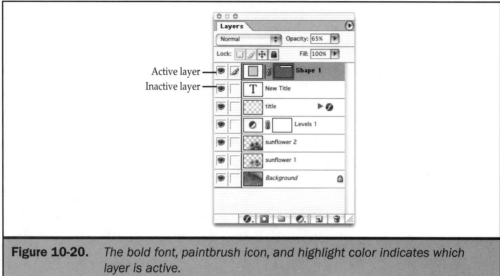

Active layer
Inactive layer

Figure 10-20. *The bold font, paintbrush icon, and highlight color indicates which layer is active.*

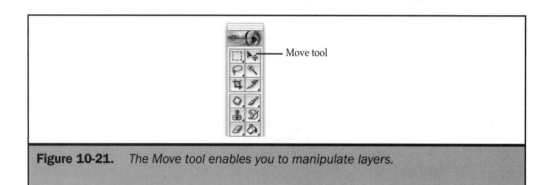

Move tool

Figure 10-21. *The Move tool enables you to manipulate layers.*

Often, you may need to select pixels inside a layer. Hold down the CTRL (Windows) or COMMAND (Mac) key and click the layer's name in the palette to select all of the pixels in the layer. You'll see the cursor, which is normally displayed as a small hand when over the layer name, change to include a dashed box when COMMAND/CTRL is held down.

The key to changing the position of a layer is the Move tool. As you can see in Figure 10-21, this is the topmost tool on the right side of the toolbox. It's used to drag entire layers around and reposition them. Unless it's locked or the Background, any Image, Type, or Shape layer can be repositioned with the Move tool.

Changing the Layer Properties

After creating a new layer, you may find that you want to rename it or change the color it displays in the Layers palette. The more complex your layer structure is, the more likely it is that you'll need to reorganize it and change layer properties. As shown in

Figure 10-22, the Layer Properties dialog box is accessible from either the Layer menu or the Layers palette menu. You can also change a layer's name by double-clicking its name in the palette and typing a new name.

Duplicating Layers

There are plenty of reasons for wanting to duplicate a layer. They run from special effects to keeping an unaffected backup copy of the layer. Since this is a pretty common function there are three ways to duplicate a layer. Select a layer and then choose Duplicate Layer command from the Layer menu. As seen in Figure 10-23, this brings up the Duplicate Layer dialog box, which contains three options: As, which enables you to change the name of the duplicated layer; Destination, which allows you to duplicate a layer into any open document; and New Name, which allows you to name the new document into which a duplicate layer is being inserted. You can also access the Duplicate Layer dialog box from the Layers palette menu, or by accessing the context menu by right-clicking/CONTROL-clicking the layer. A faster way to duplicate a layer is to use the shortcut icons. You can drag a layer over the fifth shortcut icon (page icon) to duplicate the layer. This can be quite a time saver as you work through a problem that involves layers.

By using the Duplicate Layer dialog box, you can duplicate a layer from one document to another.

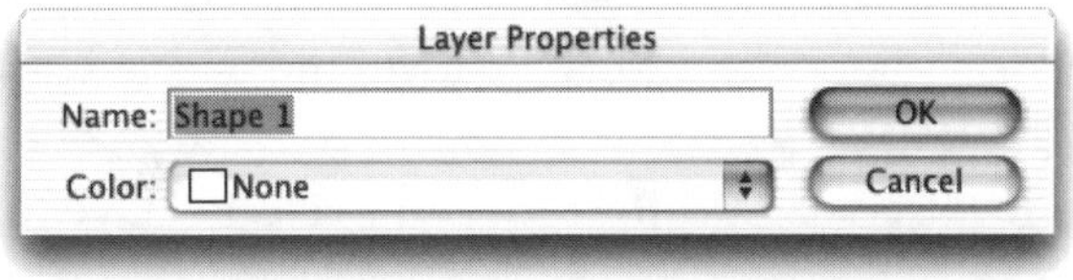

Figure 10-22.   *The Layer Properties dialog box lets you change a layer's name and color.*

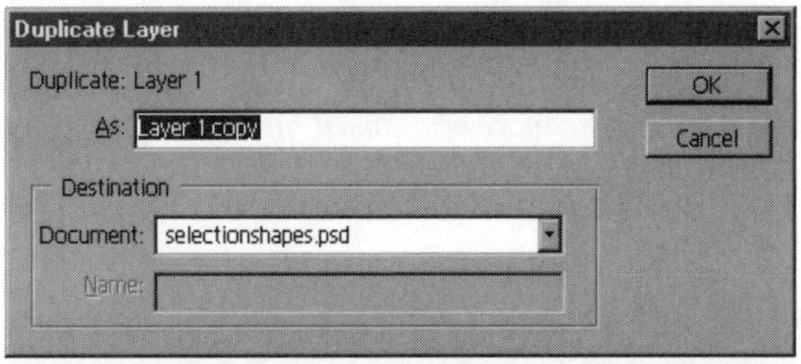

Figure 10-23.   *The Duplicate Layer dialog box can be accessed from the Layer menu.*

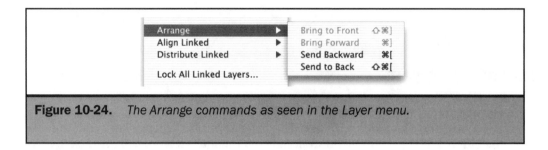

Figure 10-24. *The Arrange commands as seen in the Layer menu.*

Arranging Layers

You've seen how layers are presented as a list in the Layers palette. The order of the layers in the list makes a profound difference in how the finished image will display. The layers that are at the top of the list are closest to the viewer. As you read down the list of layers, each successive layer is beneath the previous layer in the layer structure.

Simply dragging a layer up or down the list restacks the layer. Just point and click on a layer's name, hold down the mouse button, and drag the layer to a new location in the list. Dragging a layer to the top of the list will bring the layer forward in the image. Dragging it down the list will send the layer backward. You can move any layer to any position on the list with one exception: Nothing can be moved below the Background layer, nor can you move the Background to any other position than the bottommost layer.

An alternative to stacking layers by hand is to use the Arrange commands in the Layer menu. There are four Arrange commands (see Figure 10-24), as follows:

Bring to Front (SHIFT-] or COMMAND-]) Moves the selected layer to the top of the Layers palette list.

Bring Forward (CTRL/COMMAND-]) Moves the selected layer one position higher in the list.

Send Backward (SHIFT-] or COMMAND-[) Moves the selected Layer one position lower in the list.

Send to Back (CTRL/COMMAND-[) Moves the selected layer to the bottom of the list. This doesn't move the layer below the Background layer.

During a normal working session, stacking layers by dragging them up and down the list is much faster than other restacking methods, including the alternative Layer menu Arrange commands, which are more often used for creating Actions. See Chapter 20 for more information about automating processes.

Working with Layer Locks

There are many reasons you might want to lock one aspect or another of a layer. You may want to prevent it from being edited, or you might want to affect how you are editing it. As you can see in Figure 10-25, there are several options when it comes to locking layers.

Lock Transparent Pixels   Choose this to lock all of the transparent pixels in a layer. Applying a transparency lock is the equivalent of masking the transparent pixel in the layer. You might do this so you can paint in only the pixels that contain some color—for example, on a blank layer where you created an elliptical selection and filled it with a color. You could then deselect it, lock the layer's transparency, and use the airbrush in only the filled circle. With a little effort, you could airbrush it into a sphere. This same idea could be used to paint into rasterized text layers. By locking the transparency, you don't have to deal with the distraction of the moving dashed edge that occurs when using selections.

Lock Image Pixels   Locking the image pixels in a layer enables you to paint only in the transparent pixels. You could use this to paint a glow effect around an image.

Lock Position   This choice keeps the layer from being moved. You might want to use this if you are satisfied with the position of one or more layers.

Lock All   Locks all three aspects of a layer: transparency, image, and position.

Working with the Background Layer

Almost any image you ever open will start with one layer—the Background layer. For many Photoshop operations, no other layer is needed. It's only when you combine images and create special effects that multiple layers are necessary. The Background layer, as shown in Figure 10-26, is like any other layer with a few exceptions. One of the unique limitations of Background layers is that you cannot change the layer's position. The background can be painted on and altered in most ways, but its position is locked—it can't be repositioned. Another difference between the Background and other layers is that the Background layer is opaque. You can't change the opacity of the Background in any way. It's always set to 100 percent opacity.

Every once in a while, you may run into the need to create a new Background layer. You may have moved the Background, changing it to Layer 0, or perhaps the original Background was deleted. Whatever the reason, you can change any layer into the Background layer by choosing Background From Layer from the Layer | New menu.

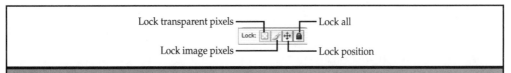

Figure 10-25.   *The lock icons lock aspects of a layer, preventing their being edited.*

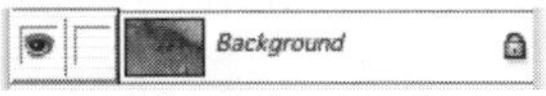

Figure 10-26. *Even complex image compositions usually have a Background layer.*

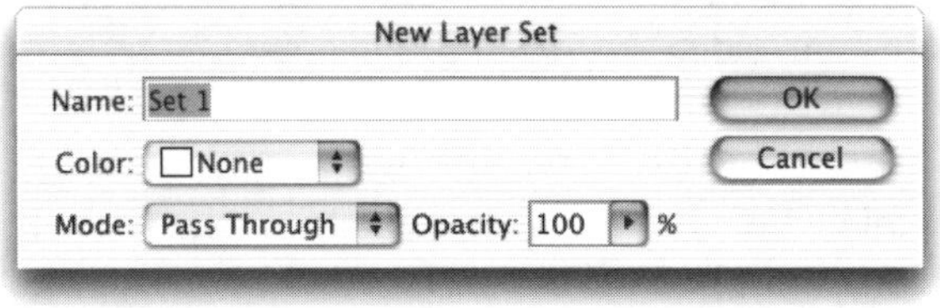

Figure 10-27. *The New Layer Set dialog box enables the creation of layer sets.*

Using Layer Sets

As you add more and more layers to your document, using the Layers palette can become very confusing. The list of layers in the Layers palette can grow so long that no matter how large you make the palette you still have to scroll up and down the list to find what you want. Even if you've taken the time to give each layer a unique name and color key, it can be hard to find the layer you're looking for quickly. Layer sets are Photoshop's solution for this problem. A layer set is a folder that can hold layers. The view of the Set can be expanded and contracted, showing and hiding its contents, to save space in the Layers palette. Naming and coloring Sets can help further organize your Layers palette, making it easier to use. You can bring up the New Layer Set dialog box, as seen in Figure 10-27, by choosing either Layer Set from the Layer | New menu or by choosing New Layer Set from the Layers palette menu. In this dialog box, you can name the new Set and assign it a color. This can really help organize your Layers palette. Also, you can apply a Blending Mode and a level of opacity to any layer put inside the layer set. The default mode of Pass Through enables layers in the Set to retain their own Blending Mode and Opacity settings.

The third shortcut icon, the folder icon, creates a new layer set but doesn't bring up the dialog box. You can always change its name and color later in one of these three ways:

- Hold down the ALT (Windows) or OPTION (Mac) key and double-click on the layer set's name.
- Choose Layer Set Properties from the Layer palette menu.
- Right-click/CONTROL-click and use the context menu.

You can add layers to the new Set by dragging them over the Set icon in the palette. Expanding and contracting your view of the Set's contents can organize and control many layers and your access to them. You can toggle the arrow icon to the immediate left of the folder icon in the Layers palette to expand and contract your view of the Set's contents.

If you have a layer set selected, clicking and dragging inside the image window with the Move tool will reposition all of the layers in the Set. What's more, any transformations applied to the layer set will affect all of the layers it contains. For example, you can scale any number of layers at the same time by placing them all in a layer set and then applying the scaling to the Set.

You can duplicate an entire layer set by choosing Duplicate Layer Set from either the Layer menu or the Layers palette menu. As you can see in Figure 10-28, the Duplicate Layer Set dialog box enables you to rename the resulting new Set and choose its destination. By selecting a destination for the new Set, you can place it in the current document, any other open document, or in a totally new document. This flexibility can help speed up the creation of a series of images that share similar elements.

Alternatively, you can duplicate a Set within a document very quickly by dragging its icon over the fifth shortcut icon, the page icon. This duplicates the Set without accessing the dialog box.

Layer sets can be linked to other Sets or other layers in exactly the same way that individual layers are linked together. Very complex layer structures can be repositioned easily his way.

Of course, if Photoshop lets you to create something it usually has a way for you to delete it, as well. Layer sets are no exception. To delete a layer set, you could select it and choose Layer Set from the Layer | Delete menu, or you could choose Delete Layer Set from the Layers palette menu. You'll be prompted to delete the Set. A faster method is to drag the layer set over the sixth shortcut icon, the trashcan icon. This deletes the layer set immediately without bringing up any prompting.

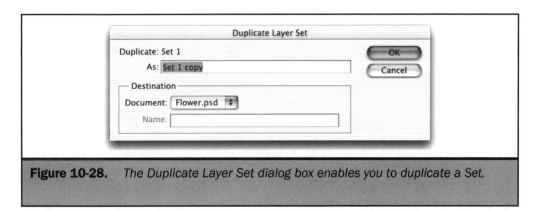

Figure 10-28.   *The Duplicate Layer Set dialog box enables you to duplicate a Set.*

Using Commands and Tools with Layers

Certain menu commands and tools work slightly differently when applied on a layer compared to the Background. For example, menu commands such as filters and color adjustments will only be applied to the active layer. Be certain which layer is active and what it contains before applying filters and color adjustments.

One Edit menu command, Copy Merged, only works with layers. The normal Copy command from the Edit menu only copies whatever is selected on the currently selected layer. Copy Merged is different in that it copies everything visible in the selected area regardless of the layer it's on.

There are several tools that can work differently in an image that incorporates layers. They are:

Move   This tool only really functions when using layers.

Eraser   The Eraser behaves differently on layers compared to the Background layer. When erasing on the Background layer, pixels are transformed into the Background color. On layers, the pixels are erased to transparency. With the exception of when the layers transparent pixels are locked, the image pixels erase to the Background color.

Several tools have the option to affect or appear to affect multiple layers. These tools all contain the options bar choice of Use All Layers:

- Clone Stamp tool
- Blur tool
- Sharpen tool
- Smudge tool
- Magic Eraser
- Paint Bucket

How to Delete Layers

Deleting a layer removes it from the image. This is usually a permanent procedure; however, during a working session it can be undone by either using Undo from the Edit menu, or backing up using the History palette. Any number of things could make this impossible to do, so be careful when deleting a layer. The Layer menu provides several options for deleting layers. As shown in Figure 10-29, they are:

Layer   Deletes the currently selected layer.

Linked Layers   Deletes the currently selected layer and any layers that are linked to it.

Hidden Layers   Deletes all hidden layers. You might want to use this to save memory. Fewer layers makes for a smaller document size.

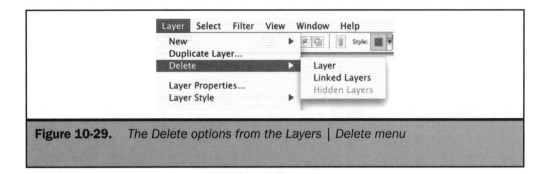

Figure 10-29.   *The Delete options from the Layers | Delete menu*

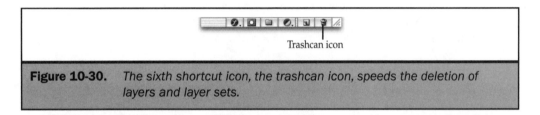

Figure 10-30.   *The sixth shortcut icon, the trashcan icon, speeds the deletion of layers and layer sets.*

Alternatively, you can choose Delete from the Layers palette menu to delete the selected layer, or by COMMAND/CONTROL-clicking on the layer and choosing Delete Layer from the context menu.

Faster than using menus is the use of the Delete shortcut icon (see Figure 10-30). Just choose a layer and then click the icon. A dialog box will appear, asking you if you want to delete the selected layer.

You can bypass the Delete dialog box by dragging a layer over the top of the Delete shortcut icon. The layer will automatically delete.

Controlling Layers

In addition to providing information about layers and giving you the opportunity to add, delete, and restack your layers, the Layers palette also provides tools for controlling your layers—their appearance and functioning within the image. Your options may seem unlimited. Photoshop supports this aspect of the product very well. Among the controls you can apply are the ability to hide layers, apply styles to their content, choose how their transparency is displayed, group your layers, and link layers so that they can be treated as a unit.

Understanding the Transparency Grid

Photoshop uses a gray checkerboard pattern as a visual metaphor for transparency. This is referred to as the transparency grid. When first using Photoshop you might find this distracting. However, with a little experience visualizing the checkerboard as transparency becomes second nature. Spending the time and effort to get used to this metaphor is well worth the effort, because it has become the industry standard for displaying transparency. To see the transparency grid, as it appears in Figure 10-31, you may have to hide some layers, most often the Background layer, to make it visible.

From the Photoshop | Preferences menu you can choose Transparency & Gamut to make changes in the transparency grid. As shown in Figure 10-32, this brings up the Transparency & Gamut Preferences dialog box. You can use this dialog box to change the following:

Grid Size   Controls at what size the transparency grid is displayed. You may want to adjust this based on your monitor size and resolution setting.

Tip   *Even though you can turn the transparency grid off by choosing None from the Grid Size drop-down list, this is a very bad idea. It will prevent you from dealing with white as a color. With the Grid off, white pixels on a layer by themselves will be invisible.*

Grid Colors   You can choose between a number of shades of gray and between several colors to use to display the transparency grid.

Figure 10-31.   *The checkerboard pattern, known as the transparency grid, indicates that the area is transparent.*

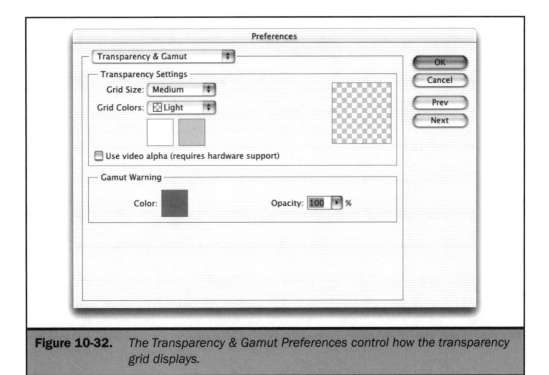

Figure 10-32.   *The Transparency & Gamut Preferences control how the transparency grid displays.*

> **Tip**   *Using Grid Colors other than a shade of gray can affect how you perceive and adjust pixel colors in the image. Keeping a medium, neutral gray selected will help your judgment of color fidelity when trying to make adjustments.*

Use Video Alpha   Replaces the Grid with a solid color. This only works with certain video cards and uses the alpha channel in a Photoshop image to matte the image directly into a video application.

Controlling Layer Visibility

The eyeball icon on the far left of the list of layers indicates whether that layer is hidden or shown. If the field contains the eyeball icon, as shown in Figure 10-33, then the layer contents are visible. If the field is blank, then the layer is hidden and its contents are invisible.

> **Tip**   *Hidden layers will not print. You can make this work for you by hiding and showing layers to print different versions of the same document. For example, if you were designing an ad and you had several different headlines for the ad, you could put each on a separate layer. That way they could be hidden/shown, and a different version could be printed from the same document. This is much easier than creating several different documents, and it can save hard drive space. Additionally, hiding and showing layers can also be used to help create graphics for animations.*

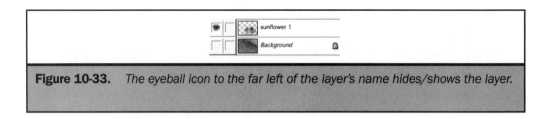

Figure 10-33. *The eyeball icon to the far left of the layer's name hides/shows the layer.*

Set the master opacity of the layer ——Opacity: 100% ▶
Set the interior opacity of the layer —— Fill: 100% ▶

Figure 10-34. *The Opacity and Fill sliders control the layer's opacity.*

In addition to hiding layers, you can set layer opacity using percentages. The lower the percentage of opacity, the more the underlying layers will show through. As shown in Figure 10-34, the Opacity control makes the layer more transparent. You can either type a number into the field or use the pop-up slider to select a percentage. This opacity setting controls not only the selected layer but also any grouped layers and attached layer styles.

*When the Move tool is selected, you can change a layer's opacity by typing numbers. Use either the keypad or the keyboard's number keys to type any number or any two numbers. Typing one number will change the opacity in units of 10—for example, typing **4** will change the layer's opacity to 40 percent. Typing two numbers in rapid succession will set the opacity to the percentage you typed—for example, typing **23** will set the selected layer's opacity to 23 percent.*

The Fill controls work just like the Opacity controls. The difference being that Fill only affects the opacity of the selected Layer's contents. Any attached styles or grouped layers are not affected.

Using the Layer Style Dialog Box

The Layer Style dialog box controls very advanced functions including options for customizing styles, individual channel opacity, level-based layer opacity, and more. You can bring up the Layer Style dialog box, as shown in Figure 10-35, a number of ways:

■ It can be accessed by selecting any Style or Blending Options from the Layer | Layer Style menu.

- You can choose Blending Options from the Layers palette menu.
- You can also choose Blending Options from the context menu.
- You can simply double-click the layer's name field in the Layers palette.

Once the dialog box opens, you can change how the layer displays using two areas of control: Styles and Blending Options. Their options are as follows:

Styles This option allows you to add and control Layer styles attached to the selected layer.

General Blending Use this option to adjust the layer's Opacity and Blending Mode settings.

Advanced Blending This section of the dialog box allows you to change the layer's fill opacity, the channels to which it's applied, establish knockout settings, and choose how the layers and any masks display and function.

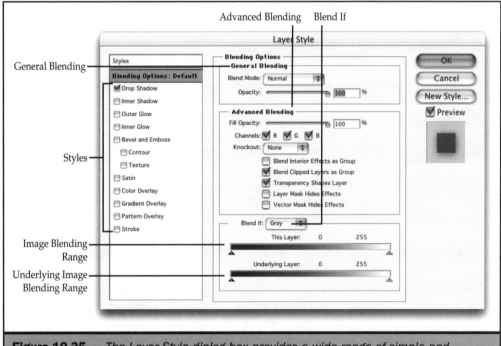

Figure 10-35. *The Layer Style dialog box provides a wide range of simple and advanced layer controls.*

Blend If   This option controls to which channels a blending range is applied. The default setting of Gray applies the range to all channels equally.

Image Blending Range   Use this option to control the range of levels displayed in the layer. Pixels out of the selected range become invisible.

Underlying Image Blending Range   This option controls which pixels in the underlying Layer display the selected Layer, based on levels.

When you've made your selections and adjusted how the layer will display, you can either click OK to continue or click New Style to save all of your choices as a style. Saved styles can be applied to other Layers using the Styles palette found in the Window menu. New Styles you create will be located at the bottom of the Styles palette list.

Applying and Customizing Styles

Using earlier versions of Photoshop, many people obtained near-mystical guru status for their ability to generate special effects using layer tricks. These days Photoshop automates many of these same layer tricks reducing them to styles that can be applied easily to any layer. This empowered many people to create new and exciting imagery, and deflated the egos of many others.

Styles are discussed in great detail in Chapter 12, however, here is the list of styles and a brief description of what they do:

Drop Shadow   Creates the illusion that the layer is floating above the background by generating a shadow effect.

Inner Shadow   Creates the illusion that the layer is cut into the surface of the background by generating a shadow effect inside the layer.

Outer Glow   Generates a glow around the image. Having a dark color on the layer beneath helps to show this effect.

Inner Glow   Generates a glow effect inside the image, either along the edge or in the center.

Bevel and Emboss   Actually several effects are available from this choice. They are inner bevel, outer bevel, emboss, and pillow emboss. All involve creating a 3D illusion.

Contour   Controls aspects of bevel and emboss.

Bevel   Controls how edges are created in the bevel and emboss effects.

Satin   Overlays a pattern of highlights atop the layer. This can look like satin cloth or highlights on chrome.

Color Overlay   Overlays the layer with a solid color.

Gradient Overlay   Overlays the layer with a gradient.

Pattern Overlay   Overlays the layer with a pattern.

Stroke   Creates a stroked line of any color and thickness around the layer. Often used with Text layers.

Styles cannot be attached to the Background layer.

Additional Styles Controls from the Layer Menu

Even though they are not part of the Styles dialog box there are eight commands in the Layer | Layer Style menu that can help you work with and manage styles, as seen in Figure 10-36. They are included here to help you further understand how styles work and help you use them more effectively. Individual and groups of styles can be copied from one layer and pasted to another. The four commands that control this time-saving function are:

Copy Layer Style   Copies the style or styles attached to a layer.

Paste Layer Style   Pastes a previously copied style or styles to another layer.

Paste Layer Style to Linked   Applies the pasted styles to the active layer and all linked layers.

Clear Layer Style   Deletes a style.

Figure 10-36.   *The Layer | Layer Style menu commands help you work with and control styles.*

The final four commands will further help you control and manage styles:

Global Light   Sets the direction of the light source used by all of the styles in the document.

Rather than use the menu commands to delete a style, you can drag its Style layer over the top of the sixth shortcut icon in the Layer palette, the trashcan icon.

Setting and using global lighting for your document will maintain continuity to the styles applied to your layers. Nothing destroys the illusion of space faster and looks more unprofessional than drop shadows that drop in different directions.

Create Layer   Converts the style into Image layers. The number of layers created depends on the style being converted. Some, like Drop Shadow, only create one Image layer, while others, like Emboss, create multiple Image layers.

Learn more about layers by using Create Layer to change a style into its component layers. Then you can examine the layers and their settings to understand how the effect was achieved.

Hide All Effects   Hides all of the styles used in the document.

Scale Effects   Enables the scaling of any effects attached to the currently active layer.

Blending Options

Blending Options enable you to have precise control over how the images of separate layers blend and interact with each other. Blending Options are divided into two categories: General and Advanced.

The General Blending commands include controls that are also available on the Layers Palette. They are:

Blend Mode   The list of 22 Blending Modes discussed earlier in this chapter in the section about the Layers palette.

Opacity   The slider that controls the percentage of opacity of the layer and any attached styles and grouped layers.

The Advanced Blending commands with the exception of Fill Opacity are not available on the Layers palette and enable very exacting controls over how layers blend. The first advanced blending option is the Fill Opacity setting. This is different then the general Opacity setting in that it only affects the contents of the selected layer and nothing else. You can further adjust the effect that the Fill Opacity setting has by controlling which channels are included.

The Knockout commands cause a layer in a layer set or clipping group to punch a hole through the layers below it in the Set or group. You'll need to change the layer's Fill Opacity to 0 percent to get the effect to work. If you are using a layer set, its Blending Mode should be set to Pass Through. There are two options when using Knockouts. They are Shallow and Deep. Shallow knocks a hole only through the layers in the layer set or clipping group. Deep knocks a hole through all of the layers all the way back to the Background.

There are five options that can be included or excluded by choosing radio buttons. They are:

Blend Interior Effects as Group   Applies blending to attached Style layers.

Blend Clipped Layers as Group   Applies the blending to all grouped layers.

Transparency Shapes Layer   This is a misleading command. At first glance it would seem to be referring to Shape layers. However it is actually allowing transparent pixels in an image to define the images edges. A better name for this command would be Transparency Defines Image Edge.

Layer Mask Hides Effects   Any Layer masking also affects attached styles.

Vector Mask Hides Effects   Any Vector Mask used to create Shape layers also affects attached styles.

The final set of controls, located at the bottom of the dialog box, are two sliders that both control opacity by limiting what tonal ranges are visible. There are three controls involved:

Blend If   Enables the selection of which channels will be affected by the tonal graphs below. The default setting of gray indicates that all channels are affected equally.

This Layer   This graph of all of the tonal values lets you set which range of tones in the active layer are visible and which are transparent. By default, the slider arrows (one white, one black) will be on the extreme right and left of the graph, respectively. With this setting, all the tonal values in the image are visible. By dragging either arrow, you can make some pixels invisible while leaving others visible. For example, if you wanted to make all of the whites and highlight colors invisible you would drag the white arrow to the left. The farther you drag, the more pixels will become transparent. You could do the same with the darkest pixels by dragging the black arrow to the right. Using this control, you can make the shadows or highlights in an image transparent. Best of all, this is not a permanent change. Unless you merge or flatten the layer, you can always return to this dialog box and make changes.

Underlying Layer   This tonal value graph is slightly harder to understand. It controls the range of tones in the underlying layer that display the selected layer. You would adjust the black and white arrows to isolate the tones in the underlying image that should be used to display the selected layer. For example, if you had black text on a white background and you added a second layer containing a photo above it, you could force the photo to only be visible where it is over the black text.

To do this you would choose the photo layer, access the Layer Styles dialog box, and then slide the white arrow of the Underlying Layer graph to the left. The pixels that are atop the white background will become transparent while those that overlap the black pixels will remain visible.

Both sliders can be further adjusted by splitting the black and white point arrows into two pieces. ALT-click/OPTION-click on the arrow and drag to split it into two halves. This creates a transition between 100 percent opaque and transparent. Dragging the halves of the arrow apart, as you can see in Figure 10-37, controls the transition. The farther apart the two halves are from each other, the smoother the transition is. Moving them closer together creates a more abrupt transition.

Working with Layer Masks

Many of the real Photoshop magic tricks are based on applying and controlling Layer masks. Layer mask pixels control the opacity of the corresponding pixels in the image. Unlike the layer's Opacity sliders, transparency is controlled by the luminosity values of the pixels filling the mask. The darker the pixels in the mask, the less opaque the corresponding pixels in the layer. So, areas of the mask that are 100 percent black appear transparent in the corresponding pixels of the image. White pixels in the mask cause the corresponding image pixel to display at 100 percent opacity. Any gray pixels in the mask will make the corresponding image pixels translucent. The darker the gray, the more transparent the image. You can create a Layer mask by selecting any layer except the Background and choose either Add Layer mask from the Layer menu or click on the second shortcut icon, the rectangle with the circle. If you use the menu option you will have to choose to either Reveal All or Hide All to decide whether the image starts out opaque or transparent. The shortcut icon always produces a mask that reveals the entire layer (i.e., an all-white mask).

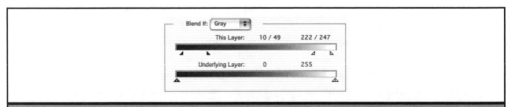

Figure 10-37. *Splitting and dragging the arrow halves creates a range of tones that create a subtle transition between opaque and transparent.*

Figure 10-38. *A layer that has an attached mask will display two thumbnail icons in the Layers palette. The icon on the right is the mask.*

As shown in Figure 10-38, attaching a mask to a layer creates a second thumbnail icon to the right of the original icon in the Layers palette. This thumbnail represents the mask. Changes you make to the mask will be reflected in the thumbnail. Since you now have two thumbnails, it's important to be sure which is selected. The selected icon will have a darker line around it. Additionally, the second icon from the left in the Layers palette list will indicate which is selected. If you see a paintbrush icon, the image is selected. If you see a gray rectangle containing a white circle, then the mask is selected. The mask and the image thumbnails are linked together by a small chain icon. You can click this icon to toggle it on and off. If it's off, the image and the mask can be repositioned independently of each other. When on, they move together.

Masks can be temporarily disabled by choosing Disable Layer Mask from the Layer menu or by holding down the SHIFT key and clicking the mask thumbnail. Either way, the mask thumbnail will display a red X through it while the mask is disabled.

Layer masks are the key to creating all the effects you've seen where one image fades away either into nothing or into another image. Try it yourself with a few simple steps:

1. Choose an image that contains several layers.

2. Select a layer and click the second shortcut icon to add a mask to the layer.

3. Choose the Gradient tool, set it to gradate between black and white.

4. Check to make sure that the mask is selected—look for the rectangle and circle icon displayed to the left of the layer thumbnails in the Layer palette.

5. Click and drag in the active window. The distance and direction you drag will control the results. The image in the active layer should appear to fade away. Any imagery on layers below will show through.

Always check your Tool settings and Foreground and Background colors before painting on Layer masks. Using gray rather than black or having a paintbrush option like Wet Edges on could produce unexpected results.

You can use tools other than the gradient tool to work on the Layer mask. The Brush, Pencil, Pattern Stamp, and any tool or process that can create or alter a grayscale image can be used to work on Layer masks

All sorts of effects can be achieved using Layer masks. For example, an almost unlimited number of edge effects, as shown in Figure 10-39, can be made using Layer masks. Try this:

1. Create a document with a white Background layer and an image floating above it on Layer 1.

2. Add a Layer mask to Layer 1.

3. With the mask selected, make a rectangular selection around the area that you wish to remain visible.

4. Choose Inverse from the Select menu and then use Fill from the Edit menu to fill the area with black at 100 percent opacity using the Normal Mode.

5. A border around your image will become transparent. Deselect your current selected area.

6. Apply any number of filters to make different edge effects. Try the Gaussian Blur or Ripple filters. Experiment with other filters and see what effects you can create using this method.

Using Grouping Layers

Grouping layers can cause a stack of layers to be visible only where they overlap the image pixels of the bottommost layer in the group. For example, you can make a photograph appear only inside the letter forms of a Text layer by grouping the Photo layer to the Text layer. As you can see in Figure 10-40, grouped layers appear indented in the list of layers and a right-angle arrow points to the layer in the bottom of the group. You can make a layer group to the layer below it in the stack by either selecting the layer and choosing Group with Previous Layer from the Layer menu, or by pointing the cursor at the line that separates the Layer names in the palette, holding down the ALT/OPTION key, and clicking. The active layer will now only be visible where its image pixels and the image pixels of the underlying layer overlap. Any number of layers can be grouped together this way. To disable the grouping, select a layer in the group and either choose Ungroup from the Layer menu or hold down the ALT/OPTION key again and click the line that separates the layer names.

Figure 10-39. *Understanding Layer masks opens up a whole range of special effects like the edge effect shown here.*

Figure 10-40.   *Layers can be grouped together so all layers in the group are only visible where they overlap the image pixels in the bottom layer in the group.*

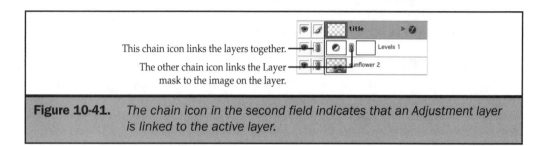

This chain icon links the layers together.
The other chain icon links the Layer mask to the image on the layer.

Figure 10-41.   *The chain icon in the second field indicates that an Adjustment layer is linked to the active layer.*

Working with Linked Layers and Layer Sets

Linking layers makes multiple layers behave as one when they're moved or transformed. Selecting any layer and changing its position with the Move tool will also move any and all linked layers. Likewise, applying a transformation, such as Scale or Rotate, will affect all linked layers. By linking layers together, you can manage large sections of a composite image on multiple layers as if they were on the same layer. You can also link layer sets to other Sets or layers, making it still easier to affect a large number of layers at one time. To link two or more layers or layer sets, select a layer or layer set, and then click on the field to the right of the eyeball icon of any other layer or Set. A small piece of chain icon should appear, as shown in Figure 10-41. To unlink the layers, just click the chain icon again.

Using Layer Alignment

Aligning layers will line up the contents of several layers along an axis that you chose. For example, if you had three boxes, each on its own layer, you could choose to have them all appear to be sitting on the same base line you by clicking on the Align Bottom Edges command. If you link two or more layers you can then align them using the Layer | Align Linked menu or by using the Align shortcut icons from the options bar. You'll need to have the Move tool selected to see these icons. As shown in Figure 10-42, the alignment shortcut icons, which give you a visual clue as to how they work, are:

- Align top edges
- Align vertical centers
- Align bottom edges
- Align left edges

- Align horizontal centers
- Align right edges

Using Layer Distribution

Distributing layers will space the contents of three or more linked layers so there is equal space between them. You can distribute linked layers by choosing commands from the Layer | Distribute Linked menu or by using the Distribute shortcut icons from the options bar, as shown in Figure 10-43. Like aligning, you'll need to have the Move tool selected to have access to the Distribute shortcut icons.

Controlling Layer Merging

As you add new layers to your document your layer structure will grow more complex and harder to manage. The file size of your document will also grow. Eventually, due to limitations in the amount of RAM your computer has available for Photoshop (or simply to make sense of a layer structure that has grown too large for its own good), you may have to merge two or more layers. You might want to do this on a copy of the document or only to images where the content pixels of the layers merging don't overlap; that way you have some options available if you need to undo the merging. Depending on what layer is active, you'll be able to merge two or more layers using the following Layer menu and Layers palette menu commands:

Merge Down   Merges the selected layer with the layer directly beneath it in the list of layers.

Merge Linked   Merges the selected layer with all layers that are linked to it.

Merge Visible   Will merge only visible layers.

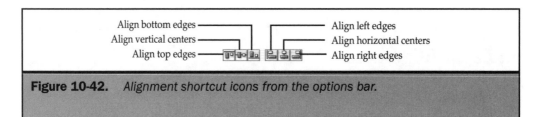

Figure 10-42.   *Alignment shortcut icons from the options bar.*

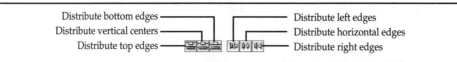

Figure 10-43.   *The Distribute icons give you a visual demonstration of their function, and you can point to them with your mouse to see their actual names.*

How to Flatten Layers

The ultimate merging is to flatten the image. This compresses all of the image's layers into one—the Background layer. You might want to do this for several reasons. Most involve wanting to save the image in a format that doesn't support layers. Additionally, flattening creates a much smaller file size. To flatten an image, choose Flatten Image from either the Layer menu or the Layers palette menu. If your layer structure included any hidden layers, you will be prompted to discard them when flattening. Choose OK to finish the process.

Merging and flattening are two different things, but they can have the same result. Merging layers results in a single layer. Merging layers with the Background layer adds them to the Background layer. Flattening merges all layers to a Background layer.

If you need to flatten an image to prepare it for the Web, print, or some other use, make a copy of the image first and flatten the copy. This takes up some extra hard drive space, but it allows you to edit the original image at a later date. There is nothing more frustrating than needing, perhaps months later, to change an image and not having access to the image's layers. If you use the File menu command Save for Web, you'll always save a copy of your original image.

Applying Rasterize Commands to Layers

You may hear rasterizing referred to sometimes as RIPing, or Raster Image Processing. It's a process where vector-based information is transformed into a bitmapped image—that is, an image made up of pixels rather than vector-based objects.

For example, you could rasterize a Type layer so it was no longer vector-based. You would lose the ability to edit the text, but since it would now be a painting of the letterforms, you could lock the layer's transparent pixels and then airbrush directly into the type, or apply filters to the letterforms.

As shown in Figure 10-44, by choosing the Layers | Rasterize menu, the following layer types can be rasterized:

- Type
- Shape
- Fill content
- Vector mask

Three other options in the same menu affect what is rasterized are:

Layer   Rasterizes the active layer.

Linked Layers   Rasterizes the active layer and any linked layers.

All   Rasterizes all layers in the document.

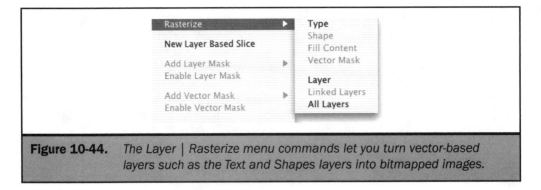

Figure 10-44. *The Layer | Rasterize menu commands let you turn vector-based layers such as the Text and Shapes layers into bitmapped images.*

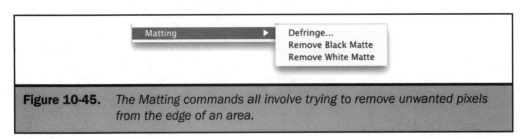

Figure 10-45. *The Matting commands all involve trying to remove unwanted pixels from the edge of an area.*

Working with Matting

A common problem when cutting and pasting images from one document to another is fringe appearing around the image. This usually happens when an image is cut out from a light-colored background and pasted on a dark background. A one- or two-pixel halo often surrounds the pasted image. The reason for the halo of pixels is because anti-aliasing is usually applied when the selection is made before copying. The partially selected pixels from the background result in the offending fringe of pixels. This also happens with the values reversed—cutting from a dark background and pasting into a light one. Being very careful when you make your selections helps, but sometime the problem happens no matter how careful you are. The Layer | Matting menu (see Figure 10-45) provides three potential solutions:

Defringe Photoshop replaces the outermost edge pixels with pixels closer to the interior. The dialog box will prompt you to set the depth that Photoshop uses to choose the interior replacement pixels.

Remove Black Matte Choose this to remove black pixels along an edge where the image pixels meet transparent pixels.

Remove White Matte Choose this to remove white pixels along an edge where the image pixels meet transparent pixels.

Remove Black Matte and Remove White Matte are particularly useful for working with stock photography; often, stock photographs are photographed in front of a black or white background.

Understanding Layer Content Transformations

Using Photoshop's Edit | Transform menu enables you to perform common transformations such as scaling and rotation, as well as more exotic transformations like distort and perspective. The Transform menu, shown in Figure 10-46, is your hub for transforming images. When using any transformation on a layer and there are no active selections, the entire layer is transformed.

Most transformations can be applied using bounding box controls in the image window, as shown in Figure 10-47, or by using numerical commands in the options bar as shown in Figure 10-48.

Transformations can cause interpolation to occur within an image. *Interpolation* is the process that Photoshop uses to make up or throw away information and degrades the image quality. This quality loss is usually seen as a blurring of the image. For example, if you scale an image to 50 percent of its original size, Photoshop throws away every other pixel in the image. If you enlarged the image to 200 percent of its original size, Photoshop would have to make up every other pixel in the image. For example, along an edge where a black pixel originally butted up against a white pixel, a new gray pixel would be created between the two—so what was originally a sharp edge where black and white met is now a softer edge, making the transition between the two colors seem less extreme.

Figure 10-46.   *The Edit | Transform menu enables you to apply transformations such as Scale or Rotate.*

Figure 10-47. *When applying transformations you can do it manually using bounding box handles.*

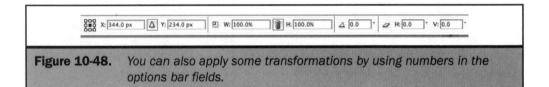

Figure 10-48. *You can also apply some transformations by using numbers in the options bar fields.*

 You can use the Unsharp Mask filter to compensate for the quality loss caused by interpolation. Be sure not to oversharpen, which can produce worse quality problems than interpolation.

Using Scaling

If you choose the Scale command from the Edit | Transform menu, a bounding box will appear surrounding the layers image pixels. This bounding box will have handles, small rectangles, in each of its four side and its four corners. You can scale the image by clicking and dragging any of the handles. If you want to scale the image proportionally so there is no distortion, you can constrain the scaling by holding down the SHIFT key while dragging one of the corner handles. Dragging one of the side handles will either scale the image horizontally or vertically. Press the RETURN key, or double-click inside the transform box, to complete the transformation.

Alternatively, you can type directly into the height and width fields in the options bar as shown in Figure 10-48. Keep the same percentage for both height and width to prevent horizontal or vertical distortion.

The ESCAPE key will cancel the transformation. This works for all transformations.

Rotating Layers

Rotation is another commonly used transformation that works in a very similar manner to scaling. Choosing Rotate from the Edit | Transform menu causes the bounding box and its handles to appear. Moving your cursor outside the bounding box, clicking, and then dragging should rotate the image to any amount you desire.

 Holding down the SHIFT key while rotating an image will constrain the rotation to 45-degree increments.

The options bar provides an alternative number-based method of performing a rotation. The advantage to this method is that you can control the precise number of degrees that you want to rotate.

You can get more out of Rotating by setting the center of the rotation. As shown in Figure 10-49, the darkened reference point on the matrix icon corresponds to a point of images bounding box. For example, clicking on and darkening the bottom-right corner point in the matrix icon would cause any transformations to be centered on the image's bottom-right corner. Rotate the image, and it will rotate around its bottom-right corner. Alternatively, you can set the center of the rotation by dragging the crosshair (target) that appears in the center of the transform box to a new location either inside or outside of the box. This crosshair indicates where the rotation or other transformation center will be located.

Applying Skew

Skewing, another Edit | Transform command, enables you to slant an image vertically and horizontally. Like Scaling and Rotating, Skewing can be accomplished by either manipulating bounding box handles or by entering information into the fields in the options bar.

Distorting Layers

There are no options bar fields to use when you choose Distort from the Edit | Transform menu. Using Distort will enable you to manipulate the corner-bounding box handles independently of each other. The image can be distorted greatly, which may also produce an equal amount interpolation distortion. You may find the need to compensate for this with the Unsharp Mask filter.

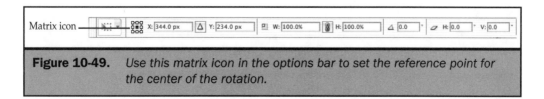

Figure 10-49. *Use this matrix icon in the options bar to set the reference point for the center of the rotation.*

You can use Distort to correct some distortions that occur in photographs. For example, some cameras will make tall buildings look bent. By selecting the building and using Distort, this problem could be corrected.

Using Perspective

Another transformation without any specific options bar features is Perspective. Accessed from the Edit | Transform menu, the Perspective command enables the use of the bounding box handles to create the illusion that the image is mounted on a flat surface that looks like it is receding in space. Manipulating any one of the four corner handles will cause a corresponding handle to move creating a symmetrical distortion. You could use this transformation to create the illusion that a painting is on a wall or that a piece of paper is actually laying on a desktop.

You cannot apply the Distort or Perspective transformations to Text layers without first rasterizing them. Since this will make them unable to be edited, you might want to work on a duplicate layer and make the original layer invisible.

Working with Preset Rotations

Photoshop includes commands, located in the Edit Transform menu, for several frequently used preset amounts of rotation:

- Rotate 180 degrees
- Rotate 90 degrees CW (clockwise)
- Rotate 90 degrees CCW (counterclockwise)

Surprisingly, these three amounts of rotation, unlike any other amounts, do not cause any interpolation to occur. When using these commands there is no need to compensate by using the Unsharp Mask filter.

Using Horizontal and Vertical Flipping

Images can be flipped across either a horizontal or vertical axis by using the command in the Edit | Transform menu. This fairly common function is used to show things like reflections and is often performed on a duplicated Image layer.

Duplicating and flipping layers can be very useful when creating new images. Many things we deal with in everyday life are bisymmetrical—that is, one side of the object is reflected across an axis to create an identical second side. For example, to create the image of a tree leaf, you could paint one half of the leaf on its own layer, then duplicate the layer and flip it across a vertical axis to create the other half of the leaf. The layers could be repositioned and then merged to create a perfectly bisymmetrical leaf.

Understanding the Again Command

The Again command from the Edit | Transform menu applies the last transformation used during the current work session. This can be used to process multiple images quickly and uniformly.

Using the Free Transform Command

The Edit menu's Free Transform command enables you to perform multiple transformations using only one command. This is a great time saver in situations where you have to apply more than one transformation.

You can use Free Transform to:

Scale   Drag any bounding box handle. Hold the SHIFT key down and drag a corner handle to perform a proportional scaling.

Rotate   Move the cursor outside the bounding box but within the image window, click, and drag in an arc.

Skew   Hold down the ALT/OPTION key, click, and drag one of the side handles on the bounding box.

Flip   Hold down the CTRL/COMMAND key and click on a bounding box handle, and drag across the image.

Summary

In this chapter, you have been introduced to the Layers palette and the Layer menu, and you have seen how they function and work together to create, organize, and manage layers. You've learned about the various types of layers, including Image, Text, Adjustment, and Shape Layers. You've learned how to create and work with these different layer types. Applying Blending Modes, styles, and masks to create special effects has been discussed. You've also learned how to manage and organize your layers and transform them to control how they will display.

BUILDING ORIGINAL
ARTWORK

The Complete Reference

Chapter 11

Adding Shapes to Photoshop Creations

P rior to Photoshop's version 6, you had to use the Marquee tool to draw shapes—you'd select an area and click inside it with the Paint Bucket. Then the shape (either a rectangle or a circle) would be filled with the current Foreground color. Now, however, you have a much stronger and more varied set of tools at your disposal for creating shapes. In this chapter, you'll learn how to create the shapes, and in the next chapter, you'll learn how to fill them.

Working with Closed Shapes

Even if most of your work in Photoshop involves retouching and restoring photographs, you'll need to draw shapes—closed geometric or freeform shapes that are filled with color or a pattern of some kind—Figure 11-1 provides an example of a shape that's been added to a photograph. If you're using Photoshop to design web graphics, you probably draw quite a few shapes and employ many of the various tools that help you create them: drawing buttons (see Figure 11-2), bars, and backgrounds of virtually any shape or size.

Figure 11-1. *A closed shape can create a frame around your image, which can be filled with a solid color or pattern.*

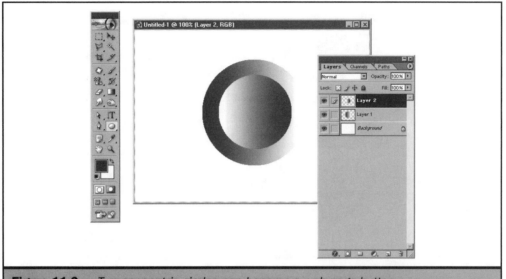

Figure 11-2.   *Two concentric circles can become a web page button.*

Closed shapes are typically filled with a color, although you can use the Pen tool to create a path and apply a stroke (outline) to it and leave the inside empty. The creation of paths was covered in Chapters 5 and 7, and you can refer to those chapters if you need to create closed, yet empty patterns. You can draw empty closed shapes with the Brush and Pencil tools, also. In this chapter, we'll focus on the selection and Shape tools for the creation of closed shapes. In Chapter 12, you'll learn how to change their fill from the Foreground color to any color you want or to any pattern or picture fill you desire.

Of course, you can use the Brush and Pencil tools to draw closed shapes (see Chapter 7). Unlike shapes created with the selection and Shape tools, however, these closed shapes won't be filled—that is, until and unless you click inside them with the Paint Bucket. If you do so and find that there's a separation between the outline and the fill, just click that space and you'll completely fill the shape.

Creating Shapes from Selections

Even though the Shape tool is there in the toolbox, I still often use the Marquee and Lasso tools to create shapes—I can quickly draw rectangles, circles, polygons, or freeform shapes, filling them with color or a pattern or painting inside them for a completely different effect. Figure 11-3 shows some shapes created with the selection tools, each filled with a solid color.

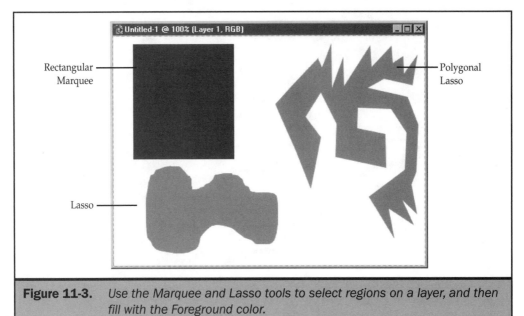

Figure 11-3. *Use the Marquee and Lasso tools to select regions on a layer, and then fill with the Foreground color.*

When you create a selection with the intention of filling it to create a shape, you need to take a few preliminary steps. First, be sure you're on the layer that should contain the shape, even if that means creating a new layer first. Second, if the shape needs to reside on a layer with other content, make sure that you know exactly where you want it to go—if you draw it and then move it, you will move whatever's behind it, leaving a big hole in its wake.

You can draw the selection first, then with the dashed border showing, go to the Layer menu or Layer palette and create and name a new layer. It's only after you fill the shape that its impact on the active layer takes effect. If you do happen to draw and fill your selection on the wrong layer, simply go back in time with the History palette to the point before you filled the selection.

A thorough discussion of all the selection tools (employed for the purpose of selecting image content) is found in Chapter 5.

Creating Shapes with the Marquee Tools

When you activate the Marquee tools, you can accept the default Rectangular Marquee or choose the Elliptical Marquee. The Single Row and Single Column Marquee tools really serve no purpose when it comes to creating closed shapes. Once either the Rectangular or Elliptical Marquee tool is selected, you can draw your shape, as shown in Figure 11-4.

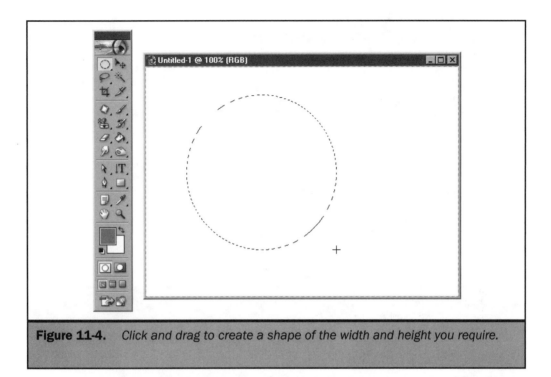

Figure 11-4. *Click and drag to create a shape of the width and height you require.*

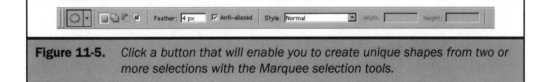

Figure 11-5. *Click a button that will enable you to create unique shapes from two or more selections with the Marquee selection tools.*

You can create interesting shapes by adding to, subtracting from, or intersecting selections. This is done, of course, before you use the Paint Bucket or the Fill command to fill the shape. On the Marquee tools' options bar (shown in Figure 11-5), you can choose how the selection will be made (from left to right). They are as follows:

New Selection   With this option turned on (it's the default), each click of the mouse starts a new selection and gets rid of the current one. Use this one to create a single, simple rectangle or ellipse.

Add to Selection   This option allows you to create multiple selections, and they need not touch. As shown in Figure 11-6, you can create interesting shapes by adding to a selection with a contiguous selection, or by creating a series of isolated selections, each ready to be filled with color.

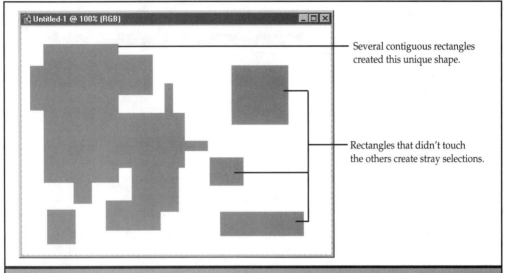

Several contiguous rectangles created this unique shape.

Rectangles that didn't touch the others create stray selections.

Figure 11-6. *Combine or simply accumulate individual selections with the Marquee tools in Add to Selection Mode.*

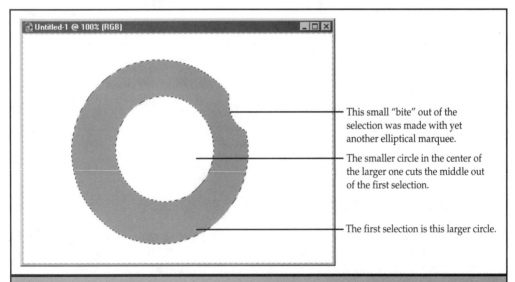

This small "bite" out of the selection was made with yet another elliptical marquee.

The smaller circle in the center of the larger one cuts the middle out of the first selection.

The first selection is this larger circle.

Figure 11-7. *Create a framing selection by subtracting a selection from the center of an existing one.*

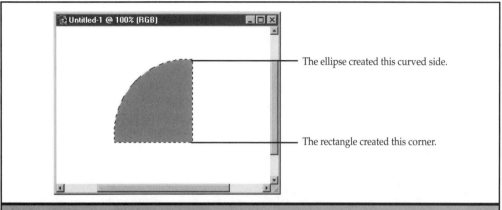

The ellipse created this curved side.

The rectangle created this corner.

Figure 11-8.   *Create interesting shapes by removing all but the intersecting portions of two or more selections.*

Subtract from Selection   Unlike the Add to Selection tool, this selection mode requires that the selections be touching. As shown in Figure 11-7, you can't take a portion of an existing selection away unless the second selected area overlaps it to some degree.

Intersect with Selection   This Marquee Mode allows you to create new shapes from the portions of two or more selections that overlap. Instead of adding to or subtracting from the existing selection(s), just the overlapping portion becomes the selection, and everything else is deselected. Figure 11-8 shows the selection result of selecting a rectangular area and then intersecting that selection with an ellipse that overlaps on the lower-right corner of the rectangle.

Tip   *To draw a perfect square or circle with the Marquee tools, press and hold the SHIFT key as you drag to draw the selection.*

Drawing Shapes with the Lasso Tool

The Lasso selection tools are great for creating selections that become shapes, because the tools give you so much more freedom than the Marquee tools do. Instead of simple geometric shapes and complex adding to/subtracting from schemes, you can simply draw the selection that creates the closed and filled shape you want.

The only Lasso tool that you might not use as often to create selections that become shapes is the Magnetic Lasso. It requires existing content on the same layer in order to work—you trace around something, and the difference in the colors of the pixels dictates the path of the selection. You can use it to create a shape by tracing content on one layer; then just prior to filling it with a color or pattern, you can add a new layer so the content you traced is never affected by the new shape. You can obscure it if the layer containing the shape is visible, but moving the shape won't destroy the content under it.

Drawing Freeform Selections with the Lasso

To draw freeform shapes with the Lasso tool, simply click and begin dragging. The mouse button should be held down during the entire process (until you close the shape, as shown in Figure 11-9); doing so ensures there are no straight sides or angles in the shape.

Unlike a path that you draw with the Pen tool, you can't edit the line that becomes a Lasso-created shape. If you don't like the selection you've drawn with the Lasso tool, you can start over by pressing CTRL-D (Windows) or COMMAND-D (Mac), which will deselect. Note that the Lasso tools' options bar includes the same New Selection, Add to Selection, Subtract from Selection, and Intersect with Selection buttons that the Marquee tools' options bar offered. You can use these to create selections such as those shown in Figure 11-10, which includes selections created by using the Marquee and Lasso tools together (in Add to Selection mode), center sections carved out with the Subtract from Selection mode used, and a new selection created by combining two intersecting selections (with the Intersect with Selection option).

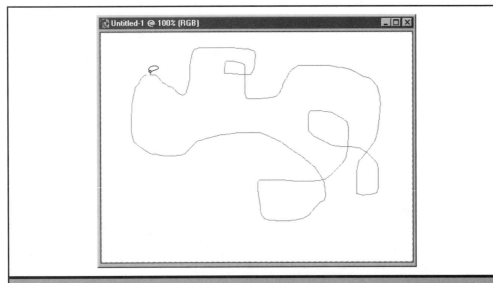

Figure 11-9.   *A freeform selection created with the Lasso can include loops—areas that won't be filled when a color or pattern is applied to the selection.*

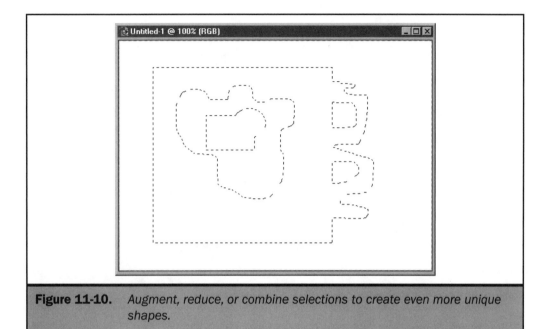

Figure 11-10.   *Augment, reduce, or combine selections to create even more unique shapes.*

As indicated in Figure 11-10, you can combine selections made with two different tools. As long as you don't have the New Selection option turned on, you can go from the Marquee tools to the Lasso tools, adding to, subtracting from, or intersecting your selections. This makes it possible to create both simple geometric and imaginative, freeform selections. You can also switch between the four selection modes as you work on your selections. If you started out in New Selection mode and realize you want to add to, subtract from, or intersect another selection, simply click the appropriate mode button before clicking your mouse again to start the next part of the selection.

You can also press the SHIFT *key while in New Selection mode to quickly switch to Add to Selection mode, and select additional contiguous and noncontiguous areas.*

Drawing Straight-Sided Selections with the Polygonal Lasso

This selection tool makes it possible to create very complex, angular shapes—much more interesting than anything you can easily create with the Custom Shape tool and its drop-down list of shapes. Figure 11-11 shows a shape you can create only with the Polygonal Lasso.

Figure 11-11. *As many sides as you want, of any length, and at any angle—that's the freedom the Polygonal Lasso gives you.*

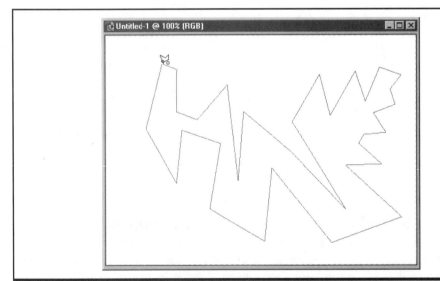

Figure 11-12. *Come home to your beginnings to bring your selection to a close.*

To draw a shape with the Polygonal Lasso, just activate the tool and click on the image window to start your selection. Of course, you want to make sure you're on the right layer (or stop and create a new one if needed) before you fill the shape using the Paint Bucket or the Fill command. (Using the Layer | New Fill Layer command will create a new layer for you.) The process of creating the selection requires simple clicking and moving the mouse. Each click of the mouse creates a corner, and the next move creates a side of the selection. When you're ready to close the shape, come back to the starting point and look for the tiny circle next to the cursor—this tells you that your last click will close the selection, as shown in Figure 11-12.

All of the selection tools—the Marquees and Lassos—offer a Feather option on their options bars. This allows you to add a diffused edge to the selection, which affects the way the fill color or pattern looks when it's applied to the selection. Instead of having a crisp, clean edge, the shape will have a soft edge—the degree of softness and diffusion dictated by the pixel level set in the Feather text box. The higher the number, the more diffused the edges will be.

Drawing Shapes with the Shape Tool

When you choose any one of the five Shape tools that create closed shapes (the Line tool doesn't, obviously), you can choose how that shape will appear in your image—on its own specialized layer as a shape, as a filled region on any layer you choose or create yourself, or as a path.

We won't be discussing paths here, as their primary use is not to create closed shapes. But you can find out about them in Chapter 5.

Figure 11-13 shows the full set of Shape tools.

The two options for drawing shapes that we will be discussing here create very different results—not solely in terms of the appearance of the shape itself, but in terms of the role the shape plays within the image. You can choose which mode you'll work in by clicking the buttons shown in Figure 11-14. You'll find them on the options bar as soon as you choose any of the Shape tools.

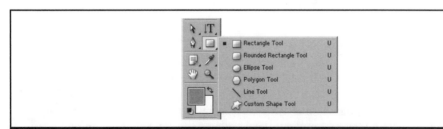

Figure 11-13. *You have five choices for the type of shape you want to create: Rectangle, Rounded Rectangle, Ellipse, Polygon, and Custom.*

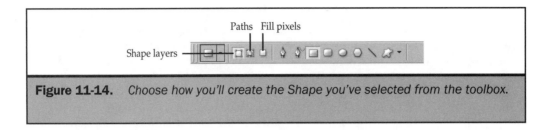

Figure 11-14. *Choose how you'll create the Shape you've selected from the toolbox.*

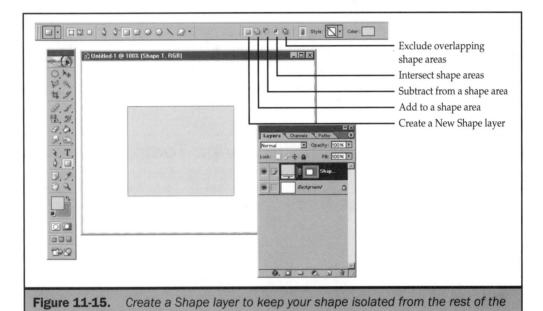

Figure 11-15. *Create a Shape layer to keep your shape isolated from the rest of the image layers.*

Shapes drawn with vector masks (using the Shape tool to create a Shape layer) will print with clean, sharp edges. Shapes created by filling selections or using the Fill Pixels option for a Shape tool will print at the resolution of the rest of the image.

Creating New Shape Layers

Shape Layers mode does three things as soon as you click your mouse and draw the shape: First, it creates the shape. The shapes outline is stored as a vector mask, and the mode then links the mask to a Shape layer. Figure 11-15 shows a new shape and its Shape layer on the Layers palette, and the Shape options bar is also displayed. Shape layers have some restrictions that make them harder to work with: you can't add anything else to the layer, and you can't erase any part of the shape. However, you can use the shape layer tools (also shown and described in Figure 11-15) to add to, subtract from, and create new shapes based on overlapping shapes.

You also have to work with the Layers palette to change the color of the shape. You can't use the Fill Bucket to change the color to a newly selected Foreground color. There is the convenience of having the shape appear on its own layer automatically, though; if you're building an image shape by shape, you may find this approach to be the most logical, preventing the accidental grouping of shapes on the same layer.

A full discussion of layers is found in Chapter 10, where you'll discover all the components of the Layers palette and Layers menu, as well as how to use these features and commands in your Photoshop creations.

Drawing Filled Regions

This option's tool tip appears as "Fill pixels" on the Shape options bar, as shown in Figure 11-16. When you use this option to draw a shape with the Shape tool, the shape you draw appears on the active layer and will be filled with the current Foreground color automatically. You can refill it with another color, a gradient, or a pattern fill by clicking inside it with the Paint Bucket, and you can use the Blending Options dialog box to apply special effects such as shadows, glows, and embossing. The shape you create with this option can be easily edited, as long as it's alone on the layer or not touching other layer content. If the shape overlaps other content on the same layer, you'll have to select the shape with one of the selection tools in order to apply a new fill color. Because there is no automatically created Shape layer added when you use this option, you have to remember to create a layer for the shape should it need to be on its own layer.

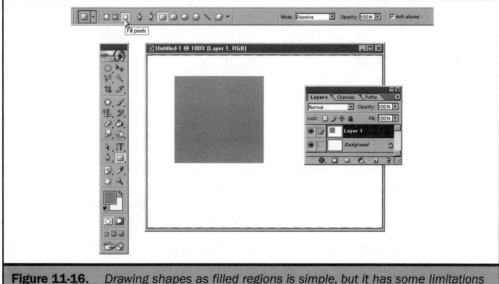

Figure 11-16.   *Drawing shapes as filled regions is simple, but it has some limitations as well.*

Choosing and Using a Shape Tool

When you realize you need a shape in your image, you probably know what shape you need—a square or rectangle, an ellipse or circle, or one of the Custom Shapes such as a heart, a checkmark, an arrow, or musical notes. When you're ready to add the shape, click the Shape tool's triangle to display the full palette of tools, and then click the one you want.

Once the tool is selected, you can make the aforementioned choice as to how the tool will work (creating a Shape layer or a filled region) and begin drawing. The technique for using all of the Shape tools is the same: click and drag diagonally. The starting point for your click should be the upper corner of the shape, and you'll drag down to dictate the shape's width and height. Don't worry if you don't get the perfect size right off the bat—you can easily resize the shape, or simply choose Edit | Undo or press CTRL/COMMAND-Z to get rid of the undesirable shape. Figure 11-17 shows a rectangle in progress.

Another thing that all shapes have in common is that they give you the ability to draw them in proportion, keeping the width and height equal. To draw a shape with equal height and width, simply press the SHIFT key as you drag. The key (pardon the expression) is to release the mouse or other pointing device *before* you release the SHIFT key. If you release the key first, the shape will snap to the proportions it would have had had you not been holding the SHIFT key at all.

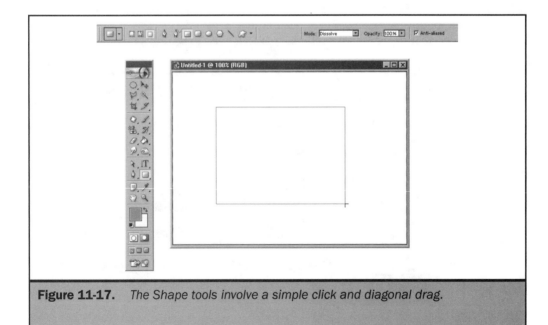

Figure 11-17. *The Shape tools involve a simple click and diagonal drag.*

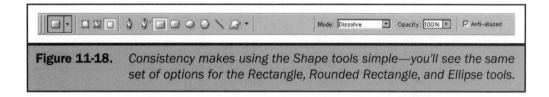

Figure 11-18.   *Consistency makes using the Shape tools simple—you'll see the same set of options for the Rectangle, Rounded Rectangle, and Ellipse tools.*

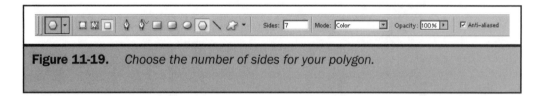

Figure 11-19.   *Choose the number of sides for your polygon.*

The Rectangle, Rounded Rectangle, and Ellipse tools all work the same way—the options bars for each of them look the same, except for the first button. They include Blending Mode, Opacity, and Anti-Aliased options, as you can see in Figure 11-18. The two Shape tools that offer additional functionality are the Polygon and Custom Shape tools. Their options bars offer you the ability to choose the shape you'll draw, giving you the potential for a new shape virtually every time you use the tools.

Drawing Polygons

When you activate the Polygon tool, a new button appears on the tool options bar—a Sides button (see Figure 11-19). The default setting is 5 sides. If left in effect, the setting of 5 sides will allow you to draw pentagons of any width or height. To reduce or increase the number of sides, simply click in the box and use the UP ARROW and DOWN ARROW keys on your keyboard, or type a new number directly.

Technically, a polygon is any multisided geometric shape. You might be confused when comparing the Polygon tool to something like the Polygonal Lasso. While the Polygon tool can be used to create regimented geometric shapes (like triangles and octagons), it is also capable of drawing shapes of any size, with any number of sides, and none of the sides need to be the same length or parallel or at certain angles to each other. The Polygon tool creates only standard geometric shapes with sides of the same length, and in the case of shapes with more than three sides, at least two of the sides will be parallel.

Obviously, if you set the Polygon tool to a setting of 4 in the Sides box, you'll draw a rectangle (or a square if you hold the SHIFT key as you draw). Better to use the tool for drawing triangles (3 sides), hexagons (6 sides), octagons (8 sides), and so on. Figure 11-20 shows an octagon in progress.

BUILDING ORIGINAL
ARTWORK

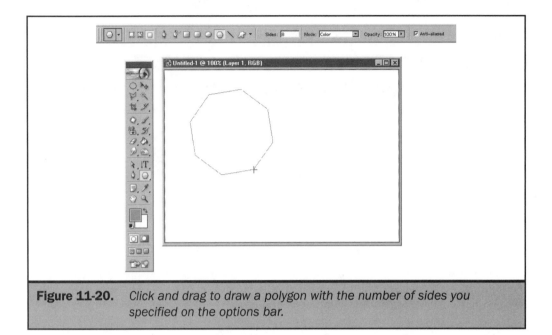

Figure 11-20. Click and drag to draw a polygon with the number of sides you specified on the options bar.

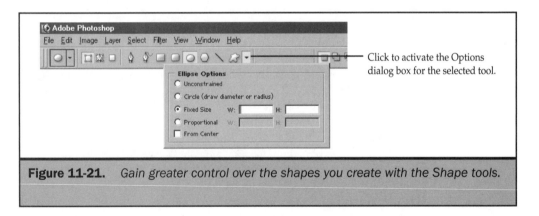

Click to activate the Options dialog box for the selected tool.

Figure 11-21. Gain greater control over the shapes you create with the Shape tools.

When drawing polygons, you can spin them into the right position before you release the mouse and fill the shape—just drag the mouse in a circle until the shape is rotated to the angle you prefer.

For each of the Shape tools, there is an Options dialog box that appears when you click the triangle to the right of the Custom Shape tool on the options bar (see Figure 11-21). The box offers settings for controlling the size and proportions of the shape and allows you to draw it from the center, rather than from a corner of the shape-to-be.

Working with the Custom Shape Tool

The Custom Shape tool allows you to choose from a series of more than 70 shapes, accessible through the Shape drop-down list that appears on the tool options bar when you activate the Custom Shape tool. Figure 11-22 shows the entire list of shapes after the drop-down list was resized (by dragging it by its lower-right corner).

Note that there's an option menu button on the right corner of the Shape drop-down list. This button opens a menu through which you can choose how the shapes will appear in the drop-down list, and to work with shape presets. You can also choose from a list of shape categories. Figure 11-23 shows the Custom Shape tool options menu, and the default Small Thumbnail setting for shape display in effect.

If you typically use only some of the shapes and don't want to be distracted by the others, right-click/CONTROL-click the shapes you don't want to see and choose Delete Shape from the context menu that appears. Once the displayed list of shapes only includes the ones you want to see, choose Save Shapes from the options menu and name the new group of shapes. After that, you can use the Load Shapes command to load the set you saved, and you'll see only the shapes you want to choose from.

You can create your own custom shapes by drawing a path with the Pen tool and then using the Edit | Define Custom Shape command. You can then name the shape you've just drawn and see it added to the palette of Custom Shapes the next time you use that particular Shape tool. Read more about drawing paths in Chapter 5.

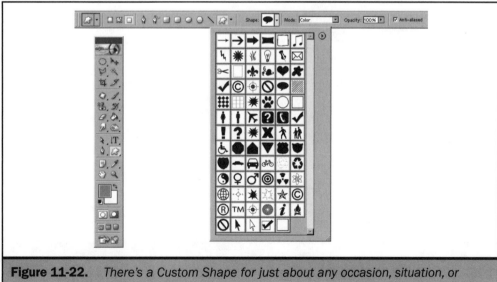

Figure 11-22.   *There's a Custom Shape for just about any occasion, situation, or editing need.*

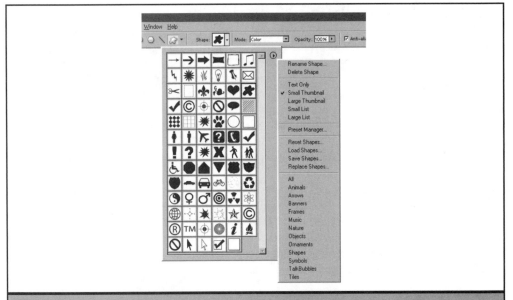

Figure 11-23. *Choose how and when you'll see Custom Shapes in the Shape drop-down list.*

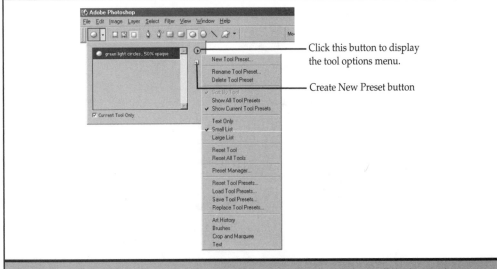

Figure 11-24. *Click the tool button on the options bar, and then click the options menu button to access more tool-related features.*

Setting and Saving Shape Tool Options

The first button on any Shape tool's options bar is the tool itself. You can click the triangle to the right of the button to display and choose any tool presets and to access the tool's options menu, as shown in Figure 11-24.

From this menu, you can choose how the tool's presets are displayed, create new presets, or return the tool to a default state. You may recognize these preset-related commands from your use of brushes and swatches (covered in Chapters 6 and 7), so this concept is probably not new to you.

The concept of creating new tool presets was covered in Chapter 1, which discussed what's new in Photoshop 7, and in Chapter 2, where you learned about the Photoshop interface. For our purposes here, the presets you create can make it easy to create shapes that have the same Mode, Opacity, and Anti-aliasing settings. If you'll be creating several shapes in the same image and you want them all to use the Dissolve Blending Mode, have an Opacity of 39 percent, and have anti-aliasing on, you can put those settings into effect, and then choose New Tool Preset from the tool options menu; or you can click the Create New Preset button. Once you've made this selection, a dialog box appears asking you to name your new preset. Be sure to give it a name that will make sense to you later, such as "Dissolving See-Through Boxes," as shown in Figure 11-25.

After you've named and saved your new preset, you'll see it in the tool palette, and also in the Tool Presets palette. Figure 11-26 shows the Dissolving See-Through Boxes preset in both locations.

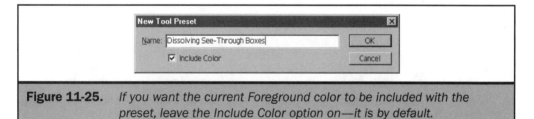

Figure 11-25.   *If you want the current Foreground color to be included with the preset, leave the Include Color option on—it is by default.*

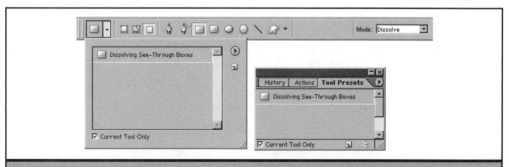

Figure 11-26.   *While the tool is in use, you can grab one of your presets from the tool's option button or from the Tool Presets palette.*

If you want to see all of your tools' presets in one place, uncheck the Current Tool Only box at the bottom of the Tool Presets dialog box.

To use your preset, simply click it in either the tool options box, or on the Tool Presets palette. Instantly, the settings you saved will be put into effect. If you elected to include the Foreground color (the one in use at the time you saved the preset), the Foreground color changes as well. Once these settings are in place, you can draw your shape. You'll know it will look just like those drawn previously with that preset—other than the size and proportion of the shape, that is; those aspects are completely unique each time you draw with the tool.

If you've created a preset for one Shape tool and wish to apply its settings to another Shape tool, simply choose the preset for the tool you created it for (after activating that tool to gain access to the preset, assuming Current Tool Only, the default, is currently checked). Then change to the tool you want to draw with now—you can choose it from the toolbox or from the options bar. The settings that were put in place by activating the preset for the earlier Shape tool will remain in effect for the second one you pick, except for the Mode— that you'll have to choose manually if you're using the Fill Pixels option for the Shape tool. Once you've done so, you can save a preset for the current tool (such as Dissolving See-Through Circles), and then you'll have the same settings for both tools.

Summary

In this chapter, you learned to draw shapes using the selection tools and the various Shape tools. In addition to drawing the shapes, you learned how to add them to layers and how to create shape layers that contain nothing but the shape. You also learned to create tool presets for the Shape tools so that you can draw consistent shapes throughout one or more images.

The Complete Reference

Chapter 12

Using Fills and Styles to Enhance Shapes and Layers

S o you've drawn a shape and now it's filled with a solid color, which may be exactly what you wanted. If, however, your image calls for something that's more visually interesting than a solid color fill, Photoshop has several options for you to choose from. You can apply gradients, patterns, and styles to your shapes. You can also use special layer style options to add shadows, glows, and 3-D embossed effects to your shapes and other layer content. In this chapter, you'll learn to apply these tools and customize them to meet your specific needs.

Filling Shapes with the Paint Bucket

Probably the simplest way to fill a shape with a solid color is to use the Paint Bucket to apply the Foreground color. If you drew your shape with the Shape tool, the Foreground color was automatically applied to the shape, and you don't have to do anything else, unless you want a different color from the Foreground color. If you drew your shape with one of the selection tools—the Marquee or Lasso tools—then you can use the Paint Bucket (or the Fill command) to fill the selection with color.

The trick to using the Paint Bucket lies in the preparation. When you use the Paint Bucket to fill a shape, selection, or layer, it applies the currently selected Foreground color (see Figure 12-1). Therefore, before you use the Paint Bucket, be sure to select a color for the Foreground. Choose either the Color Picker (which opens when you click the Foreground color button) or the Eyedropper tool to select a color that's onscreen at the time—a color from within the image, the Photoshop desktop, or any other application space that's visible onscreen.

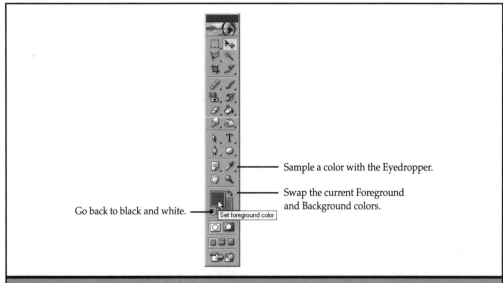

Figure 12-1.   *Click the Foreground color button to open the Color Picker.*

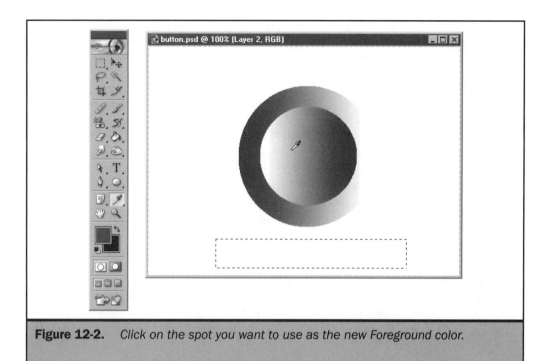

Figure 12-2.   *Click on the spot you want to use as the new Foreground color.*

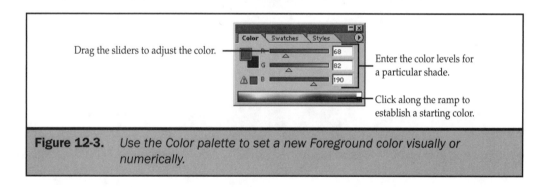

Figure 12-3.   *Use the Color palette to set a new Foreground color visually or
numerically.*

If there's a color already in use somewhere in your image and you want to apply it
to your shape, you can use the Eyedropper to sample that color (see the tool in use in
Figure 12-2). Alternatively, you can use the Color palette to set up a color, using the
sliders, color levels, or the color ramp, as shown in Figure 12-3.

How do you choose whether to use the Eyedropper or the Color palette? It depends
on what you know about the color you want to use. If you can see the color you want
right there in your image (or elsewhere in the workspace), you can quickly and simply
click it with the Eyedropper. However, if you know, for example, the RGB levels of the
color (perhaps it will be used in a web graphic, so you've selected a color you know to

be web-safe), entering those levels into the Color palette may be the way to go. If you do use the Eyedropper and want to adjust the selected color slightly, you can use the Color palette to do so, entering new color levels or dragging the color sliders to add or remove components of the color.

When you use the Eyedropper (which you can switch to quickly by pressing ALT (Windows) or OPTION (Mac) while any other tools is active), the Color palette reflects the color of the sample, displaying the color's RGB, CMYK, HSB, Grayscale, Lab, or Web Color levels— whichever you've elected to view through the Color palette's options menu.

Once you've used either the Color Picker, the Color palette, or the Eyedropper to establish a Foreground color, select the Paint Bucket to apply the color. You can click inside a shape you've drawn on any layer, or inside a selection you've made with the selection tools. Figure 12-4 shows the Paint Bucket spilling color into a rectangle created with the Marquee tool.

If you select an area that currently has other colors or patterns within it, the Paint Bucket will not necessarily fill the selection entirely; rather, it will fill an area you click on and fill the surrounding area to the extent that the Paint Bucket's Tolerance setting will allow. You can increase Tolerance to fill more of the area, or reduce it for the opposite effect.

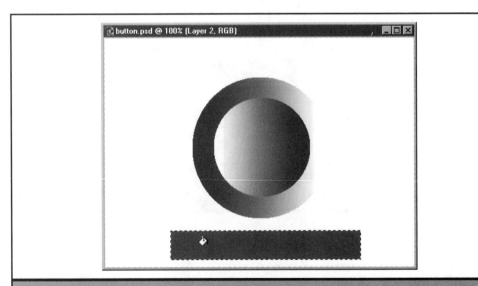

Figure 12-4. *Click inside the selection to fill it with color.*

If you want to change the color of a shape on a Shape layer, you can't click inside it with the Paint Bucket. An error prompt will tell you that the content is not directly editable (see Figure 12-5). To change the fill color of a Shape layer's shape, double-click the shape's thumbnail (see Figure 12-6), which opens the Color Picker. From there, you can select the color you want to use for the fill. When you click OK to close the Color Picker dialog box, the color you chose will fill the shape.

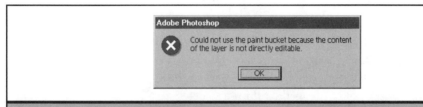

Figure 12-5.   *The Paint Bucket can't spill paint onto a Shape layer.*

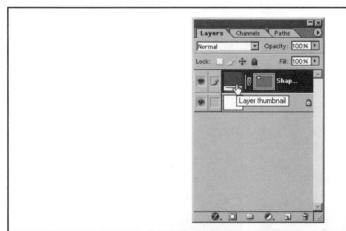

Figure 12-6.   *Double-click the Shape layer's thumbnail to open the Color Picker.*

Applying Pattern Fills and Styles to Shapes and Layers

When a solid color isn't what you need, a pattern fill or style might be more appropriate. As shown in Figure 12-7, filling a rectangle with a style can instantly create the look of a button, which would be useful if you're designing for the Web. Likewise, a pattern fill can create a variety of effects, from abstract to realistic. You can apply patterns from the Paint Bucket's options bar, and you can apply styles from the Styles palette.

Applying Pattern Fills

When the Paint Bucket tool is active, the options bar offers a Pattern button, shown in Figure 12-8. When you click the triangle to display the pop-up palette of patterns, you can choose the one you want to use as the fill for a selected area or a shape that's not on a Shape layer.

If you want to apply a pattern to a shape that you've created with the Shape tools (using the Fill Pixels option), choose the pattern first. Select the Paint Bucket, select a pattern in the options bar, and then draw your shape on the active layer.

Figure 12-7. Use a fill style to create a button (on the right), and a fill pattern to create a box of river rocks (on the left).

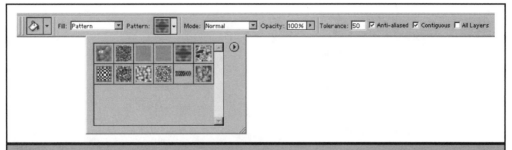

Figure 12-8.   Click the Pattern pop-up palette to choose the fill for a selection or shape.

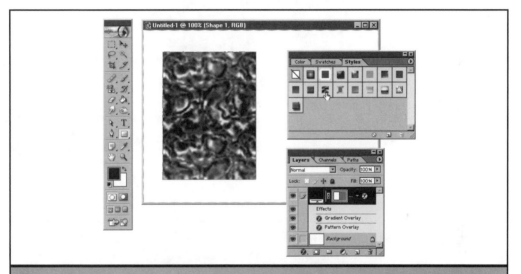

Figure 12-9.   The Styles palette offers a series of several interesting textures and patterns you can apply to Shape layers.

BUILDING ORIGINAL
ARTWORK

If you want to apply a shape to a Shape layer, you can use the Styles palette and simply click on the style you want. This, of course, requires that the Shape layer be active first, so that it's clear to which shape you want the pattern applied. Figure 12-9 shows the Styles palette and a pattern applied to a Shape layer.

You can add more patterns to the pop-up palette by clicking the Pattern options menu (see Figure 12-10). Choose one of the listed pattern preset groups, and then choose to replace the presets you have showing now or append the new group to the existing one. You can also delete and rearrange the presets in the Pattern pop-up palette, and then save that customized grouping by choosing Save Patterns from the options menu.

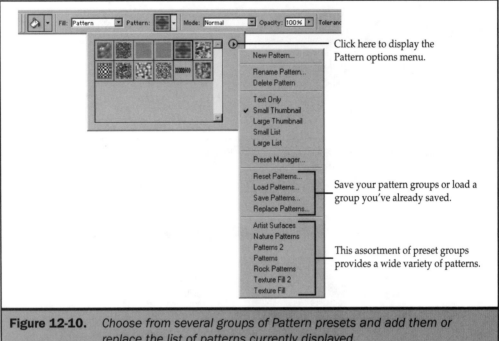

Click here to display the Pattern options menu.

Save your pattern groups or load a group you've already saved.

This assortment of preset groups provides a wide variety of patterns.

Figure 12-10. *Choose from several groups of Pattern presets and add them or replace the list of patterns currently displayed.*

The Pattern presets work very much like Brush presets. You can save customized groups, load those groups, and, if and when you want to go back to the default set, choose Reset Patterns.

Working with the Styles Palette

The Styles palette offers a list of preset fills, with names like Color Target, Nebula, and Puzzle. They're very similar to the patterns you can apply through the Paint Bucket's Pattern pop-up palette, but they generally lend themselves to a shape—some have beveled edges (see the Glass Button styles in Figure 12-11). You can apply these styles to shapes as well as to an entire layer. To apply a style to a shape, select the shape and then click the style you want in the Styles palette. If you want to fill a layer with one of the styles, simply click the layer to activate it in the Layers palette, and then click a style from the Styles palette. As soon as you click a style, activate the Paint Bucket, and then click the layer. Assuming nothing else is on that layer and there is no selection in place (which would restrict the area to be filled to that selection), the entire layer will be filled with the selected style, as shown in Figure 12-12. If the layer is not empty, a style can be applied quickly and simply when you click on another style in the Styles palette.

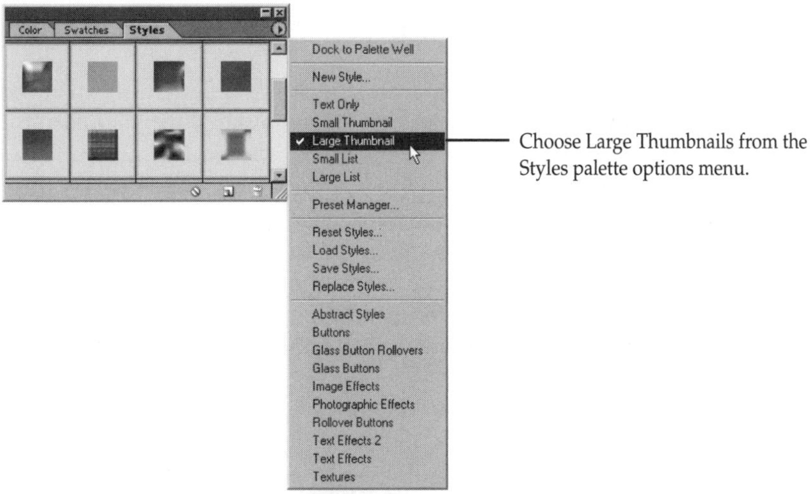

Choose Large Thumbnails from the
Styles palette options menu.

Figure 12-11.   *Set to be displayed in Large Thumbnail size, the Styles palette offers
some interesting fills that you can apply to shapes or layers.*

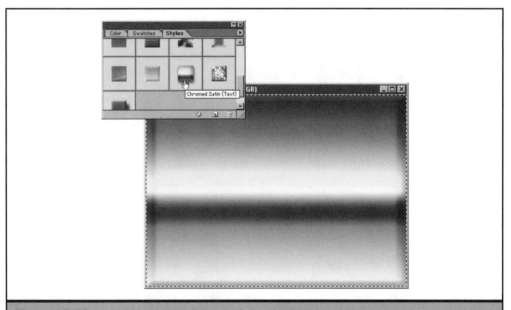

Figure 12-12.   *Apply a preset Fill style from the Styles palette.*

In order for a layer's fill to show, the layer must be above other layers in terms of stacking order, or those above it must be transparent.

Much the same as Brush and Pattern presets, the Styles palette offers a variety of preset groups that you can display in the palette and apply to your shapes and layers. You can choose different groups from the Palette options menu (shown in Figure 12-13), and you can display the groups together in the palette or choose to display the groups one at a time. If you find that you want to see and apply just a small group of styles, right-click/CONTROL-click the ones you don't want and choose Delete Style. Once the group is distilled down to just the styles you want, choose Save Styles from the Palette options menu and give the new .asl file a relevant name. Once the file is saved, you can load your custom set of styles at any time with the Load Styles command from the same options menu.

You can also create your own styles by customizing an existing style. Apply drop shadows, glows, bevel and emboss effects, textures—any of the Blending Options found in the Layer Styles dialog box. This dialog box is covered later in this chapter, in the "Setting Blending Options" section. Once you've made your shape or layer appear as you want (with the customized style applied), click the Create New Style button at the bottom of the Styles palette, or choose New Style from the Palette options menu. A dialog box appears (see Figure 12-14) through which you can name your style and choose which of its current attributes to save as part of the style itself. Be sure that Include Layer Effects is on if you used the Layer Styles dialog box to apply the special effects to the style. If you applied Blending Options such as drop shadows, textures, or glows, place a checkmark in the Include Layer Blending Options check box as well.

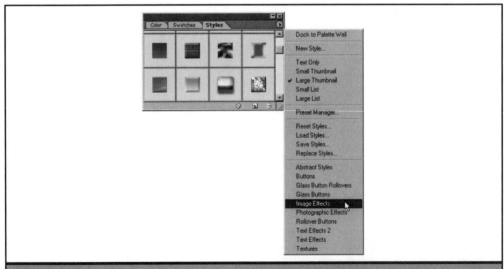

Figure 12-13. *Choose from these 10 groups of style presets and display them in the Styles palette.*

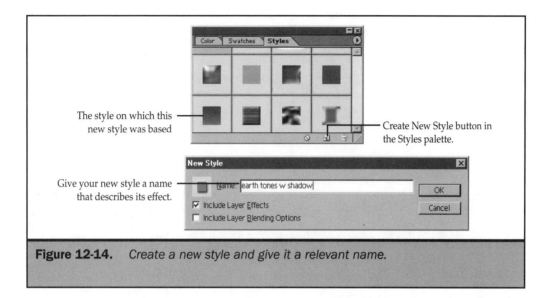

The style on which this new style was based

Create New Style button in the Styles palette.

Give your new style a name that describes its effect.

Figure 12-14.   *Create a new style and give it a relevant name.*

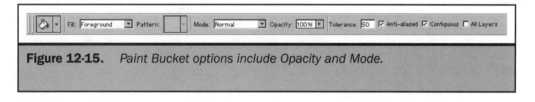

Figure 12-15.   *Paint Bucket options include Opacity and Mode.*

You can paint with a style from the Styles palette, filling in a shape or layer with the Brush tool. Click a style in the Styles palette, and then use the Brush to paint that style wherever you'd like to use it.

Customizing Fills with Opacity and Mode

Your fill colors, patterns, and styles can all be made more or less see-through by adjusting their opacity—you can fill shapes and layers with colors, patterns, or styles, and then make the effect even more interesting by controlling how much you can see through that fill. You can also choose how the color, pattern, or style will be applied by choosing a Blending Mode. If you're working with a solid color or pattern fill, the Paint Bucket's options bar (shown in Figure 12-15) gives you the tools you need to adjust the Opacity and Blending Mode for the fill—100% and Normal are the respective defaults.

If you're working with a Shape layer, you can use the Opacity slider on the Layers palette to set the master opacity—the higher the percentage, the less you'll be able to see through the fill of the layer as a whole. You can also drag the Fill slider to adjust the interior opacity. Figure 12-16 shows these two sliders set to 50% Opacity.

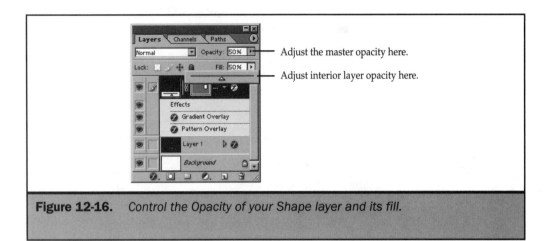

Figure 12-16.   *Control the Opacity of your Shape layer and its fill.*

> **Tip**   *All the Blending Modes and their uses have been discussed in Chapters 7, 10, and 14. You'll find that some of the Modes don't have much of an impact when you use them with patterns and styles from the Styles palette, or that their effects are not the same as they are when you're applying solid colors with the Paint Bucket or Brush tools. To find out what each of the Modes will do with individual styles, experiment and find the effect you're looking for. Combine different styles, Opacity settings, and Blending Modes—it can simply be a matter of discovering the perfect combination of effects that gives you the results you're looking for.*

Understanding the Gradient Tool

The Gradient tool applies two colors—the Foreground and Background colors by default—and makes the Foreground color slowly transition into the Background color. Figure 12-17 shows a black Foreground color transitioning into a white Background color, the fill applied to a wide rectangle.

Customizing a Gradient

The options bar, shown in Figure 12-18, includes a pop-up palette of gradient styles, five different gradient effects, Mode and Opacity settings, and the ability to reverse the direction of the gradient (so that it transitions from Background to Foreground color). You can also set Dither and Transparency settings (both on by default) to control the way the gradient fill works with other content on the same layer and the layer beneath the one containing the gradient.

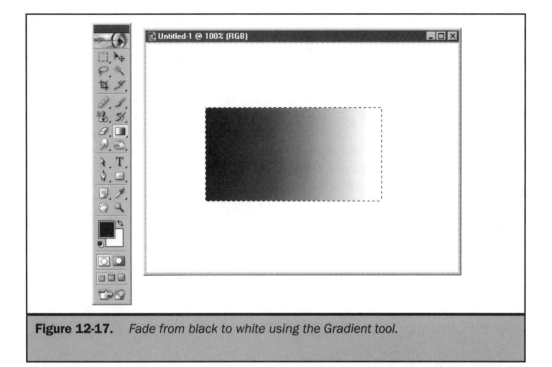

Figure 12-17. *Fade from black to white using the Gradient tool.*

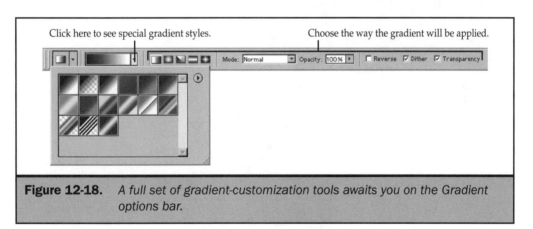

Figure 12-18. *A full set of gradient-customization tools awaits you on the Gradient options bar.*

Working with Special Gradient Styles

When you click the Gradient style pop-up palette, 15 styles appear. These gradient presets include three or more color gradients and very transparent gradient effects (low opacity applied), and you can use the Gradient options menu (see Figure 12-19) to choose from eight more groups of gradient presets.

Applying a Gradient

To apply a gradient (the simple Foreground-to-Background gradient or any of the special Gradient styles), simply select the Gradient tool, select your shape, and then drag across the selection with your pointer. If you want to use a special Gradient style, click on one in the Gradient pop-up palette, and then draw your gradient by dragging from one side of the shape to the other. You can drag from top to bottom, bottom to top, left to right, or right to left. You can also drag diagonally, from any corner or angle across the shape. Figure 12-20 shows a gradient being applied to a circular selection. When you drag, the starting point marks where the Foreground color will begin, and the end point is where the Background color ends. The midpoint along the length that you drag is where the two colors transition.

If you use a special gradient style that includes three or more colors, the colors will be distributed evenly over the distance you dragged to apply the gradient.

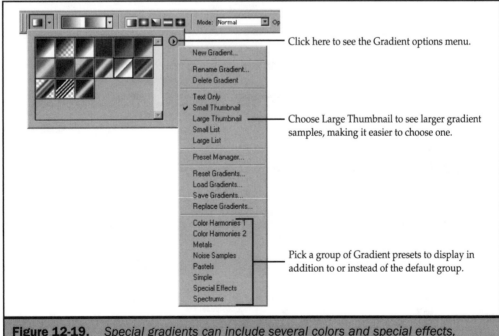

Figure 12-19. *Special gradients can include several colors and special effects, including reduced opacity and metallic finishes.*

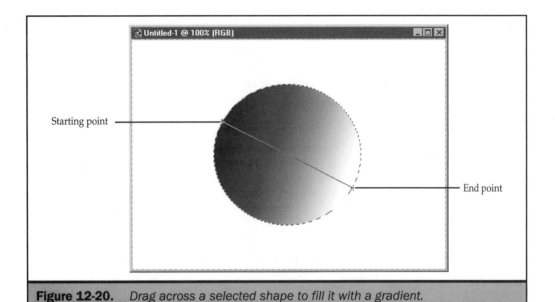

Figure 12-20. *Drag across a selected shape to fill it with a gradient.*

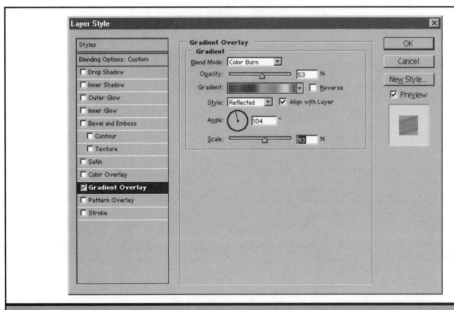

Figure 12-21. *Shape layers require the use of the Layer Style dialog box in order to apply a gradient.*

If you used the Shape tool and created a Shape layer, you can double-click the Vector Mask thumbnail for the Shape layer, and then use the Gradient Overlay option in the Layer Style dialog box (shown in Figure 12-21). You can also click the Layer Style button at the bottom of the Layers palette and choose Gradient Overlay. In either case, you can click the Gradient pop-up palette to choose a style, and use the dialog box options to dictate the way the gradient is applied.

If you drew your shape with the Shape tool and the Fill Pixels setting (on the Shape tool options bar), you can use a selection tool to select the shape before applying the gradient. Assuming the shape is currently filled with a solid color, you can use the Magic Wand to select it in its entirety, and then apply your gradient. You can also click the Lock Transparent Pixels option on the Layers palette, eliminating the need to select the shape first—you can just drag across the shape to apply the gradient.

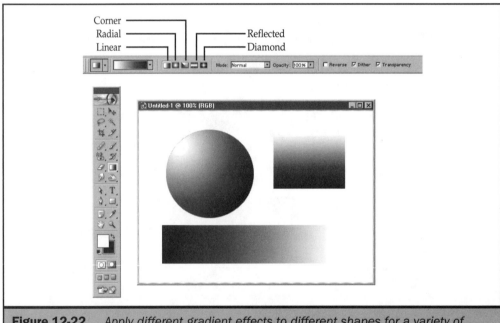

Figure 12-22. *Apply different gradient effects to different shapes for a variety of effects.*

The Linear, Radial, Corner, Reflected, and Diamond gradients allow you to make the gradient fit your shape. Notice in Figure 12-22 how the Radial gradient can make a circle look more like a sphere, and the Linear and Reflected gradients really lend themselves to rectangles and squares.

When using the Diamond gradient, it's a good idea to drag from the outside edge of the shape to the middle and stop dragging there, or to start in the middle of the shape and drag out to an outer edge. If you drag across the entire width or height of the shape, the Diamond effect won't be in the center of the shape. The other gradient effects can also be controlled by the distance you drag to apply the gradient, and the location of your drag. Figure 12-23 shows how the Radial gradient can be used to create a very small bright spot (with a Foreground color that's lighter than the Background color) by dragging a short distance. If you drag the entire width or height of the shape, the gradient effect is more subtle.

The Corner gradient can result in what looks like two solid colors—half of the shape in the Foreground color, and half in the Background. To avoid this effect, drag a very short distance, starting just off-center, in the direction toward where the lighter shade should create the look of light shining on a cone. Figure 12-24 shows the generally undesirable half-and-half effect on one shape, and the more appealing effect on another.

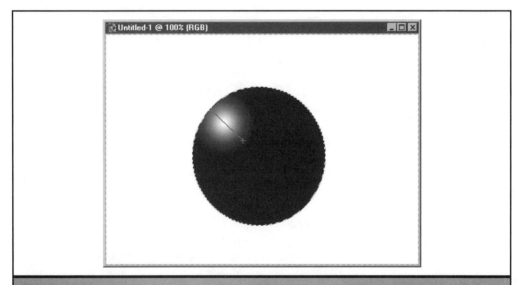

Figure 12-23.   *Drag a short distance to create a more extreme gradient effect.*

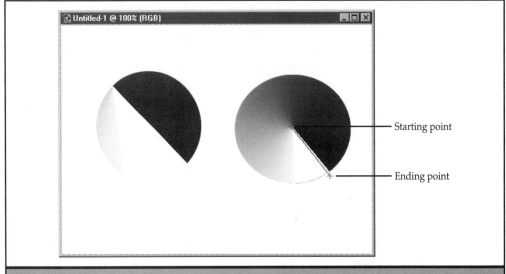

Figure 12-24. *Control the effects of the Corner gradient by dragging a very short distance.*

Working with the Pattern Maker

New to Photoshop 7, the Pattern Maker allows you to take a rectangular selection from within an image and turn it into a tiled pattern, as shown in Figure 12-25. The Filter | Pattern Maker command opens the Pattern Maker dialog box, through which you can select the portion of your open and active image that will serve as the pattern, control the size and proportions of the tiles that make up the pattern, and choose whether or not to place a border around the tiles themselves.

Creating Your Own Patterns

After you issue the Filter | Pattern Maker command, the Pattern Maker dialog box opens, displaying the active image. Figure 12-26 shows the dialog box and a selection in place. The instructions for using the dialog box appear along the top, below the dialog box title bar. These instructions get you started, and from there you can use the dialog box controls to customize the pattern your selection creates.

The original image and the selected area that became a pattern

The resulting pattern, applied to a shape

Figure 12-25. *When repeated over and over, even an insignificant object (or portion thereof) can become an interesting pattern.*

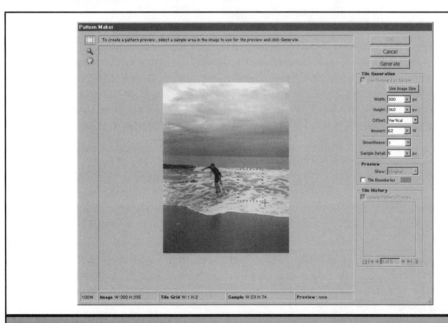

Figure 12-26. *The Pattern Maker dialog box guides you through the process of building a pattern from a selection.*

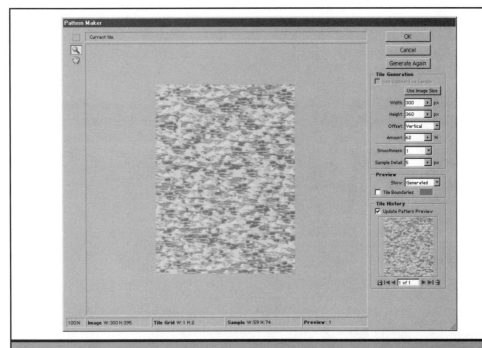

Figure 12-27. *A simple section of your image can create an interesting pattern when the selection is repeated in a series of contiguous tiles.*

As soon as you click the Generate button, the area that formerly contained your active image changes, and the pattern created by repeating your selection as an array of tiles appears (see Figure 12-27).

The controls on the right side of the dialog box become available, and you can now make the following adjustments:

Use Image Size   This makes each tile in the pattern the same size as the original image.

Width   Enter a number here, in pixels, or drag the slider that appears when you click this option.

Height   Works just like Width—enter a number or use the slider to set this half of the tiles' dimensions.

Offset and Amount   The offset is the direction that the tiles run—horizontally or vertically—and this can change the pattern subtly or significantly, depending on the pattern's content. The Amount is the percentage of the tile that runs in the selected Offset direction.

Smoothness   This option can help prevent a tiled look, if you don't want one. A higher Smoothness level reduces obvious edges where the tiles repeat, and a lower level permits some degree of obvious tiling. The need for this option is entirely dependent on the content of your Pattern.

Sample Detail   This option takes the selection and increases the detail that's preserved from it and is made part of the pattern. This can solve the problem of content that was chopped off along the edge of the selection, resulting in odd, incomplete shapes in the pattern.

Preview Show   Switch between seeing the original image and selection within it and the generated pattern.

Tile Boundaries   If you want to see where the tiles begin and end, turn this option on. If desired, click the color box to open the Color Picker and choose another color for the boundaries (the default is bright green). Be sure to pick a boundary color that's not in your pattern so that the boundaries are easier to see. Figure 12-28 shows the boundaries on a pattern in progress.

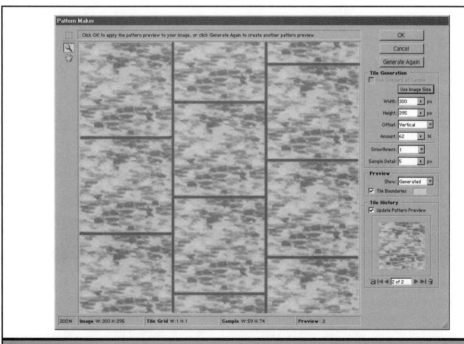

Figure 12-28.   *Tile Boundaries show each tile in the pattern.*

BUILDING ORIGINAL
ARTWORK

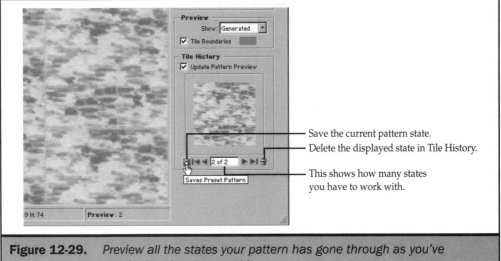

Save the current pattern state.
Delete the displayed state in Tile History.

This shows how many states
you have to work with.

Figure 12-29.   *Preview all the states your pattern has gone through as you've tweaked and regenerated it.*

Saves Preset Pattern   Click this button (shown in Figure 12-29) to bring up the Pattern Name dialog box through which you can name and save your new pattern. You can save as many states as you want, conceivably creating a new pattern each time you click the Generate Again button.

Deletes Tile from History   This trashcan button will delete the Tile History state that's currently displayed in the small preview window.

If you increase Smoothness and Sample Detail significantly, you'll also significantly increase the time it takes to generate the pattern.

As you make changes to any of these settings, the Generate button changes to a Generate Again button, which you can use to update the pattern to reflect your changes. Once you like the pattern, click OK, and the pattern you created fills the active layer in your active image. If you want to be able to use the pattern again, you can click the Save Preset Pattern button at the bottom of the Tile History section of the Pattern Maker dialog box. Alternatively, you can choose Edit | Define Pattern and save the pattern in the resulting Pattern Name dialog box. If you want to set the pattern to a smaller portion of the complete pattern, you can select a rectangular section before issuing the Edit | Define Pattern command, and only the selected area will be included in the new pattern.

Applying Your Patterns

To use a pattern you've created, switch to the Paint Bucket and choose Pattern from the Fill pop-up palette on the tool's options bar. You can also choose Edit | Fill and select

Pattern from the Use menu. This activates the Pattern pop-up palette, which will now contain your named pattern. If you point to the pattern in the pop-up palette, you'll see your pattern's name appear as a screen tip, as shown in Figure 12-30. Click once on your pattern to select it, and then go back and click inside the selection to fill it—your Paint Bucket should still be the active tool. The pattern will also be available through the Layer Style dialog box, through which shapes on Shape layers can be filled with a pattern, as shown in Figure 12-31.

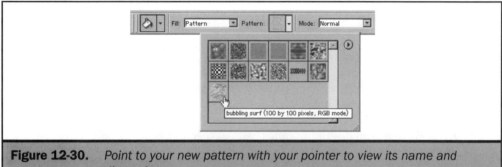

Figure 12-30. *Point to your new pattern with your pointer to view its name and dimensions.*

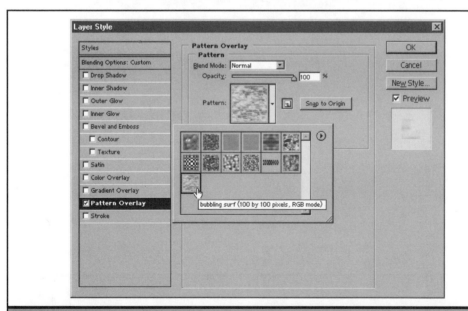

Figure 12-31. *Shape layers can be filled with your new pattern, too—just double-click the Vector Mask thumbnail and use the Pattern Overlay option in the Layer Style dialog box.*

Working with the Layer Style Dialog Box

The same Layer Style dialog box that enables you to apply a pattern to a shape on a Shape layer allows you to customize the look of shapes and layers, by applying shadows, glows, bevel and emboss effects, textures, color overlays, gradients, patterns, and strokes. You can choose these special effects (found in the Blending Options view of the dialog box, shown in Figure 12-32) and save the effects as a new style should you create one that you might reuse somewhere else in the current image or in other images.

Accessing the Layer Style Dialog Box

To open the Layer Style dialog box, double-click any layer's thumbnail or on the vector mask thumbnail on a Shape layer. The only layer that you can't double-click to open the dialog box is the Background—double-clicking the Background's thumbnail will simply open the New Layer dialog box, as Photoshop assumes you want to convert the Background into a layer. Once the dialog box is open, be sure it's set to Blending Options Mode (it should be by default). If it's in Styles Mode (shown in Figure 12-33), you'll have to choose from one of the styles usually seen in the Styles palette and apply Blending Options to it.

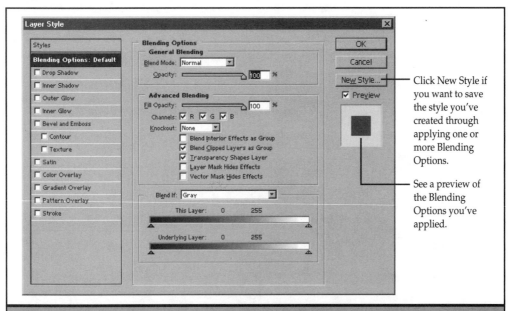

Figure 12-32. The Blending Options in the Layer Style dialog box enable you to make shapes and layers look three-dimensional.

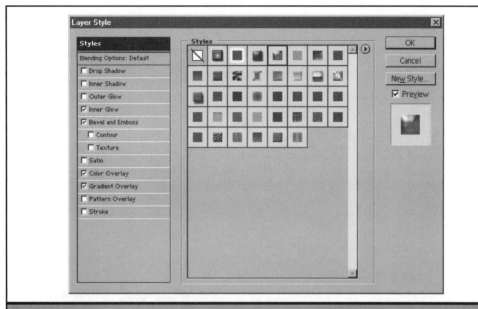

Figure 12-33.   *The Styles view of the Layer Style dialog box displays the last set of styles you chose to view through the Styles palette.*

Setting Blending Options

In Blending Options Mode, the main section of the dialog box (see Figure 12-34) is broken into three sections: General Blending, Advanced Blending, and Blend If. The General Blending section offers a list of Blending Modes, the same ones you worked with when painting with the Brush in Chapter 7. You can also set the Opacity of the Blending Options you have applied or will apply through the dialog box.

The Advanced Blending section offers a Fill Opacity option and gives you the ability to turn color channels on or off (a check box will appear for each color channel in the active image) and apply blending to individual channels. You can also choose Knockout settings (None, Deep, or Shallow) to control how the layer can be used to reveal content below it. The check boxes below the Knockout drop-down list give you further control over this.

If you're not familiar with the term knockout, check Adobe Photoshop's online help (choose Help | Adobe Online) for more information.

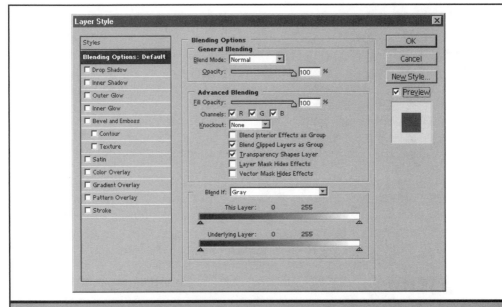

Figure 12-34.   *Establish the overall settings for how the shadows, glows, and other layer effects will be applied.*

Click here to display tools for the selected style.

Use sliders, text boxes, and check boxes to control the effects of the selected style.

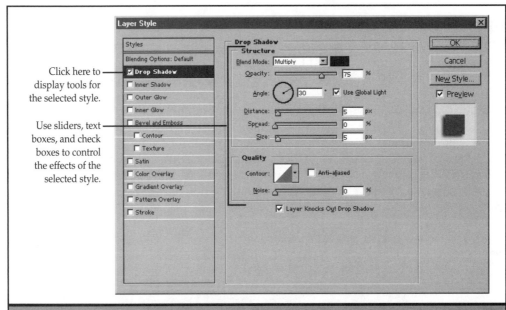

Figure 12-35.   *Each of the 12 styles has its own group of settings. These are the settings for Drop Shadow.*

In the Blend If section, you can choose from Gray and the other color components of your image, depending on its color model. For example, if your image is an RGB image, your Blend If drop-down list choices will be Gray, Red, Green, and Blue. After choosing which color to blend, you can drag the sliders for This Layer and Underlying Layer, choosing where the blending occurs.

Tip   *A complete discussion of the Blending Options and these settings can also be found in Chapter 10.*

Customizing Blending Options

As you turn on any of the 12 styles in the Blending Options version of the Layer Style dialog box, the effects will be applied according to defaults, or the way they were last applied. If you want to change how the Blending Options are applied to the active layer, click the box for the Blending Option you want to customize, as shown in Figure 12-35. The main section of the dialog box changes, offering settings for the specific effect you clicked.

The 12 Blending Option styles' names are fairly self-explanatory, as are the settings for each one. Should any of them confuse you, here's a list of the 12 options and views of the settings for each option:

Drop Shadow   This style adds a shadow that appears behind the content of the active layer. You can adjust the intensity, size, and direction of the shadow (see Figure 12-36). You can also preview the results of your tweaking in the Preview on the right side of the dialog box, or, if Preview is on, within the image window.

Tip   *Leave the Layer Knocks Out Drop Shadow option on so the shadow won't appear if the fill Opacity is transparent.*

Inner Shadow   If you want a shadow that appears within the edges of the layer's content, choose this option. As shown in Figure 12-37, an Inner Shadow makes a shape look as though it's indented or has dropped through the layer on which it sits.

Outer Glow   This option places a glow around the edges of the layer's content. Through its options (shown in Figure 12-38), you can change the color of the glow, set its Opacity, and make it a soft glow or a more precise application of light (use the Technique drop-down list in the Elements section).

Inner Glow   The opposite effect of the Inner Shadow, the Inner Glow puts a soft light on the inside edges of a layer or shape on that layer. You can choose the color of the glow, set its size and depth, and choose whether or not it will emanate from the center of the shape. Figure 12-39 shows the full set of options for Inner Glow.

BUILDING ORIGINAL ARTWORK

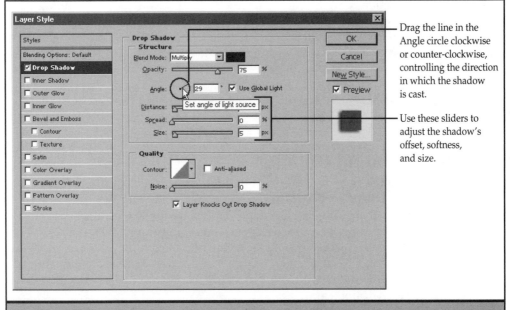

Drag the line in the Angle circle clockwise or counter-clockwise, controlling the direction in which the shadow is cast.

Use these sliders to adjust the shadow's offset, softness, and size.

Figure 12-36. *Control the appearance of your Drop Shadow.*

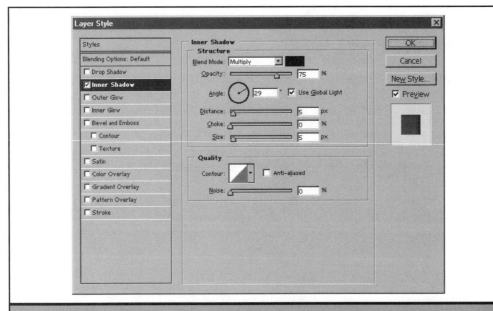

Figure 12-37. *Customize the Inner Shadow's depth and color.*

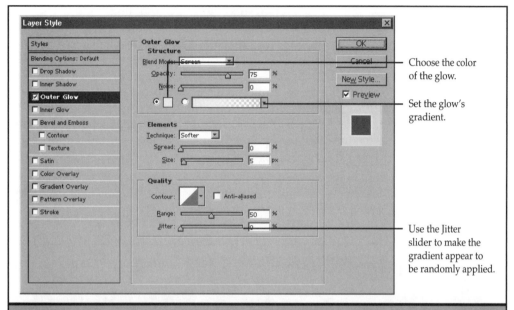

Figure 12-38.   *Control the nature of the highlights added with the Outer Glow option.*

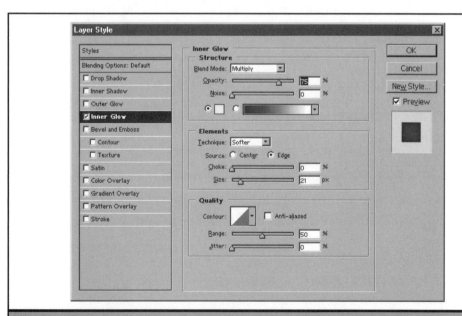

Figure 12-39.   *The Inner Glow makes the layer and its content seem to shine from within.*

Bevel and Emboss   This style has two suboptions, Contour and Texture. On its own, Bevel and Emboss makes layer content appear raised and three-dimensional. As shown in Figure 12-40, you can customize the degree of beveling and embossing, as well as control the direction from which light shines on the shape. This determines which side is shadowed, whether or not you've applied a Drop Shadow in addition to using Bevel and Emboss. If you turn on the Contour option, the bevel is exaggerated, and the edges of it have a chiseled, angular look. The Texture option adds a pattern effect to the layer and/or shape, but doesn't apply the pattern's colors—just the light and dark areas, as shown in Figure 12-41.

Satin   As the name implies, this option applies a "satin" finish to a layer or shape by applying shading to the inside of the layer and the shapes on it. The effects are subtler than an inner bevel. As shown in Figure 12-42, you can control the Opacity, Angle, Distance, and Size of the interior shading.

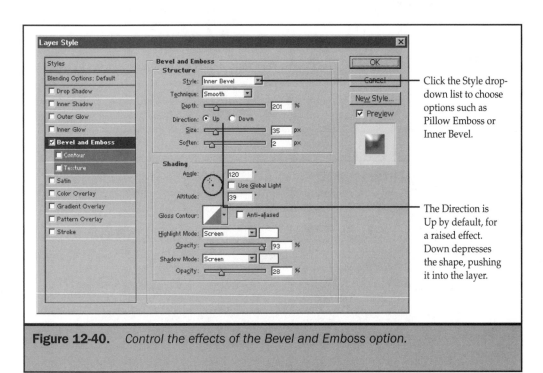

Figure 12-40.   *Control the effects of the Bevel and Emboss option.*

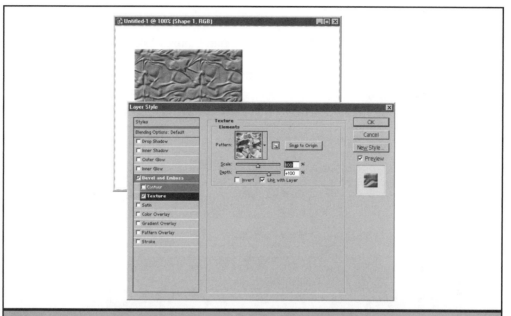

Figure 12-41.   *Turn on Texture to add more visual interest to a beveled and embossed shape.*

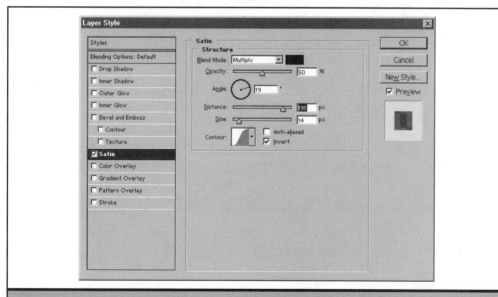

Figure 12-42.   *Apply a subtle satin finish to your layer with the Satin blending option.*

Color Overlay Handy if you want to change the color of a shape on a Shape layer, this option also allows you to change the color of any non-transparent pixels on a layer (filled pixels or shapes). As shown in Figure 12-43, the settings are simple for this option—change the color of the overlay (clicking the color box opens the Color Picker) and set the Opacity of the overlay.

Gradient Overlay If you want to change the gradient applied to a shape or Shape layer, you can use this option to choose from a series of gradient effects. The settings for this option (see Figure 12-44) include the same settings you saw on the Gradient tool's options bar.

Pattern Overlay Apply a pattern to a Shape layer or shape through this style. The settings include the palette of patterns; controls for the placement, opacity, and size of the pattern fill; and a Scale slider to make the pattern display bigger or smaller within the layer, shape, or selection (see Figure 12-45).

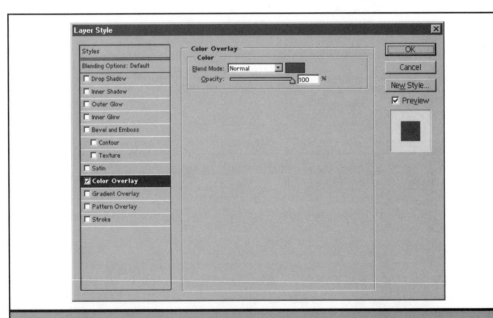

Figure 12-43. *Apply a new solid color to a layer, shape, or selection.*

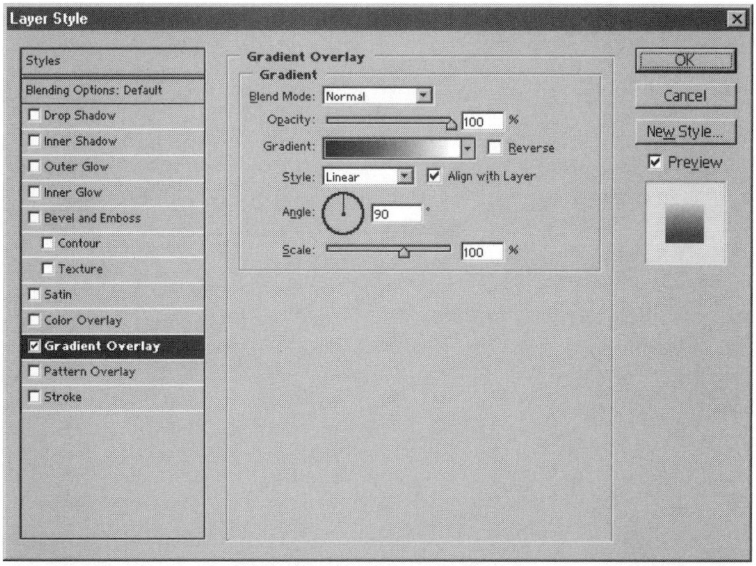

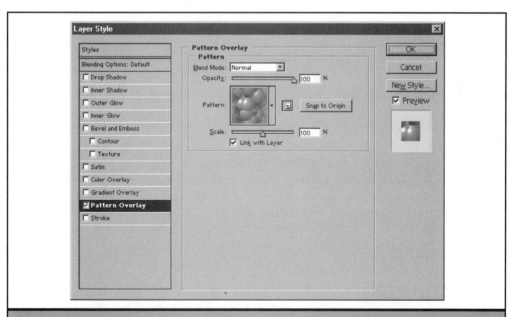

Figure 12-44.   *Customize the Gradient Overlay.*

Figure 12-45.   *Choose a Pattern fill for your Shape layer or shape.*

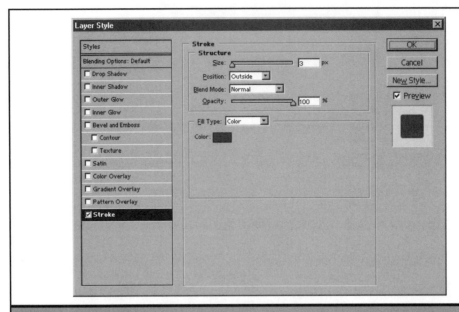

Figure 12-46. *Click the Color box to open the Color Picker and choose a different Stroke (outline) color for your layer or shape.*

Stroke   This could have been called Outline, and fewer people would have been confused by it. The Stroke settings (shown in Figure 12-46) include the Size (pixel width) of the stroke, the Position (Inside, Outside, or Center), and the ability to use a solid color, gradient, or pattern stroke. The default is Color, and the default color is Red.

Summary

In this chapter, you applied special fill effects and styles to shapes and layers. You learned to customize the way gradients, patterns, textures, and other visual effects are applied, and you learned to create your own custom fills and styles for consistency throughout your images and greater creative diversity within your creations.

Chapter 13

Transforming Images with Filters

*F*ilters are groups of special effects and formats that are applied to layers or selections within your image. Colors, texture, and patterns are applied automatically, based on the filter you choose and the settings for that filter. Each of Photoshop's filters allows you to control how the filter will be applied, and many provide a preview so that you don't have to actually commit to the filter until and unless the preview suits your needs. You have more than 12 filter categories to choose from. In this chapter, you'll learn how filters work, how to customize them, and see the results of their use on a variety of images.

Understanding How Filters Work

Photoshop has a very extensive collection of filters for you to use in enhancing, retouching, and adding visual excitement to your images. The Filter menu is the obvious home to Photoshop's filters, along with the Extract, Liquify, and Pattern Maker commands. Use of the Pattern Maker was discussed in Chapter 12, but you'll be finding out about Extract and Liquify later in this chapter.

When you open the Filter menu (see Figure 13-1), you'll see many filter categories, each accompanied by a right-pointing triangle that indicates a submenu. Each of the categories has at least four filters in its submenu (except Video, which has only two), and most of them have many, many more.

Virtually all filter commands open a dialog box through which you can usually preview the filter's effect, either in the dialog box or on the image, or both. You can also customize the filter, controlling how its effects are applied, as shown in Figure 13-2.

Figure 13-1. *Choose different filter categories in the Filter menu, and then browse their submenus.*

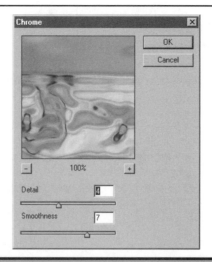

Figure 13-2.   *Use the sliders, radio buttons, check boxes, and text boxes to control how a given filter is applied to your image or a section thereof.*

If the filter's dialog box has sliders in it, but no Preview option, you can use the ALT (Windows) or OPTION (Mac) key to see a preview of the filter in the image window, showing the results of the slider adjustments in real time. If the dialog box does have a Preview option, you're seeing the filter's effects in real time—something that works better if your computer has a fast processor.

Some other filter facts follow:

- You can apply a filter only to the active layer, and only if that layer is visible.

- You can restrict the effects of a filter to a selection on the active layer by selecting the area to be filtered and then applying the filter. If you don't make a selection prior to applying a filter, the filter automatically applies to the entire active layer.

- Certain filters work only with certain file types. For example, you can't apply a filter to an image that's in Bitmap or Indexed Color Mode. Some filters only work on images that are in RGB Mode, and very few filters work with 16-bit images. You'll know if your image is one that doesn't work with a particular filter because the filter command will be dimmed in the menu.

- When you apply a filter, even if you then Undo its effects or go back to the previous state in the History palette, the last filter you applied appears at the top of the Filter menu, with the keyboard shortcut CTRL/COMMAND. If you want to reapply the filter but also see its dialog box again so you can apply it with new settings, press CTRL-ALT-F (Windows) or COMMAND-OPTION-F (Mac). Note that the last used filter command also appears in the category submenu where it was found originally.

- You can hold down the mouse button and hold the pointer on the Preview image in a filter's dialog box to see the "before" version of the image.

When you apply a filter to a large selection or to an entire layer, it can take a while to work— you'll see your mouse pointer's "busy" cursor, and you'll see a progress bar at the bottom of the workspace indicating that the filter is in progress. So that you don't wait through this time only to find that you don't like the filter's result, it's a good idea to apply the filter to a small area within the image first, and then if you like it, go ahead and apply the filter to a larger area or whole layer.

Working with Corrective Filters

Through the Sharpen, Blur, Noise, and Pixelate categories and their submenus, you can correct the appearance of your image, improving an image by illuminating lost content or softening content that you wish were less evident. You can sharpen an image to bring out detail, or blur an image to get rid of detail that's either unflattering or unnecessary. You can also get rid of spots to clean up an image that's showing wear, or add some dots to even out solid fills or remove the appearance of heavy-handed retouching.

You may find that you'll use these filters in conjunction with the retouching tools in the toolbox. For example, if you use the Blur tool to smooth out an area and then decide it's too smooth (and it's too late to Undo or go back in History), you can use the Sharpen filter or one of the Pixelate filters to bring back some of the pixel diversity your blurring eliminated.

Improving Image Clarity with the Sharpening Filters

The filters found in the Sharpen submenu work by heightening the contrast between contiguous pixels, as shown in Figure 13-3. The result is edges that stand out and a greater variety of colors or shades of gray, depending on the image itself. There are three sharpening filters (Sharpen, Sharpen More, and Sharpen Edges) and an Unsharp Mask command located in the Sharpen submenu, each devoted to creating more contrast between pixels (and therefore between adjacent objects and areas) in your image.

The Sharpen, Sharpen More, and Sharpen Edges filters work without any input from you—there are no dialog boxes to adjust how sharp the sharpening effects will be. The Unsharp Mask, however, allows you to adjust the detail along edges in your image, and to make the line added along those edges lighter or darker (see Figure 13-4).

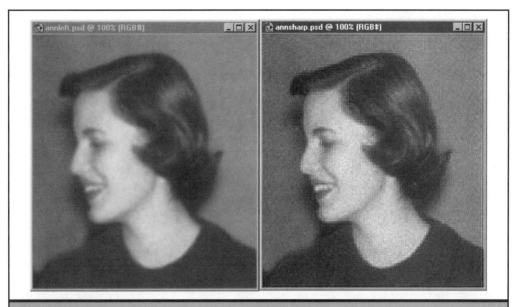

Figure 13-3.   *Add more diversity to the pixels in the sharpened area.*

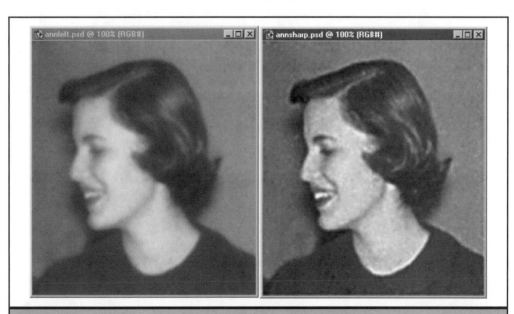

Figure 13-4.   *Give your image an overall sharper look without sharpening everything—just the edges get some focus with the Unsharp Mask filter.*

Applying Blur Filters

Blur filters work by recoloring pixels along edges and in shaded areas so that there is less contrast between the pixels. In truth, the blurring effect can be both corrective and artistic. It can be applied to soften something that's too sharp or hide content by making it so diffused that it's no longer noticeable. The content does the job of filling space and giving context, but it no longer distracts from the main subject of the image. Figure 13-5 shows an image where the Blur filter was used to take all but the central figure in the image out of focus.

For a more dramatic blur, you can use the Gaussian Blur filter, shown in use in Figure 13-6. This filter can completely blur an image beyond recognition or create a blur of any level of intensity. You do this by dragging the Radius slider, increasing or decreasing the range of pixels compared to each other and blurred to create less diversity.

The Blur filters can also be used to distort content, making static objects appear to have been moving (with the Motion Blur filter) or swirling (with the Radial Blur filter). You can control the degree of motion and the type of swirling with each filter's dialog box, and their results are quite dramatic. Figure 13-7 shows the Motion Blur in use. Note that the blurred boy also appears unblurred. This is because a copy was made of him and placed on a layer above the blurred layer, allowing him to appear clearly in front of the trail created by his motion.

Figure 13-5.   *The Blur or Blur More filters allow you to smooth out unwanted content or contrast in your image.*

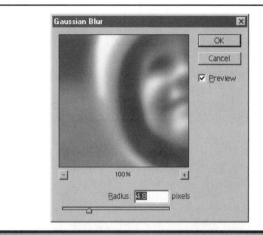

Figure 13-6.   *A low Radius setting will leave you with discernable image content; a high Radius setting will have a much more intense effect.*

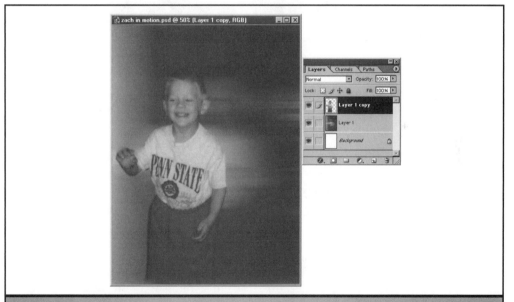

Figure 13-7.   *The Motion Blur filter makes it look as though the subject of the photo was moving at great speed when the picture was taken.*

Figure 13-8. *Get a different spin on your image content by applying the Radial Blur.*

> **Tip** *The Smart Blur filter allows you to blur the edges or the whole image, and to adjust the intensity of the effect. Use this filter when you have very specific goals for the blur effect, and you want to have more control over the results.*

Figure 13-8 has been altered with the Radial Blur filter, and this time, only the area behind the central figure is blurred—the central figure was selected with the Magnetic Lasso, and then the selection was inverted so that all but the boy would get a Radial Blur.

Making Effective Use of Noise

The Noise filter category offers four filters that add or take away visual static: Add Noise, Despeckle, Dust & Scratches, and Median. These filters give you everything from the look of a channel with no TV signal to the signs of aging and dirt that can plague older or poorly stored photographs. The Noise filters work by increasing the random application of color to pixels across an entire layer or within a selection. The extra noise can help blend contiguous or overlapping selections and mitigate the effects of dust and scratches, or you can use them simply as interesting visual effects, not necessarily improving the clarity of the image, as shown in Figures 13-9 and 13-10.

Figure 13-9. *Add some noise to an image that's too soft.*

Figure 13-10. *The Dust & Scratches filter lives up to its name, helping you get rid of the signs of your photos' aging.*

All but one of the Noise filters have dialog boxes through which you can customize the filters' effects. The Despeckle filter works without any intervention from you as it blurs everything in the selection or layer except the edges. Where the Despeckle filter finds an edge (any place with a great contrast between adjacent pixels), it heightens the color difference, bringing greater focus to the edge, as you can see in Figure 13-11.

The opposite of the Add Noise filter, the Median filter blends the brightness of pixels within a layer or selection. You can use the Median dialog box to adjust the range of pixels searched and compared to each other for the purposes of blending. Reducing the range will result in a more subtle effect, and increasing it will give you dramatic results. Figure 13-12 shows the Median dialog box and a preview of its effects on an image.

Creating Interesting Effects with the Pixelate Filters

The Pixelate filters are useful when you need to bring focus to an area of your image. They work by grouping similarly colored pixels, creating distinct edges and defined areas, as shown in Figure 13-13. In this image, you see several of the Pixelate filters in use, applied to rectangular areas of a single image for demonstration purposes. The filters can be corrective as well as artistic, restoring definition or simply adding an interesting texture to the image via the regrouping of pixels.

Figure 13-11.   *Focus on your image edges with the Despeckle filter.*

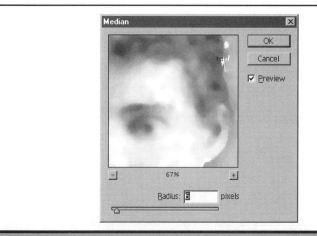

Figure 13-12.   *Increase the Radius (range) of pixels that will be blended to reduce the noise level in the image.*

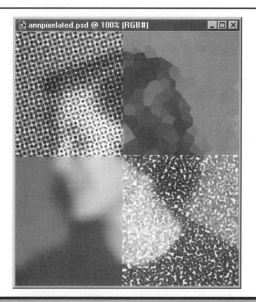

Figure 13-13.   *Clockwise from upper left: the Color Halftone, Crystallize, Pointillize, and Fragment filters are applied.*

Figure 13-14. *Choose the size of the points that will be inserted to recreate your image with the Pointillize filter.*

There are seven Pixelate filters: Color Halftone, Crystallize, Facet, Fragment, Mezzotint, Mosaic, and Pointillize. All but two of them (Facet and Fragment) offer dialog boxes that give you control over the filter's effects. The Pointillize filter's dialog box is shown in Figure 13-14. Like the other Pixelate filters', this filter offers you control over the size of the pixel effects that are applied. Each of the Pixelate filters achieves a similar end but takes a different approach. Experimentation is the best way to find out which of the Pixelate filters will give you the effect you're looking for.

Using Artistic, Brush Stroke, and Sketch Filters

When you want a photograph or electronically rendered image to look like it was created with paint, pencils, charcoal, pastels, or similar artistic media, use the filters found in the Artistic, Brush Strokes, and Sketch submenus. Over 30 filters give you the ability to turn your image into an oil painting, a watercolor, a drawing, or even a laminated piece of sculpture (using the Plastic Wrap filter).

The illusion of having used a brush, a palette knife, or a stick to apply your paint can be achieved, as can the appearance of old, faded film stock (Film Grain) or the look of a collage (Cutout filter) that turns your image into a series of shapes that appear to be cut out of paper and pasted to the page. Figure 13-15 contains a photo that's been broken into four selected areas. Clockwise from the upper left, the photo in the figure appears to have been drawn with Colored Pencil, painted with Paint Daubs, rendered with Watercolor, and smeared with a Smudge Stick.

Figure 13-16 shows a series of the Brush Stroke and Sketch filters applied to a single image. Clockwise from the upper left, the Ink Outlines, Sprayed Strokes, Photocopy, and Charcoal filters have been applied.

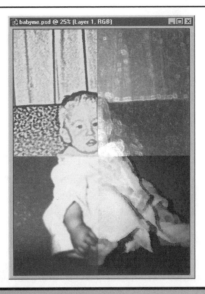

Figure 13-15.   *Each quadrant shows a different Artistic filter applied.*

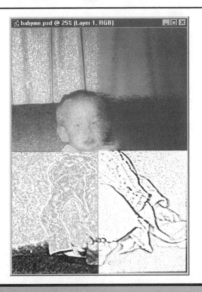

Figure 13-16.   *Brush Stroke (top sections) and Sketch filters (bottom sections) are applied to one image.*

Using the Artistic Filters

While not all of the Photoshop filters are intuitively named, the Artistic filters are. The goal in using this batch of filters is to give your images the look of being hand painted or drawn with a variety of artists' tools, from a Colored Pencil to a Palette Knife, from Fresco to Watercolor. There are similar filters in the Brush Strokes and Sketch filter submenus, but in the Artistic filters submenu, you'll find a comprehensive group of filters, representing a wide spectrum of media.

All of the Artistic filters offer you dialog boxes through which you can customize the filters' effects. You'll find the standard sliders and radio buttons and, as shown in Figure 13-17, you can preview your results in the dialog box.

The Plastic Wrap filter (see Figure 13-18) applies an interesting shiny effect to your images and is effective when you want to draw attention to the appearance of the edges in the image—the wrap highlights them by showing them as raised under the wrapping.

Using Brush Stroke Filters

The Brush Stroke filters apply the effects of various painting tools to your image, and their names describe their effects rather than naming the painting tools they mimic. For example, the Crosshatch filter applies a hatching pattern (see Figure 13-19) that looks as though it was applied with a sharp pencil. As the stroke itself and its effect on the image are paramount, the filters are named to help you choose the right one for the look you need.

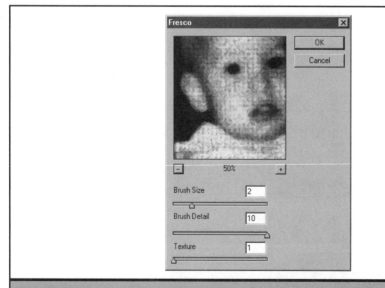

Figure 13-17.   *Give your photograph or other image the look of a Fresco, an effect achieved in real life by painting on freshly plastered walls.*

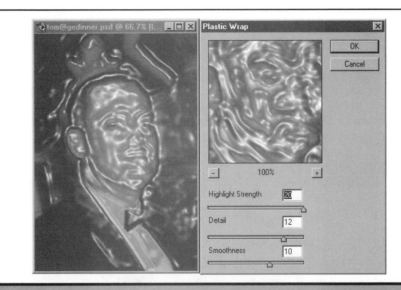

Figure 13-18. *Anything—even tightly wrapped, clear plastic—can add an artistic element to your image.*

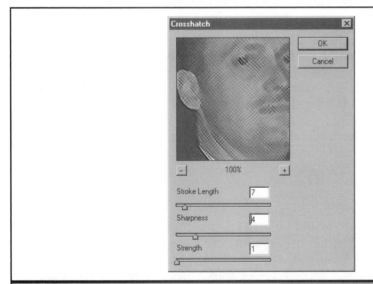

Figure 13-19. *The Crosshatch filter redraws your image with sharp, pencil-like lines.*

Figure 13-20.   *Accented Edges has a sharpening and defining effect on the left, and Ink Outlines draws attention to the fine detail on the right.*

Some of the Brush Stroke filters apply edging and outlines only. The Accented Edges filter highlights edges in bright shades, going as bright as white if you increase the brightness controls. The Ink Outlines filter, on the other hand, applies fine lines to the details of your image, not dealing with edges at all. Figure 13-20 shows these filters applied to the two halves of an image.

The Dark Strokes filter responds to the colors in your image, applying short black strokes to the darkest areas of the image, and long, white strokes to the lighter areas.

Sketching Your Images

The Sketch filters are named to match the media they appear to apply—Charcoal, Conte Crayon, Graphic Pen, and Chrome are examples (see Figure 13-21).

You'll also find filters that apply the effects of devices and papers, rather than pencils or paintbrushes, such as the Note Paper, Torn Edges, and Water Paper filters. These filters are shown in use in Figure 13-22.

Figure 13-21.   *Clockwise from upper left, four typical drawing tools at work: Charcoal, Conte Crayon, Chrome, and Graphic Pen.*

Figure 13-22.   *Note Paper, Torn Edges, and Water Paper filters give your image the appearance of being applied to a variety of surfaces.*

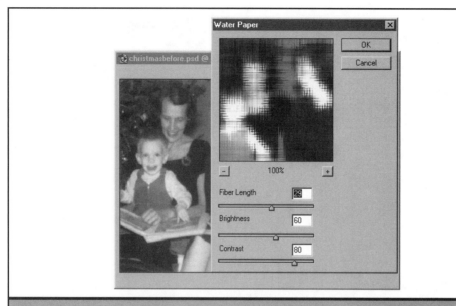

Figure 13-23. *Refine the tool or the surface that the filter creates.*

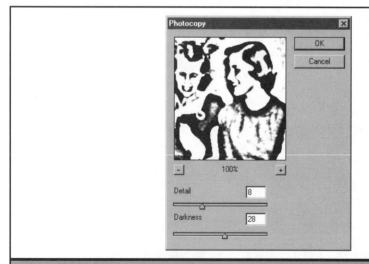

Figure 13-24. *Get the look of a low-quality photocopy with the Photocopy filter.*

The controls for the Sketch filters vary (see Figure 13-23). Does your image call for a heavy or a subtle texture? Increase the Fiber Length for a more exaggerated texture, or decrease it for results that preserve much of the clarity in your image content. The Water Paper filter's dialog box allows you to choose how fibrous the water paper is, which affects the texture applied to the image.

One Sketch filter that seems really out of place is the Photocopy filter. It generates the appearance of a copy that's a copy of a copy of a copy of a copy. Depending on the Detail and Darkness settings you apply, you can improve the quality of the alleged photocopy, maintaining some or most of the detail from your image. An image appears in the preview window of the Photocopy filter dialog box in Figure 13-24.

Rendering Images with Light and Special 3-D Effects

The Render filters are a mixed bag. Unlike some of the other filter categories, where all the filters follow a single theme, the six Render filters don't seem to have anything in common. You can choose from 3D Transform, Clouds (and Difference Clouds), Lens Flare, Lighting Effects, and Texture Fill. Figure 13-25 shows the 3D Transform and Lighting Effects in use on a single image—they're applied to the left and right sides, respectively.

Figure 13-25. *Adding a third dimension and playing with light sources make for interesting effects.*

BUILDING ORIGINAL ARTWORK

The Clouds and Difference Clouds filters don't need a dialog box—they simply apply their effects (ignoring image colors and using the current Foreground color to create the clouds) when you choose them from the Render submenu. The rest of the filters in this group, however, offer some serious tools for honing the results of the filters. Figure 13-26 shows the Lighting Effects dialog box, containing a preview of the effect it will have on the image.

Figure 13-27 shows the 3D Transform dialog box—here you can choose the type of 3-D shape that will be extruded from your image, and use tools to manipulate the shape.

Somewhat related to the Lighting Effects filter is the Lens Flare filter. This filter allows you to set up a light source and customize it. As shown in Figure 13-28, if you're trying to create the appearance of a direct light source refracted through a camera lens, the Lens Flare filter may be just what you need. You can adjust the Brightness, choose the Lens Type, and set where the flare will appear on the image.

If you add a grayscale image as an alpha channel to your image, you can choose that channel in the Texture Channel section of the Lighting Effects filter. It will add the lighting effects through the texture channel.

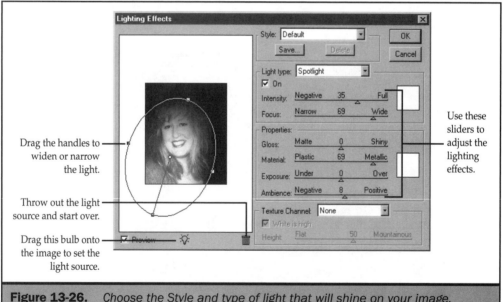

Figure 13-26. *Choose the Style and type of light that will shine on your image.*

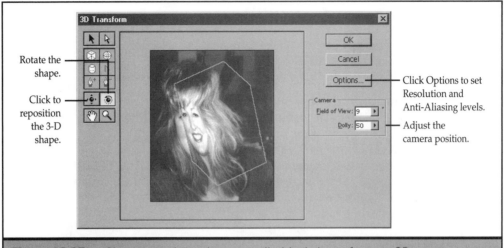

Rotate the shape.

Click to reposition the 3-D shape.

Click Options to set Resolution and Anti-Aliasing levels.

Adjust the camera position.

Figure 13-27. *Choose a cube, sphere, or cylindrical shape for your 3D Transform filter.*

Figure 13-28. *Use the Lens Flare filter to mimic the effects of a bright spot on the camera's lens.*

Working with Filters that Distort, Stylize, and Apply Textures

So far, the filters we've discussed have either improved on the quality of the image, repainted it in the style of any number of artistic tools, or changed the lighting or perspective on the image. With these filters, unless you apply the filter's attributes in the extreme, the image remains recognizable. With the Distort, Stylize, and Texture filters, however, the goal is to twist, bend, and torment your image, pulling, pushing, and stuffing it into a variety of shapes and spaces. These filters submerge your image in rough seas and flowing rivers, encase them in glass, break them into pieces, and whip them in the wind. Figures 13-29, 13-30, and 13-31 show sample filters from each of the groups. Note that in all of these figures, the filters are listed in the order they're applied—clockwise, starting in the upper left of the image.

> **Tip** *To reset your filter without leaving the dialog box, press* ALT/OPTION *as you click the Cancel button.*

Figure 13-29. *Apply (top left to right) Ocean Ripple, Spherize, (bottom right to left) Pinch, and Twirl—all dynamic distorting filters.*

Figure 13-30. *Emboss, Extrude, Wind, and Solarize are just four of the nine Stylize filters you can apply to your image.*

Figure 13-31. *Turn your image to Stained Glass, Mosaic Tiles, a fabric Texture, or a Patchwork quilt.*

Distorting Image Content

The Distort filters are a very interesting bunch. With them, you can do simple things like apply a Glass surface to an image or apply a Diffuse Glow; you can also do much more complex things like Displace an image with another image. As shown in Figures 13-32 and 13-33 respectively, the Displace filter asks you to decide how the map will be applied to your image, and asks you to choose another PSD image to serve as the Displacement Map. Once chosen, the image dictates the offset of the original image, molding it to the lights and darks within the map image, as shown in Figure 13-34.

Other filters in the Distort group include Polar Coordinates, which wraps your image around a cylinder, either on the inside of the tube or on the outside. You can choose the Option that suits your needs, as shown in Figure 13-35.

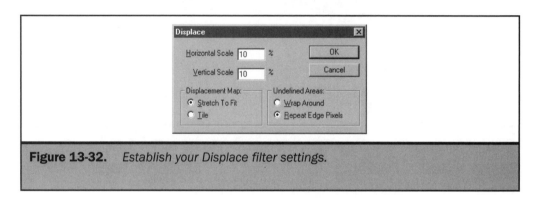

Figure 13-32. *Establish your Displace filter settings.*

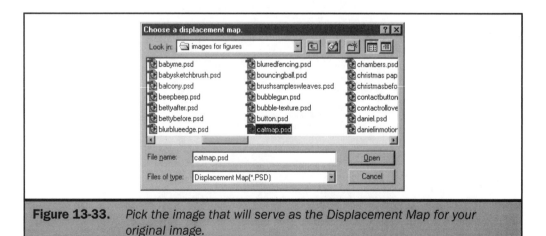

Figure 13-33. *Pick the image that will serve as the Displacement Map for your original image.*

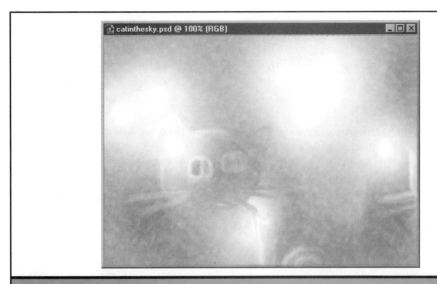

Figure 13-34. *A drawing of a cat has been used as the map for an image of the sky.*

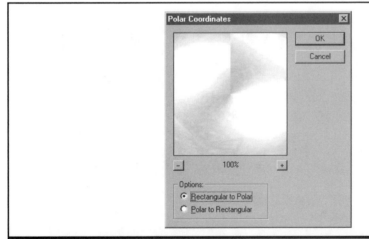

Figure 13-35. *Wrap your image around a tube and view it from a new perspective with the Polar Coordinates filter.*

Fans of wrapping or warping an image into a shape will also enjoy the Wave filter, which allows you to roll your image along a horizontal wave of varying depths and frequencies. You can use the many sliders in the Wave filter dialog box to control the wave, and then preview the results (see Figure 13-36). Clicking the Randomize button allows you to view several wave alternatives.

Using Stylized Filters

The Stylize filters include Diffuse, Emboss, Extrude, Find Edges, Glowing Edges, Solarize, Tiles, Trace Contour, and Wind. You may find some of these filters having effects that are quite similar to other filters. Motion Blur works very much like Wind, Solarize results in something that looks very much like Difference Clouds, and Extrude has an effect much like what you can achieve with 3D Transform. You can tweak the way these and the remaining filters work, however, and in doing so, create a variety of unexpected and appealing results. Figure 13-37 shows a sample—from left to right, see the Diffuse, Glowing Edges, and Tiles filters in use.

Filters that refer to light or glowing generally contain options for adjusting the brightness that the filters apply. The Glowing Edges dialog box is a perfect example (see Figure 13-38). Through this dialog box, you can adjust the width of the edges that are traced with a glow, control the brightness of that glow, and control the level of detail with the Smoothness slider.

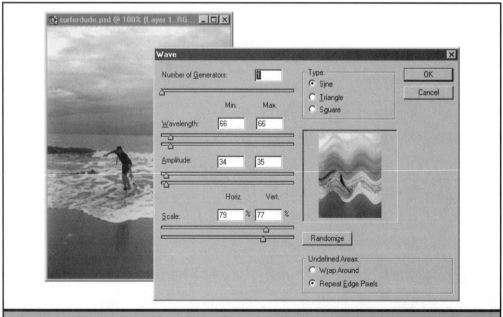

Figure 13-36. *Images containing bodies of water, shorelines, banners, or flags are good candidates for the effects of the Wave filter.*

Figure 13-37. *From subtle to dramatic, to completely unexpected, the Stylize filters have a variety of uses in all kinds of images.*

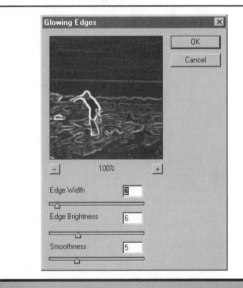

Figure 13-38. *As though wrapping your image edges in soft neon, the Glowing Edges filter draws light along the contours created by contrasting pixels.*

The Find Edges and Solarize filters have a dramatic effect on your image, yet offer no tools to control how the filter is applied. Use with care, and be prepared to Undo if you don't like the results.

Applying Texture Filters

Instead of applying color or light to your image, the Texture filters apply a sculptured look to your image with filters such as Craquelure, Grain, Mosaic Tiles, Patchwork, Stained Glass, and Texturizer. You can apply the look of cracked ceramic glaze, broken tiles grouted together on a flat surface, or a Tiffany lamp–look of leaded glass. You can also achieve the look of a variety of rough surfaces including brick, sand, and canvas. Figure 13-39 shows the Texturizer filter at work—a perfect example of this group's effect.

All six of the Texture filters require you to use a dialog box to customize the filter's effect. As you can see in Figure 13-40, you can create subtle or dramatic effects, depending on how low or high you set the levels controlling the size of the textures, which textures are applied, and the way the pieces (tiles, glass shards, and so on) are held together visually.

Figure 13-39.   *Use the Texturizer filter to give the look of your image printed on a rough fabric such as Burlap.*

Figure 13-40. *Adjust the crackled effects of your Craquelure filter by spacing the cracks.*

BUILDING ORIGINAL
ARTWORK

Applying Video Filter Effects

The Video filter group contains just two filters: De-Interlace and NTSC Colors. These filters apply effects that you would typically apply to video—smoothing the lines (interlacing) that appear on videotape, and restricting the colors included in an image to those that can be displayed effectively through a television's scan lines. For your purposes in Photoshop, you can use them on still images captured with a digital video camera (perhaps the interlaced lines appear in the still) and for images that you will be using in a video that will be presented on a television. You won't see much effect if you apply these filters to static images that were not captured by a video camera, and thus my rather brief discussion of them here.

Other Filters

A handful of filters seem to have defied categorization. Photoshop 7's Other Filters submenu contains five filters: Custom, High Pass, Maximum, Minimum, and Offset. Figures 13-41 through 13-44 show the results of these filters, applied to the same image.

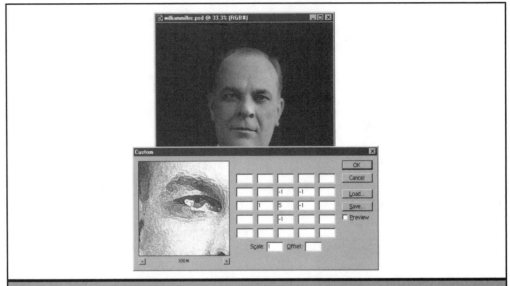

Figure 13-41. *Design your own Custom filter, adjusting pixel brightness mathematically.*

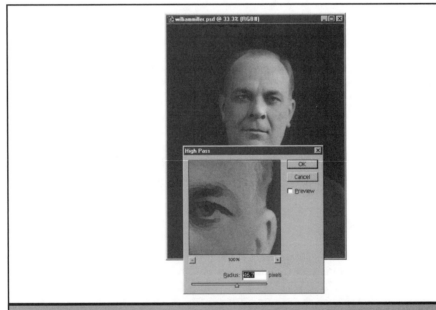

Figure 13-42. *The High Pass filter keeps your crisp edges intact and dims the rest of the image.*

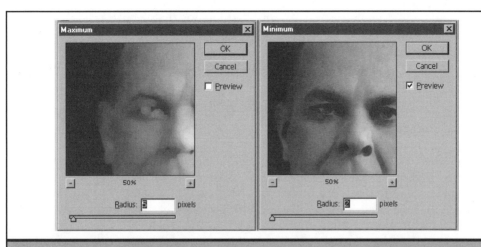

Figure 13-43. *Use the Minimum and Maximum filters (shown left and right, respectively) to choke black areas in favor of white and vice versa.*

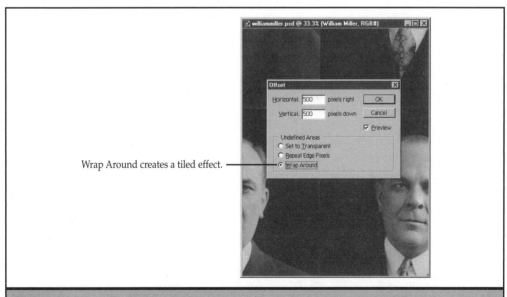

Wrap Around creates a tiled effect.

Figure 13-44. *The Offset filter moves a selected area up, down, left, or right, depending on horizontal and vertical offsets you determine.*

The Custom filter presents a very complicated-looking dialog box; certainly the math behind the filter's functioning, known as *convolution*, is quite complex. However, the process of using the dialog box is quite simple, and you can use the preview, shown in Figure 13-41, as a guide as you tweak the pixel brightness settings you enter into the array of fields.

The first step in using the Custom filter is to set the brightness value you want applied to the representative pixel. This number, ranging from –999 to +999, is entered into the center cell in the array. Next, begin entering the brightness values (using the same range) into the adjacent boxes, each of which represents an adjacent pixel. You do not have to enter values into each of the boxes, but you may find that you like the results as you adjust values and change the boxes that contain values.

The other options in the dialog box include Scale and Offset, and these play into the convolution formula. Scale is the number by which the sum of the brightness value will be divided, and Offset is the number that will be added to whatever the Scale calculation gives you. You can save your settings using the Save and Load button on the right side of the dialog box, making it possible to apply a Custom filter over and over.

Liquifying Images

Turning your image into something as pliable as a thick liquid, the Liquify command and dialog box enable you to massage your image into a variety of shapes, using tools like Warp, Twirl, Pucker, and Bloat. As shown in Figure 13-45, you can take any image and make it much more interesting by bending, expanding, and twisting content within your image.

When you issue the Filter | Liquify command, the Liquify dialog box opens (see Figure 13-46). The dialog box provides tools for distorting your image (to the left of the image) and options for controlling the effects of those distortion tools (to the right of the image). You can set the Brush Size and Brush Pressure, and add Turbulent Jitter, if desired. You can also Freeze areas to protect some of the image from distortion, and then Thaw the frozen areas to make them available for distortion again. Your View Options include whether or not you see the frozen areas, and whether or not you can see a helpful Mesh behind the image. The mesh helps you see the results of your distortions.

If you don't like the distortion you've applied, click the Revert button in the Reconstruction section of the dialog box while the Liquify dialog box is still open. You can set how the Revert process will take place, choosing a Mode from the drop-down list. Choose Modes such as Rigid (keeps right angles in the distortion where they meet frozen areas), Stiff (reduces the effects of your distortion tool of choice as you move between frozen and unfrozen areas), and Smooth (allows the distortion to continue from an unfrozen area into a frozen one). Experimentation is one of the best ways to master the Liquify tool, and there are many features to play with—different distortions, different Reconstruction Modes, and different Brush Size and Pressure settings.

Figure 13-45.   *Liquify some or all of your image for a surreal effect.*

The Freeze tool
The Thaw tool

Figure 13-46.   *The Liquify dialog box gives you all the tools you need for successful distortion.*

As you use the Liquify dialog box, keep these general tips in mind:

- If you want more dramatic results, increase the Brush Pressure. You can use the Stylus Pressure option if you have a pressure-sensitive tablet, and then the pressure setting you choose will apply to your pen. If you don't have a tablet and are using a mouse, the pressure will be simulated, working more like an intensity setting.

- The brush size you use is also key to the effects you get. Larger brush sizes make larger-scale changes, but the changes may be subtler because they take place over a larger area of your image.

- The center of your brush cursor is a vortex of sorts—it's the center point for any distortions you're creating, and the results show there first. At the center of the stroke, you'll see the most dramatic evidence of whatever distortion you're applying.

- You can select areas within your image and, by so doing, make them distortable. Unselected areas are considered frozen, which means that you can't distort them. You can use the Thaw button in the dialog box to unfreeze a frozen area. Figure 13-47 shows a frozen area designated by the gray wash drawn with the Freeze tool.

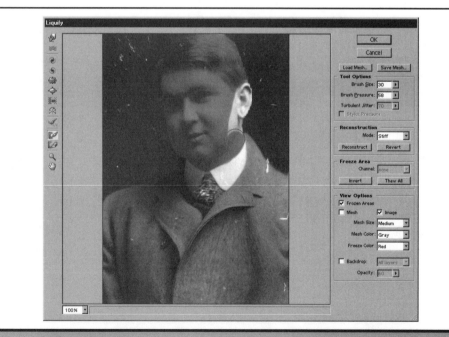

Figure 13-47.   *Paint with the Freeze tool to prevent distortion in an area of your image.*

■ You can change the color of your frozen overlay (the wash that indicates which areas are selected and which ones aren't). Choose a new color from the Freeze Color menu, located at the bottom of the Liquify dialog box.

■ If the Mesh color doesn't show within your image, change it. The mesh won't print—it's just there to help you make more precise changes and to see the results of your distortions that would not be visible or easily seen on a solid color background. The mesh also retains the distortion data when the mesh is saved.

■ The Cancel button closes the Liquify dialog box. When it's used, none of your distortions from the current Liquify session are applied to your image.

■ If you want to save your mesh so that you can apply the same Liquify effects to another image, click the Save Mesh button. You'll be prompted to choose a name for the .msh file that you can then Load (with the Load Mesh button) when you want to use that mesh again.

■ If you click OK and exit the Liquify dialog box, the changes you made are now applied to your image. If you regret them, use Undo or the History palette. If you like your distortions but want to refine them a bit, you can use toolbox tools such as the Smudge and Blur tools to make minor changes to the distortions you applied through the Liquify dialog box.

Using the Extract Command

Extracting content from an image can be done with the Background Eraser, as you erase the background around a portion of the image that you want to pull out and see without the surrounding content. Another tool that does this well is the Extract command, located in the Filter menu. When you choose Filter | Extract, the Extract dialog box opens, as shown in Figure 13-48. You can use the dialog box to perform every aspect of the Extraction process, and you'll receive help in the form of instructions that appear across the top of the dialog box.

The Extract dialog box contains tools on the left, and controls for those tools and for the overall extraction process on the right. Your image appears in a box in the center of the dialog box, and you have a Hand and Zoom tool to use in navigating and getting a closer look at the image or portions thereof.

The first step in the extraction process is to highlight (using the Edge Highlighter tool) the edges of the area to be extracted. Figure 13-49 shows this in progress. Next, click the Fill tool (looks like the Paint Bucket) and click inside the highlighted border to define the area to be retained. Figure 13-50 shows an extraction set up, with its border and interior defined.

Tip *You can change the Highlight and Fill color drop-down lists. Find them in the Tool Options section of the Extract dialog box.*

Instructions appear up here.

Tools for creating and adjusting mask

Extraction controls

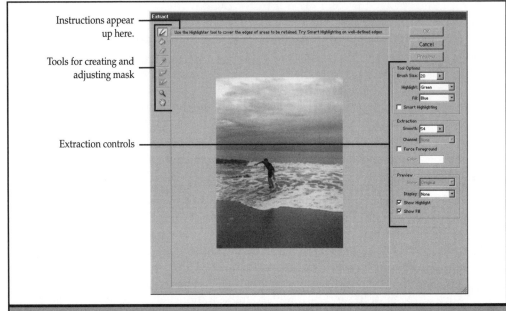

Figure 13-48. *The Filter | Extract command opens the Extract dialog box.*

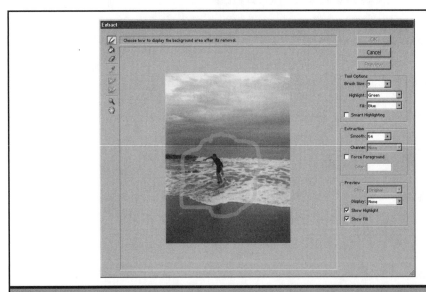

Figure 13-49. *Draw a green border (it appears gray here) to highlight the edge of the area to be extracted.*

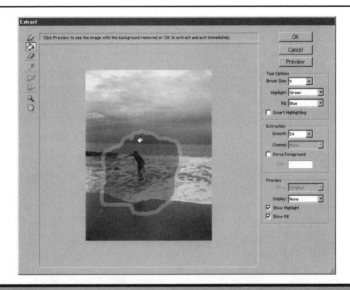

Figure 13-50. *Click inside the border with the Fill tool, resulting in a blue (gray here) wash within the border.*

> **Tip** *You can erase portions of the highlight border with the Eraser, located just below the Fill tool on the vertical strip of tools on the left side of the Extract dialog box.*

Once you've defined the area to be extracted, you can set up the way the extraction will take place. You can set the Smooth level to a higher number (it's zero by default) to remove any stray pixels from the masked area, and you can turn on the Force Foreground option if you'd like to preserve areas within your image by color—great if your image has a lot of solid color fills. If Force Foreground is on, the Eyedropper tool becomes available, and you can sample the image in the dialog box to choose the color that will be preserved.

If you need to, you can edit your mask with the Cleanup and Edge Touchup tools. The Cleanup tool makes the mask more opaque, and the Edge Touchup tool neatens the edges of the extracted area. Neither tool is available until you've clicked the Preview button to see the extraction displayed within the dialog box. Once the preview appears (see Figure 13-51), you can clean up and touch up as needed. If you like the results of the extraction, click OK to apply them to your image.

Cleanup tool ———

Edge Touchup tool ———

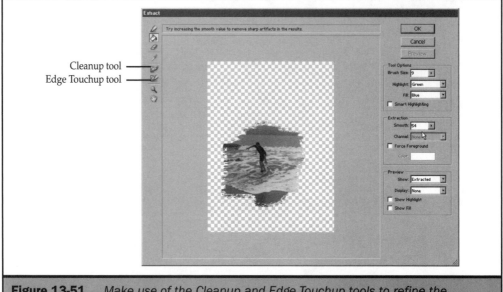

Figure 13-51. *Make use of the Cleanup and Edge Touchup tools to refine the extraction mask and adjust its opacity.*

While you can always Undo or go back to a pre-Extract state in the History palette to get rid of the extraction after you've applied it, you might want to create further backup by creating a duplicate layer for the layer you're about to Extract. You can hide the layer so it doesn't appear in the image or when printed, but you'll retain a pristine version of the layer should you decide next time you open the file that you don't like the extraction. At that point, the Undo and the History palette won't allow you to undo the extraction.

Embedding and Reading Watermarks

The Digimarc filter, located at the bottom of the Filter menu, allows you to embed an identifying watermark in your image. This can protect web graphics, which are ripe for picking by unscrupulous web surfers who'll copy your image to their computers and then reuse it, and for protecting any other sort of printed or electronically displayed image. The Embed Watermark dialog box (shown in Figure 13-52) opens when you choose Embed Watermark from the Digimarc submenu.

An important and essential first step in the watermarking process is to register with the Digimarc Corporation. Without doing so, you can't use the Digimarc filters. The corporation maintains data on artists and their creations. By registering with them, you get an ID and PIN (personal identification number) to enter before you watermark an image. The phone numbers for contacting the Digimarc Corporation appear when you click the Personalize button in the Embed Watermark dialog box. The resulting Personalize Digimarc ID dialog box (shown in Figure 13-53) provides a place to enter your ID and PIN if you have one, and also provides the URL for the Digimarc web site if you'd rather register online.

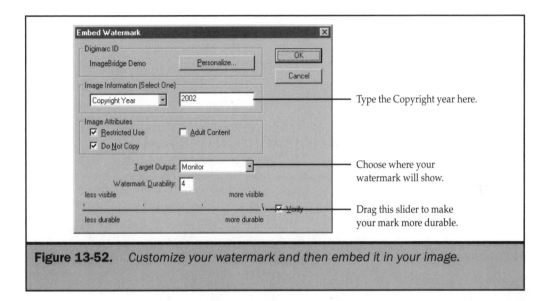

Figure 13-52. *Customize your watermark and then embed it in your image.*

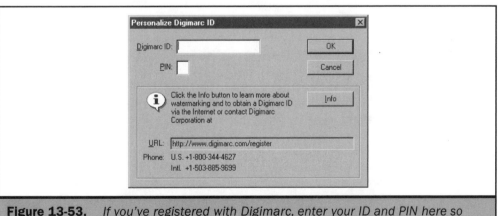

Figure 13-53. *If you've registered with Digimarc, enter your ID and PIN here so your watermark can be associated with you and referenced by Digimarc's database.*

After entering the Image Information (Copyright Year is the default), you can choose a Target Output (Web, Print, or Monitor) and then set your watermark's Durability. This number (adjusted with the slider or by entering it directly) determines how visible the watermark will be—the more visible it is, the more of a deterrent the watermark will be to would-be image bandits.

Instead of entering a copyright year, you can switch to Image ID or Transaction ID and enter those into the Image Information section of the dialog box.

If your image has multiple layers, you'll be prompted to flatten them before proceeding with the watermarking process. You can click Yes to flatten, or No to leave the image layers intact.

If you clicked the Verify option in the Embed Watermark dialog box, the Embed Watermark: Verify dialog box (shown in Figure 13-54) appears after you apply the watermark. The dialog box gives you information about the watermark, and you can check to see whether all of your settings for visibility and restrictions were applied.

To get the information on an image watermark, choose the Read Watermark command from the Digimarc submenu. You can tell if an image is watermarked by the presence of a copyright symbol (©) on the title bar for the image, right between the Photoshop logo and the file name, as shown in Figure 13-55.

You can also copyright an image with the File | File Info command. Choose Copyrighted Work from the Copyright Status menu, and a copyright symbol appears on the image title bar.

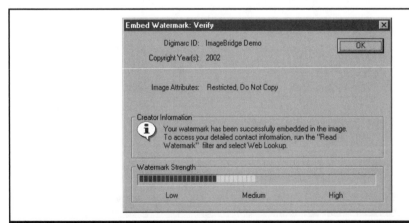

Figure 13-54.   *Check your watermark strength and make sure the right Image Attributes were put into effect.*

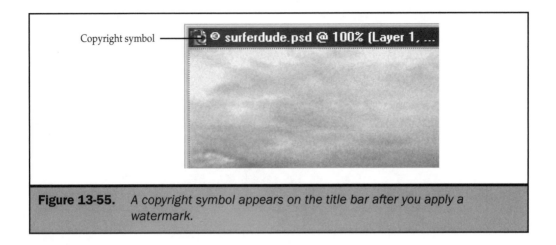

Copyright symbol

Figure 13-55.   *A copyright symbol appears on the title bar after you apply a watermark.*

Summary

In this chapter, you learned to apply and customize filters and to control where and how they affect the appearance of your images. You also learned which filters and types of filters work best in certain situations, and some of the limitations on filters that the color model and file format you're working with can impose. In addition, you learned to use the Liquify and Extract commands, and to add watermarks to your images to mark them as your own.

BUILDING ORIGINAL ARTWORK

The Complete Reference

Photoshop 7

Chapter 14

Adding Words to Pictures

P hotoshop provides you with expert typography tools that enable you to not only add type to images, but also create art with words. In this chapter, you'll learn to use the Type tools and the options that go with them.

Working with the Type Tool

Type can be placed either vertically or horizontally at any point within your image. Each time you click the Type tool and enter text into your document, Photoshop places a new Type layer in your image. A type icon in the Layer panel, shown in Figure 14-1, signifies the new Type layer.

Photoshop differentiates between two kinds of type: point type and paragraph type. With point type, as the name implies, you basically select the Type tool, click the mouse pointer at the place in the image where you want the type to start, and begin typing. This method is best used for inserting a single word or line of text. When you insert paragraph text, instead of placing the pointer in your image with a single click of the Type tool, you select the Type tool and drag out a rectangular region called a *bounding box*. The pointer appears inside this bounding box waiting for you to begin typing.

The bounding box delimits your paragraph's dimensions. When you reach the right edge of the box, your text wraps onto the following line. The bounding box provides handles similar to those you see when making transformations or using the Crop tool. These handles allow you to manipulate the entire block of text as a single unit. You can convert point type and paragraph type quite easily. Simply select the Type layer you want to convert and choose Layer | Type | Convert to Point Text or Convert to Paragraph Text.

Once you've entered text into an image, your changes are committed by either switching to a new tool, selecting a menu command, choosing an interface palette, pressing the numeric keypad's ENTER key, or pressing either CTRL-ENTER (Windows) or COMMAND-RETURN (Mac).

Figure 14-1. Type *consists of mathematically defined shapes that describe the letters, numbers, and symbols of a* typeface.

Inserting Text in an Image

If you click and hold the Type tool, you're presented with four possible options: the Horizontal and Vertical Type tools, as well as Horizontal and Vertical Type mask tools, shown in Figure 14-2.

Inserting Point Type

When you want to insert text, choose the orientation you want your text to take (either horizontal or vertical) by selecting the appropriate Type tool. Then, to enter point type, click inside your image at the point you want to insert the text. When you hover over your image, the pointer will be I-beam shaped with a small line through it. When entering text horizontally, this small line indicates the baseline of your text—in other words, the line on which the bottom of your text rests. Characters with descenders (lowercase g, j, p, q, and y) are consequently bisected by the baseline. When you're inserting text vertically, the small line instead indicates the center axis of the characters. Begin typing to enter text into the document. To begin a new line, simply press ENTER (Windows) or RETURN (Mac).

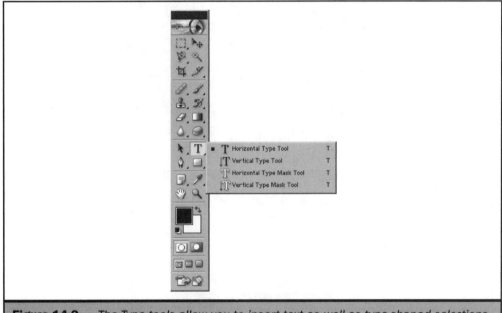

Figure 14-2.   *The Type tools allow you to insert text as well as type-shaped selections.*

Inserting Paragraph Type

When you want to insert paragraph text, instead of simply clicking and typing, you'll use the same I-beam pointer to click and drag a bounding box, as shown in Figure 14-3.

You can define your bounding box in a number of ways. The simplest method is just click and drag a diagonal swath until the box is of suitable dimension. You can also hold down the ALT (Windows) or OPTION (Mac) key while clicking, which opens the Paragraph Text Size dialog box, shown in Figure 14-4. You can then use the dialog box to enter precise dimensions for your bounding box.

Figure 14-3.   *The bounding box allows you to skew, scale, and rotate type. It also defines the point at which your text wraps onto proceeding lines.*

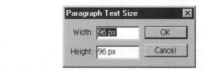

Figure 14-4.   *The Paragraph Text Size dialog box shows pixels as the unit for measuring text. Points is the default unit, but if you're designing for the Web, you may want to use pixels.*

If you want to use different units for measuring your text, refer to the "Choosing a Font Size" section later in this chapter.

Once you've defined your bounding box, the mouse pointer is located in the upper-left corner (for horizontal text), or the upper-right corner (for vertical text) waiting for you to begin typing. As you type, your text will wrap onto the following line when you reach the right edge of the bounding box. To begin a new paragraph inside the box, press ENTER/RETURN.

When your text reaches beyond the bottom edge of the bounding box, the lower-right resize handle displays a plus sign to let you know you have hidden text. You can then drag any of the three bottom resize handles to expand the bounding box and reveal the text.

Transforming a Bounding Box

You can transform a bounding box in much the same way you manipulate objects using the Transform and Free Transform commands on the Edit menu, as shown in Figure 14-5.

If you simply want to resize the dimensions of the bounding box, move your pointer over any of the handles until the I-beam changes to a double arrow. Then, drag to increase or decrease the box's area. Hold down the SHIFT key and drag a corner handle to resize the bounding box proportionally. By holding down the CTRL (Windows) or COMMAND (Mac) key, you can scale the actual size of the text within the bounding box.

You can rotate your bounding box by moving the pointer to the outside box's borders. The cursor switches to a curved double arrow, at which point you can click and drag the box around its center point. Holding down the SHIFT key in this instance limits the box's rotation to 15-degree increments. If you want to relocate the center point of a bounding box, CTRL/COMMAND-drag it to a different position, as shown in Figure 14-6.

Figure 14-5.   *The bounding box can be transformed either before or after you've entered any text into it.*

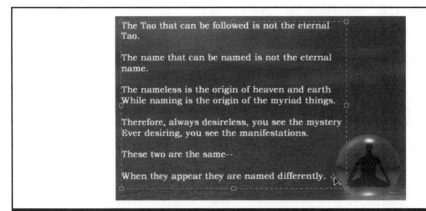

Figure 14-6. *A center point can be placed inside or outside the borders of the bounding box.*

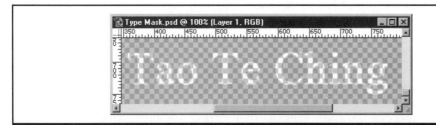

Figure 14-7. *Creating a Type mask*

Figure 14-8. *A type selection created on the active layer*

Skewing a bounding box is equally simple—hold down CTRL-SHIFT (Windows) or COMMAND-SHIFT (Mac). Your pointer again changes, this time to an arrowhead with the double arrow just beneath it. From here, grab one of the four side handles and drag.

Note *When you type text into an image, you're using Adobe's Single Line Composer method to set the type, one line at a time. This is a traditional composing method, compared to the Every Line Composer, which deals with all the text on a Type layer in total, avoiding hyphenation, and stressing the evenness of letter and word spacing above all else. You can switch Composers using the Paragraph palette's option menu.*

Creating a Type Selection

Using the Type tools to create selections is not much different from inserting ordinary text into an image. Instead of selecting the Horizontal or Vertical Type tools, you select the Horizontal or Vertical Type Mask tools. Where you were creating unique Type layers, you are now creating type-shaped selection on the current active layer.

When you initially click the active layer with one of the Type Mask tools, the layer turns transparent red to indicate a mask. The letters you type appear as open spaces in the mask, as shown in Figure 14-7.

Once you click another tool and commit your changes, the mask is replaced by a selection in the shape of the letters you've typed, shown in Figure 14-8.

Formatting Text

Photoshop's text formatting tools provide comprehensive control over your type's font, type size, color, character spacing, and paragraph alignment and justification. You can assign various type properties before you begin entering your text or modify them after your text is already inserted.

Character formatting is done in both the Type tool options bar (Figure 14-9) and the Character palette (Figure 14-10). To view the Character palette, either click the options bar palette button when the Type tool is selected, or choose Window | Character from the menu bar.

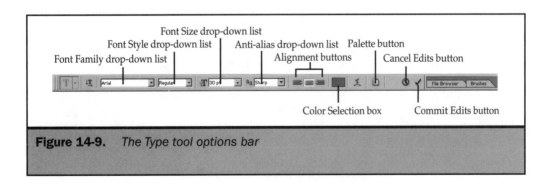

Figure 14-9. *The Type tool options bar*

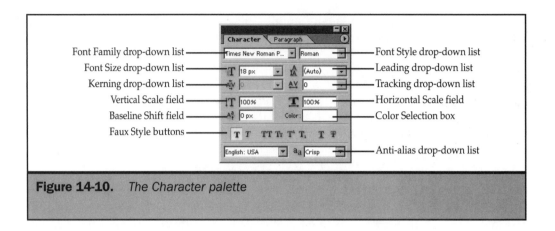

Figure 14-10.   *The Character palette*

There is high degree of overlap between the options bar and the Character palette, obviously. The options bar is there to give you fast access to the majority of basic font formatting tools, while the Character palette provides more extensive control over character spacing and font styles.

Nearly every field of these two interfaces can be typed into, or have their values increased or decreased by clicking in them to place the mouse pointer and then using the UP ARROW and DOWN ARROW keys.

    The Character palette's language drop-down list allows you to choose from several countries. When you choose one, you're asking Photoshop to use that country's spelling and hyphenation rules.

Selecting Text

The first step in formatting your text is to select it. Type can be selected a character at a time or all at once. To select individual characters, make sure the appropriate Type layer is selected. Then use the Horizontal or Vertical Type tool to place the cursor in the text flow and drag across a range of characters. You can also click at any point in the text flow, and then SHIFT-click at another to select the range of characters in between.

You can also use the arrows keys to select text, much as you do in a word processor. After placing the mouse pointer in the text flow, hold down the SHIFT key and use the arrow keys to move the pointer through the range of text you want to select. You can select entire words at a time in this fashion by holding down CTRL-SHIFT/COMMAND-SHIFT. With your text selected, you are ready to add, delete, and format it as you see fit.

If you want to select all the text in a given type layer, simply double-click the layer's type icon. You can also choose Select | All from the menu bar when the Type layer is selected. If you want to select a single word in a line of text, choose the appropriate Type tool and double-click the word. Triple-clicking will select the entire line of text. In a bounding box, quadruple-clicking selects all the text in that paragraph. You can also quintuple-click (five clicks) to select all the text in all the paragraphs.

Applying Fonts and Styles

Use the Font Family drop-down list in either the options bar or Character palette to select the desired font for your text. All fonts installed on your computer are at your disposal. Adobe applications also check the following folders for fonts:

Windows   Program Files/Common Files/Adobe/Fonts

Mac OS 9.*x* System Folder/Application Support/Adobe/Fonts

Mac OS X   Library/Application Support/Adobe/Fonts

Any fonts found in these directories are accessible only to Adobe applications.

Selecting a font style is equally uncomplicated. Simply choose a style for your text using either of the Font Style drop-down lists. Different fonts provide different styles. If your chosen font doesn't have the style you're looking for, you can use the Faux Style buttons in the Character palette. Your options include Bold, Italic, Superscript, Subscript, All Caps, and Small Caps styles.

Choosing a Font Size

You specify a font size using either of the Font Size drop-down lists. By default, Photoshop uses points as its unit of measure for text. You can change the default unit of measure in the Units & Rulers category of the Preferences dialog box, shown in Figure 14-11.

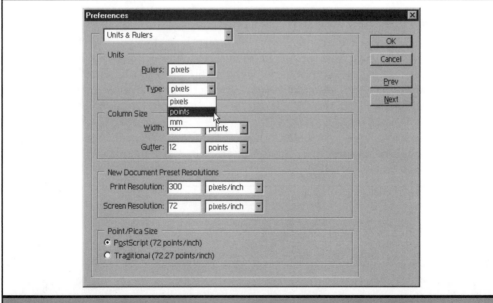

BUILDING ORIGINAL ARTWORK

Figure 14-11.   *Selecting Edit | Preferences | Units & Rulers from the menu bar brings up this category in the Preferences dialog box.*

If you prefer, you can instead enter a different unit of measure directly into the Font Size field on a case-by-case basis. Photoshop accepts the following abbreviations:

- in: Inches
- cm: Centimeters
- mm: Millimeters
- pt: Points
- px: Pixels
- pica: Picas

Applying Text Color

Text is no different than any other part of Photoshop when it comes to applying color. You simply choose a color from Photoshop's Color Picker. When working with text, you have a number of different places from which to invoke the Color Picker. The color selection boxes of the toolbox Foreground color, the options bar, and the Color palette all reflect the most recent color selected via the Photoshop Color Picker or Swatches palette. Note, however, that if you have created a Type layer and applied a different color to the text on that layer (using the Type tool options bar), the Foreground color on the toolbox will not change. To assign a text color, simply click in any one of the color selection boxes to invoke the Color Picker and select a color, or make a selection from the Swatches palette.

Changing Text Orientation

As you might guess from the Type tool options available, text can be inserted both horizontally and vertically. Once text has been inserted, however, its orientation is not set in stone—you can easily swap horizontal orientation for vertical, and vice versa. Simply select the Type layer you want to reorient by clicking the layer's text icon in the Layers palette. Then click the Text Orientation button on the options bar, shown in Figure 14-12.

You can also select Layer | Type, and then Horizontal or Vertical from the menu bar, or choose Change Text Orientation from the Character palette menu.

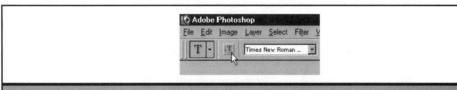

Figure 14-12.   *The Text Orientation button*

Vertical Text Rotation

Vertical text can be inserted with one of two orientations. Characters can be inserted so that each character shares a common vertical baseline running from top to bottom, as shown in Figure 14-13, or characters can be inserted in their standard upright position— each character with a horizontal baseline, but inserted from top to bottom instead of left to right, as shown in Figure 14-14.

Figure 14-13.   *Vertical text sharing a common vertical baseline*

Figure 14-14.   *Vertical text with characters inserted with an upright rotation*

Photoshop refers to the relationships to a vertical baseline as character rotation, and it only applies to vertical text. When characters are rotated they each stand horizontally while flowing from top to bottom, while characters that aren't rotated all share the same vertical baseline. To affect the rotation of vertical text, go to the Character palette menu and select Rotate Character. This places a check mark next to that menu option and rotates each vertical character to its upright position.

Adjusting Character Spacing

In working with text, the space between characters, words, and lines is just as important as the text itself. There are three traditional spacing values in typesetting: leading, kerning, and tracking.

- Leading controls the space between lines of text.
- Kerning controls the space between pairs of characters.
- Tracking controls the spacing of both characters and words in concert.

By using the tools provided in the Character palette, you have exact control of each of these measurements.

Making Leading Adjustments

The term leading (pronounced *ledding*) has an interesting history. Back when metal type was set manually, strips of lead were inserted between each line of type to fix the line spacing. In Photoshop, the leading value you apply indicates the distance between each line of text measured from baseline to baseline. If you're confused by terms like baseline, Figure 14-15 illustrates some basic typographic conventions.

Text becomes too dense and difficult to read if the leading value is too small. Decrease the leading value enough and the bottom edges of characters on the upper line of text begin to tangle with the tops of characters on the line beneath. On the other extreme, when the leading value is high, the distance between lines becomes exaggerated. Figure 14-16 offers some examples. Traditionally, a leading value of 120 percent of the text's font size is considered best for readability. Of course, in a case of text as art, no such standard exists.

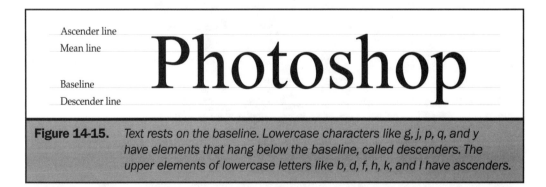

Figure 14-15.   Text rests on the baseline. Lowercase characters like g, j, p, q, and y have elements that hang below the baseline, called descenders. The upper elements of lowercase letters like b, d, f, h, k, and l have ascenders.

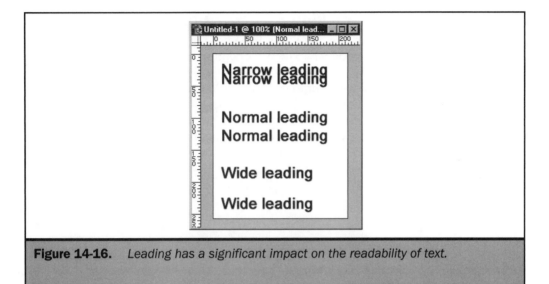

Figure 14-16.   *Leading has a significant impact on the readability of text.*

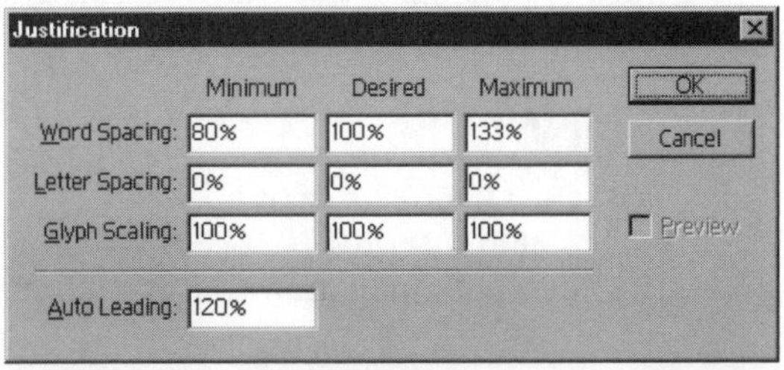

Figure 14-17.   *The Justification dialog box*

You set your leading values in the Character palette, using the Leading drop-down list. The values in the Leading drop-down list conform to the unit of measure you've set for type in the Units & Rulers category of the Preferences dialog box. If the leading value you want is not one of the choices on the menu, select the value in the leading field and enter a new one manually. If you select Auto, then Photoshop uses the default leading value of 120 percent.

If you want to change Photoshop's default auto leading value, switch to the Paragraph palette and select Justification from the palette menu. This opens the Justification dialog box, shown in Figure 14-17. Then locate the Auto Leading field at the bottom of the dialog box and enter a new value.

Making Kerning and Tracking Adjustments

Because of their shape, when some characters are evenly spaced side by side, they appear to be either too close or too far apart. Try opening up your word processor and typing **A** and **V**, then **A** and **P**, and you'll see what I mean. When you choose which type of adjustment to make, remember that kerning adds or subtracts space between two individual characters, while tracking adjusts the spacing across a range of characters.

Fonts typically have a defined kerning setting. To modify that setting, place the mouse pointer between the two characters whose kerning you want to change and make a value selection from the Kerning drop-down list, which offers you a scale of values (in metrics):

−100	−75	−50	−25	−10	−5	0
5	10	25	50	75	100	200

When you apply positive kerning values, the space between characters increases by the chosen amount; negative values decrease the space by the chosen amount. The Metrics value uses the font's built-in kerning information.

Modifying the tracking for a line of text is much the same procedure. Simply select the range of characters you want to affect, and use the Tracking drop-down list just as you would the Kerning drop-down list.

Working with Fractional Widths

In most fonts, the space between each character is not the same but instead varies. This is to counter the optical illusion created by some character pairs making our eyes think they're too far apart or too close together. The variance is sometimes in fractions of a single pixel.

When small font sizes are used, sometimes these fractional widths between characters cause them to run together or spread apart in unattractive and illegible ways. By turning off fractional width spacing, you can eliminate this tendency by separating characters by full pixel widths. Go to the Characters palette menu and locate Fractional Widths. If the option is checked, this indicates fractional widths are in use. Simply click the menu selection to remove the check mark and deselect the option.

Shifting a Character's Baseline

You can manipulate the baseline of text on a character-by-character basis using the Baseline Shift field of the Character palette. This gives you the ability to manually create superscript and subscript effects, as shown in Figure 14-18.

Use a positive value in the field to shift the character above the baseline (superscript), and a negative value to shift the character below the baseline (subscript).

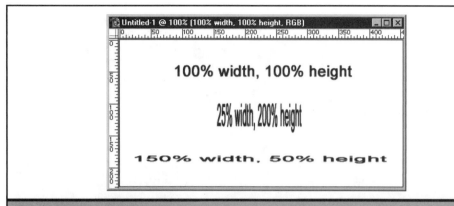

Figure 14-18.   *In this example, I've applied a negative value, shifting the baseline of the first character so that the ascender touches the mean line of the text, subscripting it as a result.*

Figure 14-19.   *Use the Horizontal and Vertical Scale fields to compress or expand selected characters.*

Scaling Text

The Horizontal and Vertical scaling fields of the Characters palette allow you to manipulate the dimensional proportions of selected text in much the same way the Scale command of the Transform submenu does. Each field defaults to a value of 100 percent, indicating the original dimension value of the font as typed. Increasing the percentage stretches the specific dimension, while decreasing that value compresses it (see Figure 14-19).

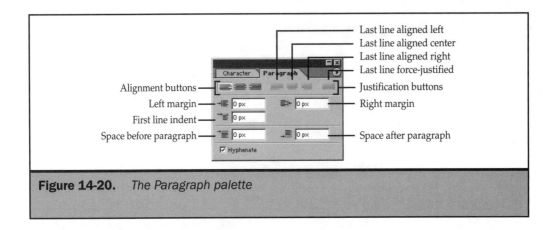

Figure 14-20. *The Paragraph palette*

Working with the Paragraph Palette

Paragraphs are formatted using the Paragraph palette, shown in Figure 14-20. The Paragraph palette lets you specify alignment, justification, indenting, spacing, and hyphenation. To view the Paragraph palette, select Window | Paragraph from the menu bar.

Aligning Text

Paragraphs with horizontal text can be aligned to the left, center, or right of the bounding box; paragraphs with vertical text can be aligned to the top, center, or bottom. Simply use the appropriate alignment button on the Paragraph palette to achieve the desired alignment.

Justifying Text

When justifying text, you are spacing text so each line fits evenly between the left and right margins. Invariably, the last line of a paragraph lacks enough words to be justified without looking awkwardly spaced. Each of Photoshop's justification options addresses this issue. You can justify each line of a paragraph, specifying how the last line of the paragraph should be formatted.

In the case of paragraphs with horizontal text, your options include justifying all but the last line, and aligning that line to the left, center, or right. You can also justify the entire paragraph, in which case the last line is force-justified, which results in odd spacing. Paragraphs with vertical text can be justified in the same manner, only the last sentence options are top, center, and bottom alignment, as well as force-justified. The Paragraph palette justification buttons are shown in Figure 14-21.

Indenting Paragraphs

The indentation settings you specify determine the margin widths between your paragraph text and the bounding box it's inside. Select the paragraph you want to format, and in the left and right margin fields enter a width value. In the case of vertical text, the left and right margin fields are relative to the top and bottom sides of the bounding box, respectively.

You can indent the first line of a paragraph using the First Line Indent field. Simply enter an indentation width value in that field. To create a hanging indent, enter a negative value.

Applying Space Before and After Paragraphs

The Paragraph palette provides spacing options so you can control the amount of space above or below each paragraph. Simply use the Space Before or Space After fields to enter a value.

Adjusting Hyphenation Options

Photoshop's hyphenation options let you determine where and how words in paragraph text can be hyphenated. You adjust Photoshop's hyphenation options in the Hyphenation dialog box, shown in Figure 14-22. To view the Hyphenation dialog box, select Hyphenation from the Paragraph palette menu. The following hyphenation options are available to you:

- In the Words Longer Than field, enter the minimum number of letters a hyphenated word can contain.

- In the After First field, enter the minimum number of characters at the beginning of a word that can be broken by a hyphen.

- In the Before Last field, enter the minimum number of characters at the end of a word that can be broken by a hyphen.

- In the Hyphen Limit field, enter the maximum number of hyphens that can appear on consecutive lines. A value of zero allows unlimited hyphens.

- In the Hyphenation Zone field, enter the distance at the end of a line that will cause a word to break in unjustified type.

- Use the Hyphenate Capitalized Words check box to specify whether capitalized words get hyphenated.

BUILDING ORIGINAL ARTWORK

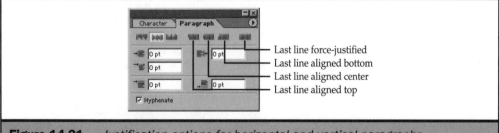

Figure 14-21. *Justification options for horizontal and vertical paragraphs*

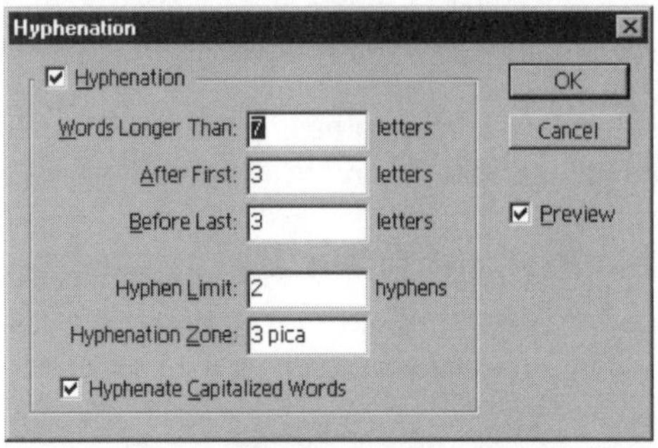

Figure 14-22. *The Hyphenation dialog box*

> **Note**
>
> *Assuming you've dealt with all the issues related to the appearance and placement of your text, don't forget to check your spelling. You can use the Edit | Check Spelling command to open the Check Spelling dialog box, which will go through the active Type layer's content and check for words not found in Photoshop's internal dictionary. The feature works very much like any word processor's spell-check facility—you can ignore things you know are spelled correctly, add words to the dictionary, and change spelling to match the suggested corrections that will be offered in the dialog box. If there are multiple Type layers in your image, the Check All Layers option will be available, and if you turn it on, you can spell-check all the text in your image rather than repeating the process for each individual layer.*

Summary

In this chapter, you learned that Photoshop differentiates between point and paragraph type, and what's involved in inserting them into an image. You learned the various methods for selecting text, and how to use the Character palette to specify fonts and font sizes, and also how to set your font color. You also learned how to modify text orientation, spacing, and scaling. Lastly, you examined the Paragraph palette and learned how to align, justify, and indent paragraph type, as well as set paragraph spacing and hyphenation options.

The Complete Reference

Chapter 15

Applying Special Effects to Text

N ot all communication in an image is done with pictures. Some images still require text to carry a message. You have already learned how to add text to your image, set its typeface and size, and add color to it. Now you are going one step beyond to work with type as artwork. You will smooth the edges of your type, change its orientation, adjust its alignment, apply blending options and shadows, bevel and emboss text, fill text, apply patterns and gradients, and work with text masks.

Working with Type Layers

By working with more than one layer, you are able to leave some elements of your image undisturbed while modifying other elements. Type is an important element and one that is frequently changed, so placing it on a separate layer makes it easier for you to edit the text or add special effects to the type. When you insert new text by clicking on your image with either the Horizontal Type tool or the Vertical Type tool, Photoshop automatically creates a new Type layer for you, as seen in Figure 15-1.

After you create the Type layer, you are able to use the layer commands to modify the layer. Just as you do with any layer, you can restack, move, copy, and change layer options for the Type layer. Layer styles also work with Type layers. There is also a special set of layer commands that applies only to Type layers: changing type orientation, creating work paths from type, converting type to shapes, applying anti-aliasing, and warping.

Figure 15-1.   The large "T" identifies the new Type layer. The first few characters of the text become the name of the layer.

The fill shortcuts work on Type layers. Press ALT-BACKSPACE *(Windows) or* OPTION-DELETE *(Mac) to fill with the foreground color; press* CTRL-BACKSPACE/COMMAND-DELETE *to fill with the Background color.*

The transformation commands on the Edit menu are applicable to Type layers, and you can use them and still edit your text, unless you try to transform just part of the Type layer. Perspective and Distort, however, as well as some filter effects and painting tools, require that you *rasterize* the type before you apply the command or tool. When you rasterize a Type layer, you convert it to a normal layer; the type is no longer considered text and, therefore, cannot be edited. Photoshop warns you if you choose a command or tool that requires a rasterized layer (see Figure 15-2). If you plan to use such an operation, you may want to duplicate your layer first and test the effect there. You can always remove the duplicate layer later. To rasterize the selected Type layer, choose Type from the Layer menu, and then Rasterize from the submenu.

For some operations the type tool must be in Edit Mode, which happens automatically when you enter new characters or you click on existing characters on a Type layer. You can tell if you are in Edit Mode if you see the Commit and Cancel buttons on the options bar. Other operations require that you commit changes to the Type layer first, which you do by clicking the Commit button on the options bar, pressing ENTER on the numeric keypad, pressing CTRL-ENTER/COMMAND-RETURN on the main keyboard, or selecting another tool or menu command.

Changing the Type Layer Orientation

One set of layer commands lets you switch the orientation of the Type layer from horizontal to vertical or the reverse. *Orientation* refers to the relation between the direction of the type lines and the bounding box or document window, depending on whether the layer contains point or paragraph type. As you can see in Figure 15-3, when the type lines are left to right in the document window, the orientation is horizontal. In a vertically oriented layer, the type goes from top to bottom.

Figure 15-2.   *When you attempt to apply a Blur filter to the Type layer, Photoshop lets you decide if you want to rasterize the type or discontinue the operation.*

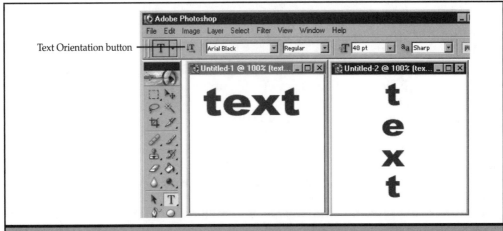

Figure 15-3. *The layer shown on the left has a horizontal orientation; the one on the right is oriented vertically.*

To change the orientation of the Type layer, start by selecting that layer in the Layers palette. Then do any of the following:

- Choose Type from the Layer menu, and then pick either Horizontal or Vertical.

- Select either of the type tools, and then click the Text Orientation button in the options bar.

- If the Character palette is visible, choose Change Text Orientation from the Palette menu.

Applying Blending Options to Type

When you work with layers, you can create a number of effects using the Blending Modes. A Blending Mode sets how a layer's pixels blend with the pixels in the underlying layers.

When you want to specify a Blending Mode for a layer or layer set, first select the layer or layer set in the Layers palette. To choose a Blending Mode, select Blending Options from the Layers palette menu or choose Layer Style from the Layer menu. Then select Blending Options from the submenu. Make your choice from the Blend Mode drop-down list in the Layer Style dialog box (see Figure 15-4).

You can also open the Blending Options dialog box by right-clicking (Windows) or CONTROL-clicking (Mac) a Type layer, or by clicking the Layer Styles button at the bottom of the Layers palette.

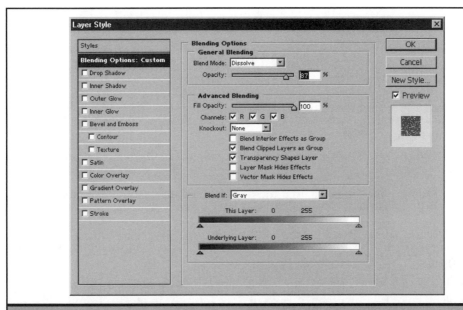

Figure 15-4.   *The Opacity slider determines how well the pixels of the underlying layer show in the final image. One-hundred percent opacity will completely obscure content on the lower layers.*

In order to understand the Blending Modes, you need to know the following terms:

■ The original color in the image is the *base color*.

■ The color being applied with a painting or editing tool is the *blend color*.

■ The color that results from the blend is the *result color*.

The base color and blend color are set by Photoshop based on the color channel information for the image.

The different Blending Modes available to you include the following:

Normal   Paints or edits each pixel to make it the result color (the default mode).

Dissolve   Paints or edits each pixel to make it the result color, which is a random replacement by the base color or the blend color (depends on the opacity of the pixel).

Darken   Replaces pixels that are lighter than the base color with the blend color.

Multiply   Doesn't change white or black but does darken other colors.

Color Burn   Increases the contrast to darken the base color to reflect the blend color. It doesn't change white pixels.

Linear Burn   Decreases the brightness to darken the base color. It doesn't change white pixels.

Lighten   Selects the lighter of the base color or blend color as the result color. It replaces any pixels that are darker than the blend color, but it doesn't change pixels that are lighter than the blend color.

Screen   Multiplies the inverse of the blend and base colors for a lighter result color. Screening with black doesn't change the pixel color, but screening with white turns the pixel white.

Color Dodge   Decreases the contrast to brighten the base color. Blending with black produces no change.

Linear Dodge   Increases the brightness to brighten the base color. Blending with black produces no change.

Overlay   Screens or multiplies the colors so patterns or colors overlay pixels without replacing them, which keeps the highlights and shadows of the base color in the image.

Soft Light   Darkens if the blend color is darker than 50 percent gray or lightens if the blend color is lighter than 50 percent gray. It produces an effect similar to a diffused spotlight.

Hard Light   Lightens the image if the blend color is lighter than 50 percent gray but darkens the image if the blend color is darker than 50 percent gray. It produces an effect similar to a harsh spotlight.

Vivid Light   Decreases the contrast to lighten the image if the blend color is lighter than 50 percent gray; it increases the contrast to darken the image if the blend color is darker than 50 percent gray.

Pin Light   Replaces pixels darker than the blend color if the blend color is lighter than 50 percent gray and doesn't change pixels lighter than the blend color. It replaces pixels lighter than the blend color if the blend color is darker than 50 percent gray, but leaves darker pixels alone.

Difference   Subtracts the blend color from the base color or the reverse, depending on which is brighter. Blending with black produces no change, but blending with white inverts the base color values.

Exclusion   Produces an effect similar to Difference, but with lower contrast.

Hue   Makes a result color that has the same saturation and luminance as the base color but the hue of the blend color.

Saturation   Makes a result color that has the same luminance and hue as the base color but has the saturation of the blend color. No change occurs in pixels with no saturation (0).

Color   Makes a result color with the same luminance as the base color, but the hue and saturation of the blend color, keeping the gray levels in the image.

Luminosity   Makes a result color with the same hue and saturation of the base color, but the luminance of the blend color, producing the opposite effect of the Color Mode.

You can quickly set the Blending Mode by making a selection from the drop-down list at the top of the Layers palette.

In the Advanced Blending section of the Layer Styles dialog box, you also see sliders that determine which pixels from the active layer and underlying layers will appear in the final image. The sliders range from 0 (black) to 255 (white). Move the white slider triangle to determine the high value of the range; the black slider triangle sets the low value. Use This Layer to determine which pixels on the active layer will blend (other pixels don't appear in the final image). Set the Underlying Layer slider to do the same for all the visible, underlying layers. Choose Gray from the Blend If drop-down list to specify the blending range from all channels or select an individual channel.

As you make your settings, you want to see what effect they will have on your image, so check Preview. When you are sure your settings produce the effect you want, click OK to close the dialog box and apply your modifications to the image.

Applying Styles to Type

There are a number of effects you can apply to change the appearance of a layer, and Photoshop links these effects to the contents of the layer. Any changes you make to the contents, such as moving or editing, causes a change in the effect. For example, if you apply a shadow effect on your Type layer and then add characters to the text on that layer, the shadow effect also applies to the new characters.

An effect or group of effects may be combined into a style you can apply to layers over and over. Photoshop has a group of preset styles for you to use. They are available on the Styles palette (see Figure 15-5), which you display by choosing Styles from the Window menu. With your Type layer selected, you click the style you want, and it is immediately applied to the layer. Some other methods for selecting styles follow:

- Drag a style from the Styles palette and drop it on the desired layer on the Layers palette. If you hold down SHIFT while you drag your mouse, the effects of the style will be added to the existing effects applied to that layer. Otherwise, the style will be replaced by the new style.

- Drag a style from the Styles palette and drop it in the document window over the layer content you want to affect.

- Open the Layer Style dialog box (see Figure 15-6) by choosing Blending Options from the Layers palette menu. Then click Styles on the left side to see the preset styles. Select one and click OK to apply it and close the dialog box.

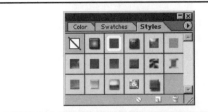

Figure 15-5.   *The first style in the top-left corner turns off any styles applied to the layer.*

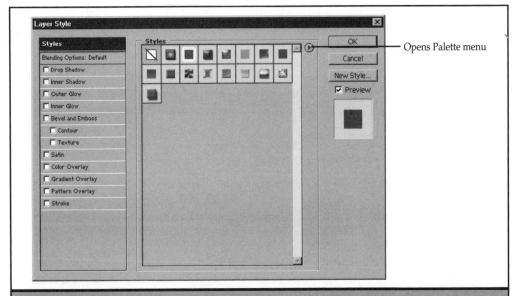

Opens Palette menu

Figure 15-6.   *In either the Layer Style dialog box or the Styles palette, select Load Styles from the Palette menu to select additional sets of styles.*

After you apply a style to a layer, an icon appears to the right of the layer name on the Layers palette (see Figure 15-7). The effects included in that style display immediately below the layer name. You can collapse or expand this list by clicking the small triangle next to the icon.

To remove a style from a layer, in the Layers palette drag the Effects bar for the layer to the trashcan icon. You may also choose Clear Layer Style from the submenu that appears when you select Layer Style from the Layer menu. There is also a Clear Style button at the bottom of the Styles palette that removes the style from the currently selected layer. To remove an individual effect from a layer, select the layer in the Layers palette and then drag the effect to the trashcan icon.

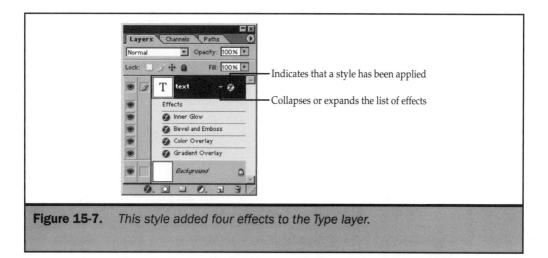

Indicates that a style has been applied

Collapses or expands the list of effects

Figure 15-7.   *This style added four effects to the Type layer.*

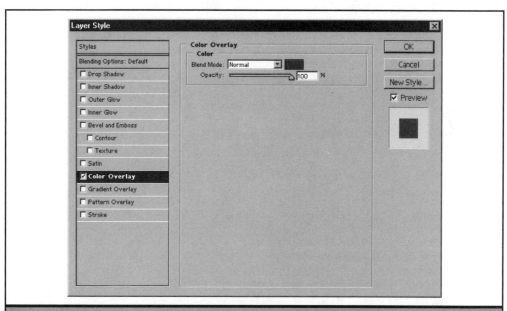

Figure 15-8.   *Select the effect under Styles to see related options for that style.*

Using Styles to Fill Type

When you create text, it takes on the color of the foreground. You already know how to change the color of selected characters. To apply color to all the type on a layer, you need to apply an Overlay style. After selecting the Type layer, choose Layer Style from the Layer menu and then, if it's not already selected (it should be by default), select Color Overlay from the submenu. This opens the Layer Style dialog box (see Figure 15-8). Check Color Overlay under Styles to see the options for coloring the type.

Click the color box next to the Blend Mode drop-down list to select the color you want to use for the overlay. Make your color choice from the Color Picker dialog box, and then click OK. You may also apply a Blend Mode to the overlay and set its Opacity. If you have Preview selected, you will see how the changes you make affect the image. Click OK to apply your modifications and close the dialog box.

   A quick way to apply styles such as Color Overlay is to click the Add a New Style button at the bottom of the Layers palette, and then choose the effect you want to apply to the layer.

Applying Pattern and Gradient Overlays

Adding a pattern or gradient to your type is a matter of selecting the appropriate overlay style for the Type layer. To apply a pattern overlay to the currently selected layer, choose Layer Style from the Layer menu and then select Pattern Overlay from the submenu to open the Layer Style dialog box (see Figure 15-9). Pattern Overlay is checked for you.

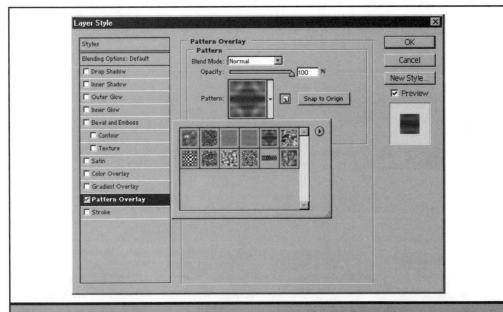

Figure 15-9.   *When you click on Pattern, a palette of predefined patterns appears.*

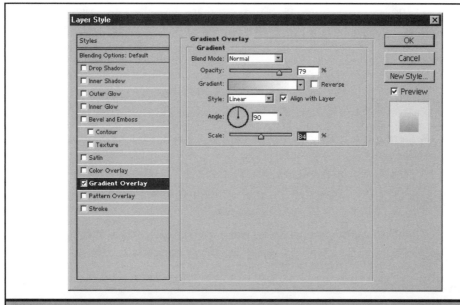

Figure 15-10. *The currently selected gradient is the Foreground to Background selection, which is based on the current Foreground and Background colors.*

As you experiment with effects, you may see several checked in the Styles list. They combine for an overall style, but the combination may confuse your current choice. Turn them off temporarily until you finish selecting the current effect.

Click Pattern to see a set of predefined patterns that are ready to use (to apply a new pattern, you must first define it). Double-click the one you want. Use the Scale slider to size the pattern within the text. Checking Align with Layer specifies that the pattern will stay with the layer even if the layer moves (the default setting). Click OK to apply the pattern overlay and to close the dialog box.

If you want to apply a gradient overlay, Photoshop does provide a set of gradient fills from which you can choose. Some of these fills use the current Foreground and Background colors, so it's a good idea to set those colors first. To apply Gradient Overlay style to the currently selected Type layer, choose Layer Style from the Layer menu and then select Gradient Overlay from the submenu to open the Layer Style dialog box (see Figure 15-10). Gradient Overlay is checked for you.

Click Gradient to see the predefined gradient fills. Three of the gradient fills rely on your Foreground and Background color choices. These include the Foreground-to-Background gradient (in the upper-left corner of the palette), the Foreground-to-Transparent gradient next to it, and the Transparent Stripes gradient. Click the gradient you want to use and see how it changes your type (if you have Preview selected). Double-click your final selection to continue setting gradient options.

To have more or different gradient fills loaded into the gradient palette, click the menu button on the right side of the palette and choose from one of the fill sets at the bottom of the menu. You can either replace the current choices or append the new ones to the existing set.

By checking Reverse, the colors in your gradient will reverse directions. For example, the Foreground-to-Background gradient will change to a Background-to-Foreground gradient.

The style of the gradient depends on where the gradient starts and ends:

Linear Shades from one side of the layer to another in a straight line (the default).

Radial Shades from the center to the outer edge.

Angle Shades in a counterclockwise sweep from the starting point.

Reflected Shades symmetrically on either side of the center.

Diamond Shades from the center out in a diamond pattern.

Where applicable to the gradient style, you can set the angle of the gradient. Use the Scale slider to set how broad the gradient is.

When you have the settings you want, click OK to close the dialog box and apply your modifications to the Type layer.

Creating New Type Styles

As you apply effects to a layer, you create its custom style. By saving the style, you make it a preset style. It then becomes available on the Styles palette.

To save a new style, select the layer that has the combination of effects you want to save, and then click the Create New Style button on the bottom of the palette or select New Style from the Palette menu. You can also drag the layer onto the Styles palette, or, if you have the Layer Style dialog box open, click the New Style button.

In the New Style dialog box (see Figure 15-11), enter a name for your new style. Decide whether you want to include just the layer effects, just the layer blending options, or both in your new style. Click OK to close the dialog box and add your new style to the presets. Figure 15-12 shows the new Blue Horizons style that was added.

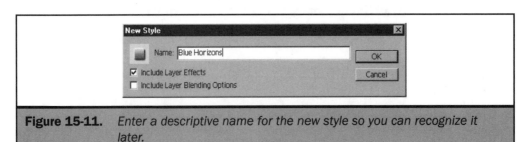

Figure 15-11. *Enter a descriptive name for the new style so you can recognize it later.*

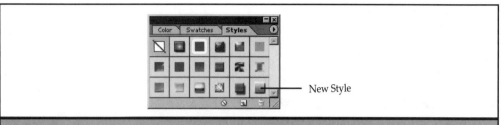

New Style

Figure 15-12.   *The new Blue Horizons style was appended to the Styles palette.*

Using Shadows to Make Text Stand Out

Shadows give your images depth. By adding shadows to your type, your text stands out from the rest of the image. A drop shadow appears behind the text to make it appear that the type is floating slightly above the layer. An Inner Shadow appears just inside the edges of the type to make it appear that the type has thickness and roundness and rises above the layer.

To apply a drop shadow to your currently selected Type layer, choose Layer Style from the Layer menu, and then select Drop Shadow from the submenu. When the Layer Style dialog box opens, Drop Shadow is selected (see Figure 15-13).

The Multiply Blending Mode is automatically applied to the drop shadow, as is the color black. The Opacity will therefore make the shadow darker or lighter. The Angle represents the angle of the light source, and you can either enter the value or drag the indicator. Select Global Light to make it appear that there is a consistent light source shining on the type. Use the sliders to set the Distance that the shadow is offset from the type (in pixels), how much Spread the shadow has (in percent), and the Size of the shadow (in pixels).

Contour controls the fading in the shadow. From the Contour drop-down list, you can select different contour curves and then view their effect on your image (if you have Preview checked). Choose the one you like by double-clicking it. Select Anti-aliased to blend the edges of the shadow. Anti-aliasing is more effective when shadows are smaller and have a complicated contour. The Noise slider makes the shadow grainier as you increase the percentage, and adding some noise can help minimize banding on the outer edges of a shadow—something you'll appreciate if you print high-resolution images to an image setter. Selecting Layer Knocks Out Drop Shadow controls the visibility of the shadow on a semitransparent layer. Click OK to apply your changes and close the dialog box.

To apply an inner shadow to the currently selected Type layer, choose Layer Style from the Layer menu and then select Inner Shadow from the submenu. When the Layer Style dialog box opens, Inner Shadow is already selected (see Figure 15-14). The Multiply Blending Mode is also selected with black as the color. Changing the Opacity makes the shadows appear lighter or darker. Check Use Global Light to set a consistent light source, and specify the Angle that you want the light to originate. Use the sliders to set the Distance (in pixels) that the shadow is offset, specify the Choke (in percent) to shrink or expand the boundaries of the matte of the shadow, and set the Size of the shadow (in pixels). Select an appropriate Contour to control the fade of the shadow. Select Anti-aliased to blend the edges of the shadow. Increase Noise using the slider to create static in the shadow. Click OK to close the dialog box and apply your settings.

Making Type Glow Inside and Out

Two interesting effects to apply to type are inner glow and outer glow. These effects make it appear that light emanates from the inside or outside edges of the type. To apply these effects, choose Layer Style from the Layer menu, and then select either Inner Glow or Outer Glow from the submenu. In the Layer Style dialog box (see Figure 15-15), Screen is set as the default Blending Mode for this effect and you can use the sliders to set its Opacity and add Noise. You also have the choice of color for the glow and can apply it as a solid or a gradient fill. Click the gradient bar to edit it.

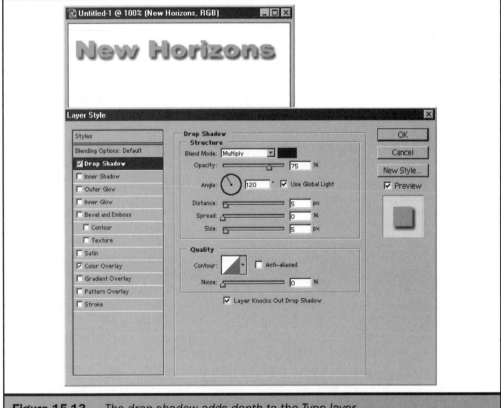

Figure 15-13. *The drop shadow adds depth to the Type layer.*

Figure 15-14. *Adding noise to the inner shadow gives a grainy texture to the shadow.*

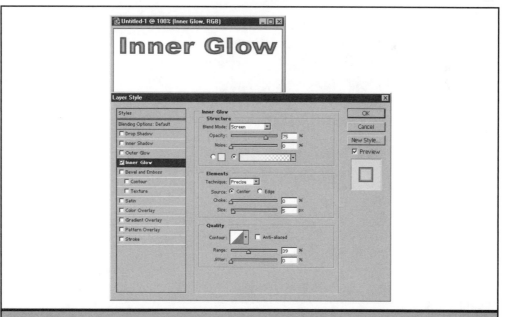

Figure 15-15. *With the Inner Glow set as a gradient, even with a precise technique, the glow appears softer.*

Under Elements, you have the option to set the Technique to Softer or Precise. Softer applies a blur but may possibly lose detailed features in larger type. Precise is more useful with hard-edged mattes such as type, and it is better at keeping detailed features than Softer. The Source option can be set to Center or Edge depending on whether the glow emanates from the center of the type or its inside edges. Use the sliders to specify the Choke (in percent) to shrink or expand the boundaries of the matte of the glow, and set the Size of the glow (in pixels). Under Quality, select an appropriate Contour to control the fade of the glow. Some of the contour choices will create rings of transparency around the type. Select Anti-aliased to blend the edges of the glow. Range controls wherein the glow the contour is applied. Jitter varies the gradient's color and opacity. Click OK to close the dialog box and apply your settings.

The Layer Style dialog box settings for Outer Glow are very similar to Inner Glow. The only difference is in the Elements section. Although you can still set the Technique to Softer or Precise and can use the slider to set the Size, you don't have Choke or Source. Instead, you have a slider to set the Spread, which controls the boundaries of the matte prior to blurring. Figure 15-16 shows a text layer with Outer Glow applied.

Beveling and Embossing Type

Applying Beveling and Embossing effects to Type layers makes the type look as if it has thickness. These effects add combinations of highlights and shadows to the type. To add these effects to a selected Type layer, choose Layer Style from the Layer menu and select Bevel and Emboss from the submenu. The Layer Style dialog box opens with Bevel and Emboss selected (see Figure 15-17).

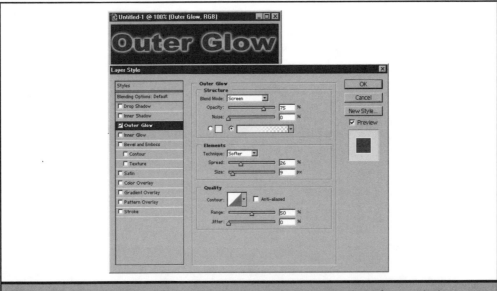

Figure 15-16.   *The Outer Glow setting helps make type stand out from a dark background.*

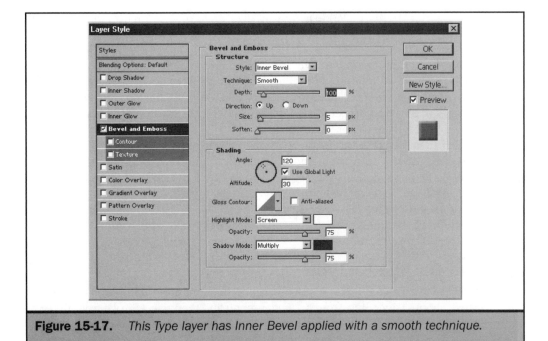

Figure 15-17.   *This Type layer has Inner Bevel applied with a smooth technique.*

There are five styles you can apply:

Outer Bevel   Adds a bevel edge to the outside of the type.

Inner Bevel   Adds ridges within the type.

Emboss   Adds height to the type making it appear higher in the center of the characters.

Pillow Emboss   Adds a rounder and fuller edge.

Stroke Emboss   Makes the stroke edgier.

For any of these styles, there are three techniques you can apply. The Smooth technique blurs the edges slightly. Chisel Hard is mostly used for hard-edged, non-aliased elements such as type. Detailed features are less likely to be lost with Chisel Hard. The Chisel Soft technique isn't as accurate as Chisel Hard, but it still keeps detailed features better than Smooth. Use the Depth slider to set the depth of the bevel. Depth is measured as a ratio of size. Select Up as the direction to see the type appear to be rising up from the layer; select Down to make it appear inset. Size sets the amount of blurring, and Soften blurs the shading.

Under Shading, you can set the Angle of the light source and its Altitude, in addition to specifying whether to use the Global Light. Select a Gloss Contour to create a glossy, metallic appearance. Check Anti-aliased to smooth the edges of the contour. Highlight Mode and Shadow Mode are blend modes applied to the highlights and shadows of the bevel or embossing. Highlight Mode is automatically set to Screen with white as the color; Shadow Mode is set to Multiply by default with black as the color. You can set the Opacity for either mode.

Below Bevel and Emboss on the Styles list are two related effects. Choose Contour to sculpt the ridges, valleys, and bumps that are shaded in embossing (see Figure 15-18). Click Contour to select the type of contour you want to apply. Check Anti-aliased to blend the edges of the contour. Set the Range slider to set the portion of the bevel or emboss to which you want to apply contouring.

Select Texture to specify a pattern to be applied to the bevel effect (see Figure 15-19). Then choose the Pattern you want to apply. The Scale slider lets you set the size of the pattern, and the Depth slider sets the degree and up-down direction of the texture. Select Link with Layer to have the texture stay with the layer if it moves. Invert turns the valleys of the pattern into ridges and the reverse.

When you finish making your setting selections, click OK to apply your modifications and close the dialog box.

Applying an Outline to Type

Another effect you can add to text is to put an outline, or *stroke*, around it. With your Type layer selected, choose Layer Style from the Layer menu and then select Stroke from the submenu. The Layer Style dialog box opens with Stroke already selected (see Figure 15-20). Use the Size slider to set the thickness of the outline in pixels. The Position of the stroke can be set Outside, Inside, or Centered over the edges of the type. You can apply the Blend Mode and Opacity to the stroke; Normal is the default setting, with 100 percent Opacity.

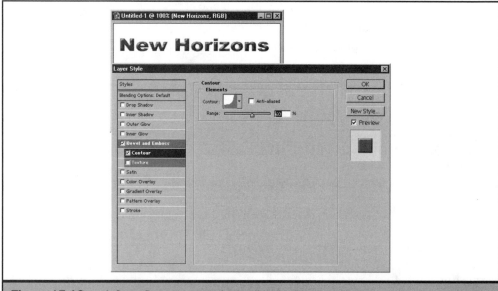

Figure 15-18.   *A Cove Deep contour is applied to the inner bevel.*

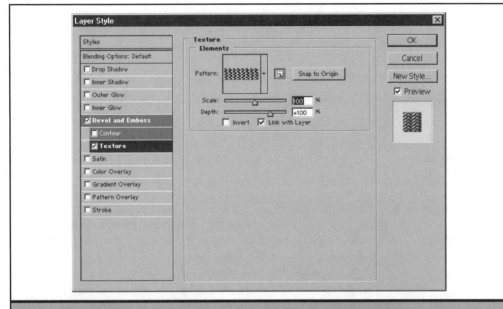

Figure 15-19.   *A Herringbone texture is applied to the inner bevel.*

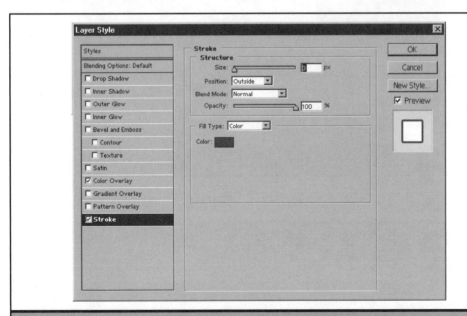

Figure 15-20.   *The three-pixel stroke combined with a white color overlay makes the type appear to be an outline font.*

The stroke doesn't have to be a solid color. From the Fill Type drop-down list, you can select Color, Gradient, or Pattern. If you choose Color, click the Color box to open the Color Picker dialog box. Select your color and click OK.

The Gradient options include:

■ Choosing a pre-set Gradient

■ Selecting Reverse to change the direction of the gradient

■ Choosing a Style to set what type of gradient to use (Linear, Radial, Angle, Reflected, Diamond, or Shape Burst)

■ Establishing an Angle to set the direction of the gradient

■ Setting the Scale to size the gradient (see Figure 15-21)

When using Pattern (see Figure 15-22), you select from predefined patterns and set the Scale of the pattern. For both Gradient and Pattern, you can choose to Link or Align with Layer so the gradient or pattern will stay with the layer even if it is moved. Click OK to apply your modifications and close the dialog box.

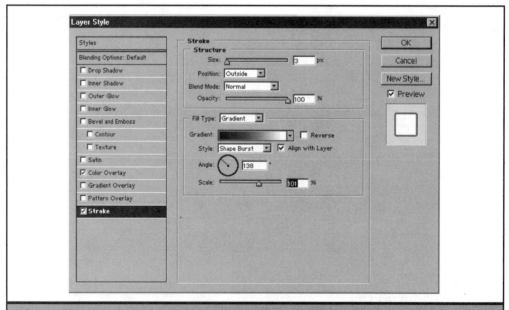

Figure 15-21. A gradient stroke is combined with a Shape Burst style on this Type layer.

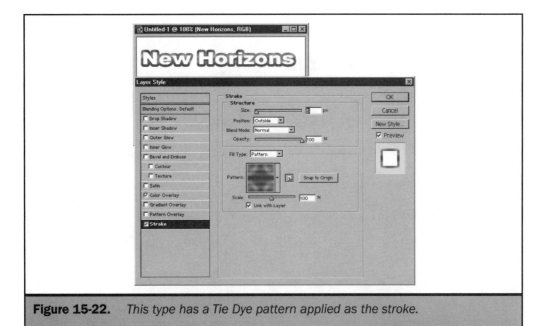

Figure 15-22. *This type has a Tie Dye pattern applied as the stroke.*

Choosing Anti-Aliasing Methods

Does the type you added to your image seem a little blurry or out of focus? When you apply anti-aliasing to a Type layer, Photoshop partially fills in the edge pixels, smoothing the edges on your type.

When you want to apply anti-aliasing to a Type layer, start by selecting that layer in the Layers palette. You can choose an anti-aliasing method from the options bar or Character palette by picking one from the drop-down list (see Figure 15-23). Alternatively, you can choose Type from the Layer menu and select a method from the submenu.

The anti-aliasing methods include the following:

None   Applies no anti-aliasing.

Sharp   Makes type appear the sharpest.

Crisp   Makes the type appear somewhat sharp.

Strong   Makes the type appear to be heavier.

Smooth   Makes the type appear smoother.

Anti-aliasing
on the
options bar

Anti-aliasing
on the Layer
menu

Anti-aliasing
on the Character
palette

Figure 15-23. *Without anti-aliasing, the type can appear jagged, especially when magnified.*

Anti-aliasing does increase the number of colors in an image. You may have difficulty reducing the number of colors and decreasing the optimized file size of the image after applying anti-aliasing, which could be a problem when the image is destined for web use. Also, stray colors may appear along the edges of the type. Although turning off anti-aliasing will result in ragged edges, it may be preferable when file size or limiting the number of colors is an issue. You might consider using larger type sizes than you would for printed images because larger type is easier to view online and gives you more leeway in the use of anti-aliasing.

Small-size type may not display consistently when you apply anti-aliasing. The same is true if the image is set for a lower resolution, as you would for an onscreen image. Try reducing this inconsistency by opening the Character Palette menu and deselecting Fractional Width.

Creating Text Masks

Once you make a selection with one of the selection tools, changing the shape of the selection is a matter of pressing keys or making options bar choices combined with using a selection tool to either add to or subtract from the selection. These operations are complicated, because they also involve hand-eye coordination. Using a mask to create or edit a selection is much easier because you can edit masks using painting and editing tools.

The mask appears as a color overlay (red by default) over the area that isn't selected (see Figure 15-24). Generally, painting with black (foreground) adds to the mask, so painting over the selection area with black reduces the selected area. Painting with white (background) adds to the selection, so painting in the overlay area with white makes the selection larger.

Selecting text using one of the selection tools would probably involve selecting part of the text using the Magic Wand or the Lasso and then increasing the selection to include all the text by making Selection commands. That's not a perfect selection method. Instead of starting with text on a Type layer, create the selection and the text in one step by using the Horizontal Type Mask or the Vertical Type Mask tools.

When you create a type selection border you start by selecting the layer where the selection will appear. That layer should not be a Type layer. Using a normal image layer yields better results. Pick either the Horizontal Type Mask tool or the Vertical Type Mask tool. Set any text options you need, such as font and size, and either click on the image where you want the text to begin, or create a bounding box. Enter the text you want in the selection. The color overlay appears outside the text area. Switch to another tool or click the Commit button to make the mask overlay disappear and to turn the outline of the text into selection boundaries. Once created, these selections are on the active layer, which means they can be filled, stroked, moved, or copied just like any other selection.

Note   *To learn more about masks, turn to Chapter 5.*

Figure 15-24.   *This mask was created using the Horizontal Type Mask. The area in red (appearing gray here) around the text is the mask.*

Moving the Text Selection

While you still have the Horizontal Type Mask tool or Vertical Type Mask tool selected, and before you commit the text (while it still displays as a mask), you can move the masked text by pointing outside the text and then dragging. When these tools are no longer selected, the mask turns into a selection boundary that you can move with the Move tool as you would any selection. While it's a selection, you can copy or cut the text and paste it to another layer, but remember—it's no longer text, and you can't edit it.

Using the Move tool will move pixels and leave the background. Use a selection tool to move the selection boundary without affecting the pixels.

Applying Fills to the Selected Text

When you create text, Photoshop automatically applies the Foreground color as the fill. To change the color, select the text and click the color box on the Character palette. On a Type layer, you apply cover overlays. For the text selection you created with the mask, you can use any painting tool to apply color. Use the Fill command from the Edit menu to select foreground, background, or pattern as the fill. The filters will apply only to the selection, which renders some filters ineligible—for example, the Gaussian Blur won't work because its effects will go beyond the selection. If you have the selection on a layer other than the background layer, the layer styles will add effects to the selection.

A fun way to fill the selection is to place an image on the layer before you add the Text mask. Then when you move the text selection it cuts out the text from the image, filling the text selection with that part of the image. Copy or move the text selection to another layer or image (see Figure 15-25).

Deleting Selected Text

Like any selected text, the easiest way to delete it is to press DELETE. However, if you do this when the selected text is on top of other content on the same layer, it cuts that underlying content, removing an area in the shape of the deleted text selection. This could be useful if you want to see through the text to the layer below (see Figure 15-26). To remove the selection boundary, choose Deselect from the Select menu.

Converting Type to a Path

There are times when you want to be a little playful with text and create new shapes from the characters. To do this, you need to create a work path from the type, which changes the type to vector shapes that you can manipulate. A work path is a temporary path. When you create one, it appears in the Paths palette (see Figure 15-27). After you save it, it works like any other path. You will not be able to edit the characters in the path as text, but the original text layer remains intact and is editable.

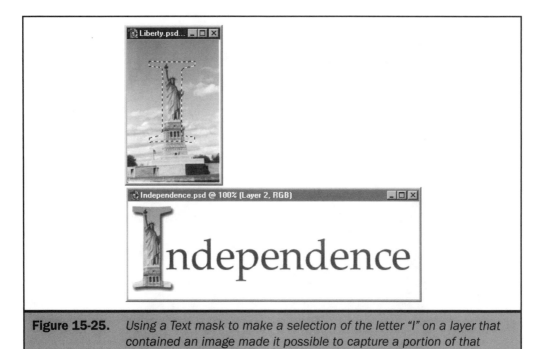

Figure 15-25.   *Using a Text mask to make a selection of the letter "I" on a layer that contained an image made it possible to capture a portion of that image within the selection and copy it to another image.*

BUILDING ORIGINAL
ARTWORK

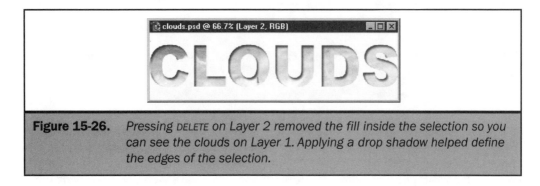

Figure 15-26.   *Pressing DELETE on Layer 2 removed the fill inside the selection so you can see the clouds on Layer 1. Applying a drop shadow helped define the edges of the selection.*

Start by selecting the Type layer. Choose Type from the Layer menu and then select Create Work Path from the submenu. To save the path, choose Save Path from the Paths Palette menu. Give the path a name and click OK. The new path can be manipulated using the pen or shape tools. You can learn more about paths in Chapter 5.

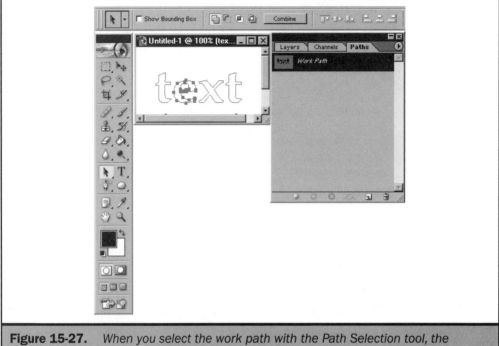

Figure 15-27.   *When you select the work path with the Path Selection tool, the anchor points appear. You use the anchor points to change the shape of the path.*

| Note | *You can create work paths only from fonts that include outline data, which means that you can't create work paths with bitmap fonts.* |

Warping Text

Have you ever seen text that appeared in a fish shape and wondered how it was done? *Warping* distorts type and makes it conform to one of several shapes. Because warping is a Type layer attribute, you can apply different warp styles at any time.

Begin by selecting the Type layer you want to warp. Then you have two ways to start the warping. One way is to choose Type from the Layer menu, and then select Warp Text from the submenu. The other way is to select a Type tool and click the Warp button on the options bar. Either way, the Warp Text dialog box appears (see Figure 15-28).

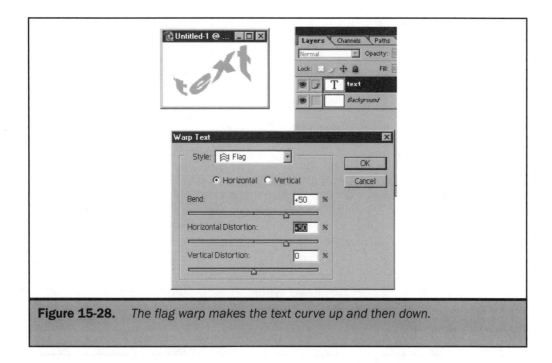

Figure 15-28.   *The flag warp makes the text curve up and then down.*

From the Style drop-down list, select a warp style such as Flag, Arch, or Rise. Then choose either Horizontal or Vertical, depending on the direction you want the warp to go. Use the Bend slider to set the amount of warp you want applied to the layer. Change the Horizontal Distortion and Vertical Distortion sliders to apply perspective to the warp. Click OK to apply your modifications and close the dialog box.

Ready to unwarp? Select the warped Type layer. Choose Type from the Layer menu, and then select Warp Text from the submenu (or select a Type tool and click the Warp button on the options bar). Change the Style to None and click OK.

If you use fonts that don't include outline data (such as bitmap fonts) or use Faux Bold formatting, you won't be able to apply warping to that Type layer.

Rendering Type as Shapes

Another way to manipulate type is to convert it to shapes. However, when you convert type to shapes you can no longer edit the text. A layer with a vector mask replaces the Type layer. You can apply styles to the layer or edit the vector mask.

To convert type to shapes, choose Type from the Layer menu and then select Convert to Shape from the submenu.

You can convert text to shapes only when the font includes outline data, which means you can't use bitmap fonts.

Aligning Text

Text alignment works best for paragraph type, where you draw a bounding box before typing. Alignment (left, center, or right for horizontal text, and top, middle, or bottom for vertical text) is then determined in relation to the edges of the bounding box. You set the alignment in the options bar or the Paragraph palette, either before you start typing or when you selected the text with a type tool (see Figure 15-29).

To align the contents of the Type layer to a selection, make a selection. Then select the layer in the Layers palette. When you pick the Move tool, you'll be able to use the buttons on the options bar to align the layer contents: Align Top Edges, Align Vertical Centers, Align Bottom Edges, Align Left Edges, Align Horizontal Centers, or Align Right Edges (see Figure 15-30).

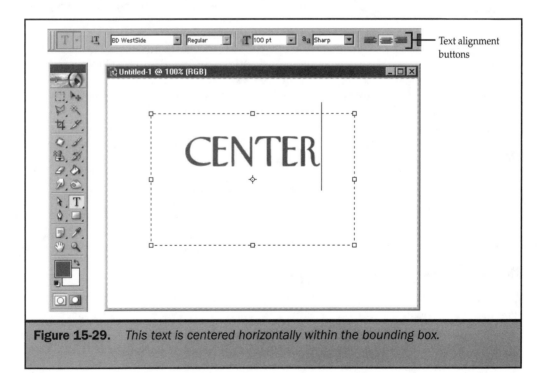

Figure 15-29. *This text is centered horizontally within the bounding box.*

If you want to align the type with the contents of another layer, you have to link the layers first. Then select the Move tool and use the alignment options to align the layers. You link layers by clicking in the left column, next to the layers you want to align. A chain link appears in the left column to show which layers are linked (see Figure 15-31). When the alignment is done, you can remove the links by clicking the link icons to toggle them off.

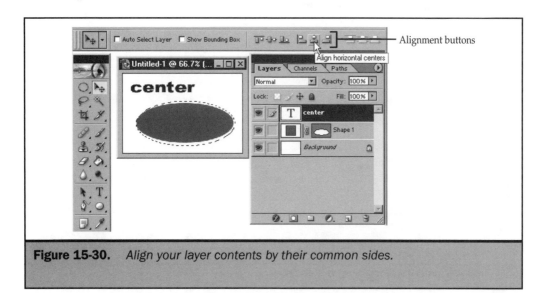

Figure 15-30. *Align your layer contents by their common sides.*

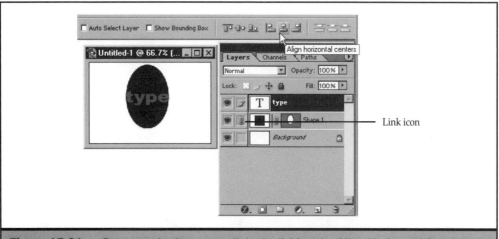

Figure 15-31. *Because the layers are linked, clicking the Align Horizontal Centers button centers text on one layer with an ellipse on another layer.*

BUILDING ORIGINAL
ARTWORK

Summary

In this chapter, you learned to add effects to text on Type layers by changing their orientation, specifying blend modes, and adding layer styles. You also learned to create text selections using masks. You made work paths from type, rendered type as shapes, warped text for special effects, and aligned text.

In the next chapter, you will learn to print your Photoshop creations.

The Complete Reference

Chapter 16

Printing Your Photoshop Creations

W hen you select File | Print from the menu bar, Photoshop sends your image to an *output device*—a printer, image setter, film recorder, or anything that generates some type of hard copy from the file.

Your printer's options may vary from those shown in this chapter's figures.

Printing Your Files

The File menu has four print-related commands, shown in Figure 16-1. Through these commands, set up page layout, preview your print job, specify the number of copies and which printer the job will be sent to, and print your file.

Page Setup

The Page Setup command, as well as other print-related dialog boxes, are available from the File menu. When you select Page Setup, the options available in the Page Setup dialog box are determined by the driver file for the output device to which you choose to send your file. For example, the Page Setup options for PostScript printers will vary greatly from those offered to users of non-PostScript printers. When I choose Page Setup, with the printer attached to the computer on which I'm writing this book, I'm first presented with the dialog box shown in Figure 16-2.

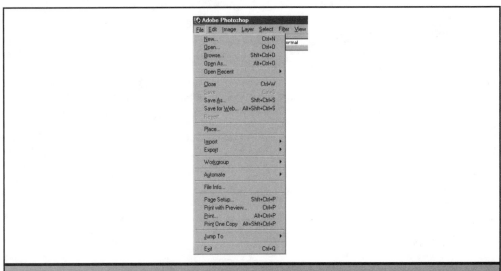

Figure 16-1. *There are four print-related commands (along with their keyboard shortcuts) located in the File menu.*

Through the Page Setup dialog box, I'd select the paper dimensions, orientation, and margin settings. If you're working on a Macintosh, your Page Setup dialog box may look like the one shown in Figure 16-3, showing the setup options for a laser printer, under OS X.

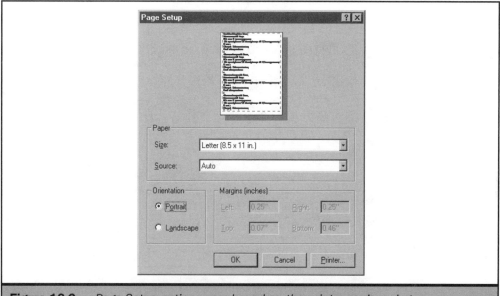

Figure 16-2.   *Page Setup options vary based on the printer you're using.*

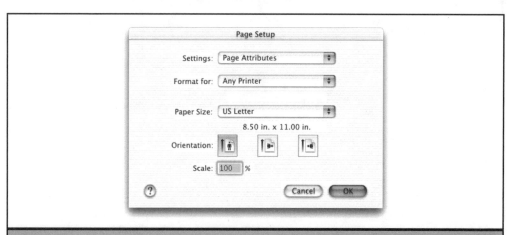

Figure 16-3.   *Macintosh users can choose from a variety of device-specific options in the Page Setup dialog box.*

If I click the Properties button, the resulting dialog box (shown in Figure 16-4) allows me to select a different printer.

This version of the Page Setup dialog box provides me with basic information about the output device, and lets me select a different printer if I choose. Clicking the Properties button in this case shows a dialog box for the specific printer and provides access to a number of options and features only this printer has, as shown in Figure 16-5.

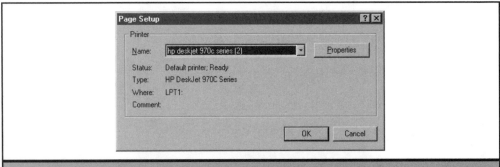

Figure 16-4. *Click the Properties button in the Page Setup dialog box to view more information about your printer.*

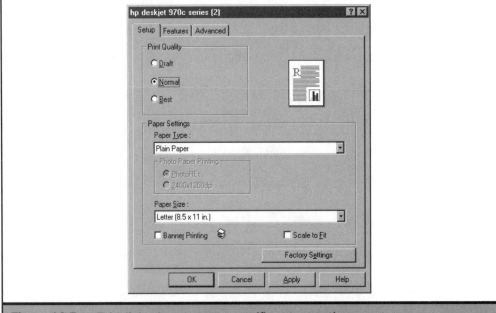

Figure 16-5. *This dialog box presents specific output options.*

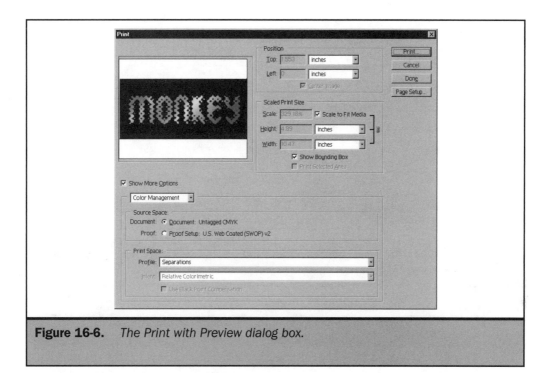

Figure 16-6.   *The Print with Preview dialog box.*

Many of the options also repeat those first shown in the first Page Setup dialog box. Again, these options vary from output device to output device.

Print with Preview

Choosing Print with Preview opens what used to be known as the Print Options dialog box, but in Photoshop 7 is now simply labeled Print, shown here in Figure 16-6. The Mac OS 9 and OS X versions of this dialog box are shown in Figures 16-7 and 16-8, respectively.

In the Position section at the top right of the dialog box, you use the Top and Left fields to specify the exact location of your image within the confines of the printed page or output medium. Alternatively, you can drag the preview window's image to set the proper position. Click the Center Image check box to secure the image in the center of the page.

Using the Scaled Print Size section of the Print with Preview dialog box has some consequences worth noting. Scaling in this dialog box affects only the printed image, not the file as a whole. This means that even though you may choose to scale the image to 80 percent of its original size, you aren't changing the document size settings like you would be if you did the same thing in the Image Size dialog box. You're simply *printing* the image at 80 percent of its actual size. Interestingly, you're also affecting the resolution of the image. As you decrease the image scale you increase the resolution proportionally. So, if you decrease the image scale by half, you double the resolution. A 300-ppi image scaled to 50 percent will print at 600 ppi.

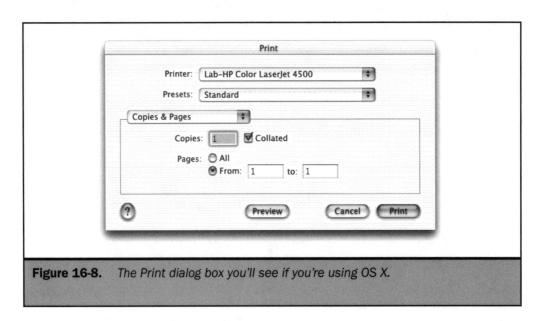

Figure 16-7.   *The Mac OS 9 Print dialog box.*

Figure 16-8.   *The Print dialog box you'll see if you're using OS X.*

If you scale an image greater than the original size, you'll reduce its printed resolution and may degrade the quality of the printout.

You can also utilize the Scale to Fit Media option to change the scaled print size so that it matches the paper size. If you're printing to paper that's 8.5 × 11 inches and your image is 9 × 12 inches, the image will fit on the letter-size paper when printed. The size of the image will not be affected, however; the scaling applies only to the printing process.

You'll also notice the Show Bounding Box option, which displays a box with corner handles. The box fits tightly around the edges of the image, and can be used to adjust the Scaled Print Size settings by dragging the handles. Figure 16-9 shows an adjustment in progress.

If you have selected a portion of your image before opening the Print dialog box, the option to Print Selected Area will be available. By placing a checkmark in that box, you restrict the printout to the portion of the image within the selection.

As I noted earlier, different output devices offer up slightly different dialog boxes (e.g., between PostScript and non-PostScript printers, and even between different inkjet printers). In some cases, you may be given a scaling option in the Page Setup dialog box as well. If you set a scaling option in the Page Setup dialog box, the Scale text box in the Print with Preview dialog box may not accurately reflect the value you set in it. You should therefore refrain from using the Page Setup dialog box to set any scaling options.

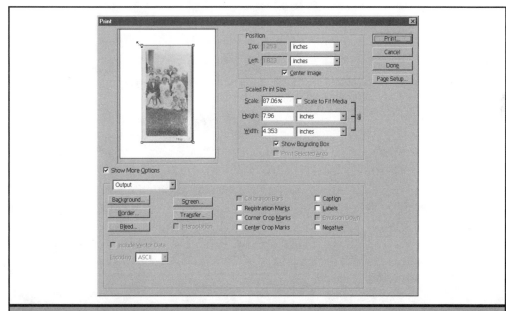

Figure 16-9.   *Drag the Bounding Box handles to scale the image.*

In the Scaled Print Size section, use the Scale field to make the image a percentage of its original size, or use the Width and Height fields to enter specific measurements. The drop-down lists beside each field allow you to set a unit of measure. Your choices are inches, centimeters, millimeters, points, or picas. Scale to Fit Media adjusts the image to fit the size of the output medium selected in Page Setup.

The Show More Options check box displays Output and Color Management options when checked. Use the drop-down list to select the category, and the bottom of the dialog box changes to offer the appropriate tools. Figures 16-10 and 16-11 show the Output and Color Management versions of the dialog box when Show More Options is checked.

Using Output Options

When working with the Output options, you'll have the following settings to choose from—each is represented by a button or a check box. When you click to place a checkmark in a check box, the item is added to the preview and, if left selected, will be included in the printout. Your options are:

Background Clicking the Background button opens the Photoshop color picker from which you can assign a colored background around the printed image.

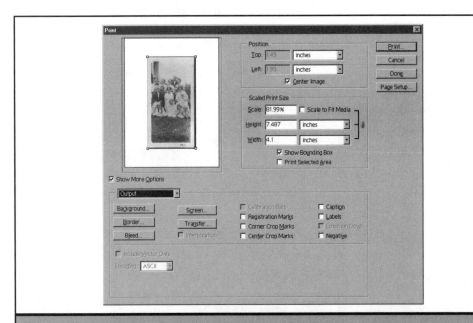

Figure 16-10. *Set the Output options for your image.*

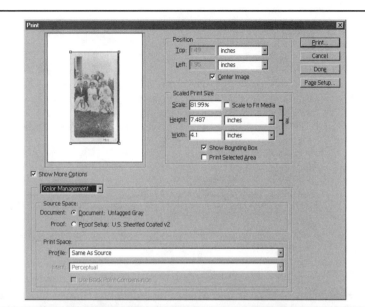

Figure 16-11.   *Use these Color Management options to control your printout.*

Border   You can define a border around your image up to 10 units in thickness. Click the Border button to access the Border dialog box, enter a border value, and choose a unit of measurement (inches, millimeters, or points). The border color will be black, despite whatever Foreground color is currently selected.

Bleed   The term *bleed* means to print an image so that the ink extends to the bounds of the page size (but not the paper size)—an effect achieved by printing and then cutting (or *cropping*) the paper down to a size within the border of the actual image dimensions. With Photoshop's Bleed option, you set crop marks inside the image dimensions. Use the Bleed dialog box to set a width value specifying the distance in from the image's edge at which you want to place the crop marks. Again, the possible units of measure are inches, millimeters, or points.

Screen   The Screen button opens the Halftone Screens dialog box. Setting halftone screens is detailed later in this chapter in the section "Halftoning Images."

Transfer   The Transfer function is only recognized if you're printing directly from the Photoshop application to a connected imagesetter, or if the file is saved in EPS format (with the Include Transfer Function option checked) and printed to a Postscript printer. The Transfer button opens the Transfer Functions dialog box, shown in Figure 16-12.

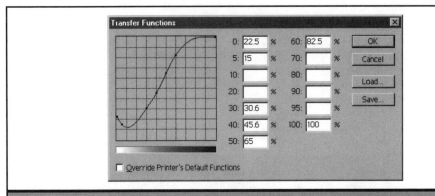

Figure 16-12.   The Transfer Functions dialog box helps you prepare your file for output to an imagesetter.

Note   *You use transfer functions when you're printing to film and trying to reconcile differences in density (dot gain or loss) between the file and the imagesetter. To adjust the transfer function values, you're going to need a transmissive densitometer. In all likelihood, you don't have one, but the technicians running the imagesetter do. They'll make an initial print of your image to film, and then use the transmissive densitometer to determine density values at specific points in your image. These points correspond to the text fields of the Transfer functions dialog box. Using Photoshop's Transfer functions, they'll use the differences in density between the film and what the file calls for to calculate the proper adjustments, and enter the appropriate values into the fields of the Transfer functions dialog box. The calculations you came up with would work something like this: If you specified a 12-percent value for a dot, and the imagesetter prints it at 10 percent, you have a dot loss of 2 percent. You'd then enter a value of 14 percent (12 percent + 2 percent) to compensate for the imagesetter's 2-percent dot loss.*

Interpolation   When you check Interpolation, the image is resampled up to decrease the jaggedness of low-res images when printing. *Resampling* means changing the dimensions of the pixels in your image, which affects the display size of the image. Resampling up adds new pixels based on the color values of pre-existing pixels in the image. The interpolation method is chosen in the General category of the Preferences dialog box. Not all printers have this capability. If your printer doesn't, then the option is grayed out.

Calibration Bars   If you want to print a grayscale or color calibration bar beside your image, select the Calibration Bars check box. Note that calibration bars, as well as registration marks, crop marks, and labels will print only if the paper size is larger than the printed image dimensions.

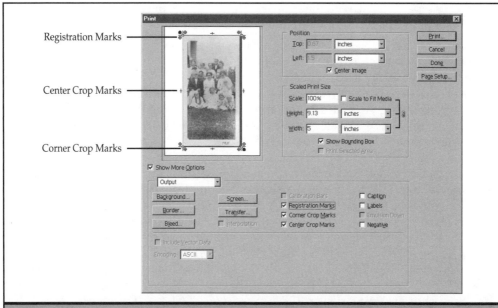

Figure 16-13.   *Helpful symbols appear around your image to assist in cropping and positioning the image for final printing.*

Registration Marks   Registration marks for aligning color separation are added to the image by selecting the Registration Marks check box. Photoshop generates both bulls-eye and star targets.

Corner Crop Marks   Checking the Corner Crop Marks check box adds corner crop marks to your image for trimming purposes.

Center Crop Marks   This check box applies center crop marks to the printed image. Figure 16-13 shows the previewed image in the Print dialog box, with Registration Marks, Corner Crop Marks, and Center Crop Marks turned on.

Caption   If the Caption check box is selected, any caption text supplied in the File Info dialog box is printed beneath the image. You have no control of the caption font or point size, which is set at 9-point Helvetica.

Labels   When you click the Labels check box, Photoshop prints the image title with the image. You'll find this to be useful if you're printing color separations, as the name will help identify the different color plates.

Emulsion Down   When printing to an imagesetter, images are typically printed emulsion down. The emulsion is the photosensitive side of the film. Emulsion down means the emulsion side is facing away from you. Selecting this option makes type readable with the emulsion down. This is the opposite of printing to photographic paper where the emulsion side is normally up, facing you.

Negative   As you might suspect, Negative inverts the image. The difference between this and the Invert command is that this option is converting the output only, not the image itself. When you print separations to film, you'll typically print negatives since the film will be used just like photographic negatives, where light is passed through them to photographic paper rendering the positive image. The print shop you use will let you know if they require positive emulsion and negative emulsion either up or down.

The Include Vector Data option (along with its Encoding drop-down list) allows you to send the vector data associated with shapes and type to a PostScript printer. If you turn this option on, you're asking Photoshop to send a separate image for each type layer and each vector shape layer to the printer, to be printed on top of the main image. This allows the edges of the vector graphics to be printed at full resolution, regardless of the resolution setting for the image itself. The Encoding options (ASCII or JPEG) apply only to PostScript printers (as does the Include Vector Data option, for that matter) and enable you to choose the encoding method that works best with your printer—some network printers can't support JPEG–encoded files, and ASCII files are larger and take longer to transfer.

Working with Color Management Options

The Color Management options in the Print dialog box include choosing Source Space (Document or Proof/Proof Setup), a Print Space Profile, and an Intent setting for PostScript printing. You can also turn on Use Black Point Compensation, which controls the adjustments for variations in black points when converting colors for different color spaces. Your choice of a Source Space depends on how you want your image colors interpreted. Choose Document if you want to use the current Color Management profile (read more about those in Chapter 6), or choose Proof if you want to use the current Proof Profile, which can be selected in the Print Space section of the dialog box.

When choosing a Print Space Profile (the options are displayed in Figure 16-14), select the one that matches your printer, or choose Same As Source to print with the Source Space profile.

You can also choose a Profile for the type of printing you'd like to do, resulting in your printer emulating the Profile of another printer.

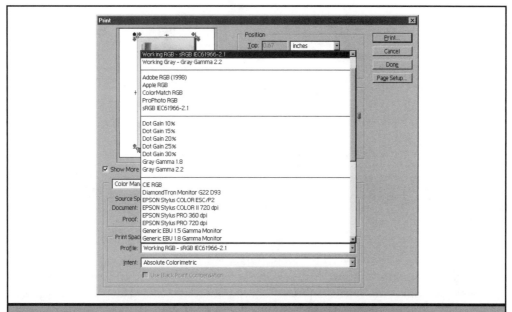

Figure 16-14. *Choose a Print Space Profile that matches your printer's capabilities.*

Halftoning Images

A *halftone image* is one that has been converted into a pattern of dots to simulate continuous tone. Traditionally, placing a screen between the image and the film, and then exposing the film, generated these dots. *Screen frequency*, or the number of lines per inch (*lpi*), controlled the amount and size of the dots and this created a better halftone image. Today, halftones are created electronically, mimicking this old photographic process. When we set a screen frequency in Photoshop, there is no longer any real screen. You can also change the shape of the dots and the angle of the virtual screens via Photoshop's Halftone Screens dialog box.

Note *In a normal print workflow, the setting of halftone screens takes place in the page layout application (InDesign, PageMaker, etc.) where the digitized images are placed. If you're printing directly from Photoshop, you can configure the halftone screens in Photoshop.*

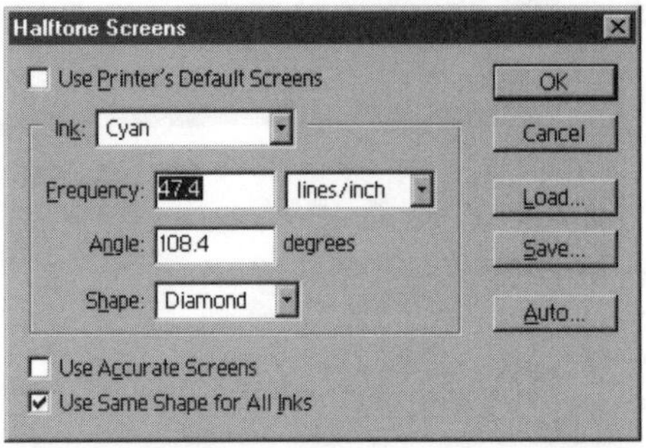

Figure 16-15. *Control the way halftone screens are printed.*

A screen angle of 45 degrees is preferable when printing a single color halftone. The human eye is less disturbed by it than, say, 90 degrees, which pulls the eye to the dots themselves instead of the image. In four-color separations (discussed later in this chapter), you must set a screen angle for four screens representing cyan, magenta, yellow, and black. You'll want to consult with your print shop prior to creating your halftone screens. They'll inform you of their preferred screen frequency, angles, and dot shape settings.

When you do set your screen options, Photoshop advises you to save the image in EPS format, which embeds your custom settings in the file itself. You must also select Include Halftone Screens in the EPS Options dialog box. You want to do this because some output devices ignore these settings in regular PSD files, and EPS files can generally override any default halftone settings the device might have.

To create your virtual screens, you need to select Print with Preview from the File menu, make sure Show More Options is selected, and then click the Screen button. This displays either of these two Halftone Screens dialog boxes, depending on whether the image is grayscale or color (including spot colors). The Printer's Default Screens option is selected by default but is turned off in Figure 16-15 so that the rest of the dialog box options are visible. When the default is left on, these settings are dimmed.

When setting your own screen options (with Printer's Default Screens turned off) on a grayscale image, the frequency range runs from 1 to 999.999. Your possible units of measurement are lines per inch and lines per centimeter. Your possible screen angle range is –180 to +180 degrees.

In a four-color separation, again, you need to define screens for each color. Use the Ink drop-down list to select the color, and then enter your screen frequency and angles. You can use the Auto button to have Photoshop select the best screen frequency and angles. Just click Auto and the Auto Screens dialog box appears, as shown in Figure 16-16.

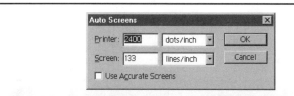

Figure 16-16.   *The Auto Screens dialog box allows you to set Printer and Screen dots and lines per inch, respectively.*

To use the Auto Screens dialog box, simply enter the resolution of your output device and your chosen screen frequency. You'll want to select Use Accurate Screens if you're using a PostScript Level 2 printer or an imagesetter outfitted with an Emerald controller. This option allows Photoshop to access the proper screen frequencies and angles for high-resolution production.

As for setting dot shape, use the Shape drop-down list in the Halftone Screens dialog box to select the appropriate dot shape for your virtual screens. In a four-color separation, the Use Same Shape for All Inks option secures a single dot shape across the four screens. If you are familiar with PostScript commands, you can choose Custom from the Shape drop-down list and enter them in the corresponding dialog box.

Color Separations

In commercial printing, images that contain multiple colors have each color separated out to an individual plate. These plates are then printed in turn to produce the full image. Printing full-color photos typically requires color separations; in process color separation, the CMYK color model is most commonly used. Photoshop enables you to control various color separation options, and these options are located in the Color Management version of the Print dialog box (formerly Print with Preview). In the Print Space section of the dialog box, make a selection from the Profile drop-down list, then click Print. Photoshop prints separations for each of the four colors.

Trapping Your Colors

Sometimes misregistration of the color plates creates small gaps that appear in between areas of distinctly different colors. To compensate for this, you set a slight overlap to ensure total coverage. This is called *trapping*. Trapping is not done in continuous tone images, but rather used in images with solid areas of color.

Figure 16-17.   *Use the Trap dialog box to control how your contiguous colors print without gaps.*

   Typically, a print shop knows if any trapping is required—after all, it's more likely you're working with a print shop's four-color output device, not your own. They'll be able to inform you of any trapping you need to set if they don't do it for you themselves.

To create a trap in Photoshop, your image can be set to CMYK, Grayscale, or Multichannel Mode. It's a good idea to save a version of the file in RGB Mode, as well, so you have it to go back to later. Before selecting Image | Trap, be sure to use the Channels palette to select the channels you want to trap (SHIFT-select them). Then you're ready to work with the Trap dialog box, shown in Figure 16-17. In the Width field, enter the value supplied from your print shop and then set the appropriate unit of measure (pixels, points, or millimeters).

Summary

In this chapter, you learned how to print your Photoshop images. You learned how to utilize the setup options for your printer. You also learned how to use the extensive options located in the Print dialog box (the version you get when you choose File | Print with Preview).

The Complete Reference

Part IV

Photoshop on the Web

The Complete Reference

Chapter 17

Optimizing Web Graphics

I n print design you have final say on how the viewer experiences the finished product. Essentially, each member of your audience will have an identical "user experience." The dimensions of the printed page, the quality of the paper the image is printed on, and the ink used to print the image are all immutable.

Designing for the Web is a very different story. When the finished product is a web site, your level of control over the final user experience is mitigated by the fact that no two site visitors have identical computer setups. Monitor resolutions, graphics cards, operating systems, and web browsers can all vary from user to user. It is your job as web designer to offer up a final product that takes each of these considerations into account, attempting to provide as uniform a user experience as possible.

Reconciling Image Quality vs. Speed of Delivery

When creating web graphics, you're attempting to produce the highest quality image with the smallest possible file size. Because your graphics are delivered to the viewer via their Internet connection, the smaller the file size the faster they receive them. In Photoshop, this display quality/file size adjustment process is referred to as image *optimization*.

If you create high quality graphics with nice tiny file sizes, some of the work is already complete. Web browsers support a limited number of file types, and each has become a web standard simply because they're capable of creating relatively high quality images with minimal file sizes. By learning the strengths and weaknesses of these file types, you can determine which format to use in the proper circumstance.

Web File Formats

At present, web browsers support three graphics file formats: the Graphics Interchange Format (GIF), the format brought about through the efforts of the Joint Photographic Experts Group (JPEG), and the Internet Engineering Task Force's answer to GIF, the Portable Network Graphics format (PNG).

Graphics Interchange Format (GIF)

GIF was created by CompuServe in the late '80s. It is an 8-bit, indexed color format, capable of displaying a maximum of 256 colors. So, what does that mean in English?

As you may or may not be aware, the bit is the smallest data unit a computer works with. Bits can be in one of two states: on or off. Your monitor also has a smallest unit of measurement, the pixel (or picture element). In an 8-bit file format each of your monitor's pixels is assigned 8 bits of data, which affects how the pixel behaves.

The file format's *bit depth* (8-bit) determines its *color depth* (256) via a simple little equation. Simply take the number of states a bit has (2) and raise it to the power indicated by the format's bit depth, which in this case is 8. This gives us 2^8, or $2 \times 2 \times 2 \times 2 \times 2 \times 2 \times 2 \times 2$, which equals 256.

The small file sizes attained via GIF are partially attributable to its color depth. By limiting the color depth, you obviously limit file size, but there's more to it than that. The GIF format, as well as JPEG and PNG, takes advantage of file compression—in this case a compression method referred to as LZW (named for its creators, Lempel, Ziv, and Welch). The LZW compression method takes advantage of inefficiencies in the file's method of data storage, essentially removing unused space within the file without discarding any of the actual image data. This makes it a *lossless* compression method.

GIF has gone through two specifications: GIF87a, the first specification published in 1987, and then GIF89a two years later, which added support from transparency, animation, and interlacing. Interlacing progressively displays a higher resolution of the image in the browser window, beginning with a very low resolution and finally ending with the full image. The purpose of this is to give the visitor an initial impression of the image while it downloads, thus preventing the document from having any blank areas during the download process.

GIF Usage

You're going to want to save an image as a GIF when you're dealing with a file that has few colors and sharp contrast. LZW compression works best on an image that devotes large areas to individual colors, where the edges of these areas are sharp and clear. Images with more than 256 colors are obviously not going to work well as a GIF, nor are images with significant gradient areas.

Figure 17-1 shows a view of the Save for Web dialog box, which we'll examine more closely later in the chapter. I've zoomed 300 percent to show the effects of JPEG compression on the edges of different regions of color. On the left is a simple four-color image with highly contrasted edges rendered as a GIF. On the right, the same image is viewed as a JPEG. Notice how trying to compress the image down to the size of the GIF distorts the image.

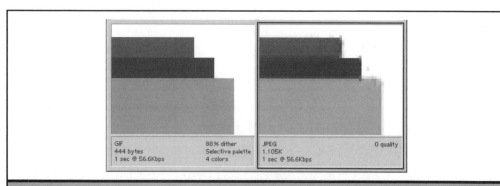

Figure 17-1. *Applying the highest degree of JPEG compression, the image on the right is still more than twice the size of the GIF on the left.*

Joint Photographic Experts Group (JPEG)

Though we use the term JPEG to refer to a specific file type, this is not technically correct. The acronym refers to the group specifically. The file format is properly called the JPEG File Interchange Format (JFIF), originally put forward by a company called C-Cube Microsystems using the compression algorithms created by the JPEG folks. Alas, JPEG's catchier pronunciation (JAY-peg) seems to have won out over JFIF (JAY-fif).

The Joint Photographic Experts Group is comprised of people nominated by standards organizations like the ISO and major companies in the field of imaging. The group is responsible for establishing standards for "continuous tone image coding." By continuous tone I mean images that have a virtually unlimited range of color or shades of gray. JPEG is a 24-bit format, which, by virtue of the equation we used previously, gives it a color depth of 2^{24} or 16,777,215 colors—a number that, for purposes of the human eye, is virtually unlimited.

JPEG compression differs from that of GIF in that it reduces file size by actually removing data from the image. JPEG relies on the fact that the images it creates are meant to be viewed by the human eye, and therefore skews its compression methods to take advantage of human visual weaknesses. The human eye registers minute changes in brightness much better than minute changes in color, so JPEG compression can throw out a great deal of color information (while still reproducing millions of colors) and still render an image you and I perceive as being highly detailed. Because this compression method removes data from the file, it is referred to as *lossy*. Unlike the GIF, however, you can adjust the level of compression when creating JPEG files, choosing how much to compress the image. The more you compress, the smaller the file size. The less you compress, the better the image quality.

JPEG Usage

The JPEG format, in contrast to the GIF format, lends itself to images on the opposite end of the spectrum, with millions of colors and detailed gradations (continuous tone). Try to avoid using JPEG in images that have large zones of a single color, as JPEG compression will introduce artifacts (distortions) when trying to render them.

Obviously, the JPEG format favors photographs and photorealistic images, as you can see in Figure 17-2. Here, the photograph of a palm tree on the beach is much more clearly rendered as a JPEG. The GIF by contrast lack sufficient color depth to do the image justice.

Portable Network Graphics (PNG)

The PNG format was created as a free and more robust alternative to GIF when Unisys, the owners of the LZW compression patent, declared they would seek royalties from software developers whose programs implemented LZW compression algorithms. Like GIF, PNG uses a lossless compression algorithm. The format supports images with bit depths of both 24 and 8, providing the color depth of JPEG with the lossless compression of GIF. PNG also supports transparency. PNG-8 supports rudimentary transparency, and PNG-24 supports full 256-level transparency.

Figure 17-2. *When compressed to a comparable file size, the GIF on the left is limited to only 13 colors, drastically reducing the detail and realism of the image.*

PNG Usage

PNG, as stated earlier, gives GIF a good run for the money at an 8-bit color depth. Depending on the circumstance, PNG generally results in slightly larger file sizes (see Figure 17-3). Granted, the differences in file size are usually only a few kilobytes, and not enough to make a significant difference in download speed. The primary reason not to use PNG in place of GIF would be if a large proportion of your audience were using browsers prior to version 4.0 of Internet Explorer and Netscape Navigator. Being that both browsers are in version 6.x it's probably safe to PNG more freely.

Figure 17-3. *Revisiting the GIF from Figure 17-1, you can see that saving this image as an 8-bit PNG with 128 colors and 88 percent dithering produces a slightly larger file size than as a GIF with identical settings.*

Preparing Images for the Web

You optimize your images for the Web via the Save For Web dialog box, where you can select the appropriate file format, set the degree of compression, determine the number of colors, adjust the dithering percentage, and choose transparency options. The Save For Web dialog box provides you with up to four simultaneous previews of an image inside which you can assign unique optimization settings.

Once you've found the best combination of settings for your needs, you can then export the image from Photoshop ready for use on the Web or other online situation. You can then quickly preview the image in any browser you have installed, as well as save the image inserted in an HTML file. In either instance, Photoshop generates all the necessary markup to display the image in the browser.

Using the Save for Web Command

The Save For Web dialog box, shown here in Figure 17-4, is invoked when you choose File | Save For Web from the menu bar.

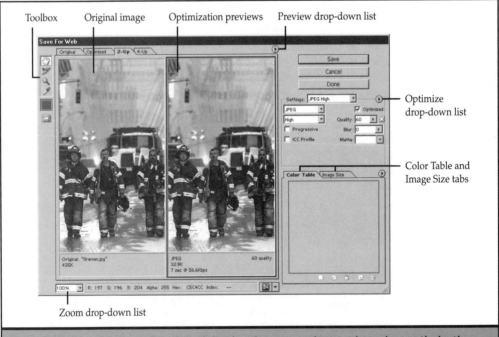

Figure 17-4. *The Save For Web dialog box lets you select and preview optimization settings for your image.*

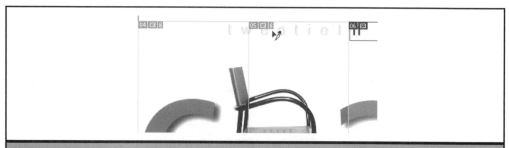

Figure 17-5. *When you link slices, link icons appear in the Save For Web dialog box.*

Once you send an image to the Save For Web dialog box, choose a preview option tab along the top of the dialog box. You can view the original image or optimized image singly, or two other variants. The 2-Up tab lets you view the original and optimized image side by side, while the 4-Up tab displays the original image and three optimized versions, usually in declining file sizes. You can click any of the three optimized views to select it and apply unique optimization settings. The selected preview is the one saved when you click the Save button.

Use the Hand tool just as you would in the Navigation palette to reposition an image in any of the preview windows. You can zoom in and out using either the Zoom tool or the Zoom drop-down menu. If you use the Zoom tool, you can zoom out by pressing the ALT (Windows) or OPTION (Mac) key. If you prefer keyboard shortcuts, CTRL-(+) and CTRL-(-) in Windows and COMMAND-(+) and COMMAND-(-) in Mac, respectively, work just as they do in the regular workspace.

If your original image makes use of slices, use the Slice Select tool to choose the individual slice you wish to optimize. If you apply different optimization settings to each slice, you'll see these reflected in the optimization information displayed at the bottom of the preview window as you move from slice to slice.

You can link any number of slices together by either pressing the SHIFT key while selecting each slice with the Slice Select tool, or by dragging the tool across the desired slices and then choosing Link Slices from the Optimize drop-down list. A link icon appears on the linked slices (see Figure 17-5), and any optimization settings are applied throughout. To unlink slices, simply reselect them and choose Unlink Slices from the Optimize drop-down list. Choose Unlink All Slice to remove all slice links within an image.

Optimizing Images as GIF and 8-bit PNG Files

As you learned earlier in the chapter, GIF and 8-bit PNG are best suited for images with limited color range and sharp, detailed edges. By default, these two file types allow a maximum of 256 colors, but that number can be reduced using the tools provided in the Save For Web dialog box, further reducing file size.

All optimization settings are made in the Settings area of the Save for Web dialog box, shown in Figure 17-6.

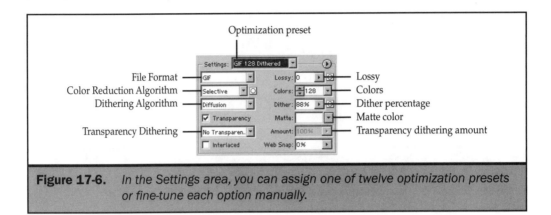

Figure 17-6. *In the Settings area, you can assign one of twelve optimization presets or fine-tune each option manually.*

Optimization Presets

On the Optimization preset drop-down list, there are seven selections for GIF, and one for PNG-8:

- GIF 128 Dithered
- GIF 128 No Dither
- GIF 32 Dithered
- GIF 32 No Dither
- GIF 64 Dithered
- GIF 64 No Dither
- GIF Web Palette
- PNG-8 128 Dithered

The numbers 128, 32, and 64 indicate the total number of colors included in the image. The GIF Web Palette option forces the image's color table to include only those found in the palette of 216 colors shared by all browsers, operating systems, and monitors when running in 8-bit, 256-color mode. Custom settings are applied using the other menus, drop-down lists, and sliders located in the Settings area.

Note *You might read the phrase "8-bit, 256-color mode" and wonder who's still running hardware with those types of limitations—at this stage in the game, probably no one. The typical graphics card in a modern computer is 32-bit, which can render 4,294,967,296 colors. However, back when 8-bit systems were the norm, 256 colors were glorious in comparison to monochrome monitors. In terms of web delivery, however, there was one small problem. The 256-color palette was not identical across operating systems and hardware platforms.*

Note   *The solution adopted by both Netscape Navigator and Internet Explorer settled on a forced color palette of 216 colors common to all operating systems and hardware configurations. Thus was born the "web-safe palette." When you stuck to this palette, you could rest assured that colors wouldn't shift or dither. Dithering creates the illusion of non-web palette colors by varying a pattern of pixels comprised of colors within the web palette. For example, a simple checkerboard of pixels using two alternating web-safe colors registers to the eye as a third color outside the 216-color palette.*

Custom Optimization Settings

To define the base file format, use the File Format drop-down list, then choose a method for determining the color table of the image by making a selection from the Color Reduction Algorithm drop-down list.

Your options fall within these three categories:

Dynamic Options   Dynamic options use your chosen color reduction algorithm to construct a color lookup table (CLUT) using the existing colors in the image as a starting point. The CLUT is reconfigured each time you modify the image or change its optimization settings.

The dynamic options include:

Perceptual   Based on how the human eye perceives color, the perceptual palette uses colors to which our eyes are more sensitive to create a customized color lookup table.

Selective   Similar to the perceptual palette, the selective palette creates a CLUT more sensitive to areas of single flat colors. Preventing them from being merged with other colors within the image, the selective palette also preserves any existing web-safe colors. This palette is generally the best for web graphics.

Adaptive   The palette created using an adaptive sampling favors the predominant colors within the image. In an image comprised mostly of reds and yellows, for example, choosing Adaptive from the Color Reduction Algorithm menu results in a CLUT weighted to those two colors.

Fixed Options   Unlike the dynamic options, which begin with the colors present in the image as a starting point from which to develop the CLUT, the fixed options start from one of five pre-existing color palettes you select and map your image's colors to it.

The fixed options include:

Web   This palette refers to the 216 colors common to Windows, Macintosh, Netscape Navigator, and Internet Explorer out of the 256 available in 8-bit mode.

Mac OS   This palette consists of the default 256 system colors of the Mac OS.

Windows   This palette consists of the default 256 system colors of the Windows operating system.

PHOTOSHOP
ON THE WEB

Custom Options   When you select Custom from the Color Reduction Algorithm menu, this maintains your current color table as a fixed palette that doesn't update with changes to the image. You can then modify the color table as you see fit using the Color Table tab of the Save For Web dialog box. If you start with a dynamic or fixed color reduction option and then make manual changes to the color table, the Color Reduction Algorithm menu will switch to Custom.

After choosing a color reduction algorithm, you can use the Colors drop-down list to select the maximum number of colors you want the image to contain. The range of colors available to you begins at a maximum of 256 and decreases incrementally by half with the lowest selection being 2 colors. You can also manually enter any number between 2 and 256 into the field.

Previously, when discussing GIF's LZW compression method, I mentioned that it was a lossless form of compression. In other words, it compressed an image without discarding any image data. You do have the option, when saving a file as a GIF, of using the Lossy drop-down list to selectively extract image data to further decrease file size. Using the Lossy drop-down list is a fairly straightforward operation: The higher you set the Lossy value, the more data you discard. This functionality is not available for PNG.

Applying Dithering Settings

The process of dithering allows you to simulate colors not found in either the color lookup table of the image, or available to the display of a particular computer by varying a pattern of pixels made up of colors within the image's existing palette. As alluded to previously, by taking two of the 256 colors available to an 8-bit image or graphics card and creating a checkerboard by alternating pixels of each color, the human eye perceives a third color that might be outside the 256 color range.

When an image devoted mainly to regions of solid color is saved as a GIF or PNG, dithering isn't usually necessary. Continuous-tone images are good candidates for dithering, as dithering helps to minimize color banding. Of course, an image largely comprised of continuous-tone and gradient regions is better saved as a JPEG. However, some images are hybrids, containing zones of solid flat color, as well as continuous-tone regions. This is where applying some level of dithering to a GIF can be advantageous.

To apply dithering, simply choose a dithering algorithm from the Dithering Algorithm drop-down list. Your choices include:

Diffusion   When you select Diffusion, the pixel pattern used to simulate a color outside the CLUT diffuses the dithering across adjacent pixels, instead of using an obvious pattern. You also apply a percentage to control the degree of dithering you want. The higher the degree of dithering, the more potential colors you simulate; however, this also increases the overall size of the image file.

Pattern   As the name implies, this dithering algorithm uses an obvious square pattern to simulate colors, as shown in Figure 17-7.

Noise   Like Diffusion, the Noise algorithm also uses a random pattern, but it does not diffuse the dithering across adjacent pixels, as shown in Figure 17-8.

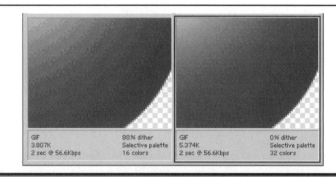

Figure 17-7. *Here you see two views of a gradient region of a GIF zoomed in at 300 percent—the left view with Diffusion, and the right using Pattern. Notice the obvious square checkerboard-like dithering in the Pattern view.*

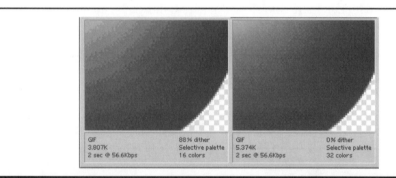

Figure 17-8. *In these two views, we see Diffusion on the left and Noise on the right. Because Noise does not diffuse the dithering across adjacent pixels, its pattern is significantly more randomized.*

Applying Transparency and Matte Settings

When you're creating a GIF or PNG-8 file with transparent areas, you need to think about how you want the transition between pixels that actually have something present and pixels that don't. Unfortunately, you can't just create an image with transparency and have it interact with the background of a web page in the same manner opaque regions do with transparent regions in your native Photoshop file.

When a Photoshop file creates anti-aliased edges or generates a drop shadow, it uses pixels of varying transparency to fool the eye by softening the jagged edges created by pixels that are fully opaque. This can't be done to GIF or PNG-8 files. A pixel is either opaque or transparent; there's no in-between. What Photoshop does in optimizing the GIF or PNG-8 is take the pixels of partial transparency and translate them into a blend of the appropriate opaque color and the color you choose for the Matte. Typically, the matte color you choose is also the background color of the web page you're inserting the image into. In this way, you're creating a small gradient along an opaque region's edge going from that region's color to the matte color. The pixels beyond that gradient are transparent and where the web page's background color will show through. Figure 17-9 shows the Save For Web dialog box with views of your various Transparency and Matte options.

The original image is shown in the upper left-hand corner of Figure 17-9. The view to the right of the original shows the image with only Transparency selected and Matte set to None. Because the drop shadow is made exclusively of semi-transparent pixels, pixels of less than 50 percent transparency are made entirely opaque with the color used to generate the drop shadow, while pixels of more than 50 percent transparency are made completely transparent.

The lower left-hand view shows how the image appears with Transparency selected and a matte color applied. This demonstrates the gradient I spoke of, blending the semi-transparent pixels with the matte color. The final view shows the image without Transparency and only a matte color selected, which is the equivalent of assigning a background filled with the matte color.

The Matte drop-down list gives you a number of options for selecting a matte color:

None   Disables matte colors.

Eyedropper Color   Uses the current color in the Save For Web dialog box's color swatch.

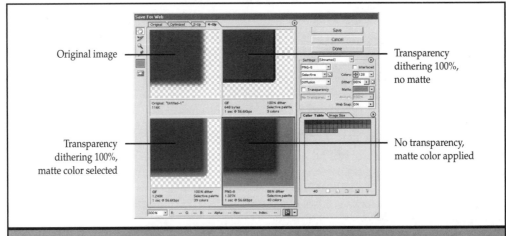

Figure 17-9.   *This figure shows a 4-Up view of an image with a drop shadow. The Transparency and Matte settings are discussed next.*

Black   Selects black for the matte color.

White   Selects white for the matte color.

Other   Invokes the Photoshop Color Picker.

You can also invoke the Color Picker by clicking directly on the Matte menu's text field itself.

Using Transparency Dithering

After you've taken those previously semi-transparent pixels and either blended them with a matte color or converted them to total transparency, you also have the ability to specifically apply a dither algorithm. Similar to regular dithering, you can apply identical dithering algorithms to those discussed previously: Diffusion, Pattern, and Noise. Figure 17-10 shows the same drop-shadowed image. Transparency is selected without any matte color applied to emphasize the dithering patterns.

Creating Interlaced Graphics

When you interlace a GIF or PNG file when the image is downloaded across a visitor's Internet connection, it initially appears at a very low resolution and gradually progresses to its full resolution over seven successive streams. Back in the days of 14.4 Kbps and

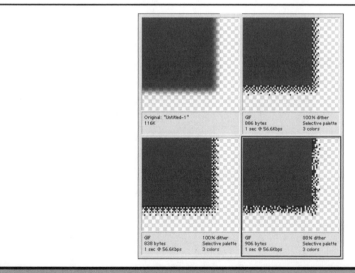

Figure 17-10.   *In this image, the view on the right of the original shows Diffusion Transparency, the lower left is Pattern Transparency, and the last is Noise Transparency.*

28.8 Kbps modems, interlacing graphics wasn't a bad idea. Though interlacing slightly increased file size, the payoff was that the site visitor at least got something on their screen right away instead of having to wait for the complete image to appear. Today, the average Internet connection is 56 Kbps or higher, so there's no real need to interlace a graphic.

Optimizing Images as JPEG and 24-bit PNG Files

JPEG and PNG-24 formats, as you recall, support 16,777,216 colors. This makes them perfect for rendering continuous-tone images. Remember that "continuous tone" means the images have a virtually unlimited range of colors or shades of gray. The sacrifice you make when using JPEG is that its compression method is lossy and achieves its reduction in file size by removing data from the image. PNG-24, on the other hand, is lossless compression. However, it can't match JPEG's level of compression simply for this reason.

The Optimization settings for JPEG and PNG-24 in the Save For Web dialog box are slightly different from those used for GIF and PNG-8, as shown in Figure 17-11.

Optimization Presets

On the Optimization preset drop-down list, there are three selections for JPEG, and one for PNG-24:

- JPEG Low
- JPEG Medium
- JPEG High
- PNG-24

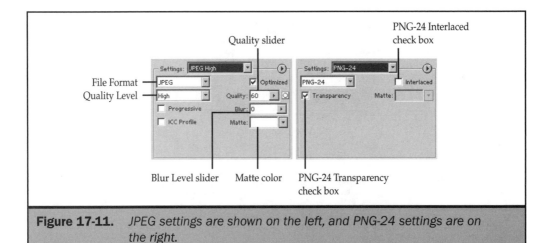

Figure 17-11.   *JPEG settings are shown on the left, and PNG-24 settings are on the right.*

When applying JPEG compression, you can adjust its level, choosing how much to compress the image. The more compression you apply, the smaller the optimized file size and the lower the image quality. The less compression applied, the larger the optimized file size and higher the image quality.

In Photoshop, JPEG compression is applied along a scale of zero to 100. The optimization presets represent points along that scale, which correspond to 10, 30, and 60.

In each of the presets, the Optimized check box is selected, Blur is set to zero, and the matte color is defaulted to white. Of course, no matte color is required if the original image has no transparent areas.

Custom Optimization Settings

The JPEG Quality Level drop-down list differs from the Optimization presets only in its offering of a Maximum setting, which places the Quality slider at 80. Of course, you can adjust the Quality slider manually to fine-tune the level of compression that best suits your quality/file size demands.

The Optimized check box is always selected in the optimization presets and shouldn't really be unchecked. This option provides enhanced color optimization and results in a smaller file size. Though older web browsers don't recognize the enhancement (prior to Netscape Navigator and Internet Explorer 4.0), these browsers have no adverse reaction to its use.

Applying Matte Colors to JPEG Files

JPEG does not support transparency. Consequently, for any situations in which your original image has transparent regions, you need to assign a matte color to fill those voids in the JPEG. Any pixel that is completely transparent is filled with your chosen matte color, while pixels of partial transparency are blended with the matte color accordingly.

The Matte drop-down list is identical to that used for GIF and PNG-8. From the Matte drop-down list, you can select any of the following options:

None   Disables matte colors.

Eyedropper Color   Uses the current color in the Save For Web dialog box's color swatch.

Black   Selects black for the matte color.

White   Selects white for the matte color.

Other   Invokes the Photoshop Color Picker.

You can also invoke the Color Picker by clicking directly on the Matte drop-down list's text field itself.

PHOTOSHOP ON THE WEB

Applying Transparency to PNG-24 Files

The PNG-24 format, just like PNG-8 and GIF, does support transparency. Unlike GIF and PNG-8 however, there is no matte color option for Transparency in the PNG-24 format. You simply have the option of keeping any transparent regions of the original image transparent by selecting the Transparency check box.

Progressive and Interlaced Graphics

From the discussion of GIF and PNG-8, you learned you can interlace an image to promote a successive download of the image to facilitate the quick appearance of at least a portion of the image across a slow modem connection. PNG-24 also allows for interlacing, and JPEG supports a similar process called Progressive JPEG.

The Progressive JPEG format reorganizes the file's data into a series of scans, each of successively higher quality. The browser displays a low-quality image almost immediately with the initial scan. The image quality gradually improves as the remaining scans are received. Unlike interlaced GIF and PNG files, progressive JPEG files are actually smaller than regular JPEG files. However, with the average modem speed being 56.6 Kbps, a non-progressive JPEG may actually display more quickly than if the image is dissected and transmitted in stages. Again, as with many technologies, older browsers do not support progressive JPEGs.

JPEG Blurring

In JPEG compression when a large region of a single color is encountered, higher levels of compression produce distortion in the image. To lesson the severity of these distortions, you can blur the image using an effect identical to that of the Gaussian Blur filter. Simply specify the amount of blur you want to introduce using the Blur slider. The available range is between 0 and 2. Typically a setting of 0.1 to 0.5 is sufficient and will allow you to further compress the image, reducing the overall file size.

Creating Your Own Optimization Presets

You can save your customized optimization settings and have them appear as options on the Settings drop-down list by choosing Save Settings from the Optimize drop-down list. This will display the Save Optimization Settings dialog box, shown in Figure 17-12.

Photoshop will ask you to save your settings files in the default location, which is in the Presets/Optimized Settings directory. If you save them anywhere else, Photoshop won't be able to display your settings in the Settings drop-down list.

You can edit your optimization presets at any time. Simply select your option from the drop-down list and make any changes you see fit. The preset name will switch to (Unnamed). When it does, just resave your preset with the Save Settings command. If at any time you want to delete a preset, select it and choose Delete Settings from the Optimize drop-down list.

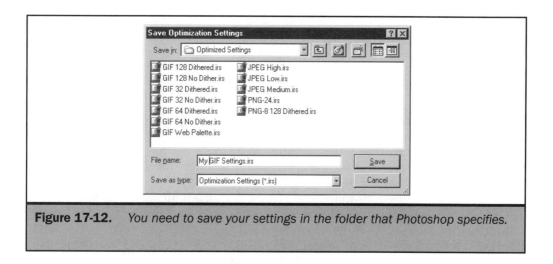

Figure 17-12.   *You need to save your settings in the folder that Photoshop specifies.*

Optimizing Images to a Preset File Size

There are times when the images you create are held to a specific file size tolerance. In the Save For Web dialog box, you can set a specific file size and have Photoshop compress the image to that size instantly. Typically, it's best to set a ballpark file size so you can then fine-tune the image after the gross reduction has been applied.

To select a specific file size to which you want an image optimized, select Optimize to File Size from the Optimize drop-down list. This opens the Optimize To File Size dialog box, shown in Figure 17-13.

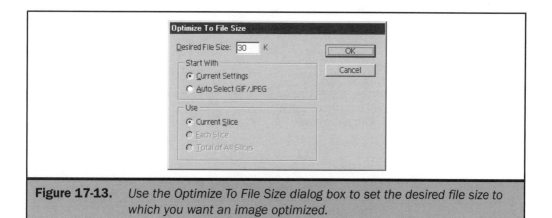

Figure 17-13.   *Use the Optimize To File Size dialog box to set the desired file size to which you want an image optimized.*

Next, enter a value in the Desired File Size field, and in the Start With field, choose either Current Settings or Auto Select GIF/JPEG. Current Settings will create an image of the appropriate file size in the file format currently selected in the Save For Web dialog box. If you choose Auto Select GIF/JPEG, Photoshop will choose between GIF or JPEG based on its analysis of the color data in the image.

Resizing an Image via the Save for Web Dialog Box

Photoshop realizes that during the optimization process it's sometimes necessary to adjust an image's dimensions. Rather than returning to the normal workspace and changing the image dimension via the Image menu, you have the ability to resize an image directly in the Save For Web dialog box.

Directly below the optimization setting controls, on the right hand side of the dialog box, sit two tabs: the Color Table tab, where the CLUT for 8-bit images is displayed; and behind that, the Image Size tab, shown in Figure 17-14.

You're given the original dimension of the image you're optimizing, and below that Width and Height fields into which you can enter new values. If you wish to change the dimensions by a percentage of their original value, the Percent field allows you to enter a scale between 0 and 100. To retain the original proportions of the image, be sure the Constrain Proportions check box is selected.

When resizing an image in Photoshop, the application uses a user-selected interpolation method, which estimates the values of any missing pixels resulting from the resizing process. This is accomplished by taking an average of known pixel values at neighboring points in the image. Below the Constrain Proportions check box sits the Quality drop-down list, where you can select from two interpolation methods:

Smooth (Bicubic) The default interpolation method, adds pixels and color values where needed based on an analysis of all pixel data in the resized image.

Jagged (Nearest Neighbor) Instead of analyzing the entire image, this method looks to the nearest pixel for information and never adds any color data that isn't already present in the image.

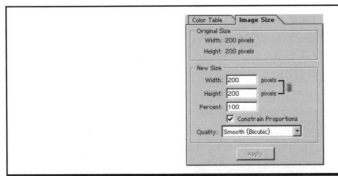

Figure 17-14. *The Image Size tab provides you with an interface similar to that of the Pixel Dimension region of the Image Size dialog box.*

Once you've made your resizing selections, simply click the Apply button located at the bottom of the Image Size tab to invoke them.

Weighted Optimization

Weighted optimization means skewing the optimization of specific regions within an image through the use of alpha channel masks. When you create an alpha channel mask for use in weighted optimizations, areas you set to white receive the highest level of optimization, black the lowest, and shades of gray are acted upon in a linear progression between the two extremes.

By employing alpha channel masks, you can

- Influence color reduction in GIF and PNG-8 files
- Modify dithering in GIF and PNG-8 files
- Modify lossiness in GIF compression
- Modify the quality of JPEG compression

GIF and PNG Color Reduction

In any alpha channel mask, the black and white areas determine the operable region of the image. When influencing the color reduction algorithm of an optimized image, white regions of the mask designate which pixels the selected algorithm should be applied to. Black regions, conversely, are ignored. By creating a series of masks, you can vary the level of influence from region to region.

To apply a mask to the color reduction algorithm, first create an alpha channel mask that corresponds to the region of the image you want to favor. Then, set your GIF or PNG-8 settings, selecting your color reduction algorithm (Perceptual, Selective, Adaptive, etc.) and maximum number of colors. Next, click the mask button to the right of the Color Reduction Algorithm drop-down list, shown in Figure 17-15.

This opens the Modify Color Reduction dialog box, shown in Figure 17-16.

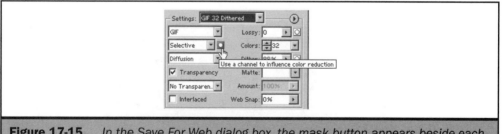

Figure 17-15.   *In the Save For Web dialog box, the mask button appears beside each setting that you can use a mask to influence.*

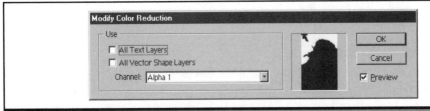

Figure 17-16.   *You aren't limited to only the alpha channel masks you create. All text and shape layers can also be used as masks.*

From here, you select the mask you want to use.

- Choose All Text Layers to create masks from the text layers in your image.
- Choose All Vector Shape Layers to create masks from the shape layers in your image.
- Use the Channel drop-down list to select any of the alpha channels you've created in your image.

By clicking the Preview check box, you can observe the results of your weighted optimization directly in the Save For Web dialog box.

Unlike alpha channels, which are saved individually, the Text Layer and Vector Shapes options create a single mask from all the text or shapes combined in your image. To remove any text or shapes from the mask, turn off their visibility first, using the Layers palette.

Modifying GIF and PNG Dithering

To use a mask to modify the dithering of a GIF or PNG-8 image, click the mask button beside the Dither text box to invoke the Modify Dither Setting dialog box, shown in Figure 17-17.

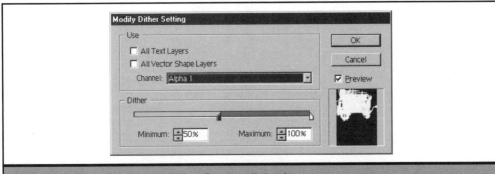

Figure 17-17.   *The Modify Dither Setting dialog box*

Tip   *When modifying Dither settings, you may find it useful to work with feathered alpha channel masks.*

You can specify the maximum and minimum range of dithering using the sliders at the bottom of the dialog box. Drag the white slider tab to control the highest percentage of dithering, and the black slider tab to set the lowest. You can also enter values directly into the Minimum and Maximum fields, or use each field's arrow buttons to change the values.

Modifying GIF Lossiness and JPEG Quality

When you use a mask to modify the lossiness of a GIF or the quality of a JPEG image, white areas receive the least amount of compression (to create higher image quality), and black areas receive the most compression (producing lower image quality). Click the mask button beside the Lossy text box (GIF) or Quality text box (JPEG) to invoke their corresponding dialog boxes, shown in Figure 17-18.

Just as you would with any of the other dialog boxes we've discussed, select the mask options you want to employ and set the quality level using the white and black sliders.

Creating Web Photo Galleries

If you've created a series of JPEG photographs and want to showcase them on the Web, Photoshop lets you generate an entire web site for that very purpose via the Web Photo Gallery command. You have eleven different design styles to choose from, to which you can make basic modifications via the Web Photo Gallery dialog box. If you are fluent in HTML or a WYSIWYG (What You See Is What You Get) HTML editor, you can modify the pre-existing style templates or create your own. Figure 17-19 shows you just one of the possible layout options you can choose from.

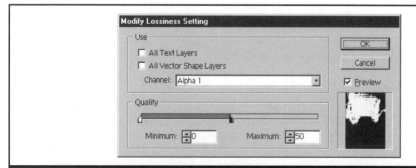

Figure 17-18.   *The Modify Lossiness Setting dialog box and Modify Quality dialog box are identical in their options.*

PHOTOSHOP ON THE WEB

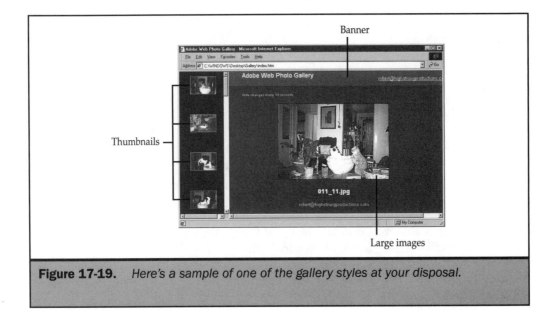

Figure 17-19. *Here's a sample of one of the gallery styles at your disposal.*

To begin the Web Photo Gallery process, you first need a folder of images (JPEG, PSD, or BMP files) you want to turn into a gallery. You also need an empty folder on your system inside of which Photoshop can generate the necessary files for the site. From here, the rest of the process is quite simple:

1. From the File menu, choose Automate | Web Photo Gallery. This launches the Web Photo Gallery dialog box shown in Figure 17-20.

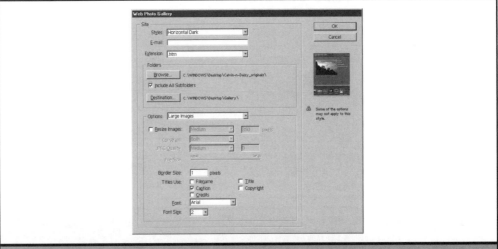

Figure 17-20. *The Web Photo Gallery dialog box*

2. From the Styles drop-down list, select the layout you wish to use. A preview appears to the right under the OK and Cancel buttons.

3. Enter an e-mail address you want displayed for contact purposes.

4. From the Extensions drop-down list, choose which HTML document extension you want to use, either .htm or .html.

5. In the Folders section of the dialog box, click Browse (Windows) or Choose (Mac) to locate and select the directory containing the JPEG files from which you want to create a Web Photo Gallery. Then click the Destination button to select the folder in which you want the Web Photo Gallery created.

6. In the Options section, choose the settings you wish to modify.

7. Click OK to generate your Web Photo Gallery.

Setting Web Photo Gallery Options

The Options drop-down list lets you select from the following categories:

- Banner
- Large Images
- Thumbnails
- Custom Colors
- Security

When selected, each category displays pertinent settings in the Options section of the Web Photo Gallery dialog box. Be aware that not every style supports each available option. The Horizontal Frame, Simple, Table, and Vertical Frame styles do; the other seven styles do not.

Banner Options

The banner appears on each site page, which displays one of the large images. When selected, the Options section reflects the choices you can modify, as shown in Figure 17-21.

- Use the Site Name text box to enter the gallery name you want displayed in the banner.

- Reference the person or group you want to give credit to for producing the images in the Photographer text box.

- Provide any appropriate contact information in the Contact Info text box.

- Enter the date you want displayed in the gallery in the Date text box. Photoshop defaults to the current system date.

- To choose a font for the banner text, use the Font drop-down list. You choices are Arial, Courier New, Helvetica, and Times New Roman.

- Use the Font Size drop-down list to select a font size value from HTML's absolute font size scale. Here, 7 is the largest and 1 is the smallest.

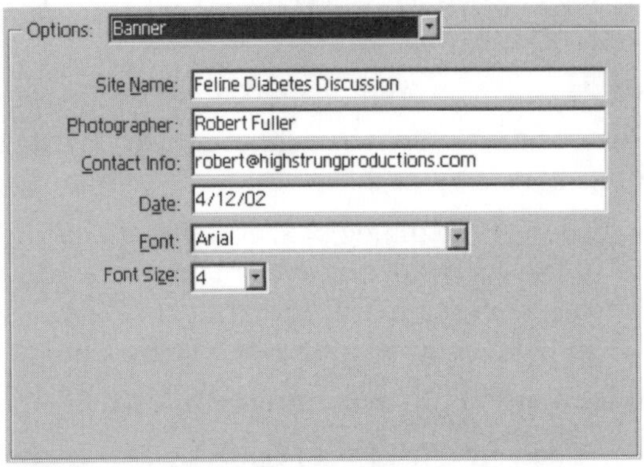

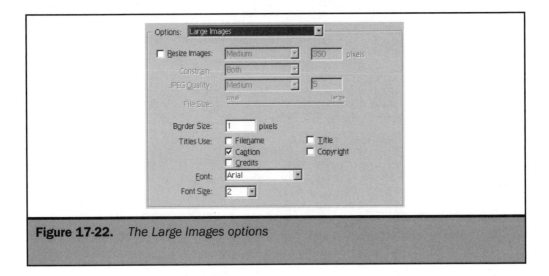

Figure 17-21. *The Banner options*

Large Image Options

The Large Images category lets you specify options for the gallery pages that display the full-size versions of your JPEGs. Figure 17-22 shows the options available when this category is selected.

Figure 17-22. *The Large Images options*

To resize the images, click the Resize Images check box, and then specify either a pixel size for the largest dimension, or choose a preset from the drop-down list (Small, Medium, Large, or Custom).

- Use the Constrain drop-down list to select which dimension to constrain: Width, Height, or Both.

- Select a JPEG Quality setting using either the drop-down list presets or the slider. The higher the value, the less compression is applied, resulting in a higher quality image, but also in a larger file size.

- If you would like borders around the images in the gallery pages, enter a value in the Border Size text box.

- Use the Titles Use check boxes to specify the style of captions. Control the font and size of the captions using the tools provided.

The caption, title, copyright, and credits information that appear represent whatever information has been stored in the File Info dialog box. If you have no information there, you won't have any with your images in the gallery, either.

Thumbnail Options

Thumbnails are the reduced versions of your images and are used as links to their larger counterparts. Figure 17-23 shows the options available for this category.

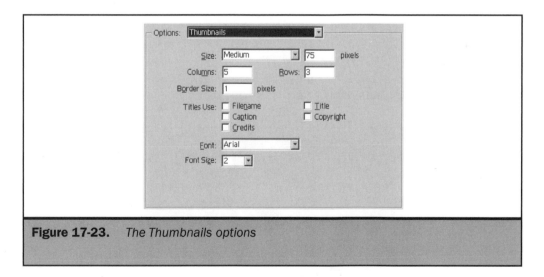

Figure 17-23.   *The Thumbnails options*

Just as with Larger Images, use Size to specify the thumbnail size using the drop-down list provided. You can also enter pixel value in the field provided. Specify the number of columns and rows in which you want the thumbnails presented, provided the style you select displays the thumbnails in columns and rows. For example, styles that use a vertical or horizontal frame to display the thumbnails are not affected. If you want your thumbnails to have borders, use the Border text box to specify their pixel width.

Custom Color Options

You can set the background, banner region, and link colors of your Web Photo Gallery using the Custom Colors category, as shown in Figure 17-24.

Simply click the appropriate color swatch to invoke the Photoshop Color Picker and change the default color.

Security Options

Security options allow you to insert text into your larger images to act as an anti-theft deterrent. Figure 17-25 shows the options available.

- From the Content drop-down list, select Custom Text, Filename, Caption, Credits, Title, or Copyright. Custom Text inserts text that you supply in the Custom Text field.

- Use the Font drop-down list to select Arial, Courier New, Helvetica, or Times New Roman, and use the Font Size pop-up to choose a point size for the text.

- Use the color tools provided to set the font color, and use the Opacity slider to affect the text's visibility.

- The Position drop-down list allows you to place the text in the center of the large images or one of their four corners.

- The Rotate drop-down list allows you to rotate text 45 or 90 degrees, both clockwise and counterclockwise.

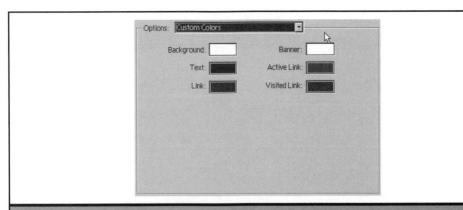

Figure 17-24. *The Custom Colors options*

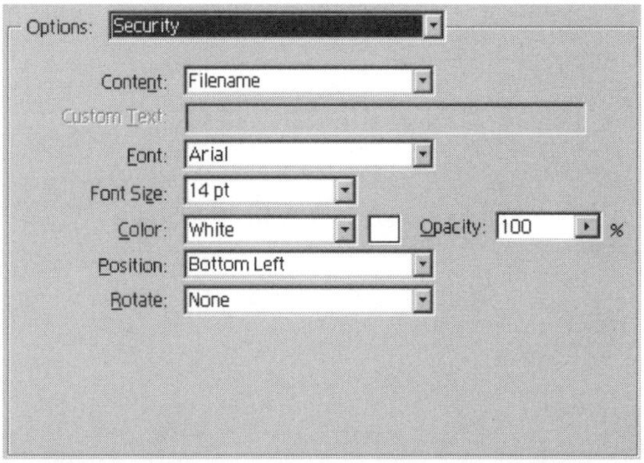

Figure 17-25.   *The Security options*

Summary

In this chapter, you learned the file types currently supported for web use (GIF, JPEG, and PNG), how to optimize images for the Web into these files types using the Save For Web dialog box, and how to use Photoshop's Web Photo Gallery feature to automatically generate a web site for displaying JPEG images.

The Complete Reference

Chapter 18

Getting to Know ImageReady

ImageReady makes images ready for the Web. While Photoshop can be used to optimize images for use online, ImageReady makes your images move, change, and link to files, web pages, and web sites. It also helps you to slice images into pieces for easier handling and faster loading on web pages, which is discussed in Chapter 19. After you create an image for the Web in Photoshop, bring it into ImageReady to make it move.

Understanding ImageReady 7.0

Photoshop 7.0 and ImageReady 7.0 have a great deal in common—menus, tools, palettes, option bars—virtually everything is the same when you compare the two applications. Why, then, is there an ImageReady? Because you need a full-fledged application to support your creation of animated GIFs, rollovers, and image maps. Of course, you can save images in web-safe formats through Photoshop, but the ability to create images that move and respond to a web-page visitor's actions is solely ImageReady's domain. In this chapter, you'll learn about these critical tools, building upon your existing knowledge of Photoshop's interface and basic tools.

Working with Animated GIF Files

When most people think of GIF files, they think of static images, usually simple in nature, consisting of solid colors and simple shapes—line art, logos, and clip art images with very simple coloring and design. You don't typically think of those same images moving around, but thanks to ImageReady, they can. Instead of storing information about the way the image looks in one static position, an animated GIF file contains information about the image in a series of frames, each one containing different parts of a single image. The GIF file itself contains all the parts of the image, but each frame has some of the image layers visible and others hidden, as shown in Figure 18-1. When the image is previewed in a web browser or through the ImageReady interface (and when it's viewed online), the frames "play" one at a time. The order in which the frames play, the duration each one is displayed before moving on to the next, and the number of times the entire series of frames plays is all stored as part of the file; when the file is displayed in a web browser window, the animation occurs as designed by the artist.

Creating Visual Interest with Rollover Images

Rollovers created in ImageReady are really multiple images that are swapped as the web-page visitor's mouse pointer moves over a graphic. You can set up rollovers through programs such as Adobe GoLive or Macromedia Dreamweaver, selecting two distinct graphics and setting one up as the image that appears when the visitor's mouse pointer is somewhere else on the page, and a second image that appears in place of the first image as soon as the visitor moves his or her pointer over the image.

ImageReady lets you go a step further, however, allowing you to create an HTML file that stores a single image in several states—Normal, where the mouse pointer isn't near the image; Over, where the pointer is on the image; and other states such as Click, which requires that the visitor click the image to make a third change occur. The rollover HTML file stores the image and its states; the file plays in a web browser window. Figure 18-2 shows a rollover's states in progress.

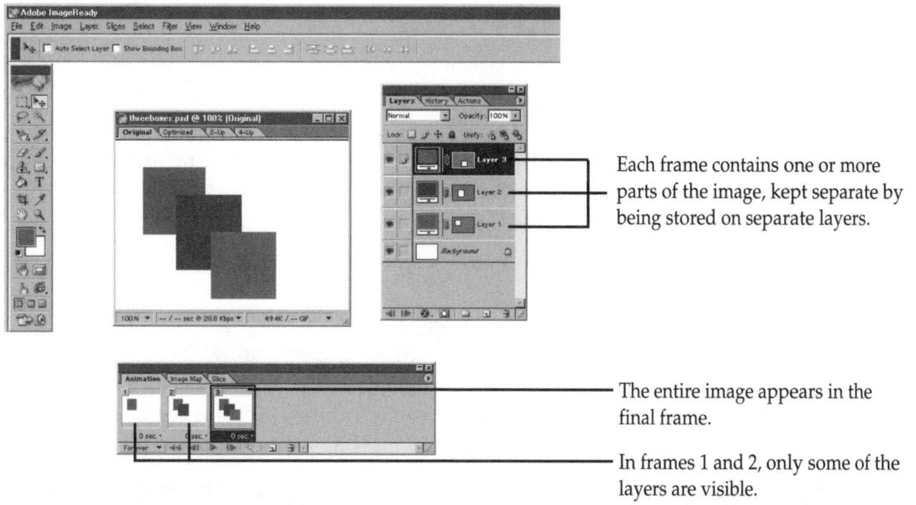

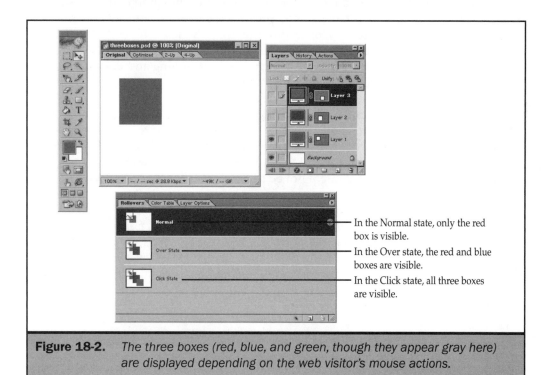

Adobe ImageReady
threeboxes.psd @ 100% (Original)
Layers
Layer 3
Layer 2
Layer 1
Background
Animation
Each frame contains one or more parts of the image, kept separate by being stored on separate layers.
The entire image appears in the final frame.
In frames 1 and 2, only some of the layers are visible.

Figure 18-1. *An image builds, one component at a time, in a series of animated GIF frames.*

threeboxes.psd @ 100% (Original)
Original
Optimized
2-Up
4-Up
Layers
History
Actions
Layer 3
Layer 2
Layer 1
Background
Rollovers
Color Table
Layer Options
Normal
Over State
Click State
In the Normal state, only the red box is visible.
In the Over state, the red and blue boxes are visible.
In the Click state, all three boxes are visible.

Figure 18-2. *The three boxes (red, blue, and green, though they appear gray here) are displayed depending on the web visitor's mouse actions.*

Integrating Animated Effects into Web Pages

When you plan to use animation in a web page, it's a good idea to make part of that planning an evaluation process—does the web page in question require animation? If you think so, how much is enough? Are you adding animation to the page simply because you can? Are you concerned that the page doesn't have enough content or interest on its own? If you're adding animation to increase visitor interaction and keep their eyes moving, that's great. If you're doing it because you're afraid you won't be exciting without it, concentrate on improving the page content before you throw a lot of animation at it.

There are several reasons you want to be conservative in your use of animation. One was expressed to me by my cousin, an intelligent, reasonable man who is new to the Internet, as many of your web site visitors may be. My cousin once referred to a web site he'd visited as an "all singing and dancing" web site. I thought his description was really quite accurate—it was a site where there was something moving or making noise on every page. This can be a good thing, if the site is for kids or pertains to something fun or silly. On the other hand, a lot of animation—things that move on their own, or things that move in response to the visitor's mouse—can be distracting and lend a frivolous tone to your site, which isn't good if your site's tone isn't supposed to be frivolous or silly.

Animation can also make a page slow to load, and the animation that moves like lightning or runs quite smoothly when you preview it on your computer may run slowly or in a jerky, halting fashion on a computer that's attached to the Internet via a slow modem. Just as you should optimize your static images for the Web so they'll load quickly (as discussed in Chapter 17), you want your singing and dancing images to load quickly, too. If they don't, or they can't due to their size and complexity, scale them back or consider sticking with static images.

Now, with all these cautions, I'm not saying you shouldn't use animated GIFs or rollovers at all. A rollover can be useful because it draws attention to a graphic or text a visitor might not have realized was a link or might not have stopped to look at or read otherwise. Animated GIFs can be useful to encourage visitors to linger on a page or to notice a portion of the page that might not be terribly eye-catching on its own.

Tip   *Another reason to use some level of animation is to compete with the many sites on the Web today that use Flash movies and similar animated content. For many visitors, any site that "just sits there" might be written off as dull. Certainly no one expects singing and dancing on a medical research site or a site devoted to financial planning information. However, using some animation to make a point or just adding some visual excitement won't hurt even those sites that pertain to sober topics.*

You can use ImageReady to create exciting and dynamic animations or very subtle animations with simple, yet effective results. An animated GIF can run through its steps quickly and then remain as a static image onscreen, or it can be looped, playing over and over so the image is never still while the page is viewed. Rollovers can swap two entirely different images so the results of the visitor's mouse movements are rather drastic, or your rollover can simply add to or take something out of an image, making a very slight change in the graphic content when the visitor moves his or her mouse. The degree and type of animation is up to you—ImageReady is poised to help you achieve your goals, no matter what they are.

Getting to Know ImageReady's Tools and Palettes

The ImageReady application window is very similar to the Photoshop application window—in fact, you might not even be able to tell them apart without looking at the title bar, where the application name appears. As shown in Figure 18-3, the ImageReady toolbox, menus, palettes, and even the image window are very similar to those that appear in Photoshop.

ImageReady on the Mac is also quite similar to Photoshop. In Figure 18-4, you can see the same tools, menus, and palettes in place, with very few contrasting items.

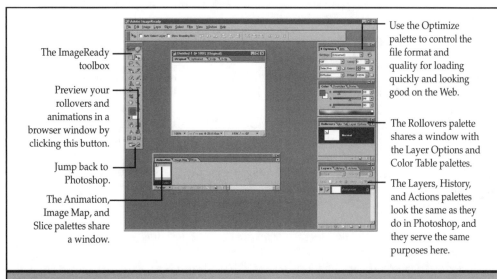

Figure 18-3.   *The similarity between Photoshop and ImageReady can work to your advantage—you can take what you know about one and use it in the other.*

PHOTOSHOP
ON THE WEB

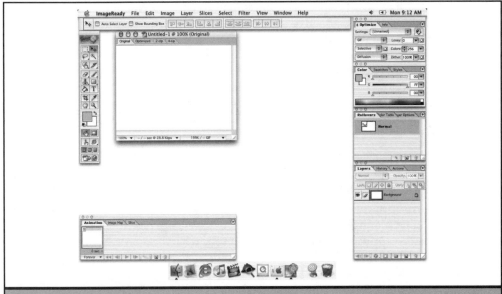

Figure 18-4. *The ImageReady interface on the Macintosh gives you many of the same tools you're accustomed to finding in the Photoshop interface.*

Getting Started with ImageReady

The easiest way to start ImageReady is from within the Photoshop application. At the bottom of the Photoshop toolbox, click the Jump to ImageReady button, as shown in Figure 18-5. Of course, if you don't have Photoshop running and don't plan to use it while you're working with ImageReady, you can also use the ImageReady icon that may be on your desktop or in your Windows Start menu Programs list.

If your computer doesn't have a lot of memory (less than 128MB), you may find that you can't run both ImageReady and Photoshop at the same time without some noticeable slowness in the operation of one or both applications. If this occurs, make sure any other non-essential applications are closed, and if the slowness continues, consider closing any applications you won't be using while you're working with ImageReady.

Once the ImageReady application is open, the next step is to open an existing image (virtually any graphic file format is acceptable, as shown in Figure 18-6), or to start a new file. Figure 18-7 shows the New Document dialog box, through which you designate the size of the new image (choose from typical monitor resolutions such as 800 × 600 or 1024 × 768), and the color of the Background layer. It's called the First Layer, but it appears as Background on the Layers palette, just as it would in a new Photoshop file.

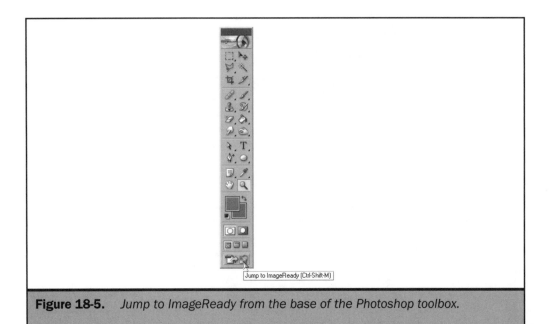

Figure 18-5.   *Jump to ImageReady from the base of the Photoshop toolbox.*

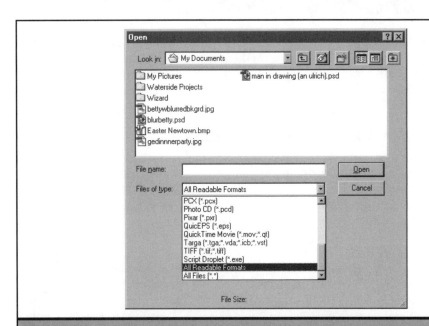

Figure 18-6.   *Open any existing PSD files from Photoshop, or open a JPEG or GIF file you've already optimized. You can also open any other bitmap or vector file that Photoshop supports.*

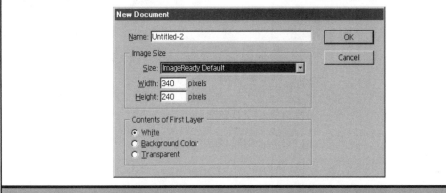

Figure 18-7.   Choose from a list of Sizes, or type your own custom dimensions for the new file.

 If you open a PSD file, your layers won't go to waste—ImageReady uses the layers from the image as you saved it in Photoshop and makes extensive use of the Layers palette. You'll use the palette to decide where and when layers and their content are visible in specific animation frames or rollover states.

After your new or existing image is open in its own window, you can begin using the toolbox, menus, and palettes to operate on the image, adding, changing, and removing content. You'll find that what you already know about Photoshop can be put to instant use in ImageReady—many of the tools are the same in appearance and functioning, and any differences are rather subtle.

Comparing Photoshop and ImageReady

The major differences between Photoshop and ImageReady are slight, but ultimately significant in that the tools that are unique to ImageReady are key to building the kind of images that ImageReady builds. You have tools for mapping sections of an image to serve as links, extensive slice-handling tools, and the ability to turn toolbox buttons with multiple buttons into floating toolbars for easy access (see Figure 18-8).

The other major difference between Photoshop and ImageReady is obvious—it's the Animation/Image Map/Slice palette, shown in Figure 18-9. This three-tabbed palette gives you the basic tools you need for creating animated GIFs and for mapping and slicing images. You'll also see a Rollovers palette (with Color Table and Layer Options tabs sharing the palette, shown in Figure 18-10) through which you'll create your interactive images. The separation of the Rollovers palette from the Animation/Image Map palette is new in Photoshop 7.

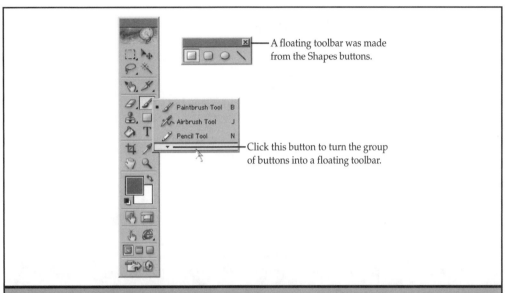

A floating toolbar was made from the Shapes buttons.

Paintbrush Tool   B
Airbrush Tool   J
Pencil Tool   N

Click this button to turn the group of buttons into a floating toolbar.

Figure 18-8.   *Slicing and mapping-specific tools are included in the ImageReady toolbox, which is otherwise identical to the Photoshop toolbox.*

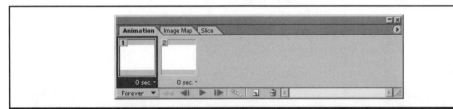

Figure 18-9.   *The Animation/Image Map/Slice palette provides access to three main ImageReady tasks.*

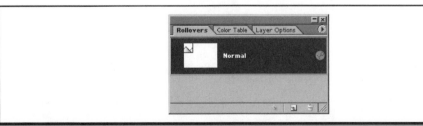

Figure 18-10.   *Squirreled away in a separate palette are the tools for building rollovers.*

PHOTOSHOP
ON THE WEB

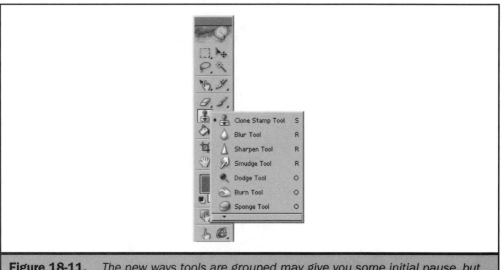

Figure 18-11.   *The new ways tools are grouped may give you some initial pause, but you'll get used to it.*

If you prefer one-stop shopping for your key ImageReady palettes, you can drag the Rollovers tab onto the Animation/Image Map/Slice palette, making a fourth tab. This can save you the trouble of keeping more palettes open than you need, and gives you more room to work when building rollovers. You learned to move tabs from palette to palette in Chapter 2, which you can review now if you need.

You'll notice that some of the tools that have button alternatives in Photoshop (indicated by the triangle in the lower-right corner of the button) don't have alternatives here. For example, the Paint Bucket (which is now on the left side of the toolbox) is the only Fill tool on that button (although you can use Brush to paint any sort of fill you want), because the Gradient tool doesn't exist in ImageReady. The Airbrush tool appears to be missing, but is now one of the Brush alternate tools (along with the Pencil).

The Eraser tool is missing an alternate, as the Background Eraser is gone. You still have the Magic Eraser and the basic Eraser tools, though. Other changes and omissions include the following:

- The Dodge, Burn, Sharpen, Blur, and Sponge tools are now alternates to the default Clone Stamp tool (see Figure 18-11).

- You can't create a Text mask with the Text tool, and there is no Quick Mask Mode.

- The History and Art History brushes don't exist in ImageReady.

- There is no Notes tool to annotate your images.

You may be thinking that these changes—and certainly the omissions—in the toolbox will limit your ability to create great images in ImageReady. Nothing could be further from the truth. Remember that you can build any image you like in Photoshop, making use of all of Photoshop's features and tools, and then save it in PSD format. Because ImageReady opens PSD files and maintains all the file details, you can open the PSD file in ImageReady and take advantage of ImageReady's tools for turning the image into a rollover, or to map areas of the image and assign links. The tools available for image editing and creation in ImageReady are aimed at more simplistic images, the sort of images that lend themselves to the GIF format. This doesn't mean you can't use photographic content, shadows, and/or embossing effects (not to mention some of the artistic patterns you can apply through Photoshop), but if you use a complex image for an animated GIF, you may see some reduction in clarity or color representation in the GIF version of the file. This isn't usually a problem, however, especially if the image remains in motion—people won't see the less-than-crisp edges or notice any color problems if an image is moving.

| Note | *When you save a file in ImageReady, you use the Save command to create a PSD version of the file, and the Save Optimized command to save a web-safe version of the file appropriate to the type of image you're creating. If you're working with an animation, the Save Optimized command automatically saves the file in GIF format. If you're saving a rollover, it is automatically saved in an HTML (HTM) format. Using the Image Map tools doesn't impose a particular format—you can choose from JPG, GIF, or PNG as the format for the image.* |

Navigating ImageReady's Animation Palette

The Animation palette is displayed when you click the Animation tab on the palette as shown in Figure 18-12. The window starts with a single frame and provides you with tools for creating new frames, duplicating existing frames, and deleting frames you no longer need. To see a ToolTip for any of the buttons on the palette, simply hover your mouse pointer over a button for a second and the tip will appear. In addition to tools for adding and deleting frames, you also have tools for controlling the speed and duration of your animation, and for playing your animation to test it.

If you're building your animation and the image that will be animated from within ImageReady, you can use the image window and the toolbox to begin drawing your animation elements right away. Note that whatever you add to the image will appear in the first frame, but you can choose later which image elements will appear in which frames, using the Layers palette in conjunction with the Animation palette's tools. You can also use an existing Photoshop image, utilizing the existing content and setting up different layers and their content to appear and disappear in different frames. You'll find out more about working with frames and actually creating animations in Chapter 19.

You can access a more extensive list of commands by clicking the palette options button on the far-right side of the Animation window. The palette options menu appears, displaying commands such as New Frame (unlike the Duplicate Frame button at the bottom of the window), Copy Frame, Delete Frame, and Select All Frames. As shown in Figure 18-13, you can access some of the same commands that are found in the Animation palette itself, plus others that don't exist anywhere else.

If you don't think you can see the content of the frames well enough, choose the large thumbnail option from the Palette Options command in the palette options menu. This will increase the displayed size of the frames in the Animation palette, potentially making it easier to see what's in each frame and make design decisions.

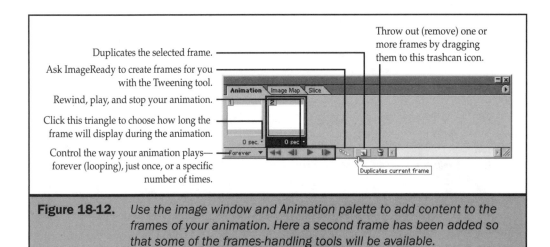

Figure 18-12.   *Use the image window and Animation palette to add content to the frames of your animation. Here a second frame has been added so that some of the frames-handling tools will be available.*

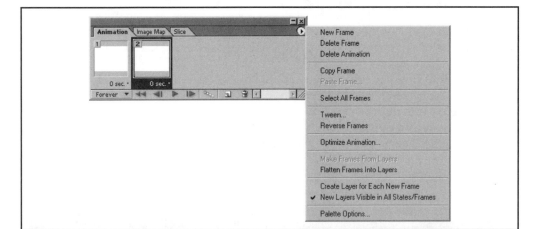

Figure 18-13.   *Access all the animation controls from the Animation palette option menu.*

Working with the Rollovers Palette

The Rollovers palette no longer shares a window with the Animation palette in Photoshop 7. You can drag it over to the same window so the palettes can live together and be accessed easily, but by default it appears in its own palette as shown in Figure 18-14. If you want to drag it into the same window as the Animation palette (shown in progress in Figure 18-15), just grab the tab and drag it with your mouse, releasing the mouse button when your mouse pointer is within the window containing the Animation, Image Map, and Slice palettes.

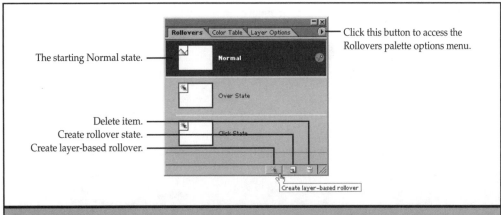

Figure 18-14.   *The Rollovers palette provides tools for taking an image and choosing how it will appear in different states, responding to web-page visitors' mouse actions. Here, two states have been added to the starting Normal state.*

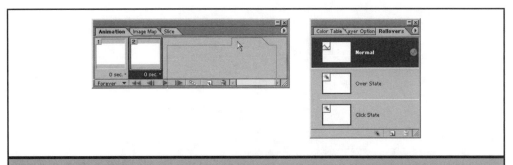

Figure 18-15.   *Move the Rollovers palette into the window where the Animation palette lives—you can simplify the workspace by keeping these palettes in the same window.*

PHOTOSHOP ON THE WEB

Like all other palettes, the Rollovers palette has a palette options menu, accessed by clicking the triangle on the right side of the palette (see Figure 18-16). The menu contains many of the same commands that are represented by buttons and drop-down lists on the palette itself, plus additional commands you'll find nowhere else. The Palette Options command allows you to choose from different thumbnail sizes (which result in smaller or larger state thumbnails in the palette), and the ability to display other palettes' content—animation frames, slices, and image maps. This dialog box is shown in Figure 18-17.

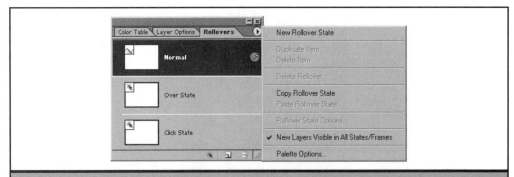

Figure 18-16. *Find all of the rollover-related commands in one place—the Rollovers palette menu.*

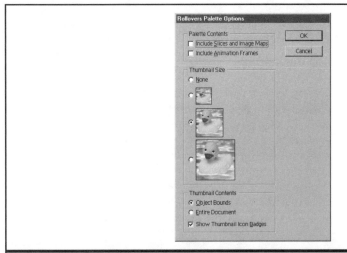

Figure 18-17. *Control the display characteristics and content of the Rollovers palette with the Palette Options command.*

The Image Map Palette

An image map makes it possible for a single image, usually a larger image containing text and/or pictures, to serve as a graphic link to more than one file or web site. For example, as shown in Figure 18-18, a series of phrases, typed and formatted in Photoshop and then opened in ImageReady, can be selected individually and associated with specific pages within a web site. This turns the simple list of phrases into a navigational tool.

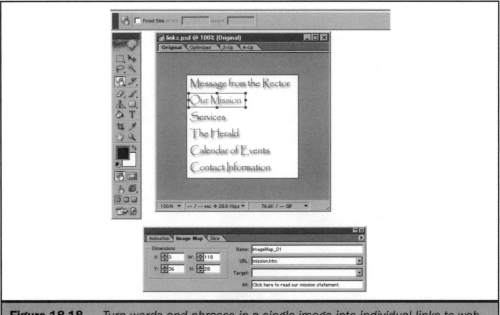

Figure 18-18. Turn words and phrases in a single image into individual links to web pages and files with ImageReady's image map tools.

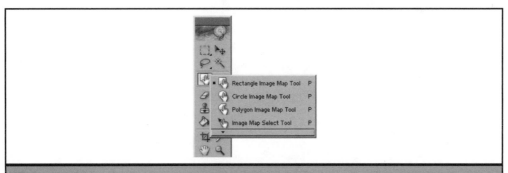

Figure 18-19. Choose from three map-drawing tools and a tool for selecting the maps you've already drawn.

Identifying the Toolbox Mapping Tools

To create an image map, you need to designate areas of the image as image maps, drawing rectangles, circles, or polygons on the surface of the image. ImageReady provides a set of tools for just this purpose, shown in Figure 18-19. Once the shape is drawn (see Figure 18-20), you can use the Image Map palette to adjust the size and location of the map and to specify the link information for that particular map.

Working with the Image Map Palette

The Image Map palette comes into play once an image map is drawn on the image. Until an image map is drawn, the palette's tools remain dimmed. Once activated, as shown in Figure 18-21, you can use them to control the size, location, and function of the image map you've drawn and selected.

The Image Map palette's option menu offers a list of commands you won't find on the palette itself—instead, you'll find commands that allow you to control the overlap, alignment, and distribution of multiple mapped areas on a single image. Figure 18-22 shows this menu and its commands, and the options bar that's available (with many of the same commands in the form of buttons) when the Image Map Select tool is active.

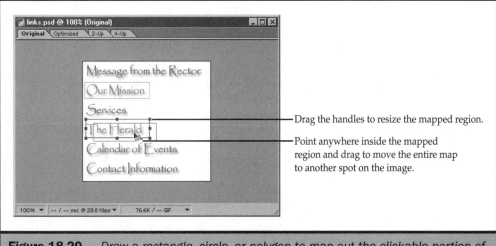

Figure 18-20.   *Draw a rectangle, circle, or polygon to map out the clickable portion of the image.*

The X and Y dimension settings control the coordinates of the image map on the surface of the image.

The W and H settings control the width and height of the selected map you've drawn.

You can name your map so it's easier to find later in the HTML code of your web page document.

The URL text box should contain the exact address of the web page to which the image-mapped area will link.

The Target option can be used to establish how the linked page displays.

Enter Alt(ernate) text into this box to provide a screen tip when the visitor hovers the cursor over the mapped area or to provide a description of the image should it not display in the visitor's browser window.

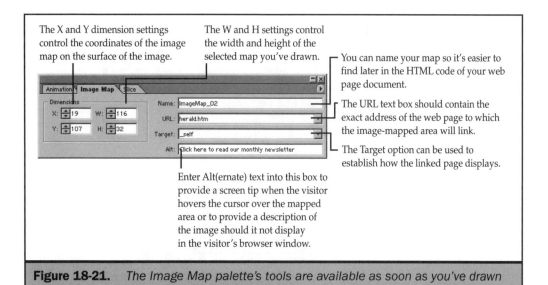

Figure 18-21. *The Image Map palette's tools are available as soon as you've drawn and selected a mapped region on your image.*

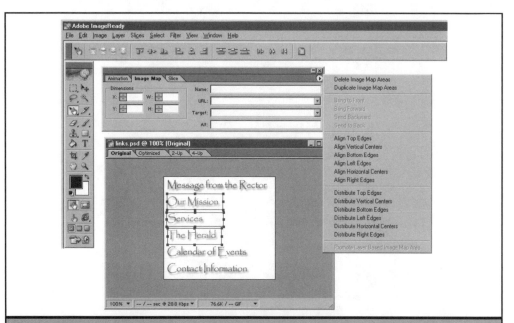

Figure 18-22. *Control the placement and special relationships between mapped areas on your image with the Image Map palette options menu. Depending on how many mapped areas you have and how they're positioned, not all of the menu items may be available.*

PHOTOSHOP ON THE WEB

The Slice Palette

Larger images are typically sliced to make them load faster on a web page. When an image is sliced, it's broken into several separate images, one per slice. The slices are then inserted into a web page (normally using a table to house the individual slices) where the individual slices are assembled to give the appearance of a single large image. Figure 18-23 shows a web page made up entirely of slices of a single large image that was created in Photoshop, sliced in ImageReady, and turned into a web page with Adobe GoLive. In the figure, it is viewed in an Internet Explorer window.

Identifying the Slice Tools in the ImageReady Toolbox

To slice an image, you need to use the Slice tool located in the ImageReady toolbox. The slice tool also exists in the Photoshop toolbox, but there is no Slice palette in Photoshop, so it's usually a better idea to do your slicing in ImageReady where there are additional slice-handling tools to work with once your image is sliced.

The Slice Tool (and Slice Select Tool, both shown in Figure 18-24) works by your clicking and dragging to draw rectangular shapes on your image, as shown in Figure 18-25. The resulting slices are numbered, and once there are slices on your image, the Slice palette can be used much like the Image Map palette to adjust their size and location, and link them to files and web pages.

Figure 18-23. *An image this size could take several minutes to load if your visitor is connected to the Internet via modem. The individual slices, however, load quickly, combining visually to create the large single image you started with in ImageReady.*

Figure 18-24.   *Use the Slice tool to draw your slices; use the Slice Select tool to activate individual slices to be edited with the Slices palette.*

Figure 18-25.   *Click and drag with the knife-like Slice tool to break your image into two or more rectangular sections.*

PHOTOSHOP ON THE WEB

Using the Slice Palette

Once a slice is created and selected, you can change its position on the image, alter its size, turn it into a link by specifying a web address to which it will point once its on a web page, and apply a background color. Figure 18-26 shows the Slice palette in its expanded display, showing its full set of tools.

You can use the Slice palette's options menu (shown in Figure 18-27) to duplicate, divide, and delete slices, as well as to control their placement and relationships to each other. You'll find out more about slices and how to manipulate them in Chapter 19.

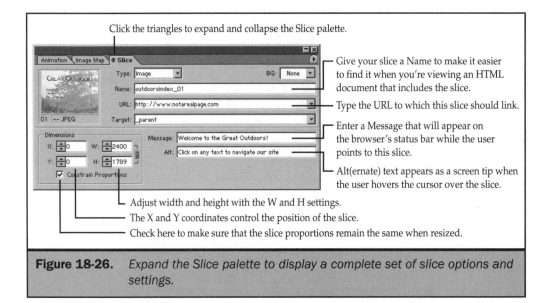

Click the triangles to expand and collapse the Slice palette.

Give your slice a Name to make it easier to find it when you're viewing an HTML document that includes the slice.

Type the URL to which this slice should link.

Enter a Message that will appear on the browser's status bar while the user points to this slice.

Alt(ernate) text appears as a screen tip when the user hovers the cursor over the slice.

Adjust width and height with the W and H settings.

The X and Y coordinates control the position of the slice.

Check here to make sure that the slice proportions remain the same when resized.

Figure 18-26. *Expand the Slice palette to display a complete set of slice options and settings.*

Figure 18-27. *Find more controls for your slices in the palette options menu.*

Summary

In this chapter, you found out what's new in ImageReady 7.0, how Photoshop and ImageReady work together, and what differences you can expect to discover when you switch from Photoshop to ImageReady. The Animation, Rollovers, Image Map, and Slice palettes were covered in detail, preparing you to use their tools as you move on to learn how to create animations, rollovers, slices, and image maps in Chapter 19.

The Complete Reference

Chapter 19

Creating ImageReady Animations, Rollovers, Slices, and Image Maps

N ow that you've been introduced to the ImageReady interface in Chapter 18, you're ready to put the tools and palettes you saw there to use. In this chapter, you'll learn to create animated GIF files, set up rollovers to add interactivity and visual interest to your web pages, and slice large images into pieces for easier and faster loading on web pages. In addition, you'll learn to create *image maps*—selected areas within a single image that serve as a visual link to multiple files and web pages.

Animating Images for Use on the Web

First, let's define the sort of animation you can create in ImageReady and discuss the other types of web-page animation you may have encountered. Some web pages are entirely animated—everything moves, either automatically or in response to the visitors' actions. These animations are often the product of applications such as Adobe's LiveMotion or Macromedia's Flash. The pages consist of actual movies that run, frame by frame, as dictated by the person who designed them. Conversely, the sort of animations you can create in ImageReady aren't movies; while they are made up of a series of frames, they're GIF files with information about individual frames stored within them. They contain instructions for when to play, how long to play, and how long to display each frame. Think of it like one of those decks of cards that you flip through and it looks like a cartoon or a quick movie—the rapid succession of changing images on the cards (like animated GIF frames) creates the illusion of motion. Animated GIFs are also simpler to create than Flash or LiveMotion movies—the same skills you use to make static GIF images are utilized, along with some added procedures to turn the static images into a series of frames.

Constructing an Animation

A new ImageReady image is a blank slate—until you start adding content to the image. The process of adding content requires a knowledge (or at least a sense) of what your animation will do, how it will look, and how it should play. This does not mean that you should build your animation one frame at a time, setting up each frame as you go in terms of when and how long it will play. Rather, it's better to create the finished image—the way the animation will look when it's completed all of its steps.

As shown in Figure 19-1, the final image, with all of its parts in place, is the goal of the animation. With each component of the image on a separate layer, you'll be ready to set up your animation frames and decide which layers are visible on which frames. It's difficult, if not impossible, to build frames and set their order and playback settings without content to work with. Figure 19-1 also shows the Layers palette, and you can see that each component of the finished image is on a separate layer.

Before you start a new animation, it's a good idea to sketch the animation on paper, a process known as *storyboarding*. The storyboarding process can be very informal or it can be more elaborate. The informal method might include simple boxes drawn on paper showing each frame of the animation. A more serious storyboard undertaking could be performed in Photoshop or an actual illustration application showing each frame of the image. I prefer the informal approach, because drawing each frame as a picture in a program like Illustrator is very much like the process of building the image in ImageReady—you're really duplicating your efforts if you do more than sketch the basic animation on paper. If, however, you have to submit your ideas to someone for approval, you should probably create something more formal, or at least a very detailed drawing.

After storyboarding your animation, you can begin creating the individual layers for your image, and then add content to the layers. Remember that every individual component of the animation should be on a separate layer, if possible. Of course, things that will appear and disappear together can be on the same layer, but anything that will be animated individually should be on its own layer.

Adding Content to Animation Layers

When you go to create an element of the animation—any line, shape, or special effect you're about to create—be sure to select the layer on which that content or effect should appear. It's a common mistake to forget to add a new layer or switch layers before drawing a new image element—an especially easy mistake to make when you're concentrating on the image itself. Always keep an eye on the Layers palette, and make sure you're on the right layer before you begin drawing or using the Brush, Airbrush, Pencil, or Pen tools.

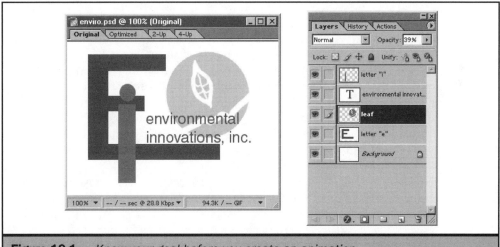

Figure 19-1. *Know your goal before you create an animation.*

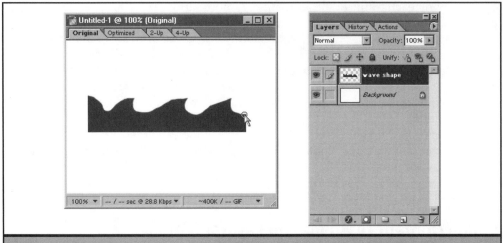

Figure 19-2. *Create layers for integral components and name the layers accordingly.*

After selecting the right layer (or adding a new one using the Layer | New | Layer command), you can begin adding that layer's content. Figure 19-2 shows a shape being drawn on a new layer—note that the layer's name is indicative of the content, and thus the role that layer will play in the animation. It's a good idea to apply meaningful names, rather than sticking with the generic "Layer #" names (where "#" is the sequential number applied automatically) that ImageReady and Photoshop give to new layers.

It's important to remember that you can build your image in Photoshop if you prefer, and then open it in ImageReady to perform the process of animating it. Even though ImageReady has virtually all the same tools you have in Photoshop, you may already have an image that you built in Photoshop, or you may simply prefer the Photoshop environment. The reason you choose one application over another doesn't matter—what does matter is that you work in the application that provides the tools you need and the comfort level that enables you to do good work. If you do build the image in Photoshop, the PSD file you create in Photoshop can be opened in ImageReady and then animated.

Note   *If you've already built an image in Photoshop, and you want to animate it but can't do so easily because each element of the image isn't on its own layer, you can move things to new layers with the help of Photoshop's selection tools. Use the Magic Wand to select solid-colored shapes and lines that need to be moved off to their own layers, and use the Marquee tool to select other areas of existing layers that need to be on new layers. You can also use the Lasso tools for more intricate selections. But if things overlap or are inextricably connected on a single layer, consider recreating those parts, each on their own layer, and then throwing out the layer that has them together. In short, if you didn't put all the parts on their own layers, all is not lost—you can split things up with the selection tools and then place the content on the appropriate layer after using the Layer | New | Layer command.*

Applying Layer Formats

Remember that animation files you build in ImageReady are animated GIF files. GIF format is best suited for line art—simple graphics with solid colors, minimal shading, and very little (if any) photographic content. That doesn't mean your animations have to look like simplistic cartoons, but you should steer clear of applying a lot of drop shadows, highlights, glows, or embossed effects. Avoid using any photographic content, unless the clarity or crispness of the image isn't integral to its role in the image. Figure 19-3 shows an image that's a good candidate for the GIF format, and Figure 19-4 shows the same image with attributes that would make it better suited to the JPG format (if it's bound for the Web) and, therefore, not a good choice for animation.

> **Tip**   *Chapter 17 discusses web-safe file formats in detail and is a good resource for more information on this topic.*

If you must animate an image that's not well suited to the GIF format, consider using another animation tool, such as Adobe LiveMotion or Macromedia's Flash. These applications provide a greater range of output options, so you're not restricted to content that doesn't go beyond the capabilities of the GIF format.

Of course, if you want to create your animation in ImageReady, you can make judicious use of all of Photoshop's and ImageReady's tools for enhancing an image, finding a happy medium between the look you want and what's possible with the GIF format. You can apply drop shadows, glows, beveled and embossed effects, even colorful styles and pattern fills, all through the Layer Style submenu, accessed by right-clicking (Windows) or CONTROL-clicking (Mac) a layer and choosing Layer Style from

Figure 19-3.   *Images that are simple in terms of color content are good candidates for the GIF format.*

Figure 19-4. *This graphic has too much color information going on in the form of photographic content and shading to be effectively turned into an animated GIF.*

the context menu. Figure 19-5 shows the submenu, which quickly applies these effects to your image. If you want to access the sometimes more powerful or more customizable tools found in Photoshop, it might be a good idea to use Photoshop's Blending Options dialog box for this sort of thing instead.

There's no limit to what you can do to an image that you intend to animate, but you should be aware that there may be sacrifices in the visual quality of the image when it appears on a web page. Of course, because the image is moving, the loss of quality isn't as obvious as it would be if the image were static—and if the animation is set to loop continuously, the image won't ever be seen sitting still. If your animation will be playing only once or some fixed number of times (ending up as a static image in the end), be sure to preview it in a web browser (using ImageReady's Preview tool) before you upload it to the Web. You may want to simplify the image a bit if the image quality is unacceptable.

Working with Animation Frames

As you can imagine, an animation must have at least two frames in order for any animation to occur. If your animation goal is a simple on/off effect, two frames will do. If you want something to happen slowly or if the animation requires several steps to complete, you'll want several frames so that the animation can occur at the speed and/or in the number of steps you want. You can build your own frames, or as you'll discover in the section "Tweening Your Animation Frames" later in this chapter, you can have ImageReady build them for you with the Tween command in the Animation palette menu, or by using the Tweens Animation Frames button on the Animation palette. In order to tween, however, you need at least two frames—one to show the image as it should start, and one to show it as it should end up—the tweening process will create the interim frames.

Inserting and Copying Frames

You can create frames by duplicating an existing frame (click the Duplicate Current Frame button, shown in Figure 19-6) or by inserting a new frame (choose New Frame from the Animation palette menu, shown in Figure 19-7).

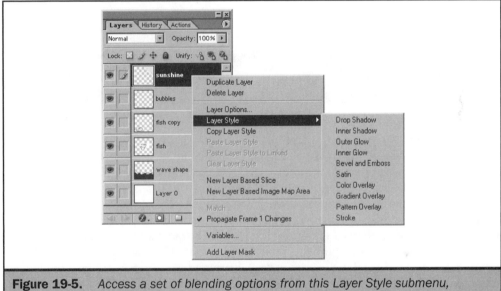

Figure 19-5. *Access a set of blending options from this Layer Style submenu, applicable to any layer you create in your animation.*

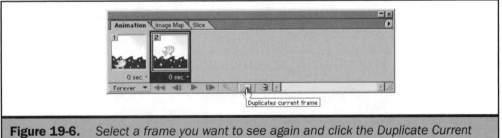

Figure 19-6. *Select a frame you want to see again and click the Duplicate Current Frame button.*

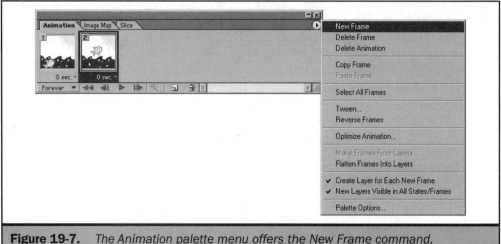

Figure 19-7.   The Animation palette menu offers the New Frame command.

Given the variety of ways to add frames to your animation, the key to creating frames effectively is choosing when to do it and what to include in the frames as they're created. This is so much more important than how you create the frames. For example, if you have all of your image layers showing in your first frame, any duplicates you create from that frame will also have all the layers showing. You'll have to go into each frame and turn things off to remove any parts that don't belong in the individual frames. If, conversely, you have only one element of the image showing in a frame and you duplicate that frame, you'll have to go to all the duplicates and turn on the layers that you want to display in each of the duplicate frames. A certain amount of hiding and displaying layers on individual frames is inescapable, but it's a good idea to think ahead and eliminate as much redundant effort as possible.

For a more efficient approach to adding a frame, start with a blank slate. If you have nothing showing in the first frame (either because your image hasn't been built yet or because all the layers are hidden in that frame), you only need to turn things on in the subsequent duplicate frames. Figure 19-8 shows a complete image represented by layers in the Layers palette, but nothing showing in the first frame. The Duplicate Current Frame button has been used to create three duplicate frames, and they, too, have nothing in them.

If you have trouble telling what's showing in individual frames, increase the size of the frames thumbnails as they appear in the Animation palette. You can control the size of the Animation palette's thumbnail display by choosing Palette Options from the Palette options menu. In the resulting dialog box shown in Figure 19-9, choose from a small, medium, or large thumbnail; your choice affects the size of the frames in the palette. The default size is medium, but if you feel you can't see everything in the thumbnail well enough to make decisions about content and timing from within the palette, choose the large size.

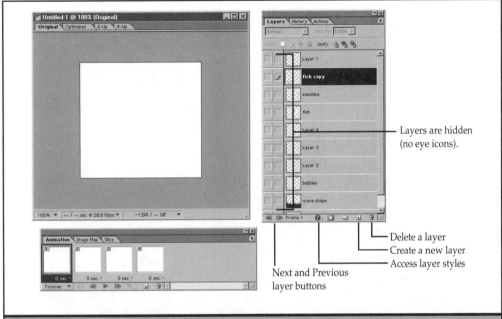

— Layers are hidden (no eye icons).

— Delete a layer
— Create a new layer
— Access layer styles

Next and Previous layer buttons

Figure 19-8. *Hide your layers in the first frame and all your duplicates of that frame will be empty as well—until you turn on individual layers in the individual frames.*

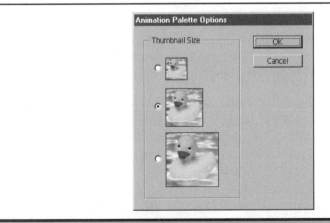

Figure 19-9. *Select a size for the frame thumbnail display in the Animation palette by choosing Palette Options from the Animation palette options menu.*

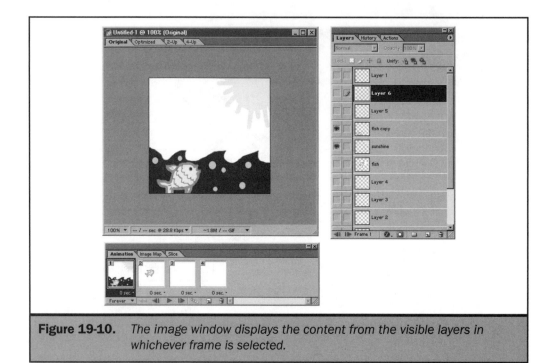

Figure 19-10. *The image window displays the content from the visible layers in whichever frame is selected.*

Of course, when you click on a frame, that frame's content is displayed in the image window. This window will change depending on which frame is active, as shown in Figure 19-10. This isn't the best way to choose content for individual frames, however, as your eye will be skipping from the Animation palette to the image window, to the Layers palette and back again, each time you go to hide or display a layer in a given frame. It's much more efficient to work in the Animation palette and use the thumbnails there to help you set up your individual frames.

When you use the Duplicates Current Frame button, everything about the current frame is duplicated—its content and its timing. If you duplicate a frame and then tinker with its content, be sure to check the timing in case you wanted the duplicate to play for more or less time than the original on which it is based. Setting frame timing is covered later in this chapter, in the section "Controlling Animation Speed and Playback."

Controlling Layer Visibility Throughout the Animation

As shown in Figure 19-11, a successful animation requires that things be different in the individual frames; otherwise, there's nothing moving or arriving or departing as the animation occurs. The frames shown in this figure show a house being built, one piece at a time. Because each wall, windows and doors, and roof are on their own layers (the lawn and trees are separate layers as well), each frame has a different set of visible and hidden layers.

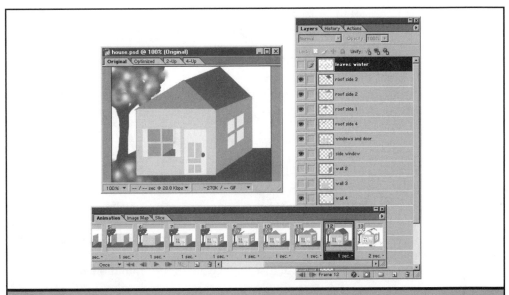

Figure 19-11.   *Build a house one wall, window, and door at a time.*

| **Tip** | *This house graphic (in PSD format) is on the CD that accompanies this book. You can see how the image was constructed and then play with the file to create your own animation.* |

The first frame shows the lawn and one tree. Then you see the foundation, then the walls, then the windows and doors, and finally the roof. Each frame builds on the frame before it—the frame containing the foundation also contains the lawn and tree, the frame containing the first wall also contains the foundation, lawn, and tree. You can apply this cumulative approach to other animations, as well—consider these scenarios:

- A flower blooms or a tree goes through the seasons onscreen, one component at a time. This works best for simple illustrations.

- A word or sentence is "written" by the animation. Each letter of the word or word of the sentence needs to be on its own layer.

- Time passing can be simulated with an animation—you can have a clock face on one layer, and the hands of the clock in progressive positions on the rest of the layers.

- Another way to make time pass through an animation is to show the sun rising, setting, being replaced by the rising moon, which also sets and is replaced by the rising sun. This animation is another that works well if looped endlessly or run just once. You can do a lot with color and light sources in the rest of the image to support the illusion of day passing into night and day returning.

Beyond making parts of the image appear and disappear by hiding and revealing them on the Layers palette, you can affect the animation by moving different parts of the image in different frames. For example, as the sun rises and sets, the flowers in the image can close at night and reopen in the morning. The colors of the grass and sky also change (by virtue of an entirely different set of shapes on their own layers) as the day progresses, as do the colors of the other objects in the image. While an animation with multiple moving and changing parts is complicated to create, it can give you a very rewarding result.

So far, most of the animations we've looked at show something building or changing over the duration of the animation. This represents a majority of the web animations you'll see (at least those created in ImageReady and similar products). But there are other types of animations—those that show movement from left to right (or right to left) and up or down within the frame. Imagine a person walking, a ball rolling or bouncing across the screen, or a car driving from the left side of the animation area to the right. The illusion of movement is achieved by moving the visible elements in each frame so that they go from point A to point B as the frames progress. Figure 19-12 shows a car moving from left to right, across the bottom of the animation area.

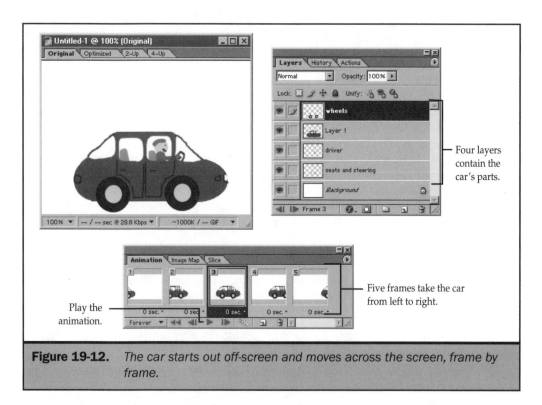

Figure 19-12. *The car starts out off-screen and moves across the screen, frame by frame.*

If you're moving some or all of your image from one place to another through a series of individual frames, don't duplicate the first frame, where the image is at the beginning of its journey, to create the frames that take the image content from point A to point B. To save yourself a good deal of work, duplicate the first frame to create the second frame, and then after moving the content in that second frame to its desired position, duplicate that frame to make the third frame. In the third frame, you need only move things slightly to show movement, rather than having to move things from the starting position to the ending position. Continue duplicating the previous frame until the image has made its entire journey, one frame at a time.

Changing the Order in Which Frames Play

After you've set up all of your frames so that the right stuff is showing in each one, you may find that you want to change the order in which things occur—either you'll discover an error in your original setup, or someone who reviews your animation may suggest a change. Whatever the reason, you can easily rearrange your frames by dragging the frames to the left or right to change their order in the animation.

You can drag frames one a time, or you can drag them in groups. Figure 19-13 shows a word that's formed by a series of frames, each containing a single letter. After rearranging the frames so that the letters appear in the proper order, the animation plays and forms the word "mystery," as shown in Figure 19-14.

Tip   *To group a series of frames, click the first one in the series, press the* SHIFT *key, and then with the key still held down, click the last frame in the series you want to group. All of the frames turn blue, indicating they're selected as a group. If your desired group is not made up of contiguous frames, substitute the* CTRL/COMMAND *key for the* SHIFT *key and click the individual frames you want to include in the group.*

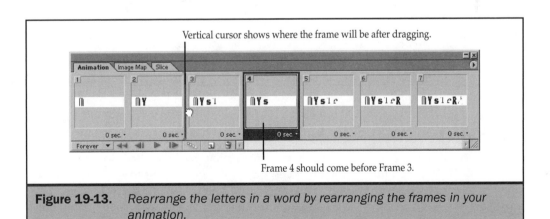

Figure 19-13.   *Rearrange the letters in a word by rearranging the frames in your animation.*

Figure 19-14. *Rearranging frames can completely alter the result of your animation.*

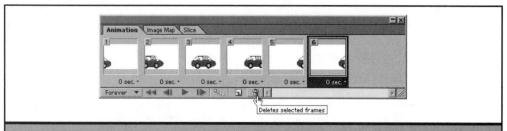

Figure 19-15. *The trash is the best place for this unwanted duplicate frame.*

Deleting Unwanted Frames

Through the process of building your own frames or having ImageReady create frames for you (as discussed in the section on tweening that follows this section), you may end up with too many frames—frames that simply aren't necessary for the animation to work, that are left over from revisions and rearrangements, or that actually get in the way of the animation's proper progression. To get rid of a frame, simply select it and drag it by its number (or anywhere across the top of the frame thumbnail) to the trash (see Figure 19-15), or click once on the frame and then choose Delete Frame from the Animation palette menu.

You can also get rid of multiple frames with either deletion technique—just select the frames to be deleted by clicking on them while pressing the SHIFT key (for a range of contiguous frames) or the CTRL/COMMAND key (for noncontiguous frames) and then dragging them to the trash. Alternatively, you can use the Delete Frames command from the palette menu. If you want to delete all of the frames in the animation, which will delete the animation itself, choose Delete Animation from the Animation palette options menu. A prompt will ask you to confirm your intention to delete all the frames in the animation, and clicking Yes will complete the deletion.

If you didn't mean to delete a frame or you deleted the wrong one, you can undo your frame deletion by choosing Edit | Undo, or you can press CTRL/COMMAND-Z. You can also use the History palette to go back in time to the point just prior to the regretted deletion.

Tweening Your Animation Frames

While you can build your animations manually, creating each frame yourself, some animations really require *tweening*. When you use the Tween command (found in the Animation palette menu), ImageReady creates frames for you, basing their content on the frames that exist at the time. You can, for example, move text or a graphic across the width of the image window without building your own frames. Simply ask ImageReady to tween the first frame (where the object is on the left side of the image window) with the second frame, where the object is on the right side of the image window. The interim frames (the frames in be*tween* the original first and second frames), where the object appears in stages across the width of the window, are created by ImageReady and the object is moved at regular intervals. The number of intervals is dictated by you when you issue the Tween command.

Controlling the Tweening Process

You can invoke the tweening process by selecting the starting or ending frame that will dictate the tweened frames' content, and then either click the Tweens Animation Frames button (see Figure 19-16), or open the Animation palette menu and choose Tween. The Tween dialog box will appear, as shown in Figure 19-17. Through it, you can choose the number of tweened frames to create, with which frame the tweens will work (the one prior to or after the selected frame), and which things to tween—all layers or just the selected layers (you'd select them ahead of time, using the Layers palette).

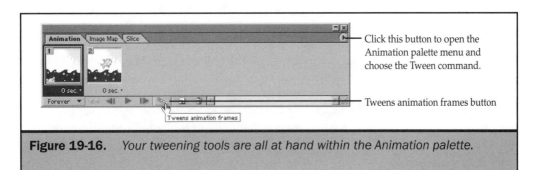

Click this button to open the Animation palette menu and choose the Tween command.

Tweens animation frames button

Figure 19-16.   *Your tweening tools are all at hand within the Animation palette.*

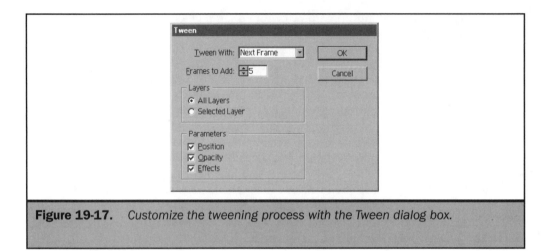

Figure 19-17.   *Customize the tweening process with the Tween dialog box.*

If you want the positions you've set for content that should move as the animation progresses to be honored, leave the Position option checked in the Tween dialog box. The Effects option refers to shadows and other layer styles you have applied to layers that are included in the tweened animation. Leaving the option on means the effects will be preserved throughout the tweening process, and any effects you had in place in the starting frame will also be in place in the frames that were created by the tweening process. The Opacity option allows you to have objects that disappear over the course of the tweening process fade out rather than simply vanish. For objects that appear over the course of the tweening process, their appearance fades in—they don't just pop up unexpectedly. Of course, if that's what you want to happen, then turn the Opacity setting off.

Using Multiple Tweens in a Single Animation

You aren't restricted to a single tween in any animation—you can use the Tween command to create the frames between two manually created frames, and then tween again at another point in the animation, creating another set of frames. As shown in Figure 19-18, you can create an animation of a bouncing ball with two separate tweens—one to take the ball from the air on the left side of the window to the ground, and then to the bounce and end up back in the air again, exiting the image window. In the first frame, you see the ball entering the image window from an unseen bounce to the left of the window, followed by frames created by tweening with the frame where the ball hits the ground. Then, the fifth frame was tweened with the frame where the ball bounces back into the air, off the screen to the right. The shadow that follows the ball through its bounce moves on its own because it's on its own layer.

Controlling Animation Speed and Playback

Whether you've built your animation frames manually or let ImageReady do it for you with the Tween command, you may want to adjust things like the speed at which the animation plays and how many times it plays at that speed. The Animation palette provides all the tools you need to control these features (see Figure 19-19).

Setting the Speed of Your Animation

By default, each frame is displayed for "0 sec" (seconds), but really it displays for only a fraction of 1 second. The result is the frame playing so quickly that if you blink, you'd miss it. For many animations, especially those with just a few frames, this is just fine—an animation that flashes some text or blinks a graphic on and off requires very little time for each of those frames to display. For more elaborate animations, however—and certainly for animations that occur in several stages—adjusting the timing of one or more of your frames is probably going to be necessary.

To change the timing of an individual frame, click the frame to select it, and then click the "0 sec" timing displayed at the bottom of the frame. A list of potential timings appears, as you can see in Figure 19-20. If you choose Other, a Set Frame Delay dialog box opens (see Figure 19-21), through which you can enter a specific number of seconds (or a fraction thereof, to $1/100^{th}$ of a second) for the selected frame to be displayed during the animation.

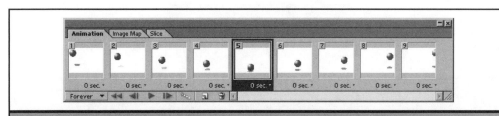

Figure 19-18.   *This bouncing ball was created with three separate tweens.*

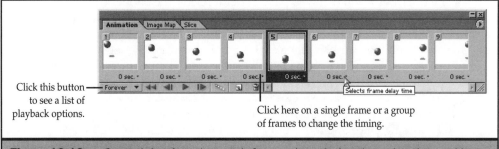

Click this button
to see a list of
playback options.

Click here on a single frame or a group
of frames to change the timing.

Figure 19-19.   *Control the time that each frame plays during the animation and how many times the animation plays.*

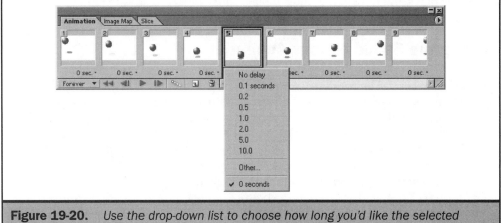

Figure 19-20. *Use the drop-down list to choose how long you'd like the selected frame to appear.*

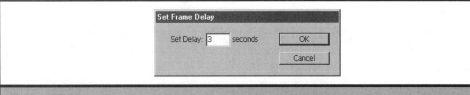

Figure 19-21. *Use the Set Frame Delay dialog box to choose a timing that's not in the frame delay drop-down list.*

Customizing Animation Playback

Some animations need to occur only once. Imagine an advertising banner, built one element at a time, at the top of a web page. After it forms, the banner can remain static as the visitor views the rest of the page. On the other hand, you might want the ad to run over and over, so that visitors to the page cannot ignore it. If your web page has frames in it and the visitors will be clicking links that display new pages in the other frames, the ad banner might have to keep moving, if only to keep being noticed.

By default, all ImageReady animations are set to run Forever, which means they'll loop over and over until the page is closed or a link is clicked, taking the visitor to a new page in the same window. You can change this Forever setting by clicking the Forever button and choosing Once or Other from the resulting drop list (see Figure 19-22). If you choose Other, the Set Loop Count dialog box appears (see Figure 19-23) through which you can enter the number of repetitions you want for the animation. If you enter "4" for example, after the fourth repetition of the animation, the image stops moving and stays in whatever condition it's in in your final frame.

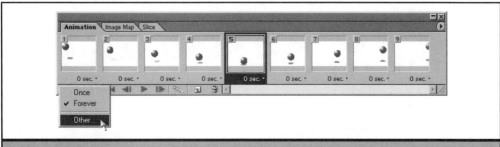

Figure 19-22.   *Set the number of times your animation will loop.*

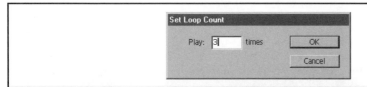

Figure 19-23.   *For a fixed number of repetitions, use the Set Loop Count dialog box.*

Note   *If your animation shows something building, growing, or going through a series of stages, you may want it to run only once; otherwise, it will build or grow and then disappear, and then build and grow again, over and over. If you want the animation to run continuously, consider creating a disintegration process in the animation—such as a flower wilting and losing its petals, only to grow from sprout to stem with bud, and blossom again. The complete cycle of birth and death is much more realistic for a continuous animation.*

Previewing Your Animation

You can test your animation by clicking the Play button at the bottom of the Animation palette, making the animation run with your current timings and repetition settings right in the image window. If you want to see how the animation will look when it's viewed on the Web, click the Preview in Default Browser button near the bottom of the toolbox (Figure 19-24 shows our bouncing ball in an Internet Explorer window). If you press and hold the Preview in Default Browser button, the two most commonly used browsers, Internet Explorer and Netscape Navigator, are listed in a submenu (see Figure 19-25), enabling you to test your animation in both applications, if both are installed on your computer.

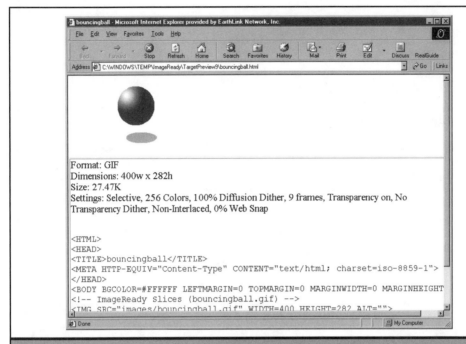

Figure 19-24. *View your animation in a browser window and see the HTML code created to run it.*

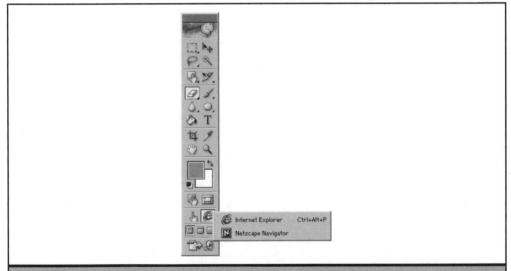

Figure 19-25. *Test your animation in either (and preferably both) of the most popular browsers.*

Tip

Never post an animation to the Web without previewing it in a browser window first. While it won't allow you to test how fast it will play online (which might be slow for people connected via modem), it will let you see whether the animation and all of its components are supported by your browser and whether you need to make any timing adjustments or adjustments to the overall size of the animation itself. Test in both Internet Explorer and Netscape Navigator, if you can, so that you've covered the two most popular bases.

Note

If your visitors are using a dial-up connection to the Internet, the first time they view a web page with your animation on it, the animation may run very slowly. On subsequent viewings of the same page, however, the animation should run more quickly, because the animation information is now in the visitor's cache (with regard to the Web, cache refers to the browser's memory of which pages it's been to before). This, of course, assumes that the visitor has not cleared their cache and deleted the cookies accumulated on their computer. If visitors are connecting to the Web via local area network (LAN), a DSL connection, or a reliable cable modem, the animation will run more quickly than it will when viewed through a dial-up modem—the first and all subsequent times it's viewed.

Working with the Animation Palette Options Menu

Open the Animation palette options menu by clicking the triangle on the right side of the palette (see Figure 19-26). The menu offers commands that you'll also find represented by buttons on the palette itself, plus a few other commands that exist nowhere else than in the menu, including:

Copy Frame   This is different from using the Duplicates Current Frame button in that it puts the frame on the clipboard, enabling you to paste the frame one or more times in the same animation.

Paste Frame   This is the command you use if you've copied a frame (or frames, if you have multiple frames selected at the time you issued the Copy Frame command) and want to place the copied frame(s) into the animation at one or more points.

Select All Frames   The command name says it all.

Reverse Frames   Again, the command name is pretty self-explanatory—the order of the frames is reversed, as though you flipped over a stack of 35-mm slides and are watching the slides of your vacation starting with the plane ride home.

Optimize Animation   This command opens the Optimize Animation dialog box (see Figure 19-27), through which you can use a Bounding Box option to crop each frame to the area that has changed since the previous frame, and the Redundant Pixel Removal option that takes all the pixels that are unchanged since the previous frame and makes them transparent. Note that for this latter option to work, you must have selected the Transparency option in the Optimize palette.

PHOTOSHOP
ON THE WEB

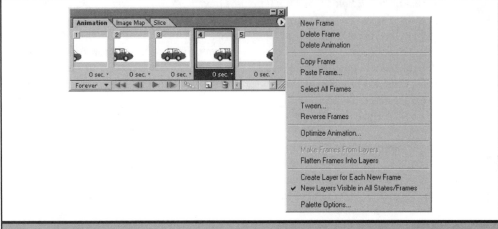

Figure 19-26. *Use the Animation palette options menu to control the appearance and function of your frames as well as their relationship to the overall image and other palettes.*

The Optimize palette is discussed later in this chapter, in the section "Saving Your Animations."

Make Frames from Layers This command will convert each of your layers (from the Layers palette) into individual frames. Depending on the animation itself, this can be a quick way to create all the frames you need—especially helpful if your animation builds or accumulates something and each of the components is on its own layer. All you'd have to do after issuing this command is go through and turn some layers on or off in specific frames.

Flatten Frames into Layers This command is the reverse of the previous one—it takes all your frames (even if just one of them is selected at the time) and turns them into layers, visible in the Layers palette.

Create Layer for Each New Frame This command is either on or off (a checkmark appears next to it if it's on) and will automatically create a new layer for each frame you add to the animation.

New Layers Visible in All States/Frames This command is on by default (a checkmark is again the indicator of the command's status), doing just what it says—makes all new layers visible in all frames. If you add a layer to your image, its content automatically appears in all of your animation's frames or rollover's states. If you find that you're going through and turning off new layers in several frames every time you add to your image, you might want to turn this command off.

Palette Options   Use this command to open the Animation Palette Options dialog box (shown in Figure 19-28) and choose the size of the thumbnails that will appear in your Animation palette. Medium is the default.

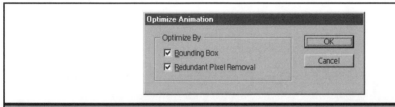

If you've opted to see large frame thumbnails, the Animation palette itself grows taller to accommodate the larger thumbnails. You may find that the Animation palette is too narrow (left to right) to see more than a few frames at once, however, in which case you can simply resize the palette to show more frames at the same time. Point to either side or the lower-right corner of the palette, and when your mouse pointer turns to a double arrow, drag outward to make the palette wider. This change in pointer appearance only occurs for Windows users, however; for Mac users, the pointer does not change, but the palette can still be resized the same way.

Figure 19-27.   *Reduce file size by optimizing the animation for use on the Web.*

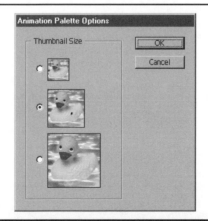

Figure 19-28.   *Choose from a small, medium, or large size for your frames' thumbnails.*

Saving Your Animation

There are really two steps to saving an animation. First, it's a good idea to save your image in Photoshop format (PSD) so that your layers are preserved, enabling you to edit the image and the animation easily in the future. This is done by choosing File | Save or File | Save As—you can also press CTRL/COMMAND-S to open the Save As dialog box by keyboard shortcut.

After you've named and saved your image in PSD format, it's time to save it for the Web, as an animated GIF. Choose File | Save Optimized and open the Save Optimized As dialog box, which is shown in Figure 19-29. You can keep the name you gave the file when saving it in PSD format and simply click the Save button in the dialog box, but first be sure that the Save As Type box (Windows) or the Format box (Mac) is set to HTML and Images (.html) if you want to maintain the HTML code that you'll need in order to add your animation to a web page. Once you save the file (by clicking the Save button in the dialog box), an images folder is created if there isn't already one in the folder you chose to store the file, and the GIF file is placed in that image's folder. In the main folder you chose, the HTML file is stored. Both the HTML and GIF versions of the file will have the same file name.

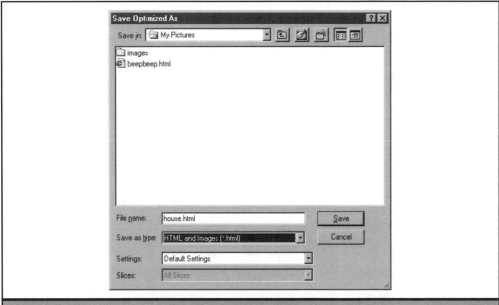

Figure 19-29.   *Save the HTML file, just the GIF file, or both the HTML and GIF files associated with your animation.*

PHOTOSHOP
ON THE WEB

Tip   *When naming files that will be uploaded to a web server and accessed by a web browser, don't use capital letters in your file or folder names, and don't use spaces or punctuation other than dashes. If you need the appearance of a space, use the underscore character. Why these restrictions? So that you know any web server and any web browser will be able to handle your files—some operating systems are case-sensitive (such as Unix) and others are not, so it's better to be safe than sorry.*

Once the animation is saved as a GIF file, you can insert it onto a web page, using the same technique you'd use to insert any other image. The animation information—its frames, their content and timing, and the overall settings for the animation's play—is stored with the file. The HTML code you may want to add to your web page document is stored in a separate HTML file. When the image is viewed live on a web page, the image file loads and the animation begins.

Note   *The Optimize palette is unique to ImageReady and is used to establish the format and quality of the images you save for the Web using the File | Save Optimized command. The default format is GIF, as this is the most appropriate format for the type of images you can animate or turn into rollovers. If you're saving a sliced image or an image with image maps on it, you can choose JPG or PNG as the file format. Depending on the format you choose, the rest of the palette's options will vary, but will generally allow you to choose colors, set dithering options, and establish the overall quality of the image.*

Building Interactive Images

Rollovers, also known as *interactive images*, can be a very useful addition to any web page. All previous warnings about not overusing animations and rollovers in your web designs aside, you'll want to use rollovers whenever there's a chance of someone not realizing that one of your graphics is actually a link, and/or when you have some information you need to convey through a graphic that you can't seem to get across if the graphic just sits there. For example, if you have a "Contact Us" button and you want the visitors to know that phone, mail, and e-mail contact information will be provided, a rollover can be an interesting way to convey that information. As shown in Figures 19-30 and 19-31, a static "Contact Us" button changes to a string of informative text on a blue rectangle.

Tip   *Rollovers can also serve simple goals. The rollover effect can be something silly and or just a funny swap of images for comedy's sake. If your web page has room for some humor, a rollover can be a subtle touch—the humor isn't always there; it only appears when someone points to a particular image.*

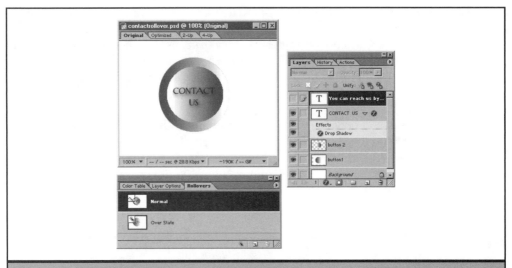

Figure 19-30. *Interactive images get the visitor involved in the web page, and can provide information as well as visual interest.*

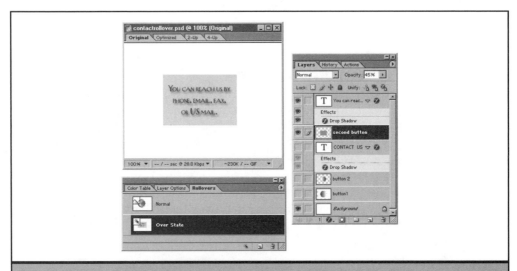

Figure 19-31. *To make sure your rollover works and fits well on a web page, keep the size of all the images for all the states the same.*

Building Rollover Content

Just like animations, rollovers require some planning, even if it's just in your head. An animation can be more complicated, and therefore the planning can be more extensive, too. Rollovers, on the other hand, tend to be much simpler, so the planning stage might simply be your mental picture of how your graphic will change in response to visitors' mouse movements. Even if your rollover has several states in it (over, click, up, down, out), you only have the equivalent of six "frames" to plan, the sixth being the Normal state when there is no mouse pointer near the graphic.

Rollovers, as you discovered in Chapter 18, are simply the swapping of one image for another when someone points to a graphic with their mouse. Through a WYSIWYG web design application such as Dreamweaver, the process of adding a rollover to the page consists of choosing two different images and setting them up to share the same space. When the visitor points to the first image, the second one is swapped in. Creating rollovers in ImageReady, however, is conceptually different. Even though the image will change in response to a visitor's mouse movements, it's just different parts of a single image that are being displayed—some layers are visible in one state and not in another.

Building Your Rollover's Layers

Just like animations, your rollover image should consist of several layers—one for each component of the image. If your rollover works by adding text when a web page visitor points to the graphic with their mouse, then the text should be on one layer, and the rest of the image can be on another layer—two states, two layers. If your rollover has more than two states, you'll need layers for all the additional states, unless the effect is more of a toggle on and off as the pointer moves onto and away from, or the visitor clicks on the graphic.

Even if your rollover is a simple one, it can pay to keep all of your image elements on separate layers, if only to make it possible to edit individual parts easily in the future, or to make it easier to create an animation from the image.

Building layers for a rollover is no different from building them for any other kind of image—use the Layer | New | Layer command. In the resulting New Layer dialog box, give your layer a name, preferably one that indicates the content of the layer or the role that content will play (see Figure 19-32). It's important to name the layers well because in the Layers palette, you can't really see what's on a particular layer (see Figure 19-33), and without selecting a layer and moving its content, you might find it hard to figure out which content is on which layer. The "Layer N" names (where "N" is the number automatically assigned) that are applied by default don't really serve you well as the image-creation process continues.

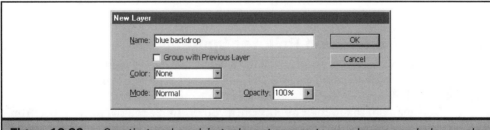

Figure 19-32.   *Creating and applying relevant names to your layers can help you plan and create a rollover in an organized way.*

PHOTOSHOP ON THE WEB

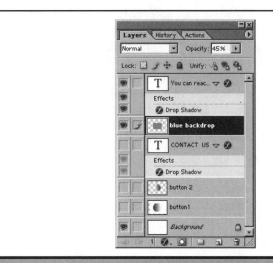

Figure 19-33. Even with a large size thumbnail, small details can be invisible on the Layers palette.

Creating Layer Content

After building your layers, you can add content to them—drawing shapes and lines, painting and drawing freeform elements, and applying fills. Be careful to activate a specific layer before creating its content. It's very easy to forget to click on a layer before drawing new content, so be prepared to use the Undo command or the History palette to remove content you've inadvertently drawn on the wrong layer. If you're using the Shape tools and have the tool set to create a new shape layer, drawing the shape will perform two tasks (drawing the shape and creating a new layer) for you. The Type tool automatically creates a new layer each time you use it, so again, you have a tool that helps keep your content on separate layers.

If the active layer is a Shape layer, you won't be able to draw or type anything else on it. This is actually a good thing, though it can seem inconvenient if you want to erase or in some other way manipulate a shape you've drawn—because you can't draw on a Shape layer, you're forced to build a new layer for whatever you want to draw next.

Using Special Effects on Rollover Content

Like animations, rollovers are saved as GIF files, and the rollover instructions, saved in an HTML file. This means that like animated images, your rollover images should remain simple from a color standpoint—photographic content and the use of shadows and special lighting effects may not retain their quality once you optimize the file for web use. You can apply drop shadows, glows, styles, or patterns if you want to, even photographic content. It's just important that you remember the image quality may be reduced when you view the image (in its various states) online.

To apply effects to any layer in your rollover, right-click/CONTROL-click the layer in question (using the Layers palette), and choose a special effect from the Layer Styles submenu that appears when you choose Layer Styles from the context menu. You can also click the layer to activate it, and then go to the bottom of the Layers palette and click the Layer Style button to access the same options. Figure 19-34 shows the submenu, as well as an image with a very simple drop shadow applied.

> **Tip**   *If you want to customize the layer styles, you'll have to use Photoshop to create the effects and then reopen the file in ImageReady. The Layer Styles submenu does not spawn any dialog box with the powers you'll find in the Blending Options dialog box that you can access from the Layers palette in Photoshop.*

> **Note**   *You can use ImageReady's Filter menu and all the filters within it to alter the appearance of your images just as you would in Photoshop. Some of the subtleties of the resulting effects may be lost when the files are saved in GIF format, but most of the filters will be effective in animations and rollovers. Feel free to experiment—try applying a motion blur to content in the Click or Over state, so the content that was motionless in the Normal state literally appears to move when the visitor points to or clicks it.*

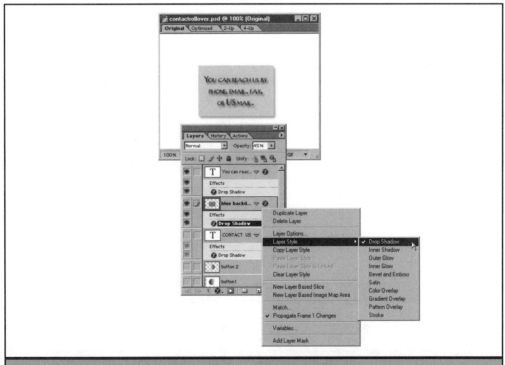

Figure 19-34.   *Use the Layer Styles submenu to apply any shadows, embossing, glows, or overlay effects.*

Understanding Rollover States

A rollover gets its name from the movement of a visitor's mouse pointer rolling over the image. When the visitor points to, clicks on, or moves in relation to the graphic, another *state* is entered, and the graphic responds by changing in some way. States are the conditions under which a graphic will change, and there are six of them:

Normal The mouse pointer is not on the image.

Over The pointer is on the image.

Down The visitor has depressed and held the mouse button while pointing to the image.

Up The visitor has released the mouse button.

Click The visitor has clicked on the image.

Out The pointer has moved off the image.

Each rollover state can have a different appearance, or you can purposely make two or more states look the same so that you maintain the way the image looks no matter what the visitor is doing with the mouse. Figure 19-35 shows a rollover with three states—Normal, Over, and Click. The Click state looks just like the Normal state, so that when a visitor clicks a graphic, it changes. Without this change, because the visitor's pointer is in the same place it was when the Over state was triggered, there would be no sign that the click had been registered. By making the Click state match the Normal state, the image reacts obviously to the visitor's click.

Adding New States

Inserting a state is very simple—just click the Create New Rollover State button in the Rollover palette (see Figure 19-36), and a new state is inserted below the active state. If you're adding states to a new rollover (which starts out with a Normal state already in place), the next new state will be Over, then Down, then Click, then Out, then Up. You can change states by right-clicking or CONTROL-clicking the state name and choosing a different state from the resulting context menu (also shown in Figure 19-36).

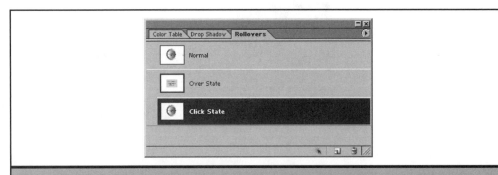

Figure 19-35. *Consider the reality of a visitor's actions in relation to the graphic as you choose what happens in each of the rollover's states.*

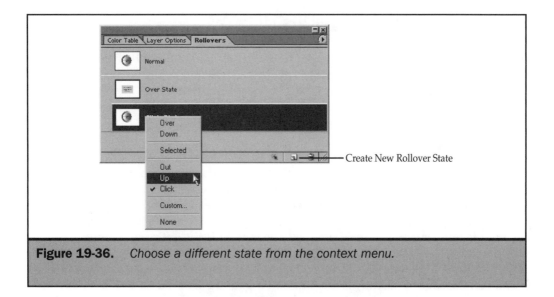

Figure 19-36.   *Choose a different state from the context menu.*

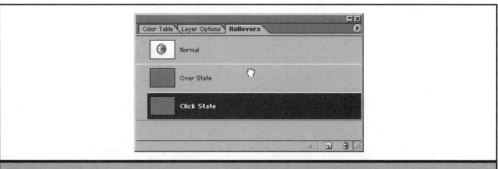

Figure 19-37.   *While their order in the Rollovers palette won't affect their play on the web page, you can put the states in an order that's logical for you.*

Rearranging Rollover States

The order that your states appear in the Rollover palette has no effect on the way the rollover works on a web page—it's the visitor's mouse actions that trigger the different rollover states to play. There is, therefore, no need to rearrange the rollover states in the Rollover palette other than to place them in some logical order for your own use—if your goal is to change the state associated with a particular view of the image, just change the state. If you do want to rearrange the order of your states as they appear in the palette, simply drag the state boxes up or down with your mouse pointer, which turns to a small fist, showing that you've grabbed the state (see Figure 19-37).

PHOTOSHOP
ON THE WEB

Establishing Rollover Layer Visibility

When deciding what will and won't show in a particular rollover state, you must use the Layers palette to turn layers on and off. Simply select a state and then use the Layers panel to hide and display specific layers. As shown in Figure 19-38, when this rollover state is selected, the layers that should be visible in that state are set to be visible (note the eye on some of the layers). The layers that should not be seen in the selected state are hidden, and no eye icon appears next to them.

Reducing Extra Space Around Rollover Images

If you look at the rollover image in Figure 19-39, it would appear that the image consists of some shapes and text in the middle of the image window. If this image were to display on a web page, you'd assume that the visitor would have to point to the shapes or text in order to trigger the rollover effect, right? Wrong. Because the shapes and text are in the middle of an image that measures 250 pixels square, the entire space within the image window is considered part of the image. As you can see in the figure, the pointer is on the edge of the window, and the Over state is displayed—simply placing the pointer on the edge of the canvas is enough to trigger the Over state.

To reduce the space around the image so that when the graphic is online the visitor must point to the actual image content, you need to do one of two things.

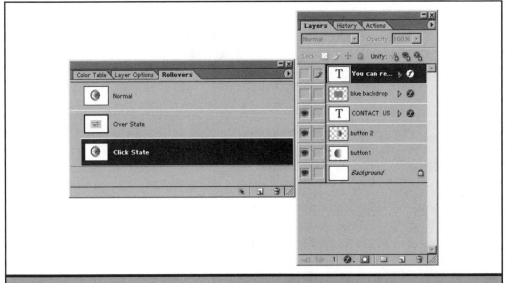

Figure 19-38. *Choosing which layers you'll be able to see in a given rollover state*

Start out with the dimensions of the finished graphic when you use the File | New command—if the graphic itself will be 75 pixels wide and 50 pixels tall, then make the image 75 × 50, and fill that space, right to the edges, with your content.

If you want some elbow room while you're creating the image, start with a bigger image window, but then crop the image to eliminate the excess background before you save and optimize the image. Figure 19-40 shows cropping in progress.

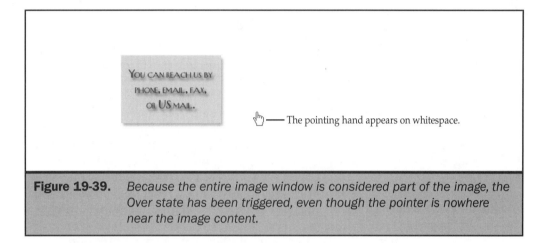

Figure 19-39.   *Because the entire image window is considered part of the image, the Over state has been triggered, even though the pointer is nowhere near the image content.*

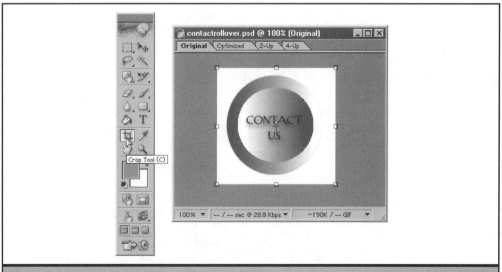

Figure 19-40.   *Crop as close to the image as possible without cutting off any of the content.*

Remember that you can crop with the Crop tool (draw a rectangle with the tool and then press ENTER/RETURN to perform the crop) or use the Rectangular Marquee tool followed by the Image | Crop command. Either technique deletes excess space around the image.

Working with the Rollovers Palette Options Menu

The Rollovers palette menu (accessed by clicking the triangle shown in Figure 19-41) offers commands that are also represented by buttons on the Rollovers palette itself, plus a few others that you won't find anywhere else:

Palette Options   While this command appears at the foot of the palette menu and would normally be discussed last, it contains settings that can affect the other menu commands, so it's a good idea to explore the resulting Rollovers Palette Options dialog box (shown in Figure 19-42) first. Through this dialog box, you can set the size of the rollover thumbnails in the palette, choosing from small (the default), medium, or large. You can also choose not to see thumbnails, but that's not a good idea—to do so would be like cooking with a blindfold on. You can also choose what the palette itself will contain—slice and image map information, and/or animation frames. By default, each state is a slice, and each slice is set to be an image map as well. You can also choose to restrict what's shown in the thumbnail to Object Bounds (the actual shapes, lines, and text with no background) or the Entire Document, which will include the background. The Show Thumbnail Icon Badges option (on by default) will remove the slice/image map indicators from the thumbnails if you turn it off.

Duplicate Item   This command changes depending on whether or not you've turned off the option to display Image Map and Slice information (in the Rollovers Palette Options dialog box). If you have Include Slices and Image Maps option turned on, then the command appears as Duplicate Slice. If you have the option off, the command appears as Duplicate Item.

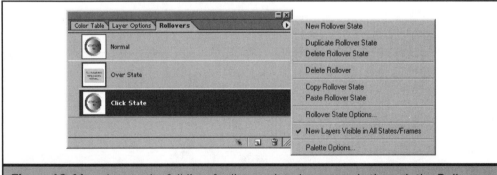

Figure 19-41.   *Access the full list of rollover-related commands through the Rollovers palette options menu.*

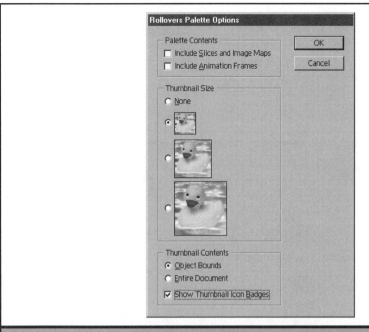

Figure 19-42.   *The Rollovers Palette Options dialog box offers several options for the appearance and functions of the Rollovers palette thumbnails.*

Delete Item   Responding to your Rollovers Palette Options dialog box settings for slices and image maps, this command appears as Delete Slice if you have the Include Slices and Image Maps option turned on.

Delete Rollover   This command gets rid of all states and displays a prompt that asks you to confirm your intention to do so.

Copy Rollover State   If you want to duplicate a state and leave the original in place, use this command. Once copied, a state can be pasted as many times as you'd like.

Paste Rollover State   If you've copied a rollover state, use this command to insert it anywhere within the rollover palette's list of states.

Rollover State Options   This dialog box (shown in Figure 19-43) allows you to change the selected state to a different state. If you choose the Selected option, the Use as Default Selected State option becomes available; if you turn it on, the state you selected will become the default state. The Custom state option activates a text box/drop-down list combo that enables you to create a new state with a name you specify. The name you type in the box will appear on the selected state in the palette and can be reused for other states in the same rollover.

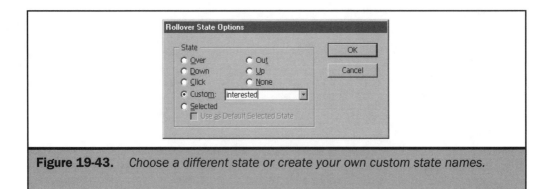

Figure 19-43. Choose a different state or create your own custom state names.

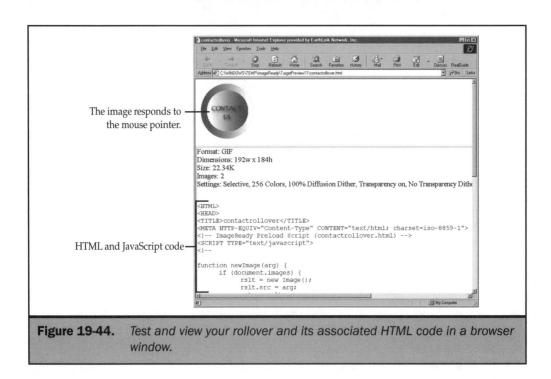

The image responds to the mouse pointer.

HTML and JavaScript code

Figure 19-44. Test and view your rollover and its associated HTML code in a browser window.

The New Layers Visible in All States/Frames command, which is on by default, simply means that when you add a new layer to the image, that layer will automatically be included (as visible) in all of your rollover's states. This can be a convenience or a burden, and if it turns out to be the latter, just turn it off by selecting it from the menu—the checkmark indicating that it's on will be removed.

Previewing Your Rollover Effects

During the creation process, and certainly when you consider your rollover to be complete, it's a good idea to test it. You can use the Play button in the Rollover palette, and then move your pointer onto the image window to test the rollover's states. Then you can click the Preview in Default Browser button to see how the image will look online. As shown in Figure 19-44, the browser preview includes the HTML code (which includes the JavaScript that runs the rollover) that you'll need to paste into your web page in order to include the rollover image.

Saving a Rollover Image

As you're building your rollover, save your image in PSD format (use the File | Save or Save As command) throughout the development process. Save early and save often to prevent losing your work to a power outage or system malfunction. You want to save your rollover image as a PSD file so that your layer information is preserved, and then when the rollover is completed, save it for the Web in HTML (.htm) format.

To save the rollover as an HTML document (including the JavaScript that makes the rollover work), choose File | Save Optimized. As shown in Figure 19-45, you can give the file a name (remember not to use capital letters, spaces, or punctuation), choose a file type (choosing from HTML and Images, Images Only, and HTML only), choose Settings (select from a list that includes Other, through which you can control the HTML code that's created with the image, as shown in Figure 19-46), and choose whether or not to include any Slices information with the file.

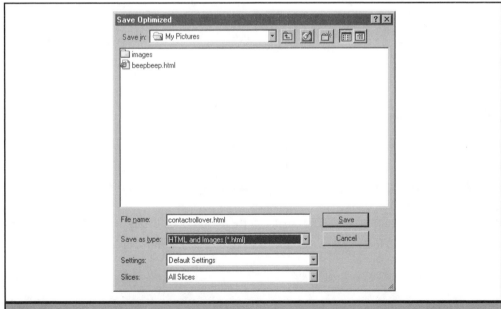

Figure 19-45.   *Save your rollover in HTML and Images format to save both the graphic and the rollover states.*

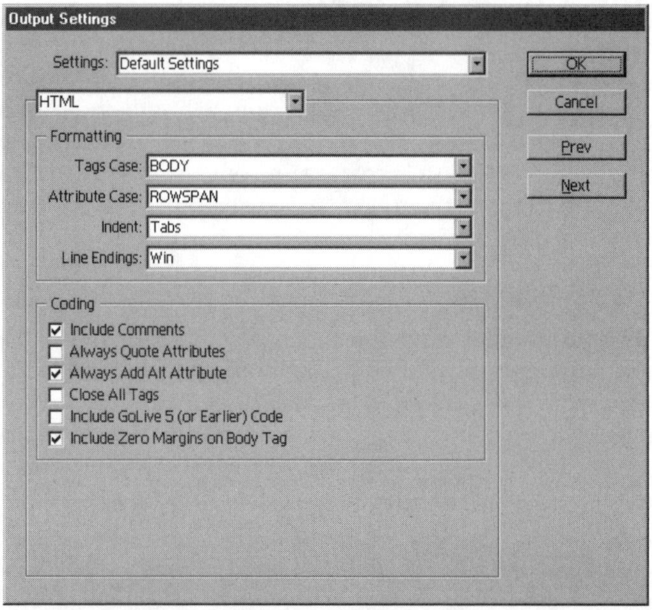

Figure 19-46. Use the Output Settings dialog box to control how your rollover's HTML code is structured and what it includes.

Use the Prev (-ious) and Next buttons in the Output Settings dialog box to view options for saving files, image maps, slices, and rollovers.

You can also access the Output Settings dialog box through the File | Output Settings menu and submenu.

When you click the Save button in the Save Optimized dialog box, if your Save As Type is set to HTML and Images, three things will happen:

- The HTML document (including the JavaScript and figure references) will be created.

- An images subfolder will be created if there isn't one already in the current folder.

- GIF files will be saved for each of the states in your rollover image.

This seems rather complex, but it's not—or at least it doesn't have to be. The name you give the HTML document is applied to the GIFs, with the state name "-over" or "-click" added to the name. So, for example, if you called your rollover contactbutton.htm, and the image has three states (Normal, Over, Click), three GIF files are created:

- contactbutton_01.gif (for the Normal state)
- contactbutton_01-over.gif
- contactbutton_01-click.gif

Note   *Once your rollover is saved and optimized, you can insert the HTML code into your web page document and place the GIF images in the appropriate folder on your web server. To save yourself time and aggravation, it's a good idea to establish the same folder hierarchy for your web files—HTML documents and images—on your local drive as you have on your web server. The common structure will make uploading files easier and eliminate potential problems as you troubleshoot your web pages.*

Slicing Photoshop and ImageReady Images

If you have a very large image in terms of dimensions and/or file size, slicing it enables you to use it as the fill for a table (one slice per table cell, reconstructing the image as though it were a very simple puzzle) or to turn the image into a web page one slice at a time. Figure 19-47 shows a large picture sliced into a tidy grid of rectangular slices, each one ready to be easily inserted into a web page table. Figure 19-48 shows a page prototype sliced into manageable chunks, bound for a web page where the slices will be arranged to fill the visitor's screen. In either case, the image slices can be turned into individual links to files or other web pages.

Slicing is really only used on web-bound images, because slicing provides significant benefits to web designers, and very few, if any, benefits to designers working with print media. A large image intended for print can be as large as the paper for which it's destined, and the file size is unrestricted by concerns about upload and download times. When it comes to the Web, however, images need to be sized to fit on the page where you intend to use them, and their file sizes need to be less than 35KB so that they don't take too long to load. For more information on web graphics and ways to make them ready for use on the Web, see Chapter 17.

Tip   *You can associate slices with web pages, turning a slice into a graphic link. Just type the web address that you want a selected slice to link to, using the URL text box in the Slice palette.*

Figure 19-47. Break an image into several rectangular slices, and then assemble them in a web page table, giving the illusion of a single large image.

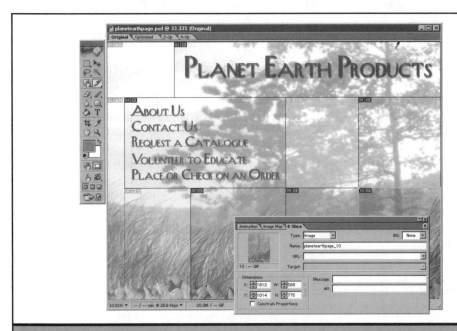

Figure 19-48. Take the prototype page you designed in Photoshop and turn it into an actual web page by slicing it and then saving the image as HTML.

Creating Slices

While you can slice images in Photoshop, the Slice palette and its buttons and commands found in ImageReady provide more support for your efforts (see Figure 19-49). You can set up everything for each slice:

■ Give your slice a name so you can find references to it easily in any related HTML and JavaScript code.

■ Enter a web address (URL) that the slice should link to.

■ Establish a Target setting to determine how the linked pages will open.

■ Provide a Message that will appear on the Status Bar in the visitor's browser window.

■ Designate Alt (-ernate) text that appears when someone points to a slice.

■ Adjust the size and position of the slice with the W and H and X and Y fields, respectively.

Note that the Slice tool works the same way in both applications, however, so you can do the slicing in Photoshop and then open the image in ImageReady to manipulate the slices.

Creating slices in ImageReady (or Photoshop) is quite simple. First, open an image, and then activate the Slice tool by clicking it. Note that the image you open can be a Photoshop (PSD) file, or an image that's already been saved in a web-safe format—JPG, GIF, or for pages you know will be viewed only through the latest browser versions, PNG. Once the tool is activated, your mouse pointer changes to a knife (see Figure 19-50), and you can begin slicing your image into blocks of varying or uniform sizes.

Figure 19-49.   *Use the Slice palette to name, resize, reposition, and associate web addresses with your slices.*

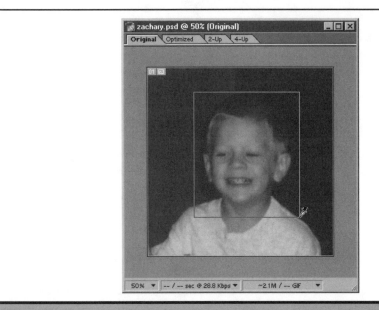

Figure 19-50. *Slice your image with a knife.*

Slicing your image is very much like drawing rectangles on the surface of the image—you click and drag diagonally away from your starting point to draw a box. The position and size of the slices are very important. You need to select your starting point carefully, and then drag only as far out and down as needed to create a slice the precise size that you need.

How do you know how big a slice you need? The size of the table cell into which that slice will be placed will dictate the slice size, or you can resize your table to match your slices after you insert them into the table. If you'll be making the table fit your slices, just slice at will, breaking the image into as many pieces as you feel will create a fast-loading group of individual image files. For example, if your unsliced image is about 500KB (in JPG or GIF format), you want to slice it into about 16 slices of approximately 30KB each. If you don't know how many slices your particular file will require in order to create individual images that will load quickly, take the total size of the file (in Kilobytes) after it's been optimized as a GIF or JPG (using the Save for Web command in Photoshop), and then divide the file size by 35 or less. The answer will tell you how many slices you need. To create the slices, use the Slice tool to divide the image into two slices, and then continue slicing the two halves until you have a grid of relatively equal-sized slices. Creating slices that are roughly uniform in size will make it easier to assemble them in a web page table later.

If you want to control the size of your slices so that they're a certain width by a certain height, display the rulers in your image window by choosing View | Show Rulers. With the rulers showing, you can watch the ruler as you make your slices, and make sure that the slice you're creating doesn't exceed or fall short of the desired dimensions.

If you need slices to be the same width and height (perfect squares rather than rectangles), you can set that control before you begin drawing. As soon as the Slice tool is activated, the options bar changes to offer slice controls. Click the Style drop-down list and choose from these three options:

Normal This slice Style applies no constraints to your slicing at all. Slices can be any size you want, enabling you to slice an image into as many slices as you can draw within the confines of the image canvas.

Fixed Aspect Ratio This option will prevent slices from being resized in such a way that their original width to height ratio is changed. For example, if a 200-pixel-wide by 100-pixel-tall slice is resized, the width will remain twice the height. To use this option, you can enter a ratio in the Width and Height boxes that appear as soon as the option is selected (see Figure 19-51). A 1:1 ratio results in slices that are the same width and height, and a 1:2 ratio results in a slice that's twice as tall as it is high. You can enter any ratio you choose, but 1 is the lowest number you can enter in either box.

Fixed Size Choose this option if you want to draw several slices of the exact same size. When this option is chosen, the W (width) and H (height) options accept measurements (rather than a ratio number), and you can enter the dimensions of the Fixed Size slices you want to draw. You can, of course, change the dimensions after drawing some slices, so your image can be diced into two or more groups of equal-sized slices. This option is very useful if your slices are bound for a web page table, where uniform slice sizes are quite helpful to the page designer as he or she reassembles the slices to create the appearance of a single, unbroken image.

If you choose the Normal or Fixed Aspect Ratio styles for your slices, you have to drag to draw them. Click a starting point and drag diagonally away from that point until the slice is the size you want. If you choose the Fixed Size style, you'll merely click on the image and move your mouse slightly, and a slice is created automatically. You then move your mouse (don't drag) to position the pre-drawn block where it belongs. Continue clicking and moving to create all the slices you need, arranging them tightly next to each other to create a tidy grid (see Figure 19-52).

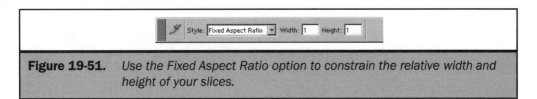

Figure 19-51. *Use the Fixed Aspect Ratio option to constrain the relative width and height of your slices.*

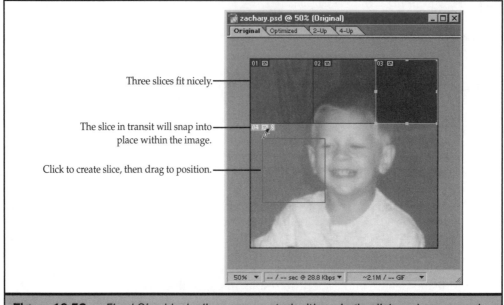

Three slices fit nicely.

The slice in transit will snap into place within the image.

Click to create slice, then drag to position.

Figure 19-52. *Fixed Size block slices are created with a single click and are moved into position, one at a time.*

Tip *If your slices don't snap right up against guides on your image, check your settings on the View menu. Make sure that Snap To | Slices is checked.*

Note that as you draw your slices, whether you're drawing them freehand in Normal or Fixed Aspect Ratio style or clicking to place Fixed Size slices on the image, numbers appear in the upper-left corner of each completed slice. These numbers will become part of the slice file names, appended to the main image name. For example, if the image is already named navigationimage.psd, the sliced images will be navigationimage01.jpg, navigationimage02.jpg, and so on. You wouldn't want to give each slice a different name, as this could become very confusing later when you position the slices in a table or directly on a web page. The full story on saving sliced images is found later in this chapter, in the section "Saving Slices and Sliced Images."

The numbering issue brings up another important thing to think about as you draw your images. If you want to make it easy for yourself later when you go to assemble your image, draw the slices in order, from left to right or top to bottom, as shown in Figure 19-53. This way, you'll know that image01.jpg goes in the top-left cell in the table or the top-left corner of the page.

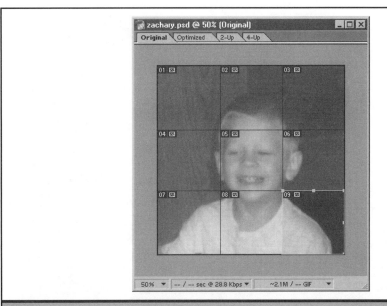

Figure 19-53.   *Use the slice numbers (a total of nine slices here) to your advantage by drawing your slices in order, starting in the upper-left corner of the image.*

Manipulating Slices

Once you've sliced your image, you may want to make changes—duplicating slices, moving slices around, making some slices bigger or smaller, or removing slices entirely. The tools provided for editing your slices are found in a variety of dialog boxes and menus, and the Slice tools' options bar in its Slice tool and Slice Select tool versions.

Rearranging Your Slices

If your slices aren't touching and a spacer slice was inserted automatically, you may want to move your slices so that they touch, resulting in the disappearance of the spacer slice. This is especially important if your slices are bound for a web page table, as some of the spacer slices and the overall slice configuration they create can't be easily recreated in a table, making it difficult to reassemble your image.

To move a slice, select it with the Slice Select tool, and drag it into the desired position. You can also use the arrow keys on your keyboard to nudge the selected slice into position. If you have guidelines displayed, slices will snap to them (or to adjacent slices, if that's your Snap To selection), making it easier to align your slices along a vertical or horizontal line. In Figure 19-54, you can tell which slice is selected by its color—a dark yellow border and handles appear around it (appearing as dark gray in this image), while the other slices remain bordered in a light gray.

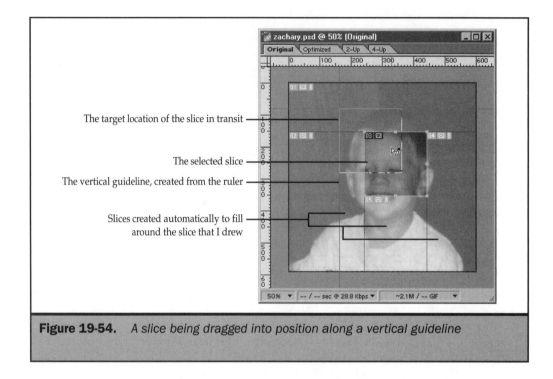

The target location of the slice in transit

The selected slice

The vertical guideline, created from the ruler

Slices created automatically to fill around the slice that I drew

Figure 19-54. *A slice being dragged into position along a vertical guideline*

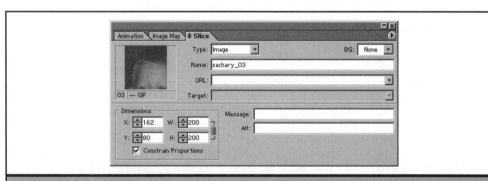

Figure 19-55. *The X and Y coordinates on the Slice palette represent the slice's position relative to its upper-left corner.*

You need to have your rulers displayed in order to quickly add guidelines to your image. If the rulers aren't showing, choose View | Rulers, and then drag out from either ruler with your pointer to position a guideline on the image.

If you prefer to work with exact measurements, you can also use the Slice palette to reposition your slices. As shown in Figure 19-55, you can enter new X (horizontal position) and Y (vertical position) coordinates and see the slice move as soon as you press ENTER/RETURN to confirm the entries. You can also click in either the X or Y box and use the arrow keys on your keyboard to increase or decrease the coordinate's current setting in 1-pixel increments. If you need to adjust the coordinates in 10-pixel increments, hold the SHIFT key as you press the arrow keys.

When the Slice Select tool is active, you can use its options bar to change the stacking order of slices; align two or more slices by their sides, tops, bottoms, or centers; and distribute the slices evenly over the surface of the image. You can also click the Hide Auto Slices button to hide any slices that were created automatically, such as spacer slices that appear to fill the gaps between user-created slices.

Creating Duplicate Slices

If you've drawn a slice and want to make another one just like it, you can duplicate it by using the ALT (Windows) or OPTION (Mac) key as you drag the existing slice into a new position. The original stays behind, and a duplicate follows you as you drag the mouse.

Of course, using the Fixed Size style for building two or more of your slices will help you make slices that are the exact same size. If you know you want at least two slices that are the same width and height, use the options bar and choose Fixed Size from the Style drop-down list; then enter the dimensions you want your slices to be. You can change the dimensions or switch to another style after your identical slices are drawn.

You can also choose Duplicate Slice from the Slice palette options menu, or right-click/CONTROL-click the selected slice and choose Duplicate Slice from the context menu.

Use the Link and Unlink commands in the Slice palette options menu (as well as in the context menu that appears if you select two or more slices and right-click/CONTROL-click them) to make two or more slices move and resize in tandem. This technique can be useful if you have two or more slices that must remain the same size or in relative positions, no matter what happens to the slices around them. Once linked, their slice numbers and link icons appear in red. To select multiple slices, hold down the SHIFT key as you click on the slices with the Slice Select tool.

If your slices overlap, you can rearrange their stacking order so that you can access the underlying slices. Select the slice that you want to move up or down in the stack (use the Slice Select tool) and choose Bring to Front, Bring Forward, Send Backward, or Send to Back from the Slice palette options menu.

PHOTOSHOP ON THE WEB

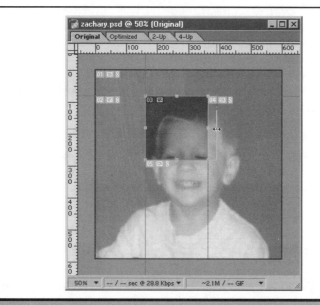

Figure 19-56. *Drag your slice handles to resize the slice.*

Resizing Your Slices

If your slices are too big or too small, you can easily drag their handles just as you would use the handles that appear around objects and layers when you use the Edit | Transform command. To resize a slice "by eye" (using the handles), select the slice with the Slice select tool and then point to any handle. When your mouse turns to a double arrow, drag outward to increase slice size, or drag inward to decrease the size of the slice (see Figure 19-56). If you work from a corner handle, you can retain current width-height proportions.

You can also use the Slice palette to change the size of your slices, entering new width and height measurements into the W and H boxes. If you want to maintain the slice's current width-to-height ratio, click to place a checkmark in the Constrain Proportions check box before entering a new measurement in either the W or H box.

Deleting Unwanted Slices

If one of your slices is no longer needed, you can delete it using any of the following methods. Note that all three require you to use the Slice Select tool to select the unwanted slice first.

- Press the DELETE key.
- Choose Delete Slice from the Slice palette options menu.
- Right-click/CONTROL-click the unwanted slice and choose Delete Slice from the context menu.

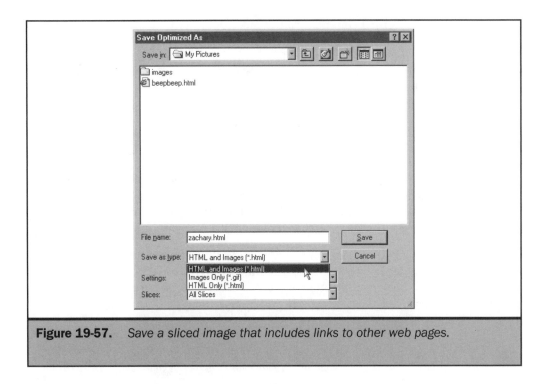

Figure 19-57.   *Save a sliced image that includes links to other web pages.*

Be careful when deleting slices; there is no confirming prompt to give you a chance to click Cancel or No. Other than using Edit | Undo (CTRL/COMMAND-Z) or the History palette, you have no recourse if you've deleted a slice in error.

Saving Slices and Sliced Images

As soon as you slice an image, you should save it in PSD (Photoshop) format so that all the slice information is saved with the file. You'll be glad you preserved a PSD form of the file if later you want to get rid of your slices and draw them again, or you simply want to resize or edit your slices and re-optimize a new version of the file. To save the sliced image for the first time in PSD format, use the File | Save or File | Save As commands, either one resulting in the Save As dialog box through which you can name your file and choose a folder in which to store it. If the file was saved previously, remember to use the File | Save As command to open the Save As dialog box.

After saving the file in Photoshop format, it's time to save the slices as web-safe files with the File | Save Optimized command. The resulting dialog box is shown in Figure 19-57.

Assuming it's the first time you're saving the file for the web, the Save Optimized As dialog box opens (which will also happen if you choose File | Save Optimized As to rename an existing optimized file), through which you can name the file and choose what type of file to save. If the image is a static one with no associated URLs, you can

PHOTOSHOP
ON THE WEB

choose Images Only (*.gif). If you did establish links for any of your slices, you can choose HTML and Images, which will generate the link information in the form of HTML code to accompany the image files created from the slices. To save a sliced image that includes links to web pages, use the URL text box in the Slice palette and choose HTML and Images from the Save As Type (Windows) or Format (Mac) drop-down list.

Once you click the Save button in the Save Optimized As dialog box, two things will happen:

- An images folder is created in the folder you chose as the place to store the sliced image(s).

- Individual files for each of the slices are created, using the filename plus the slice number. For example, if you saved the image as homephoto.psd, the default name for the slices will be homephoto_01.gif, homephoto_02.gif, and so on. These files are automatically stored in the aforementioned images folder.

After you've saved your slices as images, you can insert them into a web page just as you would any other image. Type HTML code directly, or use the commands in the WYSIWYG web design application of your choice. If your slices were linked to particular URLs and you chose the HTML and Images file type when you saved them, you can paste the HTML code into your web page document.

Use the Optimize palette to choose to save sliced images as JPG or PNG files, rather than GIFs. While GIF is the best format for animated and interactive images, there's no reason your sliced image or image with image maps needs to be a GIF. You can apply photographic content and/or special effects (shadows, embossing, filtered effects) and preserve their quality by using the JPG format to save the files for the Web.

Using ImageReady to Make Image Maps

ImageReady's Image Map tools and the Image Map palette give you the ability to draw shapes on the surface of an image and designate those areas as links to web pages and files. These mapped regions become part of the file so that when the image is inserted into a web page document, the mapped areas and their associated links come with them. The mapped areas that serve as links are also known as hotspots. The three Image Map Shape tools (shown in Figure 19-58) are found in the toolbox and are accompanied by an Image Map Select tool, which selects existing image maps.

After drawing an image map on your image, you can use the Image Map palette (shown in Figure 19-59), to change the position and size of the mapped area and set up the URL to which the map should link.

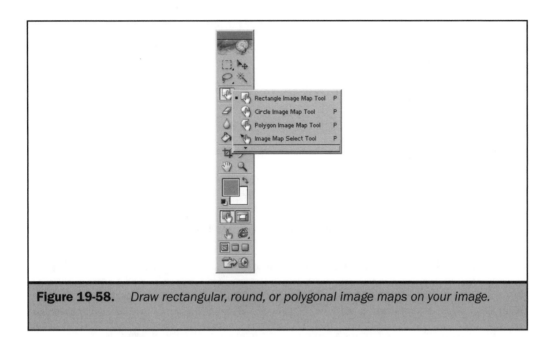

Figure 19-58.   *Draw rectangular, round, or polygonal image maps on your image.*

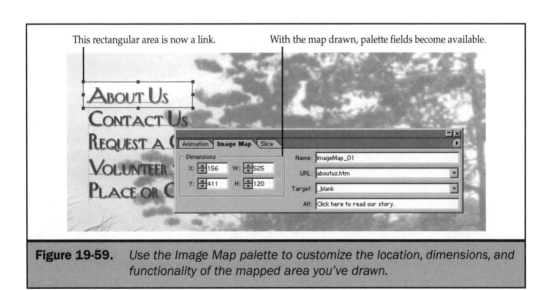

Figure 19-59.   *Use the Image Map palette to customize the location, dimensions, and functionality of the mapped area you've drawn.*

The Image Map tools' options bar allows you to control the proportions of the maps you draw (turn on the Fixed Size option and enter Width and Height settings) if you need a very specific-size map. The Fixed Size option is off by default, however, and for good reason: More often than not, you need the freedom to create the image map "by eye," dragging with your mouse to create a map that encompasses a very specific portion of the image.

An important option you can also set in the Image Map palette is the Target. The Target option allows you to choose what happens to the page that an image map links to. Your options are as follows:

_blank   Opens the linked page in a new window so that the original window (containing the mapped image) is left open in its own window.

_self   With this option, which is really the default, the window containing the mapped image replaces the current page with the linked page. If your page had frames, the linked page would appear in the same frame as the original page.

_parent   Used only if your page has frames. This option is useful if your HTML file has frames and the frame containing the mapped image is a child (frame inside a frame). The linked page appears inside the parent frame if this option is chosen.

_top   A frames-only option that enables you to replace all current frames with a single window for the page to which the mapped image (or a section thereof) is linked.

 You'll notice that the Dimensions area of the Image Map palette is blank when a polygonal mapped area is selected—this is because it would be virtually impossible to display the width and height of a freeform polygon shape in the dialog box. The dimensions appear for rectangular and circular shapes.

Creating Image Maps

To create a mapped area on an image, click the Rectangle or Circle Image Map tool, and then click and drag to draw the shape—just as you would with any of the Shape or Marquee tools. To draw with the Polygon Image Map tool, don't drag—just click and move the mouse to control the direction of the line segments you create. Keep clicking at each point where you need a corner. You'll find it works much like the Polygonal Lasso or Pen tool when you're using the click-and-move method to create paths with straight sides.

The specific image map tool you choose to draw with will be dictated by the shape you need to draw. The areas that cry out for the Rectangle or Circle Image Map tools are going to be obvious—square sections will do best with the Rectangle Image Map tool; if you need to map a circular section, the Circle Image Map tool is your clear choice. If, on the other hand, you need to create a free-form shape around a section of the image that defies easy geometric description, the Polygon Image Map tool will probably do a better job. Figure 19-60 shows an image with both rectangular and polygonal image maps.

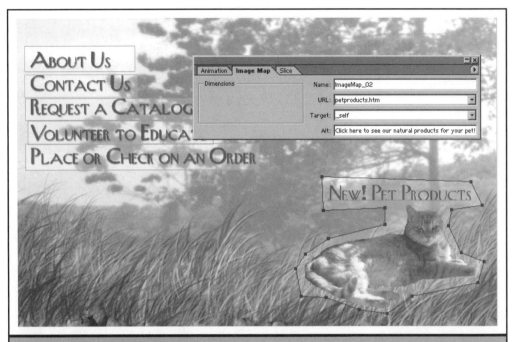

Figure 19-60.   *Different shapes within your image require different Image Map tools to map them.*

When you have a polygonal image map selected, the Dimensions portion of the Image Map palette is empty. If you want to resize it, you have to drag the handles.

Editing and Deleting Image Maps

Once you've created an image map, you can use the Image Map palette to move or resize it (as I mentioned earlier), or you can make these alterations with your mouse by dragging the map itself, or dragging its handles to make it bigger or smaller. You can also delete an unwanted map simply by selecting it (with the Image Map Select tool) and pressing the DELETE key on your keyboard.

If you want to keep your rectangular image map's proportions, drag from a corner handle when you resize the map—you'll adjust the width and height at the same time, and you can prevent changes to the width to height ratio.

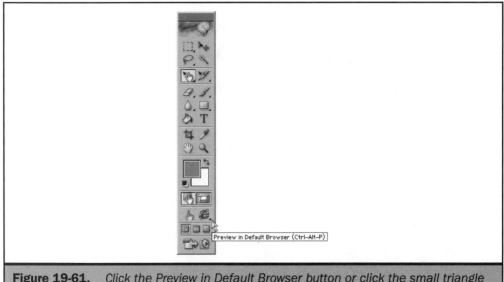

Figure 19-61.   *Click the Preview in Default Browser button or click the small triangle to its lower right to choose which browser to use for your preview.*

Testing and Saving Your Image Maps

It's a good idea to have tested an image map before you add the mapped image to a web page. You don't want to find out about errors in the map's links after you've already made the web page containing the map(s) available to potentially millions of site visitors! Instead of risking such an embarrassment, test your image maps using the Preview in Default Browser button, located on the ImageReady toolbox and shown in Figure 19-61.

When you click the Preview in Default Browser button, the image you've mapped is displayed in a browser window. You can use your mouse to click on the mapped region and see what happens. Hopefully, you'll see the page or file to which the mapped area is linked open onscreen. If you don't see the desired result, go back to the ImageReady application and check the Image Map palette for typos in the URL or errors in the choice of Target.

Once you know your image maps are working properly, you should save the file. First, as with all ImageReady creations, save the file in Photoshop format (PSD) so that all of the image information (layers, colors, frames, states, maps, and slices) are preserved for future editing. After you've done that, save the image-mapped image for the Web by using the File | Save Optimized command.

The Save Optimized As dialog box that results is no different from the one you see when you're saving a sliced image or an animation or rollover. You can name the file, choose where to store it, and then choose the type of save you want to perform: HTML and Images (which saves the HTML code controlling the image map links as well as a GIF file of the image itself), Images Only (which creates a GIF but no HTML code), or HTML only (which saves the HTML code but not the image).

HTML and Images is the default, and for good reason. The mapped image will only work on a web page if you have the HTML code to go with it. The HTML code that is generated by optimizing the file contains all the information about the image map size and position, and the web page or file to which it links. The image also needs to be saved, so you have an image to add to the web page.

Once you click the Save button in the Save Optimized As dialog box, three things will happen:

- An image folder will be created if one doesn't already exist in the folder you chose to save to.
- A GIF file will be saved to the images folder.
- An HTML file will be saved to the main folder you chose to save to.

You can then add your image (the GIF file) to any web page by using either HTML code or the Insert | Image command in the web design application of your choice. If you want to add the HTML code that was saved to the web page document, you can open the HTML document that you created when you optimized the image map file, copy the code from it, and paste it into the web page document. Again, testing is key—to make sure that the code you inserted works properly (and to make sure the image appears on the page), test your web page in a browser before posting it to the Web.

Summary

In this chapter, you learned to use the ImageReady tools to create animated GIF files and control their content, timing, and playback. You also learned to create rollovers, adding interactivity and visual interest to static graphics you create in Photoshop. The Slice tool, a tool that's also available in Photoshop but more thoroughly supported in ImageReady, was also covered in this chapter. You learned to use it to slice your images for creative use and fast loading on the Web. You also learned to create image maps, enabling a single image to link to multiple files and web pages.

Chapter 20

Using and Creating
Actions for Automatic
Special Effects

Y ou've seen how Photoshop provides a multitude of tools and solutions to empower the creative process. However, not every Photoshop project is a creative one. Many are production jobs—processing images to prepare them for use in print or on the Web. Actions are Photoshop's solution for empowering production processes. Using Actions you can automate a complex series of commands reducing them to a single keystroke or simply provide keyboard commands for frequently selected menu functions. By effectively using Actions, you will never again be burdened with repetitive tasks, and you can focus on the creative aspects of Photoshop.

Understanding Actions

The concept of Actions is an old one as far as computer programs are concerned. If you have used almost any word processing program, you may have been introduced to the concept of macros. *Macros* are a series of commands grouped into a single command. Actions are Photoshop's solution for quickly and easily creating macros.

Photoshop Actions are a simple straightforward way of recording menu commands that doesn't require anything more from you than choosing menu items. There are no special codes or a language to learn. All that is required is an understanding of basic Photoshop functions and the ability to break down a complex procedure into a series of menu commands.

You can use Actions to free yourself from performing repetitive tasks, streamline workflow, and provide a consistent application of a complex series of commands to images. Actions automate your production tasks, freeing you for other things.

The Actions palette is shown in Figure 20-1. It includes tools to create Action Sets (to hold and organize Actions); tools for recording Actions; shortcut icons to simplify the creation and use of Actions; and a palette menu for controlling, creating, editing, and managing Actions.

Figure 20-1. *Choose Actions from the Window menu to bring up the Actions palette.*

Keeping a library of Action Sets on a server can help maintain consistency and speed up production in any workplace. This can help streamline the workflow of projects like magazines and web pages while maintaining a superior level of quality and consistency.

Using Photoshop's Actions

The process of using and creating Actions can be further simplified by using the six shortcut icons located at the bottom of the Actions palette. They're identified in Figure 20-2. You'll find the palette contains everything you need to create, edit, and use Actions.

Playing Actions

Choosing Actions from the Window menu will bring up the Actions palette. This palette will include a list of installed Action Sets, a series of shortcut icons running along the bottom of the palette, and access to the Actions palette menu by using the arrow button located in the upper-right corner.

The Actions palette will include one set, Default Actions.atn, upon first use. Sets, identified by a folder icon, are containers holding one or more Actions. They're used to organize similar Actions into manageable groups. Clicking the triangle to the left of the Action's folder icon will expand the Set to show the Actions it contains.

To run an Action, first have an image open and then choose an Action from the list in the palette. For the most part, the title of the Action describes its function.

Some Actions have specific requirements that need to be met for the Action to run correctly. Adobe indicates these requirements in parentheses next to the Action's name. For example, by default the first Action in the default set should be Vignette (selection). The inclusion of (selection) in the Action's name indicates that an area of the image should be selected prior to running the Action for it to work.

With an Action selected from the palette's list and any requirements that it may indicate met, you can run the Action by either choosing Play from the Action palette menu or by clicking the third shortcut icon (triangle). The Action can be set to step through each command it contains, pausing if needed so you can select options from dialog boxes.

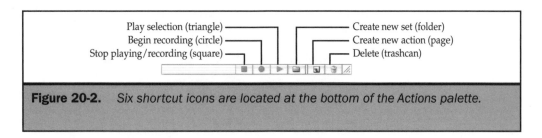

Figure 20-2.   *Six shortcut icons are located at the bottom of the Actions palette.*

In addition to the obvious functions, Actions can provide valuable insight into complex processes and how others approach a problem. Examine the steps involved in any Action and try to determine why the Action's creator made the choices they did. The method used to achieve an effect with an Action may not be the easiest due to limitations in creating Actions, but often they can help explain procedures that you don't understand.

Playback Options

You can affect how an Action plays by selecting the Action and then the Action palette menu Playback Options command (see Figure 20-3). The resulting dialog box lets you control the speed that the Action replays. By default, it will be set to Accelerated, the fastest playback speed. Alternatively, you can set the Action to play back step by step, or pause a defined number of seconds between steps.

You can even have the Action pause to play any voice annotations contained in the image. An Art Director might use this to make verbal notes on a series of images in a folder, for example. An Action could be created so that others can open each image in the folder and have the notes read aloud.

Loading Other Sets of Actions

Adobe provides an interesting selection of pre-made actions for your use. At the bottom of the Actions palette menu is a list of .atn files. These are sets of Actions Adobe provides for your use, as you can see in Figure 20-4. They cover a wide range of special effects, type effects, image adjustments, and simple Photoshop procedures. Choose one and the new Action Set will appear at the bottom of the list in the Actions palette.

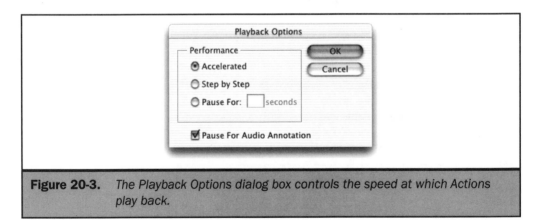

Figure 20-3. *The Playback Options dialog box controls the speed at which Actions play back.*

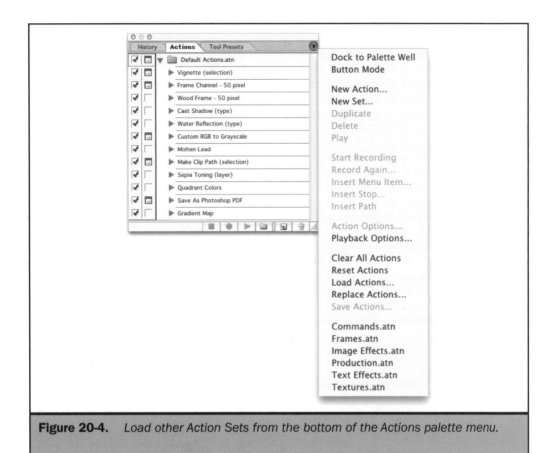

Figure 20-4.   *Load other Action Sets from the bottom of the Actions palette menu.*

Creating Your Own Actions

Actions are recordings of a series of menu commands. You cannot include as part of an Action anything other than menu commands. Excluded is any use of the tools, any sort of painting on the image itself, and many palette functions.

This limitation to only using menu commands explains a lot of redundancy built into Photoshop. If you ever wondered why there is both a cropping tool and a Crop command in the Image menu, Action's limitation of only using menu items is the answer.

When adding commands that require the inclusion of a unit of measurement, use percentages rather than pixels for Actions that will work at a variety of resolutions and image sizes.

Creating Action Sets

The first step in creating Actions is to create a new Action Set. To do this, you can either choose the New Set command from the Actions palette menu, or click the fourth shortcut icon (folder). Either will bring up the New Set dialog box, shown in Figure 20-5, which prompts you to name the Set and save it.

 While you can name Sets anything you want, two obvious strategies would be to name the Set so it either describes the function of the Actions it contains, such as Filter Effects, or name it using a job or project title, such as Jones Co. Brochure.

Creating Actions

Once you've created a new Action Set, you can begin to fill it with Actions. To create a new Action choose either New Action from the Actions palette menu, or click the fifth shortcut icon (page) to bring up the New Action dialog box (see Figure 20-6). Through this dialog box, you can do the following:

- Name your Action (give it a name that describes what it does)
- Choose the Action Set that your Action should be stored in
- Assign a Function Key (using the F1 through F15 keys)
- Assign Function Key Modifiers (to create additional keyboard shortcuts)
- Choose a Color for your Action to help organize them visually

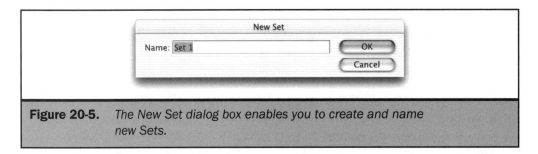

Figure 20-5. *The New Set dialog box enables you to create and name new Sets.*

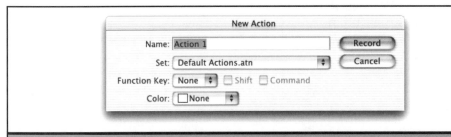

Figure 20-6. *The New Action dialog box enables the creation and customizing of new Actions.*

You will be prompted to choose a new name for the Action. While you can use any name, a name that describes the action to do is the best choice. It will allow you and others to easily identify one Action from another. In a collaborative environment, such as an ad agency or design studio, setting and maintaining a standard for naming Actions and Action Sets can help avoid confusion and duplication of work.

> **Tip** *Maintaining Adobe's naming standard for including any requirements for an Action to work in parentheses, such as (font) or (selection), will optimize ease of use in the future.*

Your next step is to assign the Action to an Action Set. Actions can be assigned to any open Action Set. If you have a large number of Action Sets open, be sure you are certain where you are saving your new Action. You can click Record to start the process of recording a new Action, or you might want to take advantage of some interesting options.

The first option is the ability to assign an Action to a Function Key. *Function Keys* are the keys at the top of most keyboards and run from F1 to F15. Even though Function Keys are included on most keyboards, not many programs take full advantage of them. Photoshop does by allowing you to set up your own keyboard commands. Additionally, you can use the Function Key modifiers SHIFT and COMMAND/CONTROL to assign additional Function Key combinations. You can assign Actions to the keys F1 through F15, SHIFT-F1 through SHIFT-F15, COMMAND/CTRL-F1 through COMMAND/CTRL-F15, and SHIFT-COMMAND/CTRL-F1 to SHIFT-COMMAND/CTRL-F15, giving you up to 60 new keyboard commands. Of course, if you have a notebook computer with only F1 through F12 available, you simply have fewer possible keyboard combinations available to you unless you attach a full-size keyboard to the notebook.

> **Tip** *Not every Action has to be a complex series of commands. With 60 different customizable Function Key combinations, you can afford to assign some to commonly used menu items. For example, neither the Gaussian Blur nor the Unsharp Mask filters have keyboard commands. You can create an Action and assign a Function Key to each.*

A second option is to assign a color to the Action. All this does is display the Action color-coded in the Actions palette. This can help you organize your actions. For example, you might want to tag all of your mode-change Actions blue and all of your filter Actions red. This may seem like an unnecessary step; however, it can simplify finding the Action you want within a long list. Taking the time to organize your actions as you create them can speed up production procedures later on. With time and practice, using an organized Action Set can become as simple as using any other keyboard command.

Recording Actions

Recording Actions is somewhat like using a tape recorder, VCR, or any other analog recording device. The basic procedure is record, stop, playback.

After creating and naming a new Action, assign it to an Action Set, and then click Record to begin automatically recording. Alternatively, you can begin recording by either selecting Start Recording from the Actions palette menu, or by using the second shortcut icon (circle). Once recording has begun, each menu item you select will be added to the Action. If, in the palette, you have the Action view expanded to show the Action's steps, you'll see the menu commands being added as you make menu selections.

Unlike a tape recorder or VCR, recording Actions doesn't happen in real time. That is, Actions record only menu commands, not the time you take to select them. So relax! If you are interrupted during the creation of an Action, the time you are away from the recording process makes no difference. Just continue where you left off making menu selections as needed.

When you are finished recording your Action, you'll need to tell Photoshop to stop recording. Choose Stop Recording from the Actions palette menu, or use the first shortcut icon (square).

Make sure to test your Actions thoroughly. You may need to edit them or adjust options to make them perform as expected. If you are working with images at a variety of resolutions, you may need to make any number of modifications.

Action Creation Strategies

Since Actions are limited to only menu commands, you may have to rethink how you would perform some otherwise simple Photoshop procedures. There are commands contained in the menus that you may have never used because using palette commands and processes are just easier and more intuitive. For example, if you wanted to rearrange the order in which layers are stacked, the simplest way would be to drag the layer to a higher or lower position in the Layers palette list. Since this wouldn't work with an Action, you would need to use one of the Arrange commands from the Layers menu.

Saving Actions and Action Sets

Individual Actions can be saved only within an Action Set. This is why setting up an Action Set first is so important. To save an Action Set, choose Save Actions from the Actions palette menu. By default, the .atn extension will be appended to the Set's name and it will be saved in the Actions folder.

You can save Action Sets to any media, taking them with you as you travel from home to office, or sending them out over the Internet. For projects that will need periodic updating, such as WebPages and newsletters, create project-specific Action Sets that can be stored with your work files. This will enable you to update projects months later with the minimum amount of effort.

Managing Action Sets

If, over time, your Actions palette becomes clogged with an excess number of Sets, you might want to clear them out. Choosing Clear All Actions will empty the entire Actions palette of all Sets and their contents. You might want to carefully read through your list of Sets and Actions and make sure you have saved those that you may want to use at a future date before proceeding to clear the palette. The Actions palette's organization tools are seen in Figure 20-7.

Rather than clearing out the list of Action Sets, you might just want to reset the palette back to its default settings. Choosing Reset Action from the Actions palette menu will enable you to do this. Choosing Append will add the default Action Set to the current set.

Action Sets that don't appear at the bottom of the Actions palette menu, such as Sets that you have downloaded from the Internet, can be loaded into the palette by choosing Load Action from the palette menu and then locating the Action Set in your hard drive. You can add a set to the bottom of the Actions palette menu by saving the set to the folder Adobe Photoshop 7/Presets/ Photoshop Actions.

Rather than simply clearing out the currently loaded Action Sets, you may want to replace them with another Set. You can do this by choosing Replace Set from the Actions palette menu. Finally, you can remove a Set from the list by selecting Delete from the Actions palette menu or by clicking or dragging it over the sixth shortcut icon (the trashcan).

Dock to Palette Well
Button Mode

New Action...
New Set...
Duplicate
Delete
Play

Start Recording
Record Again...
Insert Menu Item...
Insert Stop...
Insert Path

Action Options...
Playback Options...

Clear All Actions
Reset Actions
Load Actions...
Replace Actions...
Save Actions...

Commands.atn
Frames.atn
Image Effects.atn
Production.atn
Text Effects.atn
Textures.atn

Figure 20-7. *The Actions palette menu enables you to organize and manage your Action Sets.*

PHOTOSHOP ON THE WEB

Editing Actions

Once you've created an Action, it can still be altered to modify its function. You can temporarily exclude steps, permanently remove steps, insert new menu commands, and more (see Figure 20-8).

Each Action can be expanded to show every step/command that it contains. Each step can be expanded to show the options and settings for that step. You can toggle the arrows/triangles in the Actions palette to expand and contract the information.

You might want to duplicate Actions before editing them. That way, by working on a copy, you can always return to the unaltered original Action if needed. You can duplicate an Action by selecting it and then choosing Duplicate from the Actions palette menu or dragging the Action over the fifth shortcut icon (page).

Excluding Steps

The check box on the far left of each of the Action's steps toggles the step on or off. If you see a checkmark, then the step is included when the Action runs. If instead you see a blank field, then the step is excluded.

Definitely retest an Action after turning off any of its steps. Many steps in an Action are interdependent. Turning one off may make other steps not work or have unpredictable results.

Removing Steps

Entire steps in an Action can be permanently removed by choosing the step in the palette and either selecting Delete from the Actions palette menu or clicking or dragging the step over the sixth shortcut icon (trashcan). Be careful—this might make the Action unusable.

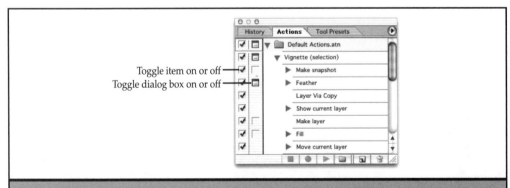

Figure 20-8.   *Each step in an Action can be toggled on or off. Some steps can be set to bring up their dialog boxes.*

Figure 20-9.   *The second icon from the left (with three dots) pauses the Action at that step and displays the step's dialog box.*

First test the Action with the step turned off. If it runs without a problem, then you can delete it.

Displaying Dialog Boxes

Any step that includes user-defined selections, such as the Gaussian Blur filter that enables you to set the amount of blurring, can be made to stop and display its dialog box. This way you can choose to make changes to the settings.

To display a dialog box for any step of any Action, click in the second field from the left of that step in the Actions palette (see Figure 20-9). You should see a small rectangle with three dots in it. Now when the Action is run, it will pause at this step and bring up a dialog box enabling you to adjust the settings.

Displaying dialog boxes to allow modification enables the Action to be used at multiple resolutions. For example, an Action that uses a Gaussian Blur set for a radius of 3 pixels when used on a 72-ppi image would need to be set to a much higher radius for a 300-ppi image.

Inserting Stops

Since Actions are dependent on using menu commands, common Photoshop functions such as using any tool in the toolbox cannot be recorded. The solution to this problem is to use the Insert Stop command from the Actions pallete menu to stop the Action at the step you choose. This can allow you to use a tool or perform some other unrecordable task. Choosing play will resume running the Action.

For example, suppose you had a group of landscape photographs and you wanted to replace the sky in each photo with a filter effect of your own creation. You could insert a Stop into your Action that would allow you to use the Magic Wand tool to select the sky in each photo and then once selected you could continue to run the Action to apply the effect and save the file.

A very useful option when inserting a Stop is to include a message. The message can include instructions or reminders of what needs to be done before the remainder of the Action can be run. Additionally, the Allow Continue option will include a Continue button in the message dialog box. Clicking it will continue the Action. This is useful if the reason for stopping is simply to check that some specific condition is met.

Using Stops that include messages can enable entry-level Photoshop users to perform tasks that normally might be above their level of understanding. This can empower users performing production tasks to produce more complex work in greater quantities.

Inserting Menu Items

You may find after testing an Action you've created that you need to insert a new step to make the Action perform to your expectations. To do this, either select the Action or select a step within the Action. Select Insert Menu Item from the Actions palette menu. This brings up the Insert Menu Item dialog box, shown in Figure 20-10. Choose any menu command and click OK to insert it into the Action. When an Action is chosen, then the new step will be inserted at the end of the Action. If a step was chosen, then the new step is inserted immediately after it. Unlike adding a command in the usual manner, inserting a command inserts a command with no preset values. The dialog box for that command will have no settings selected.

You can insert an existing Path into a selected Action by choosing Insert Path from the Actions palette menu. Then the various commands found in the Paths palette menu can be applied to the image via the Action. You can find full coverage of the Paths palette in Chapter 5.

Deleting Actions

Unwanted Actions can be deleted from any set by selecting the Action and either choosing Delete from the Actions palette menu, or clicking or dragging the Action over the sixth shortcut icon (trashcan).

Changing Action Options

If you find that you need to rename an Action, reassign its Function Key, or change its color, select Action Options from the Actions palette menu. This brings up the Action Options dialog box (see Figure 20-11) where you can make whatever changes you want.

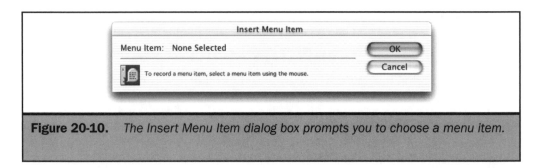

Figure 20-10. *The Insert Menu Item dialog box prompts you to choose a menu item.*

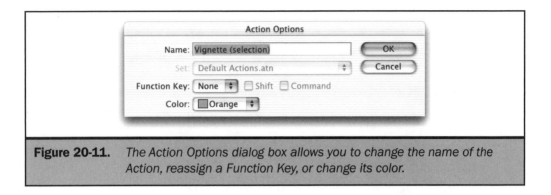

Figure 20-11.   *The Action Options dialog box allows you to change the name of the Action, reassign a Function Key, or change its color.*

Finding and Using Actions

Since Action Sets can be saved and take up little to no space, they are traded regularly across the Internet. You can search the following resources for Actions you'll need or submit Actions that you've made for others to use.

Adobe Resources

Adobe provides an online forum for users to share information about Adobe products. Adobe Studio Xchange (shown in Figure 20-12) has a large forum for Photoshop and an ever-growing collection of Actions for you to download. They are organized into categories and rated by the users, and each Action displays a small thumbnail image that shows what effect it generates. These are freeware files, and you can feel free to download any that interest you. Better still, you can upload your best Actions to the site and help out other Photoshop users and see what they think of your work.

Visit the Adobe Studio Xchange web site at http://xchange.studio.adobe.com.

Resources on the Web

The trading of Actions across the Internet is a growing phenomenon. Several sites have sprung up dedicated to promoting the use of Actions and sharing resources, including those pictured in Figures 20-13 and 20-14. Their respective addresses are:

http://www.actionfx.com

http://www.actionaddiction.com

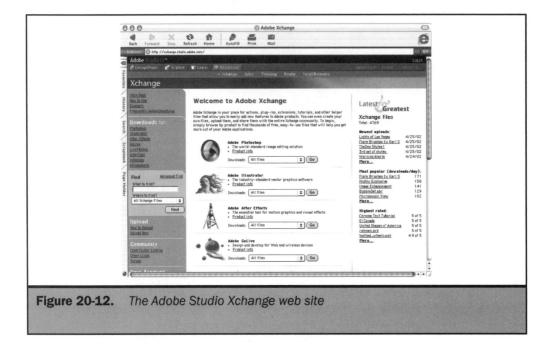

Figure 20-12. The Adobe Studio Xchange web site

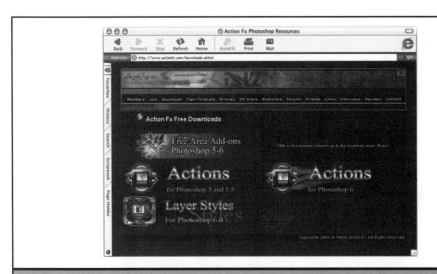

Figure 20-13. ActionFX.com (Copyright © 2001. Al Ward, ActionFX)

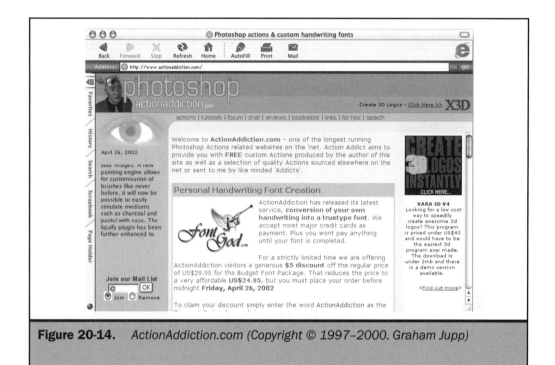

Figure 20-14.   *ActionAddiction.com (Copyright © 1997–2000. Graham Jupp)*

Newsgroups

When most people think of the Internet, they think of the World Wide Web. However, there is a wealth of information in Newsgroups. Newsgroups predate the Web and are discussion forums wherein users post messages on a wide variety of topics. The messages can be read by and responded to by any reader.

To access Newsgroups, you'll need some special software. Luckily there are many free Newsgroup readers available online. To find one, check out some shareware sites or use a search site such as www.google.com to find shareware sites. Depending on the search site you use, the way you phrase your search criteria may vary—suffice it to say that you should include the keywords "Newsgroup" and "readers" or place the phrase "Newsgroup readers" in quotes.

Newsgroups can provide an invaluable resource about Photoshop issues. Posting messages can generate answers to your questions. Here are some good general Photoshop forums:

- comp.graphics.apps.photoshop
- alt.graphics.photoshop

Automating Actions with Batch Processing

As powerful as Actions are by themselves, their effectiveness is multiplied exponentially by using batch processing. Batch processing allows you to apply an Action to the contents of an entire folder and all its subfolders. Hundreds of images can be processed swiftly and uniformly while you concentrate your efforts on more creative tasks. Photoshop does the grunt work for you!

> **Tip** *To get the most out of batch processing Actions, you'll need to set up some folders first. Create a folder to hold all of the original images that you want to process—it can contain subfolders if you so desire. Then create another new folder to hold all of the processed files.*

To set up a batch processing session, choose the Batch command from the File | Automate menu. The Batch dialog box will appear, as shown in Figure 20-15. While this might appear complicated at first, by working from top to bottom, you can set this up quickly. It's like filling out a form; with a little practice it will become second nature. The Play area of the dialog box will prompt you to choose an Action Set and an Action, and you can use the Source area to select a folder of files that you want to process. Use Destination to save the resulting images in a folder of your choice, using the naming convention you prefer, and then choose to view an Error log or pause the session if a problem occurs.

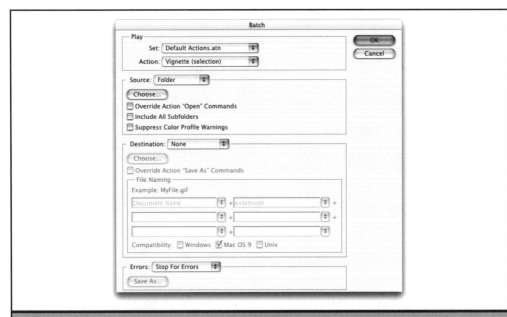

Figure 20-15. *You can use the File | Automate | Batch command to apply Actions to entire folders of images.*

You will need to have already created or picked an Action before you can set up a batch processing session.

Next, the Source area prompts you to choose the files or folder that you want to process. You can specify a particular folder (Folder), apply the Action to all of the open documents (Opened Files), import images from a scanner or digital camera (Import), or process files selected from the file browser (File Browser).

There are a few options involved in this step:

Override Action "Open" Commands   Choosing this will exclude any steps of an Action that contain Open commands, which sometimes call for specific images. If you are not sure whether to turn this on or not, read through the list of steps in the Action you are using. If it doesn't contain any Open commands, then this is not an issue.

Include All Subfolders   This option will apply the Action not only to the folder that you've selected but to any subfolder that it contains. This can be especially helpful for working with web sites that may include images divided into many subfolders. Be sure of what you are including when you choose this option. You could easily process hundreds of images unnecessarily.

Suppress Color Profile Warnings   Photoshop files often include Color Profiles to optimize and standardize color fidelity and reproduction. The problem is that if the embedded Color Profile matches the settings of other files being processed, it could generate an error or at least a warning. Choose this to turn off those warnings.

Destination   Defines where you want to save the results of your batch processing session. You can save in the same folder they originated in (None), have the images remain open (Save and Close), or be saved to a folder that you specify (Folder).

Saving the resulting new files to a separate folder allows you to keep a raw or unprocessed version. This is a really great idea and can save you a lot of work if something goes wrong during the processing or if the requirements of the job change.

There are some options involved in saving:

Override Action "Save As" Commands   Your Actions can contain embedded Save commands that may disrupt a batch session. You can choose this option to disable those commands.

File Naming   Here you can set up rules for how files are named when they are saved. You can include all manner of serial numbers, dates, times, and more. This can help in version control when dealing with files that exist in multiple states.

If you are exchanging the processed files across platforms, avoid using illegal characters in filenames.

Compatibility   Files can be saved so they are compatible with several major computing platforms including Windows, Macintosh, and Unix.

If you take it step-by-step, setting up and running a batch-processing session is fairly straightforward. However, it's always possible for something to go wrong. When that happens, you can choose two options: Either pause the session, or skip the file and generate an error log.

When creating Actions to be used in batch processing, don't insert Stops in any of the steps. It will only slow down the batch processing. If the images being processed have a variety of requirements, it's faster to divide them into separate folders, each containing similar types of images, and to run several different batches.

Clicking OK will start the batch processing session. Barring any errors, the session will run until all of the images are processed. The time it takes depends on the number of images, what's being done to them, and the speed of the computer that you are using. If everything runs smoothly, you can use the time you save to do more creative work or simply get coffee!

Creating and Using Droplets

An alternative to batch processing that takes advantage of drop-and-drag navigation is Droplets. A *Droplet*, shown in Figure 20-16, is a small application that plays back an Action. Creating a Droplet makes an icon that files and folders can be dragged onto. Those files are then processed using whatever Action you specified.

The advantage of creating Droplets is that you can create libraries of them to have access to all manner of batch-processing functions. You don't have to set up the session settings for Batch processing each time. You set up your choices once, save the Droplet, and then use it anytime you need it. You don't even have to have Photoshop running. The droplet will launch the application for you.

Creating effective Droplets can allow you turn complex product tasks over to entry-level personnel who might not otherwise possess the skill necessary to perform those tasks.

The procedure for creating a Droplet is a lot like creating a batch. In fact all of the options are the same except the first one, Save Droplet In. Use Save Droplet In to control where you are saving the Droplet to so that you can later find it and use it (see Figure 20-17). The Desktop is the most common place that people store Droplets.

Other Automated Photoshop Features

While not specifically Actions, other choices in the File | Automate menu either perform similar automated tasks or can help create some very specific Actions. The following sections discuss each of the File | Automate submenu's commands and their uses.

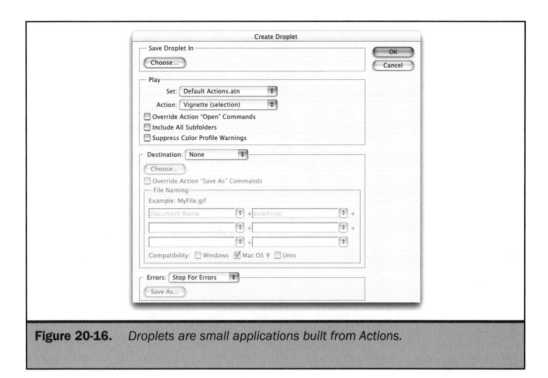

Figure 20-16. *Droplets are small applications built from Actions.*

Figure 20-17. *Dragging files or folders over a Droplet's icon will open Photoshop and run the Droplet's Action.*

Conditional Mode Change

Conditional Mode Change (its dialog box is shown in Figure 20-18) is key to batch processing certain types of Actions. You can set a Source Mode, choosing which Color Modes will be converted, and a Target Mode to select the color of the resulting files. Including this command in an Action ensures that the results will be in the correct Color Mode and can prevent some errors from occurring.

For example, if you were batch processing a folder of images for the Web, and the files in the folder were saved using a variety of Modes, you may want to convert only some of them to RGB. You may want to leave Grayscale images, Indexed Color images, and images that are already RGB unconverted. CMYK and LAB images you might want convert to RGB. The Conditional Mode Change dialog box makes these things possible.

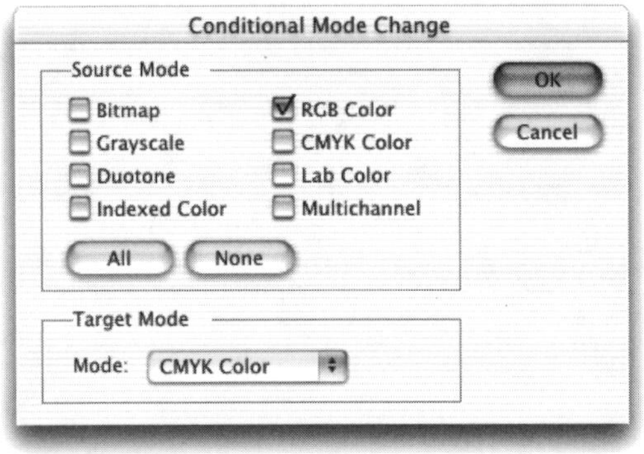

Figure 20-18. *The Conditional Mode Change dialog box*

The Source Mode area enables you to select multiple Color Modes to be converted. Color Modes not selected will remain unconverted. You specify the Mode that you want to convert to by choosing a Target Mode from the drop-down list.

Contact Sheet II

Graphic designers, illustrators, photographers, and anyone else in the growing field of digital-image manipulation share a common problem—ever-growing libraries of images. With this comes the problem of being able to store and effectively search images.

One of Photoshop's solutions to this problem is to create *contact sheets*, automatically generated pages that show a grid of thumbnail images and filenames. The Contact Sheet II plug-in dialog box, shown in Figure 20-19, enables you to choose a folder full of images and then create as many contact sheets as needed. The dialog box contains the following features:

Source Folder   Use this option to designate a folder of images from which to generate contact sheets.

Document   This feature enables you to print contact sheets, choosing the paper size and resolution.

Thumbnails   Use this setting to determine how many images you are going to fit on a page.

Use File Name as Caption   If you opt to include the file's name as a label for each thumbnail, make sure this option is left on (it is on by default) and then you can choose the Font and Font Size.

Preview   This option gives you an indication of how the page should lay out, based on the size of the thumbnails and the label font you choose.

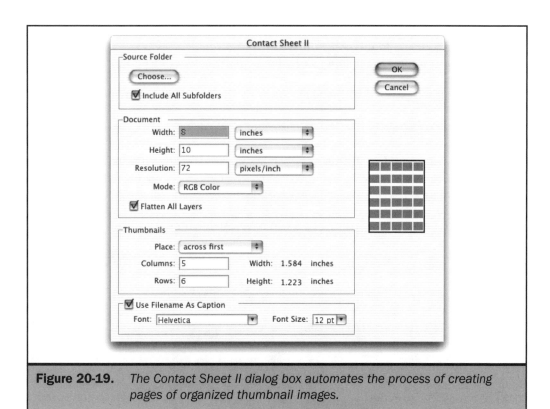

Figure 20-19.   *The Contact Sheet II dialog box automates the process of creating pages of organized thumbnail images.*

If you're including filenames on the contact sheets, you might want to look through and standardize your naming conventions. It can also be helpful to gather all of your images together into a single folder (you can use subfolders) to make them more easily accessible. This sort of prep work will generate more useful contact sheets.

The Contact Sheet II dialog box makes contact sheet generation as easy as filling out a form. The first step is to choose which folder you want to create the contact sheets from and whether or not you want to include any subfolders.

Since it's most likely that the contact sheets you're making will be printed, the next step enables you to define the printable area of the paper you plan to use. Choosing to flatten the images will create smaller files. However, leaving the layers intact allows you to edit the text layers afterward.

Next, decide how many thumbnails you want to fit on a page and whether they should read from left to right or top to bottom. The more thumbnails on a page, the smaller they will have to be. The matrix on the right side of the dialog box shows a preview of how they'll look on the page. You can also choose in what Color Mode the contact sheets will be created.

The final step is to choose whether you want to include the filenames as captions, and if so, what font and font size they'll use.

Click OK and wait as Photoshop generates as many contact sheets as needed based on the number of images in your folder (see Figure 20-20). Once it is finished, you can print out the contact sheets and create a book with all of your digital images organized and easy to find.

Fit Image

This Fit Image command (see the dialog box in Figure 20-21) is often used to create steps in Actions where an image needs to be imported at a specified size. You define the maximum height and width the image needs to be resized to. This function will resize your image but not change its aspect ratio. If your image is wider than it is high, it will remain so. It will just be scaled to whatever pixel dimension you have entered for the width.

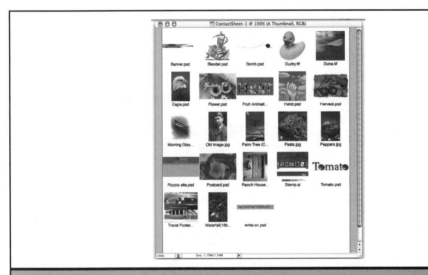

Figure 20-20. *The results of using Contact Sheet II, a useful aid to help you organize collections of images*

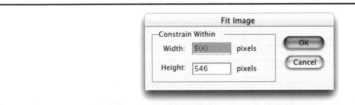

Figure 20-21. *The Fit Image dialog box allows you to constrain an image into a specific maximum width and height.*

Multi-Page PDF to PSD

The cross-platform capabilities of PDF (Portable Document Format) files make them more important in the workplace every day. Anyone with Acrobat Reader can open, read, and print PDF files. Like most Adobe programs, Photoshop can also create and open PDF files. The only problem is that PDF files created in Acrobat can contain multiple pages while Photoshop documents are only single pages.

Choosing the Multi-Page PDF to PSD command from the File | Automate submenu solves this problem by bringing up a dialog box enabling you to convert a multiple-page PDF file into a series of Photoshop documents. Within this dialog box, you can set the Source PDF (the multi-page PDF file that you want to convert to PSD), the Page Range (which pages to convert), the Output Options (so you can choose a resolution and Mode for the file), and a Destination (choose where to store the PSD files you create). The dialog box is shown in Figure 20-22.

Like many of Photoshop's automated functions, converting PDFs is as simple as filling out a form. First, in the dialog box choose the Source PDF and then locate the file you want to convert. Since PDF files can be hundreds of pages long, you'll need to select a range of pages to convert. Choosing All will convert the entire document. Be sure this is what you really want to do before continuing. Otherwise you could create many unnecessary files.

Next, you need to specify Output Options. These are the conversion options you're choosing for the format and resolution of the converted PSD files. If you simply need to read the files onscreen, choose 72 ppi. If they will be printed, choose a higher resolution. Finally, select or create a folder to save converted files in. Click OK to start the conversion process.

Figure 20-22.   *Turn a multi-page PDF into several PSD documents, making it possible to use Photoshop's tools to edit their content.*

Picture Package

Traditional photo studios often provide clients with a sheet of the same image in multiple sizes. You may have seen one generated by a portrait studio on grade-school portrait day.

Picture Package (shown in Figure 20-23) provides an automated solution to producing this sort of printed output. Located in the File | Automate menu, Picture Package enables you to easily choose either an image or a folder of images and then define how many copies of the image will be included on a single page. You'll want to choose a Source for the files or folders to be processed, and use the Document option to set the Page Size, Layout, Color Mode, and Resolution to be used. In addition, you can establish the Label settings for the fonts and font sizes used in any labels you might want to include, and you can also establish the layout of the resulting page with the Preview option.

As with the Contact Sheet II plug-in, the text is not automatically sized to fit beneath the images. If you use long filenames, large font sizes, or rotated text, the text can be cut off in the processed page.

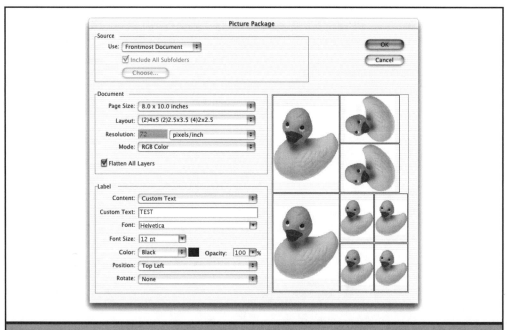

Figure 20-23. *The Picture Package dialog box creates multiple copies of an image at a variety of sizes fitted onto one printable page.*

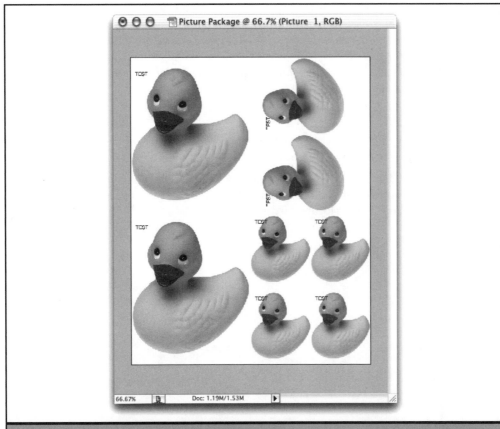

Figure 20-24.   *Picture Package creates the sort of multi-image page that many photo services provide to their customers.*

There are three steps to creating Picture Package pages. In the dialog box, step one is to choose the files or folders that you want to generate new documents from. Each image in a folder will create a separate page. Next, select the Page Size, Mode, and Resolution, and then the number of images (Layout) you want to see per page. The preview on the right side of the dialog box shows you a scaled-down version of what your final output should look like. The last step before clicking OK is to choose whether to include any labels, and if so, how and where they should be included. The new Picture Package allows you more freedom to mix the images used in a layout. You click on an individual pane in the preview layout and select a replacement image. You'll find a preview of a page of images created with Picture Package in Figure 20-24.

Note   *Picture Package creates multiple versions of a single image on a page. If you want multiple images on a single page, you need to use Contact Sheet II.*

You can use the labeling function to position a large translucent "PROOF" label or your name directly atop the images to protect against unauthorized reproduction.

The Web Photo Gallery feature (found in the File | Automate submenu) is discussed in Chapter 17.

Summary

In this chapter, you learned to automate your Photoshop activities through the use of Actions. You learned to create your own Actions and to use Actions created by other people. You read about how to locate third-party Actions online and through newsgroups. You also learned to edit Actions and to utilize additional automation features found in the File | Automate submenu.

The Complete Reference

Appendix

What's On the CD-ROM

To enhance your experience with *Photoshop 7: The Complete Reference*, a CD-ROM has been included in the back of this book. You'll find a variety of images on the CD that will assist you in exploring Photoshop 7, as well as an impressive group of applications that work well with or alongside Photoshop.

Art on the CD

You'll find PSD files for all of the copyright-free images used throughout the book's figures on the CD, as well as some additional web graphics created by the author for your use as examples and as the basis for your own work. You can freely use and edit these images for both print and web projects.

You'll also find the animated GIF files and rollovers created in Chapters 18 and 19 (on ImageReady), which you may find helpful when you build your own animations and rollover images.

A third art category included on the CD is a collection of original artwork prepared by the author specifically for this book. These files are in TIF format, and you can edit them in Photoshop as you desire. They were designed to demonstrate the major features and tool groups in Photoshop, at a level that novices can approach without intimidation and that experts can embellish using their experience and higher-level skills. These images are also copyright-free, and you can use them as they are or after you apply any kind of editing you want. You can use them for print work or save them in a web-safe format for use on the Web.

Software on the CD

The CD includes trial versions of InDesign and LiveMotion 2. If you try them and like them, you can purchase full-running versions of the software later, either from the Adobe web site (www.adobe.com), an online retailer of software (such as www.amazon.com), or a computer store near you. Of course, the trial versions of these software applications will run only for a limited time, but you'll have time to explore them and decide whether you want to purchase the full versions for your graphics and layout arsenal.

The Web Links Document

On the CD, you'll find an HTML document called PhotoshopCompleteRef.htm. This document contains links to a series of Photoshop-related web sites where you can find third-party tools to use with the software, technical advice from peers and experts, and career advice. You'll also find the names of two newsgroups where you can post questions and comments about Photoshop and receive mail from other users.

If you know of any other great Photoshop-related sites, please contact me at laurie@planetlaurie.com to let me know about them—I can then include them in future editions of the book. Thanks in advance!

Using the CD

To view the contents of the CD, simply place it in your computer's CD/DVD drive, and open the Windows Explorer or My Computer (Windows), or double-click the CD drive icon on your desktop (Mac). The contents of the CD will be displayed, and you can double-click the CD's folders to see their content.

All of the files on the CD are in logically named folders. The book's images, web graphics, and sample artwork are located in a folder called Art. The trial software applications are in their own individual folders. Photoshop 7 is in the Photoshop 7 folder. InDesign is in the InDesign folder, and so on.

If you want to copy an art file to your local hard drive, follow these operating system–specific instructions:

For Windows Users

1. With your CD in the CD/DVD drive, open the Windows Explorer or My Computer.

2. Display the contents of the CD, and right-click the file you want to copy to your local drive. If you want to copy multiple files, hold the CTRL key down as you click them.

3. Right-click the selected file(s) and choose Copy from the context menu.

4. Go to the drive (probably C:) and the folder in which you want to save the files, and right-click it, choosing Paste to place the files you copied into the desired location.

For Mac Users

1. Insert the CD into your CD/DVD drive, and double-click the icon for that device to display its contents.

2. Open the folder containing the art files, and drag the desired files onto your desktop or onto the hard drive icon.

3. Once on your desktop, you can open the files or drag them to a folder on your hard drive.

To run the installation programs for the trial software applications, open the individual folder for the application you want to install and double-click the Setup icon. The installation program will commence. When the installation is complete, you'll be prompted, and then you can jump in and give the software a test drive!

Note   *If you have any difficulty using the art files on the CD, feel free to contact me via email at laurie@planetlaurie.com. I'll be happy to send any individual files to you via email, although very large PSD files may have to be compressed or saved in a different format in order for them to be sent via email.*

Index

M

N